1 20.00
7C

D1708356

Land, labour and livestock

Land, labour and livestock:

historical studies
in European agricultural productivity

edited by
Bruce M. S. Campbell and Mark Overton

Manchester University Press
Manchester and New York

distributed exclusively in the USA and Canada by St. Martin's Press

Published by Manchester University Press
Oxford Road, Manchester M13 9PL, UK
and Room 400, 175 Fifth Avenue,
New York, NY 10010, USA

Distributed exclusively in the USA and Canada
by St. Martin's Press, Inc.,
175 Fifth Avenue, New York, NY 10010, USA

British Library cataloguing in publication data
Land, labour and livestock: historical studies in European agricultural productivity.
  1. Europe. Agricultural industries, history
  I. Campbell, Bruce M. S. II. Overton, Mark
  338.1094

Library of Congress cataloging in publication data
Land, labour, and livestock: historical studies in European agricultural
  productivity/edited by Bruce M. S. Campbell and Mark Overton.
      p.   cm.
    Papers presented to the 'Research workshop on agricultural productivity and
  the European economy in the past,' held in Mar. 1989 in Bellagio Italy.
    Includes bibliographical references and index.
    ISBN 0-7190-3171-0 (hardback)
    1. Agricultural productivity – Europe – History – Congresses.
  I. Campbell, Bruce M. S. II. Overton, Mark.
  HD1917.L33 1991
  338.1'094 – dc20   90-25477

ISBN 0 7190 3171 0 *hardback*

Set in 10.5/12.5 pt Baskerville
by Graphicraft Typesetters Ltd, Hong Kong

Printed in Great Britain
by Bell & Bain Limited, Glasgow

Contents

Contributors

Professor Robert C. Allen Department of Economics, University of British Columbia, Canada

Professor Kathleen Biddick Department of History, University of Notre Dame, Indiana, USA

Dr Bruce M. S. Campbell Department of Economic and Social History, Queen's University, Belfast, UK

Professor Gregory Clark Department of Economics, University of California, Davis, USA

Dr Paul Glennie Department of Geography, University of Bristol, UK

Dr Martine Goossens Centre for Economic Studies, Catholic University, Louvain, Belgium

Professor George Grantham Department of Economics, McGill University, Montreal, Canada

Professor Martin K. Jones Department of Archaeology, University of Cambridge, UK

Professor Patrick K. O'Brien Institute of Historical Research, London, UK

Professor Cormac Ó Gráda Department of Political Economy, University College Dublin, Ireland

Dr Mark Overton Department of Geography, University of Newcastle upon Tyne, UK

Dr K. Gunnar Persson Institute of Economics, University of Copenhagen, Denmark

Dr Robert S. Shiel Department of Agricultural and Environmental Science, University of Newcastle upon Tyne, UK

Dr Peter Solar Centre for Economic Studies, Catholic University, Louvain, Belgium

Dr Christopher Thornton Hertford College, Oxford, UK

Professor Gianni Toniolo Faculty of Economics and Commerce, University of Venice, Italy

Dr Michael Turner Department of Economic and Social History, University of Hull, UK

Dr E. A. Wrigley All Souls College, Oxford, and ESRC Cambridge Group for the History of Population and Social Structure, Cambridge, UK

Tables

Figures

Appendices

Foreword

This book was conceived in the course of a discussion during a coach trip through the Ulster countryside in April 1987. As a way of passing the time we were reviewing the current state of agrarian history in Britain, and came to the conclusion that we both regarded agricultural productivity as one of the most important yet neglected issues in our discipline. Fired by mutual enthusiasm we resolved to hold a conference on the subject. Luckily, a dozen or more historians, some geographers, an archaeologist and a soil scientist seemed to share our interest, so the project seemed possible. The possibility became a reality when the Rockefeller Foundation agreed to host the conference at their study centre in the Villa Serbelloni, Bellagio, Italy. All the papers in this volume were presented to the 'Research workshop on agricultural productivity and the European economy in the past' held in March 1989. Each paper was pre-circulated to all participants and the subject of a critical review by a discussant. Each contributor had the opportunity to revise their paper in the light of a week of intensive discussion and the revised papers were delivered to us between August 1989 and August 1990. At the time of going to press, the editors were unaware that a condensed version of Chapter 16 was to be published in *Irish Social and Economic History*, XVII, 1990, under the title 'Output and productivity in Irish agriculture from the Famine to the Great War'.

We cannot claim that the contributions to this volume provide an exhaustive geographical and chronological coverage of agricultural productivity in Western Europe. They are not intended to: indeed, it would be impossible to produce such a volume at the present moment. Our intention was simply to bring together leading scholars working in the field in English to interchange ideas both on the methodology of agricultural productivity in the past, and on the substantive historical problems associated with it. Far from being the last word on the subject, we hope that the book will encourage more research on this vitally important issue.

This venture would not have been possible without the help and support of many people. Tony Wrigley suggested that we apply to the Rockefeller Foundation and gave advice on the application. David Grigg, Alan Olmstead and Herman van der Wee acted as willing referees. The commitment and sheer hard work of the conference participants, whether as paper givers, discussants, or chairmen ensured that the conference was intellectually stimulating and highly enjoyable (the tapes of the conference sessions are punctuated by frequent eruptions of laughter). These included, in addition to the authors represented in this volume, Dr E. J. T. Collins, Professor R. A. Dodgshon, Dr S. Fenoaltea, Professor J. A. Goldstone, Professor D. N. McCloskey and Professor A. Olmstead. The staff at the Villa Serbelloni, led by Mr and Mrs Celli, ensured proceedings ran smoothly, and provided truly excellent hospitality. The British Academy assisted Paul Glennie, Martin Jones and Chris Thornton with travel grants. Anne Rook designed and drew the maps and diagrams with flair and skill and the Geography Department at Newcastle contributed towards their cost. Meemee Wong gave us invaluable help with proof reading. The staff of Manchester University Press have given enthusiastic support to the project and have transferred the text from floppy disc to printed page with care and efficiency. Annette Musker helped in compiling the index. Finally, without the direct and indirect support of the Queen's University of Belfast and the University of Newcastle neither workshop nor book would have been possible.

Belfast and Newcastle
March 1991

Abbreviations

AHR Agricultural History Review
BAR British Archaeological Reports
BPP British Parliamentary Papers
EcHR Economic History Review, 2nd series
JEH Journal of Economic History

Mark Overton and Bruce M. S. Campbell

Productivity change in European agricultural development

In all predominantly agrarian economies the productivity of agriculture is of paramount importance. Upon this depends the size and density of population which may be supported and the proportion of that population which can engage in non-agricultural activities. In the predominantly animate and organic pre-industrial world agriculture was not merely a source of foodstuffs, but also supplied most basic industrial raw materials.[1] In such economies, as Adam Smith long ago observed, of all the ways in which capital can be employed, investment in agriculture is by far the most advantageous to society.[2] Indeed, progress in agriculture provided one of the keys to economic growth, releasing the capital, raw materials, and labour to the expanding commercial and industrial sectors, and providing a vital market for their goods and services.[3] England provides the classic example of this process: the foundation of its industrial revolution of the late eighteenth and early nineteenth centuries was laid by a significant rise in the productivity of land and, more significantly, of labour in agriculture during the immediately preceding centuries. Subsequent productivity rises have been more dramatic, but none has been as far-reaching in its consequences.[4]

The capacity of modern agricultural methods to raise output almost exponentially while simultaneously reducing the agricultural

---

1 E. A. Wrigley, 'The supply of raw materials in the industrial revolution', *EcHR*, XV, 1962, pp. 1–16.
2 A. Smith, *An inquiry into the nature and causes of the wealth of nations*, ed. R. Campbell and A. Skinner, 2 vols., Oxford, 1976, I, p. 364.
3 J. P. Gibbs and W. T. Martin, 'Urbanization, technology and the division of labour', *American Sociological Review*, XXVII, 1962, pp. 667–77; J. Merrington, 'Town and country in the transition to capitalism', *New Left Review*, XCIII, 1975, pp. 452–506, reprinted as pp. 170–95 in R. H. Hilton, ed., *The transition from feudalism to capitalism*, London, 1976; J. Langton and G. Hoppe, *Town and country in the development of early modern western Europe*, Historical Geography Research Series, XI, Norwich, 1983.
4 See Table 13.1, below, p. 341; R. Shiel, below, p. 58. Compare this view with G. E. Mingay, ed., *The agrarian history of England and Wales*, VI, *1750–1850*, Cambridge, 1989, p. 971.

workforce to a tiny proportion of the total, should not obscure the fact that in historical terms these are both recent and exceptional phenomena.[5] Over many thousands of years – from the advent of sedentary agriculture in the neolithic revolution until well into the eighteenth century – output per unit of both land and labour was generally low and always prone to decline. The dilemma, as Ricardo recognised, was how to raise both total output and output per unit of land without incurring diminishing returns to labour and thereby negating economic growth in conditions of a fixed supply of land and little or no technological progress.[6] Indeed, there was a further dilemma. Attempts to expand output could disturb the ecological equilibrium conditioned by the cycle of nitrogen and other essential plant nutrients in the soil, with the consequence of jeopardising established levels of production.[7] Until these dilemmas could be resolved, and in the absence of sustained large-scale imports of food, Malthus was right in supposing that the amount of food which could be produced ultimately set the ceiling to the size of the population that could be supported and the standard at which it subsisted.[8] So long as rising food requirements could only be met by extending cultivation to inferior soils and intensifying methods of production through the application of increased labour, the inevitable tendency of population growth was to drive down the marginal productivity of labour in agriculture. This set in train a complex series of checks upon the continued growth of both the economy and its dependent population.[9]

Such ideas are central to much of what has been written on the history of European agriculture and its role in the crises and transformations by which the histories of individual regions and countries have periodically been punctuated.[10] Just as the productivity

5 R. Shiel, below, p. 58.
6 E. A. Wrigley, 'The classical economists and the industrial revolution', pp. 21–45 in *idem, People, cities and wealth*, Oxford, 1987.
7 See Shiel, below, pp. 58–69.
8 B. Thomas, 'Escaping from constraints: the industrial revolution in a Malthusian context', *Journal of Interdisciplinary History*, XV, 1985, pp. 729–53.
9 For a discussion of some of these linkages see E. A. Wrigley and R. S. Schofield, *The population history of England, 1541–1871: a reconstruction*, London, 1981, pp. 454–84.
10 For instance: E. Le Roy Ladurie, *Peasants of Languedoc*, Urbana, Ill., 1974; M. M. Postan, 'Medieval agrarian society in its prime: England', pp. 549–632 in *idem*, ed., *The Cambridge economic history of Europe*, I, *The agrarian life of the middle ages*, Cambridge, 2nd edn., 1966; V. H. T. Skipp, *Crisis and development: an ecological case study of the forest of Arden 1570–1674*, Cambridge, 1978; D. B. Grigg, *Population growth and agrarian change: an historical perspective*, Cambridge, 1980; W. Abel, *Agricultural fluctuations in Europe from the thirteenth to the twentieth centuries*, trans. O. Ordish, London, 1980.

constraints within agriculture are seen as having set the limits to economic and demographic expansion in the late third, the early fourteenth, the early seventeenth, and, again, in certain less favoured countries and regions, in the early nineteenth centuries, and are perceived as a major reason for the persistent backwardness of certain regions (such as Ireland or the Mezzogiorno of southern Italy); so the release of those constraints through technological and institutional change is recognised as crucial to the gathering pace of economic and demographic change in the more advanced parts of Europe from the seventeenth century onwards. Nevertheless, until recently, and with certain notable exceptions, accounts of agricultural development have managed to avoid explicit discussion of changes in productivity, either in terms of the ratio of output to a single input such as land, labour, or capital, or in terms of a measure which relates output to a combination of inputs such as total factor productivity.[11] Yet, whenever historians have dubbed a particular period an era of 'crisis' or 'revolution', it is always implied that a change in land and labour productivity, either for the worse or for the better, is the criterion which lends their period its special character and significance. Thus, in England, the agrarian 'crisis' of the middle ages is viewed as a decline in yields per acre, while the 'revolution' of the eighteenth and nineteenth centuries is viewed as a rise in yields per acre, and usually, by implication, as a rise in output per worker.[12]

Since it is absolute output of food per unit of land which set the spring to the Malthusian trap, there has been a tendency to equate agricultural progress with the ability to feed a growing population through rising yields. Consequently, it is this aspect of agricultural productivity which has most engaged the attention of historians. Attempts to measure land productivity directly have, however, been constrained by the availability of appropriate data sources and the methodologies employed by historians to exploit them. In the absence of such sources, or pending their fuller investigation, historians have

11 Reviews of the *Cambridge agrarian history* V focus on this point, for example: H. J. Habakkuk, 'The agrarian history of England and Wales: regional farming systems and agrarian change, 1640–1750', *EcHR*, XL, 1987, pp. 285–6; E. A. Wrigley, 'Early modern agriculture: a new harvest gathered in', *AHR*, XXXV, 1987, p. 69; M. Overton, 'Depression or revolution? English agriculture 1640–1750', *Journal of British Studies*, XXV, 1986, p. 350.

12 N. Hybel, *Crisis or change. The concept of crisis in the light of agrarian structural reorganization in late medieval England*, trans. J. Manley, Aarhus, 1989, pp. 230–6; M. Overton, 'Agricultural revolution? England, 1540–1850', pp. 9–21 in A. Digby and C. Feinstein, eds., *New directions in economic and social history*, London and Basingstoke, 1989.

often been forced into potentially erroneous circular arguments by a lack of information. For example, increases in yield have been inferred from evidence of technological change – such as the introduction of new crops or adoption of new types of rotation – by which the presumed productivity gain is in turn explained. Thus, for example, in the seventeenth and eighteenth centuries the mere presence of turnips and clover has been taken as evidence of a rise in land productivity so that the effects of the introduction of these crops have been assumed rather than demonstrated, and other mechanisms by which productivity may have increased – if increase it actually did – have virtually been ignored.[13] Conversely, the apparent absence of technological progress has been taken as evidence of the inability of medieval farmers either to raise yields or arrest their decline.[14] Such assumptions need testing against independent evidence of productivity trends if they are to have any historical validity. In so doing it is important to remember, as several of the contributors to this volume amply demonstrate, that there was a great deal more to land productivity than yields alone. Historians' concepts of land productivity have been rather narrow, and they could make more of available evidence by reconsidering how land productivity might be conceptualised and measured.

By comparison, the productivity of labour – output per worker – has been comparatively neglected. Yet it was the ability to raise output per worker in agriculture under conditions of rising population and expanding demand for agricultural products that presented the ultimate challenge in the breakthrough to sustained economic growth. Thus, it was the productivity of labour within agriculture which set the limits to urban and industrial growth and determined, other things being equal, per capita incomes within agriculture. Indeed, during certain key periods the rate of increase in agricultural labour productivity seems to have been greater than that for the industrial sector as a whole.[15] Labour productivity's central importance thus renders its relative neglect by agricultural historians all the more surprising. In part this neglect stems from the greater difficulty of deriving direct measures of labour

13 M. Overton, 'Agricultural revolution? Development of the agrarian economy in early modern England', pp. 118–39 in A. R. H. Baker and D. Gregory, eds., *Explorations in historical geography: interpretative essays*, Cambridge, 1984, p. 125.
14 M. M. Postan, *The medieval economy and society*, London, 1972, pp. 41–72; G. E. Fussell, 'Social change but static technology: rural England in the fourteenth century', *History Studies*, I, 1968, pp. 23–32.
15 N. F. R. Crafts, 'The new economic history and the industrial revolution', pp. 25–43 in P. Mathias and J. K. Davis, eds., *The first industrial revolutions*, Oxford, 1990, pp. 37–9.

productivity for periods earlier than the nineteenth century, although medieval manorial accounts possess considerable potential in this respect.[16] There is, however, much scope for estimating indirect measures of labour productivity. Wage rates for specific agricultural tasks provide one indicator, and the ratio of urban to rural population another.[17]

On the evidence of the balance between the agricultural and non-agricultural workforces, it is plain that recent centuries have witnessed a dramatic rise in the productivity of labour within European agriculture. As will be seen from Table 13.1, Britain had already reduced its agricultural workforce to 35 per cent of the total by 1800 (at which date well over half the workforces of France, Germany, Canada and the United States were employed in agriculture) and it has subsequently been reduced further to less than 5 per cent, the level now prevailing in virtually all developed countries. In fact, at the beginning of the nineteenth century it was Britain's significantly higher labour productivity, rather than any marked superiority of yields per acre, that gave it the lead over rival European economies.[18] Precisely when and how this dramatic transformation was brought about is a matter of considerable debate. Among explanations so far advanced are that it was a product of a progressive improvement in the tools and techniques of husbandry; of a more efficient, motivated, and hard-working labour force; of the substitution of first animal and then mechanical power for human labour and effort; of the creation of a system of large-scale capitalist farms; or of the replacement of open-field agriculture by farming in enclosed fields under private property rights.[19] The sheer

16 C. Thornton, below, pp. 201–7.
17 G. Clark, below, pp. 221–31; G. Persson, below, pp. 124–43; E. A. Wrigley, 'Urban growth and agricultural change: England and the Continent in the early modern period', *Journal of Interdisciplinary History*, XV, 1985, pp. 683–728, reprinted as pp. 123–68 in R. I. Rotberg and T. K. Rabb, eds., *Population and economy*, Cambridge, 1986.
18 N. F. R. Crafts, 'British industrialization in its international context', *Journal of Interdisciplinary History*, XXIX, 1989, pp. 415–28; P. M. Solar, 'Agricultural productivity and economic development in Ireland and Scotland in the early nineteenth century', pp. 70–88 in T. M. Devine and D. Dickson, eds., *Ireland and Scotland 1600–1850: parallels and contrasts in economic and social development*, Edinburgh, 1983, p. 76; R. C. Allen and C. Ó Gráda, 'On the road again with Arthur Young: English, Irish, and French agriculture during the industrial revolution', *JEH*, XLVIII, 1988, pp. 113–6.
19 G. Clark, 'Productivity growth without technical change in European agriculture before 1850', *JEH*, XLVII, 1987, pp. 419–32; *idem*, below, pp. 231–5; Wrigley, below, pp. 325–39; P. K. O'Brien and C. Keydar, *Economic growth in Britain and France 1780–1914: two paths to the twentieth century*, London, 1978; R. C. Allen,

variety of these explanations demonstrates the complexity of the phenomenon to be explained and underlines the urgent need for more explicit investigation of the determinants of labour productivity.

In urging a more systematic investigation of agricultural productivity in all its aspects – not only of land and labour, but also of other partial measures such as capital, and of combined measures such as total factor productivity – it is important to bear in mind the limitations of available evidence. Sedentary agriculture has been practised in parts of western Europe for at least eight millenia and yet it is only for the last millenium that written records are available. For most of agriculture's history it is, therefore, archaeology rather than history which must be relied upon to chart the course of productivity. For the early medieval period there are some scattered documentary references to crops and their yields, but it is not until the thirteenth century and the advent of manorial accounts that these are recorded on a systematic basis, along with information on livestock and the labour force employed on seignorial demesnes. For England these accounts are especially numerous for the period 1270–1400 and represent a treasure-trove of productivity information which has yet to yield up all its riches.[20] For most of the rest of Europe manorial accounts are altogether more sporadic in their occurrence and, instead, countries such as France and Belgium are better served by tithe records.[21] English sources for agricultural productivity are less comprehensive for the early modern period, but the story can be continued using probate inventories and tithe accounts.[22] Thereafter, as for most of Europe,

---

'The growth of labor productivity in early modern English agriculture', *Explorations in Economic History*, XXV, 1988, pp. 117–146; *idem*, below, pp. 249–52; R. Brenner, 'The agrarian roots of European capitalism', *Past and Present*, XCVII, 1982, pp. 16–113; reprinted as pp. 213–327 in Aston and Philpin, *The Brenner debate*, 1985, pp. 307–23; M. Dunford and D. Perrons, *The arena of capital*, London and Basingstoke, 1983, pp. 120–3.

20 See K. Biddick, below, pp. 95–123; B. Campbell, below, pp. 144–82; Thornton, below, pp. 183–210.

21 Examples of continental accounts include, J. M. Richard, 'Thierry d'Hireçon, agriculteur artésien', *Bibliothèque de l'école des chartes*, LIII, 1892, pp. 383–416 and 571–604; M. -J. Tits-Dieuaide, 'Cereal yields around Louvain, 1404–1729', pp. 97–105 in H. Van der Wee and E. Van Cauwenberghe, eds., *Productivity of land and agricultural innovation in the Low Countries (1250–1800)*, Leuven, 1978.

22 For England, see P. Glennie, Allen, Overton, below, pp. 247–8, 255–83 and 298–317. M. Overton, 'Probate inventories and the reconstruction of agrarian landscapes', pp. 167–94 in M. Reed, ed., *Discovering past landscapes*, London, 1984. Inventories are also available in Europe, see for example, J. De Vries, *The Dutch rural economy in the golden age, 1500–1700*, New Haven, 1974, pp. 214-24. For tithe accounts in England, see R. J. P. Kain and H. C. Prince, *The tithe surveys of England and Wales*, Cambridge, 1985, pp. 208–10.

archival resources become much richer with a growing volume of official and unofficial reports and surveys.[23] By linking evidence from these sources, and by exploiting ways of measuring productivity indirectly, there is a very real prospect that output and productivity trends can be reconstructed for the better-documented parts of Europe from the thirteenth century to the present day. This exercise naturally requires ingenuity and imagination as the sources are not without their difficulties, but their potential is considerable. Systematic investigation of them has only just begun.

The essays presented here illustrate a range of different approaches to the problem of productivity and a variety of sources with which productivity can be measured. In addition to this methodological contribution they also make a substantive contribution to several important debates in the study of western European agriculture, with particular reference to England. This chapter is therefore divided into two principal sections, each drawing on the chapters that follow. The first discusses concepts of agricultural productivity and the determinants of productivity change, and the second reviews long-term trends in the agricultural productivity of western Europe.

I Definitions of productivity

The word 'productivity' has been described as 'one of the most used, abused and mis-used words in our vocabulary', but it can be simply defined as the ratio of output to input.[24] In practice productivity indices vary considerably, depending on the combinations of outputs and inputs that are considered and the units in which they are measured. In the context of agriculture the most important inputs, and therefore the most important productivities, are usually taken to be land and labour. Thus, two of the most common measures of the agricultural productivity of a region or country are the output of agricultural products divided by the amount of land in agricultural production and by the number of workers employed in agriculture. Productivity can also be defined for specific combinations of inputs and outputs. Thus, grain output

---

23 D. B. Grigg, 'The changing agricultural geography of England: a commentary on the sources available for the reconstruction of the agricultural geography of England 1770–1850', *Transactions of the Institute of British Geographers*, XLI, 1967, pp. 73–96; J. T. Coppock, 'Mapping the agricultural returns: a neglected tool of historical geography', pp. 8–55 in M. Reed, ed., *Discovering past landscapes*, London, 1984. For examples of French sources see Grantham, below, pp. 343–4.
24 V. H. Beynon and A. M. Houston, *Productivity, the concept, its measurement and a literature review*, National Economic Development Office, 1969, p. 1.

can be related to the actual area cropped with grain in a specific year; to the area under an arable rotation; or to the total agricultural area. The output of grain can also be related to other inputs such as seed or fertiliser. For livestock productivity the 'input' can be the animal, so that productivity is defined as output (of milk, meat, wool, hides, etc.) per beast; or the output of animal products can be related to the inputs (i.e. food) put into the animal or, more crudely, to the farmed area that supports it.

A further complication is the units in which productivity is measured. Farmers usually think of the productivity of their farm enterprise in terms of physical quantities: the number of sacks of grain they can get from an acre of land under cereals, or the number of gallons of milk each cow produces. Economists usually deal in values – what in cash terms the grain and milk are actually worth – whereas ecologists relate the energy expended in producing food to the energy value of the food produced. Physical quantities are useful for investigating the sources of technical progress behind improvements in land productivity which are primarily biological or chemical, as in the chapters by R. Shiel and M. Overton.[25] Values have the advantage of reducing inputs and outputs to a common yardstick, but they also have other advantages to the economist. As P. O'Brien and G. Toniolo point out, if productivity is measured as the ratio between values of inputs used to produce a given output (or mix of commodities) and the market value of that output, then it is a measure of economic efficiency, while G. Persson shows how labour productivity may also be treated as a measure of per capita income.[26] The ratio of energy inputs to outputs is a measure favoured by archaeologists and anthropologists but has been rather neglected by historians. It has the disadvantage of failing to account for non-food crops but would seem particularly appropriate in the analysis of historical periods where output per head was close to the subsistence minimum.[27]

The contributions to this volume provide a wide range of differing applications of the basic concept of productivity. The measures employed by each contributor depend partly on the objective of their contribution and partly on the historical sources available to them. A

25 Shiel, below, p. 58; Overton, below, pp. 284–322.
26 P. K. O'Brien and G. Toniolo, below, p. 389; Persson, below, pp. 125–6.
27 Jones, below, pp. 85–7; T. Bayliss–Smith, *The ecology of agricultural systems*, Cambridge, 1982; but see P. Bairoch, 'Agriculture and the industrial revolution, 1700–1914', pp. 452–506 in C. M. Cipolla, ed., *The Fontana economic history of Europe*, III, *The industrial revolution*, London, 1973, pp. 457–60; and *idem*, 'Les trois révolutions agricoles du monde developpé: rendements et productivité de 1800 à 1985', *Annales, Économies, Sociétés, Civilisations*, XLIV, 1989, pp. 317–53.

comparison of the overall economic efficiency of the agricultural sector between countries, for example, demands calculation of the value of total output and the values of as many inputs as possible, which is the approach followed by P. Solar and M. Goossens, O'Brien and Toniolo, M. E. Turner, and C. Ó Gráda. On the other hand, investigation of the determinants of crop yields by Overton requires only a simple measure of productivity, namely crop output per sown acre. Despite their differing objectives, the most important consideration for most contributors is the availability of appropriate source material. Reasonably reliable estimates of total output and of many agricultural inputs can be made from the mid nineteenth century onwards for many European countries, but before then the necessary data are simply unavailable and the productivity measures considered are of necessity more limited. In the absence of reliable output figures some economic historians have attempted to estimate national agricultural output by the application of some basic economic assumptions. Agricultural prices are assumed to be determined by the interaction of the demand and supply of agricultural products. Thus the unknown supply (or output) can be inferred from the available information on demand (represented by population size) and on prices.[28]

Table 1.1 is an attempt to provide a guide to the various measures of agricultural productivity found in the chapters that follow so that each may be set in some sort of context. The first measure given in the Table is probably the most commonly used by historians and simply measures crop output per unit of land; it is usually calculated following contemporaries in terms of the volume of grain per unit of land sown (as bushels per acre or hectolitres per hectare), although today crop output is more commonly measured in Europe by weight rather than by volume. This straightforward measure of yield per acre is used in many chapters in this volume, particularly those covering the earlier periods when sources restrict the calculation of more sophisticated measures.[29] As E. A. Wrigley has demonstrated, yields are more useful if they can be expressed net of seed and other on-the-farm deductions, such as fodder, incurred in the maintenance of the husbandry system.[30]

28 For example, N. F. R. Crafts, 'British economic growth 1700–1831: a review of the evidence', *EcHR*, XXXVI, 1983, pp. 177–99; R. V. Jackson, 'Growth and deceleration in English agriculture 1660–1790', *EcHR*, XXXVIII, 1985, pp. 333–51.
29 See the chapters below by Biddick, Campbell, Thornton, Allen, Glennie and Overton.
30 E. A. Wrigley, 'Some reflections on corn yields and prices in pre-industrial economies', pp. 92–130 in *idem, People, cities and wealth*, 1987; Campbell, below, pp. 170–2; Thornton, below, p. 193; Overton, below, p. 304.

Table 1.1 *Some measures of agricultural productivity*

A. *Land and livestock productivity*
Individual crop yield per unit sown
Individual crop yield per unit of seed
Aggregate crop yield per unit sown
Aggregate crop yield per unit arable
Livestock output per animal per year
Total agricultural output (arable, pastoral and industrial crops) per unit
    area of farmland

B. *Labour productivity*
Output per worker employed in agriculture
Output per worker per unit of time

C. *Capital productivity*
Value of output per unit of capital

D. *Total factor productivity*
Ratio of total output to a weighted combination of inputs

Rather confusingly, medievalists commonly express them net of tithe; whereas all tithe grain was available for consumption, the profits from it did not accrue to those who produced it. Sometimes the output of grain is related to the input of seed rather than land to give a measure of productivity known as the yield ratio.[31] This has the great merit that it is impervious to customary variations in the units of area and volume, which can be a considerable problem when dealing with earlier periods. Since the weights and calorific content of the major grains (wheat, rye, barley and oats) differ, they need to be reduced to a common measure in order to be considered together. One example is the weighted index of yield used by Campbell, Thornton, and Overton, which also takes account of the differing proportion of land sown with each crop. The yields in bushels per acre for each crop are multiplied by the price of the crop relative to wheat and the proportion of land sown with it. Symbolically,

$$Y = \sum (y_i \cdot p_i / p_w \cdot a_i / \Sigma a)$$

where Y is weighted yield, y_i is the yield of crop i in bushels per acre,

---

31 B. H. Slicher van Bath, *Yield ratios, 810–1820, A. A. G. Bijdragen*, X, Wageningen, 1963; J. Z. Titow, *Winchester yields: a study in medieval agricultural productivity*, Cambridge, 1972.

p_i is the price of the crop per bushel, p_w is the price of wheat per bushel, a_i is the acreage under crop i.[32]

These measures of land productivity take no account of the frequency with which the land is cropped and can therefore be misleading. For example, high grain yields per acre on one farm might be associated with a long period of fallow, so that total grain output per acre of arable could be lower than for a comparable farm with lower yields but a shorter fallow. This problem can be avoided by relating crop output to the area of land under an arable rotation. Unfortunately, this requires detailed information on arable rotations which is rarely readily available before the eighteenth century. Some manorial accounts actually specify the names of the fields being sown and, given a sufficient number of consecutive accounts, thus permit the detailed reconstruction of rotational schemes. This is well illustrated by Thornton's meticulous reconstruction of the course of husbandry followed on the demesne at Rimpton.[33] For the early modern period the exercise is more difficult. In England, probate inventories, the most widely available and used source, offer no help, and farm accounts and tithe books survive in too small numbers to be widely representative. For these reasons the chapters by Biddick, Allen, Glennie, and Overton largely make do with output per unit sown, although Campbell and Thornton attempt to go further than this and estimate cereal output per acre of arable using reconstructions of rotations (see, for example, the comparison contained in Table 7.5). By the nineteenth century there are sufficient farm accounts available to enable reconstructions of rotations and productivities across a wide range of farms, which would not only provide a direct comparison with medieval material, but extend the analysis to more sophisticated measures. Such analysis has yet to be undertaken, perhaps because aggregate statistics are more readily available.

Crops are, of course, only one aspect of farm output, but there are very few estimates of the contribution of livestock to land and

32 Campbell, below, pp. 165–74. See also Thornton, below, p. 193, and Overton, below, pp. 302–3.
33 Thornton, below, pp. 183–210. On medieval rotations see also P. F. Brandon, 'Demesne arable farming in coastal Sussex during the later middle ages', *AHR*, XIX, 1971, pp. 126–30; B. M. S. Campbell, 'Arable productivity in medieval English agriculture', unpublished paper presented to the UC–Caltech conference, 'Pre-industrial developments in peasant economies: the transition to economic growth', 1987; M. P. Hogan, 'Clays, *culturae* and the cultivator's wisdom: management efficiency at fourteenth-century Wistow', *AHR*, XXXVI, 1988, pp. 125–31.

labour productivity, let alone of livestock productivity *per se*, before the nineteenth century. Even counting total livestock numbers is far from straightforward, since account needs to be taken of the different species, ages and sizes of the animals. This is normally accommodated by means of a system of weighting, of which those employed by Campbell, Thornton, Biddick, and Overton, by Clark, and by Turner are examples – all based on some notion of the feed requirements of the different animals.[34] The problem is, however, compounded by the fact that the weights and breeds of animals – and hence their respective feed requirements – have varied over time. Collaboration between archaeologists and historians could here prove fruitful, since only the archaeological record can provide information on carcass weights before the nineteenth century.[35] Alternatively, much could also be achieved with fuller and more sensitive price series for individual categories of animal and their products. Indeed, it is on the basis of price that Turner estimates the productivity of Irish livestock in the late nineteenth century. In this respect, one strategy would be to relate the trend in animal prices to the trend of livestock product prices to give an indication of the changing value of outputs per animal. Independent measures of the yields of meat, milk, wool and 'draught-power' are more elusive. G. Clark provides some estimates for medieval England, but as K. Biddick has shown, manorial accounts again offer the best prospect for more detailed information.[36] Once again, by the mid nineteenth century measures of the physical productivity of livestock become much more widely available.[37]

When both crop and livestock output data are available, then land productivity can be measured by dividing the total value of output by the amount of agricultural land. However, as several contributors point out, even in the relative statistical cornucopia of the nineteenth and twentieth centuries, this is not as straightforward as it might seem. In the first place, decisions have to be taken as to whether certain commodities are to be included as part of agricultural output. As Ó Gráda shows, for a country such as Ireland, the inclusion or exclusion of peat can make a significant difference to productivity estimates.

34 See also J. T. Coppock, *An agricultural atlas of England and Wales*, London, 1964, p. 213.
35 A. J. S. Gibson, 'The size and weight of cattle and sheep in early modern Scotland', *AHR*, XXXVI, 1988, pp. 162–71.
36 Clark, below, pp. 214–17. K. Biddick, *The other economy: pastoral husbandry on a medieval estate*, Berkeley and Los Angeles, 1989; *idem*, below, pp. 115–19.
37 See Clark, below, pp. 217–18; Solar and Goossens, below, pp. 366–9; Turner, below, pp. 416–24.

Secondly, gross agricultural output involves a degree of double counting. The agricultural output for one year includes the seed for the following year's crop, and crops fed to livestock are also accounted for in the value of livestock output.[38] Thus, some contributors prefer net value added as the indicator of agricultural output which allows for seed corn, crops consumed by animals, livestock products (such as milk) recycled on the farm, and animals which failed to realise their full value because of premature mortality. Moreover, to control for monetary fluctuations, output should really be valued at constant prices, and, as O'Brien and Toniolo demonstrate, in comparisons between countries there are at least two sets of prices to choose from which may yield different results.[39]

Estimates of the amount of agricultural land usually present fewer problems, although, as Solar and Goossens point out, decisions have to be made as to the area that can be counted as 'agricultural'. Land unambiguously in non-agricultural use – such as roads, buildings, and water – is easily taken account of, but land classified as 'waste' is more problematic. It is rare that land is totally unproductive of crops, animals, or fuel of some sort, so to discount it entirely would be misleading, although to include it on an equal footing with other agricultural land may be equally so. Nor can arable and pasture be treated equally, a problem encountered by Solar and Goossens in their comparison of Belgium and Ireland which have very different land-use characteristics. The problem is, again, one of weighting. Not all agricultural land is equal and this needs to be taken into account by any sensitive measure of land productivity. One solution is to employ a system of weighting based on modern soil surveys, except that this reflects soil conditions today after centuries of reclamation and improvement.[40] Another is to weight land according to its contemporary rental value, although here deficiencies of information may once more be a constraint.

As with land productivity, the main difficulty with calculating labour productivity at a national or regional level from the mid nineteenth century lies in computing the value of output rather than the number of workers in agriculture (for which censuses provide a wealth of information). Thus, once output has been estimated it can be divided by the agricultural workforce to give a measure of labour

38 Turner, below, pp. 411–14; O'Brien and Toniolo, below, pp. 393–4.
39 Solar and Goossens, below, p. 370; O'Brien and Toniolo, below, pp. 390–6.
40 O'Brien and Keydar, *Economic growth in Britain and France*, pp. 109–12; Solar and Goossens, below, p. 370.

B

productivity. The calculation can be further refined to take account of
the respective contributions of men, women, children, and seasonal
and part-time workers.[41] For earlier periods rough approximations may
be made of the size of the agricultural workforce but no direct
measurements of agricultural output are available. Even so, a very crude
index of labour productivity can be constructed by dividing the total
population by the proportion of the population working in agriculture.
If consumption per head over time remains constant, and exports and
imports can be accounted for, then the size of the population is a
direct reflection of the output of agricultural products.[42]

An alternative measure of labour productivity calculates output
per worker for much shorter periods of time. Output per worker-hour
or per worker-day is a more sensitive measure because it takes account
of the time workers actually spend working. A rise in average output
per worker per year could reflect greater efficiency, but could also
be the consequence of an increase in the number of hours or days
worked.[43] Crafts has pointed out that the 'new husbandry' in eighteenth-
century England raised output per worker-year, even though output
per worker-hour might have remained the same.[44] These fine-tuned
measures of labour productivity are most effectively calculated from
detailed farm accounts and, hence, are often the only direct measures
of labour productivity available for relatively early periods.[45]

Estimates of capital productivity in agriculture are especially
difficult to calculate for past periods because of the absence of adequate
data. Capital formation could not be estimated by O'Brien and Toniolo
in their comparison of Italy and the United Kingdom, or by Solar and
Goossens in their comparison of Belgium and Ireland.[46] Capital in
agriculture is conventionally divided into fixed and working capital,
the former being the responsibility of the landlord, and the latter
the responsibility of the tenant.[47] Fixed capital covers buildings, land
reclamation, farm roads, drainage, fencing and woodlands, while

41 Solar and Goossens, below, pp. 373–6; O'Brien and Toniolo, below, pp. 396–400.
42 Wrigley, 'Urban growth and agricultural change'.
43 For example, Persson, below, pp. 125–6; Clark, below, pp. 231–5; Solar and Goossens, below, pp. 380–2.
44 N. F. R. Crafts, 'Income elasticities of demand and the release of labour by agriculture during the British industrial revolution', *Journal of European Economic History*, IX, 1980, pp. 167–8.
45 For example, Thornton, below, pp. 201–7.
46 O'Brien and Toniolo, below, pp. 389–90; Solar and Goossens, below, pp. 379–80. But see Turner, below, pp. 431–4.
47 M. Capstick, *The economics of agriculture*, London, 1970, pp. 47–54.

working capital includes implements, machinery, livestock and standing crops. Gross capital formation is the total outlay on assets which yield a service lasting beyond the period in which they are acquired, whereas net capital formation measures the balance after the deduction of an amount to cover depreciation of the capital stock through physical wear and tear or obsolescence. Until comparatively recently the most important of these was livestock. Biddick demonstrates that medieval English kings were fully aware of the capital value of livestock and repeatedly stripped them from the estates of the Bishopric of Winchester during episcopal vacancies. Allen likewise regards livestock as the principal form of farm capital and on that basis calculates the relative capital endowment of large and small farmers in eighteenth-century England.[48] Turner, too, takes livestock as his basis for estimating the rate of capital formation on late-nineteenth-century Irish farms. Such a simplified view of farm capital nevertheless has limitations since stocking densities may have varied independently of capital considerations. Less susceptible to these kinds of ambiguity is Wrigley's emphasis upon draught animals as a specific, and perhaps key, form of working capital. The most comprehensive estimates of agricultural capital for England in an historical context, calculated by amalgamating estimates for the separate elements of capital mentioned above and dating back to 1750, have been calculated by B. A. Holderness and C. H. Feinstein.[49]

The calculation of partial indices of agricultural productivity, be they for land, labour, or some other input, are not in themselves an adequate guide to the overall level of the efficiency of agricultural production. An increase in yield per unit area, for example, could arise at the cost of a decline in one or more of the other factor productivities. Some overall measure which embraces all of the separate factor productivities is therefore required. The measure favoured by economists is total factor productivity, which relates output to a weighted

48 R. C. Allen, *The 'capital intensive farmer' and the English agricultural revolution: a reassessment*, Discussion Paper 87–11, Department of Economics, University of British Columbia, 1987; *idem*, below, pp. 244–6.

49 B. A. Holderness, 'Capital formation in agriculture', pp. 159–83 in J. P. P. Higgins and S. Pollard, eds., *Aspects of capital investment in Great Britain, 1750–1850: a preliminary survey*, London, 1971; *idem*, 'Agriculture, 1770–1860', pp. 9–34 in C. H. Feinstein and S. Pollard, eds., *Studies in capital formation in the United Kingdom, 1750–1920*, Oxford, 1988; C. H. Feinstein, 'Agriculture', pp. 267–80 in *idem* and Pollard, *Studies in capital formation*, 1988; *idem*, 'Capital formation in Great Britain', pp. 28–96 in P. Mathias and M. M. Postan, eds., *The Cambridge economic history of Europe*, VII, *The industrial economies: capital, labour, and enterprise*, part 1, Cambridge, 1978.

combination of inputs. Crafts, for example, calculates estimates of total factor productivity for eighteenth- and nineteenth-century Britain using the formula:

$$\frac{\Delta Y}{Y} = \alpha \frac{\Delta K}{K} + \beta \frac{\Delta L}{L} + \gamma \frac{\Delta T}{T} + r*$$

where Y is output, K is capital, L is labour, T is land; α, β, and γ are the shares of profits, wages and rents in national income; and $r*$ is total factor productivity.[50] Thus total factor productivity is the residual productivity increase that cannot be attributed to the recorded increase in land, labour, and capital as factors of production.[51] Estimates of total factor productivity in agriculture have been calculated in this way for the nineteenth century for the United States and for Britain, and new estimates for Ireland are included in this volume.[52]

Difficulties in obtaining data for calculating total factor productivity can be considerable; thus Solar and Goossens, lacking information on capital, calculate a partial measure of factor productivity based upon land and labour alone.[53] Another strategy is to derive total factor productivity from the ratio of input to output prices, rather than from changes in the relative quantities of factor inputs, which is the procedure followed by Ó Gráda in this volume.[54] Both methods have been reviewed by Mokyr whose revised calculations of total factor productivity in Britain during the industrial revolution provide a range of estimates which is too wide to be of much value.[55]

Compounding these problems of calculation, the concept of total

50 N. F. R. Crafts, *British economic growth during the industrial revolution*, Oxford, 1985, p. 78.
51 For a discussion of the concept see R. C. O. Matthews, C. H. Feinstein and J. C. Odling-Smee, *British economic growth, 1856–1973*, Oxford, 1982, pp. 198–213; and A. N. Link, *Technological change and productivity growth*, London, 1987, pp. 15–24.
52 R. E. Gallman, 'Changes in total US factor productivity growth in the nineteenth century', *Agricultural History*, XLVI, 1972, pp. 191–210; Crafts, *British economic growth*, pp. 83–4; C. Ó Gráda, 'Agricultural decline 1860–1914', pp. 175–97 in Floud and McCloskey, *The economic history of Britain*, II, 1981, p. 178; Turner, below, pp. 431–4.
53 Solar and Goossens, below, pp. 376–7.
54 D. N. McCloskey, 'The industrial revolution 1780–1860: a survey', pp. 103–27 in Floud and McCloskey, *The economic history of Britain*, I, 1981; G. Hueckel, 'Agriculture during industrialisation', pp. 182–203 in Floud and McCloskey, *Economic history of Britain*, I, p. 192; Ó Gráda, below, pp. 452–5.
55 Mokyr's results vary between 0.02 per cent and 0.42 per cent per annum depending on the assumptions used: J. Mokyr, 'Has the industrial revolution been crowded out? Some reflections on Crafts and Williamson', *Explorations in Economic History*, XXIV, 1987, pp. 293–391.

factor productivity is not without its critics. The measure involves a number of quite restrictive economic assumptions, including the perfect mobility of factors, perfect competition, and neutral technical progress which are unlikely to have held in many historical contexts.[56] The important point is that changes in individual factor productivities need to be interpreted in the light of changes in other factor productivities when assessing the efficiency of the agricultural sector as a whole.

II The sources of productivity growth

The classical economists did not regard increases in agricultural output as the consequence of productivity change. Ricardian theory, for example, associates a rise in aggregate output with falling output per unit area since, in the absence of technological change, extra output would be seen as the result of drawing more marginal land into agricultural use. Malthusian theory associates rising output with falling labour productivity since, again in the absence of technological change or capital investment, extra output would be seen as the result of increasing the input of labour into agricultural production.[57] Historians have not always made the distinction between a growth in output due to changes in productivity, and growth which can be accounted for in other ways, including increasing inputs. Many of the contributions to this volume shed light on the sources of productivity growth in European agriculture, but before reviewing them it is necessary to set the wider context of the ways in which total agricultural output may increase, for it may do so independently of any gain in productivity.

There are four main ways in which the agricultural output of a country or region may rise (aside from importing more food): through extension of the agricultural area; by increasing inputs, particularly of labour and/or capital; by greater farm and regional specialisation; and through a technologically-induced rise in productivity. These are not mutually exclusive, and in practice increasing agricultural output is often associated with all four operating together. Of these four, the first is by far the most straightforward and initially the solution to which resort is most immediately made.

---

56 Link, *Technological change*, pp. 11–13. See also the debate: S. Nicholas, 'Total factor productivity growth and the revision of post-1870 British economic history', *EcHR*, XXXV, 1982, pp. 83–98; M. Thomas, 'Accounting for growth, 1870–1940: Stephen Nicholas and total factor productivity measurements', *EcHR*, XXXVIII, 1985, pp. 569–75; and S. Nicholas, 'British economic performance and total factor productivity growth, 1870–1940', *EcHR*, 1985, XXXVIII, pp. 576–82.
57 Wrigley, 'The classical economists'.

Since very little land produces nothing at all, extending the agricultural area usually means increasing the intensity of land use. This is usually accompanied by a corresponding shift from pasture to arable, since crops are more productive of human food per unit area than are animals.[58] There are a multitude of examples of this strategy, whenever demands are placed upon the agricultural sector of an economy and relative prices favour arable over pastoral products. In England, for example, historical geographers have charted the reclamation of wood, marsh, and heath, which usually coincides with periods of population pressure.[59] Perhaps the most spectacular example is the repeated onslaught on the fenlands of eastern England during recurrent phases of mounting population pressure; in the Romano-British period, again during the twelfth and thirteenth centuries, and most spectacularly in the seventeenth century; although the conquest was only completed in the mid twentieth century. By dint of the expenditure of much capital and effort, an economy based on fishing, fowling, and pastoralism was eventually replaced by one in which high-yielding arable crops predominate.[60] This has proved an enduring change, but short-term changes are also evident as a response to immediate crises, such as the ploughing-up campaign of the Napoleonic War period.[61]

Extensions to the agricultural area may or may not affect productivity. At an aggregate level the usual expectation is that the extra land brought into agricultural use will be at the extensive margin of cultivation and of poorer quality, or inferior in location, than that already being farmed. If this was the case, and inputs remained constant, average output per unit area would fall, and, if labour inputs per unit area remained constant, labour productivity would also fall. But in the short term, where conversion of grassland to arable was involved, output per unit area might be higher than on established arable land, as cereal crops exploited stored-up reserves of nitrogen, although in the longer term – as Thornton's account of thirteenth-century productivity

---

58 I. G. Simmons, *The ecology of natural resources*, London, 1974, pp. 20–2 and 170–2; D. B. Grigg, *The dynamics of agricultural change*, London, 1982, pp. 68–73.
59 For example, H. C. Darby, 'The changing English landscape', *Geographical Journal*, CXVII, 1951, pp. 377–94.
60 H. C. Darby, *The changing fenland*, Cambridge, 1983.
61 M. Williams, 'The enclosure and reclamation of waste land in England and Wales in the eighteenth and nineteenth centuries', *Transactions of the Institute of British Geographers*, CI, 1970, pp. 58–69; but see the qualifications of S. Macdonald, 'Agricultural response to a changing market during the Napoleonic Wars', *EcHR*, XXXIII, 1980, pp. 59–71.

trends at Rimpton illustrates – yields would fall as the nitrogen is used up.[62] However, as the example of the English fenland shows, reclamation can change the physical quality of the land and consequently lead to an overall rise in land productivity. All else being equal, labour productivity in these circumstances would rise and fall with land productivity, but the returns to capital investment in reclamation are more uncertain.

In one sense, extending the agricultural area can be regarded as increasing the input of land as a factor of production. Output could also be raised by increasing other factors, singly or in combination. In the pre-industrial period the most important of these was labour. Output per unit area, be it of crops or animals and their products, could be increased substantially by putting more people to work on the land for more thorough ground preparation, manuring, weeding, the cultivation of fodder crops, and so on. However, increased labour inputs eventually reduce the marginal productivity of labour as the returns of food from each additional unit of labour start to fall. This phenomenon of diminishing returns also affects the other inputs into farming. Yields per unit of seed will start to fall once seeding rates exceed a certain level, output per unit area will gradually cease to rise as extra fertilisers or manure are added to the land, and, after a point, extra capital investment in the form, for example, of farm buildings or land drainage will no longer result in rising returns per unit of input.[63] The tendency for high labour inputs per unit area to result in high output per unit area but low output per unit labour has been vividly demonstrated for certain parts of England in both the middle ages and the early modern period and the phenomenon is common in the less-developed countries today.[64] On the other hand, as Thornton points out, while high labour inputs may have been agriculturally inefficient, they could have been economically efficient if cheap labour was being substituted for expensive capital inputs to the farming system.[65]

One way of both raising output and improving the efficiency of agriculture is through greater specialisation, which can occur on a

---

62 Shiel, below, pp. 62–3; Thornton, below, pp. 196–8.
63 Figure 2.1, below, p. 71.
64 B. M. S. Campbell, 'Agricultural progress in medieval England: some evidence from eastern Norfolk', *EcHR*, XXXVI, 1983, pp. 26–46; Thornton, below, pp. 208–9; P. Glennie, 'Continuity and change in Hertfordshire agriculture, 1550–1700: II – trends in crop yields and their determinants', *AHR*, XXXVI, 1988, pp. 145–61; C. Geertz, *Agricultural involution: the process of ecological change in Indonesia*, Berkeley, 1963.
65 Thornton, below, p. 210.

variety of scales ranging from the farm to the farming region. If each region concentrates its production on those commodities for which it has a natural advantage, and therefore abandons the production of those commodities for which its factor endowments are not particularly suited, overall output should rise even though farm yields per acre or output per animal do not change.[66] This presupposes a commercialised economy, whereby farmers specialise in producing certain products and exchange their surpluses on the market. In a subsistence economy, as R. H. Hilton has observed, 'everyone had to produce (on the whole) the same type of crop and tend the same sort of domesticated animals for meat, wool, and pulling power' regardless of whether they possessed any particular advantage for doing so.[67] By concentrating instead on what they produce best, given their specific endowment of land, labour, capital and enterprise, farmers are able to maximise the value of their output and thus increase the aggregate output of the entire agricultural system. Because proportionately more of a commodity is produced by those with a genuine advantage for doing so, and less by those who do not, *mean* yields of individual crop and livestock products will rise, although actual yields on individual farms may remain the same.

Much of the impetus behind this kind of development may come, not from within agriculture itself, but from the growth of large centralised markets. As the power of the market began to penetrate, economic considerations increasingly took precedence over ecological ones in determining what farmers produced in particular places. Since the transportation of goods to the market involved costs, the distance that they had to be transported determined the type of goods produced and the manner of their production. The mediating influence, as elaborated by J. H. von Thünen in his classic work, *The isolated state*, became economic rent.[68] Economic rent declines with distance from the market, resulting in a characteristic pattern of concentric land-use zones of decreasing intensity. Remoteness from major markets thus tended to be associated with low levels of economic rent, justifying

66 This describes the principle of absolute advantage, the more complicated case is comparative advantage, R. G. Lipsey, *An introduction to positive economics*, London, 1972, pp. 592–6.
67 R. H. Hilton, 'Medieval agrarian history', pp. 145–98 in *Victoria County History of Leicestershire*, II, London, 1954, p. 145.
68 J. H. von Thünen, *Der isolierte staat*, trans. by C. M. Wartenberg as *von Thünen's isolated state*, P. Hall, ed., Oxford, 1966; M. Chisholm, *Rural settlement and land-use: an essay on location*, London, 1962, pp. 20–32.

only relatively low levels of input, principally labour and capital, which thereby resulted in correspondingly low levels of agricultural output.

The depressing effect of low economic rent may have been a major reason for the low yield levels with which a number of medieval English landlords evidently acquiesced, just as the stimulating effect of high economic rent undoubtedly underpinned the highly intensive and productive husbandry which evolved in some other parts of the country.[69] Certainly, as described by Biddick, the management policy pursued by the Bishop of Winchester on his demesnes in southern England in the early thirteenth century is redolent of what von Thünen's theory would predict for an area of low economic rent. Arable crops were produced for predominantly local consumption by the bishop and his household using relatively extensive methods, while wool and dairy products – high in value relative to their bulk and thereby better able to withstand the costs of carriage to distant markets – were relied upon as the principal agricultural sources of cash. This suggests that a growth in the size and efficiency of markets and a reduction in transport costs were required before output would increase on this estate and in this part of the country.

In other regions the growth of the market does seem to have promoted output changes in the middle ages.[70] Indeed, G. Persson argues that in the more urbanised economies of thirteenth-century Tuscany and the Low Countries, greater specialisation was the principal means by which the growing towns and cities were fed. In fact, he believes that the associated gain in efficiency was such that labour productivity within agriculture also rose. Continuing changes in the transport and marketing infrastructure prompted continuing changes in economic rent and consequently in the spatial patterns of agricultural production. The phenomenal growth of London is considered by F. J. Fisher and E. A. Wrigley to have provided the driving force behind the crystallisation of specialist farming regions, growing sophistication of

69 Campbell, 'Agricultural progress'; *idem*, 'Ecology versus economics in late thirteenth- and early fourteenth-century English agriculture', in D. Sweeney, ed., *People of the plough: land and labour in medieval Europe*, State College, Pa., forthcoming.
70 Campbell, 'Ecology versus economics'; D. Keene, 'Medieval London and its region', *The London Journal*, XIV, 1989, pp. 99–111. Land-use and agriculture in the hinterland of London in the late thirteenth and early fourteenth centuries are currently the subject of a Leverhulme funded research project – 'Feeding the city, the food supplies of medieval London' – at the Centre for Metropolitan History, University of London.

markets, and the concomitant rise in agricultural output of which historians have found evidence.[71] Grantham shows the Paris food market to have exercised a decisive influence upon the type and intensity of husbandry in much of northern France during the late eighteenth and nineteenth centuries.[72] Such changes were particularly rapid in Britain during the nineteenth century, as a response to the development of the railway network, and are witnessed by the development of market gardening and the changing geography of the production of dairy products.[73]

The final process by which output can be expanded is through technological change. Agricultural historians have used the concept of technological change in rather a narrow sense, namely, in terms of specific physical innovations, such as new crops, new breeds of livestock, new implements and new machines. But in a wider sense technological change also includes intangible innovations, such as changes in the quality of inputs, improvements in knowledge, and new forms of organisation. This broader definition is often equated with changes in total factor productivity, so that technological change is considered to have taken place when more output results from a given combination of inputs, or when the same output results from a reduction in at least one input with no increase in the use of other inputs.[74]

In seeking to identify the impact of physical innovations it is most useful, at least initially, to relate them to the productivity of single factors. For example, Grantham demonstrates that in isolating the impact of specific technological developments it is helpful to study a single homogeneous commodity (in his case, wheat in northern France).[75] When other inputs are constant, changes in land productivity are the result of changes in biological and chemical technology. Some

71 F. J. Fisher, 'The development of the London food market, 1540–1640', *Economic History Review*, V, 1935, pp. 46–64, reprinted as pp. 135–51 in E. M. Carus-Wilson, ed., *Essays in Economic History*, I, London, 1954; E. A. Wrigley, 'A simple model of London's importance in changing English society and economy, 1650–1750', *Past and Present*, XXXVII, 1967, pp. 44–70; Langton and Hoppe, *Town and country*; A. Kussmaul, 'Agrarian change in seventeenth-century England: the economic historian as paleontologist', *JEH*, XLV, 1985, pp. 1–30; J. C. Chartres, 'The marketing of agricultural produce', pp. 406–502 in Thirsk, *The agrarian history of England and Wales*, Vii, *1640–1750: agrarian change*, 1985.
72 Grantham, below, p. 346.
73 M. Overton, 'Agriculture', pp. 34–53 in J. Langton and R. Morris, eds., *An atlas of industrializing Britain 1780–1914*, London, 1986.
74 C. Ritson, *Agricultural economics: principles and policy*, London, 1980, p. 95; Link, *Technological change*, p. 4.
75 Grantham, below, pp. 340–63.

agricultural historians have been accused of failing to understand the true nature of soil fertility and its maintenance, but the chapter by Shiel provides a long-term perspective on biological constraints to crop yields in north-western Europe.[76] The crucial problem was in maintaining adequate supplies of soil nitrogen, and although some technological progress was possible in the middle ages (by cultivating more pulses, for example, and making more effective use of manure and other fertilising agents), the real technological breakthrough came with rotations based on the principles of the Norfolk four-course, the key to whose success lay in the nitrogen-fixing properties of clover and other legumes.[77] Overton illustrates the stages in the adoption of this new technology for Norfolk and Suffolk from the sixteenth to the mid nineteenth century.[78] There may well have been other technological changes responsible for raising yields. Improvements in the tools and implements of husbandry facilitated cultivation of the new crops in northern France and, as Grantham shows, were a principal source of the rising wheat yields obtained during the nineteenth century.[79] Additionally, Allen suggests that the development of better strains of seed by a process of selection could have been responsible for a rise in early modern grain yields in Oxfordshire.[80] Improved breeds of animal similarly contributed to the productivity of the pastoral sector at this time.[81]

The determinants of labour productivity are more complicated and are in part a function of land productivity since,

$$\frac{Q}{L} = \frac{Q}{T} \cdot \frac{T}{L}$$

where Q is output, T is land and L is labour. Thus, if yield per acre rises, and the number of labourers per acre remains constant, labour

---

76 F. J. Banks, 'Monastic agriculture: a farmer's view, with special reference to Byland Abbey', *Ryedale Historian*, XV, 1990–91, pp. 16–20; Shiel, below, pp. 51–77.

77 G. P. H. Chorley, 'The agricultural revolution in northern Europe, 1750–1880: nitrogen, legumes and crop productivity', *EcHR*, XXXIV, 1981, pp. 71–93.

78 Overton, below, pp. 284–322.

79 G. Marshall, 'The "Rotheram" plough', *Tools and Tillage*, III, 1978, pp. 149–67; Grantham, below, pp. 353–7.

80 Allen, below, pp. 248–9.

81 For example, N. Russell, *Like engend'ring like: heredity and animal breeding in early modern England*, Cambridge, 1986; J. R. Walton, 'The diffusion of the improved shorthorn breed of cattle in Britain during the eighteenth and nineteenth centuries', *Transactions of the Institute of British Geographers*, new series, IX, 1984, pp. 22–36; A. K. Copus, 'Changing markets and the development of sheep breeds in southern England, 1750–1900', *AHR*, XXXVII, 1989, pp. 36–51.

productivity will increase. Clark, Allen and Grantham explore this relationship in their chapters, pointing out that there are two components in the labour required in farming operations: one that is constant per acre and independent of yield (e.g. ploughing), and another that varies as yield per acre varies (e.g. binding, stacking and threshing).[82] Clark argues that the rise in labour productivity in England before the nineteenth century was not due to a rise in yields per acre, but, in the absence of conspicuous technological innovation, to increased work intensity: workers worked harder – a conclusion that Solar and Goossens reach for Belgian workers in comparison with those in Ireland in the nineteenth century.[83] On the other hand, Grantham demonstrates that the major rise in French labour productivity in the two centuries after 1750 came about from increased mechanisation, a trend which was even more pronounced across the Atlantic in the United States.[84]

Gains in labour productivity arising from the introduction of machinery in the nineteenth century have been documented for England as well as for France, but there is much less certainty about the sources of improvements in labour productivity for the pre-industrial period, improvements which were to have profound consequences for the process of economic growth.[85] Substitution of animal for human labour and effort was one potential source. Grantham demonstrates the significant gain in labour productivity which accrued when northern French farmers switched from ox-ploughing to horse-ploughing, and Solar and Goossens suggest that, in the 1840s, the superior strength of Flemish horses, coupled with better ratios of horses to both land and labour, was one factor behind the higher labour productivity of Belgium when compared with Ireland.[86] Likewise, Wrigley shows that *pro rata*, English farmers had two-thirds more animal power at their disposal than their French counterparts at the turn of the nineteenth century, a factor which may go some way towards explaining the superior labour productivity of the former.[87] A comparative study of Norfolk agriculture from the thirteenth to the nineteenth centuries shows that the number

82 Clark, below, pp. 222–9; Grantham, below, pp. 350–63; Allen, below, p. 249; Glennie, below, pp. 259–71.
83 Clark, 'Productivity growth without technical change'; *idem*, below, pp. 231–5; Wrigley, below, pp. 336–9; Solar and Goossens, below, pp. 380–2.
84 Grantham, below, pp. 353–63.
85 See note 176 below.
86 Grantham, below, pp. 348–9; Solar and Goossens, below, pp. 379–80.
87 Wrigley, below, p. 329.

of beasts of traction per acre under arable crops rose by three-quarters between the middle ages and the late sixteenth century, coinciding with the period of greatest productivity increase according to Clark.[88]

Wrigley also suggests a number of other factors which may have affected labour productivity, including the under-employment of labour on family farms which would depress labour productivity – a suggestion which finds support in a recent study of the factors influencing farm productivity.[89] This would also tie in with Allen's claim that England's superior labour productivity at the end of the eighteenth century, when compared with other countries, derived from her larger farms and more rational farm layout which allowed greater efficiency in the deployment of labour.[90] Yet the issue is not clear-cut. Solar and Goossens argue that family farms allowed fuller and more effective use of family labour in early-nineteenth-century Belgium, and on Turner and Ó Gráda's figures the smaller farms of late-nineteenth- and early-twentieth-century Ireland (many increasingly run as family enterprises) fared better than their larger counterparts in England. Clearly, more detailed research is needed on exactly how hard farm workers did work, and on why rates of work varied over time and between farms, regions, and countries.

While it is convenient to distinguish those technological changes which influenced the productivity of labour from those whose primary influence was on land productivity, there are considerable interactions between the two. When weighing up the net gain of substituting animal for human labour, for example, account needs to be taken of the extra drudgery involved in cultivating the fodder crops, and especially oats, required by working horses. As E. Boserup has pointed out, the substitution of produced for natural fodder was not to be undertaken lightly for it invariably entailed a major increase in the expenditure of labour.[91] On the other hand, one of the merits of the Norfolk four-course was that the new fodder crops in the rotation required labour at seasons of the year when labour demand had previously been slack,

88 M. Overton and B. M. S. Campbell, 'Five centuries of farming: agricultural change in medieval and early modern Norfolk, *c.*1250–*c.*1750', unpublished paper presented to the Annual Conference of the Economic History Society, Liverpool, 1990.

89 Wrigley, below, pp. 335–6; National Economic Development Office, *Farm productivity: a report by the Agriculture EDC on factors affecting productivity at the farm level*, London, 1973.

90 Allen, below, pp. 249–53.

91 E. Boserup, *The conditions of agricultural growth: the economics of agrarian change under population pressure*, London, 1965, pp. 35–9.

and hence this might actually have improved labour productivity measured in terms of output per worker per year.[92]

It is understandable that historians have concentrated on conspicuous technological innovation, such as new crops or new machines, because these are clearly evident in the historical record. But the broader conception of technological change, encompassing improvements in knowledge and organisation, could result in increased output for a given level of inputs without obvious changes to farm enterprises. Such changes in farming skills and farm management undoubtedly took place but are extremely difficult to pinpoint. Thornton identifies several managerial changes on the demesne at Rimpton during the thirteenth and fourteenth centuries which may have led initially to higher and then to lower yields per unit area. The substitution of waged labour for customary labour services during this period is also likely to have exercised an influence upon the motivation and efficiency of the labour force and may help to account for the differing outputs obtained from seemingly similar labour inputs on the demesnes of Rimpton (which relied mainly on customary labour) and Martham (largely dependent upon waged labour) as documented by Thornton and Campbell. In this context, modern studies have found the practical and technical ability of the farmer, together with good labour management, to be very closely related to overall farm productivity.[93]

Changes in farming skills and management are equally difficult to pinpoint in later centuries. The supply of farming books increases from the mid seventeenth century but while some of these advocated best-practice techniques, others were quite bizarre in their recommendations.[94] One interesting change in the character of this material has been identified by K. Tribe. He points out that seventeenth-century literature was primarily concerned with good husbandry, whereas by the mid eighteenth century the emphasis had shifted to good management and an emphasis on accounting and profit.[95] The provision

---

92 C. P. Timmer, 'The turnip, the new husbandry, and the English agricultural revolution', *Quarterly Journal of Economics*, LXXXIII, 1969, pp. 375–95.

93 National Economic Development Office, *Farm productivity*.

94 For example, W. Coles, *Adam in Eden, or nature's paradise*, London, 1657, p. 117.

95 K. Tribe, *Land, labour and economic discourse*, London, 1978, pp. 53–79; R. Sullivan, 'Measurement of English farming technological change, 1523–1900', *Explorations in Economic History*, XXI, 1984, pp. 274–5. Agricultural treatises were also a feature of the middle ages when one of their main objects was to advise lords on how to avoid being defrauded by their officials: D. Oschinsky, *Walter of Henley and other treatises on estate management and accounting*, Oxford, 1971.

of formal agricultural education in England did not occur until the nineteenth century, but that is not to say that levels of skill and management were not improving. By the nineteenth century, English farmers at least had a growing range of literature advising them how to farm more profitably.[96]

Modern studies also find a positive relationship between productivity (measured as the ratio of the value of output to inputs) and farm size. The studies by Allen and Overton in this volume find no significant relationship between farm size and yields per acre in early modern England, although Allen finds that between 1600 and 1800 half of the growth in output per worker was due to the growth in farm size.[97] Larger farms were more efficient in their use of labour, and small family farms were prone, as they are today, to retain labour which is surplus to the requirements of economically efficient production.[98] This is not, however, to cost welfare benefits, which, as O'Brien and Toniolo's study of the Mezzogiorno of southern Italy shows, might be considerable when opportunities for off-the-farm employment were limited.[99]

Changes in management are often conditional on changes in the institutional environment in which farmers operate. Access to cheap, servile labour, for instance, was contingent upon the persistence of serfdom as an institution. Differences between forced and waged labour affected both supervision costs and the motivation of the workforce, in the same way that the security or otherwise of tenures evidently determined the readiness or otherwise of farmers to make capital improvements to their property. In the final analysis, Solar and Goossens consider that nineteenth-century Belgian farmers were more efficient than their Irish counterparts because they enjoyed greater security of tenure and paid a lower proportion of income in rent. Yet they recognise that to have brought the situation in Ireland more closely into line with that prevailing in Belgium 'would have required a complete

---

96 H. S. A. Fox, 'Local farmers' associations and the circulation of agricultural information in nineteenth-century England', pp. 43–63 in *idem* and R. A. Butlin, eds., *Change in the countryside: essays on rural England, 1500–1900*, Institute of British Geographers Special Publication, X, London, 1979; J. D. Sykes, 'Agriculture and science', pp. 260–72 in G. E. Mingay, ed., *The Victorian countryside*, I, London, 1981, pp. 267–70; K. Hudson, *Patriotism with profit: British agricultural societies in the eighteenth and nineteenth centuries*, London, 1972, pp. 113–29; N. Goddard, 'Agricultural literature and societies', pp. 361–83 in Mingay, *The agrarian history of England and Wales*, VI, *1750–1850*, 1989.
97 Allen, 'The growth of labor productivity'; *idem*, below, pp. 249–50.
98 Wrigley, below, pp. 335–6.
99 O'Brien and Toniolo, below, pp. 402–3.

overhaul of the political and social structures within which Irish agriculture had developed'.[100] In this context institutional factors of a primarily tenurial nature acted as a constraint upon the productivity of both land and labour. Institutional change was thus a potentially important source of productivity growth and a number of contributions to this volume allude to its significance.[101] Factors such as the commutation of labour services; break-up and leasing out of demesnes; engrossment or subdivision of holdings; security or otherwise of tenures; tenant right; level of rent; enclosure of commonfields and their pastures; and dissolution of common rights, all exercised a powerful and much debated influence upon the course of agricultural development. But as far as the mechanisms described here for raising productivity are concerned, that influence was indirect rather than direct.[102] This is not to deny the crucial significance of changing property rights or changes in the relations of production; on the contrary, they deserve a separate volume.[103]

III Trends in agricultural productivity: a long-term perspective

The archaeological record is opaque as far as agricultural productivity is concerned and consequently the trends in productivity during the long centuries prior to the advent of written records may be but dimly perceived. Changes in the efficiency with which certain basic farming tasks were undertaken may be inferred from changes in husbandry tools, and changes in the intensity and variety of farming systems may be inferred from changing crop and plant assemblages. Such developments imply corresponding changes in the productivity of land and labour. Thus, during the Roman period there is evidence that agriculture in Britain became more differentiated both in type and intensity.[104] At the same time, faunal remains imply improvements in livestock productivity via selective breeding and better management of pastoral resources.[105] Output per unit of land was consequently rising,

---

100 Solar and Goossens, below, pp. 381–3.
101 For example, Thornton, Biddick, Allen, Solar and Goossens.
102 See Grigg, *The dynamics of agricultural change*, p. 165.
103 This volume is primarily concerned with the forces rather than the relations of production.
104 Jones, below, pp. 91–3.
105 S. Bökönyi, 'The development of stockbreeding and herding in medieval Europe' in D. Sweeney, ed., *People of the plough: land and labour in medieval Europe*, State College, Pa., forthcoming.

and this, when taken in conjunction with an expansion in the agricultural area, provided the basis for a demographic expansion which took the population of England to a maximum in the late third century AD, which was not exceeded until the late thirteenth century.[106] At the same time, the foundation and growth of towns imply a relative expansion in the non-agricultural population and hence an increase in the productivity of labour within agriculture.

Nevertheless, as Shiel demonstrates, with manure-dependent technology the supply of soil nitrogen set natural ecological limits to the productivity of the land, and attempts to offset dwindling nitrogen supplies through the adoption of more labour-intensive methods would have tended to drive down the marginal productivity of labour.[107] M. Jones, in fact, believes that there is evidence of a progressive loss of soil nitrogen throughout the Roman period and that ecological stress resulted on the lighter and poorer soils.[108] Nutrients were drained away from the latter to the benefit of the richer and more intensively cultivated soils of the valley bottoms via the movement of grazing stock and transfer of produce. Thus it was at the extensive rather than the intensive margin of cultivation that the problems of maintaining crop yields were probably most pronounced, a hypothesis which is echoed in the contrasting trajectories of crop yields on some fourteenth-century manors.[109]

The level and sustainability of crop yields have long been central concerns of medieval agricultural historians. The twelfth and thirteenth centuries, like the second and third centuries, witnessed a greater elaboration and differentiation of farming systems, population growth, and an increase in the size and number of towns, and initially, at least, these developments were sustained by increases in the productivity of both land and labour.[110] The question, however, is how long both productivities were able to rise together. Persson believes that the more urbanised and developed regions of Europe – Tuscany and the 'Low

106 Jones, below, pp. 90–1; R. M. Smith, 'Demographic developments in rural England 1300–1348: a survey', pp. 25–77 in B. M. S. Campbell, ed., *Before the Black Death: studies in the 'crisis' of the early fourteenth century*, Manchester, 1991.
107 Shiel, below, pp. 51–77.
108 Jones, below, p. 90.
109 Campbell, below, pp. 174–8.
110 K. G. Persson, *Pre-industrial economic growth, social organization and technological progress in Europe*, Oxford, 1988, pp. 24–32 and 70–6; B. M. S. Campbell, 'People and land in the middle ages, 1066–1500', pp. 69–121 in R. A. Dodgshon and R. A. Butlin, eds., *An historical geography of England and Wales*, London, 2nd edn., 1990.

Countries' – experienced a genuine if modest measure of economic growth with concomitant gains in the productivity of both land and labour during the twelfth and thirteenth centuries, although these developments may have owed more to the fact that labourers worked harder and for longer hours than to any real rise in their efficiency.[111] On the other hand, increased specialisation and changes in crop and livestock mixes must have made some contribution to productivity.[112] More draught animals were employed and in the more developed areas, and, especially on peasant holdings, the horse began to be substituted for the ox.[113] Wrigley shows that these developments were to be taken a great deal further in later centuries, when they may have made a significant contribution to the post-medieval rise in labour productivity, but they were not without their benefits for the thirteenth-century economy.[114]

With time, however, it only became possible to feed the growing population by intensifying existing methods of production, and output per worker in agriculture inevitably suffered. Declining labour productivity is graphically documented by Thornton at Rimpton during the thirteenth century and is strongly implied by Campbell for Norfolk over the period 1250–1349.[115] In both cases it was only through increasingly lavish labour inputs that established levels of output per unit area were maintained or even improved. Clark estimates that *c.*1300 output per worker was only a quarter what it was to become by 1850, with, he believes, much of the improvement coming before 1600.[116] He stresses the under-employment and inefficiency of agricultural labour *c.*1300 – a time of acute population pressure – and the low living standards which must inevitably have accompanied this (of which there is strong independent evidence).[117] The problem, in part, was the retention of excess labour within agriculture, a problem shared by the

111 Persson, below, pp. 139–40.
112 Campbell, below, pp. 153–74; *idem*, 'Towards an agricultural geography of medieval England', *AHR*, XXXVI, 1988, pp. 24–39; *idem* and J. P. Power, 'Mapping the agricultural geography of medieval England', *Journal of Historical Geography*, XV, 1989, pp. 24–39; Persson, *Pre-industrial economic growth*, p. 66.
113 J. L. Langdon, *Horses, oxen and technological innovation: the use of draught animals in English farming from 1066–1500*, Cambridge, 1986.
114 Wrigley, below, pp. 325–9.
115 Thornton, below, pp. 204–7; Campbell, below, pp. 181–2; see also *idem*, 'Agricultural progress', pp. 38–41.
116 Clark, below, pp. 211–35.
117 E. Miller and J. Hatcher, *Medieval England: rural society and economic change 1086–1348*, London, 1978, pp. 240–51.

Mezzogiorno of southern Italy some six centuries later. O'Brien and
Toniolo attribute the latter to the failure of Italy's industrial and urban
economy to develop rapidly enough to pull under-employed labour
from the countryside and the same deficiency may have been true of
the English economy c.1300.[118] But in the middle ages there were
additional institutional constraints deriving from the prevalence of
feudal socio-property relations which trapped labour on the land and
handicapped the efficiency of its deployment.[119]

Important as the productivity of labour is as an issue (and much
as remains to be learnt about it), historians of the middle ages have
concentrated principally on the productivity of land. Attention has
focused on the absolute level of yield and its trend; the former because
it is generally believed to have been universally low, the latter because,
like labour productivity, it is believed, in England, to have been driven
down rather than up by population pressure.[120] In both cases it is easy,
given Shiel's exposition of the crucial importance of the nitrogen cycle,
to see why.[121] The optimal ratio between the grain and the non-grain
acreage which his model suggests was frequently exceeded and with
low levels of agricultural technology the progressive erosion of mineral
nitrogen was, seemingly, unavoidable.[122] Yet the situation was not entirely
hopeless and steps could be taken to conserve and even enhance
nitrogen supplies. These included the recycling of all available crop
wastes and manure; the reduction of soil acidity through applications of marl and lime; the importation of nitrogen in the form of
manure and crop residues from elsewhere; more effective rotations
which incorporated nitrogen-fixing crops, notably legumes; and fuller
exploitation of the nitrogen reserves stored in permanent grassland.
Most of these measures, it has been shown, were known to medieval
cultivators, but their level of application was contingent on supplies of

118 O'Brien and Toniolo, below, p. 409.
119 See the discussion in R. Brenner, 'Agrarian class structure and economic
development in pre-industrial Europe', *Past and Present*, LXX, 1976, pp. 30–75;
reprinted as pp. 10–63 in Aston and Philpin, *The Brenner debate*, 1985, pp. 31–6.
120 Campbell, below, pp. 146–8.
121 Shiel, below, pp. 58–70.
122 On the difficulty of maintaining an ecological balance within traditional
commonfield agriculture, see W. S. Cooter, 'Ecological dimensions of medieval
agrarian systems', *Agricultural History*, CII, 1978, pp. 458–77; R. S. Loomis,
'Ecological dimensions of medieval agrarian systems: an ecologist responds',
Agricultural History, CII, 1978, pp. 484–7; H. S. A. Fox, 'Some ecological dimensions
of medieval field systems', pp. 119–58 in K. Biddick, ed., *Archaeological approaches
to medieval Europe*, Kalamazoo, 1984.

labour and capital, and on environmental and economic circumstances.[123] It is for these reasons that continental historians have equated
rising population levels with rising yield levels, since with a larger labour
supply it was possible to employ the kind of labour-intensive methods
which enhanced the cycling of nitrogen within the soil.[124]

It is this issue which Campbell's study of Norfolk and Thornton's
study of Rimpton address directly. Although undertaken at different
scales, for different parts of the country operating different husbandry
systems, these two studies nonetheless yield remarkably similar and
consistent findings which together constitute a major revision to the
soil-exhaustion model advocated by M. M. Postan and J. Z. Titow.[125] In
neither case is there evidence of a demographically induced ecological
check to output per acre. On the contrary, the check to productivity
came not in the thirteenth century, when population and prices were
both rising, but in the fourteenth century when falling prices and
problems of labour supply necessitated a cut-back in labour inputs.
Indeed, the corresponding cut-back in yields was so great that, measured
by arable output alone, there was little if any compensatory gain in
labour productivity.[126] This is not to suggest that instances of ecological
distress never happened, for, on the contrary, the *Inquisitiones Nonarum*
of 1342 provide abundant evidence that they did.[127] But such distress
was far from universal and its source may have lain elsewhere than with
the shortcomings of agricultural technology *per se.*[128]

Judged by the weighted aggregate cereal yield, productivity in

123 R. A. L. Smith, *Canterbury Cathedral Priory*, Cambridge, 1943, pp. 128–45; Brandon,
'Demesne arable farming'; Campbell, 'Agricultural progress'; B. H. Slicher van
Bath, 'The rise of intensive husbandry in the Low Countries', pp. 130–53 in J. S.
Bromley and E. H. Kossmann, eds., *Britain and the Netherlands: papers delivered to
the Oxford–Netherlands historical conference 1959*, London, 1960.
124 Campbell, below, pp. 144–6.
125 Postan, 'Medieval agrarian society', pp. 556–9; Titow, *Winchester yields*; *idem*, *English
rural society 1200–1350*, London, 1969, pp. 93–6; Hybel, *Crisis or change*, pp. 230–
6.
126 Campbell, below, pp. 173–4; Thornton, below, pp. 188–95.
127 A. R. H. Baker, 'Evidence in the *Nonarum Inquisitiones* of contracting arable lands
in England during the early fourteenth century', *EcHR*, XIX, 1966, pp. 518–32,
reprinted as pp. 85–102 in *idem*, J. D. Hamshere and J. Langton, eds., *Geographical
interpretations of historical sources: readings in historical geography*, Newton Abbot, 1970.
The middle ages would appear to parallel, in part, the experience of Roman
Britain, where Jones detects signs of increasing differentiation between areas of
intensive and less-intensive agriculture, with evidence of ecological stress being
largely confined to the latter. It would be interesting to see the application to the
middle ages of the kinds of archaeological techniques for the investigation of
ecological stress which he describes: Jones, below, pp. 90–3.
128 Campbell, 'Ecology versus economics'.

Norfolk rose progressively from the 1260s to a peak in the second quarter of the fourteenth century and fell back thereafter.[129] At Rimpton, where Thornton has employed the same productivity measure but where the yield data span the greater part of the thirteenth century, the peak and decline in productivity both came somewhat earlier. Here, it was the middle decades of the thirteenth century which fared best, although yields continued to hold up well down to the 1330s, after which a decided decline in productivity and contraction in cultivation both set in.

It is the failure of the remarkable yields of the mid thirteenth century to be sustained down to the end of the century, taken in conjunction with a general contraction in the scale of demesne cultivation, which led Postan and Titow to claim that soils were becoming exhausted on the Winchester manors. Yet, in a significant revision to this view, Thornton argues that it is the high yields of the mid thirteenth century that require explanation, not their subsequent decline. In the case of Rimpton he proposes that the former are most plausibly explained by the conjunction of a spell of exceptionally favourable weather conditions – representing, perhaps, the end of the climatic optimum of the early middle ages – with the release of substantial reserves of soil nitrogen through extensive conversion of grassland to arable.[130] It now remains to be seen whether this explanation will fit any of the other Winchester manors (unfortunately, there are no others with accounts spanning virtually the whole of the thirteenth century). Certainly, the role of climatic fluctuations cannot be discounted. Glennie and Overton both draw attention to the effect of variations in the weather upon the trend of sixteenth- and seventeenth-century crop yields and a similar effect would appear to be reflected in the broadly similar fluctuations in yield identified on widely separate groups of medieval estates, with the 1350s and early 1400s, for instance, standing out as periods of particularly unfavourable harvests.[131]

A serious deficiency of these measures of land productivity, however, is their failure to take any account of livestock, which remain very much the Cinderella in the story of pre-industrial productivity trends, both medieval and early modern. Nevertheless, livestock are

129 Above, p. 10, for a description of this index.
130 Thornton, below, pp. 194–5.
131 Glennie, below, pp. 272–3; Overton, below, pp. 286–7; Campbell, below, p. 163; M. Overton, 'Weather and agricultural change in England, 1660–1739', *Agricultural History*, LXIII, 1989, pp. 77–88; H. H. Lamb, *Climate, history and the modern world*, London, 1982.

not entirely forgotten and several authors cast interesting light on this most neglected aspect of agricultural production. Clark, for instance, emphasises the subordinate role of livestock within agricultural production *c.*1300, at which time he estimates that 75 per cent of net output and no less than 93 per cent of calories produced per acre in the lowland counties of southern and eastern England came from grain.[132] This stemmed partly from low stocking densities and was compounded by low carcass weights and wool and milk yields as measured by the standards attained by the mid nineteenth century. The weights and breeds of medieval livestock remain subjects about which far too little is known – although much might be learnt from the faunal remains analysed by archaeologists – but Clark bravely hazards a set of estimates based on a range of sources and assumptions.[133] With wool and milk yields he is on surer ground, since, as Biddick demonstrates, these are matters on which manorial accounts provide much information.[134] The low stocking densities of the early fourteenth century are confirmed by Campbell's estimates of trends in the cereal acreage and livestock numbers within the demesne sector. On his figures, stocking densities virtually doubled between the late thirteenth and the early fifteenth centuries.[135] At the earlier date, when the population was approaching its medieval maximum, relative prices ensured that grain was by far the more profitable proposition but, as Biddick demonstrates, the rights embodied by feudal kingship and lordship may have operated to depress stocking densities further.[136] It is certainly widely assumed that institutional factors kept stocking densities on peasant holdings below those of demesnes, which is the very inverse of the relationship between farm size and stocking density encountered by Allen in the seventeenth century.[137]

This deficiency of livestock is considered by Postan to have been one of the central weaknesses of the medieval agrarian economy, since with too few livestock there would have been insufficient manure to

---

132 Clark, below, pp. 230–4.
133 A. Grant, 'Animal resources', pp. 149–87 in *idem* and G. Astill, eds., *The countryside of medieval England*, Oxford, 1988; P. L. Armitage, 'A preliminary description of British cattle from the late tweflth to the early sixteenth century', *Ark*, VII, 1980, pp. 405–13.
134 Biddick, below, pp. 115–18.
135 Campbell, below, pp. 153–9.
136 Biddick, below, pp. 94–104; Brenner, 'Agrarian class structure', p. 33.
137 Postan, 'Medieval agrarian society', pp. 554–6 and 602; *idem*, 'Village livestock in the thirteenth century', *EcHR*, XV, 1962, pp. 219–49, reprinted as pp. 214–48 in *idem*, *Essays on medieval agriculture and general problems of the medieval economy*, Cambridge, 1973; Allen, below, pp. 252–4.

maintain the fertility of the soil. Yet, as Biddick, Campbell, and Thornton show, the problem as far as crop yields was concerned was less the shortage of livestock than their inadequate integration with arable husbandry for it was upon this that effective cycling of soil nitrogen depended. One of the most striking features of the Winchester estate at the beginning of the thirteenth century was the tendency for pastoral and arable husbandry to be conducted as two separate enterprises with only limited linkages between them. Hence Biddick's failure to find any positive correlation between stocking densities and yields.[138] Campbell, too, finds a similar lack of correlation in Norfolk, where yields were significantly higher and stocking densities significantly lower than those on the Winchester estate.[139] In this instance it was the evolution of intensive, integrated mixed-farming systems which enabled such relatively favourable yields to be obtained in conjunction with such low stocking densities. Indeed, the greater elaboration and wider diffusion of such systems constitutes a major chapter in the subsequent story of manure-dependent technologies, of which the diffusion of the Norfolk four-course rotation – a mixed farming system *par excellence* – constitutes the climax.[140]

At Rimpton, as in the country at large, stocking densities were rising from the second half of the fourteenth century, and this trend appears to have continued with little interruption throughout the fifteenth and sixteenth centuries. In Norfolk, for instance, a county consistently in the forefront of the development of mixed-farming systems, a comparison of medieval and early modern stocking densities indicates a virtual doubling between *c.*1300 and 1660.[141] This may have been one source of the rising labour productivity which Clark attributes to this period, for he calculates that output per worker in pastoral husbandry was significantly above that in arable husbandry and, as Wrigley points out, any improvement in the ratio of working animals to labour would further have enhanced the productivity of the latter.[142]

While manorial accounts are capable of yielding fairly precise measures of the productivity of labour within the demesne sector, equivalent evidence for the early modern period is meagre in the extreme and it is not until the mid nineteenth century that some regional

138 Biddick, below, p. 115.
139 Campbell, below, pp. 172–3; also *idem*, 'Agricultural progress', pp. 29–31.
140 By 1850 Clark reckons that the pastoral sector accounted for 50 per cent of net output in the lowland counties of southern and eastern England: below, p. 230.
141 Overton and Campbell, 'Five centuries of farming'.
142 Clark, below, pp. 230–1; Wrigley, below, pp. 337–9.

estimates become available.[143] This is particularly unfortunate given the significance attached to the transformation of labour productivity between the middle ages and the nineteenth century.[144] While it is reasonably clear that labour productivity did increase between the two periods – possibly increasing by a factor of four in England – the timing of the change is uncertain. On the basis of estimates of the size of the agricultural population, Wrigley considers it is a 'virtual certainty' that two-thirds of the English labour force was engaged in agricultural production at the start of the seventeenth century and one-third by *c.*1800.[145] He reviews a number of mechanisms which could have been responsible for the rise in labour productivity which made this reduction in the proportion engaged in agriculture possible – including regional specialisation, a reduction in under-employment, and better nutrition – but in the end he plumps for an increase in energy inputs from draught animals as the most likely explanation. This hypothesis finds qualified support in evidence of a near tripling of the density of beasts of traction per cultivated acre of grain, the qualification being that the increase took place between the middle ages and the early modern period, rather than between the early modern and the nineteenth century, when the density changed little.[146] In fact, the earlier chronology agrees better with Clark's estimate of the timing of the labour productivity rise. On the evidence of harvest wage rates, he agrees that only a third of England's labour-force was employed in agriculture *c.*1800, but estimates that that proportion had already been reduced to 40–49 per cent by *c.*1570.[147]

Changes in labour productivity can in part be a reflection of changes in land productivity, but if anything yields fell during the later middle ages and hence it is to an increase in work intensity that Clark attributes the initial rise in labour productivity. This may have been encouraged by the commutation of labour services (i.e. the substitution of waged labour for customary labour) and a lessening in the burden of feudal rent, so that tenants were able to enjoy more of the fruits

---

143 P. A. David, 'Labour productivity in English agriculture, 1850–1914: some quantitative evidence on regional differences', *EcHR*, XXIII, 1970, pp. 504–14; but see E. H. Hunt, 'Quantitative and other evidence on labour productivity in agriculture, 1850–1914', *EcHR*, XXIII, 1970, pp. 515–19.

144 Above, pp. 4–6; Clark, below, pp. 211–35; Wrigley, below, pp. 335–9; Crafts, 'The new economic history', p. 29.

145 Wrigley, below, p. 335.

146 Overton and Campbell, 'Five centuries of farming'; see also Table 11.9, below, pp. 308, for statistics of horses in Norfolk and Suffolk.

147 Clark, below, pp. 228–9.

of their own efforts.[148] Certainly, if the decline of feudalism and concomitant decay of serfdom had any direct productivity benefits for agriculture it is, perhaps, in the productivity of labour that they should be sought.[149] In England the same period witnessed the break-up of demesnes and engrossing of peasant holdings, creating a smaller number of larger holdings and establishing a more favourable ratio of labour to land.[150] This would tie in with Allen's observation, based on a reworking of evidence from Arthur Young, that a close positive relationship existed between farm size and labour productivity: i.e. large farms were more efficient in their use of labour.[151] At the same time, a relative expansion in industrial and other forms of non-agricultural employment would have helped to absorb some of the surplus labour shaken out of agriculture. Nevertheless, fascinating as these speculations are, they are really no more than educated guesses. Clearly there is a crying need for studies of work practices on individual farms during the later middle ages and early modern periods. Such work would be tedious, but sufficient farm accounts exist to enable a start to be made.

With trends in output per unit of land we are on firmer, but still not solid, ground. A few farm accounts record yields per acre directly, but they form an insufficient basis for generalisation. Geographically far more comprehensive are the hundreds of thousands of inventories drawn up for the various ecclesiastical courts between the mid sixteenth and mid eighteenth centuries as part of the process of probate. Inventories provide no explicit statement of productivity although the information which they contain may be used to derive an indirect measure of yields per acre. A methodology for doing this was published by Overton in 1979 and was subsequently criticised and improved by Allen. In turn, his criticisms have been criticised by both Glennie and

---

148 Solar and Goossens, for instance, stress lower rent levels and greater security of tenure as one source of the greater work intensity which characterised Belgian as compared with Irish farmers in the 1840s: below, pp. 381–2. Subsequently, according to Turner, Irish work intensity and labour productivity improved as the Land Acts opened the door to widespread owner-occupancy: below, pp. 428–31.

149 The decay of serfdom is discussed in R. H. Hilton, *The decline of serfdom in medieval England*, London and Basingstoke, 2nd edn., 1983.

150 Case studies which illustrate the late-medieval engrossment of holdings include B. M. S. Campbell, 'The extent and layout of commonfields in eastern Norfolk', *Norfolk Archaeology*, XXXVIII, 1981, pp. 5–32; C. Howell, *Land, family and inheritance in transition: Kibworth Harcourt 1280–1700*, Cambridge, 1983; M. K. McIntosh, *Autonomy and community: the royal manor of Havering, 1200–1500*, Cambridge, 1986.

151 Allen, 'The growth of labor productivity'.

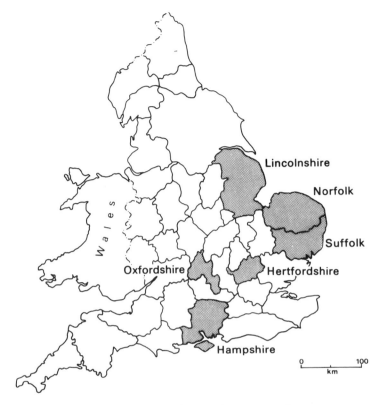

Figure 1.1 *Counties with yield estimates from probate inventories*

Overton. Refinement of the method will no doubt continue, but it now seems that the technique employed by Glennie and Overton in this volume can produce fairly reasonable estimates of absolute gross yields per acre, although assumptions involved in their calculation and the likely margins of error which they must incorporate should not be forgotten.[152]

Trends in cereal yields per acre have now been produced for the six counties shown in Figure 1.1 – Norfolk, Suffolk, Oxfordshire, Hertfordshire, Hampshire and Lincolnshire (the last two published

152 M. Overton, 'Estimating crop yields from probate inventories: an example from East Anglia, 1585–1735', *JEH*, XXXIX, 1979, pp. 363–78; R. C. Allen, 'Inferring yields from probate inventories', *JEH*, XLVIII, 1988, pp. 117–25; Glennie, below, pp. 256–71; Overton, below, pp. 298–305; *idem*, 'Re-estimating crop yields from probate inventories', *JEH*, L, 1990, pp. 931–5.

for the first time in this volume) – incorporating yields from the 1801 crop return or the Board of Agriculture Reports for *c.*1800 and from the tithe files for *c.*1836.[153] Figure 1.2 illustrates the trends in yields for five of the counties, but excludes Allen's Oxfordshire yields which are calculated on a different basis from the others and are therefore not comparable with them. In view of the century-long debate about the nature, chronology, and spatial pattern of a so-called 'agricultural revolution' based by implication on rising yields per acre, these trends are of some importance.

Although the movements in yields vary between the counties it is clear that wheat and barley yields remained at essentially medieval levels until at least the mid seventeenth century. Mean crop yields calculated for Norfolk by Campbell and Overton for farms with a minimum sown acreage of 20 acres indicate that the best medieval yields were not significantly bettered until the second quarter of the eighteenth century.[154] In Hampshire, the only county for which a similar comparison may be made, mean yields of wheat and barley were about the same in the first half of the seventeenth century as those obtained on the 24 Hampshire demesnes of the bishop of Winchester from 1209 to 1350: oats alone returned a yield which was about two-thirds higher, although this margin narrows somewhat if comparison is made with the period 1381–1410, by which time the yield of oats had significantly improved.[155]

The trends in Figure 1.2 immediately emphasise the rather obvious point that it is foolish to make claims for the existence or otherwise of a period of 'revolutionary' change on the basis of the figures for a single county. Nevertheless, all the series in Figure 1.2 show an upward trend in yields which marks a decisive break with the past at some time after *c.*1650, although the turning point differs between the counties.

153 For Norfolk, Suffolk and Lincolnshire see Tables 11.3–11.5 below; for Hampshire see Table 10.2 below; the Hertfordshire yields have been recalculated by Glennie and therefore differ from those in Glennie, 'Continuity and change'. For 1801 data are in M. E. Turner, 'Agricultural productivity in England in the eighteenth century: evidence from crop yields', *EcHR*, XXXV, 1982, pp. 489–510; and for *c.*1836 from R. J. P. Kain, *An atlas and index of the tithe files of mid-nineteenth-century England and Wales*, Cambridge, 1986, pp. 43, 72, 87, 128 and 153.
154 Table 6.8, below, p. 180.
155 Calculated from Table 10.2, below, p. 273, and Titow, *Winchester yields*. D. L. Farmer, 'Grain yields on the Winchester manors in the later middle ages', *EcHR*, XXX, 1977, pp. 560 and 565. The mean yields of the 24 Hampshire demesnes of the Bishop of Winchester for the period 1209–1349 (gross of seed and tithe) were wheat, 10.7 bushels per acre; barley, 15.8 bushels per acre; and oats, 11.6 bushels per acre.

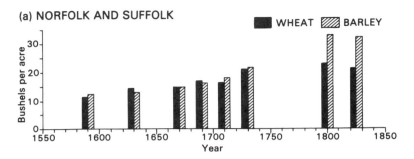

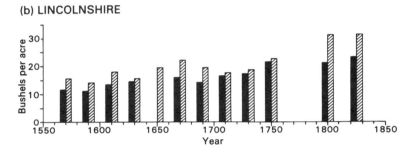

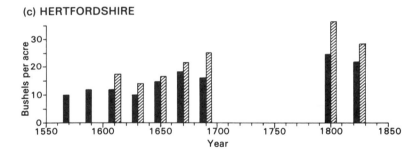

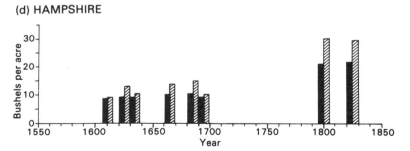

Figure 1.2 *Gross yields per acre of wheat and barley calculated from probate inventories, 1550–c.1836*

If we accept the rather narrow definition of an 'agricultural revolution' based on land productivity (which many agricultural historians seem to do) then the period before 1650 appears to be out of the running.[156] A break with medieval levels had certainly taken place by 1800, but the timing of the breakthrough seems to vary between the counties. In Hertfordshire the rise is apparent as early as the 1650s (but is subsequently interrupted by the bad weather of the 1690s); in Norfolk and Suffolk it began later, in the 1720s; in Lincolnshire, not until after the 1740s; and in Hampshire it must lie at some point between 1700 and 1800. If the trend of Allen's yields can be trusted then the equivalent turning-point in Oxfordshire dates from the last quarter of the seventeenth century.[157] In none of these counties do yields per acre change much between *c*.1800 and the mid 1830s, although a substantial rise takes place in the following twenty years.[158]

Whatever the innovations responsible for these increases in output (most of which had been available to English farmers since the sixteenth century if not earlier), part of the story of rising output per unit area both in England and in Europe as a whole must surely have been the provision of greater economic incentives to farmers to intensify and innovate. As Grantham demonstrates for nineteenth-century France, these incentives came most directly from the extension of market hinterlands via the growth of market demand, improvements in the efficiency with which markets functioned, and reductions in the unit costs of transporting agricultural goods.[159] As urban centres grew, so the geography of agricultural productivity changed, as more regions intensified, innovated, and thereby secured higher yields. The chronology of the rise in yields for the counties in Figure 1.2 seems to accord with this process. Yields first rose in Hertfordshire, in close proximity to the London market, then probably in Oxfordshire, linked to the capital by the trading artery of the Thames, subsequently in Norfolk and Suffolk, and then in Lincolnshire. Hampshire evidently

---

156 Overton, 'Agricultural revolution? England, 1540–1850'; and E. Kerridge, *The agricultural revolution*, London, 1967.

157 Allen, below, pp. 246–9; Glennie, below, pp. 272–3.

158 There is no change either for the 20 southern English counties for which data on yields exist both in the 1801 crop return and the tithe files, *c*.1836. By *c*.1850, average wheat yields in England had risen to about 28 bushels per acre.

159 Above, pp. 19–22. Grantham, below, pp. 346–7; *idem*, 'Agricultural supply during the industrial revolution: French evidence and European implications', *JEH*, XLIX, 1989, pp. 43–72; *idem*, 'Jean Meuvret and the subsistence problem in early modern France', *JEH*, XLIX, 1989, pp. 184–200.

remained outside the pull of the London market until after 1700. Eventually, as rising labour productivity in agriculture released more and more labour to an expanding urban and industrial sector, so a larger and larger area of the country was drawn within this powerful trading nexus and it became increasingly worthwhile for farmers almost everywhere to intensify and innovate. Under these circumstances spatial differentials in crop yields progressively narrowed as lower yielding areas began to catch up on those with a longer tradition of high yields.[160] Eventually the highly uneven yield map of the middle ages (whose steep productivity gradient has yet to be fully charted) was replaced by the relatively homogeneous map of today.[161]

Although the market was prompting farmers to adopt available technology, farmers were constrained in their freedom to do so by the institutional structures surrounding them. Although speculation rages, the relationships between innovation and property rights and tenure conditions need more thorough empirical investigation. Most attention has so far been directed at the role of parliamentary enclosure, although the findings are by no means conclusive.[162] In any case the breakthrough in yields for several counties came before the era of parliamentary enclosure, although this is not to argue that the process of enclosure, parliamentary or otherwise, was of no significance.

More evidence is available on the means by which these yield rises were attained, mostly from probate inventories. In evaluating their evidence, however, it needs to be remembered that inventories contain no information on fallows, and their recording of meadow and pasture is inconsistent and ambiguous. Thus, changes in pastoral farming, including yields of hay and grass, are inadequately represented. As a consequence, historians' explanations of changes in productivity in the early modern period show an inevitable bias towards arable husbandry and the innovation of conspicuous crops like turnips and clover.

These limitations mean that the *integration* of crops and stock, which was the key technological change responsible for rising yields, is particularly difficult to demonstrate. As Shiel shows, if pasture and arable were kept separate then the manure produced by livestock on

160 Grantham, below, pp. 346–7.
161 Campbell, 'Arable productivity in medieval English agriculture'; Overton, 'Agriculture', pp. 51–2; Coppock, *An agricultural atlas*, London, 1964, pp. 70, 73, 76, 80 and 81.
162 Allen, below, pp. 241–4; M. E. Turner, 'English open fields and enclosures: retardation or productivity improvements', *JEH*, XLI, 1986, pp. 669–92.

the pasture would have stayed there and been of little benefit to the arable land. Convertible husbandry, while not necessarily producing any more manure in total, redistributes it from the pasture to the arable, and grasses sown on well-prepared land are likely to give higher yields than the undisturbed 'natural' grasses of permanent pastures and meadows.[163] The system has other economic advantages in addition to raising yields, since it enables farmers to respond more flexibly to changes in the relative prices of grain and livestock, as S. Macdonald effectively demonstrates for Northumberland farmers during the Napoleonic Wars.[164] Despite their limitations inventories do indicate the gradual appearance of cultivated grass leys, which are suggestive of convertible husbandry, as well as the introduction of clovers and turnips.[165] There is clear evidence from accounts and inventories that stocking densities rose considerably between the middle ages and the early modern period, and archaeological evidence suggests that the size of livestock also increased dramatically.[166] Most telling of all is that in the middle ages there seems to have been little relationship between livestock stocking densities and grain yields; by the early modern period, as Allen and Overton both show, such a relationship had been established.[167]

By contrast, the introduction of turnips and clover, the principle elements of the famous Norfolk four-course rotation, can be charted comparatively easily. Nevertheless, as Overton demonstrates, the mere presence of these crops cannot by themselves be taken as indicating increased land productivity. Their initial introduction, in Norfolk and Suffolk at least, may have owed little to farmers' intentions of raising their grain yields, and more to a desire to increase or maintain fodder supplies as the cultivated acreage was extended in the face of deteriorating climate.[168] It was only as the crops gradually became integrated into systems of convertible husbandry that they began, in comparison with previous husbandry systems, to have revolutionary

---

163 Shiel's model underlying Table 2.1 assumes manure is transferred from pasture to arable. C. Lane, 'The development of pastures and meadows during the sixteenth and seventeenth centuries', *AHR*, XXVIII, 1980, pp. 18–30.
164 S. Macdonald, 'Agricultural responses to a changing market during the Napoleonic Wars', *EcHR*, XXXIII, 1980, pp. 59–71.
165 Glennie, 'Continuity and change'; Overton, below, p. 319.
166 Overton and Campbell, 'Five centuries of farming'; Armitage, 'A preliminary description'; Russell, *Like engend'ring like*, pp. 128–31, 176–88.
167 Biddick, below, p. 115; Campbell, below, pp. 163–4; Allen, below, p. 247; Overton, below, pp. 310–12.
168 Overton, 'Weather and agricultural change'; *idem*, below, pp. 319–20.

effects on output per acre. This point can be demonstrated both theoretically, by means of agronomic models, and empirically through evidence of yields and cropping changes from the late sixteenth to the mid nineteenth centuries.[169]

By the second half of the eighteenth century land and labour productivity were therefore almost certainly both rising, and they continued so to do notwithstanding an accelerating rate of population growth which finally took the national population above the threshold previously reached in the fourth, fourteenth, and seventeenth centuries. Hitherto it had proven impossible to reconcile the rising total output necessary to feed an expanding population with sustained rises in land and labour productivity; now, by 1800 if not earlier, all three were rising together.[170] The significance of this for European economic development as a whole is beyond question, indeed it can be regarded as the most 'revolutionary' development in European agriculture in the last two thousand years.

For England the data necessary to demonstrate that total output, output per unit area, and output per worker were all rising, have recently been assembled by B. A. Holderness. Taking his estimates of the physical output of English agriculture for 1800 and 1850, converting them to values at constant prices, and dividing by estimates of the area of agricultural land and the size of the agricultural workforce, show that total output was rising at 0.79 per cent per annum, land productivity at 0.89 per cent per annum, and labour productivity at 0.53 per cent per annum.[171] These figures are capable of considerable refinement,

---

169 Shiel, below, pp. 62–3; Overton, below, pp. 294–7.
170 Even so, the population grew faster than domestic food supply and it became increasingly necessary to import foodstuffs from elsewhere, particularly from Ireland with which the rest of Britain became politically united in 1801; B. Thomas, 'Feeding England during the industrial revolution: a view from the celtic fringe', *Agricultural History*, CVI, 1982, pp. 328–42.
171 These calculations are based on his output estimates for wheat, rye, barley, oats, potatoes, mutton, beef, pork, milk, butter, cheese and wool; cattle and horse hides have been added to the total: B. A. Holderness, 'Prices, productivity and output', pp. 84–189 in Mingay, *The agrarian history of England and Wales*, VI, *1750–1850*, 1989, pp. 144–74. Prices are from A. H. John, 'Statistical appendix', pp. 972–1155 in Mingay, *The agrarian history of England and Wales*, VI, *1750–1850*, 1989, and those used by Clark, below, pp. 214–16. Estimates of agricultural land area from H. C. Prince, 'The changing rural landscape, 1750–1850', pp. 7–83 in Mingay, *The agrarian history of England and Wales*, VI, *1750–1850*, 1989, p. 31; and the agricultural workforce from E. A. Wrigley, 'Men on the land and men in the countryside: employment in agriculture in early nineteenth-century England', pp. 295–336 in L. Bonfield, R. M. Smith and K. Wrightson, eds., *The world we have gained: histories of population and social structure*, Oxford, 1986, p. 332.

but there can be no doubt that the trajectory for both land and labour productivity was decidedly upward. Grantham's calculation of similar measures for wheat production in northern France led to a similar conclusion. He finds that land and labour productivity in wheat rose respectively by 0.5 and 0.7 per cent per annum from 1800 to 1862, 0.3 and 1.0 per cent per annum from 1862 to 1892, and no less than 0.9 and 1.8 per cent per annum from 1892 to 1929. Over the entire period 1750–1929 he calculates that output of wheat per worker-day rose by an average of 475 per cent.[172] In the absence of any reduction in the agricultural area such yield rises meant, of course, that total output was also rising.

These dramatic gains in land and labour productivity represented the culmination of manure-intensive husbandry. That its full productivity potential was only now being realised stemmed, on the one hand, from the more efficient fixing and cycling of nitrogen within the soil through wider adoption of the 'new husbandry', and, on the other, from improvements to the tools and implements of husbandry which reduced the labour required in basic farming tasks. In other words, the revolutionary biological technology of the 'new husbandry' was merged with the new mechanical technology of the industrial revolution so that for the very first time increases in the intensity of husbandry could be achieved without massive additional injections of labour. Mechanisation thus became a major source of land and especially labour productivity growth (with particular advantages accruing to areas of heavy soils where labour inputs, especially in ploughing, had always been greatest) and from the end of the eighteenth century a succession of mechanical improvements transformed first threshing, then ploughing, then finally harvesting.[173] By these means the agricultural workforce was reduced by mid-century to barely 30 per cent of the total in the more developed countries of Europe.[174]

Similar processes were at work in England during the nineteenth century. Manure-intensive husbandry reached its peak during the period of 'high farming' of the 1840s, '50s and '60s, aided and abetted by growing imports of phosphate fertilisers and cattle feed.[175] From mid-century new implements and machines became widespread, although,

172 Grantham, below, pp. 357–8. From 1800 to 1861 yields of wheat in England rose by 0.5 per cent per annum.
173 Grantham, below, pp. 354–6.
174 Table 13.1, below, p. 341.
175 F. M. L. Thompson, 'The second agricultural revolution, 1815–1880', *EcHR*, XXI, 1968, pp. 62–77.

C

as yet, we have no quantitative estimates of their impact on labour productivity except in very general terms.[176]

Not all regions and countries participated equally in these developments and several remained dogged by low labour productivity. Ireland and Italy are cases in point. Recent research has shown that, contrary to conventional opinion, both were characterised by high output per unit area, with yields of crops and animal products which compared favourably with those of Belgium and the United Kingdom.[177] Yet labour productivity was significantly lower and was associated with high rural population densities and low per capita incomes in agriculture. The poverty of the nineteenth-century Irish and Italian countrysides appalled travellers accustomed to the more prosperous rural landscapes of England and adjacent parts of northern Europe. Yet it is a mistake to equate poverty with backwardness. In both countries farmers did their best with the resources at their disposal and Turner's reworking of the Irish Agricultural Statistics suggests that during the difficult final decades of the nineteenth century Irish farmers actually adapted better than their English counterparts to the rapidly changing world market for foodstuffs.[178]

Contemporary commentators and historians have found it tempting to blame the low labour productivity of both countries on institutional constraints which depressed capital availability, inhibited technical knowledge, discouraged technological innovation, and thereby trapped too many people on the land in traditional forms of farmwork. Certainly, in the case of Ireland government became convinced that tenurial reform was an essential precondition for agricultural progress and with that object passed a series of land acts commencing in 1870 which eventually transformed Ireland from a land of tenant farms to one of owner-occupiers. The trend of recent historical opinion has been to condemn the land acts as the wrong solution to the wrong problem and R. D. Crotty has even gone so far as to claim that they

---

176 E. J. T. Collins, 'The age of machinery', pp. 200–13 in Mingay, *The Victorian countryside*, I, p. 210; J. R. Walton, 'Mechanisation in agriculture: a study of the adoption process', pp. 23–42 in Fox and Butlin, *Change in the countryside*, idem, 'Agriculture, 1730–1900', pp. 239–65 in R. A. Dodgshon and R. A. Butlin, eds., *An historical geography of England and Wales*, London, 1978.

177 Solar, 'Agricultural productivity and economic development'; *idem* and Goossens, below, pp. 366–8; O'Brien and Toniolo, below, pp. 406–7.

178 Turner, below, pp. 422–8.

bequeathed a legacy of inefficiency to Irish agriculture.[179] Yet, this harsh verdict is not borne out by the findings of Turner and Ó Gráda concerning subsequent trends in productivity.[180] The years immediately following the land acts and prior to World War I apparently saw considerable gains in land, labour, and total factor productivity and except during the worst years of the inter-war depression and trade war with the United Kingdom, the twentieth century has brought further gains. In fact, the source of Ireland's low labour productivity, like Italy's, may have lain as much outside agriculture as within.

In the case of Italy, it is the verdict of O'Brien and Toniolo, in a significant revision of established views, that low labour productivity within agriculture stemmed less from institutional and structural shortcomings within agriculture than from the lack of employment opportunities outside agriculture to soak up the under-employed and unemployed population of the countryside.[181] Significantly, both Italy and Ireland experienced large-scale emigration during the late nineteenth century at a time when, outside Lombardy in northern Italy and north-east Ulster in Ireland, industry was in a state of relative disarray. But in neither case was this sufficient to offset the high fertility of their rural populations. This serves as a salutary reminder that agriculture can be just as much constrained by the poor performance of the rest of the economy as, for so many millenia, the rest of the economy was by agriculture.

In most of western Europe, however, the twentieth century has witnessed agriculture's final demise from a position of central economic prominence. Paradoxically, it is via unprecedented productivity increases that this demise has been brought about. From the beginning of this century agricultural science has brought a deeper understanding of soil fertility and the sources of plant and animal growth.[182] This has facilitated the development of new strains of plants and breeds of animals whilst artificial fertilisers have finally broken the age-old dependence upon muck for manure. But it is since the Second World War that the development of pesticides, herbicides and new plant

179 B. Solow, *The land question and the Irish economy 1870–1903*, Cambridge, Mass., 1971; W. E. Vaughan, *Landlords and tenants in Ireland 1848–1904*, Dublin, 1984; R. D. Crotty, *Irish agricultural production: its volume and structure*, Cork, 1966.
180 Turner, below, pp. 428–9; Ó Gráda, below, p. 446.
181 O'Brien and Toniolo, below, pp. 408–9.
182 C. J. Holmes, 'Science and the farmer: the development of the agricultural advisory service in England and Wales, 1900–1939', *AHR*, XXXVI, 1988, pp. 77–86.

strains, expanded use of fertilisers, and the substitution of the internal combustion machine for horse power have raised output per worker and per unit of land to spectacular new heights and, in so doing (aided and abetted by government policies designed to encourage adoption of the new technology) have reduced the agricultural workforce in most advanced countries to barely 5 per cent of the total.[183] In agricultural if not economic terms, this has been the greatest productivity transformation of all.

IV Conclusion

Agricultural productivity provides the key to understanding both the bondage of European economies to slow economic growth throughout the pre-industrial period and their subsequent release from it in the nineteenth century. Until the end of that century the biological limitations of an organic agricultural technology set a physical limit to the output of food and raw materials from a given unit of land. Historians have demonstrated the strategies employed by past societies to raise the productivity of land in the short term, but the rate of productivity growth was invariably slow and carried an inbuilt penalty if natural ecological limits were exceeded. Sustained productivity increases were both harder and slower to achieve. For example, the technological package which constituted the so-called 'new husbandry' of the eighteen and nineteenth centuries took over 200 years to assemble and a further hundred years to become sufficiently widely adopted to make a decisive impact on overall productivity.

However, it was output per agricultural worker rather than output per unit of land on which the growth of the non-agricultural sector depended. If anything, growth in labour productivity was even harder to achieve, as witnessed by the slowness with which the urban proportion of Europe's population increased.[184] One of the principal constraints on labour productivity was a reliance on hand tools and human muscle-power rather than on machines and animal or mechanical power, but the social relations in the countryside also mitigated against improvements in labour productivity. The remedies for these limitations were

---

183 F. R. Harper, 'Crop production in England and Wales 1950–1980', *Journal of the Royal Agricultural Society of England*, CXLII, 1981, pp. 42–54; B. A. Holderness, *British agriculture since 1945*, Manchester, 1985.

184 P. Bairoch, *Cities and economic development: from the dawn of history to the present*, trans. C. Braider, Chicago, 1988, p. 201.

far from simple, and although it is fairly clear that a country such as England experienced a marked rise in labour productivity after *c*.1600, how and why this happened is far from clear. Yet without this rise in agricultural labour productivity the economic transformation of the industrial revolution would not have been possible. That transformation in turn unleashed the final and dramatic rise in labour productivity, initially through the development of labour-saving implements and machines, and subsequently through the development of artificial fertilisers, pesticides, and herbicides.

While the general outline of the course of agricultural productivity is now becoming clearer, many of its details remain opaque. The essays in this volume suggest ways of sharpening the methodological focus, and, as is often the case, research collaboration at the boundaries between disciplines proves particularly fruitful. As W. N. Parker puts it, 'The word "productivity" pushes the historian towards economics, but the phrase "productivity growth" pushes an economist towards history.'[185] Thus historians can learn much from the concepts of productivity developed by economists, but economists must turn to history to give their measures of productivity both context and meaning. Both need the insights of agronomists if they are to understand the possibilities and limitations of raising agricultural output through productivity changes. New insights can also be gained when historians venture out from the confines of their favoured period and place, as the comparisons across time and space in this volume demonstrate.

Viewing a problem from new perspectives usually raises as many questions as it provides answers. The contributions that follow pose a range of questions about agricultural productivity, and while some can never be answered, many can be taken further by fresh investigations of the historical record. Although the outline of land productivity for certain parts of Europe can be reconstructed more or less continuously from the mid thirteenth century to the present day, changes in livestock productivity are still uncertain, and the basic course of labour productivity in the pre-industrial period needs much more clarification. Speculation also outruns hard fact when it comes to explaining how these productivities changed. We have some idea of the processes behind fluctuations in the growth of land productivity, but at present our understanding of long-term changes in labour productivity

185 W. N. Parker, 'Productivity growth in American grain farming: an analysis of its nineteenth-century sources', pp. 175–86 in R. W. Fogel and S. L. Engerman, eds., *The reinterpretation of American economic history*, New York, 1971, p. 176.

are rudimentary. Thus it is hoped that the essays in this volume will encourage others to take the investigation of agricultural productivity further, while at the same time suggesting some of the issues that need to be tackled and a range of methodologies with which they may be approached. If this book promotes these ends it will have served its purpose well.

Improving soil productivity
in the pre-fertiliser era

In no other subject is it so easy to overlook a vital factor and draw from good
experiments a conclusion that appears to be absolutely sound, but is in reality
entirely wrong.

                                                                A. Wild, 1988.[1]

I The problem of improving soil fertility

The growth of plants requires an adequate level of temperature, a
supply of water, light and nutrients, an absence of toxins, pests and
diseases, and root volume sufficient to support the plant physically.
Additional constraints operate when land is managed for agriculture,
as crops must be sown and harvested at the right time. The area of
land which can be cultivated is therefore determined by the physical
nature of the soil, the power available, and the weather.

J. von Liebig realised that the productivity of crops was limited by
whichever nutrient was in 'relative minimum', and that the addition of
any other nutrient would not increase growth.[2] This principle was later
extended to all the factors influencing growth.[3] Among these limiting
factors there has long been a tendency to identify nitrogen as the
single most common source of variations in growth. Thus, G. Cooke
states that 'nitrogen is in a class alone, for in most agriculture its
supply governs yield of crops that have enough water'.[4] This may have
been largely true by the mid twentieth century, by which time reserves
of other nutrients in the soil had been increased, soils had been
limed and drained, pests had been chemically controlled, and immense

I should like to thank the editors for contributing some references to this chapter.
1 A. Wild, ed., *Russell's soil conditions and plant growth*, London, 11th edn., 1988,
  p. 3.
2 J. von Liebig, *Organic chemistry in its applications to agriculture and physiology*, ed.
  L. Playfair, London, 1st edn., 1840. A revised second edition was published in
  1842 under the title *Chemistry in its applications to agriculture and physiology*, and
  there are numerous later editions in English and German.
3 A. D. Hall, *Fertilisers and manures*, London, 1909, p. 284.
4 G. Cooke, *The control of soil fertility*, London, 1967, p. 3.

mechanical power was available. Nevertheless, at the beginning of the century the Broadbalk wheat experiment at Rothamsted showed that, after 50 years of continuous cropping, nitrogen used alone increased wheat yield by 6.9 bushels per acre, whilst used with phosphorus and potassium fertilisers, the same amount of nitrogen increased yield by 19.7 bushels.[5]

Clearly Cooke's statement needs careful qualification, and the same is true of numerous other explanations offered as to the causes of variation in plant growth. The problem for farmers has always been in deciding which, if any, changes they should make in order to increase productivity: a problem compounded by the fact that a single agricultural practice can affect a whole range of growth-controlling factors. For example, liming (or marling) alters the amount of potentially toxic soluble-aluminium, increases the supply of nitrogen from organic matter, reduces the severity of some diseases (club root of *brassicas*) and increases others (common scab of potatoes). Farmers, therefore, were not always in a position to know why a certain practice had affected growth, and they would often be given, or make, the wrong interpretation.

In the pre-industrial era there were only a limited number of changes that farmers could make in order to improve output per unit area. Better standards of ground preparation facilitated germination and were crucial to the incorporation of certain crops – such as turnips and clover, both of which required a fine seedbed – into rotations. Sowing crops in rows permitted greater weed control and was also essential before turnips could be grown. Plants were nevertheless susceptible to pests and diseases and even a rotation as renowned as the Norfolk four-course was plagued by problems such as flea-beetle in turnips and clover sickness. Yet pest and disease control was only possible by using labour to scare off predators and by rotations which separated crops in space or time. Poor drainage stunted growth on heavy and poorly drained soils, but it was not until the mid nineteenth century that really effective methods of under-drainage became available. Likewise, phosphorus and potassium were not available as fertilisers before the mid nineteenth century; until then soil supplies would have tended to decrease slowly with time. Soil acidity was a bigger problem, especially in the north and west of Britain, and marling or liming were essential in such areas before clover or turnips would grow

5 A. D. Hall, *An account of the Rothamsted experiments*, London, 1905, p. 35. The figures quoted, taken from Table XV, are for the years 1893–1902.

at all. In the drier south and east, especially on free-draining sandy and chalk soils, water was sometimes the limiting factor, and in recent years irrigation has brought significant gains to areas such as the East Anglian Breckland. Historically, however, grass was the principal beneficiary of irrigation, with the creation of water meadows in many parts of south-east England during the late seventeenth and eighteenth centuries.

Whilst implementing these various changes brought undoubted productivity gains, none is sufficient to account for the sustained rise in output per acre which appears to have taken place since the beginning of the eighteenth century, associated with the cultivation of new types of crops and evolution of novel types of rotation.[6] As noted above, the new crops required finer seedbeds, improved weed control, liming, and drainage before they would grow, with positive benefits for output per acre. But far more important for farm productivity was the effect of the new rotations into which these crops were eventually incorporated. The explanation lies in the supply of soil nitrogen. Crops use more nitrogen than any other nutrient, and unless nitrogen is replaced, a shortage in supply will limit growth after only a few years of arable cropping. The merit of the 'new' crops introduced into European agriculture from the seventeenth century onwards lay in their ability either to fix atmospheric nitrogen (legumes), or increase the amount of animal fodder, and hence recycle soil nitrogen without large losses (turnips). Nevertheless, to achieve their maximum effect these crops needed to be integrated with traditional grain crops to produce new types of rotation, of which the Norfolk four-course is the most celebrated.

Nitrogen is very labile and agricultural scientists are convinced that its supply was the main limit to crop yield in traditional agriculture. As E. J. Russell observed in 1913, 'our soils stand much in need of nitrogenous manure'.[7] Indeed, all of the 'fertilising' materials that were traditionally added by farmers to the soil contributed either directly (such as manure and nightsoil), or indirectly (such as lime, and, from the mid nineteenth century, phosphates), to the supply of nitrogen in the soil. Nor did the beneficial effects of measures adopted to enhance supplies of soil nitrogen end here. For example, crop rotations may have manipulated nitrogen budgets, but they also led to improvements in soil structure, and hence easier cultivation, whilst at the same time reducing problems from weeds, pests and diseases. Great

---

6 See P. Glennie, below, pp. 272–6; M. Overton, below, pp. 299–305.
7 E. J. Russell, *The fertility of the soil*, Cambridge, 1913, p. 13.

care must therefore be taken in attributing improvements in productivity to any single factor. Moreover, before attempting to assess the contribution to agricultural productivity of the various methods available for manipulation of soil nitrogen, it is essential to appreciate the state of knowledge which existed prior to the advent of fertilisers in the mid nineteenth century. In this case, too, care must be exercised, so as not to explain processes with the benefit of hindsight. As late as 1894, J. B. Lawes and J. H. Gilbert at Rothamsted were unsure about the role of clover in influencing soil fertility: 'there can indeed be no doubt that the leguminous crops ... have the power of taking up much more nitrogen ... *from some source* ... and the beneficial effects ... are intimately associated with this capability' [my italics].[8] Techniques may have been known to be effective, but why they were effective was often a mystery to those concerned.

II The growth in knowledge concerning nitrogen

Awareness of the value of legumes in improving the growth of a succeeding cereal crop is apparent as early as classical times. The observations of Virgil and other classical writers were subsequently collected by Crescentius and published in his *Ruralium commodorum libri duodecim* of *c.*1240, which was republished several times during the middle ages.[9] The thirteenth century seems to have witnessed a general increase in the importance of legumes as a field crop. By the end of that century manorial accounts reveal that peas and beans were widely cultivated on English demesnes, although rarely on a scale sufficient to have raised productivity. There were, however, notable exceptions. In parts of East Anglia and the south east, legumes accounted for as much as a fifth or a quarter of the cropped acreage, and reconstructions of rotations demonstrate that they were frequently sown between successive grain crops with the object of restoring fertility.[10] Elsewhere they were often sown as *inhoks* on the fallow, since they provided a much superior source of fodder to the self-seeded weeds and grasses upon which

8 J. B. Lawes and J. H. Gilbert, 'Rotation of Crops', *Journal of the Royal Agricultural Society of England*, 3rd series, V, 1894, p. 603.
9 E. W. Russell, *Soil conditions and plant growth*, London, 9th edn., 1961, p. 1.
10 H. E. Hallam, *Rural England, 1066–1348*, London, 1981, pp. 13–14; B. M. S. Campbell, 'Agricultural progress in medieval England: some evidence from eastern Norfolk' *EcHR*, XXXVI, 1983, pp. 31–3; P. F. Brandon, 'Farming techniques. South-eastern England', pp. 312–24 in Hallam, *The agrarian history of England and Wales*, II, *1042–1350*, 1988, pp. 318–20 and 323.

foraging livestock normally had to rely.[11] Vetches, too, became more widely cultivated at this time and were grown exclusively for fodder.[12] Peas, beans, and vetches, either sown singly or as mixtures, all gained in importance during the fourteenth century as greater emphasis was placed upon fodder crops and livestock, and by the opening of the fifteenth century they occupied almost a fifth of the total demesne sown acreage.[13] It was probably at about this date that experiments began to be made with new types of fodder crop across the Channel in Flanders.[14] Certainly, clover had become well established as a crop in Flanders by 1650 when R. Weston's English account of its use was published by S. Hartlib, and other accounts of the use of legumes soon followed.[15] In England the first known references to clover as a field crop date from the 1650s, and clover seed was being imported in the 1620s, although the crop had probably long been indigenous to meadows and pastures.[16] Turnips, by contrast, are recorded as a garden crop as early as the 1560s and had graduated from the garden to the field by the 1630s.[17] Nevertheless, even in as innovative a county as Norfolk, peas, beans, and vetches remained the predominant legumes grown until well into the eighteenth century.

The production of more manure from improved fodder crops, including turnips, was described by A. Speed in 1659, and W. Blith,

11 See C. Thornton, below, p. 196; H. S. A. Fox, 'Some ecological dimensions of medieval field systems', pp. 119–58 in K. Biddick, ed., *Archaeological approaches to medieval Europe*, Kalamazoo, 1984, pp. 142–5.

12 C. R. J. Currie, 'Early vetches: a note', *EcHR*, XLI, 1988, pp. 114–6; B. M. S. Campbell, 'The diffusion of vetches in medieval England', *EcHR*, XLI, 1988, pp. 193–208.

13 See B. M. S. Campbell, below, p. 160.

14 B. H. Slicher van Bath, *The agrarian history of western Europe A.D. 500–1850*, trans. O. Ordish, London, 1963, pp. 179; *idem*, 'The rise of intensive husbandry in the Low Countries', pp. 130–53 in J. S. Bromley and E. H. Kossman, eds., *Britain and the Netherlands: papers delivered to the Oxford–Netherlands historical conference 1959*, London, 1960.

15 S. Hartlib, *His legacie, or an enlargement of the husbandry used in Brabant and Flanders*, London, 1651; W. Blith, *The English improver improved*, London, 1652. See also, R. M. Garnier, 'The introduction of forage crops into Great Britain', *Journal of the Royal Agricultural Society of England*, 3rd series, VII, 1896, pp. 82–97.

16 E. Kerridge, *The agricultural revolution*, London, 1967, pp. 29 and 281. In Ireland, it has been suggested, indigenous clover grew with such profusion that there was no need to sow it: P. M. Solar, 'Agricultural productivity and economic development in Ireland and Scotland in the early nineteenth century', pp. 70–88 in T. M. Devine and D. Dickson, eds., *Ireland and Scotland 1600–1850: parallels and contrasts in economic and social development*, Edinburgh, 1983, pp. 76–7.

17 M. Overton, 'The diffusion of agricultural innovations in early modern England: turnips and clover in Norfolk and Suffolk 1580–1740', *Transactions of the Institute of British Geographers*, new series, X, 1985, pp. 209–10.

writing in 1652, recognised that clover was 'the mother of corn'.[18] On the other hand, manure had been in use since at least the Bronze Age. G. P. H. Chorley has estimated that the amount produced per hectare in the pre-legume continental rotations was small.[19] As production of arable crops was ultimately limited by the amount of manure available, then the introduction of new fodder crops, by increasing manure production, will have facilitated greater arable productivity.[20] There was, in fact, no need to make manure – it was sufficient that animals excrete on arable land – and landlords in some cases required tenants to fold animals on their land at night, when much of the excretion occurs.[21] Night housing of stock grazed during the day on common land would have had an identical result – though with manure being produced rather than land being directly fertilised. Clearly an understanding of the value of these practices had entered the farming vernacular at an early date.

Crop rotation is implied in Virgil's statement, 'sow your golden corn on land where grew legumes'.[22] The principle of rotation was enshrined in the medieval two- and three-field systems and reconstructions from manorial accounts reveal just how complex medieval rotations sometimes became.[23] Examples of ley farming, with land alternating between arable and grass, can be traced as early as the first half of the fourteenth century and in many cases were no doubt much

18 A. Speed, *Adam out of Eden*, London, 1659, pp. 18–29; Blith, *Improver improved*, pp. 184–5.
19 G. P. H. Chorley, 'The agricultural revolution in northern Europe, 1750–1880: nitrogen, legumes and crop productivity', *EcHR*, XXXIV, 1981, pp. 71–93.
20 But see Campbell and Thornton, below, p. 160 and 195–6, on the mismatch between stocking densities and yield levels, mainly due to inefficiencies in the utilisation and application of available manure supplies.
21 H. S. Bennett, *Life on the English manor: a study of peasant conditions 1150–1400*, Cambridge, 1937, pp. 77–8; K. J. Allison, 'The sheep-corn husbandry of Norfolk in the sixteenth and seventeenth centuries', *AHR*, V, 1957, pp. 12–30; B. M. S. Campbell, 'The regional uniqueness of English field systems? Some evidence from eastern Norfolk', *AHR*, XXIX, 1981, pp. 17–18 and 23–4; M. Bailey, 'Sand into gold: the evolution of the foldcourse system in west Suffolk, 1200–1600', *AHR*, XXXVIII, 1990, pp. 40–57.
22 Virgil, *Georgics*, I, line 73 *et seq.*, quoted by Russell, *Fertility of the soil*, p. 20.
23 H. L. Gray, *English field systems*, Cambridge, Mass., 1915, pp. 17–82; Thornton, below, pp. 185–6; P. F. Brandon, 'Demesne arable farming in coastal Sussex during the later middle ages', *AHR*, XIX, 1971, pp. 125–9; B. M. S. Campbell, 'Arable productivity in medieval England: some evidence from Norfolk', *JEH*, XLIII, 1983, pp. 392–4; M. P. Hogan, 'Clays, *culturae* and the cultivator's wisdom: management efficiency at fourteenth-century Wistow', *AHR*, XXXVI, 1988, pp. 125–31.

older.[24] Nevertheless, terrain, technology, property rights, and custom combined to ensure that some land remained more-or-less permanently under grass, often acquiring a mystique in the process which, in Britain, persisted until the present century. Landlords often saw permanent grassland as a storehouse of fertility – which it was, mostly of nitrogen – and constrained tenants from ploughing it and converting to arable. There was no such constraint on owner-occupiers but the requirements of mixed husbandry and the mythology surrounding old grass ensured that much land remained under permanent grass.[25] The manure which fell on it raised its fertility, but contributed little to the productivity of surrounding arable land.

All of the elements necessary for increasing the nitrogen supply – legumes, manure production from fodder crops, and rotations – were therefore in existence by the middle ages. Clover and turnips nevertheless did a more efficient job than the peas, beans, and vetches which they eventually displaced. They appeared first in Flanders and thence spread to England, where they were already being grown in the field by the time of their first appearance in print, c.1650. It nevertheless took time before these separate elements were integrated to form new types of farming system, with all the productivity benefits which thereby accrued. Integrated mixed-farming systems which incorporated legumes into rotations, and fed fodder crops to stall-fed livestock whose manure was then systematically spread upon the arable fields, may be traced as early as the late thirteenth century, but always remained circumscribed in distribution due to their labour-intensive character.[26] Subsequently, there was a lag of over a hundred years between the appearance of clover and turnips as field crops and the first documented examples of fully-fledged Norfolk four-course rotations.[27] The impact that this and other developments might have had on agricultural productivity is considered in the following sections.

24 T. A. M. Bishop, 'The rotation of crops at Westerham, 1297–1350', *Economic History Review*, IX, 1938, pp. 38–44; E. Searle, *Lordship and community: Battle Abbey and its banlieu, 1066–1538*, Toronto, 1974, pp. 272–91; E. Stone, 'The estates of Norwich Cathedral Priory, 1100–1300', unpublished University of Oxford D.Phil. thesis, 1956, p. 347; Campbell, 'Agricultural progress', p. 43. For a high-yielding, ley-farming regime in fifteenth-century Devon, see H. P. R. Finberg, *Tavistock Abbey: a study in the social and economic history of Devon*, Cambridge, 1951, pp. 74–115.
25 H. I. Moore, *Grassland husbandry*, London, 2nd edn., 1943, p. 24.
26 Campbell, 'Agricultural progress', pp. 41–4.
27 Overton, below, pp. 312–14.

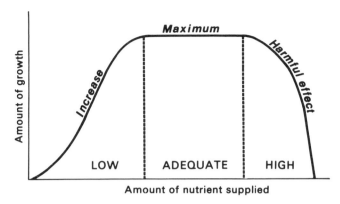

Figure 2.1 *Relationship between a particular nutrient or growth factor and amount of growth made by the plant*

III The dynamics of soil nitrogen

Nitrogen fertiliser has been the key to much of the spectacular increase in agricultural productivity of the last 40 years. During that period the use of nitrogen fertiliser in Great Britain has increased from 61,000 tons in 1939 to 1,416,000 tons in 1982.[28] As a result there has been intense study of the behaviour of nitrogen in the soil. Most of the transformations of nitrogen which occur are biological – either within plants or in micro-organisms. This complex of transformations is conventionally described as the nitrogen cycle.[29] For crops such as cereals, grain yield can increase by 15 kilograms for every kilogram of nitrogen supplied to the plant.[30] This gives farmers a 300 per cent return on investment in fertiliser (based on 1989 prices for the European Economic Community), an opportunity not available to earlier farmers. Wheat responds spectacularly to nitrogen, giving yields of over 10 tons per hectare (4 tons per acre) provided all other limits to crop growth are removed by scientific management.

The shape of the nitrogen : yield response curve is typical of that of other nutrients and exhibits a form which can be explained by Liebig's Law of the Minimum (Figure 2.1). There is an initial phase of nitrogen deficiency over which there is a largely linear increase in

28 Wild, *Soil conditions*, p. 26.
29 For example, see M. Alexander, *Introduction to soil microbiology*, New York, 1961.
30 Hall, *Fertilisers and manures*, p. 90, quotes an increase of 14.4 for the Broadbalk wheat experiment at Rothamsted over the range from 0 to 43 lbN per acre.

growth – the section of curve where nitrogen is limiting – followed by a flat section over which some other factor is limiting. The level at which this plateau occurs will depend on the 'other factors', such as acidity and phosphorus deficiency, which must be corrected before a further nitrogen response can be obtained.[31] Finally, yield falls as nitrogen supply increases: for instance with barley, excessive nitrogen can cause 'lodging' (the straw becomes weak causing the plant to topple over).[32] The most economically efficient area of the response curve is clearly the portion of linear increase, and today the farmer's objective should be to get as close as possible to the top of this section, so that the effects of area-dependent costs such as rent and soil cultivation are minimised. The Law of Diminishing Returns does have an impact towards the top of this section, but as the response is so near linear over such a large region it will be treated as exclusively so for the purposes of this discussion.[33] To get near the top of this portion it is necessary to generate in the soil large amounts of inorganic nitrogen – ammonium or nitrate ions – which appear to be the dominant types of ion taken up by plants. The nitrate ion was, in fact, the cause of the spectacular growth increases noted in the seventeenth century when saltpetre was applied to the soil.[34]

One problem with nitrate and ammonium ions is that they can be lost. Ammonium is lost by volatilisation from animal manures, while nitrate can be washed out of soil in wet weather.[35] An efficient system of nitrogen management should attempt to minimise these losses (hence the superiority, recognised by certain medieval farmers, of spreading and ploughing-in manure, over the casual droppings of grazing livestock).[36] The conversion of ammonium ions to nitrate occurs subsequent to, and faster than, the formation of ammonium ions from organic nitrogen sources – mostly manure or plant remains. Both ammonium and nitrate ions are used by plants and can therefore be considered together as mineral nitrogen (M). The amount of mineral nitrogen produced depends on the amount of organic nitrogen (N) in the soil and its decay rate (k). There are actually a wide range

31 For an example see Overton, below, p. 322.
32 H. C. Pawson, *Cockle Park Farm*, Oxford, 1960, pp. 137–8.
33 An agricultural example is given in Hall, *Fertilisers and manures*, pp. 283–4.
34 E. J. Russell, *A history of agricultural science in Great Britain*, London, 1966, pp. 26–33, notes several reports of improvements in crop growth due to saltpetre.
35 J. C. Ryden, 'The flow of nitrogen in grassland', *Proceedings of the Fertiliser Society*, CCXXIX, London, 1984.
36 Campbell, 'Agricultural progress', pp. 33–6.

of forms of organic nitrogen, each with its own characteristics, so that in strict terms

$$M = \sum k_a N_a$$

For most practical purposes this can be simplified so as to consider only two nitrogen fractions, a readily decomposable fraction (N_r) which is rapidly degraded (at a rate k_r which is 0.400 year^{-1}) and a stable fraction (N_s) which is much more slowly degraded (at a rate k_s of 0.02 year^{-1}). There is probably also a much more stable fraction ($k = 0.0003$ year^{-1}) which can be ignored. Fresh organic material, such as grass, can be considered to consist of 70 per cent N_r and 30 per cent N_s but clearly these proportions will change rapidly in the soil. After five years just over 13 per cent of N_r will remain as compared with slightly less than 90 per cent of N_s. N_r can therefore have a large, but short-term, effect, while N_s may accumulate, becoming the dominant fraction in terms of total quantity in the soil.

The relationship between the annual input (I_r and I_s) of readily and slowly degraded fractions and the mineralisation (M_r and M_s) gives the change in N_r and N_s:

$$dN_x/dt = I_x - k_x N_x$$

where I_x is the annual addition of fraction X, and $k_x N_x$ is the amount of nitrogen mineralised (M_x) of fraction x in the soil. The amount of fraction x after time t is then given by:

$$N_x = I_x/k_x - (I_x/k_x - N_o)e^{-kxt}$$

where N_o is the amount of nitrogen at time t_o. This expression shows that N_x will reach an equilibrium level at I_x/k_x as time increases and as e^{-kxt} approaches zero. With initial conditions of $N_o = 0$ and $t = 0$, I/k would be within 5 per cent of its equilibrium value after eight years for $k = 0.4$, and after 150 years for $k = 0.02$. In order to evaluate N_x it is necessary to estimate the input of nitrogen (I). For grassland this can be estimated from the harvested crop, uneaten grass, and roots. The last is often assumed to be half the shoot production for low output systems.[37] For the unfertilised natural grassland at Palace Leas leaf production was measured as 4,770 kg ha^{-1} giving a total drymatter of 7,150 kg.[38] Assuming the average nitrogen content to be 1.8 per cent, then the input, allowing for 25 per cent losses under a grazing

37 Chorley, 'The agricultural revolution', pp. 71–93.
38 R. S. Shiel and J. C. Batten, 'Redistribution of nitrogen and phosphorus on Palace Leas meadow hay plots as a result of aftermath grazing', *Grass and Forage Science*, XLIII, 1988, pp. 105–10.

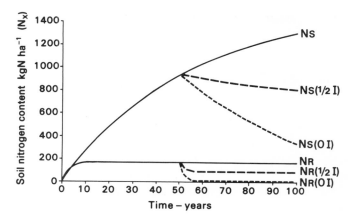

Figure 2.2 *Change in soil nitrogen over time*

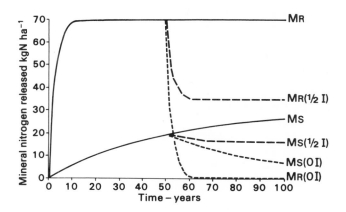

Figure 2.3 *Change in mineralised nitrogen over time*

regime, is 97 kgN ha^{-1}. Values for N_r and N_s, assuming 70 per cent of the added organic material is N_r, are shown in Figure 2.2. The accumulation of soil nitrogen over 80 years is 1,400 kgN ha^{-1}.

A change in nitrogen input will result in an abrupt deviation of N_x from its equilibrium value, with a subsequent progressive approach to a new equilibrium. At equilibrium, 90 per cent of the organic nitrogen in the soil would be in the N_s form, justifying the earlier comment on its quantitative dominance; however, 70 per cent of the mineral nitrogen (M) would originate from the N_r fraction. If, on the other hand, the input of N_r and N_s were to cease, then after five years M would have declined to 36 per cent of its original amount but 74 per cent of this would be coming from the N_s fraction (Figure 2.3).

IV Manipulating the nitrogen cycle to increase mineral nitrogen (M)

A number of strategies are available to increase the supply of mineral nitrogen to crops, the simplest of which is to reduce weed competition. Weeds compete for mineral nitrogen and hence effectively reduce the amount available to the crop. At least part of the success of drilling crops in rows was the superior control of weeds in corn and turnips. Improved seedbed preparation associated with drilling also means that crops develop a more extensive root system and hence are able to intercept more mineral nitrogen, which might otherwise be unused or lost.[39] Three other types of strategy are available, namely, to exploit total supplies of soil nitrogen (N_t), to accelerate the decay rate (k), or to raise annual inputs (I). All of these will increase mineral nitrogen, at least in the short term.

Where the soil has a large nitrogen content, this accumulated store can be exploited; but, as has been shown earlier, mineral nitrogen will fall rapidly unless annual inputs are large enough to replace the lost nitrogen. Ploughing out old grassland – as in the Highfield experiment at Rothamsted – provided all the nitrogen for wheat for a period of six years, and for a further ten years the response of wheat to fertiliser was less on the ploughed-out grass than on 'old arable' land.[40] This was for twentieth-century yield levels, so that at lower yields, benefits from the ploughed-out grass would have been noticeable for a longer period. The progressive reduction in mineral nitrogen at Highfield during the first six years would mostly have been due to a reduction in readily decomposable nitrogen (N_r), whilst in the latter part of the period decline in the more stable forms of nitrogen (N_s) would have progressively narrowed the difference in mineral nitrogen between old grass and old arable land. If manure were applied to such ploughed-out grassland then the benefits of its cultivation would have been felt over a much longer period as the fall in total nitrogen (N_t) would have been delayed.

By the mid nineteenth century much of the old arable land in Britain appears to have lost two-thirds of the soil nitrogen which was present before farming began, and experiments at Rothamsted suggest that when grass is sown on old arable land the nitrogen content more than doubles in a hundred years.[41] This rate of change is in reasonably

---

39 Russell, *Fertility of the Soil*, pp. 54–6.
40 Cooke, *The control of soil fertility*, pp. 213–14.
41 D. S. Jenkinson, 'Soil organic matter and its dynamics', pp. 589–91 in Wild, *Soil conditions*.

good agreement with the period suggested earlier for nitrogen recovery. Thus, exploited land has a long recovery period, and although the more readily decomposable nitrogen (N_r) will increase rapidly, its more slowly degraded counterpart (N_s) will change only slowly.[42] Hence, if after a short period under grass the land is ploughed again, yields will decline much more rapidly, although there will be a good first-year crop. This is the situation in a rotational system where N_s is small and N_r larger. The apparently temporary nature of E. Kerridge's English 'agricultural revolution' of the sixteenth and seventeenth centuries based on ley or 'up and down husbandry' may be due to changes in N_r and N_s.[43] The initial gains from ploughing out permanent grassland may have been quite high, but in the longer term, given the difficulties of re-establishing grass, and the long period required for N_s to recover, it is understandable that the practice may have been discontinued.[44]

An alternative strategy is to maximise the decay rate (k). This will certainly increase mineral nitrogen, but will lead to a rapid diminution of total nitrogen (N_t). Such a strategy depends on the possibility of increasing decay rates. The micro-organisms (and mesofauna such as earthworms) which bring about organic-matter breakdown depend on warmth, oxygen, water, and a moderate acidity (pH of over five). The values for k used so far have assumed such conditions, but if acidity or poor drainage depress decay rates a large amount of readily decomposable nitrogen (N_r) can accumulate, eventually forming peat if conditions become extreme.[45] The benefits of correcting soil acidity have long been known but the vast labour of digging and spreading marl meant that it was most widely used during periods of relative labour abundance, such as the thirteenth and eighteenth centuries.[46] At other times its use was probably only justified by a life-long lease. When liming, which is much less labour-intensive, became popular late in the

42 An argument implicit in M. M. Postan's interpretation of the inevitability of the late-medieval economic and demographic downswing once soil fertility had been depleted in the thirteenth century: M. M. Postan, 'Medieval agrarian society in its prime: England', pp. 549–632 in *idem*, ed., *The Cambridge economic history of Europe*, I, *The agrarian life of the middle ages*, Cambridge, 2nd edn., 1966.

43 E. Kerridge, *The agricultural revolution*, London, 1967.

44 J. Broad, 'Alternate husbandry and permanent pasture in the midlands 1650–1800', *AHR*, XXVIII, 1980, pp. 77–89. See Overton, below, pp. 293–4.

45 R. S. Shiel, 'Variation in amounts of carbon and nitrogen associated with particle size fractions from the Palace Leas meadow hay plots', *Journal of Soil Science*, XXXVII, 1986 pp. 249–57.

46 Russell, *Fertility of the soil*, pp. 53 and 80–2, quotes Pliny the Elder on the use of marl and lime in Britain and Gaul; Campbell, 'Agricultural progress', pp. 33–4; H. C. Prince, 'The origins of pits and depressions in Norfolk', *Geography*, XLIX, 1964, pp. 15–32.

seventeenth century in England, not only did it improve the growth of acidity-sensitive crops such as barley, but it would also have produced a sudden spurt in nitrogen mineralisation.[47] Unless a thick layer of peat had accumulated, such an effect would have been only temporary (similar to ploughing out old grass) but could nevertheless have unleashed a spectacular, if short-lived, spurt in productivity.[48] Drainage has a similar benefit, and the high yields of the Fenland area are still obtained with relatively little fertiliser, due to rapid mineralisation of the limed, drained peat.[49]

Another method of increasing decay rates is to accelerate the decomposition of organic material by feeding it to livestock. The digestion of herbage by ruminants occurs at high temperature, and in an optimal environment. The fermentation of manure with straw also accelerates decomposition, as does any form of composting which elevates the temperature. Compared with adding the plant remains directly to the soil, such treatment can be considered to be equivalent to compressing two years' decay into one. Thus, a given amount of nitrogen in the form of manure ploughed into the soil will give a larger growth effect in the year of application, and a more rapid decay of residues, than will an equal amount of nitrogen added as undigested plant remains. Bare fallowing has a similar effect to manuring in that mineralisation occurs in the absence of a crop 'sink', so that a subsequent crop has the benefit of more than one year's nitrogen supply.[50] Both manure and bare fallowing can result in problems of nutrient losses, which can be reduced by applying manure in spring as growth begins, and in the case of fallowing by ensuring that a crop is established before autumn becomes too far advanced and leaching occurs.

The final method of increasing mineral nitrogen is by increasing inputs (I). This may be done in three main ways. First, inputs may be increased by 'fixing' more atmospheric nitrogen. Second, by reusing

47 M. A. Havinden, 'Lime as a means of agricultural improvement: the Devon example', pp. 104–34 in *idem* and C. W. Chalklin, eds., *Rural change and urban growth*, London, 1974.

48 For the initial dividends accruing from systematic liming see A. Young's description of the improving activities of Chief Baron Anthony Foster at Collon, Co. Louth in the mid eighteenth century: A. Young, *A tour in Ireland with general observations on the present state of that kingdom made in the years 1776, 1777, and 1778 and brought down to the end of 1779*, 2 vols., Dublin, 1780, I, pp. 146–50.

49 Tables of fertiliser recommended for different soils are included in Ministry of Agriculture and Fisheries and Food, *Fertiliser recommendations*, London, 1973.

50 W. Fream, *Elements of agriculture*, 2nd. edn., London, 1892, p. 24; J. A. S. Watson and J. A. Moore, *Agriculture: the science and practice of British farming*, Edinburgh, 9th edn., 1949, pp. 154–5.

and conserving existing supplies more effectively and reducing losses of nitrogen by selling a different product – for example changing from grain to cattle. Third, nitrogen may be transferred from elsewhere, at the cost of creating soils with different nitrogen contents.

The most obvious source of non-soil nitrogen is the atmosphere. This nitrogen source can be utilised by legumes, which under good conditions fix over 100 kgN ha^{-1} a^{-1}, but a very wide range of values have been reported.[51] Because of their ability to fix nitrogen, legumes are very good pioneer species, but tend not to be good competitors with strongly growing species, such as the grasses, and hence tend to disappear progressively unless grass is mown or grazed regularly.[52] This means that legumes are more successful in a rotation than in a permanent grassland system, unless they are carefully managed. The modern solution is to avoid such management problems by using chemical energy to fix atmospheric nitrogen.

Reusing the soil nitrogen depends on returning the maximum possible amount of crop waste. Animals only retain a small fraction of the nitrogen consumed yet provide a valuable product to sell. Increased animal production apparently results in a decrease in total cereal area, but if cereal yields can be increased, as a result of keeping more stock which produce more manure, total grain output may not decline.[53] Over 75 per cent of the nitrogen consumed by stock is returned directly as excreta or becomes part of farmyard manure, although 50 per cent of the nitrogen in manure can be lost in storage.[54] The problem is that much of the excreta falls on the grass field and hence only some of the nitrogen is available in manure.

From the middle ages onwards, farmers made great efforts to ensure that manure was used to maximum effect. In East Anglia, for example, sheep were folded on arable land during the night – a system known as the 'fold course'.[55] Other East Anglian farmers went to even

---

51 Most authors (e.g. R. E. White, *Introduction to the principles and practice of soil science*, Oxford, 1979, pp. 132–5; J. M. Lynch and M. Woods, 'Interaction between plant roots and micro-organisms', pp. 534–50 in Wild, *Soil conditions*) quote very wide ranges for nitrogen fixation. Presumably, a figure of 50 kgN ha^{-1}, rather than the modern mean rate, would be more reasonable for the earlier periods.

52 Moore, *Grassland husbandry*, pp. 29–37, describes how grazing and mowing alter the proportions of different species. Continued mowing can lead to the total loss of clover.

53 See Overton, below, pp. 295–7.

54 Hall, *Fertilisers and manures*, pp. 207–17.

55 Allison, 'Sheep-corn husbandry'; Campbell, 'Regional uniqueness'; Bailey, 'Sand into gold'.

greater lengths and gathered up manure from marshland sheep cotes.[56] This helped to transfer some nitrogen to the arable land, but much of the excreta still fell on the grassland during the day. Only when the grassland was ploughed up and used for arable cropping did the nitrogen locked in the soil become available. Clearly, rotation of grassland with arable cropping ensures that the maximum amount of nitrogen from excreta and manure is made available to the arable crops; although if their yield increases, as it presumably should, then the removal of nitrogen in arable crops will be increased. The strategy of recycling nitrogen quickly through crops therefore still depends on a separate source of nitrogen, and on the extent of the loss of nitrogen (or sink) in the form of crop sales. If the sink is too large the amount of manure produced will progressively decline, resulting in the reverse of the upward spiral of fertility noted by Weston in seventeenth-century Flanders where manure was in excess.[57] If increased forage production therefore leads to an increase in sale of arable crops there may only be a short-term benefit from the improved nitrogen reuse.

One method of reducing the 'sink' is to recycle urban waste as 'nightsoil'. This was certainly carried out in the vicinity of towns, although transport costs usually ensured that its use was restricted to within a few kilometres of its source.[58] Significantly, cultivation was often more intensive in such locations. Such use constitutes transfer of nutrients rather than reuse, as the nutrients are unlikely to be returned to the farm they came from. Alternatively, a green manure effectively stores up all the nitrogen it takes up and this is released when the crop is ploughed down. Unfortunately it produces no income, but is more efficient in conserving nitrogen in a wet area than is a bare fallow.[59]

Where grassland and arable are kept separate permanently, only some of the nutrients from the grassland can be transferred to the arable land through manure. This is because summer grazing of stock will result in much excreta being returned directly to the pasture. Night housing and winter housing would allow 25–50 per cent of the excreta to be collected, but in spite of this there would be a progres-

56 Campbell, 'Agricultural progress', pp. 34–5.
57 Russell, *History of agricultural science*, pp. 37–8.
58 Hall, *Fertilisers and manures*, pp. 263–7, describes the agricultural value of nightsoil. For a specific example see J. Anderson, *General view of the agriculture of Aberdeenshire*, Edinburgh, 1794. In the late thirteenth and early fourteenth centuries substantial purchases of urban manure were restricted to demesnes within a five-mile radius of Norwich and were strongly influenced by the availability of cheap water transport: Campbell, 'Agricultural progress', p. 34.
59 Fream, *Elements of agriculture*, p. 24.

sive accumulation of nitrogen in the grassland (due to the addition of excreta and unconsumed grass) and depletion from the arable land (due to the removal of cereals for consumption elsewhere). Such a problem can only be avoided if the ratio of grassland area to arable is very large, so that heavy dressings of manure can be used on the arable. This system of separate grassland and arable compartments can therefore be seen as being relatively inefficient in transferring nitrogen to the nitrogen-exhausting crops such as cereals.

During the nineteenth century, as transport improved, complex animal diets developed containing imported foodstuffs – often by-products of industry, such as cotton cake – which served to increase the stock of nutrients in the soil, but at the cost of depleting nutrients elsewhere.[60] Liebig became very excited about the transfer of phosphorus to Britain from the continent in the form of bones. He accused Britain of hanging 'like a vampire ... on the neck of Europe'.[61]

V Manure production and systems of managing mineral nitrogen (*M*)

Traditional systems of European farming have depended on the integration of animals with crops and, in the more sophisticated systems, the manuring of land.[62] Yield of extractive grain crops was considered to depend on manure supplies obtained from forage crops via livestock: 'a full bullock yard and a full fold yard means a full granary'.[63] Hence it is important to ascertain how much manure can be extracted from a particular land-use system.

The supply of manure depends on the number and type of animals, their housing system and diet. The situation can be simplified by considering only the period when stock are housed and fed conserved feeds during the winter. W. Somerville indicates that a ton of hay fed to stock will result in the production of about two tons of manure, assuming that straw is supplied for bedding, for dietary supplementation, and to soak up the urine.[64] Hay yields on the unmanured plots of the two existing British classical meadow hay experiments, Palace Leas at Cockle Park (from 1897) and Park Grass at Rothamsted (from

60 A. D. Hall, *The feeding of crops and stock*, London, 1911, pp. 178–82, describes imported animal feeds.
61 Liebig is quoted by Russell, *Fertility of the soil*, p. 58.
62 G. Barker, *Prehistoric farming in Europe*, Cambridge, 1985.
63 Moore, *Grassland husbandry*, p. 12.
64 W. Somerville, *Agriculture*, London, *c.*1910, pp. 177–8.

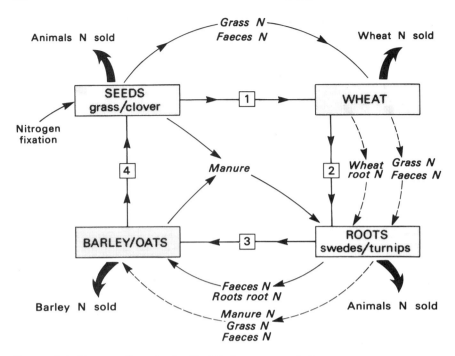

Figure 2.4 *Nitrogen flows in the Norfolk four-course rotation*

1854) are 18 and 9 hundredweight (cwt.) per acre respectively.[65] The difference in yield arises partly because Palace Leas is in a wetter area which is better suited to grass production and is further benefited by the grazing of stock on the hay aftermath, whereas at Park Grass a second grass cut is taken. If half the grass area is cut for hay, and the other half used for pasture while the hay field is 'shut up', then every acre of grassland would produce just under 1 ton of manure. If the remainder of the grass produced is grazed (about two-thirds of the total grass production, after allowance for hay) and one quarter of the manure is collected by night-housing the stock, then an additional 1 ton of manure per acre of grassland could be obtained. This system therefore gives a maximum of 2 tons of manure per acre of forage.

   In the Norfolk four-course rotation the 'roots' (turnips or swedes) could be 'carted' and fed to housed stock, or be 'eaten off' in the field.

65 Pawson, *Cockle Park Farm*, pp. 124–40, refers to Palace Leas; R. G. Warren and
   A. E. Johnson, *Rothamsted Experimental Station annual report for 1963*, Harpenden,
   1964, pp. 240–62, refer to the Park Grass experiment.

Yields for manured roots from the experimental rotations at Cockle Park (15 tons of manure per acre) and at Rothamsted (fertiliser equivalent to 15 tons of manure per acre) were 13 and 20 tons per acre respectively.[66] The Rothamsted yield was higher probably because of the use of fertiliser, which arguably contained more available nitrogen than it should have. On a pro rata basis with the dry matter in hay, the roots at Cockle Park would supply about 4 tons of manure per acre of crop. If half of the grass at Cockle Park (45 cwt. per acre) was made into hay, then this would give 2 tons of manure per acre of grass whilst, on the same basis, the clover at Rothamsted (32 cwt. per acre) would give 1.5 tons of manure per acre. Even if all the oats (or barley) were fed to horses on the farm, manure would only be increased by about 2 tons per acre. The best case for manure production at Cockle Park would give 8 tons per acre, and at Rothamsted, just under 10 tons per acre. The yield of manure at neither site would equal the amount applied to the experimental plots, even if all the grass were fed indoors. If the roots were eaten off *in situ* manure production would actually reduce by half, although nutrients would still be available in the soil for the succeeding crop. The sources of the additional manure needed for these rotations must either be nightsoil, purchased industrial feed for the livestock, or an increased area of grass relative to crops. In many real rotational systems the solutions adopted were either to use an area of less suitable land for permanent grass, or to extend the grass break to three years.[67] Historically, mixed farming employing a combination of permanent arable and permanent grass was widely practised in north-western Europe. It was, for instance, intrinsic to the two- and three-field systems, with their permanent, subdivided, and commonly regulated arable fields and their common pastures and hay meadows, whose status, like that of the fallow grazings on the arable, usually remained inviolate. An alternative system, developed during the late eighteenth century and gaining wide currency thereafter, largely dispensed with permanent grassland and integrated arable and pastoral husbandry through the cultivation of fodder crops such as turnips and clover. Known in its classic form as the Norfolk four-course rotation, contemporary advocates of agricultural improvement were loud in its praise. It is therefore interesting to consider the productivity benefits

66 The data for the Cockle Park and Rothamsted rotation experiments are given, respectively, by Pawson, *Cockle Park Farm*, pp. 124–40; Lawes and Gilbert, *Rotation of crops*, pp. 585–646.
67 Somerville, *Agriculture*, pp. 188–218.

of the Norfolk four-course over the older and more traditional alternative of mixed farming with permanent arable and grass.

VI Mixed farming with permanent arable and permanent grass

In this system the only inputs of nitrogen to the arable land come from the atmosphere, manure or nightsoil, from 'weed' legumes growing in the fallow, or from a pea, bean, or vetch crop. It is assumed that the arable is cropped according to a three-course rotation of winter-corn, spring-corn, and fallow. A bare fallow provides no extra nitrogen, although there will be nitrogen mineralised and unused as a result of the fallow, which will increase the growth of one crop albeit at the cost of losing a crop. With some exceptions the cultivation of peas, beans, and vetches does not appear to have been widespread on farms with reasonably substantial reserves of permanent pasture, and in any case these crops are often considered less efficient nitrogen sources than the forage legumes.[68] Night-soiling would only have been practical if there was a town nearby and, judging by the middens in medieval towns, such sources do not appear to have been used very efficiently.

Atmospheric inputs, other than from nitrogen fixation, seem to have been small.[69] This leaves manure from the grassland as a source of nitrogen. If it is assumed that fallowing (E) increased yield by 5 bushels per acre; a fraction (F) of one-third of the arable area is fallowed; there is a linear increase in yield (B) of 2 bushels for each ton of manure applied per acre from a base level of 5 bushels per acre, as manure use increases from zero to 10 tons per acre on the grain; and each acre of grassland produces an amount of manure (M) of 2 tons; then the productivity of an area of land can be modelled as the proportions devoted to grass and arable change. To make an economic assessment it can be assumed that animals and grain produce output of equal value per unit area (Os) when the grain yield is 10 bushels per acre, and that the output from animals depends only on the area of grassland. By derivation from this model, Table 2.1 gives the maximum total output (O_T) when the area under grain (Gm) is 15 per cent of the total area (A).

---

68 Russell, *Soil conditions*, pp. 343–7, points out that the large-seeded legumes, such as peas, only increase soil nitrogen content if the seeds are returned in manure. The crops do fix atmospheric nitrogen, but this frequently is only equal to the amount removed in the crop.

69 According to Wild, *Soil conditions*, p. 654, the amount of atmospheric nitrogen input in the pre-industrial era was only 5 to 6 kg ha^{-1}.

Table 2.1 *The effects of the relative area of grass and grain on the output of a 100-acre 'farm'*

Area grass (acres)	Area grain (acres)	Area fallow (acres)	Manure (tons per acre)	Grain yield (bushels per acre)	Total grain (bushels)	Stock output[a] (bushels)	Total output[a] (bushels)	Total output[b] (bushels)
100	0.0	0.0				1,000	1,000	500
80	13.3	6.7	>10.0	27.5	366	800	1,166	766
77	15.3	7.7	10.0	27.5	421	770	1,191	806
60	26.7	13.3	4.5	16.5	441	600	1,041	741
40	40.0	20.0	2.0	11.5	460	400	860	661
20	53.3	26.7	0.7	8.9	474	200	674	574
0	66.7	33.3	0.0	7.5	500	0	500	500

Notes
[a] Output from stock per acre assumed to be equal in value to 10 bushels of grain.
[b] Output from stock per acre assumed to be equal in value to 5 bushels of grain.

Source See text.

As will be noted, output of grain per unit area declines very rapidly as the proportion of grain expands beyond Gm, with the result that total grain output increases relatively slowly with expanding grain acreages (G). If the relative values are altered, for example the value of animals per acre (Os) is halved, or the yield function (B) is changed so that yield only increases by 1 bushel per ton of manure (for both models of relative crop value), maximum total output is attained with 15 per cent of the land under grain.[70] It is at this proportion of grain that all of the manure produced can be efficiently utilised at 10 tons per acre (O). With less than 15 per cent of arable under grain, the manure produced cannot be spread without exceeding 10 tons per acre, probably resulting in crop loss due to lodging. This suggests that the maximum production from the system will be obtained at exactly that proportion of grain cropping (Gm) where the manure produced from the remaining area can all be spread so as to obtain the maximum yield per unit of area over the whole grain-producing area (assuming that maximum grain productivity per unit area exceeds maximum animal productivity per unit area).

This effect can be explained by examining the changes that occur as the grain area increases. Up to the point where manure application

70 Historically, the ratio of arable to grassland was often very much higher than this. In the east midlands, the core area of English medieval commonfield farming, H. S. A. Fox has demonstrated on the evidence of Inquisitions *Post Mortem* that as much as 40–50 per cent of total farmland was regularly sown with grain: Fox, 'Some ecological dimensions'. In areas of non-commonfield farming this proportion was sometimes even higher.

falls below its maximum application rate (D) of 10 tons per acre, the loss of 1 acre of grass results in an increase of 27.5 bushels of grain. Provided the 27.5 bushels are worth more that the outputs from the acre of grass, total output must rise. Once manure production falls below the level necessary to fertilise the entire arable area at 10 tons per acre, mean output per acre of grain declines with every acre of grass lost.

A general set of expressions can be obtained for a farm of (A) acres on which the area of grassland is given by:

$$A - G/(1 - F)$$

The output of grain depends on the area (G), the base level of yield without fertiliser defined as (Z), the effect of fallowing given by $FE/(1 - F)$ where $F \leq 0.5$, and the other parameters as defined earlier. This gives Equation 1 when G is less than or equal to Gm and Equation 2 when G is greater than Gm:

$$O_T = Os\left(A - \frac{G}{1 - F}\right) + G\left(Z + BD + \frac{FE}{1 - F}\right) \tag{1}$$

$$O_T = (Os + BM)\left(A - \frac{G}{1 - F}\right) + G\left(Z + \frac{FE}{1 - F}\right) \tag{2}$$

For the situation in Table 2.1 these simplify to,

$$O_T = 1000 + 12.5G$$

and

$$O_T = 1400 - 13.5G$$

respectively. For the general model there is a maximum at:

$$Gm = \frac{MA(1 - F)}{M + D(1 - F)}$$

which simplifies to $Gm = 15.4$ acres for the situation in Table 2.1. This last equation shows that yield maximisation depends on manure production per acre of grass, the proportion of land fallowed, and manure application per acre of arable.

When the area of grass is suddenly decreased, by ploughing and conversion to grain production, there will be a reduction in the amount of manure, but due to its stored-up reserves of nitrogen the ploughed-out grassland will initially give a high yield without manure or fallowing, which will progressively decline to the yield of the old arable land over,

Table 2.2 *Mixed farming with permanent grass and permanent arable: the effect on total output of an expansion in grain acreage from 16.7 to 33.3 per cent of total farmland*

Year	Old arable		New arable		Crop output (bushels)	Stock output[a] (bushels)	Total output (bushels)
	Manure (tons per acre)	Grain yield (bushels per acre)	Manure (tons per acre)	Grain yield (bushels per acre)			
0	9.0	25.5	0.0		425	750	1,175
1	6.0	25.5	0.0	27.5	1,113	500	1,613
4	6.0	23.0	0.0	23.5	963	500	1,463
7	6.0	21.5	0.0	23.0	725	500	1,225
10	4.0	20.5	2.0	20.5	683	500	1,183
12	4.0	17.5	2.0	18.0	591	500	1,091
14	3.0	15.0	3.0	15.0	500	500	1,000
16	3.0	13.5	3.0	13.5	450	500	950

Note
[a] Stock output is assumed to be equal in value to 10 bushels of grain per acre.

Source See text.

say, ten years.[71] As the yield on the new arable land is initially higher than that on the old arable land, it can be assumed that no manure will be used on this land, nor will it be fallowed, until its yield falls to that of the old arable. In the meantime the yield on the old arable land will also have declined, because of reduced manure input due to the reduction in grass area. It appears that the yield on the unmanured new arable will fall to that on the old arable after four years, after which fallowing may be introduced. This will temporarily increase output, at the cost of reducing the cropped area. After between seven and ten years it will become worthwhile to reallocate the manure to, say, a 4-tons-per-acre application to the old, and a 2-tons-per-acre application to the new arable. This will reduce the yield on the old arable but slow the rate of decrease on the new. By year 14 it will be necessary to allocate the manure equally. This model is shown in Table 2.2 for a change from 25 to 50 per cent arable, and uses the assumptions in the earlier model used in the derivation of Table 2.1. Initially there is a marked rise in yield when the arable area is increased, but thereafter total output declines progressively until, after nine years, it has fallen back to its original level. Decline subsequently continues until total output stabilises at 81 per cent of the original.

71 Support for this model of yield decline after ploughing out old grass is provided by the Highfield Experiment at Rothamsted.

Table 2.3 *The production of manure and its equivalents, and yields per acre using the Norfolk four-course rotation*

Crop	Area	Manure	Faeces	$N_R + N_S$ in excess of old arable	Traditional varieties		19th-century varieties	
					Yield[a]	Total yield	Yield	Total yield
	(acres)	(tons per acre)	(tons per acre)	(tons per acre)	(bushels per acre)	(bushels)	(bushels per acre)	(bushels)
Wheat	25		4	3	19	475	28	700
Roots	25	3		2	15	375	15	375
Oats	25		3	1	13	325	27	675
Seeds	25				15	375	15	375
Total	100					1,550		2,125

Note
[a] Stock output is assumed to be equal in value to 15 bushels of grain per acre.

Source See text.

VII The Norfolk four-course rotation (Figure 2.4)

Calculations of output and productivity are complicated here by the integration of short-term forage crops with grain crops, there being no permanent grass. As the manure for the two grain crops is produced indirectly, with the farmyard manure from the clover-hay being applied to the roots, it is essential to make assumptions about the amount of 'manure' available, and about the effects of the grass and root residues. If the hay from half the clover or artificial-grass area and half the oats are used for feeding housed animals, there will be 3 tons per acre of manure produced for the roots. The wheat, which follows the clover/grass, will receive excreta produced by animals eating the 'grass', equivalent to 4 tons of manure per acre, plus the unconsumed grass 'residues'. This latter component can be assumed as equivalent to 3 tons of manure, giving 7 tons of 'manure' in total. The roots get 3 tons of manure, plus part of the residue carried over from the 'grass' equivalent to perhaps 2 tons, giving a total of 5 tons. From this it might be expected to grow 10 tons of roots per acre, giving excreta equivalent to 3 tons of manure, plus a ton-equivalent of carried-over root residues.

Using the earlier production criteria produces the output estimates given in Table 2.3. In this model the output value of stock produced from the forage has been increased by 50 per cent per acre because of the higher quality nutrition provided by the grass/legume mix and the root crops, compared with old permanent pasture. As will be seen, total productivity is 25 per cent higher than from the optimal proportion of 15 per cent grain in the mixed-farming system described in Section VI (Table 2.2), but is 63 per cent higher if equivalent proportions of permanent grass and grain are assumed. This increase is due both to improved output from the 'grass' and particularly from the cereals.

An extension in the length of grass break in the Norfolk rotation to two years would increase farmyard manure available for the roots to 5 tons per acre, and hence the root crop yield would be improved. Nitrogen in the soil organic matter would also be increased, giving wheat and oat yields at least 3 bushels per acre higher. This would result in a 7 per cent gain in cereal yields, but a small reduction in total grain output. If nineteenth-century varieties and machinery are used then yields comparable with Cockle Park or Rothamsted could be realised. This results in a near-doubling of output compared with mixed farming based on permanent arable and permanent grass.

VIII Conclusions

It appears that improved management of soil nitrogen has made a major contribution to increased agricultural productivity. Several of the components of nitrogen management depended on other developments, such as liming and improved soil cultivation, although these 'other' developments cannot in themselves account for the scale of productivity increases which occurred. Such ancillary developments make it clear that improved productivity arose from a complex of interrelated factors, none of which was of decisive importance in itself, but which in combination produced a system which in total represented far more than the sum of the individual parts. This is as true of the intensive, high-yielding, mixed-farming systems evolved during the middle ages as it is of the new farming systems which succeeded them.[72]

Partly because these integrated mixed-farming systems comprised so many mutually dependent components, their evolution took time. Hence the long lag between the appearance in England of clover, turnips and the other components of the Norfolk four-course system and the perfection of the system itself, whose widespread diffusion must be dated to the late eighteenth and nineteenth centuries.[73] Much

72 Campbell, 'Agricultural Progress'; M. Mate, 'Medieval agrarian practices: the determining factors?', *AHR*, XXXIII, 1985, pp. 22–31.
73 See Overton, below, pp. 306–13.

trial and error was involved and there were economic as well as ecological risks to be faced. Nevertheless, of the superiority of the new
system there can be no doubt, at whose root quite literally lay the
improved management of soil nitrogen.

Enhanced nitrogen fixation, exploitation of accumulated nitrogen in old grassland, a greater rate of turnover of the existing soil
nitrogen pool, and a reduction in unproductive 'fallow' land, all served
to increase the nitrogen budget available for arable and fodder crop
growth under the Norfolk four-course system. Thus, increased use of
leguminous crops as fodder for animals resulted in a greater input
of nitrogen to the soil, and this facilitated an increase in the growth
of extractive crops such as cereals. Perennial forage legumes fix about
twice as much nitrogen as pulses and, together with the switch from
grass-dominated permanent grassland to rotational grasses and clover,
resulted in a massive rise in the recurrent input of nitrogen. The
nitrogen incorporated in such swards was no longer allowed to accumulate over a long period, but was exploited for cereal production
within one or two years. This was achieved not only by transferring
nutrients via manure, which was a long-established practice, but also
by sowing cereals on land which had recently grown legumes. This
exploited the rapidly-mineralisable residues in the crop wastes, much
of which had not formerly been used. As a result the organic-matter
content of land in rotational farming may not have become any higher
than the mean of a permanent grass/permanent arable system, but the
nitrogen available to the cereals in the former system was much superior.
Coupled with the greater amount of animal manures produced per
unit area of fodder crop, the rotation system has a clear advantage in
terms of nitrogen management.

In addition, when old grassland is ploughed out, there is at first
rapid release of the nitrogen accumulated in such land. For a period
of about ten years from the changeover from fixed grass and arable
areas to a rotational system the farmer would benefit substantially from
this component. Fallowing had a number of functions, including weed
control and the accumulation of mineralised nitrogen, but did not
provide an income. Its replacement with a non-legume fodder crop –
such as turnips – allowed efficient weed control and accumulated
mineralised nitrogen in the manure from the crop, as well as producing
a saleable product in the form of meat.

Although systems such as the Norfolk four-course rotation increased output of both stock and crops, their major contribution may
have been that optimum output occurred with a larger proportion of

arable crops than under a permanent-grass/permanent-arable system. The much-increased amounts of manure from more efficient fodder crops, and the rotational use of crop residues, allowed this substantial increase in grain area, while still maintaining, or even boosting, yields. Nevertheless, it has been suggested here that the 50 per cent of land conventionally devoted to cereal crops in the classic Norfolk system may have been rather too large, and that variants of the rotation with 40 per cent cereal cropping may have resulted in slightly better yields of grain.

D

Agricultural productivity in the pre-documentary past

Archaeological endeavour has yielded numerical data in abundance, and yet ideas about agrarian change in the pre-documentary past remain predominantly qualitative. That past can be filled with 'revolutions', 'crises', and periods of continuity and change, but when it comes to attempting population numbers, yield measurements and such like, there is little alternative to speculation. It is the purpose of this chapter to take an example at the edge of the written record, that of Roman Britain, and against the background of a qualitative model for agrarian change, consider the potential for complementing that model with some notion of quantity and scale. In the course of this exercise the methods available within archaeology (and, especially, environmental archaeology) for the study of agrarian change will be reviewed. As a second theme, attention will also be given to the potential such methods hold for the study of more recent periods.

In archaeology the word 'revolution' is used more to focus academic minds on a common problem, than to convey any contemporary experience of radical transition. Such periods of change are by nature qualitative, so for example, the 'neolithic revolution' marks the transition from food procurement to food production, and the 'secondary products revolution' marks the transition from use of domesticates solely at the end of their life cycle, to the management and exploitation of them during growth.[1] It will be argued below that the period 1000 BC to 1000 AD encompasses a further 'revolution' of this kind. Such usage of the term does not in itself imply evidence of abrupt transition, indeed, the above examples may have been drawn out over centuries, or even millenia.[2] Neither does it imply evidence of quantitative change in productivity. Nevertheless, if the quantitative

---

1   Originally developed by V. G. Childe, *New light on the most ancient near East: the oriental prelude to European prehistory*, London, 1934: see also S. Cole, *The neolithic revolution*, London, 1970. A. G. Sherratt, 'Plough and pastoralism: aspects of the secondary products revolution', pp. 261–305 in I. Hodder, G. Isaac and N. Hammond, eds., *Pattern of the past*, Cambridge, 1976.

2   Compare E. S. Higgs, ed., *Papers in economic prehistory: studies by members and associates of the British Academy major research project in the early history of agriculture*, Cambridge,

aspect of these trajectories is to be explored through time, it is necessary to consider how well suited archaeological method is to the quest.

I A review of archaeological method

Five potential aspects of quantification are considered here: areas under cultivation; the balance of crops, livestock and other resources within those areas; productivity per acre; productivity and ecosystem stress; and population estimates.

The major archaeological means of providing an area survey of past land use are pollen analysis, remote sensing (including aerial photography), and ground-based survey. Since the onset of agriculture, the climax vegetation of much of Europe has been some form of woodland.[3] For this reason, palynologists have used the ratio of non-tree pollen to tree pollen to provide a broad indication of the extent of agricultural clearance. Although this can be achieved in a fully quantitative manner, there are numerous problems in moving from numbers of pollen grains to areas of past landscape under agriculture, and in delineating with precision the land area supplying pollen to a particular site.[4] The approach is therefore better suited to relative quantification, to determining which regions experience an increase or decrease through time in cultivated area, and comparing the scales of different changes.

While there is no intrinsic constraint to using pollen analysis in the historic period, much of the existing work has been conducted at levels of precision more compatible with prehistoric time-scales, with individual samples incorporating a century or more of vegetation change.[5] However, recent work has involved the selective close sampling

1972, in relation to the onset of agriculture, and J. C. Chapman, 'The "secondary products revolution" and the limitations of the neolithic', *Bulletin of the Institute of Archaeology, University of London*, XIX, 1982, pp. 107–22, in relation to the secondary products revolution.

3 H. Godwin, *History of the British flora*, Cambridge, 2nd edn., 1975.

4 See P. D. Moore and J. A. Webb, *An illustrated guide to pollen analysis*, London, 1978, for a useful discussion of constraints on reconstruction.

5 J. Turner has been largely responsible for bringing pollen analysis into the historical period: see, for example, J. Turner, 'The anthropogenic factor in vegetational history', *New Phytologist*, LXIII, 1964, pp. 73–90; *idem*, 'A contribution to the history of forest clearance', *Proceedings of the Royal Society*, series B, CLXI, 1965, pp. 343–54. Also M. K. Jones and G. Dimbleby, eds., *The environment of man: the iron age to the Anglo-Saxon period*, BAR, British series, LXXXVII, Oxford, 1981; and B. K. Roberts, J. Turner and P. Ward, 'Recent forest history and land use in Weardale, northern England', pp. 207–21 in H. Birks and R. West, eds., *Quaternary plant ecology: 14th symposium of the British Ecological Society*, Oxford, 1973.

of a millimetre or less of sediment, with each sample containing a few years' pollen rain.[6] In conjunction with the development of small-sample radiocarbon dating, and of pollen analysis in direct association with archaeological stratigraphy, the potential for application to historic periods is growing.[7] Both remote sensing (in particular aerial photography) and ground-based survey (in particular field-walking) can provide quantitative evidence of changes in settlement density, but both are subject to considerable sampling problems.[8]

The analyses described above provide a great deal of data with which to subdivide the various areas of humanly-disturbed landscape, but if attention is focused on the different *categories* of land-use, such analyses become constrained in a number of ways. This is largely due to the variable release of pollen from different plants.[9] With the exception of rye, cereals release very little pollen to the wind, and the same applies to insect-pollinated crops, such as the legumes. Two recent publications have collated the possibilities of subdividing humanly-disturbed landscapes, and notable among these are attempts to generate 'arable–pastoral' ratios from pollen and insect evidence.[10]

Two approaches are possible in the attempt to estimate productivity per unit area: the identification of the particular crops and animals used, and consideration of their potential productivity; and theoretical reconstruction of complete farming units. In the first approach, skeletal

---

6 See Turner, 'The anthropogenic factor'; *idem*, 'Forest clearance'; R. G. Scaife, 'The elm decline in the pollen record of south-east England and its relationship to early agriculture', pp. 21–33 in M. K. Jones, ed., *Archaeology and the flora of the British Isles: human influence on the evolution of plant communities*, Oxford University Committee for Archaeology monograph, XIV, and Botanical Society of the British Isles conference report, XIX, Oxford, 1988.

7 J. A. J. Gowlett and R. E. M. Hedges, eds., *Archaeological results from accelerator dating: research contributions drawing on radiocarbon dates produced by the Oxford radiocarbon accelerator based on papers presented at the SERC sponsored conference 'Results and prospects of accelerator dating' held in Oxford in October 1985*, Oxford University Committee for Archaeology monograph, XI, Oxford, 1986.

8 J. W. Mueller, *Sampling in archaeology*, Tucson, Arizona, 1975; J. F. Cherry, C. Gamble and S. Shennan, *Sampling in contemporary British archaeology*, BAR, British series, L, Oxford, 1978; C. C. Haselgrove, M. Millett and I. Smith, *Archaeology from the ploughsoil: studies in the collection and interpretation of field survey data*, Sheffield, 1985; D. R. Wilson, *Aerial reconnaissance for archaeology*, London, 1975.

9 See G. Erdtman, *Handbook of Palynology*, Copenhagen, 1969, and a briefer discussion in Moore and Webb, *Pollen analysis*.

10 K. E. Behre, *Anthropogenic indicators in pollen diagrams*, Rotterdam, 1986; M. K. Jones, ed., *Integrating the subsistence economy*, BAR, supplementary series, CLXXXI, Oxford, 1983 (especially D. J. Macguire, 'The identification of agricultural activity using pollen analysis', pp. 5–18, and M. A. Robinson, 'Arable/pastoral ratios from insects?', pp. 19–55).

evidence of animals and charred remains of grains and chaff form a rich data base, and one that allows the identification of considerable genetic precision, which is much greater than is currently feasible from pollen. In conditions of severely-arrested decay (waterlogged conditions being a principal case), skeletal evidence may be accompanied by evidence of hair, wool and skin, and charred remains accompanied by waterlogged seeds, fruits, leaves, etc.[11] Experimental cultivation of those species of cereal found in archaeological deposits has shown the yield range of individual species of prehistoric cereal to be high.[12] Research at the reconstructed prehistoric farmstead at Butser Hill in Hampshire has demonstrated in several successive harvests the physiological upper limit for yields for such cereals as emmer, *Triticum dicoccon*, and spelt wheat, *Triticum spelta*, approaches and perhaps exceeds 1 ton per acre.[13] Of equal significance, however, is the effective lower-yield limit. The more primitive species of cereals are also more hardy than modern cultivars, and better able to compete with weeds. They are consequently genetically well adapted to producing low, yet dependable yields, and this may be of relevance to, for example, the high-altitude prehistoric farms recovered in such areas as Dartmoor, the Pennines and the Cheviots.[14]

This evidence can be extended to infer that, just as there is considerable genetic range in prehistoric domesticates, so there may have been a similar variety in the yields they produced. The possibility of assessing yields on the basis of genetics is consequently limited to establishing their yield potential. This is of value in that it disposes of spurious conjectures about an upper limit on the yield potential of 'primitive' varieties constraining early productivity.[15]

11 Jones and Dimbleby, *The environment of man.*
12 See R. Shiel, above, pp. 51–77 for a discussion of the constraints upon crop yields, independent of seed quality.
13 P. J. Reynolds, *Iron age farm: the Butser experiment*, London, 1979. 1 ton of wheat roughly corresponds to 37 bushels.
14 A. Fleming, *The Dartmoor reaves*, London, 1988; Roberts, Turner and Ward, 'Recent forest history'; D. Spratt and C. Burgess, eds., *Upland settlement in Britain: the second millennium BC and after*, BAR, British series, CXLIII, Oxford, 1985; J. C. Chapman and H. C. Mytum, eds., *Settlement in north Britain 1000 BC–AD 1000: papers presented to George Jobey, Newcastle upon Tyne, December, 1982*, BAR, British series, CXVIII, Oxford, 1983.
15 On the other hand, such high potential yields conform with M. M. Postan's belief that yields were significantly lower in the late thirteenth century, lower than in some remote, but unspecified, period in the past: *The medieval economy and society*, London, 1972, p. 62.

The second approach to productivity involves attempts to re-construct the quantity of farm produce and the area from which it derived. Buildings and structures associated with storage have been much used in efforts to quantify early harvest sizes.[16] This is in part because data can be derived even from partly-excavated and poorly-excavated sites, and in part because of the ease of relating storage capacity to harvest size. Projected volumes of underground silos and raised granaries can be multiplied by effective crop densities, and byre areas can be related to species norms acquired from current livestock records.[17]

The area of the catchment, that is the land from which most of the primary produce reaching the site derives, may be directly discerned from physical boundary features, such as major walls or banks, roads and natural boundaries, and from funerary and some ritual sites.[18] In the absence of such evidence, site catchments can be constructed on the basis of supposed cross-cultural norms of mobility from a home base.[19] Reconstruction exercises of this kind have been conducted for sites of a wide range of periods, from pre-agricultural sites with minimal evidence of anything but a site location, to farming estates of the Roman period with site and field plans, and in some cases detailed evidence from excavation.[20]

The two approaches outlined above lead directly to figures of output per unit area. An alternative approach is the direct examination of soils which have been sealed at some definable point in the past (by,

16 S. Applebaum, 'Roman Britain', pp. 3–277 in Finberg, *The agrarian history of England and Wales*, Iii, AD *43–1042*, 1972; B. W. Cunliffe, *Danebury: an iron age hillfort in Hampshire*, 2 vols., Council for British Archaeology Research Report, LII, London, 1984.

17 G. Bersu, 'Excavations at Little Woodbury, Wiltshire. Part I: the settlement as revealed by excavation', *Proceedings of the Prehistoric Society*, VI, 1940, pp. 30–111; Reynolds, *Iron age farm*; Applebaum, 'Roman Britain'.

18 M. K. Jones, 'Towards a model of the villa estate', pp. 38–42 in D. Miles, ed., *Archaeology at Barton Court Farm, Abingdon, Oxon.*, London, 1986; K. Branigan, *Gatcombe*, Oxford, 1977; S. Applebaum, 'The agriculture of the British early iron age, as exemplified at Figheldean Down, Wiltshire', *Proceedings of the Prehistoric Society*, XX, 1954, pp. 103–14; *idem*, 'Roman Britain'.

19 For the original formulation: E. S. Higgs and C. Vita-Finzi, 'Prehistoric economies: a territorial approach', pp. 27–36 in Higgs, *Papers in economic prehistory*, 1972. For a more recent review: D. C. Roper, 'The method and theory of site catchment analysis: a review', pp. 119–40 in M. B. Schiffer, ed., *Advances in archaeological method and theory*, II, London, 1979.

20 E. S. Higgs, ed., *Palaeoeconomy: being the second volume of papers in economic prehistory by members and associates of the British Academy major research project in the early history of agriculture*, Cambridge, 1975; Branigan, *Gatcombe*; Jones, 'Towards a model of the villa estate'; Applebaum, 'Roman Britain'.

for example, human constructions or natural slope processes), since this reflects upon the closely associated impact upon the soil system of productivity levels approaching the ecological limit for those soils. Despite the fact that such information cannot be directly translated to yield figures, it does provide a parallel approach to studying the *scale* of global productivity, and one whose empirical base is more secure.

'Buried soils' can retain a considerable amount of physical, chemical and biological information relating to their condition and ecology prior to burial, both at the macro and micro scale. In relation to past productivity, areas of key potential include: the state of genesis at time of burial, which has implications both for past levels of fertility and past levels of agricultural use; the flora and micro-fauna at time of burial; and direct evidence of soil disturbance and cultivation by humans prior to burial.[21] Buried soils have, for instance, provided the major source of data for study of the development of heathland soils in relation to past human activity. In a classic work, G. W. Dimbleby examined the degeneration of brown earths to podsols in the context of human exploitation, by plotting the downward movement of minerals in soils sealed by prehistoric burial mounds, a study of considerable importance in the understanding of the development of upland marginality in Britain.[22]

Fragments of early agricultural soils have been found beneath funerary monuments, field walls, banks and Roman roads, Hadrian's Wall and the Antonine Wall, and a range of natural accumulations, such as slope deposits and blown sand.[23] In addition to information on soil genesis and contemporary biota, these soils have retained evidence of cultivation by hoe and hand-tool, and by ard and plough. These

21 For a general discussion of the method and its application see S. Limbrey, *Soil science and archaeology*, London, 1975; also G. W. Dimbleby, *The palynology of archaeological sites*, London, 1985; J. G. Evans, *Land snails in archaeology*, London, 1972; P. J. Fowler and J. G. Evans, 'Plough marks, lynchets and early fields', *Antiquity*, XLI, 1967, pp. 289–301.

22 G. W. Dimbleby, *The development of British heathlands and their soils*, Oxford, 1962.

23 For example, P. Ashbee, I. F. Smith and S. Evans, 'Excavations of three long barrows near Avebury', *Proceedings of the Prehistoric Society*, XLV, 1979, pp. 207–300; A. Everton and P. J. Fowler, 'Pre-Roman ard-marks at Lodge Farm, Falfield, Avon: a method of analysis', pp. 179–85 in Bowen and Fowler, *Early land allotment*, 1979. Several instances of cultivation marks beneath Hadrian's Wall are recorded in *Archaeologia Aeliana*: for example, J. Bennett, 'Examination of turret 10A and the wall and *vallum* at Throckley, Tyne and Wear, 1980', *Archaeologia Aeliana*, 5th series, XI, 1983, pp. 61–78. See also D. Breeze, 'Plough-marks at Carraburgh on Hadrians Wall', *Tools and Tillage*, II, 1974, pp. 188–90. C. Thomas, 'Types and distributions of pre-Norman fields in Cornwall', pp. 7–15 in Bowen and Fowler, *Early land allotment*, 1979.

types of evidence can be discerned at the micro as well as the macro level, and micromorphological analysis of buried soils may provide greater detail than is feasible from studying gross morphology alone. This applies not just to cultivation methods, but also for example to methods of water management and irrigation.[24]

As well as influencing soil development *in situ*, cultivation may also stimulate and enhance soil erosion, and the eroding sediments may in some cases be redeposited within a stratigraphic sequence. Colluvial and alluvial sequences of this kind have been analysed and dated by M. Bell, providing information on the time-scale of past erosion, and its implications for contemporary land use.[25] The precise relationship between valley infilling and contemporary land use may, however, be less straightforward than it first appears. Whilst intensive land use undoubtedly encourages erosion, valley-bottom accumulations may relate less to the general intensity of agriculture at the time than to discrete periods of landscape reorganisation which released sediments ponded up at field edges.[26]

The examination of soil stress can be complemented by associated vegetation studies. This may entail pollen evidence, as in the case of the expansion of *Calluna* (ling) which reflects, in turn, an increase in soil acidity. A second important source of such evidence is charred seeds. An archaeological assemblage of crop seeds may be accompanied by upwards of 50 species of weeds, each with its own physiological range, which combine to determine the ecological range of particular plant assemblages. As monitors of contemporary field conditions, such weed assemblages have enabled changes in soil type, hydrology, nutrient status, sowing time, and cultivation method to be recorded.[27] These can be related to areas under cultivation and the intensity of their management.

The main approach to population estimates involves some assumption about living space.[28] Such assumptions are founded in supposed cross-cultural norms of ground area requirement derived from ethnography, and then applied to settlement plans preserved in

---

24 M. A. Courti, P. Golberg and R. Macphail, *Soils and micromorphology in archaeology*, Cambridge, 1990.
25 M. Bell, 'Valley sediments and environmental change', pp. 75–91 in Jones and Dimbleby, *The environment of man*, 1981.
26 S. Limbrey, personal communication.
27 M. K. Jones, 'The ecological and cultural implications of selected carbonised seed assemblages from southern Britain', unpublished University of Oxford D. Phil thesis, 1985; *idem, Flora.*
28 F. A. Hassan, *Demographic archaeology*, London, 1981.

the archaeological record. Additional routes to settlement populations include calculations from the size of communal gathering places, such as meeting halls and amphitheatres, and of the size, growth, and detailed demography of their cemeteries.[29] Prehistoric population estimates have been highly conjectural, and in Britain it is not until the Roman period that such estimates acquire a cohesive empirical basis.[30]

II The reliability of archaeological quantification

There is little doubt that differences in the scale of agricultural productivity can be discerned from archaeological evidence and examined independently from qualitative change. The question is, what types of quantitative change may be discerned in this way, in what form, and at what level of precision? One possible way of proceeding is with reference to the framework of the *landscape,* and the areas occupied by different land-use, different populations, and different yields. Another is to employ the framework of the *ecosystem* and the pathways of energy and cycles of minerals and nutrients which it comprises. In principle, questions of agricultural productivity can be phrased in terms of either; in practice, different forms of evidence may lend themselves to one approach or the other.

There are various reasons why, from an archaeological standpoint, the framework of the ecosystem probably has greater potential in this respect. First, the major part of the relevant archaeological data base is biological, and such material generally retains clearer evidence of what it consumed, or was consumed by, than where it lived. Second, the clearest correlate of agricultural change within biological fragments of past ecosystems is through stress within the food chain and the soil system. Third, it may be argued that an ecological framework lends itself well to discussions of changing productivity in any period, as crops and livestock are biological organisms which follow the laws and dynamics of ecology.

The main constraint upon precision within either framework is not the precision of measurement, since, as indicated at the outset, archaeological reports abound in tables of precise *quanta.* The constraint, instead, relates to unknowns in the processes of formation of the archaeological record. For instance, although, within a given period of time, the cereal pollen rain falling on a particular surface

29 For example, G. C. Boon, *Silchester: the Roman town of Calleva*, Newton Abbot, 1974.
30 See below, pp. 90–1.

can be precisely determined, it cannot be established where, or how much, cereal was growing in the vicinity. Differential pollen productivity, release, mobility, and deposition dynamics pose too many problems, and equivalent problems constrain other categories of data.[31] However, as many of the unknowns, particularly those relating to natural processes, recur between data sets, there is a much greater potential for *relative* quantification, comparing the same ecosystem at different points in time, or different ecosystems at the same points in time. Moreover, as well as considering relative *quanta*, the archaeological evidence may reflect a passage through ecological thresholds which indicate that an ecosystem was subjected to critical levels of stress. Such thresholds include the onset of peat growth, podsolisation, and valley infilling.[32] With these various approaches in mind, it is now time to turn to the example of agrarian change in Roman Britain.

III Agriculture in Roman Britain: qualitative change

The major feature relating to productivity in this period is the growth of intensive valley-bottom agriculture. This, in turn, has three facets: the deep ploughing of clay-rich soils for intensive cultivation of bread wheat; the creation of hay meadows; and the development of horticulture and allotment cultivation within towns and on rural estates.[33] The archaeological evidence associated with this transition is summarised in Table 3.1.

In broad terms, this substantial transition relates to a trend that has long been evident in the historical geography of Britain, namely, an apparent contrast between the density of prehistoric sites on higher ground, and the density of medieval sites on lower ground.[34] The details of this contrast have been continuously modified by newly gathered data. It is now clear, for example, that the valley bottoms were by no means devoid of prehistoric settlement, and that clay-rich soils were

31 See Moore and Webb, *Pollen analysis*, chapter 7, for a resumé.
32 P. D. Moore, 'The development of woodlands and upland mires', pp. 116–22 in Jones, *Archaeology and the flora of the British Isles*, 1988; Limbrey, *Soil science*; M. Bell, 'Pedogenesis during the later prehistoric period in Britain', pp. 114–26 in A. F. Harding, ed., *Climatic change in later prehistory*, Edinburgh, 1982.
33 M. K. Jones, 'Agriculture in Roman Britain: the dynamics of change', pp. 127–34 in M. Todd, ed., *Research on Roman Britain 1960–1989*, Britannia Monograph, XI, London, 1989.
34 Compare the Ordnance Survey maps of *Ancient Britain* and *Britain before the Romans*.

Table 3.1 *Evidence of agricultural transition in the Roman period*

	Before	*After*
Major cereals		
	Emmer wheat	Bread wheat
	Spelt wheat	Rye
	Six-row barley	Six-row barley
		Oats
Minor cereals		
	Bread wheat	Emmer wheat
	Rye	(other tetraploids)
	Oats	Spelt wheat
Status of clay-rich soils		
	Marginal	Optimal
	(poor drainage)	(nutrient-retentive)
Cultivation method		
	Wooden ards	Turning ploughs
	(crook and bow)	(with metal parts)
Horticulture		
	No evidence	Plots in town
		and country
Animal fodder		
	Woodland fodder	Hay meadows
	Rough pasture	Woodland fodder
		Rough pasture

Source See text.

both settled and, to some extent, amenable to prehistoric cultivation techniques.[35]

The chronology of change is most clearly evident in the metal-technology and plant evidence. Less archaeologically visible, but also of great significance, are the more intensive use of animal power that deep cultivation demands, the more intensive use of manure required to justify the creation of a deeper soil, and the more intensive use of manpower and animal power involved in weeding and draining a richer soil. In other words, the trend is to a number of substantial yet invisible investments, at least on the clay-rich soils. All the elements required for those investments had existed for some time. Metal technology

35 B. W. Cunliffe and R. T. Rowley, eds., *Oppida, the beginnings of urbanisation in barbarian Europe: papers presented to a conference at Oxford, October 1975*, BAR, supplementary series, XI, Oxford, 1976; Everton and Fowler, 'Pre-Roman ard-marks'.

existed in Britain from the early second millenium BC, yet it was another 1,000 years before metal implements appear that show signs of agricultural usage, and later still that metal is used in cultivation equipment.[36] The crops that grew in importance had been present for many centuries but as minor components of the crop record. The valley bottoms had been settled in prehistory, both on and off the clay-rich soils, hence the ability to clear supposedly 'thick impenetrable woodland' was clearly not a constraint. It would appear that the factor limiting the transition was the need and ability to invest human and animal resources in the land. Early signs of this investment are the indications of extensive ditch-digging and drainage towards the end of the pre-Roman iron age, and, on some sites, a shift in the suite of crops.[37] This may be observed in detail at Bierton in Buckinghamshire, where a late iron age site, set in a landscape rich in clay soils, had switched fully to a bread-wheat-based agriculture.[38] By this point metal tools had been used in agriculture for several centuries, but the items involved – short sickles and share tips – were little bigger than a dinner knife. The late Iron Age sees the first balanced sickles in Britain, which by their design are bound to involve a greater weight of metal.[39]

While incorporation into the Roman Empire seems to have stimulated iron production, its immediate impact on methods of agricultural production appears to have been limited to the provision of animal fodder.[40] It is in this period that sickles suitable for harvesting hay are first recorded, alongside biological evidence for hay in a variety of forms.[41] Even these may have been limited in impact at first, since most of the evidence is associated directly with military contexts.

36 S. Rees, '*Agricultural implements in prehistoric and Roman Britain*, 2 vols., Oxford, 1979.
37 M. K. Jones, 'The development of crop husbandry', pp. 97–107 in *idem* and Dimbleby, *The environment of man*, 1981.
38 D. Allen, 'Excavations in Bierton, 1979. A late iron age "belgic" settlement and evidence for a Roman villa and a twelfth-to eighteenth-century manorial complex', *Records of Buckinghamshire*, XXVIII, *1986*, pp. 1–120, especially contribution by M. K. Jones, pp. 40–5.
39 Rees, *Agricultural implements*.
40 W. H. Manning, 'The native and Roman contribution to the development of metal industries in Britain', pp. 111–21 in B. C. Burnham and H. B. Johnson, eds., *Invasion and response: the case of Roman Britain*, BAR, British series, LXXIII, Oxford, 1979.
41 Rees, *Agricultural implements*; J. Greig, 'Some evidence of the development of grassland plant communities', pp. 39–54 in Jones, *Archaeology and the flora of the British Isles*, 1988; G. Lambrick and M. Robinson, 'The development of flood-plain grassland in the upper Thames Valley', pp. 55–75 in Jones, *Archaeology and the flora of the British Isles*, 1988; see also J. Greig, 'The palaeoecology of some

In the arable sphere, the occupying force was clearly well equipped to handle, process, and transport grain in large quantities, but there is no evidence that they significantly changed the way that it was produced, which is in contrast to their late-third-century and fourth-century successors.[42] It is in the later-Roman period that a substantial change is seen in cultivation and harvesting equipment, and this is also a period in which evidence for allotments, planting holes, and horticultural crops increases in quantity.[43] The late-third- and fourth-century metal implements include sizeable coulters, indicating the cutting of a deep furrow, and asymmetrical share tips, suggesting the existence of a mouldboard and turning plough. It also includes scythes of a size not equalled hitherto or since, which, together with the *vallum* (an animal-drawn harvester known from contemporary accounts and stone reliefs), reflect a concern with labour intensification at harvest time.[44] These developments are, perhaps, a corollary of concentration on a narrower genetic range of cereals, bread wheat in particular, and the resultant compression of crop-ripening into a shorter period.

The two pollen-related *quanta* discussed above, the tree to non-tree ratio and the arable to pasture ratio, are generally computed for individual sites. R. Bradley has attempted to collate data from a number of sites to produce composite graphs for both ratios to cover all of England, Scotland and Wales, though unfortunately stopping at the start of the Roman period.[45] His computed proportion of tree pollen drops steadily during the first millenium BC from around 60 per cent to 25 per cent of the total pollen. J. Turner's qualitative account sees this trend continue through the Roman period particularly in the north of England, suggesting that global productivity must have grown throughout the Iron Age and Roman periods, whatever happened to yield per hectare.[46] In Bradley's data, there is no such clear shift in the arable to pastoral ratio during the first millenium BC, but, instead,

British hay meadow types', pp. 213–26 in W. Van Zeist and W. Casparie, eds., *Plants and ancient man*, Rotterdam, 1984, for consideration of the possibility of prehistoric hay production.

42 Jones, 'The development of crop husbandry'.

43 Jones, 'The development of crop husbandry'; R. Macphail, 'Soil and botanical studies of the "Dark Earth"', pp. 309–31 in Jones and Dimbleby, *The environment of man*, 1981.

44 Rees, *Agricultural implements*.

45 R. Bradley, *The prehistoric settlement of Britain*, London, 1978, Figures 2.7 and 3.5.

46 J. Turner 'The vegetation', pp. 67–73 in Jones and Dimbleby, *The environment of man*, 1981.

fluctuations around a steady value. It would certainly be interesting to extend such an analysis into the Roman period.

The record for colluviation and alluviation is more difficult to generalise across Britain as the well-recorded sites are more localised. Bell's summary of colluviation and alluviation suggests that the former was more intense and widespread in the first millenium BC than the first millenium AD, while the reverse is true for the latter.[47] However, his examples of colluviation are heavily concentrated in the south of England, whereas those of alluviation are spread through the Midlands and the North. In other words, the pattern of valley sedimentation would seem to follow the northerly wave of clearance suggested by the pollen evidence.

The evidence of contemporary arable weeds also depicts a progressive ecological stress in this period.[48] In southern England, weed floras indicate a progressive loss of soil nitrogen from the middle of the first millenium BC onwards, together with an extension of agriculture on some very poorly drained soils.[49] In Wales and northern England weed evidence suggests the cultivation of some heath-like soils.[50]

Such discussion that exists about prehistoric population sizes has envisaged exponential growth in the first millenium BC.[51] While such a picture is convincing in terms of settlement evidence, it should be emphasised that its empirical basis is a great deal less secure than in subsequent periods. M. J. Millett has recently examined the evidence for England and Wales in the Roman period.[52] The data which have been used include documentary evidence for military strength; settlement size in conjunction with living space estimates and, in one case, recorded settlement population; and field survey evidence of rural settlement density. Taking two contrasting conjectural figures for rural-

---

47 M. Bell, 'Pedogenesis', Figures 1 and 3.
48 Jones, 'Carbonised seed assemblages'.
49 On the significance of soil nitrogen see Shiel, above, pp. 53–70.
50 G. Hillman, 'Interpretation of archaeological plant remains: the application of ethnographic models from Turkey', pp. 1–47 in Van Zeist and Casparie, *Plants and ancient man*, 1984; M. Van der Veen and C. Haselgrove, 'Evidence for pre-Roman crops from Coxhoe, Co. Durham', *Archaeologia Aeliana*, 5th series, XI, 1983, pp. 23–5. Both articles provide evidence of *Seiglingia decumbens* growing as a weed.
51 Compare D. Brothwell, 'Palaeodemography and earlier British populations', *World Archaeology*, IV, 1972, pp. 75–87; B. Cunliffe, 'Settlement and population in the British iron age: some facts, figures and fantasies', pp. 3–24 in *idem* and R. T. Rowley, eds., *Lowland iron age communities in Europe: papers presented to a conference of the Department for External Studies held at Oxford, October, 1977*, BAR, supplementary series, XLVIII, Oxford, 1978.
52 M. J. Millett, *The Romanisation of Britain*, Cambridge, 1990, chapter 8.

settlement occupancy, Millett puts forward estimates of 1.8 ± 1.2 million, and 4.6 ± 2.9 million respectively. Other estimates published over the last 25 years range between 2.0 and 6.0 million.[53]

The data as currently assembled hardly justify any subdivision of the Roman period in terms of demographic estimates. It is, however, possible to draw some comparisons between the population of Britain in the Roman period and at the time of the Domesday Book. The latter figure is also subject to large areas of uncertainty, but a population in the region of 1.5–2.0 million has been suggested.[54] Suffice it to say that, while both the archaeological and historical data can accommodate substantial demographic fluctuation between the fourth and eleventh centuries AD, they do not easily accommodate a substantial net increase over the period as a whole. This is corroborated by the well-dated pollen evidence of this period, which fluctuates in both directions, at different times, and in different parts of the country.[55]

This is in contrast to the environmental evidence for the preceding millenium, which, as outlined above, is consistent with steady and substantial population increase. In other words, the full development of valley-bottom agriculture did not herald a permanently enhanced carrying capacity and itself developed in tandem with the growth of population. The culmination of the agricultural changes which have been described was therefore also the culmination of an extended period in which Britain's carrying capacity grew.

While the valley bottoms were being drained and put down to hay and bread wheat, the concurrent growth in the prominence of two other crops in the archaeological record calls for a different kind of explanation. While bread wheat is well suited to intensive cultivation, rye and oats are well adapted to less-intensive cultivation on poorer soils.[56] They may have emerged slowly as crops in their own right, having previously been part of crop mixtures with bread wheat. As the intensity of cultivation became more varied in space, so the dominant crops within these mixtures would also have varied, producing a geography of cropping which reflected differences in both the

53 Millett, *Romanisation*, Table 8.1.
54 Estimates have generally been derived by applying a multiplier to the recorded population of 275,000 (assumed to have been male heads of household) and then correcting up for areas and groups left out of the survey. See H. C. Darby, *Domesday England*, Cambridge, 1977, pp. 57–94; S. Harvey, 'Domesday England', pp. 45–138 in Hallam, *The agrarian History of England and Wales*, II, *1042–1350*, 1988, pp. 46–9.
55 M. K. Jones, *England before Domesday*, London, 1986, chapter 10.
56 Jones, 'The development of crop husbandry'.

environment and the intensity of cultivation.[57] In other words, just as
bread wheat was adapted to the optimal soils that had developed in the
valley bottoms, so rye and oats were adapted to the more marginal soils
that had developed on higher ground and in coastal and sandy areas.
Integral to the overall process of change is the wholesale transfer of
nutrients from the latter to the former, which, at its simplest level,
would have resulted from the intensive use of manure in the valley
bottoms derived from animals grazing in the broader landscape.[58] In
a less direct manner, it would have resulted from progressive segregation
of those farmers more and less able to invest energy and other resources
in their land.[59]

The changes outlined above were not confined to Britain. All of
temperate Europe made the same transition in terms of crops and
technology at some stage between 1000 BC and 1000 AD, though the soil
types involved and the precise timing varied from place to place. In
other words, there was a general switch from a highly versatile and
diverse crop repertoire which was in widespread use, to a more differentiated pattern characterised by greater crop specialisation and
a clearer demarcation between areas of intensive and less-intensive
agriculture. The latter was underpinned by the lateral transfer of natural
resources from soils that become poor to soils that become rich.[60]

This mosaic of intensive and non-intensive agriculture existed at
both the regional and local level. At the macro-scale it shows up in the
changing crop record of Europe as a whole, in which progressive
specialisation can be seen throughout the first millenium AD and into
the early middle ages.[61] At the micro-scale, a contrast can be seen
between neighbouring farmsteads in a single region, varying in their

57 G. Hillman, 'On the origins of domestic rye – *secale cereale*: the finds from a ceramic Can Hasan III in Turkey', *Anatolian Studies*, XXVIII, 1978, pp. 157–74; Jones, 'Carbonised seed assemblages'.
58 Shiel, above, pp. 56, 66 and 76.
59 I have discussed elsewhere the relationships between the wealth evident from artefacts, coinage, etc. of later-prehistoric/Romano-British farmsteads and the form of agriculture which they individually practised: M. K. Jones, 'Crop production in Roman Britain', pp. 97–107 in D. Miles, ed., *The Romano-British countryside: studies in rural settlement and economy*, BAR, British series, CIII, Oxford, 1982; idem, 'Carbonised seed assemblages'; idem, Flora.
60 Jones, Flora.
61 U. Willerding, 'Zum Ackerbau in der jüngeren vorrömischen Eisenzeit', pp. 309–30 in *Festschrift Maria Hopf*, Cologne, 1979; idem, 'Anbaufrüchte der Eisenzeit und des frühen Mittelalters, ihre Anbauformen, Standortsverhältnisse und Erntemethoden', pp. 126–96 in H. Beck and H. Jankuhn, eds., *Untersuchungen zur eisenzeitlichen und früh-mittelalterlichen Flur in Mitteleuropa und ihrer Nutzung*, Göttingen, 1980.

ability to make the necessary investments that intensification required.[62]

Against the background of this changing mosaic of differential prosperity, qualitative change can be viewed as a change in *access* to ecological productivity, not necessarily demanding a net change in global productivity. The major source of enhanced global productivity may well have been woodland clearance alone, with the agricultural changes which have been discussed merely affecting the movement, rather than the quantity, of ecological resources within that cleared landscape.[63]

IV Conclusions

While there are substantial constraints on the precision with which archaeological methodology allows past productivity to be quantified, the example of Roman Britain shows how that methodology does allow the relative progress of quantitative and qualitative change to be examined. The results obtained possess sufficient clarity to allow inferences to be drawn on the broader dynamics of agrarian change. While historians might regard archaeological evidence rather crude in comparison with their own, there is great potential for the two disciplines to work together in the the study of agricultural change in more recent centuries. To give just two examples: historians have very little direct evidence of livestock weights, or of the extent of weed competition with growing crops before the nineteenth century. Archaeological methods could provide such evidence.[64]

While archaeology's lack of precision is a constraint, its great potential for studies of agricultural productivity is twofold. First, it can provide considerable detail of the agricultural activities of those farthest removed by either time or social status from the written record. Second, it allows agrarian change to be placed in the context of an extended time-scale, such that, for example, Roman Britain can be understood in the context of the ecological changes of the previous millenium. The earliest direct evidence of land productivity in England is not

62 Jones, 'Agriculture in Roman Britain'. Compare, for example, the contrasting productivity performance of neighbouring manorial demesnes during the thirteenth and fourteenth centuries: K. Biddick, below, pp. 106–19, and B. M. S. Campbell, below, pp. 174–8.

63 Although, as Shiel demonstrates, the reserves of nitrogen released by woodland clearance would have become progressively depleted: above, pp. 58–61.

64 A. J. S. Gibson, 'The size and weight of cattle and sheep in early modern Scotland', *AHR*, XXXVI, 1988, pp. 162–71, combines historical and archaeological methods.

available until 1208, and is fragmentary until the 1270s.[65] At most, therefore, historians have only seven hundred years in which to chart land productivity changes, although very few such attempts have been made.[66] It could be that medieval agricultural historians might gain new insights by setting their work in the context of the changes archaeologists have revealed for Roman Britain.

65 Biddick, below, pp. 183–4.
66 Campbell, below, pp. 149–52.

Agrarian productivity on the estates of the Bishopric of Winchester in the early thirteenth century: a managerial perspective

Much of our evidence about medieval cereal yields, livestock herds, wages and prices comes from the Winchester archive of annual manorial accounts (1208–1454).[1] Only a handful of accounts from other English manors exist prior to 1270 (which is also the case for the estate of the priory of Winchester, the manors of which often lay adjacent to the Bishop's manors), and it is only after this date that comparable

The generous support of the National Science Foundation Economics Panel (SES85-08539) made the research for this paper possible. The additional support of the Institute for Scholarship in the Liberal Arts, University of Notre Dame, enabled me to travel to the Bellagio Conference. Bruce Campbell and Mark Overton and the Bellagio participants provided invaluable suggestions and editorial advice. I am also grateful to colleagues at the economic history workshops at the University of Chicago, Northwestern University, and the University of Texas at Austin, who commented on earlier versions of this paper. Catrien Bijleveld, the co-author, enlarged my understanding of some of the relationships discussed in this paper through the use of the statistical technique she has designed called Linear Dynamic Systems Analysis. We will publish those results elsewhere.

1 Systematic use of manorial accounts was pioneered by J. E. Thorold Rogers in his magisterial *A history of agriculture and prices in England*, 7 vols., Oxford, 1866–1902. Sir William Beveridge drew attention to the importance of the Winchester archive in 'The yield and price of corn in the middle ages', *Economic History* (a supplement of *The Economic Journal*), I, 1927, pp. 155–67; *idem*, 'The Winchester rolls and their dating', *Economic History Review*, II, 1929, pp. 93–114; *idem, Prices and wages in England from the twelfth to the nineteenth century*, I, London, 1939. The Winchester accounts have also been used in the following selected studies of medieval agrarian productivity: B. H. Slicher van Bath, *The agrarian history of western Europe AD 500–1850*, trans. O. Ordish, London, 1963; J. Z. Titow, *Winchester yields: a study in medieval agricultural productivity*, Cambridge, 1972; *idem, English rural society, 1200–1350*, London, 1969; D. L. Farmer, 'Grain yields on the Winchester manors in the later middle ages', *EcHR*, XXX, 1977, pp. 555–66; G. H. Dury, 'Crop failures on the Winchester manors, 1232–1349', *Transactions of the Institute of British Geographers*, new series, XIX, 1984, pp. 401–18; D. Keene, *Survey of medieval Winchester*, Winchester Studies, II, Oxford, 1985.

sequences of accounts become available for other seignorial estates.[2] Hence, for the first two-thirds of the thirteenth century the agrarian history of England is perforce largely based on the evidence of the Bishop of Winchester's demesnes.[3] Institutionally and geographically, however, the Winchester estate is far from representative of demesne agriculture at large. The Bishop was one of the greatest and wealthiest of ecclesiastical magnates and his manors were spatially concentrated in the southern counties of England with a specific focus on Hampshire (Figure 4.1). This makes it particularly important to establish the links which existed with the state, local markets, and the regional economy, since these provided the specific context within which husbandry was conducted and are therefore integral to any evaluation of productivity levels on this estate.

It is now clear that cereal yields on the Winchester demesnes were low in both relative and absolute terms.[4] As B. M. S. Campbell demonstrates, arable husbandry on Norfolk demesnes was on average roughly twice as productive per unit of land as that attained on the Winchester demesnes.[5] Such below-average yield levels persisted for the county of Hampshire – in which over half of the Bishop's manors lay – until well into the early modern period.[6] Hampshire also ranked comparatively low among medieval counties for population, market density and land values. At the time of Domesday, with a recorded rural population of six people per square mile, it fell within the lowest

2 On the availability of manorial accounts see P. D. A. Harvey, ed., *Manorial records of Cuxham, Oxfordshire, circa 1200–1359*, Oxfordshire Record Society, L, London, 1976, p. 17. The accounts of Winchester Cathedral Priory await study. Runs of accounts for priory manors in Hampshire first appear in 1248, then 1261, 1267, 1270, 1272, 1280, 1282, 1283 and 1299. The papers of John Summers Drew, who worked on some of the priory accounts, are currently stored in the Institute of Historical Research, London.

3 This applies particularly to M. M. Postan, 'Medieval agrarian society in its prime: England', pp. 549–632 in *idem*, ed., *The Cambridge economic history of Europe*, I, *The agrarian life of the middle ages*, Cambridge, 2nd edn., 1966; *idem, The medieval economy and society*, London, 1972. For an attempt to redress this imbalance see H. E. Hallam, ed., *The agrarian history of England and Wales*, II, *1042–1350*, Cambridge, 1988.

4 See B. M. S. Campbell, P. Glennie and C. Thornton (below, pp. 160–1, 271–6, and 188–95) for comparative data on Winchester yields, yields from the county of Hampshire, and yields on the Winchester manor of Rimpton in Somerset. The findings for Rimpton in this paper which identify it as a manor with market-orientated strategies in the early thirteenth century confirm Thornton's conclusions in an interesting way.

5 Campbell, below, pp. 172–3.

6 See Figure 1.2, above, p. 58.

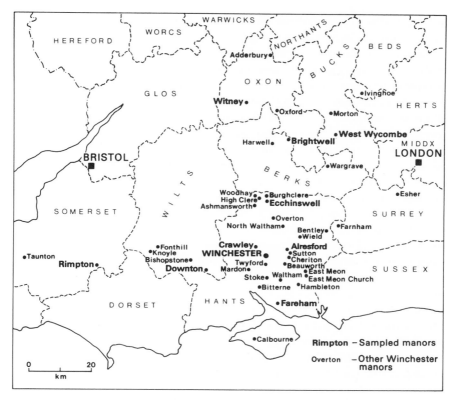

Figure 4.1 *Distribution of Winchester manors*

third of English counties.[7] Before the Black Death the county enjoyed only one market per 35 square miles in contrast to East Anglia with one market per 17 square miles.[8] Moreover, southern England's urban network had undergone some realignment during the late twelfth and early thirteenth centuries, as Winchester and Oxford contracted relative to both London and the inland and port towns of East Anglia, a contraction accompanied by decline in the absolute size of these two

---

7 For maps of population density by county, based on Domesday Book and the Poll Tax returns of 1377, see R. M. Smith, 'Human resources', pp. 188–212 in G. Astill and A. Grant, eds., *The countryside of medieval England*, Oxford, 1988.

8 For comparative statistics of chartered markets see R. H. Britnell,'The proliferation of markets in England, 1200–1349', *EcHR*, XXXIV, 1981, pp. 209–21.

towns.[9] Rural land values as revealed by *'Inquisitions Post Mortem'* were correspondingly below average.[10] Compared with other counties, Hampshire demesnes also husbanded comparatively few horses, whose speedier transport might have provided some compensation for the region's comparatively poor access to major markets.[11]

This regional context cautions against using the evidence of the Winchester estate as some disembodied benchmark of agrarian productivity and raises an important set of new questions. For instance, if cultivation techniques capable of raising yields were known and used in other regions, why did the managers of the Winchester demesnes not employ them?[12] Moreover, were low productivity levels merely the product of unsatisfactory cultivation methods or were demesne managers pursuing a deliberate strategy of which low productivity was the logical outcome? What, in fact, was the management strategy of the estate and to what extent was it determined by the role of the Bishop as a leading magnate within the feudal state?

I The state and the framework of agrarian productivity

The medieval state provided a political context for agrarian productivity, yet there are no studies of how its growing extractive powers in twelfth- and thirteenth-century England influenced the institutional and economic arrangements of demesne agriculture. Agrarian lords bore the burden of the growing demands of the Crown during the twelfth century as the state realised real increases in revenues which exceeded the steep inflation of the later part of the century. Figure 4.2 illustrates such demands on the bishopric, an estate comparatively favoured by the Crown.

9 For Winchester's twelfth-century urban decline see Keene, *Survey of medieval Winchester*, pp. 95–8; M. Biddle, ed., *Winchester in the early middle ages*, Oxford, 1976, pp. 498–506. For the decline of Oxford see A. Crossley, ed., *The Victoria history of the county of Oxford*, IV, Oxford, 1979.

10 County maps of the per-acre value of meadow and pasture are given in B. M. S. Campbell, 'People and land in the middle ages, 1066–1500', pp. 69–121 in R. A. Dodgshon and R. A. Butlin, eds., *An historical geography of England and Wales*, London, 2nd edn., 1990, p. 82.

11 For data on work horses see J. L. Langdon, *Horses, oxen and technological innovation: the use of draught animals in English farming from 1066–1500*, Cambridge, 1986.

12 For spatial variations in medieval husbandry systems see B. M. S. Campbell and J. P. Power, 'Mapping the agricultural geography of medieval England', *Journal of Historical Geography*, XV, 1989, pp. 24–39.

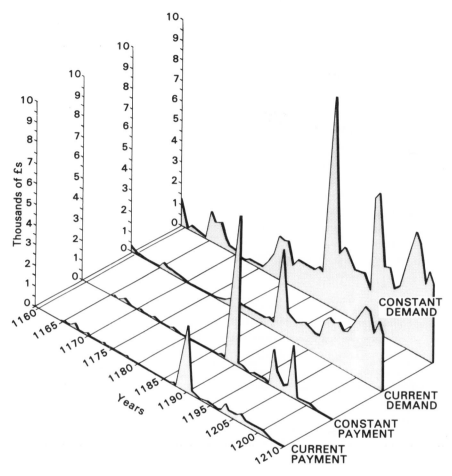

Figure 4.2 *Demands of the Crown on the Bishop of Winchester and payments by the Bishop to the Crown, 1155–1210*

The Crown induced indebtedness among its tenants-in-chief over the century and increased its power by dispensing its patronage through pardons of debt and interest. The King had alternative means of pressing debts owed by ecclesiastical estates, since by his regalian right he held custody of these estates during vacancies (the period between the death of a Bishop or Abbot and the elevation of the successor). This allowed the Crown to expropriate estate rents, fines and fees of justice, and agricultural profits, and to use the revenue-yielding resources of fields,

Table 4.1 *Receipts of Winchester vacancies, 1171–1244*

	Henry II 1171–72 1 year	Richard I 1189–90 0.75 year	John 1204–05 0.75 year	Henry III 1238–44 6 years
Total receipts				
shillings	31,101[a]	19,221	63,797	519,624
oxen[b]	10,367	6,623	11,341	9,444
Rents (shillings)		12,318[c]	15,166	126,365
% receipts		64.0	23.7	24.3
Aids, Courts (shillings)			24,359	52,940
% receipts			38.2	10.2
Grain (shillings)			9,187	173,596
% receipts			14.4	33.4
Livestock (shillings)		6,000	8,647	22,399
% receipts		31.2	13.5	4.3
Wool (shillings)		903	2,533[d]	22,275
% receipts		4.7	4.0	5.0
Dairy (shillings)				9,914
% receipts				2.0

Notes
[a] Receipts lumped together as farm of the manors.
[b] Prices from D. L. Farmer, 'Some price fluctuations in Angevin England', *EcHR*,
IX, 1956–7, pp. 34–43; J. Z. Titow, *English Rural Society, 1200–1350*, London, 1969,
pp. 97–102. Rates converted to twelve months where necessary for comparability.
[c] These 'rents' include courts and aids.
[d] Amount includes sales of cheese.

Source
Pipe Rolls: 18 Henry II; 1 Richard I; 6–7 John; Public Record Office E 372/85; 87
and 88.

herds, pasture and woodlands.[13] Clerical chroniclers of the twelfth and
thirteenth century complained of royal abuse during such vacancies. A
study of the Winchester evidence can help us both to evaluate their
claims that the King 'spoiled' vacant sees and to establish the precise
effects of such depredations.

Data extracted from the Pipe Rolls for the Winchester vacancies
demonstrate considerable royal depredation of agrarian resources, as
Table 4.1 shows. When Henry II took custody of the See of Winchester

13 M. Howell, *Regalian right in medieval England*, London, 1962; D. Sutcliffe, 'The
     financial condition of the See of Canterbury 1279–1282', *Speculum*, X, 1935,
     pp. 53–68.

in 1171–72, the Bishop was still leasing or 'farming' his manors to
middlemen in exchange for money rents and food renders. For the
period of this vacancy the Pipe Rolls list only the total collected from
the farm rents of the manors. Not only did the revenues collected
from this vacancy exceed the Bishop's outstanding debt as calculated
from the Pipe Rolls (Figure 4.2), but the King failed to make any
reduction in the scale of the debt after the vacancy.

By the reign of Richard I the Pipe Rolls offer more details on the
management of vacancies. The entry for the Winchester vacancy of
1189–90 breaks down the income collected from rents, and from the
sales of the livestock and wool. Calculated according to that year's
price of oxen, livestock sales alone during the vacancy brought in a
sum equivalent to the sale of 1,550 oxen (a number in turn equivalent
to 95 per cent of the total number of oxen herded by the Bishop just
a quarter of a century later, when manorial accounts become available).[14]
This comparison shows just how much capital the Crown diverted from
production through such sales of livestock. Likewise, when the See
next fell vacant, in 1204–05, livestock sales yielded a revenue equivalent
to the sale of 71 per cent of all the oxen stocked on the Winchester
demesnes a few short years after the vacancy, in 1208–09. It is on the
occasion of this vacancy that the Pipe Rolls itemise sales of grain from
the estate for the first time, most no doubt emanating from those
demesnes which the Bishop had already brought under direct
management.[15] Following the death of Bishop Peter des Roches on 9
June 1238 the royal keepers' accounts for the ensuing vacancy, entered
on the Pipe Rolls from 1238 to 1244, document in even greater detail
the King's drain on local estate capital.[16] On this occasion a comparison
can be made between the local manorial accounts for the year preceding
the vacancy (1236–37) and the opening year of the reign of the new
Bishop (1244–45) with the keepers' accounts to assess losses of productive capacity.[17]

Table 4.1 shows (in annual units derived from current oxen prices)
that Henry III collected revenues at an annual rate comparable to

14 The prices used to calculate 'oxen equivalents' come from D. L. Farmer, 'Some
   price fluctuations in Angevin England', *EcHR*, IX, 1956–57, pp. 34–43.
15 The late twelfth and early thirteenth centuries mark a crucial transition towards
   direct management of estates: P. D. A. Harvey, 'The Pipe Rolls and the adoption
   of demesne farming in England', *EcHR*, XXVII, 1974, pp. 345–59; M. Mate, 'The
   farming out of manors: a new look at the evidence from Canterbury Cathedral
   Priory', *Journal of Medieval History*, IX, 1983, pp. 331–43.
16 Public Record Office E372/85, 87 and 88.
17 Hampshire Record Office, Winchester Pipe Rolls, 158285, 159287.

vacancies under Henry II, Richard I and King John. Nevertheless, although Henry III did not expropriate at a higher annual rate, he did keep the See vacant for a period five times longer than his predecessors. The keepers' accounts for the vacancy show changes in the sources of vacancy revenue. A dramatic increase in grain sales undoubtedly reflects the completed shift to direct management on the estate together with the expanding scale of demesne husbandry during the first decades of the thirteenth century. Over the six years of the vacancy, the King sold livestock equivalent to 2,440 oxen at their current price, representing an increase of almost two-thirds as compared with 1189-90. Either higher stocking levels under direct management made more livestock available for sale, or flocks and herds were being depleted at a higher rate during this vacancy. The four keepers' accounts preserved for the Winchester manors (less the Somerset manors of Taunton and Rimpton, which had their own keepers' accounts) show quite clearly that the King made the bulk of livestock sales in the last year of the vacancy, with 35 per cent of revenue from this source (£376 7s 0d out of £1,058 12s 0d) being received during this final year. The King thus maintained the sheep flocks and dairy herds of the Bishop and profited from them until the last shearing and milking, after which they were sold off for cash.

The King apparently stripped the Bishop's granary as well. In the last account, extending from Michaelmas (29 September) 1243 to 11 September 1244, the royal keepers recorded the sale of crops from the preceding harvest year. They also reported that they sold the *hibernagium* or winter corn stored in the granary. Presumably this sale included the winter wheat (the chief cash crop) and rye (the grain used to pay manorial servants) harvested just a month before the new Bishop took over the estate. Such sales undermined the productive capacities of the estate for some time by simultaneously stripping it of seed grain and depleting its capacity to buy seed grain. When William de Ralegh finally took over the Bishopric, he endeavoured to redress the damage by raising rents and doubling court fines: thereby, in turn, draining capital away from his tenants.[18] Nevertheless, these exactions could not make good the losses and cereal cultivation contracted by almost 1,000 acres in the immediate aftermath of the vacancy.

It was, however, the King's management of livestock resources

18 A recent study of St Alban's Abbey shows other ecclesiastical lords raised court fines after vacancies for probably very similar reasons: L. Slota, 'Law, land transfer and lordship on the estates of St Albans Abbey in the thirteenth and fourteenth centuries', *Law and History Review*, VI, 1988, pp. 119–38.

which most devastated the estate. Although sales of livestock, wool and dairy products brought in only a modest 11 per cent of total receipts during the vacancy, livestock provided an essential capital base for the estate. Their traction enabled demesne fields to be cultivated, their manure enriched the soil, and the Bishop sold dairy products and wool for a modest but steady annual income. Yet the King removed one-third of the Winchester sheep flock during the vacancy. Since it was the wethers which bore the heaviest fleeces and commanded the highest prices, their numbers were depleted most. The resultant two-thirds reduction seriously curtailed the incoming Bishop's chances to make cash on wool sales. Unimproved sheep flocks grow at an annual rate of about 15 per cent.[19] Since the King had reduced overall flock size by a third and breeding ewes by just under two-thirds, the Bishop would have had to wait at least four years for natural replacement to have made good these losses.

Even more devastatingly, the King sold approximately 90 per cent of the estate's breeding cows (as compared with 17 per cent of its oxen). Without a breeding herd of cows the Bishop could not even replace his dead oxen without outside purchases, much less restore the ox herd to its former numbers. In selling off the cows, the King essentially destroyed the herd by curtailing its reproductive capacity. Cattle herds grow more slowly than sheep flocks. Under optimum biological circumstances the herd would have taken at least a decade to reach its former levels, unless resort was made to the purchase of replacements. The King also wiped out the Bishop's pig herd, and in so doing removed a major source of calories from the episcopal household (which normally ate several thousand pigs a year).[20] Nevertheless, the Bishop was left his horses, an exception which raises interesting questions about their status as chattels.

The See of Winchester endured a vacancy in every generation throughout the thirteenth century. Since the King physically removed seed grain and livestock which resulted in serious reductions of the factors of production and consumption, vacancies cannot merely be equated with a form of income tax. Simple restoration of pre-vacancy production levels required both cash and time. The Bishops' tendency

---

19 Reproduction rates for sheep and for cattle come from G. Dahl and A. Hjort, *Having herds: pastoral growth and household economy*, Stockholm Studies in Social Anthropology, II, 1976, pp. 96–101 and 49–71.

20 K. Biddick, 'Pig husbandry on the Peterborough Abbey estate from the twelfth to the fourteenth century AD', pp. 161–77 in J. Clutton-Brock and C. Grigson, eds., *Animals and archaeology*, BAR, supplementary series, CCXXVII, Oxford, 1985.

to invest elsewhere in ritual symbols of power – churches and palaces – might very well be related to, and, indeed, an attempt to mask, the discontinuous nature of their power over agrarian resources. For these reasons data from the account rolls of particular estates provide a far from unproblematic source for examining linear trends in economic growth.

II The marketing framework and cereal productivity

Agrarian historians have regarded the thirteenth century as the golden age of demesne cultivation for the market without an adequate study of manorial accounts for evidence of the relative scale of market involvement. Manorial accounts record the proportions of the harvests marketed by seignorial lords and those consumed by their households, feudal officials, labouring staff, and livestock, together with the local sale prices of those commodities that were sold.[21] With this information it is possible to evaluate the extent to which cropping practices were determined by production for exchange or production for consumption. Decisions about the proportion to market and the proportion to conserve for seed, animal feed, and home consumption affected a farmer's vulnerability to fluctuations in prices. The greater the proportion of their harvest farmers consumed, the less their income varied with market price fluctuations and therefore they were less vulnerable to harvest fluctuations. Expectations of consumption versus marketing could thus shape a farmer's attitude toward yields.[22]

This relationship has been investigated for a sample of nine of the Winchester manors with reference to the accounting years 1209–37. Data were extracted from the accounts concerning the respective amounts of harvested grain consumed by the household, itinerant officials, demesne workers, and livestock, and reserved as seed for the following year, together with local sale prices for wheat, oats, barley, rye, and rye mixes (mancorn).[23] The period 1209–37 spans the episcopal

21 For the most comprehensive introduction to manorial accounts as sources see Harvey, *Manorial records of Cuxham.* For an introduction to agricultural manuals and accounting guides of the period consult D. Oschinsky, ed., *Walter of Henley and other treatises on estate management and accounting,* Oxford, 1971.

22 For consideration of these points see E. A. Wrigley, 'Some reflections on corn yields and prices in pre-industrial economies', pp. 92–130 in *idem, People, cities and wealth: the transformation of traditional society,* Oxford, 1987; W. Kula, *An economic theory of feudalism,* trans. L. Garner, London, 1976.

23 The following Winchester accounts were used in this study and are the sources for the tables: Hampshire Record Office, Winchester Pipe Rolls, 159270–85. See Appendix 4.1 for notes on data collection.

reign of Peter des Roches and also coincided with a revolution in agrarian lordship. Over the period 1180–1220, English lords, with few exceptions, took over direct management of their estates. Presumably direct seignorial control of agricultural production enhanced their capacities to respond to the commercial opportunities of the new medieval world economy in which they found themselves producing.[24]

The nine Winchester manors were chosen to represent a range of demesne sizes and locations on the estate (Figure 4.1). Four manors – Alresford, Crawley, Ecchinswell and Brightwell – were chosen from four of the administrative units of the estate located in the counties of Hampshire and Berkshire, where the bulk of the Bishop's manorial holdings lay. Downton and Rimpton were selected to represent the western holdings of the Bishop, and Fareham, located on an inlet of Portsmouth Harbour, to represent his southern coastal holdings. Finally, Witney in Oxfordshire and West Wycombe in Buckinghamshire were included as examples of outlying northern holdings of the estate used by the Bishop for access to Oxford and the east midlands.

Chalk and loam soils predominated on the manors of Alresford, Crawley, Downton, Ecchinswell, Fareham and West Wycombe, as they did on the majority of the Bishop's manors which clustered on the chalklands of southern England. Fertile loam and greensands formed the soils at Brightwell, whereas clay soils predominated at Rimpton and Witney.[25] In terms of market access, the manors of Downton, Alresford and Witney had market towns attached to them. Fareham was a mesne borough of the Bishop. The manor of Crawley lay within walking distance of the Winchester market and its great fair of St Giles held on September 1. Ecchinswell enjoyed access to the nearby market of Kingsclere as did Rimpton to the market town of Yeovil and the

24 See the following articles for discussion of the change in estate management: Harvey, 'Pipe Rolls'; M. Mate, 'The farming out of manors'. G. Duby labelled the period around 1180 as one of 'take-off' in *The early growth of the European economy*, trans. H. B. Clarke, Ithaca, NY, 1974. For a discussion of realignment of the medieval world economy during this time see also P. Nightingale, 'The evolution of weight standards and the creation of new monetary and commercial links in northern Europe from the tenth century to the twelfth century', *EcHR*, XXXVIII, 1985, pp. 192–209; K. Biddick, 'People and things: power in early English development', *Comparative Studies in Society and History*, XXXII, 1990, pp. 3–23.

25 Descriptions of soils and geology may be found as follows: L. Dudley-Stamp, ed., *The land of Britain: the report of the land utilisation survey of Britain*, London, part 56, 1943 (Witney), part 78, 1936 (Brightwell), part 86, 1938 (Rimpton), part 87, 1940 (Downton), part 89, 1940 (Alresford, Crawley, Ecchinswell), part 54, 1942 (West Wycombe).

ecclesiastical centre of Sherborne Abbey.[26] London cornmongers came to middle-Thames villages, such as Brightwell, to purchase wheat for transport by river to London.

II.i *Marketing and consumption of the grain harvest*

A simple tabulation of the evidence for marketing and home consumption of Winchester demesne grains shows high consumption rates for grain harvests (Tables 4.2 and 4.3), notwithstanding the traditional portrayal of these demesnes as 'federated grain factories' producing grain for the market. In fact, the rates of grain consumption on the Winchester demesnes were much higher than the consumption rate of 10 per cent assumed by the historical 'rule of thumb'. Tables 4.2 and 4.3 show that the Bishop, his household, and manorial staff consumed 72 per cent of his oat harvest on average, followed by barley at 65 per cent, and wheat – the most commercialised of grains – at the lower rate of 44 per cent.

II.ii *Local grain prices and their influence on consumption and cultivated acreages*

Even though the Bishop preferred to dispose of the bulk of his grain outside of the market, changing cereal prices may nonetheless have influenced his decisions about what portion of his demesne to cultivate with the chief cereal grains: wheat, barley, oats and rye. A study of the interrelationships between cereal consumption, cultivated acreage, and cereal prices in the early thirteenth century can shed light on the Bishop's interests in the grain market and serve as the basis for considering links between better yields and marketing.

Conventional economic wisdom maintains that farmers respond to a rise in the price of grain by sowing more grain. Economists and historians know very little about the dynamics of crop supply and the historical nature of farmers' responses to prices in their cultivation practices. M. Nerlove, a chief researcher of twentieth-century North American farmers' responses to grain prices, argued that farmers respond to price changes they expect to be permanent.[27] He called that price the 'expected normal price' or 'the average level about which future prices are expected to fluctuate'. Nerlove experimented with

---

26 See Thornton, below, pp. 187–8.
27 M. Nerlove, *The dynamics of supply: estimation of farmers' response to prices*, Johns Hopkins University Studies in Historical and Political Science, series LXVI, II, 1958, pp. 82–6 and 210–15. I am grateful to Winifred Rothenberg for this reference.

Table 4.2 *Total acreage, proportion of demesnes sown with grain, and proportion of grain consumed, on nine Winchester manors, 1209–37 (means and standard deviations)*

Manor	Mean acreage	Wheat		Oats		Rye[a]	Barley	
		[b]	[c]	[b]	[c]	[b]	[b]	[c]
Alresford	340.5	25.2	50	34.6	78	15.8	24.5	46
s.d.	71.9	8.4	27	6.2	21	12.5	5.4	17
Brightwell	228.8	69.6	37	18.7	91	5.8	10.6	100
s.d.	11.7	6.9	22	2.9	38	4.2	7.6	96
Crawley	366.5	17.3	46	47.0	83	18.5	19.5	65
s.d.	39.2	3.5	29	6.4	24	4.7	5.3	15
Downton	760.6	43.3	52	33.4	65	7.4	19.4	44
s.d.	89.4	8.0	29	3.9	25	5.7	8.3	13
Ecchinswell	212.5	47.4	34	38.0	65	14.8	3.4	55
s.d.	29.4	13.1	25	6.7	46	7.8	3.5	28
Fareham	364.6	46.2	62	41.6	85		12.1	58
s.d.	43.1	5.3	30	4.1	41		4.1	29
Rimpton	196.2	44.3	43	36.2	53	15.5	4.1	49
s.d.	39.9	6.6	38	5.8	17	7.5	4.2	36
West Wycombe	398.2	39.0	34	44.5	52	10.5	6.8	78
s.d.	58.0	5.7	10	6.7	19	7.1	4.1	68
Witney	460.6	46.5	34	34.7	73		18.8	89
s.d.	85.6	14.7	23	14.5	23		11.4	36

Notes
s.d. is the standard deviation.
[a] The rye data are erratic: see Appendix 4.1.
[b] Mean percentage of acreage sown
[c] Mean percentage of harvest consumed

Source
Hampshire Record Office, Winchester Pipe Rolls (1209–1237), 159270A and 159270–85.

price lags of one, two, and three years in his study of changing responses to cultivation of corn and wheat acreages and found varying strengths of correlations depending on the lags introduced in the equation.

Significantly, Table 4.4 – which lists Pearson correlation coefficients for cereal consumption, cultivated acreage, and prices (the latter with lags of one, two, and three years) – reveals no such tendency for the Winchester demesnes to alter their sown acreages in response to local

Table 4.3 *Yields and consumption of grain per acre on nine Winchester manors,
1209–37 (bushels per acre, means and standard deviations)*

Manor	Wheat			Oats			Barley		
	Yield	*Eat*	*%*	*Yield*	*Eat*	*%*	*Yield*	*Eat*	*%*
Alresford	7.5	2.7	36	10.8	7.9	73	12.0	6.5	54
s.d.	2.7	1.6		2.5	1.5		4.6	2.3	
Brightwell	13.4	3.6	27	12.2	10.3	84	24.1	19.2	80
s.d.	4.0	0.8		5.2	4.3		5.3	14.0	
Crawley	9.1	3.7	41	12.3	9.2	75	16.5	10.3	62
s.d.	2.5	2.5		2.0	2.5		2.0	2.8	
Downton	6.6	2.7	41	12.1	7.3	60	16.1	6.9	43
s.d.	4.9	0.9		2.2	3.7		4.0	3.3	
Ecchinswell	8.2	1.7	21	12.2	5.6	46	12.9	6.6	51
s.d.	4.0	0.8		4.1	1.5		5.9	4.0	
Fareham	8.4	4.6	55	13.7	10.0	73	23.2	12.5	54
s.d.	1.5	3.4		1.5	4.3		3.2	8.1	
Rimpton	7.2	1.8	25	11.4	5.4	47	12.4	4.6	37
s.d.	4.2	0.9		3.8	1.2		8.3	3.9	
West Wycombe	11.5	3.6	31	16.0	6.4	40	20.5	9.6	47
s.d.	2.3	0.8		3.4	1.5		5.3	8.4	
Witney	6.7	2.2	33	11.2	10.1	90	17.0	11.1	65
s.d.	1.8	1.4		3.5	6.0		4.3	4.2	
Mean rate of consumption of yield per acre	34 (±10)			65 (±17)			55 (±12)		

Note
s.d. is the standard deviation.

Source As Table 4.2.

price fluctuations. The highest correlation of 0.250 for oat acreages
lagged three years against oat prices, is far too low to justify postulat-
ing a causal link between the two. Indeed, in the case of barley the
equivalent correlation is negative at −0.235, implying that higher barley
prices resulted in less planting. On this evidence short-term price
changes had virtually no influence on planting strategies. By contrast,
decisions to plant wheat, rye, barley and oats reveal strong correlations
with consumption patterns. The acreage sown with spring barley

Table 4.4 *Pearson correlations of sown acreage with consumption and lagged prices on nine Winchester manors, 1209–37*

	Consumption	Prices (lag 1)	Prices (lag 2)	Prices (lag 3)
Wheat	0.660	0.001	−0.180	0.147
Oats	0.686	0.124	0.045	0.250
Rye	0.602	−0.191	−0.208	−0.102
Barley	0.791	0.081	−0.085	−0.235
n	153	153	76	39

Note n is the number of harvests for which data is available.

Source As Table 4.2.

correlates most strongly (0.791) with consumption. This is not surprising as barley was the grain used for brewing and a grain typically used to pay manorial servants. The acreage sown with oats also correlates fairly closely with consumption (0.686), as does that of winter wheat (0.660), whereas the correlation with rye is somewhat weaker (0.602). Considered together, the data from the nine manors show the strong effects of consumption on decisions to plant demesne acreages with different cereals. Such results suggest that the Bishop was primarily interested in subsistence agriculture on his demesnes.

The consumption of grain had a specific structure on the estate, in so far as the Bishop used different grains for specific forms of consumption. He produced the bulk of the hay and oats fed to his own cattle and horses as well as the considerable number of horses of itinerant officials who rode through his manors. Particular provision for stabling and fodder was made on manors such as Witney, which served the Bishop as a chief staging point to the midlands. Manorial servants were paid with rye or spring barley. Some manors paid their staff exclusively in one or the other grain, such as Fareham which paid in barley or Ecchinswell which paid almost wholly in rye. Other manors, such as Alresford, paid some staff with rye and others with barley. The Bishop's household also used barley for brewing and wheat for baking bread.

II.iii *Grain consumption, acreages, and prices at the local level: manor by manor analysis*

The regional structure of the Bishop's consumption habits, his cultivation practices, and his response to the market become clearer by examining the correlations between consumption, prices, and acreages

E

Table 4.5 *Pearson correlations of sown acreage with harvest consumption and prices on nine Winchester manors, 1209–37*

	Wheat		Barley		Rye		Oats	
	prices	cons.	prices	cons.	prices	cons.	prices	cons.
Alresford	.165	.437	.391	.415	−.335	.741	−.194	.517
Brightwell	−.225	.492	.440	.693	−.413	.418	−.208	.570
Crawley	−.177	.228	−.033	.613	−.108	.759	−.416	.513
Downton	.191	.248	−.053	.843	−.383	.897	.118	.020
Ecchinswell	−.131	.360	.142	.773	.304	.210	.090	.548
Fareham	−.180	.693	.404	−.148	.357		−.381	.542
Rimpton	.162	.228	−.101	.243	.473	−.260	.585	.876
West Wycombe	.259	.020	−.003	−.080	−.194	.737	−.365	.468
Witney	−.349	.345	.303	.289	.221	.092	.103	−.106

Source As Table 4.2.

on the individual manors (see Table 4.5). High correlations between acreage and consumption on the individual manors show that both large and small manors practised consumption strategies. With few exceptions, then, consumption had a stronger relationship to planting decisions than did prices. Even in those few instances – wheat at West Wycombe, oats at Downton and Witney, rye at Ecchinswell and Rimpton, barley at Fareham – where correlations between prices and acreage were higher than the correlations between consumption and acreage, they did not exceed 0.40. Thus, the Bishop seems to have practised a 'satisfier' strategy; which means that he protected his consumption base, rather than maximising his income through participation in grain markets.

Satisficing strategies guided choices about crop mixes on the nine Winchester demesnes in the study. In order to understand why these demesnes cultivated different crop mixes it is necessary to examine how each demesne served as a node with its own specific consumption role within this sufficing framework. This entails finding a way to depict the complex interactions between consumption, prices, and acreages on each of the different manors. The method employed has been to plot (in Figure 4.3), for each of the major grains cultivated by the Bishop, the manor-by-manor correlations between prices and acreages (horizontal axis) and between consumption and acreage (vertical axis). The resultant patterns help to illustrate the point that each of

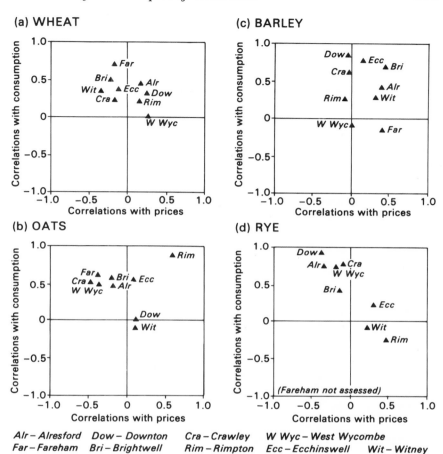

Figure 4.3 *Correlations of acreage with prices and consumption on nine Winchester manors, 1209–37*

the manors occupied a specific position within the consumption framework of the estate's cereal economy.

The pattern for wheat, Figure 4.3(a), shows that the correlations between acreages and consumption, and acreages and prices, were lower than those for other grains. These results make sense if wheat is thought of as the crop the Bishop marketed most. He constrained manorial consumption of wheat more than any other grain. Manorial servants, feudal officials, and demesne livestock were least likely to receive this grain for pay, gift, or sustenance. Such restraint on manorial consumption of wheat undoubtedly explains the lower correlations of wheat consumption with acreages. The weak correlation of prices with acreage also becomes more understandable if the Bishop is thought of as a target producer of his cash crop. Constrained by the requirements to grow oats for fodder, and rye or barley for wages in kind and other consumption necessities, the Bishop had to fix his winter wheat acreage. Such fixed acreages would not drive prices, thus producing a marketing situation where there are low correlations between prices and sown acreage. Among the manors, Fareham has the highest correlation for wheat consumption and acreage. Brightwell, Witney, Ecchinswell and Crawley all have moderate positive correlations between acreages and consumption and moderate to low negative correlations between acreages and prices. Alresford, Rimpton, Downton, and, in a lone position, West Wycombe, represent different types of wheat cropping strategies with moderate positive correlations between acreages and consumption and low positive correlations with prices.

Generally, correlations of oat consumption with acreage are higher, Figure 4.3(b), reflecting pressures to match oat acreage with fodder consumption. At Downton and Witney correlations of oat consumption and acreage are particularly low. Both manors served as staging points for the Bishop and his officials and substantial consumption of oats occurred there. Witney was also a manor where Bishop and peasants engaged in much assarting, or land clearance. The practice of planting assarted land with oats could account for the weak negative correlation of oat consumption with acreage at Witney. Certainly, Table 4.2 shows that the highest standard deviations for acreages sown with wheat, oats, and barley occurred at Witney, possibly reflecting a cycle of woodland clearance, involving first oat cropping and subsequent incorporation of cleared areas into field systems for winter and spring cropping cycles. In contrast, the oats acreage at Downton varied little from year to year, unlike the consumption of oats by the Bishop's household which varied a good deal. During the troubled years of 1209–18 the Bishop spent much time at Downton and his horses consumed a great deal of fodder. Afterwards, his political itinerary changed, and the Bishop's consumption of oats there became negligible. With its residence and larder for the Bishop, Downton served as one of the chief household centres of the estate. Accordingly, there is little correlation between prices and consumption, and prices and oat acreage, on this manor simply because oats were only sold when they were left unconsumed by the household.

The picture for oats in Figure 4.3(b) depicts a spectrum of responses of acreages to prices. At Rimpton, acreage correlates positively with prices and consumption. This manor balanced responsiveness to both consumption and prices: a strategy which can be termed innovative. Crawley, in contrast, displays a negative correlation of oat acreages with prices (−0.416). When oat prices rose it could plant a smaller acreage and still achieve its income target, while releasing space in its fields for other crops. This response to prices can be termed adaptive. The manors of Crawley, Fareham, West Wycombe, Ecchinswell, and Rimpton, can be imagined as ordered on an adaptive–innovative continuum according to their cropping strategies. Crawley appears the most adaptive, Ecchinwell assumes an intermediate position, and Rimpton anchors the innovative end of the continuum.[28]

The correlations of barley with acreages in Figure 4.3(c) show mostly innovative strategies, with consumption also appearing as a relatively important factor. This underlines barley's dual role as a commercial brewing grain and as a grain used to pay manorial servants in kind. Adaptive strategies are consequently less prevalent for barley and Crawley (−0.033), Downton (−0.053), Rimpton (−0.101), West Wycombe (−0.002) all register very low negative correlations between sown acreages and prices. At Fareham the signs of a 'commercial' strategy might be appearing, since barley prices correlate positively with acreages, whereas consumption correlates negatively. In its restraint of barley consumption Fareham resembled Rimpton in its restraint of rye consumption.

Interpretation of the picture for rye in Figure 4.3(d) requires some caution, since several manors grew little or no rye during this period and purchased rye on the market to pay their manorial servants. The manors of Alresford and Downton showed adaptive strategies to the cropping of rye. Rimpton is the one manor where a commercial tendency emerges. The rye acreage at Rimpton correlates positively with rye prices (+0.473) but weakly and negatively (−0.260) with rye consumption. No manor showed evidence of innovative responses to rye cropping.

This study of grain consumption shows that, although the Bishop sold grain on the market, planting strategies on the estate were at this date more influenced by the requirements of consumption. Manors traded off acreages in different winter and spring crops and a manor's position in the consumption structure of the estate probably influenced such trade-offs. Such patterns also overrode environmental factors so that cropping strategies differed between demesnes within the same

28 For Rimpton see Thornton, below, pp. 183–210.

ecological zone, as in the cases of Downton and Crawley, both large chalkland manors. The choice of grain customarily used on a manor as pay for manorial staff also explains some of the differences in crop choice which have been observed. Traditionally some manors, such as Witney, paid servants with barley, others such as Rimpton, paid them with rye, whereas yet others paid with both. The expectations of manorial servants for payment in a certain kind of grain constrained the trade-offs a manor could make between winter and spring crops.

The importance of consumption to planting strategies has broad implications for evaluating the associated productivity levels. The configurations of responses to prices and consumption found for each of the grains suggest that overall sufficing strategies mattered for cereal cultivation on the estate of the Bishop of Winchester in the early thirteenth century. The Bishop chose balance and flexibility to meet production targets for consumption and income.[29] Such an argument does not, however, intend to link typologically high consumption rates with low productivity. The intensive high-yielding cultivation practices, typical on certain Norfolk demesnes, and adopted, presumably, in response to the lure of urban markets, occur elsewhere, as, for instance, on the home manors of the Peterborough Abbey estate, which fed the monastic household and sold virtually no grain. Likewise, the monks of Battle Abbey used progressive convertible husbandry on their home demesne at Marley to integrate intensive market-oriented pastoral husbandry with the consumption of grain from the demesne.[30] In short, the local nature of subsistence agriculture and marketing on the Winchester demesnes cannot alone explain their low productivity. Account

29 This conclusion suggests that the Bishop took over direct management of his estate in order to protect consumption whilst he engaged in the market. Agrarian lords knew from their long familiarity with power that 'they were what they ate', and their priority in the early thirteenth century was hence to protect consumption. Whether they persisted in such consumption strategies, or subsequently became, instead, 'what they marketed' will be the subject of future studies.

30 The Norfolk evidence is discussed in B. M. S. Campbell, 'Agricultural progress in medieval England: some evidence from eastern Norfolk', *EcHR*, XXXVI, 1983, pp. 26–46; *idem*, 'Arable productivity in medieval England: some evidence from Norfolk', *JEH*, XLIII, 1983, pp. 379–404. Peterborough Abbey used high-yielding techniques similar to those employed in Norfolk on manors whose grain was mostly destined for the Abbey's consumption: K. Biddick, *The other economy: pastoral husbandry on a medieval estate*, Berkeley and Los Angeles, 1989. E. Searle describes convertible husbandry on Battle Abbey's manor of Marley in the early fourteenth century and argues that the principal object of this technological innovation was greater 'animal produce': *idem, Lordship and community: Battle Abbey and its banlieu, 1066–1538*, Toronto, 1974, p. 286.

must also be taken of the inter-regional links of local economies. For the county of Hampshire this requires a consideration of the Bishop of Winchester's involvement in the inter-regional wool market.

III The framework of pastoral production

The regular depletion of flocks and herds during royal vacancies depressed pastoral productivity on the Winchester estate. Since the cereal acreage also tended to contract as a result of vacancies, total livestock units and total sown acreage tended to move in sympathy with one another.[31] The numbers of livestock herded by the Bishop had little effect, however, on the yield per acre of the different cereals. The highest correlation (−0.308) occurred for livestock units and gross wheat yields per acre. The fact that this correlation is negative – which suggests that more animals meant lower yields – hints at the possibility that the Bishop considered his pastoral farming as a parallel enterprise to his grain farming, rather than the two as an integrated enterprise.

Sheep served as the Bishop's chief pastoral cash crop. He relied on the sale of sheep cheese and wool as his main sources of pastoral income and consequently endeavoured to expand flock numbers. Between 1209 and 1237 sheep numbers rose by 15 per cent on the nine sampled manors, the bulk of this increase being accounted for by biological growth rather than market purchases. Indeed, at a time when the combined flock of these nine manors numbered some 4,400–5,000 animals, an average of only 85 sheep were purchased each year. Compared with sheep, cows and horses played a minimal role in the Bishop's pastoral economy. During the period 1209–37, oxen outnumbered cows by over two to one and horses by anywhere between 12 and 19 to one. Cows were thus comparatively insignificant as dairy stock and horses had yet to be incorporated into cultivation or transport.

Agrarian historians lack convenient methods for comparing cereal and pastoral productivity. One partial solution is to compare the relative contribution of the chief sources of the Bishop's income – rents, grain

---

31 The method used to calculate livestock units is similar to that employed by Campbell and Thornton (below, pp. 153, 156–7 and 198–9), with the exception that 3–4-year-old cattle and 2–3-year-old cattle are grouped together and multiplied by a factor of 0.5 to arrive at the units for these cohorts. Correlation coefficients of livestock units against sown acreage on the nine manors for the period 1209–37 yield results of 0.550 for wheat, 0.672 for barley, and 0.666 for oats.

sales, and sales of cheese and wool – per cultivated acre on the nine manors. For the period 1209–37 income from grain sales by no means predominated, a finding to be expected from a satisficer strategy. Pastoral income amounted on average to 25 per cent of grain sales per cultivated acre, and rental income to 64 per cent.[32] Pastoral income from cheese and wool is actually more highly correlated with total cultivated acreage (+0.611) than is grain income (+0.454). Since the Bishop consumed far less of his pastoral output than his grain output such a relation makes sense.

Methodological problems also face historians wishing to assess the relative importance of sheep dairying and wool growing in the estate economy. Unfortunately, important as pastoral husbandry was to the Bishop, standardised ways of measuring dairy productivity had not fully penetrated his accounting practices. In this period the accounts reported weights for marketed cheeses only, and simply counted the unmarketed cheeses. Since the weight of cheeses varied enormously it is not possible to devise any reliable factor for converting enumerated cheeses into weights. Without the figure for the total weight of cheeses produced, the dairy productivity of ewes cannot be fully assessed. Instead, measures of dairy and wool productivity have to rely upon the quantities that were marketed since it is only these for which weight information is available.

In the case of wool, the pounds of marketed wool per acre closely approximates total wool production, since the Bishop kept back only a few fleeces from the market to pay shepherds and dairy maids, and tithes on some manors. With cheese the disparity is greater, for the Bishop consumed some cheeses and paid others in wages and in tithes. Even so, Table 4.6 shows that on the nine sampled manors the Bishop produced more cheese per cultivated acre than wool. Textbooks frequently disparage sheep dairying; it is therefore important to emphasise that this labour-intensive activity provided the Bishop with a valuable source of income.[33] Dairy income per ewe varied between 66 and 100 per cent of the wool income per ewe and wether of the sheep flock. The several thousand cheeses produced yearly on the manors thus amounted to a lucrative income for the Bishop.

Estate policy was thus chiefly one of consuming the products of the grain sector and selling the pastoral products of sheep husbandry.

---

32 On average, rent contributed 1.04 shillings per cultivated acre, grain sales 2.12 shillings, and pastoral sales 0.45 shillings in the early thirteenth century.
33 The labour would have been predominantly female.

Table 4.6 *Pounds of marketed cheese and wool per cultivated acre on nine Winchester manors, 1209–37 (means and standard deviations)*

	Cheese	Wool
1209	2.41	1.29
s.d.	1.33	0.85
1211	3.19	
s.d.	2.17	
1212	2.19	1.53
s.d.	1.28	0.79
1214	3.24	1.75
s.d.	2.60	1.30
1216[a]		
1218[a]		
1219	2.66	1.56
s.d.	1.40	1.05
1220	2.70	1.58
s.d.	1.88	1.25
1221	5.18	2.47
s.d.	3.56	2.00
1224	4.26	1.87
s.d.	2.69	1.47
1225	3.29	1.91
s.d.	1.45	1.41
1226	4.36	1.76
s.d.	2.12	2.07
1227	4.75	1.64
s.d.	2.80	1.82
1232	3.73	2.46
s.d.	1.24	1.81
1233	4.99	2.62
s.d.	2.91	1.88
1236	4.26	2.69
s.d.	2.36	1.92
1237	4.41	2.65
s.d.	3.30	2.11

Notes
s.d. is the standard deviation.
[a] Data too erratic during the Civil War.

Source As Table 4.2.

Table 4.7 *Pearson correlations between the prices of wheat, oats, cheese, wool, and livestock numbers on nine Winchester manors, 1209–37*

| | Price per quarter | | Price per pound | |
	Wheat	Oats	Cheese	Wool
Sheep flock	.137	.120	.243	.117
Horse herd	−.067	.648	−.040	.010
Cattle herd	.042	−.038	.101	.232
Cheese price per 1b.	.188	.051		.371
Wool price per 1b.	−.075	−.060	.371	

Source As Table 4.2.

Interestingly, local cereal and livestock product prices do not correlate strongly, a result which seemingly reflects the separation of the pastoral and cereal sectors within the regional economy. Table 4.7 lists correlations of grain prices with cheese and wool prices as well as correlations between grain prices and herd sizes. Only local oat prices correlate strongly with horse herd size (+0.648), a finding which underscores the dichotomy which existed between the Bishop's reliance on the market to replace horses, as opposed to his reliance upon biological reproduction to maintain his sheep flocks and cattle herds.

Historians have taken for granted that the medieval livestock sector depended upon the cereal sector without exploring the relationships between them. Given the importance of the Bishop's pastoral husbandry, it is useful to conceptualise relationships between the pastoral and cereal sectors on the nine manors of our study. The Bishop co-ordinated pastoral and cereal activities along a spectrum, as Figure 4.4, which plots the correlations between pastoral income and grain income with cultivated acreage, illustrates. On the manors of Fareham and Alresford, cultivated acreage declined slightly between 1209 and 1237 as their sheep flocks increased. These manors grew more 'pastoral' over time. Crawley and Ecchinswell mirrored Fareham and Alresford: acreage cultivated remained stable at Crawley and Ecchinswell as the sheep flock increased. Crawley and Ecchinswell thus maintained their cropping strategies as they intensified the pastoral sector. The manors of Downton and Rimpton, the largest and smallest demesnes respectively, lie along the cereal axis. Downton's sheep flocks declined as its acreage remained stable and its grain sales increased. It thus became more 'arable'. Rimpton, too, improved its arable acreage

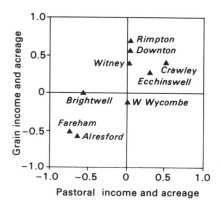

Figure 4.4 *Correlations of pastoral and grain income with cultivated acreages on nine Winchester manors, 1209–37*

and grain income per acre.[34] Brightwell, a manor with no pastoral marketing component, lies, not surprisingly, along the negative pastoral axis. Its practice of selling much of its winter wheat crop and consuming most of its spring crops from its two-field system probably accounts for the very low correlation of grain sales with cultivated acreage.

IV Conclusion

M. M. Postan and J. Z. Titow have argued on the evidence of the Winchester estate that a high point in demesne productivity reached in the first half of the thirteenth century diminished toward the end of the century due to the excessive demands of agriculture upon the soil.[35] This study has shown that the intensely extractive pressure of the emerging medieval English state complicates any simple notion of a golden age for early-thirteenth-century demesne agriculture. Over the opening four decades of the thirteenth century the King, by virtue of regalian right, twice stripped the Winchester estate of important livestock capital, which resulted in the loss of draught energy and pastoral income. Productivity on the estate and the agrarian strategies of the Bishop must be evaluated within this broad framework of cyclical state disinvestment.

34 See Thornton, below, pp. 186–7.
35 Postan, 'Medieval agrarian society'; *idem, The medieval economy and society*; Titow, *Winchester yields; idem, English rural society*. For an assessment of the situation at Rimpton see Thornton, below, pp. 197–8.

Within this political framework the estate consistently opted for diversity and flexibility in its cultivation practices as the fan-like patterns which depict the relations between consumption, prices, and cereal acreages in Figure 4.3, and the scores for pastoral and cereal income correlated with total cultivated acreage in Figure 4.4, illustrate. The high consumption rates for cereals on the estate buffered the Bishop from fluctuations in market prices. The Bishop's good returns from sales of cheese and wool – the prices of which do not seem to have fluctuated with local wheat and oat prices – further cushioned the Bishop's need to maximise income in the cereal sector. Such high consumption rates of cereals in a comparatively non-urbanised regional economy undoubtedly reinforced the low commercial returns to marketed grain.[36] Surprisingly, then, the relatively and absolutely low yields of Winchester demesne cultivation may have seemed optimal to the Bishop who subsisted on his grain and relied on the inter-regional wool market for a modest but steady source of cash.

These detailed findings for the early thirteenth century point to wider issues requiring further study. The changing levels of population density, market development, and urbanisation, as well as the specific links of a regional economy to inter-regional markets and the state, are crucial to understanding the local decisions which determined demesne cultivation practices. If the bulk of the Bishop's manors had lain in a more urbanised area, differently articulated with livestock markets, then undoubtedly his attitude toward cereal yields would have been different. Hence, on any individual demesne, agrarian practices were as much shaped by links with the wider political and economic world as they were by custom and other specifically local conditions. Closer studies of the institutional articulation of production and consumption and the nature and degree of integration between cereal and livestock markets will therefore prove crucial to a better understanding of spatial and temporal differences in levels of pre-industrial agrarian productivity.

36 See G. Grantham, below, p. 346.

Appendix 4.1 *Notes on the collection of data for prices, consumption, and storage from the Winchester account rolls*

Some difficulties were encountered in collecting these Winchester data. In spite of its reputation as a continuous series, the Winchester accounts have only six decades – 1310–19 and 1340–89 – with complete sets of accounts. No decade in the thirteenth century has more than seven accounts preserved. Seventeen accounts survive from the 28 year episcopal reign of Peter des Roches (1209–37) and these are the only known extant documents of their type for England for this time.

The period had its share of political unrest which had an impact on seignorial agriculture. Upon the death of King John is October 1216, baronial rebellion flared. In the early spring of 1217 members of the baronial party marched on the strongholds of Peter des Roches, a leading royalist and guardian of the young King Henry III. Intermittent rebellion continued in the autumn of 1217. The accounts for the years 1215–16 and 1217–18 thus cover a period of turmoil. Grain prices rose in 1217–18. During that year the Bishop routed grain from his manors to provision his castles at Wolvesey in Winchester and Farnham outside London. On many manors he sold the autumn harvest as it stood in the fields. He occasionally sold grain in that way during the 1220s as a response to taxation demands, such as the Fifteenth of 1225, and to military campaigns, such as the Welsh campaign of 1221. When grain was sold as a standing crop valuable information is lost about the total harvest, since the accountants simply recorded the sum received for the sale. Other problems arise because in the early thirteenth century the accountants did not usually break down the amount of grain sold at different prices over the course of the year, a practice which became common by the end of the century. Generally, there is only one annual price for a grain. When accountants did record more than one grain price the highest was chosen for this study. If no local grain price was available, due to lack of sales or damage to the document, the current grain price was used from the closest neighbouring manor. Failing that, the sale price for that grain at Crawley, a manor just outside the episcopal seat of Winchester, was used.

The collection of information on acreage also presented some problems. The Bishop of Winchester did not convert customary acres, which varied from manor to manor, to statute acres until 1232.[37] Historians have therefore tended to neglect the early Winchester accounts. In this study a conversion factor derived from the sowing rate was used to convert customary acres to standard acres for each manor. Sowing rates per customary acre and per measured acre showed little variation over the first half of the thirteenth century. It was therefore possible to use the difference between the two seeding rates to calculate the manor's conversion factor. The manors of Downton, Rimpton and West Wycombe were among the minority of Winchester manors already using statute acres when the accounts begin. Statute acres ranged from 1.32 to 1.55 times larger than customary acres.

Local grain storage, which could shape planting strategies if manors regularly stored some of their winter or spring crops, also required consideration. Out of a potential maximum of 153 cases, reserves of more than 10 per cent of the demesne harvest remained in the barn at the end of the accounting year in the following instances:

	cases	*per cent*
Wheat	11	7.0
Oats	10	6.5
Rye and rye mixes	1	1.3
Barley	4	2.6

In only four instances did the volume of wheat reserves on a manor exceed the storage capacity of a small barn measuring 30 feet by 15 feet by 10 feet, roughly the size of a medieval peasant house.[38] Barley

---

37 Titow, *Winchester yields*, p. 9. Peter des Roches also established the Soke of Winchester at this time as part of a major reorganisation of rural and urban properties: Keene, *Medieval Winchester*, pp. 72–3.

38 This empirical evidence contributes to the debate between D. N. McCloskey and S. Fenoaltea over *seignorial* grain storage: D. N. McCloskey and J. Nash, 'Corn at interest: the extent and cost of grain storage in medieval England', *American Economic Review*, LXXIV, 1984, pp. 174–87; S. Fenoaltea, 'Transaction costs, Whig history, and the common fields', *Politics and Society*, XVI, 1988, pp. 171–240; D. N. McCloskey, 'The open fields of England: rent, risk, and the rate of interest, 1300–1815', pp. 5–51 in D. W. Galenson, ed., *Markets in history: economic studies of the past*, Cambridge, 1989. The estimate for the size of a barn capable of storing 40 quarters (320 bushels) of grain comes from Oschinsky, *Walter of Henley*, p. 475: 'Ad estimacionem grangie. Memorandum quod una meya frumenti in grangia que grangia est latitudinis xxx pedum in uno spacio inter duo furcos longitundine xv pedum et altitudine parietum x pedum continebit communiter xl quarteria.'

reserves exceeded such capacity on a manor once, and oat reserves, twice. Except for the manor of Alresford, which carried reserves of oats into the next harvest more than twice in the 17 accounting years, no manor practised a policy of regular storage. Even Alresford stored oats less than 25 per cent of the time over the 17 accounting years. Storage was too irregular and contingent to shape manorial planting strategies.

The measure of consumption used in the study comprises each grain itemised in the accounts as sent to the Bishop's household, seed for sowing, pay for manorial staff and feudal officials, harvest meals for customary labour, and feed for livestock. Manors purchasing grain for consumption, which happened frequently with rye (a grain chiefly used as wages in kind for manorial servants), received a consumption value of zero, since they did not use their own manorially-grown grain for consumption purposes.

Labour productivity
in medieval agriculture:
Tuscany and the 'Low Countries'

I The rationale of productivity measurements

Attempts at productivity measurement are usually inspired by the implicit assumption that changes in productivity also provide information about changes in income, or even better, welfare. The problem to be faced in analysing medieval Europe, however, is not only that the documentation is poor, but also that direct information pertaining to productivity concerns the product of single factors of production other than labour. The ingenuity which medievalists have displayed in the analysis of, for example, yield ratios in terms of seed corn or land, has greatly increased knowledge of agriculture in this period, but yield ratios have no unambiguous income or welfare implications. For instance, an increase in yield per seed may represent a genuine increase in total factor productivity or may, alternatively, have derived from a switch in production methods so that more land and/or labour were used in production.[1] The problem is that control for variations in all factors of production is not normally possible. Similarly, an increase in yields per unit of land may be part of a total factor productivity increase but may also be related to higher inputs of seed corn and/or labour.

Research for this chapter was made possible by a generous research grant from the Carlsberg Foundation. Centre Culturel Suèdois provided me with a 'studio' while working in Paris. Professors Alain Derville and Gérard Sivéry of Université de Lille III, have been most helpful in correspondence and conversations. Mr Jens Buus Christensen has given me computer assistance. Numerous participants at the Workshop on Agricultural Productivity in the European Past, Rockefeller Center, Bellagio, Italy, March 1989 and the Second World Congress of Cliometrics, Santander, Spain, June 1989 suggested improvements which I have tried to incorporate in this version. Participation in these conferences was made possible by travel grants from the Danish Social Science Research Council.
1 Total factor productivity is the residual productivity increase that cannot be attributed to the recorded increase in factors of production such as labour, capital and land. It is thus dependent on improvements in technology, knowledge, quality of inputs and organisation.

Problems do not end here, however, because yield statistics do not normally cover all types of agrarian output. Since the relative weight of non-recorded products varied over time – industrial plants were becoming increasingly important in the medieval period – it is difficult to predict changes in total output. And even if there was information on all agrarian products, the problem of aggregating different physical units to an income measure – something which has yet to be attempted for the medieval period – remains to be solved.

Another frequently-used source for output and productivity measurements is tithe data. It is possible to estimate income from tithe data interpreting the tithe as an income tax provided that, (a), income from all types of output was covered by the tithe, (b), the exact magnitude of the tithe is known, and finally, (c), the taxed unit remained the same throughout the period under investigation. Unfortunately, the frequency of – or changes in – fraudulent behaviour of the tithe-paying units cannot be ascertained. Nor is it possible to be sure about the percentage of the output ascribed to the tithe, or that the unit to be taxed remained unchanged. The magnitude of the tithe varied between 5 and 15 per cent, and the incidence of fraud is, by the very nature of such behaviour, difficult to assess.

To compound matters, the bulk of surviving documentation relates to the agricultural activities of landlords and especially of estates in clerical ownership. If an independent peasantry or tenantry played an increasingly important role in agricultural production, as it undoubtedly did by the end of the medieval period, then available documentation may be more and more out of tune with what actually happened. Any attempt at measuring agricultural productivity in this period will of course face the problem of scarcity of information. Nevertheless, the method that is offered here uses other types of data and can, to some extent, be supplemented by theoretical considerations. Moreover, the method is very 'economical' in its use of those data, in so far as it demands only limited quantities and types of information. It also has the merit of focusing directly on a productivity concept which is at the same time an income measure, that is, a labour productivity measure.

While labour productivity can easily be interpreted as per capita income (see Appendix 5.1), it is not a perfect welfare index. Thus, although it is possible to assess product per labourer, changes in hours worked per labourer cannot be controlled for. It is perfectly possible that what is recorded as a stagnant income may conceal an increase in product per hour of labour while producers decided to remain on the same income level and increase their leisure. In that case income per labourer has not increased, but welfare has, considering leisure time as a contribution to welfare. Conversely, what is recorded as an augmentation in productivity (as product per labourer) may be due in whole or in part to an increased number of hours worked per labourer. Is such an increase in income also generating an increase in welfare? The answer to that question must take the particular circumstances in which labour is expanded into consideration. If it is a matter of unrestrained choice in doing so, then it can without hesitation be called an increase, not only in income, but also in welfare. In fact, it will be argued in the concluding paragraphs of this chapter that a significant part of the recorded increase in income can probably be ascribed to an increase in labour effort, that is hours per labourer.

II Method

Appendix 5.1 contains a formal presentation of the method used in estimating labour productivity growth. In this section, therefore, an attempt is made to provide an intuitive understanding of it. The data requirements of the method are also outlined.[2]

The basic idea is fairly simple and uncontroversial and can be summarised as follows. In a basically two sector economy producing food (i.e. agrarian goods) and non-food (i.e. industrial or urban goods), the share of per capita income devoted to food will decline as income increases. This is known as Engel's law and was established on the basis of cross-sectional data in the middle of the last century and has since also been confirmed as a time-series phenomenon.[3] Indeed, it seems to be a fairly general property of consumer behaviour.

If per capita income is increasing then a change may be expected, not only in the consumption pattern (so that food is now absorbing a smaller fraction, and non-food or 'urban' goods, a larger proportion of total income), but also in the production structure of the economy, generating a greater proportion of non-food producers. This change in the occupational structure can be taken to be roughly indicated by

---

2 The present method is a generalisation and formalisation of an approach first applied by E. A. Wrigley, 'A simple model of London's importance in changing English society and economy, 1650–1750', *Past and Present*, XXXVII, 1967, pp. 44–70.

3 For a modern appraisal of Engel's findings see G. J. Stigler, 'The early history of empirical studies of consumer behaviour', *Journal of Political Economy*, LXII, 1954, pp. 95–113.

the urbanisation ratio, i.e. the proportion of the urban (or industrial) population in the total population. The problems in so doing are discussed in Section III.

Exactly how much an income increase will affect urbanisation depends first and foremost on the particular shape of the consumption function, and more specifically on the marginal propensity to consume food, in other words, the proportion of a given increase in income spent on food. The larger the marginal propensity, the smaller the impact of a given increase in income on urbanisation. This simple relationship between income, consumption pattern, and production or occupational structure is complicated by two major independent influences; changes in relative income and productivity levels between the agrarian and urban sectors, and the pattern of external trade. If, for example, urban per capita income is higher than rural income, it takes a larger rise in per capita income to increase the urbanisation ratio by a given amount than if per capita income was equal in both sectors. Conversely, if relative urban income declines, it may well be because urbanisation is occurring independently of productivity or income increases. To turn the argument round: if there is an inflow of labour to urban occupations, but – in the absence of any increase in income – no increase in demand for urban products, the economy will consequently experience unemployment and/or a downward pressure on urban wages.

It is, of course, possible that urban employment is generated by foreign demand for industrial products, which the urban population exchanges for imported food. In that case an increase in the urbanisation ratio cannot be interpreted as associated with an increase in income. Allowance must therefore be made for the contribution of food imports if a proper assessment of changes in income and labour productivity is to be derived from changes in the occupational structure. It is also important to isolate the effects of agrarian productivity (or income) on urbanisation (the subject of this study), from the effects of productivity changes originating in the urban sector. That is done by controlling for changes in the urban/agrarian income difference as the occupational structure changes.[4]

The sorts of information needed to perform the relevant calculations can be summarised as follows:

a) The parameter in the consumption function – the marginal propensity to consume food – denoted by m.

4 See Appendix 5.1 for the formal resolution to this problem.

b) The urbanisation ratio or, more generally, the occupational distri-
    bution between agrarian and non-agrarian (i.e. industrial and
    urban) trades. These variables are denoted by l_a for the propor-
    tion of agrarian population in total population and l_i for the
    industrial (or urban) proportion (note that $l_a + l_i = 1$). Assuming
    that household size and participation rates are the same in both
    sectors, arguments relating to sectoral proportions of the population
    apply equally well to sectoral proportions measured in terms of
    the labour force.
c) The urban/agrarian per capita income ratio, denoted s.
d) The net import of food or, more precisely, the ratio of net import
    of food to total production of food, denoted by k.

As explained in Appendix 5.1 (Equation 15), agrarian labour productivity in period 1 (q_{a1}) can be indexed on labour productivity for
period 0 (q_{a0}) by the following expression:

$$\frac{q_{a1}}{q_{a0}} = \frac{l_{a0}(1 - m) - ml_{i0}s_0 + k_0 l_{a0}}{l_{a1}(1 - m) - ml_{i1}s_1 + k_1 l_{a1}}$$

This is the expression used in the growth accounting reported in Section
IV.

III Values of the variables and the parameter

Few would dispute that the most advanced regions in medieval western
Europe experienced a significant shift in their occupational structure
away from agriculture and in favour of trade and industry in the
period from the mid to late eleventh century up to the end of the
thirteenth century and, perhaps, even until the outbreak of the Black
Death.[5] Cities which had decayed and stagnated in the post-Roman era
experienced revival and new cities were formed. The regions most
affected by these economic changes included northern France together
with present-day Belgium, the areas bordering on the Rhine, south-
east England, plus northern Italy and parts of southern France and
Spain. In this paper, however, attention will be focused on northern

---

5 There is some evidence that the bigger cities in Flanders peaked at the beginning of the fourteenth century, while smaller ones continued to grow. In Brabant
  and Hainaut most cities continued their growth. See W. Prevenier, 'La
  Démographie des villes du comté de Flandre aux XIVe et XVe siècles. Etat de la
  question. Essai d'interpretation', *Revue du Nord*, LXV, 1983, pp. 255–75.

France and Belgium – hereafter called the 'Low Countries' – and northern Italy.

III.i *The urbanisation ratio*[6]

There are, of course, obvious shortcomings in using the urbanisation ratio as an indicator of the relative size of the non-agrarian labour force. Since many urban dwellers spent some time in agrarian work and vice versa, ideally knowledge is required of the distribution of time between urban and agrarian tasks of each producer, industrial and agrarian, and changes therein. To some extent urbanisation may simply have occurred because tasks previously performed by peasants were transferred to specialists in the cities, so that peasants spent more time in agriculture than before. This implies that neither per capita income nor the consumption pattern altered as radically as is indicated by the change in locational structure. Some economic gains must certainly have been present in such a transformation but they are exaggerated by the present accounting method. However, to the extent that urban dwellers responded in a similar way, by decreasing their food-producing activities, there may be little or no effect in terms of urbanisation, since the increased demand for urban goods was satisfied by the existing urban dwellers working more hours in industrial occupations and less in agrarian. Part of the attraction of the present method therefore lies in the way that it reinforces an interpretation of urbanisation which is closely related to real changes in occupational structure, consumption, and production.

Nevertheless, it might also be argued that urbanisation stemmed in part from the progressive relocation of rural craftsmen in cities

6 Apart from sources explicitly referred to in the ensuing text the following sources have been consulted: P. Bairoch, *De Jéricho à Mexico. Villes et économie dans l'histoire*, Paris, 1985; P. Desportes, 'Les Communes picardes au moyen âge: une évolution originale', *Revue du Nord*, LXX, 1988, pp. 265–84; R. Fossier, *La Terre et les hommes en Picardie jusqu'à la fin du XIIIe siècle*, Paris, 1968; A. Higounet-Nadal, 'La Démographie des villes françaises au moyen âge', *Annales de démographie historique*, 1980, pp. 187–211; R. Mols, *Introduction à la démographie historique des villes d'Europe du XIVe au XVIIIe siècle*, 3 vols., Louvain, 1954–56; D. Nicholas, *Town and countryside: social, economic and political tensions in fourteenth-century Flanders*, Bruges, 1971; H. Pirenne, *Les Villes flamandes avant le XIIe siècle*, Paris, 1905; Y. Renouard, *Les Villes d'Italie de la fin du Xe siècle au début du XIVe siècle*, 2 vols., Paris, 1969; G. Sivéry, *Structures agraires et vie rurale dans le Hainaut à la fin du moyen âge*, 2 vols., Lille, 1973; A. Verhulst, 'La Laine indigène dans les anciens Pays-Bas entre le XIIe et le XVIIe siècle', *Revue historique*, DIV, 1972, pp. 281–322; *idem, Neue Ansichten über die Entstehung der Flämischen Städte am Beispiel von Gent und Antwerpen, Studia Historica Gandensia*, CCLV, Ghent, 1983.

during this period. If this were the case the implication would be that the current method underestimates the real urban or industrial character of the European economies at the beginning of the period under investigation. This, however, is offset by the growth accounting method being employed, which gives a downward bias to the productivity growth inferred from a given rise in urbanisation, equivalent to starting at a higher urbanisation ratio. Since the object has been to give a conservative and, hence, robust estimate, this bias strengthens the argument that the present estimates represent minimum values. It is also worth mentioning that although rural craftsmen may well have tended to settle in cities, the growth of cities was itself paralleled by a rise in rural industries, with the result that urbanisation *per se* may well underestimate the true growth in non-agrarian occupations. Unfortunately, the limited information at hand means that it is impossible to evaluate the net balance between these two countervailing tendencies. Estimates of growth derived from the urbanisation ratio must therefore be regarded as upper-bound estimates of the change in occupational structure. For this reason allowance has been made in the actual calculations for the possibility that recorded urbanisation is a potentially misleading surrogate for changes in occupational structure, in the sense that it tends to overestimate occupational change.

Northern Italy possesses the best, and most extensively investigated, records of urban growth. J. C. Russell has made an attempt to measure levels of urbanisation in various European regions and has suggested an increase in the urbanisation ratio, l_i, in Tuscany – with Florence as the main urban centre – from 0.11 to 0.26, or from 11 per cent to 26 per cent, over a period of some 90 years during the thirteenth century.[7] Russell was unable to trace the development of urbanisation in a detailed way for other regions, although parts of northern Italy obviously had an urbanisation ratio at the end of the thirteenth century similar to that witnessed in Tuscany.

Sources are less abundant for the 'Low Countries' before the end of the thirteenth century. This region (essentially present-day Belgium and the modern French region of Nord Pas-de-Calais) includes the following areas: Brabant, with the cities of Louvain and Brussels; Flanders, with the cities of Lille, Douai, Ghent and Bruges; Artois, with Arras and St Omer; Picardy; and Hainaut. In the early eleventh century, cities in this area were small and often comprised an administra-

---

7 J. C. Russell, *Medieval regions and their cities*, Newton Abbot, 1972, p. 42.

Table 5.1 *The growth of St Omer,* AD *1000–1300*

AD 1000	'un bon milliers', i.e. 1,000–1,400
AD 1100	4,000
AD 1200	12,000
AD 1300	35,000

Source A. Derville, *Histoire de Saint-Omer*, Lille, 1981,

tive/military centre with a commercial suburban population outside
the walls. The area of the city within the walls might cover a mere 5
to 10 hectares and contain a total population of a few thousands, with
perhaps 5–10,000 in the larger centres. In the ensuing 200–250 years
urban growth was considerable. The city of St Omer probably grew
faster than most and provides a striking example of the changes experienced during this period, as Table 5.1 shows.

It would appear that urban population tripled every century,
whereas it took the entire period 1000–1300 AD for the total population to increase by as much. By the mid fourteenth century there were
several cities in the area with a population above or close to 50,000,
notably Bruges and Ghent, while Ypres was a little smaller, with a
population of approximately 30,000. A. Derville argues that there were
three or four other cities in the southern part of Flanders, for instance
Lille, Arras and Douai, with around 30,000 inhabitants.[8] On the assumption that urban population multiplied by a factor of 2.5 every
hundred years, a city such as Ghent – with about 50,000 inhabitants in
1300 – would have had 4,000 inhabitants in 1000 and 10,000 in 1100,
which seems plausible. In fact, on the same assumption, and assuming
that the total population tripled or quadrupled from 1000 to 1300 and
that an urbanisation ratio of 0.05 applied in 1000, the urbanisation
ratio in 1300 can easily be calculated. The result, l_i, is 0.26, or 26 per
cent. If the total population grew at a faster rate than that of the rest
of western Europe and quadrupled, the urbanisation ratio would be
0.20. These figures are higher than the one suggested by J. C. Russell
for what he calls the Ghent region (an area which includes the present-
day Netherlands which were not as urbanised at that time as they were
to become in the fifteenth and sixteenth centuries). Russell's lower

8 A. Derville, 'Le Nombre d'habitants des villes de l'Artois et de la Flandre Wallone
1300–1450', *Revue du Nord*, LXV, 1983, pp. 277–99.

figure also reflects the fact that he underestimated the populations of several of the larger cities compared with recent assessments.[9]

How does an estimate of the urban proportion of the population in the range 20–25 per cent *c.*1300 compare with other estimates? For smaller sub-regions such as the diocese of Arras, B. Delmaire has suggested an urbanisation ratio between 0.32 and 0.35 *c.*1300.[10] W. Prevenier has proposed a 1469 figure as high as 0.34 for the Low countries as a whole.[11] At that date the urban population may have reached or come close in absolute size to its pre-plague level, but the rural population had not, so the level of urbanisation at the beginning of the fourteenth century must have been lower. But an overall figure as high as 30 per cent *c.*1300 cannot be ruled out, although the more conservative estimate of 20–25 per cent will be employed here.[12]

III.ii *The net import of food*

Available evidence concerning the net import of food, *k*, is qualitative rather than quantitative, but with the aid of inferential reasoning we can specify certain reasonably narrow limits. The 'Low Countries' as a region seems to have been more-or-less self-sufficient in food. Although the northern and most urbanised part of the region imported food, this mostly came from elsewhere within the region, especially those

9 The most recent estimates made by W. Prevenier ('La Démographie des villes du comté de Flandre'), improving those he made in *idem*, 'Bevolkingscijfers en professonele strukturen der bevolking van Gent en Brugge in de XIVde eeuw', pp. 269–303 in *Album offert à Charles Verlinden à l'occasion de ses trente ans de professorat*, Ghent, 1975, suggest higher numbers for the towns of Flanders and it seems clear that J. C. Russell (based on H. Van Werveke, *Miscellanea mediaevalia*, Ghent, 1968) did not take all towns into consideration. For some particular cities, such as Ghent, Van Werveke in fact points out that he has established a minimum figure (*Miscellanea mediaevalia*, pp. 348–9). Before the Black Death Russell estimates the population of the textile cities of Flanders at 130,000, while Prevenier reaches the figure 158,000 for the cities in 'Flandre wallone' only. If the cities in 'Flandre gallicante' are added – with rather large cities such as Lille, Arras, and Douai and many smaller ones – an urban population close to 250,000 is not unlikely.
10 B. Delmaire's calculations stem from his unpublished thesis and the results have been made available to me in a private communication by Professor A. Derville, Université de Lille III.
11 Prevenier, 'La Démographie des villes du comté de Flandre', pp. 261–3.
12 In a private communication Professor A. Derville proposes a figure between 20 and 25 per cent for that part of the area under scrutiny which is now the French region Nord-Pas de Calais, but was not the most urbanised part of the area at that time. Professor G. Sivéry suggests an urbanisation ratio of 35 per cent for Flanders and 25 per cent for Hainaut *c.*1300 and an insignificant ratio of 1 or 2 per cent *c.*1000.

parts that fall within present-day France.[13] There is also evidence of imports from northern and eastern Europe but they may only have been of importance after the fourteenth century. On the other hand, Tuscany does appear to have developed into a net importer of food. Yet although its trade relations were widespread, the bulk of its supplies do nevertheless seem to have come from within the region and adjacent districts. In fact, evidence for the Florence region – with an urbanisation ratio around 30 per cent – suggests that it was mostly in years of crisis that food was supplied from areas far away.[14]

Can these rather vague indications be of any help in suggesting a figure to be used in the calculations? Their tenor suggests that although there may in both cases have been an increasing dependency on food imports, it had yet to become very great, but it is difficult to be more precise. There is, however, an alternative approach by which the magnitude of this variable may be specified. If there were net imports of food, these imports must have been paid for by exports from the urban sector. The urban sector itself comprised two parts, namely trade and production for the domestic market, and trade and production for both the domestic and foreign markets. The latter, which may be termed the B sector, almost certainly involved not more than half and probably less of all urban producers.[15] Assuming that the net import of food was 5 per cent of aggregate food production, $k = 0.05$, and assuming further that the proportion of imports in urban production value was 10 per cent, the B sector can be expected to have had an export ratio (i.e. exports as a proportion of total production) of about 50 per cent. If some 10 per cent of total food production was imported, the export ratio of the B sector would be around 80 per cent. Sectoral export ratios higher than 60 to 70 per cent are seldom found in modern economies so it does not seem plausible that the net import of food was higher than 5 to 10 per cent of total production. From a theoretical point of view it can be argued that most export-oriented industries also keep a considerable (but proportionally decreasing) home market, for the simple reason that a home market is the prerequisite for developing the specialisation advantages which eventually make it possible to enter foreign markets.

13 See A. Derville, 'Les Greniers des Pays-Bas médiévaux', *Revue du Nord*, LXIX, 1987, pp. 267–80, and H. Van Werveke, *Miscellanea mediaevalia*, pp. 104–22.
14 C.-M. La Roncière, *Prix et salaires à Florence au XIVᵉ siècle*, Rome, 1982, p. 547.
15 D. Nicholas, 'Structure du peuplement, fonctions urbaines et formation du capital dans la Flandre médiéval', *Annales, Économies, Sociétés, Civilisations*, XXXIII, 1978, pp. 501–27.

III.iii *The marginal propensity to consume food*
Judging from recent studies of developing countries the value of the
marginal propensity to consume food, m, seems to be around 0.5. As
such it is influenced by the nature of production in the agrarian sector.
Thus, if agrarian production also includes processing, transporting,
and marketing goods it is reasonable to suggest a fairly high figure. As
economies develop, however, some agricultural tasks – such as brewing
– become urban trades, hence the equivalent figure is lower. Plainly,
what is actually being estimated as agrarian productivity must be
acknowledged. To take account of this, two alternative values of
$m = 0.5$ and $m = 0.25$ are both employed.[16]

III.iv *Remaining variables*
As this chapter only concentrates on agrarian productivity, information is not required on the price of urban goods relative to agrarian
goods (p). Unfortunately, the same does not apply to the ratio of
urban to agrarian per capita income (s), for which direct information
is not abundant. What matters here, however, is not the level but
rather the trend. Given labour mobility as an equilibrating force there
are normally no reasons to suppose strong variations in this variable.
Nevertheless, under feudal socio-property relations, a priori reasoning
would suggest that there was a risk premium on mobility to urban
agglomerations because it was restricted and punished by lords. On
the other hand, there were obvious non-economic attractions of urban
life in terms of personal freedom which may have compensated for the
risks of deserting the manor, although these would have diminished
once freedom began to penetrate peasant life. For these reasons the
level and trend of s both remain ambiguous over the period in question. If the ratio of urban to agrarian per capita income increased over
time a given rise in urbanisation would imply a higher increase in
agrarian productivity, and vice versa. On the other hand, there are
grounds for arguing that late-thirteenth-century cities were becoming
increasingly overcrowded and experiencing mounting under- and
unemployment. Under these circumstances the ratio of urban to
agrarian per capita income would have been depressed, requiring a

16 These problems are discussed at some length in chapter 4 of K. G. Persson, *Pre-
industrial economic growth, social organization and technological progress in Europe*,
Oxford, 1988. See also *idem, Aggregate output and labour productivity in English
agriculture 1688–1801. A novel approach and comforting new results*, Discussion
Papers from the Institute of Economics, 89-06, University of Copenhagen, 1989.

Table 5.2 *Tuscany and the 'Low Countries': values taken by the variables and the parameter in the estimates of growth*

Tuscany		
	1200–10	*1290–1300*
t	0	1
l_a	0.89	0.74–0.80
l_i	0.11	0.26–0.20
k	0.00	0.00–0.10
s	1.00	0.80–1.20
$m = 0.50$ alternatively 0.25		
The 'Low Countries'		
	1000–50	*1250–1300*
t	0	1
l_a	0.95	0.75–0.80
l_i	0.05	0.25–0.20
k	0.00	0.00–0.10
s	1.00	0.80–1.20
$m = 0.50$ alternatively 0.25		

Source See text.

downward adjustment in *s*. For these reasons a range of values has been employed on s_1 between 1.2 and 0.8.

What has been argued so far is summarised in Table 5.2, above.

IV Results and interpretations

A wide range of results ensue depending on the particular combination of values of the parameter (other things being equal, $m = 0.5$ will make for higher growth than $m = 0.25$) and the variables at the end of the period under scrutiny (i.e. time 1). In the case of Tuscany the estimated annual growth in labour productivity falls in the range 0.15–0.35 per cent, while for the 'Low Countries' the corresponding values are 0.1–0.25 per cent. Given not only the uncertainty in assessing the variables but also the problems of interpretation (as in the case of relating occupational distribution to the physical location of the population), a few conservative estimates are to be preferred. These estimates must be robust in the sense that plausible values of the variables should not affect the growth results in a downward direction, but only upwardly. The method employed here has been to construct a series of 'equal growth' surfaces in a three dimensional space. Each point on the surface represents the same rate of growth of labour productivity at a given value of m (marginal propensity to consume food) and is associated with a specific configuration of values of the three coordinates, which are the three variables k_1, l_{a1}, and s_1, i.e. the import of food, occupational structure ($l_{a1} = 1 - l_{i1}$), and the urban/agrarian income differential.

There is an 'equal growth' surface of 0.1 per cent per year at $m = 0.25$ in Figure 5.1(a). Interpretation of that diagram requires consideration of two things. Firstly, it has been argued that plausible values on k_1 lie in the range 0.0–0.1, hence this will be used as a sort of control variable. Second, for reasons spelt out below, there are reasons for believing that a high proportion of agrarian population (and consequently a low urbanisation ratio) goes with high or moderate values on the urban/agrarian income ratio, s_1.

The west corner of the surface in Figure 5.1(a) indicates that a growth of 0.1 per cent is compatible with a l_{a1} value of 0.75, and, consequently, an urbanisation ratio of 0.25, a s_1 value of 0.8, and a value of k_1 of 0.06. The north corner has corresponding coordinate values of $l_{a1} = 0.75$, $s_1 = 1.2$, and $k_1 = 0.10$. The 'corner values' for all figures can be found in Table 5.3, and by using that information the reader can get an approximate impression of the coordinate values for any specific point on the surface outside the corners.

Are the two 'equal growth' surfaces for the 'Low Countries', Figures 5.1(a) and 5.1(b) (the latter exhibiting a growth of 0.15 per cent at $m = 0.5$), robust in the sense discussed above? In both cases the import of food variable (k_1) is higher than expected in the area around the north corners of the 'equal-growth' surfaces. Provided that the other variables, l_{a1} and s_1, are correct, this implies that actual growth was higher than indicated by the diagram. An alternative interpretation is, of course, that the specific combination of high s and low l_a values is implausible. Why should this be so? Primarily because high urbanisation (and low l_a) would have been associated with downward pressures on urban wages since there is evidence that urban populations became swollen by the ranks of the under-employed. At the opposite, south, corner the configuration of coordinate values becomes less robust as, on the face of it, the import of food variable (k_1) is rather too low. However, if the proportion of the agrarian population was as high as 0.8 (i.e. equivalent to an urbanisation ratio, l_{i1}, as low as 0.2) and the urban/agrarian income ratio was low, then the need for food imports is unlikely to have been great. A more modest urbanisation figure can also be interpreted as a reflection of the fact that the increasing urban population spent some of its time in food production. Each urban

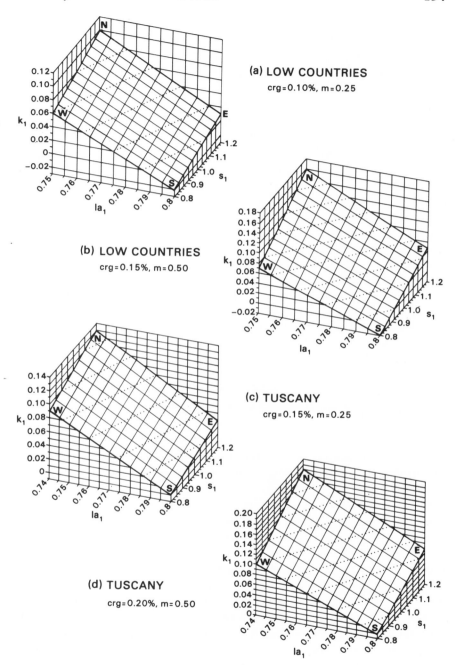

Figure 5.1 *Equal growth surfaces for labour productivity in the 'Low Countries' and Tuscany*

Table 5.3 *'Corner' values for Figure 5.1*

The 'Low Countries'

Figure 5.1(a) $m = 0.25$; growth rate 0.10 per cent per year

	West	North	East	South
l_{a1}	0.75	0.75	0.80	0.80
s_1	0.80	1.20	1.20	0.80
k_1	0.06	0.10	0.01	−0.02

Figure 5.1(b) $m = 0.5$; growth rate 0.15 per cent per year

	West	North	East	South
l_{a1}	0.75	0.75	0.80	0.80
s_1	0.80	1.20	1.20	0.80
k_1	0.07	0.16	0.05	−0.02

Tuscany

Figure 5.1(c) $m = 0.25$; growth rate 0.15 per cent per year

	West	North	East	South
l_{a1}	0.74	0.74	0.80	0.80
s_1	0.80	1.20	1.20	0.80
k_1	0.09	0.13	0.03	−0.01

Figure 5.1(d) $m = 0.5$; growth rate 0.2 per cent per year

	West	North	East	South
l_{a1}	0.74	0.74	0.80	0.80
s_1	0.80	1.20	1.20	0.80
k_1	0.10	0.18	0.07	0.01

Note

A negative sign on k_1 implies net export of food.

Source See text.

dweller thus counts as only a fractional urban producer, the fraction of time spent on urban production being smaller than 1.

The particular combination of low s_1 and high l_{a1} values represented by the south corners can also be disputed from an economic point of view. If cities did not grow very fast (i.e. with a high l_{a1} and consequently a low urbanisation ratio, l_{i1}), a strong downward pressure on urban wages is unlikely to have occurred hence s_1 should not decline markedly. In other words, low values on l_{a1} go with low values on s_1 and vice versa. The most plausible combinations of s and l_a coordinates can consequently be expected to be found in a fairly wide 'corridor' along a straight line between the west and east corners of the surfaces, which also happens to indicate values on k_1 that are acceptable. A cautious estimate of labour-productivity growth in agriculture for the 'Low Countries' would thus be 0.1–0.15 per cent per annum.

In Figures 5.1(c) and 5.1(d) similar 'equal growth' surfaces are constructed for Tuscany. Figure 5.1(c) has a growth rate of 0.15 per cent per year with m at 0.25, and Figure 5.1(d) a 0.2 per cent growth with m at 0.5. These surfaces seem slightly more robust compared to those for the 'Low Countries', since the occupational variable has a wider margin of variation (35 per cent compared with 25 per cent for the 'Low Countries'). Once more, the south corners are the least robust with their low k_1 values, but for much the same reasons as those given above this specific combination of circumstances may be considered unlikely. Concentrating on the 'corridor' between the west and east corners, it is evident that these growth rates are compatible with a wide variety of variable values, including plausible k_1 values. The plausibility of a growth rate of 0.25 per cent at $m = 0.5$ cannot be ruled out, since it is not on the whole associated with unrealistically low food import figures, although a more conservative estimate of annual labour productivity growth in Tuscan agriculture would place it somewhat lower.

Do these estimates appear reasonable in the sense that they can be supported by independent evidence? Obviously, at these kinds of rates rapid or sudden technological or scientific breakthrough is not at issue. Rather, they reflect a sort of piecemeal accumulation and diffusion of new knowledge gained in production, which included, amongst other things: new and/or better crops, especially legumes, with their nitrogen-fixing qualities; systematic rotation, which helped to control pests and diseases; manuring, which performed an essential role in recycling nitrogen; and liming and marling, which helped control soil acidity. In these respects the agricultural developments which characterised this period were not so very different from those normally associated with the so-called 'agricultural revolution' of the eighteenth century. Yet the implied productivity growth is only half or a third of what is usually ascribed to eighteenth-century English agriculture. Measured by that yardstick these estimated medieval growth rates do not seem excessively optimistic. Indeed, a substantial part of the medieval productivity rise may have derived from an increase in the hours worked, as market opportunities promoted the adoption of more labour-intensive methods of husbandry and the cultivation of industrial and horticultural plants with their greater labour demands. An increase of 25 per cent in the hours worked per labourer would be sufficient to account for approximately half of the recorded productivity increase per worker. This is by no means implausible given what is known about the increased frequency of labour-intensive undertakings such as marling, manuring, and the suppression of fallows. We should expect, of course, documented increases in the traditional physical output measures such as yield ratios and it does, indeed, appear to have been the case that the 'Low Countries' obtained higher yields per unit of seed and land in the late thirteenth century than in many subsequent centuries.[17]

Whatever their respective merits and shortcomings it would be quite unproductive to present the traditional 'single factor' physical output measures, and this approach, as mutually exclusive. In fact there are excellent opportunities for their peaceful and fruitful co-existence. One of the problems with the traditional method is that productivity growth of single factors, as observed for example in the thirteenth century, cannot be interpreted as unambiguous evidence of a growth of income. Such an interpretation is, however, supported by the results presented here. In short, indirect evidence suggests that significant but slow growth of labour productivity and income occurred in the most advanced regions in Europe at least up to the early fourteenth century.

Appendix 5.1 *The formal presentation of the growth accounting model for labour productivity*

Consider an economy with two sectors, an agrarian and a non-agrarian, denoted by subscripts, a, for agrarian and, i, for industrial = non-agrarian = urban. There is balanced foreign trade and L is the total labour force:

$$L = L_a + L_i \tag{1}$$

National income is

$$Y = L_a q_a p_a + L_i q_i p_i \tag{2}$$

where q_a and q_i are per capita output and p_a and p_i are prices of agrarian and industrial goods respectively. q_a and q_i are the unknowns: all other variables and the parameter introduced below must be derived empirically, sometimes supported by a little a priori reasoning.

17 See, for example, A. Derville, 'Dimes, rendements du blé et révolution agricole dans le nord de la France au moyen age', *Annales, Économies, Sociétés, Civilisations*, XLII, 1987, pp. 1,411–32. Also, B. M. S. Campbell, below, pp. 144–6.

Dividing (2) through with L gives the per capita income, y:

$$y = l_a q_a p_a + l_i q_i p_i \qquad (3)$$

l_a and l_i are the proportions of agrarian and industrial labour force in the total labour force, with $l_a + l_i = 1$. Define

$$y_a = y/p_a \qquad (4)$$

and

$$p = p_i/p_a \qquad (5)$$

Divide (3) through with p_a

$$y_a = l_a q_a + l_i q_i p \qquad (6)$$

y_a can be interpreted as the per capita income expressed in terms of agrarian goods. An Engel-type consumption function is chosen to be expressed in terms of the income measure y_a. Prices will affect the income of the urban population but prices will not affect the consumer's choice between urban and agrarian goods. Only income will. The consumption function states that the average propensity to consume agrarian goods, c, declines with increasing income.

$$cy_a = b + my_a \qquad b > 0, \qquad 0 < m < 1 \qquad (7)$$

b and m are constants. b is the income-independent consumption of food and m the marginal propensity to consume agrarian goods. A relative industrial/agrarian income ratio may now be defined, s,

$$s = q_i p/q_a \qquad (8)$$

which gives another expression for industrial per capita income

$$q_i p = s q_a \qquad (9)$$

and an expression for q_i

$$q_i = (s/p) q_a \qquad (9')$$

By solving for q_a (how that can be done will be explained below) q_i can be obtained, provided empirical information is available on s and p. But s is a problematic variable since it is functionally related to both of the unknowns. Can s be known without knowing $q_i p$ and q_a? One solution is to use a priori reasoning to determine plausible values on s, without knowing the *levels* of sectoral per capita income. Equilibrating forces will keep s close to 1.

F

Turning now to the problem of deriving q_a, this will be done by elaborating an identity stating that demand for agrarian goods will equal supply. This identity can be expressed as follows, with demand on the left hand side and supply on the right hand side:

$$Lb + L_a m q_a + L_i m s q_a = L_a q_a + M_a - X_a \tag{10}$$

where X_a is export of food and M_a is import of food and where b and m will be recognised as the parameters from the consumption function. Net import of food per capita is denoted n:

$$n = (M_a - X_a)/L \tag{11}$$

Divide (10) through with Lq_a and rearrange

$$b/q_a = l_a(1 - m) - ml_i s + n/q_a \tag{12}$$

To solve for b/q_a in (12) empirical information is necessary on the parameter m, the marginal propensity to consume agrarian goods, and the following variables: l_a and l_i (i.e. the sectoral composition of the labour force), and, s, the industrial/agrarian income ratio. Both s and n/q_a are functionally related to q_a, but will be treated as empirically and independently derived variables. n/q_a can be difficult to estimate directly but there is empirical information on the entity

$$(M_a - X_a)/L_a q_a \tag{13}$$

i.e. the ratio of net import of food to total production of food. Dividing numerator and denominator of (13) with L and recalling (11) a variable, k, may be defined to the effect that

$$(M_a - X_a)/L_a q_a = n/l_a q_a = k \tag{14}$$

Since $k = n/l_a q_a$ it follows that kl_a can be substituted for n/q_a in (12) and hence

$$b/q_a = l_a(1 - m) - ml_i s + kl_a \tag{12'}$$

So far a time subscript has been evaded for expositional reasons but all the variables are of course time-dependent. By solving b/q_a for two points in time, say time 1 and 0, the level of agrarian per capita output will be obtained at time 1 relative to product in year 0 since

$$\frac{(b/q_{a0})}{(b/q_{a1})} = \frac{q_{a1}}{q_{a0}} = \frac{l_{a0}(1 - m) - ml_{i0}s_0 + k_0 l_{a0}}{l_{a1}(1 - m) - ml_{i1}s_1 + k_1 l_{a1}} \tag{15}$$

Having now solved for q_{a1} it is possible to derive the corresponding value of q_{i1} with the additional empirical information p_1, the ratio of industrial to agrarian prices. Consider expressions (8–9)

$$q_{i1} = (s_1/p_1)\, q_{a1} \qquad\qquad (9'')$$

Notation

L	total labour force
L_a	agrarian labour force
L_i	non-agrarian labour force
l_a	proportion of agrarian labour force in total labour force
l_i	proportion of non-agrarian labour force in total labour force
Y	national income
y	Y/L
q_a	output per agrarian producer
q_i	output per non-agrarian producer
p_a	price of agrarian goods
p_i	price of non-agrarian goods
p	p_i/p_a
y_a	y/p_a
b	income-independent consumption of agrarian goods, a constant
m	marginal propensity to consume agrarian goods, a constant
c	average propensity to consume agrarian goods
s	ratio of non-agrarian to agrarian per capita income, $q_i p/q_a$
M_a	import of food
X_a	export of food
n	net import of food per capita, cf. (11)
k	ratio of net import of food to total production of food
t	time subscript
crg	compound rate of growth

Land, labour, livestock, and productivity trends in English seignorial agriculture, 1208–1450

I The historiography of pre-industrial agricultural productivity

Accounts of agricultural productivity change on opposite sides of the English Channel during the pre-industrial centuries present an historiographic contrast. In northern France and the Low Countries, for instance, analysis of tithe data has suggested a predominantly positive relationship between population trends and output per unit of land, but an essentially negative relationship between population trends and output per unit of labour, during the five-century period between the start of the thirteenth and the end of the seventeenth centuries.[1] Thus, an initial peak in the gross output of agriculture has been identified which coincides with the medieval demographic maximum of the opening decades of the fourteenth century. Not only was the cultivated area at full stretch at this time, but grain yields also appear to have reached a secular high under the stimulus of such labour-intensive techniques as manuring and marling, weeding, and the cultivation of fallow *inhoks* with legumes and rape. Their collective effect was to raise

I am grateful to Jenitha Orr and John Power for research assistance, to John Langdon and Mark Overton for supplying data, and to the participants of the Bellagio workshop for their helpful comments on an earlier version of this paper. Part of the research upon which this paper is based was undertaken whilst in the tenure of a Research Fellowship of the Economic and Social Research Council of the United Kingdom.

1 H. Van der Wee, 'Introduction – the agricultural development of the Low Countries as revealed by the tithe and rent statistics, 1250–1800', pp. 1–23 in *idem* and E. Van Cauwenberghe, eds., *Productivity of land and agricultural innovation in the Low Countries (1250–1800)*, Leuven, 1978; E. Le Roy Ladurie, 'The end of the middle ages: the work of Guy Bois and Hugues Neveux', pp. 71–92 in *idem* and J. Goy, *Tithe and agrarian history from the fourteenth to the nineteenth centuries: an essay in comparative history*, Cambridge, 1982.

supplies of soil nitrogen, which, according to R. Shiel, was the single greatest constraint upon yields at this time.[2]

In the Low Countries H. Van der Wee has argued that adoption of these labour-intensive techniques was promoted by the subdivision of holdings, so that on average the smaller the size of holding, the higher the productivity of land, although the attendant low labour productivity has led B. H. Slicher van Bath to describe this as 'scarcely controlled poverty'.[3] With respect to yields, H. Neveux has demonstrated for the Cambrésis region of northern France that the distinctive feature of this period was not that high yields became universal, but that the range of yields moved significantly upwards to 10–21 hectolitres per hectare.[4] Certainly, yields per unit of seed (yield ratios) obtained at this time by Thierry d'Hireçon on his estates in Artois were impressive by any standard of pre-industrial agriculture.[5] Such high yields were, however, very much the product of an abundance of cheap labour and as, with the late medieval demographic recession, labour became progressively scarcer and dearer, so yields fell.

In France the fall in yields was both immediate and pronounced, although offset, it is believed, by a rise in labour productivity. Land fell out of cultivation and – notwithstanding a retreat from poorer soils and an enhanced ratio of grassland to arable – even that which remained under the plough became less productive as husbandry declined in intensity.[6] By the mid fifteenth century yields in the Cambrésis had fallen to 4–18 hectolitres per hectare.[7] Although there was some recovery in the late fifteenth and early sixteenth centuries, again under the stimulus of population growth, Neveux maintains that yields did not

---

2 R. Shiel, above, p. 51.
3 Van der Wee, 'Introduction', p. 4; B. H. Slicher van Bath, 'The rise of intensive husbandry in the Low Countries', pp. 130–53 in J. S. Bromley and E. H. Kossmann, eds., *Britain and the Netherlands: papers delivered to the Oxford–Netherlands historical conference 1959*, London, 1960.
4 H. Neveux, *Les Grains du Cambrésis, fin du XIVe–début du XVIIe siécles. Vie el déclin d'une structure économique*, Paris, 1980, cited in Le Roy Ladurie, 'The end of the middle ages', pp. 83–5. For a comparable upward shift in maximum yields within English agriculture during the seventeenth century see P. Glennie, below, pp. 271–4. A yield of 10–21 hectolitres per hectare is equivalent to $11\frac{1}{2}$–24 bushels per acre.
5 J. M. Richard, 'Thierry d'Hireçon, agriculteur artésien', *Bibliothèque de l'Ecole des Chartes*, LIII, 1892, pp. 383–416; B. H. Slicher van Bath, *The agrarian history of western Europe AD 500–1850*, trans. O. Ordish, London, 1963, pp. 175–6.
6 Shiel, above, pp. 65–6.
7 Equivalent to $4\frac{1}{2}$–21 bushels per acre.

regain their early-fourteenth-century level until the second half of the eighteenth century, and it was only in the nineteenth century that they rose significantly higher.[8] In the Low Countries the story was rather different. First, the decline in yields was postponed until the second half of the fifteenth century and was relatively muted. Second, based upon a range of new husbandry techniques, the recovery of the sixteenth century soon matched the productivity achievement of the earlier demographic peak, while during the course of the following century crop yields were pushed progressively higher, constituting – according to certain definitions – a veritable agricultural revolution.[9]

This equation of rising population with an increased intensity of production and thus higher yields at the price of lower labour productivity, and vice versa during periods of population decline, contrasts sharply with English accounts of the same period which have tended to stress the adverse effects of population growth for both land and labour productivity, especially under feudal socio-property relations.[10] M. M. Postan, for instance, sees population growth as having promoted a Ricardian extension of cultivation on to inferior soils during the thirteenth century, thereby depressing mean yields per acre; a view echoed by R. B. Outhwaite for the sixteenth century.[11] Concomitantly, the conversion of grassland to arable reduced supplies of pasturage, with adverse consequences for stocking densities and hence the manure

8 Le Roy Ladurie, 'The end of the middle ages', pp. 81–3.
9 Van der Wee, 'Introduction', pp. 2 and 9–10.
10 On the relationship between population density and agricultural intensity see E. Boserup, *The conditions of agricultural growth: the economics of agrarian change under population pressure*, London, 1965. On the adverse consequences of feudal socio-property relations for agricultural productivity see R. Brenner, 'Agrarian class structure and economic development in pre-industrial Europe', *Past and Present*, LXX, 1976, pp. 30–75, reprinted as pp. 10–63 in Aston and Philpin, *The Brenner debate: agrarian class structure and economic development in pre-industrial Europe*, 1985.
11 M. M. Postan, 'Medieval agrarian society in its prime: England', pp. 548–632 in *idem*, ed., *The Cambridge economic history of Europe*, I, *The agrarian life of the middle ages*, Cambridge, 2nd edn., 1966, pp. 556–9; R. B. Outhwaite, 'Progress and backwardness in English agriculture, 1500–1650', *EcHR*, XXXIX, 1986, pp. 1–18. Outhwaite postulates the following scenario: 'farmers, faced with a compelling need to grow grains in a time of expanding population, extended their cultivation onto marginal lands; they also extended grain cultivation at the expense of grazing land, in some places rotations became more intensive, with consequent reductions in fallowing; livestock holdings diminished, particularly among the lesser cultivators. Wherever these developments occurred they tended to have depressing influences on arable productivity' (pp. 5–6).

supplies which were a major source of soil nitrogen.[12] J. Z. Titow and
D. L. Farmer are alike in attributing low grain yields in the late
thirteenth and early fourteenth centuries on the estates of the Bishops
of Winchester and Abbots of Westminster to this kind of ecological
imbalance.[13] The peak in gross agricultural product output at this time
through the expansion of the agricultural sector as a whole thus masks
a deterioration in the per unit product of land, a development which
exacerbated the inherent Malthusian tendency for the marginal
productivity of labour in agriculture to fall and, consequently, for the
growth of food supply to lag behind the growth of population.[14]

To compound matters Outhwaite believes that, far from promoting
higher yields, the subdivision of holdings which was such a feature of
the thirteenth century and, to a lesser extent, of the sixteenth, may
actually have had the opposite effect, since '[the smallholder's] poverty,
his limited acreage, and his family consumption requirements may
have militated against the most effective means of raising his yields –
decreasing his arable acreage, purchasing more livestock and increasing
his dunging'.[15] Labour productivity in peasant agriculture consequently
suffered, and accordingly Postan believes that it was the larger cultivators, and especially the demesne lords, with advantages of land and
capital, who fared best.[16]

For subscribers to this pessimistic scenario the effects of population
decline in the later middle ages were thus more beneficial than adverse.
Lowered population levels allowed the concentration of cultivation on
to the better soils and the abandonment of marginal land, to the

12 M. M. Postan, 'Village livestock in the thirteenth century', *EcHR*, XV, 1962,
   pp. 219–49, reprinted as pp. 214–48 in *idem, Essays on medieval agriculture
   and general problems of the medieval economy*, Cambridge, 1973. Shiel, above,
   pp. 67–8.
13 J. Z. Titow, *Winchester yields: a study in medieval agricultural productivity*, Cambridge,
   1972, p. 30; D. L. Farmer, 'Grain yields on Westminster Abbey manors, 1271–
   1410', *Canadian Journal of History*, XVIII, 1983, p. 342.
14 J. D. Chambers, *Population, economy and society in pre-industrial England*, Oxford,
   1972, pp. 24–5.
15 Outhwaite, 'Progress and backwardness', pp. 15–16.
16 'The higher quality of the lord's land, his superior command over capital,
   equipment, pastures and folds were bound to tell, and his yields were bound to
   be higher': Postan, 'Medieval agrarian society', p. 602. Yet H. Neveux argues that
   in the Cambrésis in the sixteenth century the emergence of substantial,
   commercialised farms retarded the growth of agricultural productivity: Le Roy
   Ladurie, 'The end of the middle ages', pp. 90–1. See also R. C. Allen, below,
   pp. 253–4, who questions whether stocking densities on small holdings were
   necessarily lower than those on demesnes.

benefit of mean yields. At the same time, with a better ratio of land to labour and a shift away from the more intensive techniques of production, labour productivity should have risen.[17] Moreover, both trends should have been reinforced by a swing back towards pastoralism as the demand for grain abated and rising per capita incomes promoted higher per capita consumption of meat, dairy produce, and other livestock products. Better ratios of grassland to arable and livestock to crops would have redressed the ecological imbalance within agriculture and released increased supplies of manure to the soil so that yields should eventually have risen to reach a higher mean level than either earlier or later.[18] Within the peasant sector declining levels of feudal rent should further have reinforced these trends.[19]

Whereas continental historians thus regard gains in productivity per unit area as only possible at the expense of productivity per unit labour, English historians argue that simultaneous increases in both were attainable once declining population created conditions of relative land abundance. The ultimate challenge, therefore, was to raise land and labour productivity together in conjunction with a general expansion of agricultural output and growth of population. Only when this had been achieved would the productivity constraints within agriculture cease to impede the progress of the economy at large. It is the resolution of this fundamental dilemma which constituted the so-called agricultural revolution. At its core in England's case lay, on the one hand, structural and tenurial changes in the units of production – notably the size and layout of farms and terms on which they were held – which transformed the productivity of labour, and, on the other, an ecological transformation of the methods of production, which yielded significant gains in the productivity of land.[20]

17 A. R. Bridbury, *Economic growth: England in the later middle ages*, London, 1962, pp. 52–3, claims that land and labour productivity both rose after 1350 but offers no direct evidence.
18 On the time taken to rebuild supplies of soil nitrogen see Shiel, above, pp. 60–3. High grain yields under conditions of grassland abundance are reported for the late fifteenth century from the estates of Tavistock Abbey in Devon: H. P. R. Finberg, *Tavistock Abbey: a study in the social and economic history of Devon*, Cambridge, 1951, pp. 86–128.
19 R. H. Hilton, *The decline of serfdom in medieval England*, London and Basingstoke, 2nd edn., 1983.
20 Brenner, 'Agrarian class structure'; D. B. Grigg, 'Breaking out: England in the eighteenth and nineteenth centuries', pp. 163–89 in *idem, Population growth and agrarian change: an historical perspective*, Cambridge, 1980; J. R. Walton, 'Agriculture 1730–1900', pp. 239–66 in R. A. Dodgshon and R. A. Butlin, eds., *An historical geography of England and Wales*, London, 1978; M. Overton, 'Estimating crop yields

The key to the latter, it has long been believed, lay in an enhanced cycling of nutrients facilitated by the incorporation of improved fodder crops into new types of rotation, which allowed higher stocking densities, heavier dunging rates, higher arable yields, more fodder crops, more livestock, and so on in a progressively ascending spiral of progress.[21] Such a line of reasoning naturally reinforces the arguments of those who claim, conversely, that it was a deficiency of livestock which had hitherto, at times of population pressure, jeopardised arable productivity. Fortunately, the medieval data are of a quality which allow equations of this sort to be put to the test. These data relate exclusively to the demesne sector, which obviously combined land, labour, and capital in very different proportions from the peasant sector, and on the evidence of the Hundred Rolls of 1279 probably accounted for between a quarter and a third of the arable area.[22] It is therefore less representative of agriculture at large than the tithe data so widely employed by continental historians but capable of providing a more direct insight into productivity and its determinants. Nor are its lessons without relevance for the peasant sector.

II Productivity in medieval England: data and methods

Traditionally, medieval seignorial agriculture has been investigated via case studies of individual well-documented manors or estates.[23] Nevertheless, there are very few manors, and still fewer estates, for which there is a sufficiently long run of accounts to be able to chart trends in production and productivity over a period of more than just a few decades. The well preserved archive of the estates of the Bishops

---

from probate inventories: an example from East Anglia, 1585–1735', *JEH*, XXXIX, 1979, pp. 363–78; E. A. Wrigley, 'Urban growth and agricultural change: England and the continent in the early modern period', *Journal of Interdisciplinary History*, XV, 1985, pp. 683–728; Allen, below, pp. 236–54; Shiel, above, pp. 67–77; Overton, below, pp. 284–322.

21 E. Kerridge, *The agricultural revolution*, London, 1967; J. D. Chambers and G. E. Mingay, *The agricultural revolution 1750–1880*, London, 1966, pp. 54–62. See E. A. Wrigley, below, pp. 321–39, for the role of draught animals in the growth of labour productivity.

22 E. A. Kosminsky, *Studies in the agrarian history of England in the thirteenth century*, Oxford, 1956, pp. 87–95.

23 Examples include F. J. Davenport, *The economic development of a Norfolk manor, 1086–1565*, Cambridge, 1906; R. A. L. Smith, *Canterbury Cathedral Priory*, Cambridge, 1943; Finberg, *Tavistock Abbey*; J. A. Raftis, *The estates of Ramsey Abbey*, Toronto, 1957; P. D. A. Harvey, *A medieval Oxfordshire village: Cuxham 1240–1400*, Oxford, 1965.

of Winchester, with its almost continuous series of Pipe Rolls
documenting agricultural production over the period 1208–1453 is
quite alone in this respect.[24] Its evidence thus tends to loom disproportionately large in all discussions of medieval productivity change,
although as an index of general trends its utility is circumscribed by its
exceptional status as the possession of one of the wealthiest and most
powerful ecclesiastical magnates in the land, together with the fact that
the bulk of its constituent manors were concentrated in Hampshire
and adjacent counties in southern England on land which, for the
most part, was of below average quality and productivity (Figure 4.1).[25]
Other well preserved archives similarly relate to the properties of large
ecclesiastical institutions, with all the problems of representativeness
which this implies, but there is additionally a great mass of miscellaneous
documentary material for a whole range of other classes of estate, lay
as well as ecclesiastical, which is much more fragmentary in its temporal coverage.[26] The latter is capable of adding very considerably to
knowledge and understanding, but requires a type of approach akin to
that developed by early modernists in conjunction with probate
inventories.[27]

The approach adopted in this paper has therefore been to draw
upon the full range of extant documentation and reconstruct trends
in demesne husbandry for a cross-section of estates by means of a
sample of accounts (a methodology analogous to that employed in this
volume by R. C. Allen, P. Glennie and M. Overton in analyses of probate
inventories).[28] This has been undertaken at two scales, that of the
country as a whole and that of an individual county, Norfolk. For the
former, a sample of 1,904 different accounts has been assembled
representing some 873 separate demesnes, 41 per cent of them in lay
ownership and 59 per cent in ecclesiastical. These are drawn from all

24 Titow, *Winchester yields*; D. L. Farmer, 'Grain yields on the Winchester manors in the later middle ages', *EcHR*, XXX, 1977, pp. 555–66.
25 K. Biddick, above, p. 97.
26 These sources are surveyed in J. L. Langdon, *Horses, oxen and technological innovation: the use of draught animals in English farming from 1066–1500*, Cambridge, 1986, pp. 82–5; B. M. S. Campbell, 'Towards an agricultural geography of medieval England', *AHR*, XXXVI, 1988, pp. 88–9. For the range of grange accounts extant for one particularly well-documented part of England, see B. M. S. Campbell, 'Agricultural productivity in medieval England: some evidence from Norfolk', *JEH*, XLIII, 1983, pp. 381–2.
27 M. Overton, below, pp. 300–3; P. Glennie, below, pp. 265 and 272–4; Allen, below, p. 247.
28 Below, p. 247, pp. 265, 272–4 and 300–3.

parts of the country, but with a bias towards the better documented and more densely populated counties of the south and east. Within this sample the vast majority of demesnes are represented by just one or two accounts.[29] In contrast, the sample assembled for Norfolk is altogether more comprehensive and solid.

Norfolk is one of the best documented counties in the country and in the middle ages was further distinguished by a high density of population and relatively intensive systems of husbandry.[30] Its data set comprises information extracted from all known extant grange accounts for the county, namely 1,900 accounts representing some 216 different demesnes (effectively a 10 per cent sample of all demesnes in the county). All classes of landlord are represented, from the mightiest magnates down to humble lords of a single manor, but with an inevitable bias towards the former and especially the estates of the greater ecclesiastical landlords, which account for 69 per cent of surviving records and 48 per cent of recorded demesnes. Because of its comprehensive nature this data set can be disaggregated to provide detailed information on individual demesnes, estates, and farming regions. The estate of the Prior of Norwich is, however, alone in retaining reasonably complete records from the whole of the period in question, although even its best documented demesnes cannot match those of the Bishopric of Winchester in their consistency of coverage.[31]

On the basis of this sample information, trends in the mean cereal acreage, the mean number of livestock, and the mean ratio of livestock to cereal acres per demesne can be charted over the 200-year period 1250–1449. The relevant statistics are summarised in Table 6.1

29 This sample was largely assembled by John Langdon of the University of Alberta in conjunction with his major study of the technology of haulage and traction in the middle ages and I am most grateful to him for making it available to me.
30 The Norfolk account rolls used in this study are drawn from the following public and private archives: Public Record Office; Norfolk Record Office (NRO); North Yorkshire Record Office; Nottinghamshire Record Office; West Suffolk Record Office; Bodleian Library, Oxford; British Library; Cambridge University Library; Canterbury Cathedral Library; Chicago University Library; Harvard Law Library; John Rylands Library, Manchester; Lambeth Palace Library; Nottingham University Library; Eton College; Christ's College, Cambridge; King's College, Cambridge; Magdalen College, Oxford; St George's Chapel, Windsor; Elveden Hall, Suffolk; Holkham Hall, Norfolk; Raynham Hall, Norfolk; Pomeroy and Sons, Wymondham. I am grateful to the relevant authorities for granting me access to these materials. For a full discussion of Norfolk agriculture based on a comprehensive analysis of these accounts, see my forthcoming book, *The geography of seignorial agriculture in medieval England*, in preparation for Cambridge University Press.
31 For example, C. Thornton, below, pp. 183–4.

and are weighted to take account of inconsistencies in spatial coverage. Thus, the Norfolk figures are the product of four regional sub-totals and the national figures of six (the weighted total for Norfolk being one of them).[32] These sub-totals are the mean of the individual manorial means which are in turn the mean of the annual means for those years for which relevant data are available.[33] The final aggregate figure for England has been derived by weighting each regional sub-total according to its respective shares of lay wealth in 1334 and population in 1377.[34] Other inconsistencies in the structure of the data are, however, less easily corrected. For instance, the diffusion of annual accounting as an administrative device means that small estates and manors are initially underrepresented with the result that the results for 1250–99 are likely to be inflated.[35] The selective impact of leasing has a similar effect upon the results for 1375–1425 and 1400–49, rendering those demesnes which remained in hand and for which production information is available less and less representative of the demesne sector at large.[36] This is further compounded by small sample size. The results for the first and last time periods thus need to be treated with

32 The six regional groupings are as follows: the north (Berwickshire, Northumberland, Durham, Yorkshire, Cumberland, Westmorland, Lancashire, Cheshire, Shropshire, Staffordshire, Derbyshire, Nottinghamshire), the south-west (Herefordshire, Worcestershire, Gloucestershire, Monmouthshire, Wiltshire, Dorset, Somerset, Devon, Cornwall), the south-east (Hampshire, the Isle of Wight, Surrey, Sussex, Kent), the midlands (Leicestershire, Rutland, Northamptonshire, Warwickshire, Bedfordshire, Buckinghamshire, Oxfordshire, Berkshire), the eastern counties (Lincolnshire, Huntingdonshire, Cambridgeshire, Suffolk, Essex, Hertfordshire, Middlesex, and Norfolk).

33 Glennie, however, would advocate the calculation of individual annual means as an intermediate step, below, p. 265.

34 These regional weightings are as follows: the north × 0.213, the south-west × 0.209, the south-east × 0.120, the midlands × 0.164, the eastern counties × 0.214, Norfolk × 0.081.

35 F. B. Stitt, 'The medieval minister's account', *Society of Local Archivists Bulletin*, XI, 1953, pp. 2–8; P. D. A. Harvey, 'Agricultural treatises and manorial accounting in medieval England', *AHR*, XX, 1972, pp. 170–82; P. D. A. Harvey, 'Introduction, Part II, accounts and other manorial records', pp. 12–71 of *idem*, ed., *Manorial records of Cuxham, Oxfordshire circa 1200–1359*, Oxfordshire Record Society, L, 1976.

36 On the farming of demesnes see F. R. H. Du Boulay, 'Who were farming the English demesnes at the end of the middle ages?', *EcHR*, XVII, 1965, pp. 443–55; B. Harvey, 'The leasing of the Abbot of Westminster's demesnes in the later middle ages', *EcHR*, XXII, 1969, pp. 17–27; R. A. Lomas, 'The priory of Durham and its demesnes in the fourteenth and fifteenth centuries', *EcHR*, XXXI, 1978, pp. 339–53; J. N. Hare, 'The demesnes lessees of fifteenth-century Wiltshire', *AHR*, XXIX, 1981, pp. 1–15; M. Mate, 'The farming out of manors: a new look at the evidence from Canterbury Cathedral Priory', *Journal of Medieval History*, IX, 1983, pp. 331–44.

Table 6.1 *England and Norfolk: demesne production trends, 1250–1449 (weighted 50-year staggered means)*

Years	Mean cereal acreage		Mean livestock units[a]		Livestock units per 100 cereal acres	
	England	Norfolk	England	Norfolk	England	Norfolk
1250–1299	176.7	149.2	64.2	45.6	41.9	30.5
1275–1324	176.7	140.8	67.7	46.5	44.1	33.0
1300–1349	155.7	126.6	64.8	45.9	47.9	36.3
1325–1374	134.7	115.3	63.8	47.2	55.8	41.0
1350–1399	124.9	110.6	75.0	49.3	62.8	44.6
1375–1424	123.9	120.1	78.6	43.3	69.9	36.1
1400–1449	117.4	140.7	89.3	43.5	78.6	30.9

Note
[a] (Horses × 1.0) + (oxen, cows, and bulls × 1.2) + (immature cattle × 0.8) + (sheep × 0.1) + (swine × 0.1).

Source See notes 29 and 30.

circumspection and especially so in the case of Norfolk, whose more comprehensive documentation renders it highly sensitive to such structural shifts in the composition of the data.

III The changing ratio of livestock to crops

As the figures summarised in Table 6.1 and graphed in Figure 6.1 indicate, the period 1250–1449 witnessed significant changes in the ratio of livestock to crops (identified by so many authors as one of the keys to arable productivity).[37] On the arable side the mean cereal acreage declined from a high point at the opening of the fourteenth century to a low point towards its close. This decline amounted to some 20 per cent in Norfolk – notwithstanding the county's natural bias towards arable husbandry – and 30 per cent within the country as a whole, and approached 40 per cent in the counties of the south west. Such reductions were achieved partly by the transfer of land via leasing to the non-demesne sector, partly by an increase in the frequency and duration of fallows, and partly by the conversion of arable to pasture.

37 Below, p. 155.

In much of the country it is also plain that this contraction in demesne cultivation had already begun well before the demographic hiatus of the mid fourteenth century. In Norfolk the mean cereal acreage shrank by an estimated 10 per cent during the decades prior to the Black Death and this was matched by a reduction of approximately 12 per cent within the country as a whole. An important contributory factor was the slump in grain prices of the 1330s which precipitated an acute agricultural depression for commercial cereal producers.[38] This is the first major set-back they had experienced in more than half a century. For most of the second half of the thirteenth century and the opening decade or so of the fourteenth century, rising grain prices and depressed real wages had encouraged demesne managers to bring as much land as possible under cultivation, hence the high mean cereal acreages of Norfolk and England at the start of the period under consideration. In fact, given the method by which these results have been derived, it is reassuring that the trends obtained for Norfolk and England should be so similar, especially for the central part of the period for which the data are structurally most consistent. In this context, it should be noted that Norfolk demesnes exhibited a mean sown acreage which was consistently below the national average (except in the very final period when, as already observed, the samples are least representative), as is consistent with the county's fragmented manorial structure and the consequent predominance within it of small demesnes.[39] Moreover, the credibility of these results is further reinforced by their correspondence to the specific experience of individual estates, such as that of the Prior of Holy Trinity Cathedral, Norwich (Figure 6.1).

The Prior of Norwich's estate comprised sixteen manors, three of them in the north-west of Norfolk, four in the centre, two in the east, and seven around Norwich.[40] As grain prices rose during the second

38 M. Prestwich, 'Currency and the economy of early fourteenth century England', pp. 45–58 in N. J. Mayhew, ed., *Edwardian monetary affairs, 1279–1344*, BAR, British series, XXXVI, Oxford, 1977. See also the observations of M. Mate in 'The agrarian economy of south-east England before the Black Death: depressed or buoyant?', pp. 78–109 in B. M. S. Campbell, ed., *Before the Black Death: studies in the 'crisis' of the early fourteenth century*, Manchester, 1991.
39 B. M. S. Campbell, 'The complexity of manorial structure in medieval Norfolk: a case study', *Norfolk Archaeology*, XXXIX, 1986, pp. 228–32.
40 NRO, DCN 40/13, 60/4, 60/10, 60/13, 60/14, 60/15, 60/18, 60/20, 60/23, 60/26, 60/28, 60/29, 60/33, 60/35, 60/37, 61/35–6, 62/1, 62/2; L'Estrange IB 1/4, 3/4 and 4/4; NNAS 20 D1–3; Raynham Hall, Norfolk, Townshend Manuscripts; Bodleian Library, Oxford, MS Rolls, Norfolk 20–45. A full handlist of the Norwich Cathedral Priory archive is available at the Norfolk Record Office.

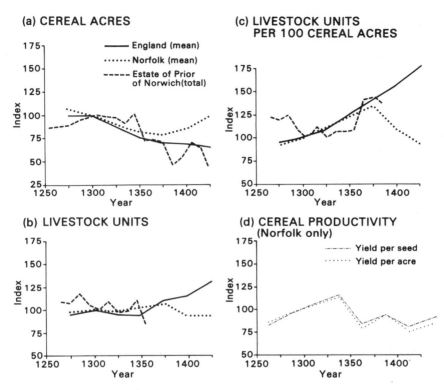

Figure 6.1 *England and Norfolk, 1250–1450: cereal acreages, livestock units, livestock units per 100 cereal acres, and cereal productivity*

half of the thirteenth century, successive Priors pursued a policy of expansion on their demesnes: additional land was purchased, further land was expropriated from their tenants, and fallows were reduced so that an enlarged proportion of the arable was brought under cultivation. By these means approximately 350 acres were added to the sown acreage between 1260 and 1310, amounting to an expansion of roughly 15 per cent. These developments were especially marked on the demesnes closest to Norwich, and most conspicuously of all on the demesne at Newton, to which approximately 150 acres were added between 1260 and 1340. Across the estate as a whole, however, the peak in cultivation came – as probably in the country as a whole – in the opening decade of the fourteenth century, by which time the Prior had almost 3,000 acres under cultivation.

During the 1310s and '20s cultivation fluctuated at around the c.1300 level, expanding or contracting according to the state of the grain market but not rising significantly higher, until in the 1330s there was an abrupt cut-back in the total sown acreage by 9.5 per cent, mainly because a decision was taken to lease the demesnes at Thornham, Hindringham, and Hindolveston (although on many of the other demesnes cultivation was maintained at more-or-less its existing level, and at *Heythe* near Norwich a wholly new demesne farm of some thirty sown acres was created). This was an unprecedented step, but by the mid 1340s, with a revival in grain prices, all three demesnes were back in hand and the sown acreage on the estate briefly returned to the level of some forty years earlier. Nevertheless, this recovery was short-lived, and from the 1350s cultivation on this estate underwent a long secular decline. Thereafter two or three of the demesnes were always at farm, with the result that during the 1350s, 1360s and 1370s the total acreage under cultivation was never more than approximately 75 per cent its previous maximum level. Then, in the late 1370s, a further price fall precipitated a renewed spate of leasings which reduced the acreage under the Prior's direct control to just 45 per cent of its *c.*1300 level. After a brief recovery in the 1390s and 1400s, the Prior finally abandoned direct management on all his demesnes in the 1420s and early 1430s. From this time on, demesnes which remained in hand became a relative rarity within the county, most of them the home farms of religious houses or minor gentry families.

These trends in cereal acreage had obvious implications for the numbers of livestock, since they were the product in part of the conversion of pasture to arable and vice versa. Counting livestock is, however, a much more complicated exercise than counting sown acres since some method has to be found of equating the different ages and categories of farm animal – horses, oxen, cows and other cattle, sheep, and swine. Historical opinion is divided as to how this should be done. Medieval historians such as Titow and Farmer have omitted swine from their calculations and employed weightings of 1.0 for horses, oxen, and cattle and 0.25 for sheep.[41] Apart from the fact that such weightings are obviously very crude, the omission of swine is unjustifiable, and a weighting of 0.25 is arguably too high for sheep. In contrast, early modern historians, notably J. A. Yelling in his analysis of seventeenth-century probate inventories, have employed weightings derived from

41 Titow, *Winchester yields*; Farmer, 'Grain yields on the Winchester manors'; *idem*, 'Grain yields on Westminster Abbey manors'.

those utilised by T. R. Coppock in his agricultural atlas of 1964 and based upon modern animal feed requirements.[42] A version of these is employed here and shown in Table 6.1. These weightings give lower absolute results than those obtained by Titow's method and – when the results for individual farms are mapped – a more coherent spatial pattern, although their relative trend remains much the same.

In both England and Norfolk the mean number of livestock units per demesne remained essentially static throughout the period 1250–1350, with the number of livestock on Norfolk demesnes well below the national average, partly because demesnes were themselves smaller, but also because of a natural bias towards arable production. After 1350 there was a brief and very marginal increase in livestock numbers in Norfolk, and a much more substantial and sustained increase in their numbers in the country as a whole. By the end of the fourteenth century demesnes carried on average 16 per cent more livestock than they had done at the beginning of the century, a trend which is if anything understated since flocks were increasingly accounted for separately and herds farmed out. This is no doubt one reason why livestock numbers appear to have fallen back to late-thirteenth-century levels in Norfolk, although this trend is also attributable to a decline in Norfolk's traditionally intensive, arable-based livestock husbandry. Certainly, for reasons of both accounting and economics, livestock numbers registered little absolute increase on the estates of the Prior of Norwich, in contrast to the country at large where demesne flocks and herds grew steadily in size until well into the fifteenth century (Figure 6.1(b)). Underpinning the latter development was a sustained rise in the absolute and relative importance of sheep, from roughly a fifth to a third of the total, a more modest increase in the importance of dairy cattle, and, concomitantly with the contraction in the arable sector, a decline in the relative importance of draught animals. The net result was a transformation in the livestock profile of many demesnes between the end of the thirteenth and the beginning of the fifteenth centuries.

Significantly, neither in Norfolk, nor in the country at large, did

42 J. A. Yelling, 'Probate inventories and the geography of livestock farming: a study of east Worcestershire, 1540–1750', *Transactions of the Institute of British Geographers*, LI, 1970, p. 115; R. C. Allen, *The 'capital intensive farmer' and the English agricultural revolution: a reassessment*, Discussion Paper 87–11, Department of Economics, University of British Columbia, 1987, pp. 27–33; *idem*, below, pp. 245–6; T. R. Coppock, *An agricultural atlas of England and Wales*, London, 1964, p. 213. For a variant on these weightings see G. Clark, below, p. 213.

the timing of the rise in livestock numbers synchronise with the contraction in cultivation. Demesnes may have been cultivating less land between 1300 and 1350, but the resources thus released do not seem to have been transferred to the pastoral sector. The explanation may be that the land was simply being cultivated less intensively or, more probably, that much of it was being leased out to tenants and thus transferred to the hard-pressed peasant sector. Only after 1350 did the withdrawal of land from cultivation coincide with a rise in the average number of livestock per demesne. As in later periods, this swing from corn to horn was most pronounced, neither in the traditionally arable east, nor in the traditionally pastoral north and west, but in an intermediate group of counties in the midlands and the south east which possessed comparative advantages for both arable and pastoral husbandry.[43] Within these counties the balance struck between these two sectors was determined by the prevailing terms of trade and when, as in the later fourteenth century, these shifted in favour of pastoral products, a substantial increase in livestock numbers was the result. Moreover, since at this time it was sheep numbers that expanded most dynamically, it was in the various downland counties of the south and east which possessed particular advantages for sheep farming that the rise in livestock units was most marked, averaging 50 per cent or more in Hampshire and the Isle of Wight, Surrey, Sussex and Kent.[44]

Given the contraction in mean cereal acreage which took place during the first half of the fourteenth century, and the expansion in mean livestock numbers which took place during the second half, it follows that mean stocking densities (livestock units per 100 cereal acres) must have improved steadily throughout the century. Table 6.1 and Figure 6.1(c) demonstrate that this was indeed the case. Stocking densities rose by almost a third *c.*1275–1350 and by a further 40 per cent *c.*1350–1425. Over the period as a whole stocking densities rose by an estimated 88 per cent and in real terms, given the problems of under-recording, the increase must have been even greater.[45] This trend was, however, far from universal.

The rise in stocking densities was least pronounced in the counties

---

43 A. Kussmaul, 'Agrarian change in seventeenth-century England: the economic historian as paleontologist', *JEH*, XLV, 1985, pp. 1–30.
44 Compared with other livestock the attraction of sheep lay in their lower unit costs due to their amenability to extensive forms of management.
45 The equivalent increase using Titow and Farmer's weightings of horses and cattle × 1.0 and sheep × 0.25 is 91 per cent.

north of the Trent, where the coverage of the sample is most sparse and no clear trend emerges in either the mean cereal acreage or mean livestock numbers. Here, stocking densities appear to have been much the same at the end of the period as they had been at the beginning. Much the same applies in Norfolk. In this county, a modest reduction in the mean cereal acreage in the middle decades of the fourteenth century, coupled with a small but real increase in livestock numbers after 1350, resulted in stocking densities which were 23 per cent higher in the period 1350–99 than they had been 1300–49 (a trend which is echoed on the estates of the Prior of Norwich where the equivalent increase was approximately 29 per cent). Nevertheless, this improvement was not maintained, and after 1375 stocking densities, at least on demesnes, gradually reverted to their original low level. Norfolk's comparative advantage lay mostly in intensive, arable-based pastoralism, and except in certain specific districts was ill-equipped to convert to the extensive, grass-based pastoralism which economic trends were increasingly favouring.[46] Elsewhere in the eastern counties the rise in stocking densities was more sustained, amounting to some 40 per cent over the fourteenth century as a whole, but was still significantly below the national average. By contrast, it was in the counties of central and southern England that the improvement in stocking densities was most pronounced, for it was here that cereal acreages contracted, and livestock numbers expanded, most markedly. The gain in potential nitrogen supply should therefore have been considerable with all that this implies for grain yields.

IV The productivity response

Other things being equal, the general contraction in arable cultivation and associated improvement in stocking densities which took place during the fourteenth century should have had beneficial consequences for arable productivity, especially in central and southern England

---

46 The exceptions were the Fens and Broadland (where there had always been much permanent pasture); the light, sandy soils of the west of the county (where there was a significant expansion of sheep farming); and the heavy clay soils of central and south-eastern Norfolk (where there was much conversion of arable to permanent grass, although probably more at the initiative of tenants than of landlords). The greatest changes occurred, however, in the fifteenth rather than the fourteenth century. For the distinctive features of pastoral husbandry in Norfolk see B. M. S. Campbell and J. P. Power, 'Mapping the agricultural geography of medieval England', *Journal of Historical Geography*, XV, 1989, pp. 28–37.

where these developments were most pronounced. If Titow is right in supposing that arable fields were suffering from a 'chronic state of under manuring' at the end of the thirteenth century, the opposite should have been the case by the close of the fourteenth century: more grassland and more livestock should together have enhanced the supply of mineral nitrogen to crops and resulted in better harvests.[47] Moreover, grain yields should further have benefited from increased sowings of legumes, which accounted for 7.0 per cent of the sown area at the beginning of this period and 17.5 per cent at the end.[48] Legumes – peas, beans and vetches – fixed nitrogen from the atmosphere and their incorporation within rotations thereby enhanced rather than depleted soil fertility. When fed to livestock they led to a significant improvement in the nitrogen content of manure and in their role as a fodder crop their increased cultivation further reinforced the trend towards higher stocking densities, especially in those regions and localities which were otherwise deficient in pasturage. Climatic changes apart, therefore, ecological circumstances would appear to have been broadly conducive to a significant improvement in yields over this period.[49] To what extent this was actually the case nevertheless remains very much to be seen. We are still, unfortunately, a long way from having a national series of yield data by which such relationships might be tested, although in the long term, given the temporal and spatial range of extant manorial accounts, construction of such a series ought to be feasible.[50] In the meanwhile it is necessary to make do with the long series of Winchester yields calculated by Titow and Farmer, which mostly relate to Hampshire and adjoining counties in southern England; the somewhat shorter series of Westminster yields calculated by Farmer, which relate to a wider scatter of demesnes with concentrations near London, in Essex and Hertfordshire, and on the Gloucestershire/ Warwickshire border; and the series of yields for Norfolk which is presented here for the first time (Table 6.2).[51]

47 Titow, *Winchester yields*, p. 30; Shiel, above, pp. 70–2.
48 B. M. S. Campbell, 'The diffusion of vetches in medieval England', *EcHR*, XLI, 1988, p. 204.
49 H. H. Lamb, *Climate, history and the modern world*, London, 1982; Shiel, above, pp. 65–9.
50 Yield figures from a variety of published sources are collected together in B. H. Slicher van Bath, 'The yields of different crops, mainly cereals in relation to the seed c.810–1820', *Acta Historiae Neerlandica*, II, Leiden, 1967, pp. 78–97.
51 Titow, *Winchester yields*, disaggregates the yields by manor and year, but Farmer, unfortunately, publishes only mean figures for the Winchester and Westminster estates as a whole: Farmer, 'Grain yields on the Winchester manors'; *idem*, 'Grain

Table 6.2 *Mean gross yields per seed on the estates of the Bishops of Winchester and Abbots of Westminster, and in Norfolk, 1225–1453*

Years	Wheat	Barley	Oats
A. *Winchester*[a]			
1225–1249	4.09	4.69	2.68
1250–1274	3.87	4.03	2.52
1275–1299	3.75	3.25	2.18
1300–1324	3.90	3.57	2.21
1325–1349	3.96	3.74	2.25
1350–1380	3.66	3.53	2.43
1381–1410	3.88	4.13	2.93
1411–1453	3.66	3.64	3.03
B. *Westminster*[b]			
1271–1299	3.27	3.63	2.37
1300–1324	2.86	3.82	2.14
1325–1349	2.98	4.38	2.54
1350–1380	2.84	3.99	2.57
1381–1410	3.25	4.13	2.75
C. *Norfolk*[c]			
1250–1274	3.83	3.17	2.37
1275–1299	4.57	3.06	2.40
1300–1324	4.78	3.24	2.62
1325–1349	4.96	3.36	2.78
1350–1374	3.93	3.09	2.38
1375–1399	4.11	3.58	2.80
1400–1424	4.18	3.20	2.86
1425–1449	3.77	3.21	2.94

Source
[a] J. Z. Titow, *Winchester yields: a study in medieval agricultural productivity*, Cambridge, 1972; D. L. Farmer,'Grain yields on the Winchester manors in the later middle ages', *EcHR*, XXX, 1977, pp. 555–66.
[b] D. L. Farmer,'Grain yields on Westminster Abbey manors, 1271–1410', *Canadian Journal of History*, XVIII, 1983, pp. 331–47.
[c] See note 30.

yields on Westminster Abbey manors'. For case studies of the Winchester demesne of Rimpton, Somerset, and Westminster demesne of Kinsbourne, Hertfordshire, see Thornton, below, pp. 183–210, and D. V. Stern, 'A Hertfordshire manor of Westminster Abbey: an examination of demesne profits, corn yields, and weather evidence', unpublished University of London Ph.D. thesis, 1978. Disaggregations of the Norfolk data will be given in my forthcoming book, *The geography of seignorial agriculture*.

The yield series for Winchester and Westminster have the merit that they derive from specific groups of demesnes, although in practice not all individual demesnes are consistently well recorded and represented. Such inconsistencies of coverage particularly affect the Westminster series due to the wide geographical scatter of demesnes – each with potentially divergent productivity trajectories – from which it is composed. By contrast, the Winchester series is more geographically concentrated, as well as longer and more completely documented. Geographically, the Norfolk series is most sharply focused of all, since it is constructed solely from accounts relating to that county. All three series incorporate yield ratios entered as marginal notes by the medieval auditors along with those calculated from information of seed sown and grain harvested given in consecutive accounts.[52]

For Norfolk, information of varying degrees of completeness is available for 121 different demesnes, representing a total of 1,085 individual harvests and a variety of different crops (i.e. an average of roughly nine harvests per demesne and five demesnes per year over a 200-year period). The Norfolk yield data are therefore substantial in volume, if fragmented in nature, and, if inferior in quality to those available for the Winchester estate, are nevertheless superior to those estimated from probate inventories where individual farms are never represented by more than a single harvest.[53] Spatially, most parts of the county and its constituent farming regions are covered, although this coverage is far from even. The biggest gaps occur in the central and western parts of the county, both of them areas of medium-to-poor soils. Conversely, information is fullest for the immediate environs of Norwich, as well as more generally in the north-west and extreme south of the county, partly because of the survival of particular estate archives. To try and minimise the impact of these variations in the spatial coverage of the data, and especially the fact that this does not remain consistent over time, each aggregate yield figure is the weighted product of four regional sub-means. Chronologically, there are no yield statistics for any date earlier than 1264–65, and there is a pronounced diminution in the quantity of surviving data after 1430. Between these two extremes there is a reasonably consistent coverage:

52 For the calculation of yields from consecutive accounts see Titow, *Winchester yields*, pp. 5–9. The yields entered by medieval auditors as marginal notes are discussed in J. S. Drew, 'Manorial accounts of St Swithun's Priory, Winchester', *English Historical Review*, LXII, 1947, reprinted as pp. 12–30 in E. M. Carus-Wilson, ed., *Essays in Economic History*, II, London, 1962, p. 22. See also Campbell, 'Agricultural productivity', p. 382.
53 Glennie, below, pp. 279–80.

the period from 1290–1340 is especially well recorded, with the 1300s standing out as by far the single best represented decade.

Given the very different documentary and arithmetic basis of the yield series for Norfolk as compared with those for the Winchester and Westminster estates, it is reassuring to note a quite high degree of correspondence between them. This is most marked in the case of barley, correlation coefficients producing results of 0.6164, 0.7222 and 0.9141, respectively, for Norfolk against Westminster, Winchester against Westminster, and Norfolk against Winchester over the period 1275–1399. Equivalent correlations for wheat yield results of 0.0860, –0.1303, and 0.6875 respectively, indicate a fair degree of correspondence between Norfolk and Winchester only, whilst in the case of oats there is no correspondence whatsoever, except that the lowest yields all tended to occur towards the beginning of the period, and the highest at the end. It should be noted that the correlations are consistently strongest between the two geographically most focused series, notably Norfolk and Winchester, which is heartening given that they are constructed from such contrasting assemblages of data and are calculated so differently.

In all three series gross yield ratios fluctuated between fairly narrow limits which never exceeded five-fold.[54] Certain of these fluctuations were shared in common – the upturn in the yield of all crops in the second quarter of the fourteenth century, the downturn in yield in the third quarter, and the recovery of the final quarter – which implies the influence of some over-arching factor such as climate.[55] But although the yields of barley and especially oats generally fared rather better after 1350 than before, wheat, the crop most responsive to nitrogen supplies, if anything fared worse. Nor is there much sign of an overall improvement in yields on a scale commensurate with the contemporary rise in stocking densities. The experience of Norfolk is a case in point. The abundance or otherwise of its harvests seems to bear little or no relation to the relative trend in livestock numbers. Impressive wheat yields were obtained in the first half of the fourteenth century in the face of stocking densities which were both absolutely and relatively low, and when stocking densities finally registered a modest improvement in the third quarter of the fourteenth century

---

54 Yet the thirteenth-century author of the *Husbandry* expected yield ratios of fourfold for oats, fivefold for wheat, and eightfold for barley: D. Oschinsky, *Walter of Henley and other treatises on estate management and accounting*, Oxford, 1971, p. 419.

55 Lamb, *Climate*; H. E. Hallam, 'The climate of eastern England 1250–1350', *AHR*, XXXII, 1984, pp. 124–32; Thornton, below, p. 194.

the yields of wheat, rye, barley and oats all fell (that of wheat, it would appear, irredeemably).

The post-1350 rise in stocking densities was more marked on the Westminster manors, and on the Winchester manors the improvement was dramatic, stocking densities more than doubling on the most favoured manors.[56] Yet on neither estate was any dramatic increase in mean yields forthcoming. Yields of barley and oats were generally rather better than they had been, but wheat yields, at least on the Winchester manors, tended to sag. This is not to deny that stocking densities had an influence upon yields, for at a local scale they patently did. Farmer has pointed out that after 1350 those Winchester manors which secured the best grain yields were those which raised their stocking densities most, and on the downland manors which operated a sheep-corn system of husbandry M. Stephenson has demonstrated a close correlation between sheep numbers and the yield of oats.[57] Nevertheless, at a general level the beneficial effects of high stocking densities were less dramatic than some historians have supposed. Manure may have become more abundant, but labour was becoming scarcer and dearer and farming systems were themselves changing, with the result that crops did not necessarily benefit from the potential increase in nitrogen supplies. Nor are the gross yield ratios of individual crops necessarily the most sensitive measure of productivity changes.

According to the seeding rate, the same yield ratio can be translated into very different yields per acre, and yet it was the latter in which medieval cultivators were most interested.[58] The yield of a particular crop was also to some extent dependent on the scale on which it was grown and the position which it occupied in rotations. For instance, Norfolk's superior wheat yields were a direct function both of the limited scale on which that crop was grown and the privileged position which it occupied in rotations, whereas its inferior barley yields reflected the reverse. A change in the scale on which a crop was grown could thus alter its mean rate of output independently of any real change in yields. Related to this is the fact that the various crops can hardly be regarded as equal since they possessed very different monetary and nutritional values. Wheat was consistently the most valuable crop

---

56 Farmer, 'Grain yields on Westminster Abbey manors', 1983, p. 342.
57 D. L. Farmer, 'Crop yields, prices and wages in medieval England', *Studies in Medieval and Renaissance History*, VI, 1983, p. 136; M. J. Stephenson, 'The productivity of medieval sheep on the great estates, 1100–1500', unpublished University of Cambridge Ph.D. thesis, 1987, pp. 176–87.
58 Campbell, 'Arable productivity'.

and throughout the period under consideration worth per bushel more than twice the value of oats, the least valuable crop.[59] One strategy which farmers might employ to raise the productivity of their land was therefore the substitution of higher for lower value crops.[60] Much the same applied to the frequency with which the land was sown, with, at constant yields, the higher the frequency of cropping the greater the productivity.[61] It might even be worth accepting lower yields per acre if these could be offset against a greatly increased frequency of cropping. Finally, there is also the question of the precise proportion of the harvest that was required to service the production system, in the form of seed corn, fodder for the livestock, and payments in cash and kind to the farm workers. Hence, as E. A. Wrigley has persuasively argued, historical discussion should focus on the net rather than the gross yield.[62]

V Aggregate cereal productivity

As P. Solar and M. Goossens demonstrate in their contribution to this volume, more satisfactory and comprehensive indicators of land productivity are required than the yield of any one crop.[63] In the case of arable productivity such measures should ideally take account of the proportion of the total sown acreage accounted for by each crop, the net yield of each crop after allowance for tithes, seed corn, and other on-the-farm deductions, the respective value of each crop, and the proportion of the total arable area that was sown each year.[64] Fortunately, virtually all the information required for the calculation of

59 Their different values in part reflected their different weights. In the early nineteenth century wheat weighed *c.*56–60 lbs. per bushel, rye *c.*53–55 lbs., barley *c.*49–50 lbs., and oats *c.*38 lbs. J. C. Loudon, *An encyclopaedia of agriculture*, London, 6th edn., 1866, p. xxiii; J. S. Bayldon, *The art of valuing rents and tillages*, London, 1827, p. 188.
60 P. Solar and M. Goossens, below, p. 372.
61 Glennie, below, p. 279.
62 E. A. Wrigley, 'Some reflections on corn yields and prices in pre-industrial economies', pp. 92–130 in *idem, People, cities and wealth: the transformation of traditional society*, Oxford, 1987.
63 Solar and Goossens, below, p. 372.
64 On the relationship between yields, cultivated area, and total output see M. Overton, 'Agricultural revolution? Development of the agrarian economy in early modern England', pp. 118–39 in A. R. H. Baker and D. Gregory, eds., *Explorations in historical geography: interpretative essays*, Cambridge, 1984, pp. 125–7. For productivity comparisons based on monetary value see G. Clark, below, pp. 214–9; Solar and Goossens, below, pp. 376–7, and P. O'Brien and G. Toniolo, below, pp. 390–6.

such weighted aggregate net yields is contained within manorial accounts. Most of these record the acreage sown with each crop, along with information relating to seeding rates, yields, and the price of grain. It is only the amount of land left unsown each year that presents a problem.

On some demesnes the fallowed area was actually recorded, but this was not always done consistently and in Norfolk it generally speaking was not done at all until after 1350. Even when the documents record fallow it is in the very specific sense of land subject to summer ploughing and due for cultivation the following year: arable land lying unsown as part of a convertible husbandry system (*friscus*) is not included. Of course, when, as at Rimpton, the arable was subject to a fixed and regular rotation of crops the proportion left unsown may be readily estimated, but outside the bounds of the regular commonfield system and in a county such as Norfolk this was rarely the case.[65] Estimates of the respective areas sown and unsown therefore require the painstaking reconstruction of crop rotations, an exercise which is itself only possible when there is a sufficient run of consecutive accounts naming the individual fields and plots being sown. Unfortunately, these conditions are rarely satisfied: there are, for instance, only 12 such cases out of the 216 Norfolk demesnes for which accounts are extant. It is for this reason that weighted aggregate yields are most conveniently calculated per sown acre rather than per arable acre, and, since recorded yields of legumes are prone to distortion due to the occasional practice of feeding them to livestock green and unthreshed, they may be further restricted to cereal crops alone.

Estimates for England and Norfolk of the percentage of the total cereal acreage accounted for by the principal grain crops – wheat, rye, maslin, barley, oats and dredge – are summarised in Table 6.3. These reveal a pattern of cropping which for 200 years remained remarkably stable in Norfolk but which changed significantly within the country as a whole. Nationally, wheat remained the pre-eminent cereal crop throughout the period 1250–1449, its share of the total cereal acreage varying within narrow limits and reaching a peak of almost 40 per cent during the first half of the fourteenth century. By comparison, the other winter grains – rye and maslin (a wheat–rye mixture) – were of relatively minor significance, and a significance which tended to diminish after 1350. As a result the winter sown grains, which had gradually expanded in importance during the period 1250–1349,

65 Thornton, below, pp. 185–6.

Table 6.3 *England and Norfolk: percentage of total cereal acreage under different crops, 1250–1449 (weighted 50-year staggered means)*

Years	Wheat	Rye	Maslin	Barley	Oats	Dredge
England						
1250–1299	34.3	5.9	1.0	15.0	40.7	2.6
1275–1324	36.2	6.1	1.4	16.2	35.6	3.5
1300–1349	39.2	5.8	2.6	16.7	30.3	4.7
1325–1374	38.7	4.7	2.1	18.4	27.9	7.0
1350–1399	36.0	4.0	1.1	21.9	28.2	7.5
1375–1424	36.7	2.2	0.7	24.4	25.2	7.8
1400–1449	38.2	1.6	0.4	27.4	23.7	6.9
Norfolk						
1250–1299	16.8	10.8	0.6	51.3	20.1	0.4
1275–1324	16.0	12.1	0.8	52.3	18.5	0.3
1300–1349	14.9	13.8	1.2	53.7	16.0	0.4
1325–1374	17.3	11.2	1.0	53.8	16.0	0.7
1350–1399	17.2	6.5	1.0	58.3	16.5	0.5
1375–1424	14.8	5.2	1.1	61.5	17.3	0.0
1400–1449	16.8	5.4	0.7	59.0	18.1	0.0

Source See notes 29 and 30.

occupied a steadily contracting share of the cereal acreage in the period 1350–1449. Overall, however, it was the spring grains – barley, oats and dredge (a barley–oats mixture) – which always had the edge, and it was within the spring sector that the greatest changes occurred.

Initially oats was by far the most important spring crop, rivalling even wheat in its share of the cereal acreage, but over time that share was progressively reduced as barley rose gradually to prominence. In the mid thirteenth century oats accounted for more than two-and-a-half times the area occupied by barley, yet by the opening of the fifteenth century it was barley which occupied the larger area. The rise of barley was paralleled by a growth in the relative importance of dredge, so that by the close of the period under consideration they together accounted for fully a third of the total cereal acreage. These developments were, of course, partly related to the fact that land was being withdrawn from cultivation, so it is no surprise to find that rye and oats – the crops most closely associated with the cultivation of poorer soils – should have declined in relative importance. But the rise of barley and dredge represent more than this, for their gains were absolute as well as relative. In effect, higher-value crops were being substituted for lower-value crops, since barley commanded a price significantly higher than oats. In Norfolk, by contrast, barley had always been the pre-eminent crop and all that happened was that this pre-eminence became more pronounced after 1350, so that by the close of the fourteenth century no less than 60 per cent of the county's cereal acreage was devoted to barley, a proportion unequalled anywhere else in the country. Unusually, this expansion seems to have been mainly at the expense of rye – a winter grain whose share of the total cereal acreage was halved during the second half of the fourteenth century – as barley rose to prominence as the leading crop on the light sandy soils in the south-west of the county.[66] By contrast, the respective shares of wheat and oats remained little changed, at just under a fifth of the total cereal acreage.

Associated with these changes in the relative importance of different crops were changes in their relative value (see Table 6.4). Over the entire period 1250–1449 the value per bushel of wheat, rye, barley and oats stood in the ratio 1.00, 0.71, 0.66, and 0.40 respectively. Thus, the winter grains were more valuable than the spring grains, with wheat the most valuable of the former and barley the most valuable of the latter. On the whole, the gap in relative value between the winter and spring grains tended to narrow before 1350, under the stimuli of expanding population and declining per capita incomes which encouraged the dietary substitution of lower- for higher-value grains, and to widen thereafter for more-or-less the opposite reasons.[67] The post-1350 decline in the relative value of individual cereal crops eroded the productivity of the arable sector in monetary terms and provided cultivators with a major incentive to modify their enterprise in favour of the more valuable crops. Equivalent ratios calculated for Norfolk from the unpublished price data collected by Lord Beveridge reveal similar, if more pronounced, trends.[68] Thus, the post-1350 decline in relative values was in excess of 20 per cent for oats and 25 per cent for barley as compared with 12 and 14 per cent respectively for the country as a whole, a differential deterioration which significantly reduced the

---

66 M. Bailey, *A marginal economy? East Anglian Breckland in the later middle ages*, Cambridge, 1989, pp. 282–4.
67 C. C. Dyer, *Standards of living in the later middle ages: social change in England, c.1200–1520*, Cambridge, 1989.
68 Lord Beveridge made extensive unpublished tabulations of regional price data which are now housed in the library of the London School of Economics and Political Science. Those for Norfolk – Box G9 – draw heavily upon the records of Norwich Cathedral Priory.

Table 6.4 *England and Norfolk: trends in grain prices relative to wheat,*
1250–1449

Years	Wheat	Rye	Maslin	Barley	Oats	Dredge
England[a]						
1250–1299	1.00	0.79	0.89	0.68	0.38	0.53
1275–1324	1.00	0.75	0.87	0.70	0.41	0.55
1300–1349	1.00	0.77	0.88	0.71	0.40	0.55
1325–1374	1.00	0.68	0.84	0.68	0.42	0.55
1350–1399	1.00	0.66	0.83	0.61	0.39	0.50
1375–1424	1.00	0.64	0.82	0.65	0.41	0.53
1400–1449	1.00	0.68	0.84	0.61	0.37	0.49
Norfolk[b]						
1250–1299	1.00	0.65	0.82	0.72	0.40	0.56
1275–1324	1.00	0.72	0.86	0.77	0.44	0.60
1300–1349	1.00	0.67	0.83	0.74	0.49	0.61
1325–1374	1.00	0.61	0.80	0.65	0.46	0.55
1350–1399	1.00	0.68	0.84	0.55	0.36	0.45
1375–1424	1.00	0.71	0.85	0.56	0.43	0.49
1400–1449	1.00	0.58	0.79	0.53	0.38	0.45

Source
[a] Calculated from J. E. Thorold Rogers, *A history of agriculture and prices in England*,
I, Oxford, 1884.
[b] Calculated from unpublished Beveridge price data (Box G9) held in the library
of the London School of Economics and Political Science. I am grateful to the
London School of Economics for permission to use this information.

value of the grain harvest in the county and exacerbated the agricultural
depression of the closing decades of the fourteenth century.

The combined effect of these changes in the composition of the
cereal acreage and the relative value of the various grains, as Table 6.5
demonstrates, was to alter the relative value of the cereal acreage.
Converted into wheat equivalents on the basis of relative prices, the
cereal acreage registered a 5 per cent gain in value in Norfolk over the
period 1250–1349 (where it was already worth more than the national
average) and an 8 per cent gain within the country as a whole.
Thereafter, however, the value of the cereal acreage declined. The
substitution of higher- for lower-valued crops meant that nationally
this decline was only of the order of 5 or 6 per cent, but in Norfolk
the decline, was catastrophic and amounted to no less than 20 per
cent. Only by devoting a much larger share of its arable to wheat could
Norfolk have countered this decline, and yet such a change was not

Table 6.5 *England and Norfolk: changing relative value of the cereal acreage,*
1250–1449

	1250–1299	1275–1324	1300–1349	1325–1374	1350–1399	1375–1424	1400–1449
England	66.8	69.9	72.4	71.7	67.7	69.0	68.5
Norfolk	69.5	74.0	73.0	67.6	60.7	61.4	58.7

Note
Each figure is calculated according to the formula $\sum(a_i \cdot p_i)$ where a_i is the proportion of the cropped acreage under crop i (Table 6.3) and p_i is the price of crop i relative to wheat (Table 6.4).

Source Tables 6.3 and 6.4.

readily reconciled with rotational schemes whose successful operation relied upon a heavy spring emphasis.[69] The only other alternative was to offset the decline in the relative value of its produce by significantly increasing its per unit output (such as was to occur under somewhat less extreme circumstances in the second half of the seventeenth century), but as the yield statistics summarised in Table 6.2 illustrate, this does not appear to have happened.[70]

By combining information on the relative value and area of the individual grain crops with weighted estimates of their yields it is possible to derive an estimate of the weighted aggregate net yield per seed and per acre, measured in wheat equivalents.[71] The results are summarised in Table 6.6 and graphed in Figure 6.1(d). They are net in the sense that tithe and seed corn have both been deducted, although no allowance has been made for fodder, food liveries, or other on-the-farm deductions which collectively could be at least as considerable.

69 Wheat eventually became the leading crop of east Norfolk, but probably not until the sixteenth century: M. Overton and B. M. S. Campbell, 'Five centuries of farming: agricultural change in medieval and early modern Norfolk, *c.*1250–*c.*1750', unpublished paper presented to the annual conference of the Economic History Society, Liverpool, 1990.
70 E. L. Jones, 'Agriculture and economic growth in England, 1660–1750: agricultural change', *JEH*, XXV, 1965, pp. 1–18, reprinted as pp. 67–81 in *idem, Agriculture and the industrial revolution*, Oxford, 1974.
71 The yields per acre are calculated by multiplying weighted mean yields per seed (Table 6.2) by weighted mean seeding rates computed for all demesnes with seeding information (the weights are by geographical location but *not* harvest year). The resultant yields are thus more widely representative of conditions within the county than if they had been derived solely from the rather limited population of demesnes and accounts with direct information of per-acre yields.

Table 6.6 *Norfolk: weighted aggregate net cereal yields, 1250–1449 (wheat bushel equivalents, net of tithe and seed)*

Years	n	Yield per seed	Yield per acre
1250–1274	19	1.46	5.69
1275–1299	36	1.68	6.47
1300–1324	42	1.85	6.95
1325–1349	56	2.05	7.68
1350–1374	45	1.48	5.32
1375–1399	39	1.64	6.30
1400–1424	25	1.44	5.08
1425–1449	10	1.59	5.58

Note

Figures are calculated according to the formula $Y = \sum (y_i \cdot p_i/p_w \cdot a_i/\Sigma a)$ where Y is weighted yield, y_i is the yield of crop i as yield per seed or in bushels per acre, p_i is the price of the crop per bushel, p_w is the price of wheat per bushel, a_i is the acreage under crop i.
n is the number of demesnes with yield information.

Source Tables 6.2 and 6.4.

On the evidence of five well-documented demesnes of varying levels of productivity, seed corn accounted for 51–88 per cent of total deductions in the case of wheat, 37–65 per cent in the case of rye, 48–63 per cent in the case of barley, and 28–48 per cent in the case of oats. In each case additional grain was set aside to meet other essential, recurrent commitments, notably food liveries for the farm workers and fodder for the livestock. As these figures indicate, the extent to which this was the case varied between crops and it will be noted that the proportion was smallest in the case of wheat, the most valuable crop, and greatest in the case of oats, the least valuable. The true net yield which was free for disposal after the immediate requirements of husbandry had been met was thus even smaller than the estimates of aggregate yield imply. On the intensively cultivated and high-yielding demesne at Hemsby, for instance, over the period 1261–1335 the net disposable surplus amounted to 78 per cent of the wheat harvest, 69 per cent of the rye, 49 per cent of the barley (the chief crop), and none of the oats, the whole of whose produce was consumed on the demesne as seed, fodder, and liveries.[72] On less productive demesnes these proportions were lower: respectively 25 per cent, 0 per cent, 29 per cent, and 0 per

72 NRO DCN 60/15/1–16.

cent on the low-yielding demesne at Thorpe Abbotts over the period 1336–79.[73]

To set these Norfolk estimates of aggregate yield in context an equivalent figure has been calculated for the Winchester manors over the period 1209–1349. This is based upon the yield information contained in Appendices B and L of Titow's *Winchester Yields*; details of the percentage cropped for eight randomly selected years, and data on prices derived from the Winchester Pipe Rolls and published by Farmer.[74] The result is a mean weighted aggregate net yield per acre of 5.13 bushels, a figure some 19 per cent lower than the mean figure for Norfolk over the period 1250–1349. Norfolk thus enjoyed a considerable productivity advantage over the Winchester manors, an advantage, moreover, which would have been even greater had it been possible to take the frequency of fallowing into account. For, whereas on most of the Winchester manors between a third and a half of the arable lay fallow each year, in much of Norfolk this proportion was considerably lower and in those parts of the county where cultivation was most intensive, much of the arable was under a continuous succession of crops. On the most productive and intensively cropped of these demesnes, such as Hemsby, Martham, Flegg and Ormesby, the weighted aggregate net yield per arable acre attained approximately 6–9 bushels. In contrast, at Brightwell and Harwell, the most productive demesnes on the entire Winchester estate, adherence to a two-course rotation of crops restricted the net yield per arable acre to approximately 4.2–5.0 bushels. On the estate as a whole the equivalent of 2 to 4 bushels of wheat were produced per arable acre per year after allowance for seed corn and tithes. In Norfolk the range of yields was much wider: the highest yielding Norfolk demesnes were twice as productive as their Winchester counterparts and at a crude estimate, arable land

---

73 NRO WAL 478/274x6. Compare the equivalent proportions calculated by Thornton for Rimpton, below, p. 193.
74 The yield data are drawn from Titow, *Winchester yields,* and from the unpublished researches of E. A. Wrigley, to whom I am grateful for supplying information. The years for which crop data have been obtained are 1265, 1274, 1284, 1286, 1296, 1302, 1321 and 1345. The data for five of these years was extracted from Table 6.VI of J. Z. Titow, 'Land and population on the Bishop of Winchester's estates 1209–1350', unpublished University of Cambridge Ph.D. thesis, 1962. A transcript of the data for 1286 was kindly supplied by John Langdon and the data for 1274 and 1296 was extracted from the relevant Pipe Rolls in the Hampshire Record Office, 159302 and 159315. The price data is drawn from D. L. Farmer, 'Some grain price movements in thirteenth-century England', *EcHR*, X, 1957–8, pp. 207–20.

in Norfolk was on average 50 per cent more productive than that on the Winchester manors.[75]

Arable productivity thus attained an impressive level in Norfolk, notwithstanding stocking densities which were well below the national average and significantly lower than those prevailing on the Winchester manors. On the evidence of Table 6.6 cereal productivity appears to have risen progressively from the mid 1260s to reach a peak in the first half of the fourteenth century, when it was boosted in the 1330s by a fortuitous run of good harvests. This trend was in part buoyed up by a steady improvement in relative prices, so that during the period 1325–49 the value of a bushel of Norfolk malted barley reached 95 per cent the value of a bushel of wheat, but it was also underpinned by a progressive increase in the intensity of husbandry. By the opening of the fourteenth century cultivation methods in the more fertile and densely-populated parts of the county had reached an extraordinary pitch of intensity and required lavish inputs of labour in the preparation of the seed bed and weeding and harvesting of the crop.[76] These methods were sustained by high grain prices, low wages, and an abundance of labour, but as labour became progressively scarcer and dearer following the demographic collapse of the mid fourteenth century, and then as prices fell from the late 1370s, so husbandry methods became correspondingly less intensive.

On the Prior of Norwich's demesne at Martham in east Norfolk the number of man-days per sown acre worked by the permanent staff of farm servants was reduced from 10.42 in the period 1300–24 to 8.21 in the period 1400–24, a reduction of 21 per cent.[77] Over the same period the employment of casual labour was curtailed even more drastically so that total labour inputs per acre were probably reduced by a third or more.[78] The net result at Martham was a significant reduction in arable productivity, for by 1400–24 the weighted aggregate

75 See Thornton, below, pp. 191–2, for a detailed comparison of arable productivity at Martham and Rimpton, which reveals the former to have been almost exactly twice the latter.
76 B. M. S. Campbell, 'Agricultural progress in medieval England: some evidence from eastern Norfolk', *EcHR*, XXXVI, 1983, pp. 26–46.
77 Labour inputs per sown acre at Rimpton, as calculated by Thornton, were in fact consistently higher: below, Table 7.7, pp. 204–7. This discrepancy narrows when labour inputs are calculated per *arable* acre, and shifts in Martham's favour when casual labour is taken into account. There is also the question of the relative efficiencies of the customary labour relied upon by Rimpton and hired labour which predominated at Martham.
78 Campbell, 'Agricultural progress', pp. 38–9.

G

net yield per cereal acre was some 40 per cent lower than it had been in 1300–24. Over the same period the reduction in productivity within the county as a whole was some 27 per cent. In both cases the general deterioration in relative grain prices, especially those of barley, the crop in which Norfolk specialised, accounted for a large part of the decline, but a genuine reduction in yields, particularly of wheat, also played its part. As will be seen from Table 6.6, aggregate productivity fluctuated considerably over the period 1350–1449, no doubt reflecting the impact of weather conditions on the quality of the harvest, but with lowered labour inputs it never regained the high level of the early fourteenth century. Two additional developments further reinforced the decline in arable productivity. First, as the intensity of husbandry was lowered, so the frequency of fallowing increased, with the result that a reduced proportion of the arable was under crops in any one year. Second, as part of the general improvement in working conditions, farm workers were given an increasingly generous allowance of food, thus raising production costs.[79] In effect, the net yield shrank.

VI Productivity trends at the intensive and extensive margins of cultivation

The discrepancy in the scale of the productivity decline between Martham and Norfolk serves as a reminder that aggregate trends invariably subsume a considerable diversity of experience. This is exemplified by five demesnes of Norwich Cathedral Priory, each of which possesses a good run of accounts for both the early fourteenth and the early fifteenth centuries.[80] As will be seen from Table 6.7, four of these five demesnes registered a decline in aggregate productivity in excess of the county average, and at Martham and Hindolveston this decline was in excess of 40 per cent. On both these demesnes the net yield per acre of wheat, barley, and legumes was substantially lower in 1400–24 than it had been in 1300–24 and only oats fared as well or better. Wheat had always occupied the most privileged position on these two demesnes, occupying the first course in rotations and thus

79 C. C. Dyer, 'Changes in nutrition and the standard of living in England, 1200–1500', pp. 35–44 in R. W. Fogel, ed., *Long-term changes in nutrition and the standard of living*, Section B7, the proceedings of the Ninth International Economic History Congress, Bern, 1986.
80 NRO DCN 40/13; DCN 60/18/15–24 & 53–62; DCN 60/23/11–20; NNAS 5905–15 20 D2 & 5916–17 20 D3; DCN 60/29/15–20 & 40–46; DCN 60/33/14–24 & 31; L'Estrange IB 1/4 & 3/4; DCN 60/35/14–22 & 43–52.

Table 6.7 *Productivity on five Norfolk demesnes of the Prior of Norwich, 1300–24 and 1400–24*

	Hindolveston	Martham	Plumstead	Sedgeford	Taverham	Mean
Wheat – net yield per acre (bushels)						
1300–24	16.5 (14)	16.5 (16)	13.1 (11)	13.3 (16)		14.8
1400–24	10.7 (8)	9.2 (11)	8.7 (6)	11.6 (16)	7.91 (7)	10.1
% change	−35.2	−44.2	−33.6	−12.4		−32.2
Rye – net yield per acre (bushels)						
1300–24	8.5 (8)		8.8 (8)	5.1 (16)	5.9 (14)	6.6
1400–24			7.6 (4)	4.3 (14)	6.4 (9)	6.1
% change			−13.1	−15.8	+8.7	−7.3
Barley – net yield per acre (bushels)						
1300–24	13.8 (14)	13.0 (16)	9.5 (11)	11.7 (16)	6.9 (14)	11.0
1400–24	8.3 (8)	11.4 (11)	10.5 (7)	9.7 (17)	12.1 (9)	10.4
% change	−39.6	−12.5	+10.8	−17.4	+75.9	−5.1
Oats – net yield per acre (bushels)						
1300–24	6.9 (14)	13.0 (16)	8.5 (11)	6.3 (16)	4.6 (13)	7.8
1400–24	7.0 (8)	16.4 (8)	9.4 (5)	5.5 (17)	7.9 (9)	9.2
% change	+1.9	+25.9	+10.8	−12.1	+70.9	+17.7
Legumes – net yield per acre (bushels)						
1300–24	5.5 (14)	7.5 (15)	6.9 (11)	3.7 (16)	3.4 (13)	5.4
1400–24	4.7 (8)	4.0 (9)	5.3 (5)	3.7 (17)	1.5 (7)	3.8
% change	−14.8	−46.3	−22.8	0.0	−54.7	−28.0
Weighted aggregate net yield per acre[a]						
1300–24	9.064	10.191	7.312	7.214	4.450	7.646
1400–24	4.701	5.989	5.049	5.382	5.142	5.253
% change	−48.1	−41.2	−31.0	−25.4	+15.6	−31.3
Mean sown acreage						
1300–24	165.3	194.3	218.5	410.8	132.1	224.2
1400–24	132.3	177.2	198.7	293.1	83.0	176.9
% change	−20.0	−8.8	−9.1	−28.7	−37.2	−21.1

Notes
[a] See Table 6.6.
Figures for each manor following the productivity measure are the number of recorded harvests.

Source See note 80.

receiving the maximum benefit from ploughings and manurings. When the latter were reduced as husbandry became less intensive its harvest was consequently disproportionately affected. What, however, was wheat's loss was oats' gain. The latter had always been penalised by being placed at the end of a long and demanding sequence of cropping, hence it actually benefited from the lowered intensity of husbandry. Significantly, this pattern is repeated to some degree across all five demesnes, with wheat exhibiting the greatest absolute decline in yield and oats the greatest relative improvement.

Nevertheless, it will be noted that at Sedgeford the overall yield decline was a relatively modest 11.5 per cent across all five main crops, and at Taverham there was actually a 15.6 per cent gain, with rye and especially barley and oats performing significantly better in the later than in the earlier period. Significantly, it was on these two demesnes that the contraction in cultivation was greatest and it was at Taverham, the least productive of the five, that there was most scope for an improvement in yields. Nor was the experience of Taverham unique. On Ely Cathedral's demesne at Brandon on the Norfolk–Suffolk border a 50 per cent reduction in the area under cultivation between 1340 and 1390 was accompanied by a 45 per cent improvement in aggregate cereal productivity, as part of which the yields of rye, barley and oats all increased substantially.[81] Brandon, like Taverham, was located on poor sandy soils and obtained yields in the first half of the fourteenth century which were both absolutely and relatively low. Under these circumstances genuine productivity benefits do appear to have accrued from a withdrawal of tillage to the better soils and a lengthening in the duration of fallows.

What the contrasting experience of these various demesnes appears to be demonstrating is the divergence of the productivity response at the intensive and extensive margins of cultivation. In this respect, Martham, Hindolveston, Plumstead and Sedgeford all represent versions of the former, since on all four demesnes individual crop yields and aggregate productivity were both at a peak when labour inputs and sown acreages were at a maximum in the first half of the fourteenth century. Thereafter, as the population declined and wage rates rose, so labour inputs were reduced and productivity suffered. In fact, so great was the reduction in output per acre that on occasion, as at Martham, there was little if any concomitant gain in labour productivity. On this demesne the weighted aggregate net yield per 1,000 man days worked by the *famuli* declined by 20 per cent from 0.5127 bushels in 1300–24 to 0.4116 bushels in 1400–24 (at constant prices the equivalent figure is 0.5292 bushels), although this fails to take account of the substantial decline in the employment of casual labour between these two periods.[82] The normal expectation, however, is that with a reversion to more

81 Chicago University Library, Bacon Roll 643–59; Public Record Office SC 6/1304/ 22–36; Elveden Hall, Suffolk, Iveagh Collection 148, Phillipps 26523.
82 Thornton, below, p. 209.

extensive methods of production, labour productivity should have improved. The predominantly positive relationship between physical productivity and population trends exhibited by these four demesnes is much the same as that envisaged by Le Roy Ladurie for northern France and Van der Wee for the Low Countries over the same period, both of which, like much of Norfolk, were areas of relatively intensive arable husbandry.[83] Yet as the experience of Taverham and Brandon demonstrate, this was by no means the universal response.

Taverham and Brandon were situated at the extensive margin of cultivation, on light soils which were incapable of sustaining intensive methods of production. As wage rates rose and, in due course, prices fell, cultivation was substantially curtailed on both demesnes. In Ricardian fashion, cropping became increasingly concentrated on to the better land, with corresponding benefits for individual crop yields, and associated with this went an improvement in the ratio of high- to low-value crops which constituted a source of aggregate productivity growth. The performance of these two demesnes conforms much more closely to the expectations of those English historians who have stressed the productivity benefits of a reduction in the intensity of arable husbandry and a contraction in the area under cultivation. At Taverham and Brandon it was, indeed, as Postan, Titow, Farmer, and Outhwaite have argued, when cultivation was at its fullest stretch in the early fourteenth century that mean yields were lowest, although this does not mean that soils were necessarily becoming exhausted.[84]

Nevertheless, although Norfolk contained a variety of productivity responses, in aggregate the relationship between yields and population trends was more positive than negative. The county was one of the most intensively cultivated in the country and, accordingly, it was the experience of the intensive margin of cultivation which prevailed. Except possibly on the lightest and poorest soils, output per acre was highest when labour inputs were greatest and not when livestock were most numerous. The net result, as Neveux found in the Cambrésis region of France, was that the range of yields narrowed as population declined and labour inputs were reduced.[85] There may have been gains at the

83 Van der Wee, 'Introduction'; Le Roy Ladurie, 'The end of the middle ages'.
84 Postan, 'Medieval agrarian society'; J. Z. Titow, *English rural society 1200–1350*, London, 1969, pp. 52–4; Farmer, 'Grain yields on Westminster Abbey manors', 1983; Outhwaite, 'progress and backwardness'. Compare also productivity trends on the Westminster demesne at Kinsbourne, Herts.; Stern, 'A Hertfordshire manor'.
85 Le Roy Ladurie, 'The end of the middle ages', p. 85.

lower end of the yield spectrum but, at least in Norfolk, these were
more than offset by losses at the upper. How representative Norfolk is
of the country at large is, however, a moot point and one deserving of
further investigation. By the early fourteenth century England had
evolved a variety of different types of agricultural system of differing degrees of intensity, each of which will have responded to the
demographic and economic changes of the fourteenth century in its
own unique way.[86] Norfolk was certainly unusual in the relatively small
scale on which cultivation contracted and stocking densities increased
in the period 1350–1449 and its productivity history may consequently
yet prove to have been more the exception than the rule.

VII The duration of Norfolk's late medieval productivity decline

If the high yields sustained in early-fourteenth-century Norfolk
subsequently declined, as methods of husbanding soil nitrogen became
less careful, when did productivity begin to recover? In the Low
Countries the sixteenth century appears to have been the key period,
although it was not until the seventeenth century that the medieval
productivity peak was exceeded. The sixteenth century was also a time
of recovery in northern France, although the early fourteenth century
continued to set the standard for productivity until the latter part of
the eighteenth century. For Norfolk a partial answer is provided by
comparing medieval gross yields per acre calculated from manorial
accounts with a series of yield estimates for the period 1584–1739
made by M. Overton from valuations of standing crops contained in
probate inventories.[87] To facilitate comparison, the latter have been
calculated for farms with a minimum sown acreage of twenty acres and
aggregated to produce county means using the same system of regional
weighting as that employed with the accounts. Weighted aggregate
gross yields per cereal acre have also been calculated using information on crop proportions and prices contained in the inventories and
the results indexed, taking 1250–74 as the base period, to produce an

86 Campbell and Power, 'Mapping'; B. M. S. Campbell, 'People and land in the
   middle ages, 1066–1500', pp. 69–121 in R. A. Dodgshon and R. A. Butlin, eds.,
   An historical geography of England and Wales, London, 2nd edn., 1990, pp. 89–92.
87 See M. Overton, below, pp. 298–305. Gross yields are employed in the comparison
   because of the absence of reliable information on seeding rates for the early
   modern period. Tithes are assumed to have comprised 10 per cent of yield
   throughout.

overall index of cereal productivity.[88] Also included are a series of yield estimates for the late eighteenth and early nineteenth centuries assembled from various sources.

Apart from the major gaps in the resultant time series – most notably 1450–1584 but also 1600–27, 1641–59, and 1740–69 – several problems, mostly unresolvable, attend its interpretation. In the first place the estimates themselves are based upon different sources of evidence and have been calculated in different ways: the medieval yields by measurement, the early modern by estimation, and those for the late eighteenth and early nineteenth centuries by observation. Methods of estimating absolute yields from probate inventories are themselves a matter of debate and the results subject to margins of error of the order ± 2 bushels an acre.[89] In the case of the lesser crops – rye and oats – this error is likely to be one of overestimation, due to problems of small sample size, likely price undervaluation by the appraisers, and distortions arising from the inclusion of straw in the valuations. Additional, largely unresolvable, problems arise from the employment of customary as opposed to statute measures of area and volume and from differences in the sizes of farm being compared.[90] Caution must therefore be exercised in making comparisons. Nevertheless, given available data sources, this yield series is the best obtainable and the first to present statistics for the same unit area over such a long span of time.[91]

On the evidence of Table 6.8, neither the high wheat and barley yields nor the high aggregate productivity of the first half of the fourteenth century were significantly bettered until the early eighteenth century. When yields and aggregate productivity rose over the period

88 As P. O'Brien and G. Toniolo observe: 'how much produce a medieval peasant obtained from a 50-hectare plot of land compared with his modern successor cultivating the same plot is a question that can only be tackled by valuing the mix of crops harvested at prices prevailing in medieval and modern times' (below, p. 390).
89 Glennie, below, pp. 256–71.
90 Several contributors to this volume note, however, little correlation between yields and farm size: Overton, below, pp. 309–11; Allen, below, pp. 246–9.
91 It improves upon M. Whitney, 'The yield of wheat in England over seven centuries', *Science*, CVIII, 1923, pp. 320–4; M. K. Bennett, 'British wheat yield per acre for seven centuries', *Economic History* (a supplement of *The Economic Journal*), III, 1935, pp. 12–29, reprinted as pp. 54–72 in W. E. Minchinton, ed., *Essays in agrarian history*, I, Newton Abbot, 1968; and G. Stanhill, 'Trends and deviations in the yield of the English wheat crop during the last 750 years', *Agro-Ecosystems*, III, 1976, pp. 1–10. The Norfolk series is further discussed in M. Overton and B. M. S. Campbell, 'Five centuries of farming'.

Table 6.8 *Norfolk: gross cereal yields per acre, 1250–1854*

Years	Wheat (bushels)	Rye (bushels)	Barley (bushels)	Oats (bushels)	WACY[a]	Index[b]
1250–1274	13.2	8.8	15.7	13.5	9.3	100
1275–1299	14.9	10.3	15.8	13.8	10.3	111
1300–1324	14.9	10.0	16.1	13.3	11.0	118
1325–1349	15.6	10.5	17.2	15.0	11.9	127
1350–1374	11.4	8.9	15.3	11.9	8.6	92
1375–1399	12.9	10.1	17.3	14.0	9.7	104
1400–1424	12.7	9.9	14.9	13.9	8.0	86
1425–1449	10.7	12.0	15.4	14.5	8.9	96
1584–1599	11.7	11.9	11.7	15.4	8.2	85
1628–1640	17.3	11.6	11.9	18.4	9.4	98
1660–1679	12.8	14.1	13.9	13.1	8.2	85
1680–1709	14.7	9.0	15.3	20.0	8.5	89
1710–1739	16.9	14.4	22.0	26.4	12.9	134
1760s[c]	25.5	25.0	30.9	38.3		
1790s[d]	24.0		32.0			
c.1800[e]	20.0					
c.1800[f]	24.0		36.0	40.0		
c.1836[g]	23.3		32.0	36.3	20.7	216
1854[h]	30.0		38.0	46.0	25.5	266

Notes
Unlike those for Norfolk and Suffolk in Overton, below, p. 302, inventory yields are for farms with 20 or more cropped acres, and are not weighted by harvest year. Inventory averages conceal wide fluctuations as well as being subject to error.
[a] Weighted aggregate cereal yield, see Table 6.6.
[b] Index of weighted aggregate gross yield per cereal acre. 1250–74 = 100.

Source
1250–1449, from manorial accounts (see note 30); 1584–1739 from probate inventories (see Overton, below, pp. 298–305).
[c] Calculated from A. Young, *The farmer's tour through the east of England*, 4 vols., London, 1771, IV, pp. 230–45.
[d] N. Kent, *General view of the agriculture of the county of Norfolk with observations for the means of its improvement*, London, 1796, pp. 56 and 59.
[e] W. Marshall, *The review and abstract of the county reports to the Board of Agriculture, III, Eastern Department*, York, 1818, p. 349.
[f] A. Young, *General view of the agriculture of the county of Norfolk*, London, 1804, p. 303.
[g] R. J. P. Kain, *An atlas and index of the tithe files of mid-nineteenth-century England and Wales*, Cambridge, 1986, p. 72.
[h] *Reports by the poor law inspectors on agricultural statistics (England)*, BPP, LIII, 1st series Cd.1928, London, 1854–5.

1584–1640 they were therefore recovering to an essentially medieval level of productivity and, as Glennie has suggested for Hertfordshire, may have done so via the employment of medieval-type methods of land management.[92] Moreover, the economic incentives for an intensification of husbandry techniques were much the same: high prices and a cheap and abundant labour supply. Thereafter, as prices sagged and wages rose, cereal productivity – in late medieval fashion – fell (a development reinforced by worsening climatic conditions).[93] Yields and cereal productivity remained below the best medieval standards for the remainder of the seventeenth century, but from the opening of the new century they began to rise again and to do so more vigorously than ever before. By the 1720s and '30s mean yields of Norfolk's two principal crops were back on a par with the record set almost exactly four centuries earlier, while the harvests obtained on some individual farms began to better the medieval best. The spectrum of yields was once more moving upwards and evidently continued to do so for the remainder of the eighteenth century, since by that century's close mean wheat and barley yields were respectively 40 and 70 per cent higher.[94] The steepness of this rise in productivity was unprecedented and, for the first time, the rise in yields ante-dated rising prices and falling wages. As such it reflected the adoption of new types of husbandry system which harnessed and cycled larger quantities of nitrogen.[95]

Chronologically, the experience of Norfolk thus falls midway between that of the Low Countries, where the medieval productivity peak was exceeded in the seventeenth century, and northern France, where it was not exceeded until the later eighteenth century. As has been noted, all three of these areas lay at the intensive margin of cultivation where labour inputs were patently a major determinant of the rate at which land yielded so that, contrary to much English writing on the subject, the correlation between land productivity and population

92 'The higher crop yields of the later seventeenth century cannot be seen as indicating a decisive break between medieval and modern agriculture, but rather continuity in the techniques by which land productivity could be raised': P. Glennie, 'Continuity and change in Hertfordshire agriculture, 1550–1700: II – trends in crop yields and their determinants', *AHR*, XXXVI, 1988 pp. 155–6.
93 M. Overton, 'Weather and agricultural change in England, 1660–1739', *Agricultural History*, LXIII, 1989, pp. 77–88.
94 This contrasts with R. C. Allen's chronology for Oxfordshire, based on a much smaller sample of inventories, which places the bulk of the yield increases firmly in the seventeenth century: below, pp. 247–8.
95 Shiel, above, pp. 68–79, 74–5; Overton, below, pp. 319–22.

levels was essentially positive.[96] Elsewhere the story may have been very different, although C. Thornton's meticulous analysis of Rimpton in Somerset, where husbandry was at an altogether lower pitch of intensity, reveals some striking Norfolk parallels.[97] Nevertheless, Norfolk is not England, and much work remains to be done before it can be established how representative or otherwise it is of the country at large. Of the complexity of the productivity equation, however, it leaves no doubt. Strategies for raising productivity included substituting higher-yielding for lower-yielding and higher-value for lower-value crops, reducing fallows and cultivating the land more frequently, and adopting more efficient seeding techniques which increased the net as a proportion of the gross yield. These were all ways in which an increased return could be obtained from the land irrespective of any improvement in yield levels *per se*. Having an adequate supply of fertiliser to keep the land in good condition of course helped, but livestock manure was not the only source of fertiliser, and large numbers of livestock were no guarantee that arable fields would be adequately manured.[98] Throughout the medieval period and probably much of the early modern, keeping land in good heart required labour as much as livestock – to supervise herds; pen flocks in movable folds; gather and spread manure; dig marl; cart night soil, sea sand, and any other extraneous sources of fertiliser that might be available; plough and harrow the land; eliminate weeds, and harvest with care – and it was consequently when labour was cheapest and most abundant that the most intensive arable farming systems attained their peak of productivity. Under medieval technological and economic conditions, however, high output per unit area was bought at the expense of low output per worker and it was to require a structural and technological transformation of agriculture before both were able to expand together.

96 See above, pp. 146–8.
97 Thornton, below, pp. 193–5.
98 Biddick, below, p. 115.

The determinants of land productivity on the Bishop of Winchester's demesne of Rimpton, 1208 to 1403

I Winchester yields

The Pipe Rolls of the Bishopric of Winchester provide much the earliest and most continuous series of crop yields relating to medieval English agriculture. J. Z. Titow's analysis of Winchester yields per seed up to 1349 concluded that there had been a 'general deterioration' by the late thirteenth century, a trend which he linked to the increasing cultivation of marginal land under population pressure and to a fall in manure supplies as animal grazing was ploughed up. D. L. Farmer's extension and re-evaluation of this material up to 1453 also supported a direct link between soil fertility and the availability of animal manure. These findings underpinned the interpretation of productivity change contained in M. M. Postan's influential 'population-resources' model of the medieval economy, which stressed the ecological imbalances within agriculture and the generally adverse effects of demographic growth on both land and labour productivity.[1]

Nonetheless, the Winchester yields derive from an exceptionally powerful ecclesiastical estate and one situated in a relatively poor farming region. These qualifications are important, because little attempt has been made to examine the yields within their institutional and agricultural context. This chapter aims to redress this deficiency

My thanks to all the workshop contributors, plus Harold Fox, Nigel King, Lynn Marston, Andrew Butcher and Paul Ell, for their help and encouragement. I retain full responsibility for the opinions expressed here. The research was funded by the William Gibbs Trust Fund. The British Academy provided a travel grant.

1 J. Z. Titow, *Winchester yields: a study in medieval agricultural productivity*, Cambridge, 1972, pp. 1–33; D. L. Farmer, 'Grain yields on the Winchester manors in the later middle ages', *EcHR*, XXX, 1977, pp. 563–4; M. M. Postan, 'Medieval agrarian society in its prime: England', pp. 549–632 in *idem*, ed., *The Cambridge economic history of Europe*, I, *The agrarian life of the middle ages*, Cambridge, 2nd edn., 1966, pp. 556–9; *idem*, *The medieval economy and society*, London, 1972, pp. 23–5 and 61–72.

by investigating the level and trend of land productivity within a detailed reconstruction of husbandry on the Winchester demesne of Rimpton. The first surviving Pipe Roll suggests that Rimpton had just been brought into direct management in 1208–09.[2] It remained directly managed until 1402–03, except for a short lease during the episcopate of Nicholas of Ely (1268–80). Rimpton has 143 Pipe Roll accounts for the period of direct management, irregular in survival for the first three quarters of the thirteenth century and then virtually continuous. Although these are enrolled accounts, rather than original reeves' returns, they still surpass any other series of documents in the quantity of economic information they contain.[3]

II Demesne farming at Rimpton[4]

The parish of Rimpton is situated near the head-waters of the river Yeo in south-east Somerset adjacent to the county boundary with Dorset, thus being somewhat detached from the main focus of the Winchester estate in Hampshire.[5] Approximately one-third of Rimpton's land lies astride an oolitic escarpment which forms a southern extension of the Cotswolds, the other two-thirds descending into a region of rolling lias and clay hills (Figure 7.1). The higher lands consist of clayey soils over siltstone and shale, quite irregular in parts due to landslips, whilst the lower lands comprise clays and loams with some alluvial deposits near a central brook. With adequate drainage most of the parish is suitable for a mixture of farming activities including cereals, grassland and dairying.

    Rimpton was a small 'classical' manor of 'midland' type in which the manor and parish were coterminous and a servile tenant population dwelt in a nucleated village and farmed a commonfield system. In the early thirteenth century the commonfields occupied almost all of the south of the parish, with some recently-assarted fields lying north of the brook running through the village. Further north survived considerable quantities of woodland pasture near a newly-assarted

---

2 Hampshire Record Office (HRO) Eccl. Comm. 2, 159270. A general trend amongst landowners; P. D. A. Harvey, 'The Pipe Rolls and the adoption of demesne farming in England', *EcHR*, XXVII, 1974, pp. 345 and 355.

3 All references to Rimpton (unless otherwise stated): HRO Eccl. Comm. 2, 159270–407. The accounts are dated by the closing Michaelmas.

4 A summary based on: C. C. Thornton, 'The demesne of Rimpton, 938 to 1412: a study in economic development', unpublished University of Leicester Ph.D. thesis, 1989.

5 See K. Biddick, above, Figure. 4.1, p. 97.

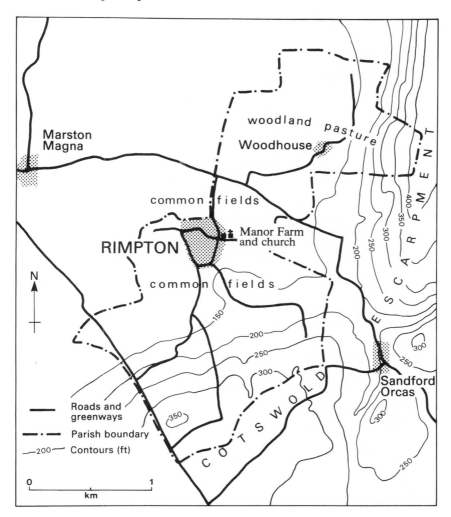

Figure 7.1 *The manor of Rimpton*

hamlet at Woodhouse (Figure 7.1). The arable in the south of the parish may once have comprised a regular open-field system, but this had become modified and irregular by the thirteenth century. There were no longer two or more great open-fields, and the three-course rotation of winter crop, spring crop, and fallow was instead accommodated within three distinct 'seasons' of furlongs. Each of these 'seasons' was similar in function to an open-field but had its constituent furlongs scattered across the parish rather than concentrated in a single block. Although some demesne lands lay in separate enclosures outside of this system, most lay intermixed with bondland strips, the agricultural land of *c.*1,000 acres being about equally shared between the tenants and the manor farm. The latter was managed by a professional bailiff and a local tenant chosen as reeve, the workforce chiefly deriving from the heavy labour service rents of the tenantry.

The amount of land recorded as sown each year can be translated into an estimate of the total demesne arable acreage by adding an extra 50 per cent to represent the fallow, based on the knowledge from cropping plans that a similar three-course rotation and ratio of cropped to fallow land existed throughout both centuries. Cultivation clearly greatly expanded in the first half of the thirteenth century, with one major addition *c.*1223–24 and further growth *c.*1244–45 (Figure 7.2(a)). Overall, the total area of the demesne furlongs (including fallow) probably doubled from around 230 acres between 1208–09 and 1213–14 (with two plough-teams) to around 420 acres between 1244–45 and 1267–68 (with four plough-teams). After the lease of the manor (1268 to 1280) the arable had become slightly reduced, but it then remained relatively stable at just under 400 acres until the 1320s. A sharp reduction occurred during the next decade, followed by a second period of stability at just above 300 acres until the 1370s (with three plough-teams). By the last quarter of the century cultivation had declined towards 200 acres, which was similar to the situation two centuries earlier.

The main crops sown on Rimpton's demesne were wheat and oats, a typical pattern in the region, also being found on the east-Somerset demesnes of Glastonbury Abbey.[6] Beans were also sown throughout, and barley too – except for a period between 1307–08 and 1340–41. Rye ceased to be cultivated after 1262–63, the same year in which peas were introduced as a field crop. Another legume, vetch, was first sown in 1283–84.[7] Demesne livestock comprised sufficient horses and oxen for carting and ploughing respectively, a cow herd of up to 26 adult beasts, a flock comprising a maximum of 250 ewes and wethers and a herd of up to 100 pigs.

6 I. Keil, 'The estates of the Abbey of Glastonbury in the later middle ages', unpublished University of Bristol Ph.D. thesis, 1964, pp. 77–8. See also B. M. S. Campbell and J. P. Power, 'Mapping the agricultural geography of medieval England', *Journal of Historical Geography*, XV, 1989, pp. 31–5.
7 B. M. S. Campbell, 'The diffusion of vetches in medieval England', *EcHR*, XLI, 1988, pp. 193–208.

(a) **CROPPED ACREAGE**

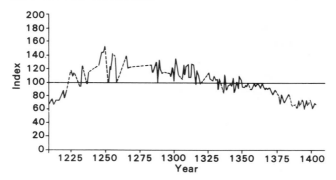

(b) **CROP PRODUCTIVITY**

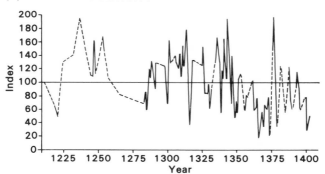

Figure 7.2 *Rimpton, 1209–1403: cropped acreages and crop productivity*

Two major external influences on the manorial economy were the institutional requirements of the Winchester estate and the economic stimuli provided by the growth and decline of the regional market. K. Biddick's analysis of the Bishop as a consumer has emphasised just how much each manor's economy was affected by its role within the estate's 'consumption structure'.[8] Rimpton's isolated location limited integration into the estate's internal organisation and it was thus among the most market-orientated of the manors; a somewhat ironic situation, as it lay in an area of relatively small-scale urbanisation quite distant from any major town or port (Figure 4.1).

Although some sales of the harvest *in grosso* to merchants are recorded, the majority of Rimpton's sales were piecemeal in small

8 Biddick, above, pp. 113–14.

quantities at varying prices, surely indicating a preponderance of local marketing. This argument is supported by more detailed references to purchases which seem to have been largely confined to Somerset markets. The pattern is similar to that for the Deverill manors of Glastonbury Abbey in Wiltshire, which were too far from the Abbey for consumption and also isolated from major centres of demand.[9] Rimpton's most important local markets were probably Ilchester, Castle Cary, Yeovil and Sherborne, places no more than six or seven miles distant to which the tenantry owed carrying services c.1250.[10] Yet the strenuous marketing efforts which coincided with the peak of Rimpton's arable expansion suggest that considerable commercial opportunities could derive from the growth of population even within this limited catchment area. Before 1220–21 less than half of the annual grain harvest had been sold, but this increased to nearly two-thirds thereafter with sales of the market-orientated wheat crop rising most quickly. Not until after a reduction in the demand for grain brought about by the demographic reverse of the Black Death did the proportional significance of marketing over consumption decline.

III The level and trend of land productivity

Rimpton's mean yields per seed (bushels, net of tithe) were comparable to the gross yield level recommended in the *Anonymous Husbandry* for wheat (5.0), but were lower than that author's expectation for oats (4.0) and barley (8.0) (Table 7.1). Compared with other medieval examples collected by B. H. Slicher van Bath, and to those calculated by Titow and Farmer for all Winchester demesnes, they appear quite high. In contrast, Rimpton's mean yields per acre (bushels, net of tithe) were quite dismal in relative terms, especially for the crops with the lowest sowing densities, wheat and rye. Indeed, Rimpton's seeding rates were unusually low for all crops and their association with high yields per seed and low yields per acre is given further consideration below in Sections V and VI.[11]

9 Thornton, 'The demesne of Rimpton', pp. 254–9; Keil, 'The estates of the Abbey of Glastonbury', p. 104; D. L. Farmer, 'Two Wiltshire manors and their markets', *AHR*, XXVII, 1989, pp. 1–11.
10 British Library, Egerton MS 2418.
11 D. Oschinsky, ed., *Walter of Henley and other treatises on estate management and accounting*, Oxford, 1971, pp. 418–19; B. H. Slicher van Bath, *Yield ratios, 810–1820*, A. A. G. Bijdragen, X, Wageningen, 1963, *passim*; Titow, *Winchester yields*, pp. 13–14; Farmer, 'Grain yields', p. 559.

Table 7.1 *Rimpton: mean yields per seed and per acre, 1211–1402 (bushels, net of tithe)*

Crop	n	Yield per seed	n	Yield per acre
Wheat	113	4.7	109	7.2
Rye	16	4.3	16	7.9
Barley	89	4.2	87	12.3
Dredge	4	3.2	4	10.5
Oats	113	3.3	109	10.2
Beans	109	3.8	106	14.8
Peas	23	6.9	22	8.3
Vetch	75	5.1	73	6.3

Notes
n is the number of harvests.
No compensation has been made for uncertain changes in grain measurement, although harvests might be somewhat under-recorded before 1262–63.

Source
See above note 3.

The trend of productivity at Rimpton has been analysed using weighted aggregate net yields in order to facilitate comparison with trends for Norfolk and England.[12] The first stage of this calculation involves the changing percentage of the arable acreage occupied by the different principal crops (Table 7.2). The chief feature at Rimpton was the greater bias toward winter-sown crops than in the Norfolk and England samples. Crop choice was itself remarkably stable on the manor, the only major change being the eclipse of rye in favour of more wheat in the thirteenth century. This represented the replacement of a consumption-orientated crop with a commercial crop, the poorer part of the expanded wheat harvest (*currallum*) now replacing rye in the food liveries to the regular manorial workers. Oats somewhat expanded in use before 1350, against the general picture, but this was partly at the expense of barley which was Rimpton's other consumption-orientated crop. A revival of barley after 1340 was linked to a new emphasis on its sale. The only other notable trend was a peak in the use of legumes in the period 1275–1324.[13]

Calculations of land productivity also need to take account of

12 B. M. S. Campbell, above, p. 171.
13 Thornton, 'The demesne of Rimpton', pp. 150–5.

Table 7.2 *Rimpton: percentage of cropped acreage under different crops, 1209–1403*

Years	Wheat	Rye	Barley	Dredge	Oats	Beans	Peas	Vetch
1209–1249	43.2	13.6	5.2		35.4	2.7		
1225–1274	46.1	9.8	6.2		33.7	3.6	0.6	
1250–1299	53.3	2.6	4.0	0.1	33.3	4.7	1.3	0.7
1275–1324	53.2		1.3	0.1	37.1	5.7	0.7	2.0
1300–1349	51.8		1.4	0.9	37.5	6.0	0.5	1.8
1325–1374	51.0		3.0	0.9	37.7	5.5	0.4	1.6
1350–1403	50.7		4.2		38.5	4.7		1.9
1209–1403	50.4	2.7	3.3	0.4	36.5	4.9	0.5	1.3

Source See note 3.

Table 7.3 *Rimpton: trends in crop prices relative to wheat, 1209–1403*

Years	Wheat	Rye	Barley	Oats	Beans	Peas	Vetch
1209–1249	1.0	0.90	0.66	0.33	0.78		
1225–1274	1.0	0.99	0.61	0.37	0.70	0.59	
1250–1299	1.0	0.83	0.54	0.39	0.68	0.59	0.50
1275–1324	1.0		0.52	0.42	0.66	0.46	0.48
1300–1349	1.0		0.59	0.40	0.73	0.43	0.50
1325–1374	1.0		0.62	0.37	0.62	0.41	0.44
1350–1403	1.0		0.58	0.37	0.44		0.38
1209–1403	1.0		0.59	0.37	0.61	0.47	0.47

Note
[a] These calculations slightly overestimate the relative price of wheat because the poorer part of the wheat harvest (*currallum*) has deficient price information.

Source See note 3.

changes in relative crop values. Over the period 1209 to 1403 the value per bushel of wheat, barley, oats and beans at Rimpton stood in the ratio 1.0, 0.59, 0.37, 0.61, respectively (Table 7.3). These price differentials reveal one reason why large-scale cultivation of low-yielding wheat was undertaken: it was Rimpton's most valuable commodity and much of the profit of the manor stemmed from its cultivation. As with the Norfolk and England examples, the relative price gap between wheat and oats narrowed under rising market demand prior to 1350 and relaxed thereafter, but there is no such clear picture for the other

Table 7.4 *Rimpton: changing relative value of the cropped acreage, 1209–1403*

Period	1209–1249	1225–1274	1250–1299	1275–1324	1300–1349	1325–1374	1350–1403
Value	72.6	74.9	74.9	74.7	73.2	71.1	70.2

Note

Each figure is calculated according to the formula $\sum(a_i \cdot p_i)$ where a_i is the proportion of the cropped acreage under crop i (Table 7.2) and p_i the price of crop i relative to wheat (Table 7.3).

Source Tables 7.2 and 7.3.

crops. Part of the explanation may lie with the particular use of each crop at Rimpton, the small amounts of legumes and barley being sown before 1350 most often being used for food liveries rather than being sold.

Combining crop choice with relative prices allows the calculation of the changing relative value of Rimpton's demesne arable acreage in wheat equivalents. This showed a slight gain of 2 to 3 per cent by the mid thirteenth century, followed by a stable peak until the 1320s. Thereafter the index fell, but only by around 5 per cent by 1350 to 1403 (Table 7.4). These changes were of the same magnitude as for England as a whole, but were less than for Norfolk. In contrast to Norfolk's dependence on barley which fell in value post 1350, Rimpton's economy was protected by the continued dominance of wheat within its rotation: the relative value of this crop improved as per capita incomes and diets improved in the late fourteenth century.

Comparison of weighted aggregate net yields per acre at Rimpton with those at two other well-documented manors, Martham in Norfolk and Cuxham in Oxfordshire, gives some indication of Rimpton's comparative productivity performance (Table 7.5). Here the degree of fallowing can be taken into account, as well as crop choice and relative prices, because of the detailed reconstructions of husbandry available for these three manors. The use of legumes to eliminate fallow at Martham, together with concentration upon highly-priced barley, made that demesne very much more productive than the regular three-course rotations employed at Cuxham and Rimpton. Output at Martham was 300 per cent that of Rimpton and 150 per cent that of Cuxham. The large gap in performance between Rimpton and Cuxham chiefly derived from the former's very much poorer wheat yields per acre, which may be explained by soil type. These calculations seem to show that whilst

Table 7.5 *Comparison of weighted aggregate net yields per acre (bushels, net of tithe and seed) at Cuxham, Oxfordshire (1294–1359), Martham, Norfolk (1294–1340), and Rimpton, Somerset (1283–1349)*

Crop	Mean net yield per acre (bushels)[a]			Relative crop prices[b] (wheat = 1.00)		
	Cuxham	Martham	Rimpton	Cuxham	Martham	Rimpton
Wheat	14.4	18.0	6.5	1.00	1.00	1.00
Maslin		16.2			0.83	
Barley	19.8	15.4	10.4	0.65	0.74	0.57
Dredge	15.0		9.0	0.52		0.47
Oats	9.2	16.6	7.5	0.42	0.49	0.40
Legumes	12.2	8.6	8.7	0.65	0.62	0.59

Crop	Mean percentage of arable acreage			Weighted aggregate net yield per 100 acres (bushels)[c]		
	Cuxham	Martham	Rimpton	Cuxham	Martham	Rimpton
Wheat	33.3	16.5	35.0	479.5	297.0	226.8
Maslin		1.8			24.2	
Barley	4.1	52.9	1.2	52.8	602.9	7.1
Dredge	7.3		0.4	57.1		1.7
Oats	16.2	2.9	24.5	62.5	23.6	73.5
Legumes	5.8	17.8	5.5	45.8	94.9	28.3
All crops	66.7	91.9	66.6	697.7	1042.6	337.2

Crop	Rimpton's output (R) as percentage of Cuxham (C) and Martham (M)		
	R as % of C	R as % of M	C as % of M
Wheat	47.3	76.4	161.5
Maslin			
Barley	13.5	1.2	8.8
Dredge	3.0		
Oats	117.7	298.2	264.7
Legumes	61.8	29.8	48.3
All crops	48.3	32.3	66.9

Notes
[a] Calculation of yields: Rimpton: Hampshire Record Office Eccl. Comm. 2, 159270 to 159407; Cuxham and Martham: B. M. S. Campbell, 'Arable productivity in medieval England: some evidence from Norfolk', *JEH*, XLII, 1983, pp. 390–4.
[b] Calculation of relative prices: Rimpton: HRO Eccl. Comm. 2, 159270 to 159407; Cuxham: J. E. Thorold Rogers, *A history of agriculture and prices in England*, I, Oxford, 1884, pp. 44–139; Martham (the figure is for Norfolk): Campbell, this volume, Table 6.4, column 1300–1349.
[c] See the note to Table 7.6.

Source After Campbell, 'Arable productivity in medieval England'.

Table 7.6 *Rimpton: weighted aggregate net crop yields, 1211–1403 (wheat equivalents, net of tithe and seed)*

Years	n	Yield per seed		Yield per acre	
		All crops	Cereals	All crops	Cereals
1209–1249	12	2.436	2.437	5.213	5.142
1225–1274	12	3.186	3.234	6.306	6.247
1250–1299	18	2.856	2.879	5.016	4.884
1275–1324	31	2.917	2.976	5.154	4.990
1300–1349	41	2.970	3.089	5.335	5.221
1325–1374	46	2.193	2.300	4.002	3.960
1350–1403	42	1.777	1.824	3.326	3.285
1209–1403	113	2.439	2.489	4.338	4.240

Notes

n refers to the number of years for which yields for some or all crops may be calculated. Figures are calculated according to the formula $Y = \sum (y_i \cdot p_i / p_w \cdot a_i / \Sigma a)$ where Y is weighted yield, y_i is the yield of crop i as yield per seed or in bushels per acre, p_i is the price of the crop per bushels, p_w is the price of wheat per bushel, a_i is the acreage under crop i. Figures for cereals are thus directly comparable with the data in Table 6.6.

Source Tables 7.1, 7.2 and 7.3.

Martham's agricultural system was certainly advantageous, the comparative potential of the standard medieval system, as it was practised at Cuxham for example, should not be underestimated.

Trends in land productivity at Rimpton are revealed by weighted aggregate net yields per seed and per acre measured in wheat equivalents (Figure 7.2(b) and Table 7.6). Before proceeding to describe these trends, however, two factors affecting the interpretation of these yield calculations must be discussed. First, although the calculations are net of tithe and seed, no other allowances have been made. Of course, the amount left over for sale after the deduction of liveries and fodder was even less, Rimpton's mean net disposable surplus amounting to 69 per cent for wheat, 63 per cent for oats, 35 per cent for barley, and 34 per cent for beans between 1209 and 1403. These are still relatively high figures, closer to those on intensively-cultivated Norfolk demesnes such as Hemsby rather than low-yielding ones such as Thorpe Abbotts.[14] This contrast underlines Rimpton's paradoxical nature as a market-orientated demesne with a low level of productivity.

14 Campbell, above, pp. 171–2.

The second factor to keep in mind when interpreting Figure 7.2(b) and Table 7.6 is the impact of climatic change. Despite the fierce debate which has raged over this question, the impact of the weather remains extremely difficult to measure. It may have been confined to the introduction of an additional cyclical trend to the yield figures: for example, over the fourteenth century Rimpton's yields clearly fit the general weather-influenced pattern of an upturn in the second quarter of the fourteenth century, a downturn in the third, and an improvement in the fourth quarter. Nevertheless, this cycle was not powerful enough to override other factors producing a very significant long-term decline in productivity over the fourteenth century. Yet the contribution of weather conditions cannot be entirely dismissed, especially the possibility that the higher level of yields at Rimpton in the mid thirteenth century was influenced by the tail end of a recognised 'climatic optimum' in the early middle ages.[15]

The underlying yield trends revealed by Figure 7.2(b) and Table 7.6 appear quite straightforward. Yields were comparatively unimpressive in the early years of the thirteenth century, but this seems understandable given the low levels of stocking, equipment and labour before the 1220s. Peak yields occurred in the period 1225–74, precisely at the high-tide mark of Rimpton's arable exploitation. Although productivity certainly fell back thereafter, a real 'crisis' in land productivity had not occurred by 1325. This evidence reinforces the suspicion that Titow's 'general deterioration' of the late thirteenth century may only represent the aftermath of an exceptional high point in land productivity on the estate in the middle of the century. One possible explanation for this productivity 'blip' may lie with favourable weather conditions, but another alternative is explored below in Section IV. An even greater problem for the orthodox 'population-resources' model is provided by the very severe decline in land productivity that occurred at Rimpton after 1325. This cannot be attributed to anything but a direct fall in yields because both crop choice and relative prices

15 For the climate in general: H. H. Lamb, *The changing climate*, London, 1966, pp. 170–95. For the Winchester estate: J. Z. Titow, 'Evidence of weather in the account rolls of the Bishopric of Winchester 1209–1350', *EcHR*, XII, 1960, pp. 365–91; J. Z. Titow, 'Le Climat à travers les rôles de compatibilité de l'évêché de Winchester (1350–1450)', *Annales, Économies, Sociétés, Civilisations*, XXV, 1970, pp. 312–50; G. H. Dury, 'Crop failures on the Winchester manors 1232–1349', *Transactions of the Institute of British Geographers*, new series, IX, 1984, pp. 401–18; H. Osmaston, 'Crop failures on the Winchester manors 1232–1349 AD; some comments', *Transactions of the Institute of British Geographers*, new series, X, 1985, pp. 495–8.

were fairly stable. The trend clearly runs contrary to Postan's Ricardian expectation that yields would rise when production contracted to better soils and when increased grazing resources and animal numbers improved manure supplies. Rimpton's yields therefore support B. M. S. Campbell's revision of our view of late-medieval productivity trends on intensively cultivated demesnes.[16]

IV The ecology of the field system

R. S. Shiel has demonstrated that the supply of nitrogen was the most important factor for land productivity in the 'pre-fertiliser era', and has identified four ways that the nitrogen budget of commonfield systems could be manipulated: (i) increased fixation by use of pulses; (ii) the release of stored-up nitrogen by conversion of old grassland; (iii) increased nitrogen turnover rates through better livestock stocking and management; (iv) reduction of unproductive fallowing.[17] The application of these policies at Rimpton is considered here, in juxtaposition to the traditional emphases upon 'natural' limitations deriving from soil quality and gross manure levels, in order to understand the ecological factors that lay at the root of productivity change.

Shiel's first point concerning the deliberate use of leguminous crops to increase the fixation of atmospheric nitrogen in the soil is a disputed point among medievalists, despite the very suggestive evidence from Norfolk that this was indeed the case.[18] Rimpton's cultivation of legumes increased from 2.67 per cent of the cropped acreage between 1209 and 1249 to a peak of 8.41 per cent between 1275 and 1324 (Table 7.2). New types were also added in the form of peas and vetches. Although these levels are much lower than with the later Norfolk four-course rotation (25 per cent), the possible impact of this trend on maintaining nitrogen levels at Rimpton during the thirteenth century should not be ignored. Declining yields were also later paralleled by a reduction in legumes: peas were abandoned and beans and vetch declined to 6.59 per cent between 1350 and 1403.

16 Campbell, above, pp. 159–78.
17 R. S. Shiel, above, pp. 62–7.
18 For different interpretations: J. Z. Titow, *English rural society 1200–1350*, London, 1969, pp. 41–2; H. E. Hallam, *Rural England 1066–1348*, London, 1981, pp. 13 and 136; D. L. Farmer, 'Crop yields, prices and wages in medieval England', *Studies in Medieval and Renaissance History*, VI, 1983, pp. 132–3; B. M. S. Campbell, 'Agricultural progress in medieval England: some evidence from eastern Norfolk' *EcHR*, XXXVI, 1983, pp. 31–3; M. Mate, 'Medieval agrarian practices: the determining factors?', *AHR*, XXXIII, 1985, pp. 27–31.

Moreover, the administration was clearly aware of their yield-enhancing properties: in 1370–71, 1371–72 and 1382–83 there are references to the seeding of vetches on the fallow, or in addition to oats, in order to 'compost' the land for future years. These were not isolated experiments peculiar to Rimpton, a similar phrase being used at Taunton as early as 1328–29, and vetches being sown on the fallow of Winchester demesnes in Wiltshire in the thirteenth century.[19]

Detailed cropping plans in Rimpton's accounts suggest other aspects of legume production related to 'nutrient cycling' – the structural relationships which determine how inputs affected different crops in a rotation.[20] Regular sowings of legumes were confined to about one in three furlongs, all of which seem to have benefited as this group also comprised those fertile enough to step out of the rotation for an extra year of cultivation (an *inhok*). Furthermore, to benefit from the nitrogen fixed in the soil, the sowing of a cereal crop must follow as quickly as possible after the legumes. If this factor was significant for yields at Rimpton, the trend of legume production should exhibit more influence on the wheat yield than the oats yield (following a three-course rotation). Although no such difference is visible for the thirteenth century when all crops yielded well, fourteenth-century trends for wheat were more steeply negative than those for oats, perhaps revealing a drop in available nitrogen as legume production contracted.

Shiel's second point concerning the nitrogen-rich qualities of old pasture when first ploughed may also explain certain features of the productivity trend at Rimpton. Titow proposed a strong correlation between 'marginal colonisation' and declining productivity on at least twelve Winchester demesnes, the 'more-successful' yielding manors in the thirteenth century, including Rimpton, usually being small with little colonisation.[21] Yet this classification of Rimpton is misleading, for the cessation of peasant assarting derived from the Bishop's appropriation of all remaining land resources. The new demesne assarts then created were probably not as marginal as those on some other Winchester demesnes, as revealed by stability in the production of oats – the least ecologically demanding crop often associated with expansion

19 HRO Eccl. Comm. 2, 159380, 159454, 159389 (Rimpton), 159341 (Taunton); R. C. Payne, 'Agrarian conditions on the Wiltshire estates of the Duchy of Lancaster, the Lords Hungerford and the Bishopric of Winchester in the thirteenth, fourteenth and fifteenth centuries', unpublished University of London Ph.D. thesis, 1940, p. 118.
20 Shiel, above, pp. 65, 70.
21 Titow, *Winchester yields*, pp. 32–3.

on to poorer lands.[22] But even so, Rimpton's expansion still involved creating a large 'breach' (Middle English *breche*) of nearly 100 acres in a large block of common pasture lying towards Woodhouse and conversion of meadows to arable as shown by the field name element *mede* in cropping plans.[23] The very high yields produced between 1225 and 1274 might therefore be interpreted as arising from a sudden influx of nitrogen when the arable area encroached upon ancient pasture (Table 7.6).

Some later arable contraction during or after the lease of the manor (1268–80) could be explained by the gradual shedding of those assarts which produced decreasing returns. This earliest stage of contraction may only represent a return to more normal levels of production and land productivity in the period 1275 to 1324. None-theless, most of the new lands remained in successful cultivation for over a century, with large-scale contraction not beginning until the 1320s. Thereafter, most of the earlier assarts were quickly shed, a decline which was a mirror image of the earlier expansion: only a core of ancient fields in the centre and south of the parish remained in cultivation throughout both centuries. Thus, almost the opposite relationship to that proposed by Postan is revealed, for when 'marginal' land was cultivated, so yields were high, but when the same land was shed, so yields declined (Figure 7.2(b) and Table 7.6).

When Postan discovered that newly-colonised land often had a higher value than anciently cultivated land it led him to presume 'that the older lands, though situated on what should have ranked as better soil, were worth less because their productive power had been sapped'.[24] Yet Shiel's theoretical work and the evidence from Rimpton combine to suggest that such differences in value were instead a function of higher yields on new furlongs as their stored-up nitrogen was released.[25] It seems at least possible, therefore, that high yields across much of the Winchester estate in the first half of the thirteenth century may have been associated with an unusually early peak of cultivation and assarting.

22 See T. A. M. Bishop, 'The rotation of crops at Westerham, 1297–1350', *Economic History Review*, IX, 1938, p. 42.
23 For other examples of 'breaches' and ploughed meadows see: H. P. R. Finberg, *Tavistock Abbey: a study in the social and economic history of Devon*, Cambridge, 1951, p. 105; R. H. Hilton, *A medieval society: the west midlands at the end of the thirteenth century*, London, 1966, p. 117; C. C. Dyer, *Lords and peasants in a changing society: the estates of the Bishopric of Worcester, 680–1540*, Cambridge, 1980, p. 96.
24 Postan, *The medieval economy and society*, p. 64.
25 For a similar suggestion: M. Mate, 'Profit and productivity on the estates of Isabella de Forz (1260–92)', *EcHR*, XXXIII, 1980, pp. 332–3.

Any later decline in mean yields to a lower but stable level may have been the result of a drop-off in productivity from certain assarts, being variable from manor to manor depending on their quality and the inputs made, rather than the shedding of anciently cultivated land which had become exhausted.[26]

The impact of animal stocking upon the turnover rate of nitrogen within a field system is one of Shiel's points that has already received some research attention. Previous analyses of Winchester yields have related the manure potentials of livestock to the cropped acreage, Titow discovering that a fall in this ratio correlated with lower productivity on 26 Winchester demesnes. The relationship was not clear-cut, however, for the ratio had a reverse or negligible effect in another 11 instances.[27] This finding may well suggest that the detrimental effect of a reduction in manure production is confused in the short term by the initial release of large amounts of soil nitrogen as the arable area expands on to old grassland.

At Rimpton, Titow argued that a fall in the ratio by the late thirteenth century may have caused the drop in yields per seed he detected. Nevertheless, these calculations are unreliable because of their total confidence in the 'livestock' section of Rimpton's accounts. Sheep are only included therein up to 1264–65, their subsequent absence being largely responsible for the declining ratio. Yet a reorganisation of sheep farming across the whole estate had only removed control of the flock from the local reeve.[28] Indeed, the 'exits of the manor' and 'sales of pasture' sections still reveal the presence of quite large flocks – the pastures now being occupied by sheep from other demesnes or being leased to the villagers.[29]

The complex relationship between animal numbers and land productivity can still be explored by concentrating on the period with complete stock accounts up to 1264–65. Animal ratios have been calculated using weightings of horses × 1.0, oxen, cows and bulls × 1.2, immature cattle × 0.8, sheep and swine × 0.1.[30] These weightings produce a mean of 40.38 livestock units per 100 acres of grain between 1209 and 1265, a figure lower than Campbell's general sample for England but similar to the area of intensive arable cultivation in

26 See Farmer, 'Crop yields, prices and wages', p. 131.
27 Titow, *Winchester yields*, pp. 30–1.
28 A tendency noted on other Winchester manors: Payne, 'Agrarian conditions', pp. 190 and 212–13.
29 Thornton, 'The demesne of Rimpton', pp. 180–7 and 314–17.
30 Campbell, above, pp. 156–7.

Norfolk.[31] If Rimpton's livestock are related to the acreage of both grain and legumes, as in Titow's original calculation, the mean ratio falls to 35.92. This figure is below the average for the Winchester estate which Titow already considered too low for adequate manuring.

One explanation may be that Rimpton's tenantry were heavily involved in pastoral farming and provided more of the commonfield animals. Yet Rimpton was exceptional amongst the Winchester demesnes for its degree of commitment to arable farming and it may be significant that its animal ratio is quite similar to those prevalent on the more arable-orientated estate of Westminster Abbey.[32] Moreover, demesne animal numbers at Rimpton actually increased alongside the arable expansion and the ratio per 100 acres of all crops hardly changed over time: it stood at 35.80 units before the expansion of the arable (1209 to 1221), rising to 43.51 units when the biggest assarts were made (1224 to 1237), and then levelled out at 32.82 units at the peak of arable exploitation (1245 to 1268) at a time when many livestock had been lost through episcopal vacancies (below, Section V). Thus, despite the conjunction of intensive arable husbandry and low animal stocking rates at Rimpton, shrinking grazing resources could be used more intensively when required. Such changes in the intensity of grazing brought about improvements in the transfer rates of nitrogen to the arable and may indicate that Postan and Titow actually overestimated the number of animals required for the recycling of nutrients within such field systems.

In addition, the employment of carters for the collection and spreading of manure increased, a change so important that it required expensive investment on new horse-drawn manure-carts. This represented a technological advance for a demesne which had previously depended upon ox-hauled vehicles.[33] Significantly, these carts were first purchased in 1223–24, the very point at which the demesne arable expanded by about 100 acres. Although the acreages manured were never very large, typically 10 acres per annum, such intensive applications on top of the dung left by fallow-field animals may have improved nitrogen levels. This evidence demonstrates that simple animal numbers are an insufficient guide to how livestock could improve the turnover of nitrogen within a field system.

---

31 Campbell, above, p. 153.
32 Titow, *Winchester yields*, pp. 135–9; Farmer, 'Crop yields, prices and wages', p. 137.
33 See J. L. Langdon, 'Horse hauling: a revolution in vehicle transport in twelfth-and thirteenth-century England', *Past and Present*, CIII, 1984, pp. 37–66.

The limited renaissance of livestock farming after the Black Death, combined with the gradual decline in cultivation, must have greatly improved Rimpton's animal ratio. In the orthodox population-resources model such a development could have been expected to improve land productivity, and Farmer has indeed argued that yields improved in response to similar circumstances on some other Winchester demesnes.[34] Yet despite the very numerous references to the presence of large inter-manorial flocks of sheep at Rimpton, land productivity still declined. One explanation lies with the impact of the Black Death on the availability and the costs of hiring workers to take advantage of potential compost, thus curtailing the return of nitrogen from the farmyard manure-heaps. This may have occurred long before the advent of plague, for fewer carters were being employed after 1320 and labour-service accounts also show very few customary 'works' then being used for manuring. In addition, the changing nature of Rimpton's pastoral economy may have contributed to the decline of yields. During the thirteenth century most livestock were grazed upon the arable in moveable folds, the stated purpose of the sheep flock being the provision of manure.[35] In contrast, by the late fourteenth century cattle and sheep were increasingly being farmed for meat, hides, and wool, and although folding still took place many livestock were grazed in newly-enclosed pastures and meadows. Thus diversification toward pastoral farming, perhaps in an attempt to offset declining incomes from grain production, could have further reduced nitrogen turnover rates and compromised the productivity of the commonfields.

Finally, the nitrogen budget could also be improved by reducing the amount of unproductive fallow land. Reductions in fallowing did occur on some Norfolk demesnes in the middle ages, but these were exceptional cases: such improvements did not generally appear in Britain until the introduction of clover and the evolution of the Norfolk four-course system during the late seventeenth and eighteenth centuries. The elimination of Rimpton's fallow field was not an economically viable option within the prevailing structure of landholding and system of husbandry. All that was managed in this direction were occasional seedings of legumes on the fallow and occasional *inhoks* on demesne lands lying in severalty. Yet the Winchester administration was able to

34 Farmer, 'Grain yields', pp. 563–4; Farmer, 'Crop yields, prices and wages', pp. 136–7.
35 When village sheep temporarily replaced the lord's flock in 1267–8 they were grazed there *propter compostationem*: HRO Eccl. Comm. 2, 159298.

develop one way of manipulating existing field arrangements to increase the nitrogen budget, which once again involved the cultivation of old pasture. In 1310–11, a group of well-manured headland and pathway grazing strips surrounding cultivated furlongs were added to the arable, and other parts of those furlongs laid down to rest in turn, probably as part of a continuing process of renewal. This 'furlong rejuvenation' of 1310–11 may have helped to produce the following four good harvests (which were against the general trend on the Winchester estate), a sequence only halted by the weather-related catastrophes of 1315 and 1316. Significantly, much less interest was later shown in such matters, with no more 'furlong rejuvenations' and reduced cropping flexibility: further evidence of the decline in available nitrogen and thus crop growth in the later middle ages.[36]

V Management and labour

It is also important to examine the administrative and social context of productivity change, not the least because the medieval treatises on husbandry stress the need for competent estate management if demesne exploitation was to be successful.[37] Biddick has highlighted the problems faced by important ecclesiastics in maintaining a secure financial base for their estate organisations. Episcopal vacancies, for example, could lead to serious difficulties because the Crown had gained the right to administer ecclesiastical temporalities. Widespread asset-stripping took place, chiefly through the sale of livestock, leaving each new Bishop of Winchester to engage in a massive reinvestment campaign.[38] At Rimpton the royal officials maintained those beasts essential for agriculture, such as plough-oxen and cart-horses, but usually sold off the entire cow herd and sheep flock. In addition, a royal vacancy account of 1259–60 reveals that Rimpton's arable was deliberately over-cultivated with extra wheat being sown upon lands which should have lain fallow: this must have further strained the ecology of the field system.[39] Yet even a run of vacancies over the mid thirteenth century did not prevent the arable expansion, and neither did the long episcopates of the late fourteenth century prevent eventual decline. Moreover, the

36 For similar 'metabolic changes' on some other Glastonbury and Winchester manors: Postan, *The medieval economy and society*, pp. 64–6.
37 Oschinsky, *Walter of Henley*, pp. 65–74.
38 Biddick, above, pp. 98–104.
39 Public Record Office SC6 1142/25; Thornton, 'The demesne of Rimpton', pp. 219–22.

administration always appears to have been able to find the capital needed to restock the manor within a few years. the chief effect of the vacancies, therefore, was to introduce a further cyclical tendency into agricultural production.

Probably more important on such isolated manors were changes in administrative structures and controls at the local level, where more opportunity existed for inefficiency, idleness and fraud. To begin with the local reeve was responsible for the everyday conduct of husbandry (albeit under the supervision of the Constable of Taunton). Then, from 1224 to 1308, the reeve was joined by a stipendiary bailiff. This important and highly-paid official probably exercised particular authority over the harvest and the manorial court, the latter often being used to regulate labour services and protect demesne farm assets. The bailiff's employment reflects a general managerial revolution during 'the age of high farming' when extra tiers of supervision were required for supporting expansionist policies.[40]

In contrast, management structures weakened later in the fourteenth century. The post of bailiff was discontinued in 1308–09, probably because of the impact of inflation upon his salary, the everyday management of agriculture returning to the reeve.[41] Very short terms of service for most fourteenth-century reeves compared with their predecessors may indicate either a reluctance to serve or that the administration was less than satisfied with their unsupervised performance. Another cost-cutting switch from stipendiary to tenant haywards after 1323–24 also had dangerous implications: far lower reimbursements to the latter provided greater incentives for fraud at harvest time. A gradual multiplication of leases of demesne assets and fixed returns from livestock over the century may partly reflect such problems of control. Increasing surcharges (*oneratio*) in the grain account from 1329–30, like those on the estates of St Swithun's Priory, also reveal the uphill struggle of the administration to influence the trend of land productivity.[42]

Whilst it is quite simple to trace changes in administrative structure, it is less easy to link them directly with changing agricultural practice. One area which holds some promise, however, is the basic management

---

40 See J. S. Drew, 'Manorial accounts of St. Swithun's Priory, Winchester', *English Historical Review*, LXII, 1947, pp. 22–3; reprinted in E. M. Carus-Wilson, ed., *Essays in economic history*, II, 1962, pp. 12–30.

41 M. Mate, 'High prices in early fourteenth-century England: causes and consequences', *EcHR*, XXVIII, 1975, pp. 15–16.

42 Drew, 'Manorial accounts', pp. 29–35.

task of deciding the seeding density. As has already been mentioned Rimpton's seeding rates were unusually low, a situation compounded by a reduction of about 25 per cent in bushels per acre seeded for wheat (2.0 to 1.5), rye (2.0 to 1.5), and oats (4.0 to 3.0) over the first half of the thirteenth century. These were real changes, not a function of changing grain measures, for the barley rate remained stable and that for beans actually increased. Two explanations can be suggested for these interesting changes. First, a lower seeding rate at Rimpton allowed a smaller number of plants to get a bigger share of available nitrogen, a policy which may have increased yields where the animal ratio and nitrogen soil content were low. Second, the reductions at Rimpton could be linked to the rising ratio of labour to land which improved cultivation conditions, for other studies have suggested that higher seeding rates were a response to the weed-infested nature of medieval arable.[43] These labour improvements included extra workers at boon-days for harrowing and fallow-ploughing and piece-work labourers for weeding the more valuable crops. In contrast, consumption-orientated crops like barley and beans were concentrated on a smaller area by high seeding rates which smothered weed development and reduced labour requirements.[44]

The apparently deliberate policy of obtaining higher yields per seed of the most valuable crops may have later run into difficulties. Low seeding rates for wheat and oats were disadvantageous by the fourteenth century because investment in weeding fell quite substantially. This decline was alluded to in 1320–21, the last year in which labourers were hired for intensive weeding of selected crops, when extra workers were required 'because of the many thistles'.[45] In addition, labour-service accounts reveal very few services being utilised for weeding by the mid fourteenth century. Although an obvious response would have been to increase seeding rates once more to smother weed-growth, it would have been a tough administrative decision to reduce the proportion of saleable grain when the market was already in decline, and perhaps one beyond the capacity of the local reeve.

Purchase of seed stock is another management decision which can be seen to have had an effect on land productivity. There was

43 For example: P. F. Brandon, 'Cereal yields on the Sussex estates of Battle Abbey during the later middle ages', *EcHR*, XXV, 1972, pp. 409–10; W. Harwood-Long, 'The low yields of corn in medieval England', *EcHR*, XXXII, 1979, pp. 468–9.
44 Thornton, 'The demesne of Rimpton', pp. 155–8 and 304–7.
45 HRO Eccl. Comm. 2, 159334.

clearly great variation between crop types, wheat and rye having 20 per cent of their seed purchased, barley 15 per cent, oats a mere 1 per cent (a scale perhaps linked to their value per quarter). Moreover, for the commercially-orientated wheat crop there was a tremendous increase in seed purchases from 8 to 73 per cent between the periods 1209–14 and 1224–37. Although seed was generally only purchased when it could be bought at a price lower than the sale price of the manor's harvest, there was probably a deliberate policy to find better seed.[46] An order sent to the keepers of the vacant See of Winchester in 1238 shows that the comparative benefits of local, purchased, and exchanged seed were then under discussion, and seed was also purchased to raise productivity on royal manors at this time. Annual seed purchases of 10 per cent in the period 1283–1349 probably reflects both the general advice found in Walter of Henley's treatise and the specific instruction to the bailiffs of John of Pontoise, Bishop of Winchester in the late thirteenth century, to obtain seed from elsewhere by purchase or exchange.[47]

In contrast, seed purchases for most crops collapsed after the Black Death as demand for grain decreased. The only exception were those for wheat, the price of this crop remaining more buoyant. When general demand and prices fell further in the mid 1370s, so seed purchases for wheat also trailed off. In these conditions the reeve probably found it difficult to buy replacement seed at a lower price than the sale value of the manor's large harvest. Comments concerning the quality of seed were also disparaging: in 1356–57, for example, the seeding rate of oats was lower than usual because the seed was debilitated.[48] Although other factors were involved, the correlation between declining seed quality and poorer yields may well show that the earlier instructions of Walter of Henley and Bishop Pontoise had real practical value.

The size and management of the workforce is a most important issue for understanding the dynamics of this manor's very labour-intensive system of husbandry. Rimpton had an unusual rent and labour-service structure in which partial rent acquittances were given to those tenants performing services. This allows an estimate of available labour to be calculated from the rent section of the accounts over a century

---

46 Thornton, 'The demesne of Rimpton', pp. 155–8 and 304–7.
47 R. C. Stacey, 'Agricultural investment and the management of the royal demesne manors, 1236–1240', *JEH*, XLVI, 1986, pp. 928–30; Oschinsky, *Walter of Henley*, pp. 174–5 and 324–5.
48 HRO Eccl. Comm. 2, 159367.

Table 7.7 *Rimpton: manorial labour ratio and yield per 1,000 man-days, 1209–1403*

Years	Mean days work[a]		Mean sown acreage	Days' work per acre	Yield per acre per 1,000 man days
	famuli	services			
1209–1249	2,071	1,179	223	14.57	1.6040
1225–1275	2,407	2,083	266	16.88	1.4044
1250–1299	2,168	2,709	260	18.76	1.0285
1275–1324	2,169	2,967	252	20.38	1.0035
1300–1349	1,983	2,214	230	18.25	1.2711
1325–1374	1,727	1,445	208	15.25	1.2616
1350–1403	1,652	1,139	176	15.86	1.1916
1209–1403	1,918	1,778	219	16.88	1.1737

Note
[a] Labour of all administrative officials, smith and miller omitted. Amendments made for participation in pastoral husbandry, festivals and holidays and commutations (sales) of labour services.

Source See note 3.

before detailed labour-service accounts become available in the 1320s. Furthermore, a ratio of labour to land can be calculated, in much the same fashion as an animal ratio, because all types of manorial worker, both tenants performing regular labour services and waged farm servants (*famuli*), can have their work expressed in a number of days worked per annum. Only tenants called to extra boon-day works and piece-work labourers are excluded, but this is not critical because their relative importance was very minor compared with the extremely large pool of regular manorial workers.[49]

At the very start of the thirteenth century the manorial labour supply was relatively low (about 10 days per sown acre), but its intensity increased quickly as the arable expanded. The mean figure for the first half of the century was 14 days and it had already reached 16 days by the period 1225 to 1274 (Table 7.7). During this period much emphasis was placed upon soil improvement. For example, marling first occurred at Rimpton in 1224–25 when 2s 0d was paid for a new horse-hauled marling cart and two carters were paid 6s 6d for marling in the summer. Thereafter four carts and four carters were regularly employed in this

49 For further details of the labour supply and complex labour-ratio calculations: Thornton, 'The demesne of Rimpton', pp. 223–53 and 321–9.

H

activity up to 1257–58. Although the amount of land treated was probably never very extensive it may have helped to improve the quality of the poorest assarts, for marling increases the rate of breakdown of organic matter in the short term, thus reducing the soil store of nitrogen but increasing yields at the same time.[50] Slight shrinkage of the arable, combined with intense exploitation of labour-service obligations, provided an even greater ratio of 20 man-days in the period 1275 to 1324. It is possible to state, therefore, that the greatest labour intensity coincided with the peak of the general demographic expansion, and was probably an important factor in the maintenance of output per acre. Notably, however, higher labour ratios in the periods 1250 to 1299 and 1275 to 1324 compared with the period 1225 to 1274 did not prevent a slight decline in yields and a contraction of the arable. This may either have been the result of worsening weather conditions or of a drop-off in the fertility of assarts as their extra nitrogen was expended – or of both those factors.

Annual commutations of labour services began in the 1320s, some *famuli* being laid off and fewer wage labourers and boon-workers employed. This decline was proportionately greater than the arable contraction, resulting in a reduction to 15 days' work per sown acre from 1325 onwards. In addition, some evidence concerning the employment of the *famuli* suggests that the real labour supply may have fallen much lower. After 1350 there developed a suspiciously high ratio of one plough-team per 70 acres (far higher than that recommended in the treatises), suggesting that in spite of their job descriptions the ploughmen and drovers were also engaged in other work, perhaps supervising the growing numbers of young cattle.[51] One ploughman was certainly undertaking 'diverse work' for half of the year as early as 1346–47.[52] Neither does the ratio take account of the lost flexibility in production resulting from the decision not to employ any more piece-work labourers after 1357–58 probably in response to local labour shortages and rising wage rates. All of these trends could have affected yields, especially for wheat which was most reliant on cultivation standards.

Real problems also existed for the management and control of the forced labour on such manorialised farms. For example, Rimpton's thirteenth-century expansion depended on a powerful assertion of the

---

50 HRO Eccl. Comm. 2, 159278–93. Shiel, above, pp. 63–4.
51 Oschinsky, *Walter of Henley*, pp. 264–5 and 312–13.
52 HRO Eccl. Comm. 2, 159356.

Bishop's right to exact full labour service of four days' work per week from all of his tenants and to coerce those unwilling or inefficient through the manorial court. It thus seems possible that Rimpton's yields were later undermined by a general decline in manorial labour efficiency during the fourteenth century, when the performance of services suffered from the rising tide of peasant grievance against this expression of servility.[53] This was certainly the opinion of a Commons petition in the 1377 Parliament which claimed that 'in many parts of the realm the corn lies unharvested ... and is lost for all time' because of the withdrawal by villeins of 'the customs and services due to their lords'.[54] Customary tenants on some Winchester demesnes refused to perform services in both the build-up and aftermath of the 1381 rising, news of the revolt also triggering some disturbances in Somerset.[55] At Rimpton, the Bishop's denial of any wage rise to the *famuli* in the fourteenth century and the policy of altering their food liveries to include the least valuable of crops cannot have endeared them to his interests, for elsewhere workers' living standards were rising.[56]

VI Conclusions

The history of land productivity at Rimpton in the middle ages was characterised by a high point in the mid thirteenth century and a prolonged decline from the mid fourteenth century. These findings cannot be easily accommodated by interpretations of the medieval agrarian economy which stress a general decline of yields over the thirteenth century arising from the infertility of 'marginal' land brought into cultivation and/or the overcultivation and exhaustion of the ancient arable core. High productivity at Rimpton in the period 1225 to 1274 most probably resulted from the ploughing-up of fertile nitrogen-rich

53 R. H. Hilton, 'Peasant movements in England before 1381', *EcHR*, II, 1949, pp. 122–30.
54 R. B. Dobson, ed., *The Peasants' Revolt of 1381*, London, 2nd edn., 1981, pp. 76–8.
55 E. Robo, *Medieval Farnham: everyday life in an episcopal manor*, Farnham 1935, p. 96; B. F. Harvey, 'Draft letters of manumission and pardon for the men of Somerset in 1381', *English Historical Review*, LXXX, 1965, pp. 89–91; R. J. Faith, 'The "Great Rumour" of 1377 and peasant ideology', pp. 43–73 in R. H. Hilton and T. H. Aston, eds., *The English rising of 1381*, Cambridge, 1984, pp. 44–5 and 53–7.
56 Thornton, 'The demesne of Rimpton', pp. 227–30; N. Kenyon, 'Labour conditions in Essex in the reign of Richard II', *EcHR*, IV, 1932–4, pp. 429–51; reprinted as pp. 91–111 in E. M. Carus-Wilson, ed., *Essays in economic history*, II, London, 1962, pp. 92–4; Dyer, *Lords and peasants*, pp. 142–3 and 146.

assarts and the latter years of a climatic optimum. The underlying forces behind this development can be identified as the pressure of population growth and rising prices, perhaps also influenced by the growing taxation burdens of the bishopric.[57] The real peak did not last much more than a generation for as prices stagnated mid-century, and as the productivity 'bonus' of some assarts declined, so the arable started to contract in the 1260s. The situation might well explain why Rimpton's demesne was leased between 1268 and 1280, although direct management returned as prices recovered an upward aspect in the last quarter of the century.[58]

Although there had been a slight fall in yields and production levels by the 1280s, these were then maintained up to the 1320s. This trend both reflects the generally high market demand for grain and the continuing effects of the complete overhaul of the demesne's management which had occurred from 1223–24. Long-term policies had then been enacted to raise cultivation standards, to increase nitrogen fixation in the soil with legumes, to provide more manure and marl, and to improve seed quality, associated with an intensified application and management of manorialised labour. Thus, land productivity was maintained by a combination of factors, perhaps none individually dominant but which together supported an agricultural system operating near its limit.

These inputs continued, albeit with some short-term fluctuations, until *c.*1320, but thereafter many yield-enhancing policies were undermined or discarded: soil preparation and weedings were reduced, legume cultivation declined, applications of marl and manure were abandoned, seed purchases cut back and the supply and management of labour reduced. Not surprisingly, mean yields were immediately reduced in the period 1325 to 1374. Although it has been suggested that the general stagnation of demesne agriculture in this period may have been associated with a halving of the money supply by 1350, the timing is also indicative of a change in demand deriving from the much debated pre-plague famines.[59] Further, the general correlation in the movement of land productivity, arable cultivation, and crop prices suggests that most of Rimpton's improvements in arable

57 Biddick, above, pp. 98–104.
58 N. J. Mayhew, 'Money and prices in England from Henry II to Edward III', *AHR*, XXXV, 1987, p. 127.
59 M. Prestwich, 'Currency and the economy of early fourteenth-century England', in N. J. Mayhew, ed., *Edwardian monetary affairs, 1279–1344*, BAR, British series, XXXVI, 1977, pp. 45–58; R. M. Smith, 'Demographic developments in rural England 1300–48: a survey pp. 25–77 in B. M. S. Campbell, ed., *Before the Black Death: studies in the 'crisis' of the early fourteenth century*, Manchester, 1991.

technique were not permanent but followed the growth and decline in the demand for grain (Figure 7.2). This study of Rimpton thus supports the Boserupian view of a generally positive relationship between population trends and land productivity in areas of intensive arable husbandry.[60]

Finally, some comment is warranted concerning the relationship of land productivity to other elements of total factor productivity, namely output per units of labour and capital. As regards the former, Table 7.7 indicates that output per 1,000 man-days at Rimpton fell quite sharply over the thirteenth century. Clearly, whilst higher output per acre or per seed could be achieved it was only at the cost of decreasing returns per worker. This was the major limitation for agricultural development before the application of new techniques in the agricultural revolution of the eighteenth century enabled both land and labour productivity to rise together. The failure of output per 1,000 man-days at Rimpton to recover very much over the fourteenth century, parallel to the trend at Martham in Norfolk, strongly suggests that the decline in yields per acre was so severe that even a reduction in the intensity of arable production was unable to improve labour productivity.[61]

Yet arable output was only one aspect of labour productivity, and low returns per worker from arable production could well have been matched by increasing returns from those involved in pastoral production. Rimpton's livestock fertility and mortality rates had greatly improved by the fourteenth century through better animal management, more forceful accounting practices, proper culling, and the provision of adequate sires. In addition, more young cattle were available for marketing as the arable contracted, and from the 1340s Rimpton's wooded pastures were utilised as specialised fattening ground for flocks of debilitated sheep from the Bishop's downland manors in Wiltshire.[62] Such specialisation reflects redistributions of per capita wealth and improvements in diet after the plagues and the first stages of the transformation of south-east Somerset into an important region for fattening, dairying, wool, and clothmaking.[63]

---

60 E. Boserup, *Population and technology*, Oxford, 1981; Campbell, above, pp. 144–9.
61 Campbell, above, pp. 176–7.
62 Thornton, 'The demesne of Rimpton', pp. 185–7.
63 C. C. Dyer, 'English diet in the later middle ages', pp. 191–216 in T. H. Aston, P. R. Coss, C. C. Dyer and J. Thirsk, eds., *Social relations and ideas: essays in honour of R. H. Hilton*, Cambridge, 1983, p. 214; J. Thirsk, 'The farming regions of England', pp. 1–112 in *idem, The agrarian history of England and Wales*, IV, *1500–1640*, 1967, pp. 4, 71–4 and 79–80.

Measurement of output per unit of capital requires further detailed analysis of the economic information within account rolls, but some limited comment can be made concerning gross levels of investment at Rimpton. A number of studies have argued that such expenditure was very low on medieval demesnes – typically 5 per cent of gross income, a pattern repeated at Rimpton where a similar level of arable income was reinvested.[64] Yet the heavy nature of customary labour-service obligations at Rimpton may have allowed the substitution of extra unskilled workers for capital investment: the manor's labour ratios were clearly much higher than those calculated for other demesnes, such as Martham, which placed more reliance upon skilled *famuli* and other waged labourers. These workers were more costly but probably also more efficient and hard-working. But although Rimpton's farming system may have been comparatively agriculturally inefficient, as suggested by the very low level of land productivity, at the same time it may have been economically effective for the Bishop because the labour services were worth very much more than the fixed customary land rents which could be taken in their place. Thus, whilst the manor's distance from major markets precluded high inputs of capital and skilled waged labour to raise land productivity, the Winchester administration could still farm profitably through the intensified use of the existing manorial labour force.[65] This conclusion underlines the significance of the institutional framework for any assessment of the economic performance of manorial farms recorded in medieval account rolls.

64 M. M. Postan, 'Investment in medieval agriculture', *JEH*, XXVII, 1967, p. 579; R. H. Hilton, 'Rent and capital formation in feudal society', pp. 174–214 in *idem*, *The English peasantry in the later middle ages*, Oxford, 1975, pp. 184–96; Thornton, 'The demesne of Rimpton', pp. 356–8.
65 For comments: Campbell, 'Agricultural progress', pp. 41–4; R. Brenner, 'The agrarian roots of European capitalism', *Past and Present*, XCVII, 1982, pp. 16–113, reprinted as pp. 213–327 in Aston and Philpin, *The Brenner debate: agrarian class structure and economic development in pre-industrial Europe*, 1985, p. 232–6.

Labour productivity in English agriculture, 1300–1860

I Introduction

One of the key elements in the emergence by the nineteenth century of the modern European economy was the growth of output per worker in agriculture. Increases in output per acre may well have allowed a larger population to be supported per unit of land, but of itself this would have done little to advance incomes per capita. With low output per agricultural worker most of the population would still have been employed in the agricultural sector, keeping overall output per capita low. In pre-industrial Europe it is generally reckoned that one farm worker supported only one-third of a non-farm worker.[1] Consequently, had output per worker not increased in agriculture the productivity advances of the industrial revolution would necessarily have had a limited effect on economies as a whole. Most of the population would still have been required to labour in agriculture merely to produce food for subsistence. The development of Europe until the late nineteenth century is hence as much the story of increasing output per worker in agriculture as it is the story of industrial advance.

Total output per agricultural worker was substantially higher by the mid nineteenth century in the advanced economies of the United States and United Kingdom than in eastern Europe. This can be shown in a crude but convincing way if statistics of output per worker are examined for those agricultural products for which comparative data are available: notably, grains and animals of various types, potatoes and wine. Table 8.1 shows output per worker of all grains combined (including maize), and the stock of cows, cattle, sheep and pigs. It also shows an index of net output per worker which consists of the sum of outputs of wheat, rye, barley, potatoes, wine and animal products per worker weighted by their relative 1850 British prices.[2] The net output

---

1 C. Cipolla, *Before the industrial revolution*, New York, 1976, pp. 40 and 75.
2 In the index of net output per worker it is assumed that all the maize was consumed by farm animals, and that net output of oats is gross output times the fraction of the population not in agriculture.

calculation assumes cattle, sheep and pigs were the same size everywhere and produced the same amount of milk and wool. This biases the calculation against the more advanced agricultures of the United States and western Europe.[3] Also, the index excludes vegetables, fruits, and other speciality crops which were probably grown more in America and western Europe. P. Bairoch's estimates of output per worker for the same dates are also shown, where the weighting is not by prices but by the total number of calories produced per worker.[4] These estimates show even larger gaps between the poor and the advanced economies. Yet why was output per worker in Britain much higher than in most European countries, and when did this increase take place? Differential rates of mechanisation are unlikely to be the explanation, for by 1851 the only operation substantially mechanised in British agriculture was threshing, which had always been a task of the slack season when labour was abundant in any case.[5]

Estimating output per worker in English agriculture before 1851 is difficult due to the lack of information on both output and labour inputs for most periods. Manorial sources, which nevertheless provide a good idea of output per worker in the period 1250–1350, suggest that at that point it was at or below the level of the least developed countries in Europe in the nineteenth century (see Table 8.1).[6] Thus, sometime between 1300 and 1850 output per worker must have risen substantially. In fact, there are indications that output per worker was unusually high in England by the late sixteenth century – higher even than in eastern Europe in the nineteenth century – and that this rise in output per worker preceded the increase in yields per acre. This implies that the English economy was substantially developed long before the industrial revolution. Indeed, it would seem that there were two distinct agricultural revolutions in England: an increase in output per acre which occurred between 1650 and 1850, and an increase in

3 M. G. Mulhall, *A dictionary of statistics*, London, 1892, pp. 15 and 23–7, for example, assumes that the average cattle carcass in Britain in the late nineteenth century yielded 600 lb. of beef, compared with 500 lb. in Russia, Germany, Austria and Hungary.
4 P. Bairoch, 'Les trois révolutions agricoles du monde développé: rendements et productivité de 1800 à 1985', *Annales, Économies, Sociétés, Civilisations*, XLIV, 1989, pp. 317–53.
5 But see the observations by G. Grantham on mechanical improvements to northern French agriculture after 1750, below, pp. 353–7.
6 The very small weight of medieval animals implies that Table 8.1 greatly overstates the output per worker in medieval England.

Table 8.1 *Output per agricultural worker for selected countries in the nineteenth century*

Country	Year	Grain (bushels)	Animals (cattle-equivalent)	Net output (US = 1)	Net output (Bairoch)
USA (North)	1850	297	8.54	1.00	0.99
Britain	1851	223	5.66	0.95	1.00
France	1850	98	2.84	0.59	0.48
Netherlands	1849	74	3.49	0.48	0.46
Belgium	1851	74	2.06	0.37	0.41
Ireland	1851	98	3.10	0.47	0.46
Germany	1850	86	3.00	0.47	0.45
Sweden	1850	70	3.34	0.43	0.30
Austria	1854	72	2.66	0.39	0.25
Hungary	1854	114	2.00	0.40	0.25
Romania	1870	92	3.67	0.46	0.30
European Russia	1870	108	1.89	0.36	0.26
S. England c.1300	1300	78	2.83	0.38	

Notes
Grain in the index of grain per worker is simply the total bushels of grain harvested (including peas, beans and maize). Animals in the index of animals per worker is calculated by giving a weight of 1.0 to cows and cattle, 0.1 to sheep, and 0.3 to pigs.

Source
G. Clark, 'Productivity growth without technical change in European agriculture: reply to Komlos', *JEH*, XLIX, 1989, p. 980; P. Bairoch, 'Les trois révolutions agricoles du monde développé: rendements et productivité de 1800 á 1985', *Annales, Économies, Sociétés, Civilisations*, XLIV, 1989, p. 329.

output per worker, much of which occurred before 1600. Respecting the latter, there is evidence that, even controlling for yields, various tasks in agriculture were performed at a slower rate in the medieval period than in the years after 1561, contributing importantly to the low output per worker. Indeed, it will be argued here that one component in the rise of output per worker in England from 1300 to 1851 was an increase in the intensity of labour which occurred sometime between 1460 and 1560.

II Labour productivity, *c.*1300 and *c.*1850

Labour productivity in 1300 and 1850 has been calculated using the identity,

$$Q/L \equiv (Q/T) \cdot (T/L)$$

where Q/L is output per worker, Q/T is output per acre, and T/L is acres per worker. For 1300 measures of output per acre can be obtained from manorial accounts in conjunction with *inquisitiones post mortem*, while the number of acres per worker can be estimated from a variety of different sources. For 1851 acres per agricultural worker can be derived from the population census, and output per acre can be estimated by extrapolating back from the later agricultural censuses with the aid of farm handbooks.

II.i *Output per acre*

Tables 8.2 and 8.3 summarise the calculation of output per cultivated acre in 1300 on a typical manor in the south of England. Output is given both in terms of prices of that period, and also, for comparison, in terms of the equivalent value in bushels of wheat. Table 8.2 shows the proportions of cultivated acreage devoted to each arable crop, and to fallow and pasture, in a national sample of demesne accounts from 1300 to 1349.[7] It also shows the estimated gross yield of each crop (including tithes), the estimated seed inputs, and the estimated uses of crops for animal feeds. The yield estimates are an unweighted average of the yields reported for the Winchester manors, the Westminster manors, and for Norfolk.[8] From this information it is possible to calculate the net output per cultivated acre of each crop, and the value per acre of arable output.

Animal outputs in 1300–49 are calculated in Table 8.3. The average weight of sheep fleeces per animal on the Winchester manors from 1300 to 1324 was 1.50 lb., which is about the same as J. Thorold Rogers' estimate of fleece weights.[9] Net milk production per cow is

7 I am grateful to Bruce Campbell for supplying land-use information from his own national sample of inquisitions *post mortem* and crop data from John Langdon's national sample of manorial accounts.
8 J. Z. Titow, *Winchester yields: a study in medieval agricultural productivity*, Cambridge, 1972; D. L. Farmer, 'Grain yields on the Winchester manors in the later middle ages', *EcHR*, XXX, 1977, pp. 555–66; *idem*, 'Grain yields on Westminster Abbey manors, 1271–1410', *Canadian Journal of History*, XVIII, 1983, pp. 331–48; B. M. S. Campbell, above, pp. 160–5.
9 M. J. Stephenson, 'Wool yields in the medieval economy', *EcHR*, XLI, 1988, p. 377.

Table 8.2 *England: crop output per acre of cultivated land, and prices, 1300–49 and c.1850*

Crop	Area (%)	Gross output (bush./ sown acre)	Seed (bush./ acre)	Animal feed (bush./ acre)	Net output (bush./ acre)	Price (d/bush.)	Value of net output (d/acre)
1300–1349							
Wheat	18	11.8	2.6	0.0	1.66	9.12	15.2
Rye	3	11.8[a]	2.6	0.0	0.27	7.02	1.9
Barley	9	18.0	4.4	0.0	1.16	6.47	7.5
Oats	18	12.4	4.4	0.6	0.85	3.77	3.2
Legumes	4						
Fallow	29						
Grass	19						
All							27.8
All (bushels)							3.05[b]
1850						(s/bush.)	(s/acre)
Wheat	18.3	26.0	2.5	0.0	4.30	6.54	28.1
Barley	10.7	33.0	3.0	0.0	3.21	3.84	12.3
Oats	(13.2)	36.0	4.0	2.9	1.31	2.68	3.5
All							44.0
All (bushels)							6.73[b]

Notes

[a] For lack of information rye yields are assumed equal to wheat yields, though they were probably lower.

[b] Output per acre measured as the equivalent in bushels of wheat.

Source

1300–49: B. M. S. Campbell, above, pp. 149–70; D. L. Farmer, 'Grain yields on the Winchester manors in the later middle ages', *EcHR*, XXX, 1977, pp. 555–66; J. Z. Titow, *Winchester yields: a study in medieval agricultural productivity*, Cambridge, 1972; J. E. Thorold Rogers, *A history of agriculture and prices in England*, I, Oxford, 1866; *1850: Returns relating to the acreage of crops in the United Kingdom*, BPP, LX, 1st series 3727, London, 1866; P. Dodd, 'The agricultural statistics for 1854: an assessment of their value', *AHR*, XXXV, 1987, pp. 159–70; B. R. Mitchell and P. Deane, *Abstract of British historical statistics*, Cambridge, 1962.

taken to have been 100 gallons per year, and milk production per ewe 8.5 gallons.[10] Evidence of the meat produced per carcass is much scantier. Some idea of relative meat production per animal can be obtained from the prices of mature animals of each type. The maximum value of the meat content of the animal is the residuum left after deducting the value of its hide or fleece (see Table 8.4). Of course, the

10 R. Trow-Smith, *A history of British livestock husbandry to 1700*, London, 1957; R. A. L. Smith, *Canterbury Cathedral Priory*, Cambridge, 1943; I. Kershaw, *Bolton Priory: the economy of a northern monastery, 1286–1325*, Oxford, 1973.

Table 8.3 *England: animal output per acre of cultivated land, and prices, 1300–49 and c.1850*

Animal	Numbers/ acre	Grain fed/ capita (bush.)	Product	Producers (%)	Output/ animal	Price (d)	Value (d/acre)
1300–49							
Cattle	0.0557	0.0	milk	49	100 gal.	0.55	1.50
			meat	13	168 lb.	0.59	0.72
			hides	13	1	25.50	0.19
Sheep	0.4505	0.0	milk	34	8.5 gal.	0.55	0.72
			meat	26	22 lb.	0.59	1.52
			wool	100	1.5 lb.	5.60	2.38
Pigs	0.0613	1.27	meat	49	64 lb.	0.59	1.13
Oxen	0.0593	1.25	meat	13	225 lb.	0.59	1.02
			hides	13	1	25.50	0.20
Horses	0.0227	20.0	hides	13	1	25.50	0.08
All							9.45
All (bushels)							1.04[a]
1850						*(s)*	*(s/acre)*
Cattle	0.1308	0.0	milk	50	450 gal.	0.50	10.84
			meat	20	600 lb.	0.43	6.71
			hides	20	1	20.0	·0.51
Sheep	0.9831	0.0	meat	40	70 lb.	0.55	15.18
			wool	100	4.1 lb.	1.06	4.30
Pigs	0.1013	0.0	meat	100	100 lb.	0.46	4.68
Horses	0.0363	80.0	hides	13	1	20.0	0.09
All							42.31
All (bushels)							6.56[a]

Notes
The percentage producers shows the proportion of animals of each type that contributed to that product. The percentage of animals slaughtered is estimated from the number of each type of animal born each year as a proportion of the year's end stock.
[a] Output per acre measured as the equivalent in bushels of wheat.

Source
K. Biddick, 'Pig husbandry on the Peterborough Abbey estate from the twelfth to the fourteenth century AD', pp. 161–77 in J. Clutton-Brock and C. Grigson, eds., *Animals and archaeology*, BAR, Supplementary series, CCXXVII, Oxford, 1985; F. G. Davenport, *The economic development of a Norfolk manor, 1086–1565*, Cambridge, 1906; C. C. Dyer, *Lords and peasants in a changing society: the estates of the Bishopric of Worcester, 680–1540*, Cambridge, 1980; P. D. A. Harvey, *A medieval Oxfordshire village: Cuxham 1240–1400*, Oxford, 1965; G. A. Holmes, *The estates of the higher nobility in the fourteenth century*, Cambridge, 1957; I. Kershaw, *Bolton Priory: the economy of a northern monastery, 1286–1325*, Oxford, 1973; M. Morgan, *The English lands of the Abbey of Bec*, Oxford, 1946; J. A. Raftis, *The estates of Ramsey Abbey*, Toronto, 1957; R. A. L. Smith, *Canterbury Cathedral Priory*, Cambridge, 1943; J. Z. Titow, *Winchester yields: a study in medieval agricultural productivity*, Cambridge, 1972; R. Trow-Smith, *A history of British livestock husbandry to 1700*, London, 1957; B. R. Mitchell and P. Deane, *Abstract of British historical statistics*, Cambridge, 1962; J. C. Morton, *A cyclopaedia of agriculture*, 2 vols., Glasgow, 1851 abd 1855.

Table 8.4 *England: meat output per animal, c.1300*

| Animal | Price | Raw hide | Fleece | Maximum meat value | Weight of meat[a] |
	(d)	(d)	(d)	(d)	(lbs)
Oxen	161	28		133	225
Cows	122	23		99	168
Pigs	38			38	64
Sheep	16		5.6	13	22

Notes
[a] Assuming meat from a sheep weighed 22 lb. The price for sheep is an average of shorn and unshorn; half the value of the fleece is therefore deducted to get the maximum meat value. The weight of a full-grown sheep is derived by comparison with mountain sheep in the mid nineteenth century (see text). The Table implies that a pound of meat would have cost 0.59*d.*

Source
D. L. Farmer, 'Some livestock price movements in thirteenth-century England', *EcHR*, XXII, 1969, pp. 1–16; J. E. Thorold Rogers, *A history of agriculture and prices in England*, I, Oxford, 1866, pp. 344–5, 395 and 451.

value of the meat was worth less than this in those cases where animals were purchased for traction, or for milking, wool-producing or breeding purposes.

In 1850 mountain sheep with about the same wool yield per fleece as medieval sheep yielded about 22 lb. of meat, and this is taken to be the carcass weight of sheep *c.*1300.[11] On this assumption, the relative value of sheep *vis à vis* other animals implies that fatted pigs weighed about 64 lb., oxen 225 lb., and cows 168 lb. *c.*1300. Archaeozoological evidence for the fourteenth and fifteenth centuries suggests that sheep had about half the shoulder height of cattle, which would imply, if everything were proportional, that cattle had a carcass weight about 8.7 times that of a sheep, or about 191 lb., which is very close to the estimated average of 196 lb. per head of cattle given in Table 8.4.[12] Another way of approaching the same problem is to note that cattle in this period were about 80 per cent the height of cattle in the late eighteenth century, which would imply that they were about 49 per cent of their weight.

Tables 8.2 and 8.3 also show the net outputs per acre of crops and livestock in *c.*1850. On the evidence of the 1854 Poor Law Returns

11 J. C. Morton, *A cyclopaedia of agriculture*, 2 vols., Glasgow, 1851 and 1855.
12 A. Grant, 'Animal resources', pp. 149–87 in *idem* and G. Astill, eds., *The countryside of medieval England*, Oxford, 1988, p. 176.

combined with the 1866 crop returns, 18.3 per cent of an estimated 13.86 million acres under cultivation in south-east England at about this date were devoted to wheat, 10.7 per cent to barley, and 13.2 per cent to oats and legumes.[13] However, 1884 is the earliest date for which there are comprehensive yield statistics for Great Britain. Before then the 1801 crop returns and various estimates made by J. Caird for individual English counties in 1850–51 provide the best and most comprehensive evidence of grain yields.[14] These indicate mean yields per acre for wheat, barley, and oats, respectively, of 21.0, 32.0, and 32.5 bushels in 1801, as compared with 30.6, 34.1, and 38.0 bushels in 1884–88 and 27.5 bushels for wheat only in 1850.[15] Averaging these results provides an estimated yield for 1851 of 26 bushels for wheat, 33 bushels for barley and 36 bushels for oats. As Table 8.2 shows, this implies a substantially greater grain output per acre in 1851 than *c.*1300 despite the smaller proportion of land sown with grain.

Estimating animal stocks from the 1866 Agricultural Returns and then projecting back to 1851 using information for the selected counties in the 1854 Poor Law returns, implies 0.131 cattle, 0.983 sheep, and 0.101 pigs per cultivated acre, which is about 25 per cent higher than the medieval ratio.[16] Moreover, animals were larger and more productive by 1850. For instance, in 1850–54 estimated wool production per sheep in Britain and Ireland was 4.1 lb. per year, i.e. over 2.5 times the medieval yield.[17] Likewise, *c.*1850 milk output per cow was 450 gallons per year, more than four times the medieval output.[18] For the nineteenth century as a whole M. G. Mulhall estimates that the meat content of the average carcass was 600 lb. in the case of cattle, 70 lb. for sheep, and 100 lb. for pigs, with respective slaughter rates of 20 per cent, 40 per cent, and 100 per cent.[19]

Combining these output estimates of crops and livestock yields a total net output per acre of farmland (Q/T) in wheat equivalents of

13 *Returns relating to the acreage of crops in the United Kingdom*, BPP, LX, 1st series Cd.3727, London, 1866.

14 M. E. Turner, 'Agricultural productivity in England in the eighteenth century: evidence from crop yields', *EcHR*, XXXV, 1982, pp. 489–510; J. Caird, *English agriculture, 1850–1*, London, 1853, p. 474.

15 All bushels are Winchester bushels.

16 *Returns relating to livestock in the United Kingdom*, BPP, LX, 1st series Cd.3655, London, 1866.

17 B. R. Mitchell and P. Deane, *Abstract of British historical statistics*, Cambridge, 1962, pp. 82-4 and 190; P. Dodd, 'The agricultural statistics for 1854: an assessment of their value', *AHR*, XXXV, 1987, pp. 159–70.

18 Morton, *Cyclopaedia*, I, pp. 606–20, and II, pp. 369 and 403–6.

19 Mulhall, *Dictionary*, p. 15.

4.1 bushels *c.*1300 and 13.2 bushels *c.*1850. On these figures output per acre rose by 3.2 times during the intervening five-and-a-half centuries.

II.ii *Output per worker*

To derive output per worker from output per acre requires an estimation of the number of cultivated acres per worker. In 1851 the population census makes this straightforward.[20] At this date there were approximately 18.7 cultivated acres per worker in south-eastern England. The calculation for 1300 is much more uncertain and may be inferred in three different ways.

The first method is to make an upper-bound estimate using aggregate data for 'south-eastern' England on the probable total area of farmland and total agricultural labour force *c.*1300.[21] In 1866 it is known that the former comprised some 13.85 million acres and for the purpose of estimation it is assumed that the farmed area had been as great *c.*1300 even though there may well have been more unreclaimed land such as woodland, marsh and heath. For the same region the 1377 poll tax returns record 1.06 million taxpayers aged fourteen years or older.[22] On a group of Essex manors the decline in population from 1300 to 1377 was about 50 per cent.[23] Assuming a 10 per cent evasion rate in 1377, this implies an adult population in 1300 of 2.34 million. If 75 per cent of the population were employed in agriculture, this in turn implies a male agricultural labour force in 1300 of approximately 0.88 million.[24] The amount of farmland per male agricultural worker in 1300 would thus have been 15.7 acres.

A second method of estimation is to use data from individual manors on the number of sown acres per capita, or per tenant. Table

---

20 *Census of Great Britain, 1851. Population tables II, BPP*, LXXXVIII, 1st series Cd.1691, London, 1852–53.

21 The area comprises the counties of Bedfordshire, Berkshire, Buckinghamshire, Cambridgeshire, Dorset, Essex, Gloucestershire, Hampshire, Hertfordshire, Huntingdonshire, Kent, Leicestershire, Lincolnshire, Middlesex, Norfolk, Northamptonshire, Nottinghamshire, Oxfordshire, Rutland, Somerset, Suffolk, Surrey, Sussex, Warwick, Wiltshire, Worcestershire, and the East Riding of Yorkshire. It was chosen since, as well as comprising the more densely populated parts of the country, it is to this area that most of the information on outputs and animal stocks relates.

22 J. C. Russell, *British medieval population*, Albuquerque, New Mexico, 1948.

23 L. R. Poos, 'The rural population of Essex in the later middle ages', *EcHR*, XXXVIII, 1985, pp. 515–30.

24 The agricultural labour force may have been 70 per cent or 80 per cent of the workforce but at this level of participation neither of these alternative figures would change the result much.

Table 8.5 *England: sown acres per worker, c.1300*

Year, location	Sown arable acres	Population	Male farm workers	Sown acres per worker
1279, S. England	319,117	148,415	41,556	7.7
1311, Taunton	8,093		1,315	7.7
1260–1315, Elloe, Lincs.	8,850	6,059	1,697	5.2
1300–49, Cuxham	251		44	5.7

Notes
It is assumed that 80 per cent of the population was engaged in agriculture. The acres per worker for the south of England in 1279 are derived from E. A. Kosminsky's analysis of the Hundred Rolls, assuming each tenant represented a household of five people. This is subject to two upward biases: the acres used may be smaller customary acres, and landless families and manorial servants in residence in the grange are not counted.

Source
H. E. Hallam, 'Some thirteenth-century censuses', *EcHR*, X, 1958, pp. 340–61; J. Z. Titow, 'Some evidence of thirteenth-century population increase', *EcHR*, XIV, 1961, pp. 216–31; E. A. Kosminsky, *Studies in the agrarian history of England in the thirteenth century*, Oxford, 1956, pp. 100, 216 and 232; P. D. A. Harvey, *A medieval Oxfordshire village: Cuxham 1240–1400*, Oxford, 1965.

8.5 summarises a variety of such estimates. These imply a somewhat lower ratio of 14.8 acres per worker.

The third method of estimating the number of acres per worker is to consider the implications of the previous two estimates for per capita calorific intake in 'south-eastern' England *c.*1300. At this date the number of calories produced per acre may be estimated at 761 per day (93 per cent of which were from grains). If there were 15.7 acres per male worker, then each worker produced 11,941 calories per day. If all calories were consumed by people, and the agricultural labour force was 75 per cent of the employed, this would imply an average intake of 3,129 calories per day per person.[25] E. Smith's dietary survey of agricultural workers' families in Britain in 1862 shows most consumed fewer calories per person per day than this, the average in the poorer southern English counties being only 2,100–2,300 calories per day.[26] Thus, since the late thirteenth century is generally regarded as

25 Not all of these calories would be available for direct or indirect human consumption since some of the oats would have been used to feed horses outside of agriculture. Calories derived from fowl, fish, wild game, honey, fruits, and garden vegetables have not been included, but their overall contribution would presumably have been small.

26 Consumption per capita was less than 2,300 calories in 6 of the 37 English counties Smith visited, namely: Cornwall (2,240); Devon (2,290); Somerset (2,176); Wiltshire (2,222); Norfolk (2,282); and Berkshire (2,190). In another ten counties consumption per capita was 2,300–2,500 calories. Calculated from the diets

a period of population stress and low living standards, there may well have been significantly fewer than 15.7 acres of farmland per worker. To generate an average consumption per capita per day of 2,500 calories would have required only 8.5 acres per male worker.

On the evidence of these three methods of estimation, the number of acres of farmland per worker in 'south-eastern' England *c.*1300 is likely to have been between 10.1 and 15.7. In the calculations which follow a figure of 13.6 acres has been employed – of which seven would have been sown – equivalent to a daily consumption of 2,720 calories per person and a gross output per worker of 56 bushels. By comparison, there were about 18.7 acres per worker *c.*1850, yielding a gross output of 246 bushels. Thus output per worker in 1850 was 4.4 times output in 1300. Over the same period the number of bushels of grain harvested per male worker rose by 2.6 times, from 93 bushels to 243 bushels.

III Labour productivity, yields per acre, and the composition of output

One interpretation of the fourfold rise of output per worker in English agriculture between 1300 and 1850 is that much of it was a consequence of the increase in yields per acre. Suppose, for example, that there was only one type of agricultural output, grain, which required labour inputs only in proportion to the area cultivated and independently of the yield per acre. Then,

$$L = b \cdot T , \quad \text{so}$$

$$L/Q = b \cdot (T/Q), \tag{1}$$

where L/Q is the labour input per unit of output, Q/T is yield per acre, and b is a constant. Since grain yields per acre net of seed increased more than twofold from 1300 to 1850 this implies that the rise in yields explains much of the increase in output per worker. It has been seen, for instance, that harvesting rates more than doubled from 93 to 243 bushels over this period. Yet, since gross output per acre rose from 13.3 to 30.9 bushels, the number of acres actually harvested per worker increased only slightly from 7.0 to 7.9.

There were, in fact, many different types of output in agriculture, but if labour inputs per acre for each of them were fixed and the

---

given in E. Smith, *Food of the lowest fed classes, appendix VI, conditions of nourishment,* pp. 216–329 in *Sixth report of the medical officer of the Privy Council, BPP,* XXVIII, 1st series Cd.3416, London, 1864.

proportion of different types of output did not change, then the rise in output per worker would still be proportional to the increase in yields. Such a view implies, in turn, that yield increases would indeed be the major independent determinant of the rate at which overall productivity rose in agriculture, since they would also determine output per worker. Further, since the proportion of the population which has to be employed in agriculture at a given level of food consumption is largely determined by output per worker, the timing of yield increases from 1300 to 1850 should also be a strong predictor of the rate at which population shifted out of agriculture into trade and manufactures.

On the other hand, many of the labour inputs in agriculture depended more on the quantity of output than on the area cultivated. Such inputs included binding sheaves, carting crops, threshing grain, manuring (since the volume of manure depends only on the quantity of animal feed), and marketing output.[27] The labour per acre required in cutting grains and grass would also have depended in part upon the yield per acre. Thus the labour required in agriculture would have been,

$$L = \sum (a_i Q_i + b_i T_i)$$
$$= a \cdot Q + b \cdot T, \tag{2}$$

where $a_i Q_i$ is the labour input for task i that depends on output, and $b_i T_i$ is the labour input that is fixed per acre. Labour input per unit of output, from (2), would thus have been,

$$(L/Q) = a + b(T/Q)$$

so,

$$(Q/L) = 1/[a + b(T/Q)]. \tag{3}$$

Equation 3 indicates that the labour required per unit of output would have contained a constant component (a), and a part which declined as yields increased. The effect that increasing yields would have had on output per worker can, in fact, be calculated (assuming a constant composition of output) provided that the values of a and b can be estimated. A zero value for a indicates that output per worker will have been proportionate to yield per acre, whereas a zero value for b means that output per worker will have been independent of yields.

Table 8.6 gives the relative importance of labour costs on various tasks in arable agriculture in 1771, 1808 and 1846 under different

27 See G. Clark, 'Yields per acre in English agriculture 1266–1860: evidence from labour inputs', *EcHR*, XLIV, 1991; and Grantham, below, p. 353.

Labour productivity in English agriculture

223

Table 8.6 *England: percentage labour costs in arable cultivation, 1771–1846*

Source	Young (1771)	Batchelor (1808)		Raynbird (1846)
Rotation	wheat barley clover beans	fallow wheat beans	roots barley clover wheat	roots/fallow barley/oats clover/beans wheat
Area				
Ploughing	11.4	14.2	9.4	12.8
Harrowing, etc.	0.7	5.8	5.9	3.0
Sowing	2.4	0.8	0.9	3.7
Water-furrowing	3.8	0.0	0.0	3.9
Weeding, hoeing	11.2	7.7	17.0	12.8
Ditching	7.2	0.0	0.0	0.0
All	36.7	28.5	33.2	36.2
Yield				
Pulling roots			3.4	1.4
Carting	7.3	13.6	10.9	10.2
Thatching	0.0	2.4	2.2	2.1
Threshing	17.2	23.4	22.2	18.7
Manuring	12.0	1.1	3.5	9.0
Various[a]	1.3	5.3	4.0	1.5
All	38.8	45.8	46.2	42.9
Area and yield				
Reaping	17.7	25.9	11.9	9.3
Mowing	5.2	0.0	8.6	9.3
Cutting stubble	2.5	0.0	0.0	2.1
All	25.4	25.9	20.5	20.7

Note
[a] includes marketing grain, and preparing animal feed.

Source
A. Young, *The farmer's guide in hiring and stocking farms*, I, Dublin, 1771, pp. 123–6, 148–52, 220–4 and 286–9; T. Batchelor, *General view of the agriculture of the county of Bedfordshire*, London, 1808, pp. 118–21; W. and H. Raynbird, *The agriculture of Suffolk*, London, 1849, pp. 136–9.

types of rotations: grain, grain, fallow; grain, grain, clover, beans; and grain, grain, clover, roots. These costs are divided into those which were fixed per acre cultivated, those which depend only on the yield, and those which depend both on the area and on the yield.[28] The switch to new rotations involving clover and roots did not seem to change greatly the proportion of different types of costs. Labour costs which depended only on yields were always about 40 per cent of total labour costs, and those which depended at least in part on yields accounted for another 25 per cent.

To get an estimate of *a* and *b* in Equation 3 it is necessary to divide up the harvest costs which depend on both area and yield into their respective components. This can be done by comparing the piece rates paid for reaping grain with day wages as yields increase. In general, if *w* is the day wage and *h* is the payment per unit of the task, the amount of labour required for a task *L*, in man-days, will be given by,

$$L = h/w.$$

Thus, the labour input per bushel for threshing and winnowing wheat, in man-days, will be,

$$L_t = h_t/w_w,$$

where w_w is the winter day-wage and h_t is the payment per bushel for threshing and winnowing wheat. Similarly, the man-days required to reap an acre of wheat will be,

$$L_r = h_r/w_h,$$

where w_h is the harvest day-wage and h_r is the payment per acre for reaping and binding wheat.[29] Table 8.7 shows for reaping and threshing the labour inputs required over time in English agriculture calculated on this basis.

28 Note that the tasks listed as being fixed per acre and independent of yields were nevertheless linked to yields indirectly, since more labour inputs per acre in ploughing, harrowing, weeding, and ditching will have resulted in larger yields. For evidence of the relationship between labour-inputs and yields see Campbell, above, pp. 176–7.

29 Since there are many more quotations of winter wages than of harvest wages, it is assumed throughout when calculating the reaping rate that, $w_h = k \cdot w_w$, so that the harvest wage is some fixed multiple of the winter wage. What data there are for harvest wages confirm this assumption. In all calculations that follow *k* is taken as equal to 2. The fact that it was probably, on average, slightly less than this does not affect the results about the change in labour inputs per task over time.

Table 8.7 *England: task-level labour requirements in reaping and threshing implied by piece-work payments and day wages, 1266–1860*

Period	Threshing		Reaping wheat	
	N	Man-days per bushel	N	Man-days per acre
1860			70	3.07
1850	80	0.259	116	2.92
1790–1810	40	0.233	44	2.82
1768–1771	68	0.240	105	2.59
1700–1733	8	0.248	7	2.28
1675–1724	9	0.242	9	2.34
1650–1699	11	0.244	14	2.19
1625–1674	16	0.240	13	2.02
1600–1649	16	0.239	8	1.90
1575–1624	18	0.232	12	1.87
1561–1599	18	0.221	15	1.82
1400–1463		(0.240)	19	1.73[a]
1349–1399		(0.240)	36	1.67[a]
1300–1348		(0.240)	47	1.71[a]
1266–1299		(0.240)	16	1.76[a]

Notes

The man-days required in threshing is the average of the implied labour inputs for threshing wheat, barley, and oats, normalised to the labour inputs for wheat.

N is the number of observations.

[a] This is the man-days required for reaping assuming that the rate at which threshing was performed from 1266 to 1463 was 4.17 bushels a day, i.e. the average threshing rate from 1561 to 1850.

Source
G. Clark, 'Yields per acre in English agriculture 1266–1860: evidence from labour inputs', *EcHR*, XLIV, 1991.

Labour inputs in threshing, predicted as largely independent of yields, remained roughly constant from 1561 to 1860. Higher yields did not reduce the labour inputs per unit of output in threshing over this period. By contrast, labour inputs per acre in reaping increased substantially as yields rose. Estimated wheat yields of 28 bushels per acre in 1860 and 12 bushels per acre in 1561–99 imply that in reaping wheat,

$$(L/T)_r = 0.88 + 0.078(Q/T)_w,$$

and thus,

$$(L/Q)_r = 0.078 + 0.88(T/Q)_w. \qquad (4)$$

That is, reaping and binding wheat entailed an input of 0.88 man-days per acre irrespective of the yield, whereas all other labour inputs were dependent on the number of bushels harvested. It follows that the substantial gain in yields from the medieval levels of pre-1600 to those of 1850 did not produce a proportionate labour saving in cutting and binding wheat.

Using Equation 4 to allocate the harvest labour inputs given in Table 8.7 between those fixed per acre and those dependent on yields, it is found that,

$$(Q/L) = 1/[a + b(T/Q)]$$
$$= 1/[0.57 + 9.46(T/Q)] \qquad (5)$$

where output per acre is measured in terms of bushels of wheat, and is assumed to have been 22 bushels per acre in 1771–1808. Table 8.8 shows the relationship that (5) implies as having existed between yields and output per man-day. As can be seen, the more than doubling of grain yields from the medieval levels of *c.*1300 and 1550–1600 to those of 1850 resulted in a gain in labour productivity of only 45 per cent, since the labour inputs per acre increased by 49 per cent.

For the predominantly arable husbandry of 'south-eastern' England it can be argued that the single most important constraint on output per worker was the amount each worker could harvest. Labour demands on the arable were seasonally highly peaked, with the harvest month absorbing at least twice as much labour as the average month in the rest of the year in most areas. Figure 8.1, for example, shows the payments per week to workers on a Norfolk farm employing convertible husbandry in 1733–34. The payments peak very sharply in August so that, even considering the higher wages paid per hour at the harvest, probably 2.5 times as many man-hours per week were worked then as in the slackest seasons.[30] Most of the labour required in the harvest month was for cutting and carting the standing crops (that is, wheat,

30 On an estate in Durham in 1733 (probably employing traditional techniques) there were over three times as many man-days worked in August as in any of the six winter months. Considering the longer summer working day, this implies more than four times the number of man-hours worked in August as in any of the winter months. P. Brassley, *The agricultural economy of Northumberland and Durham in the period 1640–1750*, New York, 1985, p. 37.

Table 8.8 *England: labour costs and output per man-day versus yields per acre*

Yield (bushels/acre)	Date	Total output per man-day (1790 = 100)	All labour per acre (1790 = 100)	Harvest output per man-day (bushels)
10		66	69	4.8
12	1580, 1300	74	74	5.2
14		80	79	5.5
16		86	84	5.7
18		91	90	5.9
20		96	95	6.1
22	1790	100	100	6.3
24		104	105	6.4
26	1850	107	110	6.5
28	1860	110	116	6.6

Note
Yields are shown in terms of wheat yields, assuming all other yields changed in proportion.

Source Equations 5 and 6.

rye, barley, oats, beans and peas). The implied relationship between yields per acre and output per worker, taking these activities only, is, from Equation 5 and Table 8.7,

$$Q/L = 1/[0.12 + 0.88(T/Q)], \qquad (6)$$

where output per worker is measured in bushels of wheat per man-day. According to this formula, at an assumed wheat yield of 22 bushels per acre in 1790, a harvest worker would have been able to harvest 6.3 bushels of wheat per man-day. Table 8.8 also shows how output per worker in harvesting changed with grain yields. At medieval yield levels harvested output per man-day was about 5.2 bushels per acre. Thus, from 1600 to 1850 rising yields per acre led to a 25 per cent gain in harvest output per man-day, as compared with the more than doubling of output which actually took place. The contribution of higher grain yields was modest because most of the labour inputs in the agricultural sector during the harvest period were independent of yields.

On the evidence of both harvest labour inputs and total labour costs over the whole year, output per worker should have increased by only 25–45 per cent from 1600 to 1850 as yields rose from medieval to nineteenth-century levels. This has implications for the share of the

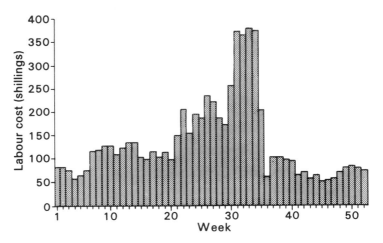

Figure 8.1 *Weekly labour payments on a Norfolk farm, 1733–34*

labour force retained within the agricultural sector in the years before 1850. The latter, L/L_T, is given by,

$$L/L_T = (L/Q) \cdot (Q/L_T)$$
$$= (L/Q) \cdot (Q/N) \cdot (N/L_T)$$
$$= (L/Q) \cdot [(C - I)/N] \cdot (N/L_T), \qquad (7)$$

where N is the population, C is total consumption of agricultural products, I is imports of agricultural products, and L_T is the total labour force. Suppose, for instance, that the share of the population employed and the consumption of domestic agricultural products per capita, $(C - I)/N$, were constant. Then the share of the labour force in agriculture would be proportionate to the labour input per unit of output in agriculture. Periods when real wages in terms of agricultural produce were constant are also those in which Q/N can be expected to have been roughly constant. Table 8.9 identifies some such periods.

Evidence from Tables 8.7 and 8.8 that labour inputs per acre were comparatively low in the period 1561–1600, at a time when yields per acre were still relatively low, implies that the share of the English labour force in agriculture was already below that observed in eastern Europe in the late nineteenth century. In 1570 perhaps no more than 40–49 per cent of the population was engaged in agriculture, as compared with 33–34 per cent on the eve of the industrial revolution, in 1770, and 25 per cent in 1850. This further implies the English economy was relatively developed as early as 1570. At constant food consump-

Table 8.9 *Estimates of English grain production, 1565–1855*

Years	Grain wage (1860 = 100)	Assumed yield (bushels wheat)	Food imports (%)	Share of labour in agriculture	
				All labour (%)	Harvest labour (%)
1565–75	84	12	0.0	49	40
1735–45	90	18	−3.9	41	37
1785–95	64	22	+2.4	34	33
1825–35	89	24	+9.4	31	30
1845–55	90	26	+22.8	25	25

Notes
Yields per acre are given in bushels. Labour per unit of output is from Table 8.8.

Source
H. Phelps Brown and S. V. Hopkins, 'Seven centuries of building wages', *Economica*, XXII, 1955, pp. 195–206; *idem*, 'Seven centuries of the prices of consumables compared with builders' wage-rates', *Economica*, XXIII, 1956, pp. 296–314; E. A. Wrigley and R. S. Schofield, *The population history of England, 1541–1871: a reconstruction*, London, 1981; B. R. Mitchell and and P. Deane, *Abstract of British historical statistics*, Cambridge, 1962.

tion per capita, the larger the share of the population outside the agricultural sector, the higher the real income. Indeed, on these calculations the fall in the share of labour in agriculture from 1790 to 1850 was mainly the result of increased imports of food.

The finding that output per worker in English agriculture was approaching the levels of 1850 by the 1560s contradicts widely-held assumptions about the large size of the agricultural sector in England prior to the industrial revolution. E. A. Wrigley, for instance, assumes that 76 per cent of the population was employed in agriculture in 1520, 70 per cent in 1600, 55 per cent in 1700, and 36 per cent in 1801.[31] In effect, he assumes that levels of labour productivity in English agriculture in the sixteenth century were equivalent to those of eastern Europe in the nineteenth century. On this assumption, given that real incomes in 1850 were higher than in any period since 1540,

31 E. A. Wrigley, 'Urban growth and agricultural change: England and the continent in the early modern period', *Journal of Interdisciplinary History*, XXV, 1985, p. 700.

Equation 7 implies that output per worker in late-sixteenth-century agriculture was only 45 per cent or less that in 1850.

Yet there is independent evidence that agriculture's share of the labour force in England was much smaller by the seventeenth century than Wrigley and others assume, and hence that labour productivity in agriculture was much higher. A detailed muster roll for Gloucester in 1608 shows only 46 per cent of males aged twenty or older employed in agriculture, even excluding Bristol.[32] This proportion is equivalent to that recorded in the 1811 census, notwithstanding the halving in agriculture's share of the workforce which is supposed to have occurred during this interval.[33] P. Lindert, estimating the occupations of the population from 1688 onwards from burial records and local censuses, similarly finds a relatively small proportion of the population employed in agriculture.[34] By his reckoning, in 1688 only 19 per cent of adult males who were not indigent were occupiers of land and at most only a further 17 per cent were agricultural labourers or servants. A maximum of 36 per cent of able-bodied males was thus employed in agriculture at this time. He calculates the equivalent proportions in 1700, 1740 and 1755 as 35, 47 and 44 per cent respectively.

In calculating the effect of yield increases on output per worker it has, of course, been assumed that the composition of output was unchanging. Yet one way of raising output per worker was by shifting production towards types of output, such as beef or wool, which employed less labour per unit of output. *Circa* 1300 arable products represented 75 per cent of net output in 'south-eastern' England, while by 1850 this proportion had fallen to 50 per cent. Taking this into account, labour per unit of output in 1300 and 1850 would be,

$$(L/Q)_0 = 0.75(L/Q)_{a0} + 0.25(L/Q)_{p0}$$

and

$$(L/Q)_1 = 0.50(L/Q)_{a1} + 0.50(L/Q)_{p1} \qquad (8)$$

where *a* indexes arable and *p* pasture. The approximate output of arable and pastoral products and the total labour input can be estimated for each English county in 1851. This allows an estimate of the labour input required per unit of arable output (measured in bushels of wheat)

32 A. J. and R. H. Tawney, 'An occupational census of the seventeenth century', *Economic History Review*, V, 1935, pp. 98–103. At this date, however, the manufacture of woollen cloth was Britain's chief industry and Gloucester was one of its principal centres.
33 Wrigley, 'Urban growth', p. 702.
34 P. Lindert, 'English occupations, 1670–1811', *JEH*, XLV, 1980, pp. 685–712.

and per unit of animal output (again measured in bushels of wheat) to be derived. The result suggests that output per worker in animal husbandry was about 80 per cent greater than in arable cultivation.[35] If it is supposed that labour per unit output of arable and pastoral products did not change significantly between 1300 to 1850, then the shift in the composition of output towards a greater share of animal products would have increased total output per worker. Nevertheless, the effect would have been small. Deriving from Equation 8,

$$(Q/L)_1 = 1.15(Q/L)_0 \qquad (9)$$

Essentially, this change in the composition of output would have contributed only 15 per cent to the increase in output per worker.

IV Medieval labour productivity and work intensity

Sections II and III present a conundrum. In Section II. ii it was estimated that output per worker *c.*1300 was only about a quarter that in England *c.*1850. This calculation was made on the assumption that 75 per cent of the population was employed in agriculture. But in Section III consideration of how labour requirements varied with yields suggests that the low yields of medieval England, and the concentration of output on arable products, should not have depressed labour productivity by anything like this large amount. Improvements in yield and changes in the product mix during the intervening period were certainly sufficient to promote a 70 per cent gain in output per worker, but otherwise are an inadequate explanation of the 300 per cent increment in labour productivity which is estimated as actually having occurred.

Table 8.7, for example, shows that if the threshing rate *c.*1300 was the same as in the period 1561–1850 then the payments to harvesters suggest that only 1.72 man-days would have been needed to reap and bind an acre of wheat in 1300 compared with 2.92 man-days in 1850. With 13.6 acres per worker in 1300 there would have been 7 acres per worker to harvest each year. Assuming all grain was cut with the sickle, the total labour required in 1300 for cutting, binding and carting each acre, if workers were as efficient as those of 1850, would have been 2.2 man-days per acre. Thus, total labour requirements in harvest would have been 15 man-days per male worker or just over two-and-a-half weeks.[36] Since in the medieval period women were extensively employed

35 But compare M. Turner, below, p. 417, n. 19.
36 If barley and oats were mown, as was the case by the sixteenth century, the total labour requirement at harvest would drop to 14 man-days.

as reapers the total labour demanded of each male worker would have been less even than this.[37]

By contrast, in 1850 each acre of wheat, peas, or beans would have required 2.9 man-days per acre to reap and bind and 1.0 man-days to cart, and each acre of barley and oats 1.9 man-days to reap and bind and 1.2 man-days to cart. There were 4 acres of wheat, peas and beans to harvest per worker in the 'south-eastern' England *c.*1850 and 3.9 acres of barley and oats. Hence the total labour requirement was 28 man-days per male worker, or nearly five weeks' work. In addition, in this later period there would have been some roots to hoe in the harvest period and, of course, there were more animals to be tended per worker.

It follows that if agricultural workers in 1300 and 1850 were of equal efficiency, those in 1850 would have been called upon to supply almost twice as much work as those in 1300. Either there were many more acres per worker *c.*1300 than calculated in Section II, so that output per worker was twice as high, or workers *c.*1300 were under-employed and significantly less efficient. If the former, less than 75 per cent of the workforce would have been required in agriculture since, if output per worker in harvesting was twice as great, there would have been about 27 cultivated acres per male worker in 1300, requiring the employment of only 38 per cent of the population in agriculture. The small size of average land-holdings and the low level of material culture in England *c.*1300 both argue against this possibility. Perhaps, therefore, output per worker was indeed unexpectedly low in early-fourteenth-century England. If so, either agricultural workers were under- or unemployed for much of the year, including much of the harvest period, or they were less efficient at performing farm tasks than workers in 1561 and later. Since there is strong evidence that low output per worker in Eastern Europe in the nineteenth century owed much to the inefficiency of workers there, it is interesting to consider the relevance of this possibility to medieval England.[38]

Evidence for the inefficiency of workers in Eastern Europe comes in the main from the fact that they threshed and reaped grain at a much lower rate per day than it was threshed and reaped in England

---

37 S. Penn, 'Female wage-earners in late fourteenth-century England', *AHR*, XXXV, 1987, pp. 1–14.
38 See G. Clark, 'Productivity growth without technical change in European agriculture before 1850', *JEH*, XLVII, 1987, pp. 419–32; *idem*, 'Productivity growth without technical change in European agriculture: reply to Komlos', *JEH*, XLIX, 1989, pp. 979–91.

from 1561 onwards. Workers in nineteenth-century Eastern Europe threshed only 2.0–2.5 bushels of wheat per day, as compared with an average of 4.2 bushels in England from 1561 to 1850.[39] Unfortunately, equivalent medieval rates are less easily computed. If information were available on the day-wage of agricultural workers in winter the efficiency of workers in reaping and threshing could easily be calculated by the methods used in Table 8.7 for the period 1561–1850. But medieval sources rarely specify the day-wages of agricultural workers, and only exceptionally state in which season workers were employed. In the period 1300 to 1348 the average payment for threshing and winnowing a bushel of wheat was 0.37*d*, and for reaping an acre of wheat it was 5.58*d*. For workers to have been as efficient as those of 1561 and later, the daily winter wage would have had to have been 1.55*d* – equivalent to 0.17 bushels of wheat – with a corresponding harvest wage of 3.1*d* per day (harvest day-wages commonly being double winter wage rates). Similarly, for workers in the period 1400–63 to have been as efficient as those from 1561 on, they would have had to have been paid at a rate of 0.29 bushels of wheat in winter and 0.58 bushels at harvest. These are remarkably high rates of pay by comparison with later periods. For example, the daily winter wage was 0.18 bushels of wheat *c.*1770, 0.17 bushels *c.*1794, and 0.24 bushels *c.*1850. Given that output per worker in agriculture was apparently so much lower in the fourteenth and fifteenth centuries, why were wage rates so much higher then?

In fact, there are good reasons for believing that daily winter wage-rates were lower than 1.55*d* (0.17 bushels of wheat) in the period 1300–49, with the implication that medieval labour was relatively inefficient at performing simple farm tasks. First, manorial servants such as ploughmen, carters, and shepherds, who in later years were somewhat better paid than day labour, earned the equivalent of only 30 bushels of wheat per year *c.*1300, or 0.11 bushels per day on the assumption that they worked 300 days per year. Second, Walter of Henley's treatise on agriculture, probably written between 1276 and 1290, assumes a harvest wage of 1.5–2.0*d* per day, a rate significantly below the 3.1*d* calculated as the appropriate rate of enumeration if medieval harvesters worked as efficiently as those after 1561.[40] Walter evidently presumed a cutting and binding rate of 0.4 acres per day, which compares favourably with a rate of 0.3–0.4 acres derived from the average contract

39 Clark, 'Productivity growth', p. 427; *idem*, 'Reply to Komlos', p. 982.
40 D. Oschinsky, *Walter of Henley and other treatises on estate management and accounting*, Oxford, 1971, pp. 144 and 445.

price of 5*d* paid for reaping and binding wheat in 1266–99. Yet by 1561–99, as Table 8.7 shows, 0.55 acres per day were being cut and bound, at presumably the same yield levels. Finally, dietary evidence suggests woefully low wage rates.

Section II demonstrated that arable crops accounted for 80 per cent by value of total food output *c.*1300, with a mere 20 per cent contributed by meat and dairy products (Tables 8.2 and 8.3). Such proportions are symptomatic of desperately low living standards among society as a whole. To be sure, households of the wealthier classes consumed arable and pastoral products in roughly equal proportions, but at the opposite extreme landless labourers dependent only on wage income must have spent 85–100 per cent of their food budget on arable products.[41] By comparison, a study of food expenditures by agricultural labourers in 1862 found that even the poorest of them, earning a mere 0.2 bushels of wheat per day in winter, spent no more than 70 per cent of their income on corn products and potatoes.[42] Furthermore, virtually all these workers consumed the more expensive wheat flour, instead of the cheaper rye, barley and oats which tended to prevail before 1350. By implication, their medieval counterparts must have been paid even less, with all that this implies for corresponding levels of efficiency.

One test of the supposition that the agricultural workforce was less efficient *c.*1300 than between 1561 and 1851 can be made using information on the day-wages and piece-rates of sawyers. From an early date it was customary to employ sawyers both on a flat daily-wage and at a piece-rate paid per 'hundred' feet (at this date commonly a long-hundred of 120 feet) of board sawn. The ratio of the piece-rate to the day-wage thus indicates how many feet of board a sawyer would typically saw in a day. Unfortunately, sawyers were rarely engaged on both a piece-rate and a per diem basis by the same institution in the same year, but the day-rate of carpenters is widely given and from this may be inferred the day-rate of sawyers, since from 1265 to 1713 the two stood in a fairly constant relationship to each other. On this basis, Table 8.10 shows the cutting-rate implied by piece-rates from 1265 to 1713. As can be seen, in the period 1550 to 1713 the cutting-rate of sawyers remained roughly constant, whereas before 1450 they worked at a rate some 27 per cent lower. There are other possible explanations

41 C. C. Dyer, *Standards of living in the later middle ages: social change in England, c.1200–1520,* Cambridge, 1989, p. 56.
42 *Agricultural labourers: return of the average rate of weekly earnings of agricultural labourers in the unions of England and Wales, BPP,* L, HC.14, London, 1861.

Table 8.10 *Hundred feet sawn per day per two sawyers, 1265–1713*

Years	Number of sources	Number of reports	Hundred feet per day
1265–99	5	5	0.69
1300–49	15	21	0.82
1350–99	2	2	0.78
1400–49	14	33	0.76
1450–99	10	22	1.04
1500–49	10	38	1.01
1550–99	10	34	1.07
1600–49	7	24	1.04
1650–99	3	28	1.09
1700–13	1	6	1.02

Source
J. E. Thorold Rogers, *A history of agriculture and prices in England*, 7 vols., 1866–1902.

for this finding – improvements in saws, or changes in what constituted a 'hundred' feet of board, for example – but it is consistent with the notion that there was an increase in the intensity with which agricultural workers laboured between 1400–63 and 1561.

Much remains to be learnt about medieval wage-rates and working practices, but in the meanwhile it would appear that if yields per acre were low *c.*1300, output per worker was yet lower and compared unfavourably with the situation in English agriculture from the late sixteenth century on. At the core of this low labour productivity lay low levels of work intensity due to inefficiency and under-employment. If before 1349 the daily wage normally paid in winter was merely the 0.11 bushels of wheat received by manorial servants, then, on the evidence of the method elaborated above, the rate at which grain was reaped and threshed was only two-thirds that which prevailed in 1561–99.

The two English agricultural revolutions, 1450–1850

The productivity of English agriculture increased substantially between the middle ages and the nineteenth century. That increase has usually been attributed to the enclosure of the open fields and to the amalgamation of peasant holdings into large capitalist farms. The purpose of this paper is to reassess the importance of those institutional changes in raising efficiency. In contrast to the standard story, it will be argued that most of the productivity growth in early modern England was accomplished by small farmers in the open fields during the seventeenth century. This was the yeomen's agricultural revolution. Enclosure and the amalgamation of small farms into large capital farms, which may be called the landlords' revolution, made only a modest contribution to the growth in productivity.

The view that the landlords' revolution raised agricultural efficiency originated in the early modern debates about enclosures and large farms. As early as the fifteenth century, critics of enclosure argued that it led to the conversion of arable to pasture and reduced employment. In 1539 Mr Fitzherbert countered that enclosure promoted convertible husbandry which implied greater employment and higher corn yields.[1] These views were refined by many writers in the seventeenth and eighteenth centuries.[2] Two distinct interpretations emerged, which for convenience may be called 'marxist' and 'tory'. According to the 'marxist' view, enclosures and large farms modernised agriculture, in part by reducing employment and in part by increasing yields. Output per worker increased and the redundant population moved to the towns to become the industrial work force. According to the 'tories', enclosures and large farms led to a more capital-intensive agriculture that raised both employment and output. Output increased

---

1 Fitzherbert, *Surveyenge* (1539), pp. 22–5 in R. H. Tawney and E. Power, eds., *Tudor economic documents, being select documents illustrating the economic and social history of Tudor England*, III, London, 1924.

2 M. Beresford, 'Habitation versus improvement: the debate on enclosure and agreement', pp. 40–69 in F. J. Fisher, ed., *Essays in the economic and social history of Tudor and Stuart England in honour of R. H. Tawney*, Cambridge, 1961.

yet further as labour productivity rose. Arthur Young, who was a proponent of this view, was a proto-Malthusian and argued that the rise in per capita food availability would induce a rise in population with the increment finding employment in manufacturing. Thus, the 'tories' and 'marxists' agree that enclosures and large farms raised farm efficiency and contributed to economic development, although they disagree on the manner in which these institutional changes brought about their beneficial results.

These positions are widely held by historians today. For instance, they remain an important example of the 'marxist' belief that capitalism is a progressive phase of history. C. Hill, for instance, brands the seventeenth century as 'backward-looking' and calls for 'an agrarian law, partible inheritance, stable copyholds': reforms aimed at preserving small scale, open-field farming. In his view: 'The economic arguments against those who merely defended commoners' traditional rights in the waste are overwhelming. England's growing population could be fed only by more intensive cultivation, by bringing marginal land under the plough. Enclosure by men with capital, brutally disregarding the rights of commoners, did at least do the job.'[3] Likewise, the 'tory' view is widely held. In 1983, for instance, P. Mathias contended that: 'Enclosure of open fields, engrossing of smaller plots and holdings into larger agricultural units (units of production and tenure rather than units of ownership) established the basis of improvement ... The break-up of the peasantry was the price England paid for the increased supplies of corn and meat to feed her growing population.'[4] And, following Young rather than Marx, added: 'local migration from the rural areas to industrial, mining centres and ports came from increments in population being born in the countryside, not from the effects of enclosure in driving people off the land.'[5] Whether with a 'marxist' or a 'tory' twist, enclosure and large-scale farming remain the institutional prerequisite for agricultural productivity growth in many accounts of English economic development.[6]

3 C. Hill, *The world turned upside down*, London, 1972, p. 104.
4 P. Mathias, *The first industrial nation*, London, 2nd edn., 1983, pp. 55–6.
5 Mathias, *The first industrial nation*, p. 57.
6 See, for instance, A. Toynbee, *Lectures on the industrial revolution in England*, London, 1884; P. Mantoux, *La révolution industrielle au XVIIIᵉ siécle*, Paris, 1905; Lord Ernle, *English farming, past and present*, London, 1912; C. Wilson, *England's apprenticeship 1603–1763*, London, 2nd edn., 1984; C. Clay, *Economic expansion and social change: England 1500–1700*, Cambridge, 1984; J. D. Chambers and G. E. Mingay, *The agricultural revolution 1750–1880*, London, 1966; E. L. Jones, *Agriculture and economic growth in England, 1650–1815*, London, 1967.

J

Not all writers on English farming have regarded these developments as indispensable for progress. In 1848, John Stuart Mill concluded from a review of available evidence that peasant farming in Europe was often technically progressive.[7] Economists studying small-scale farming in other parts of the world have frequently come to the same conclusion.[8] As far as English history is concerned, several writers have challenged the importance of enclosure.[9] M. A. Havinden's classic investigation of the adoption of sainfoin by open-field farmers in Oxfordshire was the pioneering study.[10] E. Kerridge has claimed that 'whether fields were open or enclosed has little bearing on the agricultural revolution'.[11] This revisionist research suggests the need for a general review of the evidence underlying the orthodox claim that enclosures and large farms were prerequisites for the modernisation of English farming during the early modern period.

Assessments of the relative performance of open and enclosed farms have usually focused on the adoption of new crops and methods, or have attempted to infer relative efficiency from rents paid.[12] This chapter, however, will concentrate on yield per acre and output per worker. These indicators approximately doubled between the late middle ages and the early nineteenth century.[13] The contributions of enclosure and large farms to that productivity growth are assessed using statistical evidence, beginning with a comparison of yields in open and enclosed villages and on large and small farms. These comparisons show that neither enclosure nor farm amalgamation was responsible for the growth in yields: almost all of the yield increase was accomplished by small farmers in the open fields. Next, attempts to

7 J. S. Mill, *Principles of political economy*, ed. W. J. Ashley, New York, 1965.
8 C. J. Dewey, 'The rehabilitation of the peasant proprietor in nineteenth-century economic thought', *History of Political Economy*, VI, 1974, pp. 17–47.
9 R. A. Berry and W. R. Cline, *Agrarian structure and productivity in developing countries*, Baltimore, 1979; A. Booth and R. M. Sundrum, *Labour absorption in agriculture*, Oxford, 1985.
10 M. A. Havinden, 'Agricultural progress in open-field Oxfordshire', *AHR*, IX, 1961, pp. 73–83.
11 E. Kerridge, *The agricultural revolution*, London, 1967, p. 19.
12 Havinden, 'Agricultural progress'; J. A. Yelling, *Common field and enclosure in England, 1450–1850*, Hamden, Ct., 1977; D. N. McCloskey, 'The enclosure of open fields: preface to a study of its impact on the efficiency of English agriculture in the eighteenth century', *JEH*, XXXII, 1972, pp. 15–35; R. C. Allen, 'The efficiency and distributional consequences of eighteenth-century enclosures', *Economic Journal*, LXII, 1982, 937–53.
13 B. M. S. Campbell, above, pp. 178–82; M. Overton, below, pp. 301–4; G. Clark, above, pp. 214–21; E. A. Wrigley, below, p. 327.

measure the impact of enclosure and farm size on employment per acre are discussed. Enclosure that led to the conversion of arable to pasture lowered employment as did increases in the size of farms. Finally, a simulation is undertaken of the growth in labour productivity between 1600 and 1800. This exercise shows that half of the growth in output per worker was due to the rise in yields and the other half to enclosure and the growth in farm size. Together these investigations establish that most of the rise in yields and half of the rise in labour productivity was the result of the yeomen's agricultural revolution. The remaining boost to output per worker was provided by the landlords' agricultural revolution. Since the rise in corn yields and much of the growth in labour productivity was accomplished by small-scale, open-field farmers, the true hero of English agricultural history was the yeoman, not the improving landlord or his rich tenant.

I Productivity growth in English agriculture

On the available evidence grain yields and labour productivity both grew about 100 per cent between the middle ages and the nineteenth century. Grain yields in medieval England were low but not unusually so. The best performance was achieved in north-eastern Norfolk where wheat yields of 20 bushels per acre were common.[14] Elsewhere, 10 bushels per acre was the norm.[15] Such a yield is common for backward farmers in poor countries today.[16] Most medieval English farmers were operating at the same low level of efficiency as recently prevailed among traditional farmers in India, China and the Middle East. By the end of the eighteenth century, however, English wheat yields were twice their medieval level. Young's tours in the 1760s, the Board of Agriculture reports of 1790–1815, and the 1801 crop returns all point to a wheat yield of 20–22 bushels.[17] Yields of other grains also doubled over the

14 B. M. S. Campbell, 'Agricultural progress in medieval England: some evidence from eastern Norfolk', *EcHR*, XXXVI, 1983, pp. 26–46.
15 J. Z. Titow, *Winchester yields: a study in medieval agricultural productivity*, Cambridge, 1972; B. M. S. Campbell, 'Arable productivity in medieval English agriculture', unpublished paper presented to the UC–Caltech Conference, 'Pre-industrial developments in peasant economies: the transition to economic growth', 1987.
16 H. Hanson, N. E. Borlaug and R. G. Anderson, *Wheat in the Third World*, Colorado, 1982, p. 4.
17 M. E. Turner, 'Agricultural productivity in England in the eighteenth century: evidence from crop yields', *EcHR*, XXXV, 1982, 489–510; R. C. Allen and C. Ó Gráda, 'On the road again with Arthur Young: English, Irish, and French agriculture during the industrial revolution', *JEH*, XLVIII, 1988, pp. 93–116.

period. Nevertheless, until recently, there was no evidence to pin down when that doubling occurred.[18]

Labour productivity was also twice as high by the close of the eighteenth century as it had been in the middle ages. Assuming no trade in food grains, E. A. Wrigley has suggested that the ratio of the total population to the agricultural population indicates output per worker in farming.[19] Using this ratio as his guide, he found that labour productivity grew 90 per cent in England between 1500 and 1800. G. Clark has used wage data to gauge levels of labour productivity, and his calculations show output per worker increased by 40–96 per cent.[20] Both Wrigley's and Clark's calculations involve debatable assumptions, but it is significant that both imply a doubling in output per worker.[21]

It was high labour productivity, rather than land productivity, that made English agriculture unusually productive at the beginning of the nineteenth century.[22] Thus, English wheat yields were apparently no higher than yields per acre in Ireland (22 bushels), Holland (21 bushels), and north eastern France (22 bushels). Nor, probably, was output per acre in north-western Germany and Belgium dissimilar.[23] Yet output per worker was 40–50 per cent greater in England than in

18 There has been unending debate on this issue. See G. E. Fussell, 'Population and wheat production in the eighteenth century', *The History Teachers' Miscellany*, VII, 1929, pp. 65–8, 84–8, 108–11, 120–7; P. Deane and W. A. Cole, *British economic growth, 1688–1959*, Cambridge, 2nd edn., 1967, pp. 67–8; Turner, 'Agricultural productivity'; *idem*, 'Agricultural productivity in eighteenth-century England: further strains of speculation', *EcHR*, XXXVII, 1984, pp. 252–7; M. Overton, 'Agricultural productivity in eighteenth-century England: some further speculations', *EcHR*, XXXVII, 1984, pp. 244–51; N. F. R. Crafts, *British economic growth during the industrial revolution*, Oxford, 1985, p. 44; R. C. Allen, 'Inferring yields from probate inventories', *JEH*, XLVIII, 1988, pp. 117–25; M. Overton, 'Re-estimating crop yields from probate inventories', *JEH*, L, 1990, pp. 931–5.
19 E. A. Wrigley, 'Urban growth and agricultural change: England and the continent in the early modern period', *Journal of Interdisciplinary History*, XV, 1985, pp. 683–728.
20 G. Clark, 'Productivity growth without technical change in European agriculture before 1850', *JEH*, XLVII, 1987, p. 428.
21 See K. G. Persson, above, pp. 129–30, for a discussion of the approach taken by Wrigley. J. Komlos, 'Agricultural productivity in America and eastern Europe: a comment', *JEH*, XLVIII, 1988, pp. 655–64, critiques Clark's method.
22 Crafts, *British economic growth; idem, British industrialization in an international context*, University of Leeds, School of Economic Studies, Discussion Paper Series A:87/7, 1987, especially has urged this view.
23 Allen and Ó Gráda, 'On the road again'; J. L. Van Zanden, *De economische ontwikkeling van de Nederlandse landbouw in de negentiende eeuw,1800–1914*, A. A. G. Bijdragen, XXV, Wageningen, 1985; G. P. H. Chorley, 'The agricultural revolution in northern Europe, 1750–1880: nitrogen, legumes, and crop productivity', *EcHR*, XXXIV, 1981, pp. 71–93.

these other countries.[24] Moreover, productivity, as indicated by both measures, was higher in north-western Europe than elsewhere on the continent.[25]

This doubling of land and labour productivity is taken as the yardstick for measuring the importance of enclosures and large farms as causes of productivity growth. If the spread of enclosure and engrossment of farms explains most of this growth, then they were important; otherwise, they were not.

II Enclosure and the growth in grain yields

Did enclosure lead to a doubling of crop yields? The answer is certainly no. In the past decade, economic historians have assembled several data sets that allow the comparison of yields in open and enclosed villages. M. E. Turner abstracted information from the Home Office returns of the 1790s and the 1801 crop returns.[26] His revised, national figures indicate that yields in enclosed villages exceeded those in open villages by 23 per cent for wheat and barley and 11 per cent for oats.[27] R. C. Allen and C. Ó Gráda abstracted the information that Young obtained about yields on his tours of the late 1760s.[28] These data show smaller gains: 8 per cent for wheat, 7 per cent for barley, and 12 per cent for oats. While the data concur that enclosed villages reaped higher yields than open ones, an even more important implication of the figures is that the apparent rise in yields at enclosure was much less than the rise in yields between the late middle ages and the nineteenth century: even Turner's 23 per cent increase in the yields of wheat and barley is far short of the doubling that took place.

Furthermore, both data sets suffer from two important limitations. First, they cover the greater part of the country and thus include regions where 'open' and 'enclosed' had different meanings. Only in the

24 P. Bairoch, 'Niveau de développement économique de 1810 à 1910.' *Annales, Économies, Sociétés, Civilisations*, XX, 1965, p. 1091–6; P. K. O'Brien and C. Keyder, *Economic growth in Britain and France, 1780–1914: two paths to the twentieth century*, London, 1978, pp. 102–45; Wrigley, 'Urban growth', p. 720; C. Ó Gráda, *Ireland before and after the famine: explorations in economic history, 1800–1925*, Manchester, 1988, chapter 2; Clark, 'Productivity growth'; P. Solar and M. Goossens, below, pp. 372–6.
25 P. O'Brien and G. Toniolo, below, pp. 401–3 compare Italian and British land and labour productivity.
26 Turner, 'Agricultural productivity'.
27 M. E. Turner, 'English open fields and enclosures: retardation or productivity improvements', *JEH*, XLI, 1986, p. 691.
28 Allen and Ó Gráda, 'On the road again', p. 98.

midlands did the scattering of land result in regular, classical open-field systems. Elsewhere, enclosures and 'irregular' open fields were frequently interspersed.[29] Farmers outside the midlands who had both enclosed and open-field land had more flexibility than open-field farmers in the Midlands who had the vast majority of their land constrained by the rules of the field system. It might be expected, therefore, that enclosure would have more impact on methods and yields in the Midlands than elsewhere. To assess that possibility, yield comparisons should be done within (or without) that region. Second, neither Turner nor Allen and Ó Gráda standardise the villages for soil characteristics, so it is not clear to what extent variations in fertility are confounded with the effects of enclosure.[30]

To address both problems, a further data set has been assembled. These data relate solely to the south midlands and are derived from the Board of Agriculture county reports, the 1801 crop returns, and the Home Office returns for Northamptonshire *c.*1795.[31] To control for environmental variation the villages concerned have been divided into three natural districts: heavy arable, light arable and pasture. The heavy arable district includes villages on the boulder clays of Huntingdonshire, Cambridgeshire and Bedfordshire. After enclosure, most land in that district remained under grain but with the major improvement of the installation of hollow drainage. Likewise, there was no conversion of arable to pasture in the light arable district. Here the main improvement that enclosure allowed was the introduction of the Norfolk four-course rotation and improved sheep to convert the expanded output of fodder to mutton and wool. In the pasture district, by contrast, enclosure led to significant conversion of arable to grass. New crops and improved livestock were also adopted where feasible.

Table 9.1 compares yields of open and enclosed villages in the three natural districts. As with the other data sets, yields of enclosed villages were usually higher than those which remained open, but the differential was small except for the spring grains in the heavy arable district. The latter is shown, by a regression analysis of C. Vancouver's 1794 data for Cambridgeshire, to have been principally associated with

29 H. L. Gray, *English field systems*, Cambridge, Mass., 1915; A. R. H. Baker and R. A. Butlin, eds., *Studies of field systems in the British Isles*, Cambridge, 1973; Yelling, *Common field and enclosure.*

30 Turner, 'English open fields'; Allen and Ó Gráda, 'On the road again'.

31 I am grateful to Dr Turner for making available his transcripts of the latter source.

Table 9.1 *English midlands: corn yields and enclosure, c.1800*

	Open (bush. per acre)	Enclosed (bush. per acre)	Enclosed relative to open (%)	Enclosure gain relative to medieval–19c. advance
A. The heavy arable district				
Wheat	19.5	20.1	3.1	6.4
Spring corn	22.8	26.4	15.8	26.4
B. The light arable district				
Wheat	20.8	20.4	−1.9	0.0
Spring corn	26.3	27.6	4.9	9.4
C. The pasture district				
Wheat	21.8	22.1	1.4	2.6
Spring corn	27.7	29.5	6.5	11.1

Notes

'Enclosed relative to open (%)' equals the yield of enclosed farms divided by the yield of open farms minus 1 and multiplied by 100.

'Enclosure gain relative to medieval–19c. advance' equals the difference between the yield of open and enclosed farms divided by the difference between the yield of enclosed farms and medieval yields. These were taken to be 10.7 bushels per acre for wheat, 16.8 for barley, 11.7 for oats and 10.0 for peas and beans. The yields for wheat, barley and oats are the average yields on the Winchester demesnes: J. Z. Titow, *Winchester yields: a study in medieval agricultural productivity*, Cambridge, 1972. See also P. F. Brandon, 'Cereal yields on the Sussex estates of Battle Abbey during the later middle ages', *EcHR*, XXV, 1972, pp. 403–20; D. L. Farmer, 'Grain yields on the Winchester manors in the later middle ages', *EcHR*, XXX, 1977, pp. 555–66; B. M. S. Campbell, 'Agricultural progress in medieval England: some evidence from eastern Norfolk', *EcHR*, XXXVI, 1983, pp. 26–46; *idem*, 'Arable productivity in medieval English agriculture', unpublished paper presented to the UC–Caltech conference, 'Pre-industrial developments in peasant economies: the transition to economic growth', 1987, for discussions of medieval yields. The figures for spring corn are computed from weighted averages of the yields of barley, oats and beans: the weights are shares of arable planted with these crops. For the heavy arable district, the shares were computed for villages enclosed by act; for the light arable district, the shares were computed for non-sheepfolding villages enclosed by act. For the pasture district, the shares were the averages of the shares for the heavy and light arable districts.

Source

Computed from R. C. Allen, 'Enclosure, farming methods, and the growth of productivity in the south midlands', pp. 69–88 in G. Grantham and C. Leonard, eds., *Agrarian organization in the century of industrialization: Europe, Russia, and North America*, Research in Economic History, Supplement V, Greenwich, Ct. and London, 1989, pp. 71, 72 and 76.

the installation of hollow drainage after enclosure.[32] The diffusion of the Norfolk rotation (turnips, barley, clover, and wheat) in the light arable district and the widespread conversion of arable to grass in the pasture district had little impact on yields. These comparisons provide no support for the common hypothesis that enclosure increased the production of fodder and forage, which in turn led to high livestock densities and, ultimately, higher corn yields. Indeed, regression analysis of the underlying data consistently rejects a correlation between livestock density, new crops, and yield.[33]

The final column of Table 9.1 shows the difference in the yields of open and enclosed villages relative to the medieval yield for the same crop. Again, except for the spring crops in the heavy arable district, the gain in yield at enclosure was small compared with the advance between the middle ages and the nineteenth century. Enclosure was not the cause of the rise in early modern grain yields.

III Farm size and farm capital

In addition to enclosure, the advent of the large farm and capitalist agriculture are traditionally emphasised as a cause of rising yields. There is no doubt that the average size of farms rose in the eighteenth century. A large sample of estate surveys in the south Midlands showed the average open field farm was 59 acres in the early seventeenth century, 65 acres in the early eighteenth, but 145 acres *c.*1800. This increase in average size meant that, by the early nineteenth century, most of England's farmland had effectively passed from family farmers to large-scale capitalist tenants.[34]

32 R. C. Allen, 'Enclosure, farming methods, and the growth of productivity in the south midlands', pp. 69–88 in G. Grantham and C. Leonard, eds., *Agrarian organization in the century of industrialization: Europe, Russia, and North America*, Research in Economic History, Supplement V, Greenwich, Ct. and London, 1989.

33 Compare Overton, below, pp. 310–14.

34 R. C. Allen, 'The growth of labour productivity in early modern English agriculture', *Explorations in Economic History*, XXV, 1988, pp. 117–146. For detailed information on farm sizes and lease terms, see also G. E. Mingay, 'The size of farms in the eighteenth century', *EcHR*, XIV, 1962, pp. 469–88; J. R. Wordie, 'Social change on the Leveson-Gower estates', *EcHR*, XXVII, 1974, pp. 593–609. Their findings are consistent with the chronology adopted in this paper. M. Spufford, *Contrasting communities: English villagers in the sixteenth and seventeenth centuries*, Cambridge, 1974, finds that farm sizes in Chippenham increased before the eighteenth century. J. P. Cooper, 'In search of agrarian capitalism', pp. 138–91 in Aston and Philpin, *The Brenner debate: agrarian class structure and economic development in pre-industrial Europe*, 1985, gives a provocative discussion of these issues.

Young believed that this change raised yields for two reasons.[35] First, he claimed that no farmer had access to credit, so farm capital depended entirely on the personal wealth of the farmer. This claim is hard to reconcile with the substantial evidence of lending in the countryside during the eighteenth century.[36] Second, he maintained that large farmers were wealthier in proportion to the size of their farm than small farmers. This claim is prima facie implausible. It can, however, be made more plausible if Young is simply taken as having meant that large farmers were wealthier than small farmers and, hence, had access to credit on cheaper terms. Consequently, large farmers deployed more capital (in particular more livestock) per acre and reaped higher yields as a result. Reformulating Young's position like this makes it coherent and consistent with the issue as it has emerged in the economic development literature.

Young's beliefs about farm size and capitalisation can be tested with reference to three definitions of farm capital using his own sample of farms.[37] Finance refers to the cost of rent, taxes, seeds, labour, implements and livestock that a farmer incurred in stocking a farm. Capital cost refers to the interest (at 5 per cent) and depreciation of livestock and implements. Animal density refers to a weighted sum of the livestock on the farm, where the weights indicate relative food consumption (and hence relative manure output).[38] On the basis of these three definitions, the relationship between farm size and capitalisation was explored by regressing capital per acre on farm acreage and farm acreage squared. The coefficients were generally significant. Table 9.2 summarises the results by tabulating the predicted values of farm capital per acre as a function of size. Generally, pasture farms had more capital per acre when animal density or capital cost are used as the indicator. Arable farms had more capital per acre when the finance definition is used, since that measure incorporates wage advances, whilst employment per acre was higher on arable farms than on pasture farms. Whichever definition was chosen, Table 9.2

---

35 A. Young, *Political arithmetic*, London, 1774, pp. 287–8.
36 B. A. Holderness, 'Credit in a rural community, 1660–1800', *Midland History*, III, 1975–76, pp. 94–115; *idem*, 'Credit in English rural society before the nineteenth century, with special reference to the period 1650–1720', *AHR*, XXIV, 1976, pp. 97–109.
37 These data are described in Allen, 'Inferring yields'. They were taken from A. Young, *Six weeks' tour through the southern counties of England and Wales*, London, 1768; *idem*, *A six months' tour through the north of England*, London, 2nd edn., 1771; *idem*, *The farmer's tour through the east of England*, 4 vols., London, 1771.
38 The weights are from Yelling, *Common field and enclosure*, p. 159.

Table 9.2 *English midlands: capital per acre for arable and pasture farms, c.1770*

	Farm size (acres)					
	25	50	100	150	200	250
Arable farms						
Finance	£4.93	£4.78	£4.51	£4.27	£4.06	£3.88
Capital	£0.97	£0.96	£0.93	£0.89	£0.86	£0.83
Animal density	0.28	0.27	0.25	0.23	0.22	0.20
Pasture farms						
Finance	£4.76	£4.51	£4.05	£3.66	£3.34	£3.07
Capital	£1.85	£1.75	£1.57	£1.42	£1.30	£1.20
Animal density	0.46	0.44	0.39	0.35	0.32	0.29

Source See text.

contradicts Young's views, since with all three definitions, farm capital per acre declined with size.

Rejection of Young's theory is to be expected in view of the history of developing countries.[39] As in early modern England, large farmers in poor countries usually have access to cheaper credit than small farmers. As a result, large farmers in the developing world frequently (but not invariably) use more *purchased* fixed capital (tractors and tillers) and circulating capital (fertiliser) per acre than small farmers. For capital inputs that are not purchased but are produced on the farm, however, capital intensity declines with size. This is true both of improvements that use otherwise unemployed family labour and also of livestock. As A. Booth and R. M. Sundrum observe, 'certainly the data on livestock by holding size indicates an almost universal tendency for per hectare numbers to decline as the holdings become larger'.[40] Aside from the payment of wages in advance of receipts from the harvest, livestock were the principal type of capital on early modern English farms. Capital per acre declined with size in eighteenth-century England just as it does today in Brazil or India.

IV Farm size and yields per acre

Since Young's views on farm size and farm capitalisation were incorrect, it would be no surprise if his views on size and yield were also in error.

39 Berry and Cline, *Agrarian structure and productivity*, pp. 52–3, 111 and 116; Booth and Sundrum, *Labour absorption*, pp. 186–99.
40 Booth and Sundrum, *Labour absorption*, p. 197.

Table 9.3 *English midlands: crop yields and farm size, 1550–1750 (bushels per acre)*

	Wheat			Barley		
Size (acres)	1550	1650	1750	1550	1650	1750
59	9.0	16.4	24.8	12.1	17.5	23.7
65	9.0	16.5	24.9	12.1	17.5	23.7
145	10.2	17.7	26.1	12.1	17.6	23.8

Note
The calculations assume that each farm had half of its acreage under grain and pulses. This is consistent with each farm having three-quarters of its land arable, two-thirds of that planted with grain and pulses and the remaining one-third fallow.

Source See text.

Probate inventories are the best source for testing the hypothesis that yield increased with farm size.[41] A sample of inventories has been assembled for 35 farms in Oxfordshire from the period 1550 to 1727. Their apparent yields per acre have been correlated with farm size, livestock density, and some other variables that might be expected to influence yield. The coefficients of livestock density were substantial, so Young was right that more livestock could raise yields. However, livestock densities seemingly did not increase with time or size, so that biological possibility was not realised historically. The share of land planted with legumes was included as a possible explanatory variable, since legumes are nitrogen-fixing crops and G. P. H. Chorley has recently suggested that their diffusion raised yields.[42] This hypothesis receives no support from the data. Nevertheless, the most important implication of the probate inventories is that farm size had little impact on yields, for in none of the regressions that were run did size emerge as a significant variable.

On the other hand, regressing farm size against yield often produced a small, positive coefficient, which raises the possibility that increases in farm size were more beneficial than adverse. To explore that possibility, Table 9.3 was constructed, which shows predicted wheat and barley yields for various sizes of farm in 1550, 1650 and 1750. The sizes used were the average size of open-field farms in the early

41 M. Overton, 'Estimating crop yields from probate inventories: an example from East Anglia, 1585–1735', *JEH*, XXXIX, 1979, pp. 363–78, pioneered this method. See Allen, 'Inferring yields', for a refinement. P. Glennie, below, pp. 255–71, and Overton, below, pp. 298–300, extend discussion of the method.
42 Chorley, 'The agricultural revolution'.

seventeenth century (59 acres), early eighteenth century (65 acres), and *c.*1800 (145 acres).[43] At any date and with either crop, yields tended to increase with farm size, although the increments were small. With barley, the increment was negligible (0.1 bushels). With wheat, the increase in farm size from 59 acres to 145 acres was associated with a yield increase of just over 1 bushel per acre, but this is a small increment when compared with the significant productivity gains which the same table reveals as having accrued over time. Wheat yields, for instance, increased by 15.8 bushels from 1550 to 1750 and barley yields by 11.6 bushels.[44] These observations again accord with contemporary experience of poor countries, where most investigations have shown the yields of the main field crops to be independent of farm size.[45]

On the evidence of Table 9.3, something other than growing farm size or enclosure (since the farms in the sample of probate inventories were virtually all open-field farms) was responsible for the rise in yields per acre in early modern Oxfordshire. What was it? This is a question that requires further research, but a strong contender is better seeds. In his *Natural history of Oxfordshire*, published in 1677, R. Plot reports that a high-yielding variety of wheat: 'was first propagated from some few ears of it pickt out of many *Acres*, by one *Pepart* near *Dunstable*, about fifty years ago, which sowed by it self till it amounted to a quantity, and then proving *Mercatable*, is now become one of the commonest grains of this County.' Pepart's selecting was done about 1625, in other words, just before the inventories show a rapid rise in the yield of wheat. Nevertheless, by the time of Plot's *History*, this seed had already been displaced by an even more productive variety which was also 'first advanced like the former from some few *ears*'. This variety yielded 'sometimes *twenty for one*,' which was about 45 bushels per acre. It was widely grown 'all along the *Vale* under the *Chiltern* Hills', which is the region from which most of the sample of Oxfordshire probate inventories was drawn.[46] It is likely that these improved seeds were responsible for a significant proportion of the rise in yields exhibited in Table 9.3.

If better seed was the basis for the growth in yields, it is not so

43 Allen, 'The growth of labour productivity', p. 122.
44 Compare Overton's conclusion on the same point, below, pp. 309–11.
45 Berry and Cline, *Agrarian structure and productivity*; K. Bharadwaj, *Production conditions in Indian agriculture*, Cambridge, 1974; C. J. Bliss and N. H. Stern, *Palanpur: the economy of an Indian village*, Oxford, 1982; C. H. H. Rao, *Technological change and distribution of gains in Indian agriculture*, Delhi, 1975.
46 R. Plot, *The natural history of Oxfordshire*, Oxford, 1677; Overton, below, p. 290.

surprising that open-field farmers were innovative. Individual farmers could choose their seed without reference to the village community, so the need for collective decision-making did not bar changes in seed as it sometimes did for certain new crops like turnips. Moreover, as will be argued, the incentives for raising productivity were especially strong in the seventeenth century since most farmers held their land for very long terms on beneficial leases or copyholds.

V Enclosure, farm amalgamation and employment

The growth in yields was one aspect of progress in early modern English agriculture; the growth in labour productivity was another. The two developments were related. Since the hours of work required for many activities in arable husbandry were independent of the yield, the rise in yields immediately raised output per worker.[47] Enclosure and the shift to large farms may also have made an independent contribution, raising labour productivity by lowering employment per acre or by increasing it at a lower rate than the expansion of output. The first possibility is the 'marxist' view, the second is the 'tory' view.

To investigate the validity of these views, employment per acre of men, women, and boys, and total employment (as measured by wages paid) were regressed on farm size using Young's sample of farms.[48] Table 9.4 shows the predicted levels of employment per 1,000 acres of farmland when that land is divided into farms of the sizes indicated.[49] Evidently, larger farms led to lower employment of all types of labour. The conversion of arable to pasture reduced the employment of men, although it slightly raised the employment of women, and had no effect on the employment of boys. The overall result was a reduction in total labour earnings and, thus, employment. Aside from its impact on the balance of tillage and grass, the regressions show that enclosure had no other effect on employment. The overall impact of the landlords' agricultural revolution was to shake labour out of agriculture. The amalgamation of farms lowered employment, and enclosure did likewise

47 But see Clark, above, pp. 221–31, and G. Grantham, below, pp. 353–7. W. N. Parker and J. L. V. Klein, 'Productivity growth in grain production in the United States, 1840–60 and 1900–10', pp. 523–80 in *Conference on research in income and wealth, output, employment, and productivity in the United States after 1800*, National Bureau of Economic Research, Studies in Income and Wealth, XXX, New York, 1966.

48 Allen, 'The growth of labour productivity'.

49 Since 1,000 acres corresponds to a small village, Table 9.4 suggests the social impact of farm amalgamation and enclosure.

Table 9.4 *English midlands: employment per 1,000 acres, arable and pasture farms, c.1770*

	Farm size (acres)					
	25	50	100	150	200	250
Arable farms						
Men	46	44	40	36	34	31
Women	32	28	22	17	13	9
Boys	33	29	22	16	11	7
Total	£1,631	£1,520	£1,319	£1,143	£994	£807
Pasture farms						
Men	32	30	26	22	19	17
Women	34	31	25	19	15	11
Boys	32	28	22	16	11	7
Total	£1,298	£1,188	£987	£812	£662	£538

Note
The farms are assumed to be open-field. Arable farms are 80 per cent arable and pasture farms 20 per cent arable.

Source
Computed from R. C. Allen, 'The growth of labour productivity in early modern English agriculture', *Explorations in Economic History*, XXV, 1988, p. 132.

when it led to the conversion of arable to pasture. Young's data refute his opinions on these matters and sustain the 'marxist' theory in this regard.

VI Simulating the rise in labour productivity

Several changes were occurring in early modern agriculture that all tended to raise labour productivity: yields were rising under the yeoman system and they also rose modestly at enclosure; employment fell as farms were amalgamated, and was further reduced when enclosure resulted in the conversion to pasture. To sort out the relative importance of these factors in raising output per worker between 1600 and 1800, a simulation has been undertaken of their probable effects, concentrating upon grain-growing areas where enclosure did not result in the conversion of arable to pasture.

Tables 9.5 and 9.6 show two simulations using different assumptions about yields. Table 9.5 uses Turner's estimates of yields in open

Table 9.5 *England: labour productivity in grain farming, c.1600–c.1800: Turner's yields*

	c.1600 (open)	c.1700 (open)	c.1800 (open)	c.1800 (enclosed)
Output per acre	£2.55	£3.49	£3.49	£3.92
Labour per acre	1.24	1.17	0.91	0.91
Output per worker	£2.05	£2.97	£3.83	£4.30
Index	1.00	1.45	1.87	2.10

Source See text.

Table 9.6 *England: labour productivity in grain farming, c.1600–c.1800: Young's yields*

	c.1600 (open)	c.1700 (open)	c.1800 (open)	c.1800 (enclosed)
Output per acre	£2.55	£3.90	£3.90	£4.11
Labour per acre	1.24	1.17	0.91	0.91
Output per worker	£2.05	£3.33	£4.29	£4.52
Index	1.00	1.62	2.09	2.20

Source See text.

and enclosed villages.[50] These estimates provide an upper-bound measure of the yield-boosting effect of enclosure. With Turner's yields, enclosed farms produced 12 per cent more than open farms, and open farms accomplished 69 per cent of the advance from the c.1600 output level of £2.55 per acre to the c.1800 output level of £3.92 per acre. Table 9.6 uses Young's reported yields. The differential between yields on open and enclosed farms is much smaller in this sample. The revenue per acre of enclosed farms c.1800 is only 5 per cent greater than for open farms. Further, open farmers accomplished 87 per cent of the advance in output per acre. As shown earlier, the impact of enclosure on yield varied with soil type, and Tables 9.5 and 9.6 probably indicate the corresponding range of output responses.

50 Turner does not report yields for beans or peas, so the yields for beans in the heavy arable district given in Table 9.1 have been used. The differential between open and enclosed yields is of the same order as the differential in the grains Turner reports. The values computed here for revenue per acre using Turner's revised yields are identical to those previously reported, although slightly different yields have been used: Allen, 'The growth of labour productivity', p. 140.

Output per worker is the ratio of output per acre to labour per acre. Labour per acre is the same in both simulations. It declined because of the growth in farm size, but did not change with enclosure, since the farms under consideration are those which remained in arable. In both cases, output per worker increased slightly more than twofold. With Turner's yields, open farmers accomplished 79 per cent of the growth in output per worker between 1600 and 1800. With Young's yields, they accomplished 91 per cent. Depending on the table and the method of reckoning, about half of the growth in output per worker was accomplished by small-scale, open-field farmers before 1700.

Expanding the simulation to take account of the conversion of arable to pasture, which often followed enclosure, does little to change this basic conclusion, because, although conversion to pasture reduced employment, output suffered as well. For instance, Young's data indicate that pastoral farms in the eighteenth century produced £2–3 per acre versus £4 for arable farms.[51] Thus, pastoral farming was a less intensive form of agriculture than arable farming, and the conversion of arable to pasture reduced farm employment, although it did not raise output per worker.[52]

VII Lessons of history

The usual lesson drawn from English history has been that enclosure and capitalist agriculture caused productivity growth. During the nineteenth century English institutions were held up as models for modernisation, and as late as the 1950s it was imagined that farm amalgamation was the way to raise output in the developing world. Subsequent experience, however, has shown that small farmers are capable of being highly innovative. Japanese history suggested this, and results from the early Indian Farm Management Studies were another great shock, for they suggested that small farms were more efficient than large farms.[53] Much research on this issue has established that peasant agriculture is frequently efficient and, moreover, capable of modernisation. In light of that research, English history, with its apparently contrary lessons, has become increasingly anomalous.

51 Allen, 'The growth of labour productivity', pp. 128–9.
52 See Allen, 'The growth of labour productivity', pp. 141–2.
53 K. Ohkawa and H. Rosovsky, 'The significance of the Japanese experience', pp. 617–84 in T. Ogura, ed., *Agricultural development in modern Japan*, Tokyo, 1963; A. K. Sen, 'Size of holdings and productivity', *The Economic Weekly*, XVI, 1964, pp. 323–6.

Not only are the conventional lessons drawn from English history poor guides for development, but they are a great misrepresentation of what happened in England itself. The results presented here show that small, open-field farmers were primarily responsible for the rise in yields in early modern England, and also for half of the growth in labour productivity. In the eighteenth century, the landlords' agricultural revolution shook some labour out of agriculture (when surplus population was already becoming a social problem), and thereby pushed English agricultural labour productivity above continental levels. Nevertheless, most of the advance in agricultural efficiency had been accomplished in the yeomen's revolution a century before.

This conclusion has some bearing on other issues in English economic history, in particular, the question of the relative efficiency of peasant and demesne agriculture in the high middle ages.[54] M. M. Postan and J. Z. Titow have argued that demesnes were more productive than peasant holdings on the grounds that livestock densities were highest on the demesnes.[55] The regression analysis of probate inventories undertaken here does confirm that more livestock meant higher yields (although analysis of the data underlying Table 9.1 shows no such correlation), but whether livestock densities were, in fact, higher on demesnes is an empirical matter about which there is currently little evidence.[56] Indeed, the finding that small farmers in the eighteenth century had higher livestock densities than large farmers calls the Postan/Titow assumption into question. It would not be surprising, in the light of these results, if peasant farms in the twelfth and thirteenth centuries had more animals per acre and reaped higher yields than the demesnes.[57]

On the other hand, these results from the seventeenth and eighteenth centuries suggest a new way in which demesnes may have been more productive: namely, in the use of labour. Demesnes were frequently several hundred acres and were thus large enough to realise

54 Campbell, above, p. 147.
55 M. M. Postan, 'Medieval agrarian society in its prime: England', pp. 549–632 in *idem*, ed., *The Cambridge economic history of Europe*, I, *The agrarian life of the middle ages*, Cambridge, 2nd edn., 1966; Titow, *Winchester yields*.
56 The most important study remains M. M. Postan, 'Village livestock in the thirteenth century', *EcHR*, XV, 1962, pp. 219–49, reprinted as pp. 214–48 in *idem*, *Essays on medieval agriculture and general problems of the medieval economy*, Cambridge, 1973. No attempt, however, is made to calculate stocking densities on different types of holding.
57 If not, a revolution in stocking densities must have occurred among the small farmers of England between the thirteenth and the seventeenth centuries.

the labour savings achievable with large work gangs.[58] These gains were more likely to have been realised when wage labour was used rather than when servile labour was employed. As with the question of livestock densities, this is also a matter for further research.

Finally, the results discussed in this paper raise a fundamental question about open fields and enclosures. If, as has been argued, open-field farmers were efficient, why were the open fields enclosed? There were several reasons. First, open-field farmers were never as willing as enclosed farmers to convert their land to pasture since that change reduced the demand for their labour. Hence, enclosure was a prerequisite to large-scale conversion of tillage to grass. Second, the innovativeness of open-field farmers in grain growing probably declined over time. In the Midlands, enclosure to improve arable farming only became common in the eighteenth or nineteenth centuries. There was no need for enclosure for that purpose earlier since open-field farmers were progressive grain growers. In the middle ages they shifted, on occasion, from two-field to three-field systems, and in the seventeenth century they adopted better seeds and incorporated new crops like pulses and grasses into their rotations.[59] If they could make these changes earlier, why was there a problem with turnips in the eighteenth century? The answer possibly lies in new forms of leases adopted after 1700. In the seventeenth century, many open-field farmers held their land as copyholds or beneficial leases. Hence, their rents did not rise as they improved their efficiency. In contrast, during the eighteenth century, these tenures were replaced by tenancies-at-will or for very short terms of years. Under the new circumstances, improvements in productivity resulted in higher rents, not higher incomes for the farmers. This change in tenancy may well have reduced the innovativeness of the open fields and led to their enclosure.

58 Allen, 'The growth of labour productivity'.
59 H. S. A. Fox, 'The alleged transformation from two-field to three-field systems in medieval England', *EcHR*, XXXIX, 1986, pp. 526–48; Gray, *English field systems*; W. G. Hoskins, 'The Leicestershire farmer in the sixteenth century', pp. 123–83 in *idem*, ed., *Essays in Leicestershire history*, Liverpool, 1950; *idem*, 'The Leicestershire farmer in the seventeenth century', pp. 149–69 in *idem*, ed., *Provincial England*, London, 1963; Havinden, 'Agricultural progress'.

Measuring crop yields in early modern England

New methods of estimating trends in crop yields from data in English probate inventories, first proposed in 1979, promise greater understanding of crop yields in the period *c.*1550–1750. This knowledge is of considerable potential significance because of the virtual absence of direct evidence on the chronology, geography, and causes, of improved yields. Instead, agrarian historians, geographers and economists have used innovations as surrogates for yield increases, becoming locked into circular arguments in which the presence of innovations indicates yield increases which are explained by the innovations.[1] This circularity can be bypassed if yields can be calculated directly and systematically. Moreover, new findings on these topics have consequences beyond the agricultural sector, and beyond this historical period. Knowledge of past agricultural productivity and the (pre)conditions for agricultural development can inform wider development debates, both historical and contemporary.

In evaluating methods of yield estimation, this chapter has both methodological and substantive goals. Its primary aim is to consider claims that absolute yield levels can be calculated from probate inventories. Different versions of the method and their results are compared using a large sample of inventories from the southern English county of Hampshire. New data on yields in this important area of commercial agriculture are analysed, and compared with yield trends in various parts of early modern England, recalculating yields for several areas by a single method. In combination, an investigation of method, a substantial volume of new data, and the comparison of results, enable an exploration of interpretative questions raised by earlier studies.

I thank the staff of the Hampshire County Record Office, Winchester, and the Hertfordshire County Record Office, Hertford, for their assistance, and the Straker family of Petersfield and Winchester for their hospitality. This paper benefited from comments by Mike Turner, Bob Allen and Mark Overton.
1 A circular argument is not necessarily incorrect, of course, but its causal mechanisms are not articulated independently.

Various schemes for estimating trends and levels of yields are summarised in Section I. Several methodological problems are identified in Section II, and refinements are suggested. Section III presents a new analysis of yields in seventeenth-century Hampshire, establishing long-term trends and short-term variations in arable yields per sown acre, and exploring their relation to innovations, farm type and location. Section IV considers the scope for uncovering the regional geography of changing crop yields, and Section V highlights the important distinction between crop yields and land productivity. In conclusion, some implications for views of English agricultural change are considered.

I Estimating crop yields from probate inventory valuations

Studies by M. Overton, R. C. Allen and P. Glennie investigate yields in East Anglia, Oxfordshire and Hertfordshire respectively.[2] Since each uses a different version of the same method, it is, however, unclear to what extent their differing results reflect real differences in experience among the areas, and how far they are artefacts of differences in procedure. Overton's pioneering work was concerned with yield trends, aiming to identify the chronology of yield increases within the early modern period, rather than with absolute yield levels. Subsequently, Allen has adapted Overton's method to estimate absolute levels of crop yields, enabling yields during 'the inventory period' (c.1550– c.1750) to be compared with those calculated from earlier and later sources.

The starting point for all versions are valuations of grain made by appraisers of probate inventories, whose tasks included assessing the

2 M. Overton, 'Estimating crop yields from probate inventories: an example from East Anglia, 1585–1735', *JEH*, XXXIX, 1979, pp. 363–78; *idem*, 'Agricultural revolution? Development of the agrarian economy in early modern England', pp. 118–39 in A. R. H. Baker and D. J. Gregory, eds., *Explorations in historical geography: interpretative essays*, Cambridge, 1984; *idem*, 'Agricultural productivity in eighteenth-century England: some further speculations', *EcHR*, XXXVII, 1984, pp, 244–51; *idem*, 'Weather and agricultural change in England, 1660–1739', *Agricultural History*, LXIII, 1989, pp. 77–88; *idem*, 'Re-estimating crop yields from probate inventories', *JEH, L*, 1990, pp. 931–5; *idem*, below, pp. 298–305; R. C. Allen, 'Inferring yields from probate inventories', *JEH*, XLVIII, 1988, pp. 117–25; *idem*, 'The growth of labour productivity in early modern English agriculture', *Explorations in Economic History*, XXV, 1988, pp. 117–46; P. Glennie, 'A commercialising agrarian region: late medieval and early modern Hertfordshire', unpublished University of Cambridge Ph.D. thesis, 1983, chapter 10; *idem*, 'Continuity and change in Hertfordshire agriculture, 1550–1700: II – trends in crop yields and their determinants', *AHR*, XXXVI, 1988, pp. 145–61.

value of a dead farmer's crops. In an ideal world (for historians), appraisers would have made an explicit estimate of how much grain would be obtained from the crop on specified areas. In reality, appraisers hardly ever specified the weight or volume of grain on an area. For example, in a sample of more than 1,500 farm inventories from seventeenth-century Hampshire, only two contain this information. In October 1660, the four appraisers of the estate of Thomas Barrett of Shorwell in the Isle of Wight listed 'for 3 acars of Barly 12 quarters ... £12 0s 0d' and 'for 2 acars of Wheate 2 quarters ... £4 0s 0d'.[3] And in September 1685, appraisers at Northwood, also in the Isle of Wight, noted 'three ackers and a halfe of wheate by Judgement aboute fiftie bushels ... £6 5s 0d'.[4] In these cases the calculation of bushels per acre is straightforward. Usually, however, appraisers gave at most the area and value of a crop, for example 'for 6 acres of Rye ... £4 16s 0d'.[5]

Appraisers valued growing crops either according to the costs which the farmer had already incurred (such as seed and ploughing) or by estimating the revenue that would be received when the grain was sold after harvesting.[6] These will be referred to these as 'cost of production' valuations (COPVs) and 'anticipated sale price' valuations (ASPVs) respectively. ASPVs are central to all the methods to be discussed because, as Overton realised, they contain implicit estimates of yields. Problems may arise in eliminating COPVs, since appraisers often do not state which valuation method they have used. These are discussed below.

In making ASPVs appraisers made two estimates: first, the likely quantity of grain to be produced, and second, its value per bushel (based on their expectation of the grain's eventual selling-price). So their stated valuation per acre (v) was the product of estimated bushels per acre (y) multiplied by estimated price per bushel (p):

3 Hampshire County Record Office (HCRO) inventory 1664/B/4. The units of measurement for grain are bushels and quarters. Eight bushels made one quarter, although there were regional and local variations, and a quarter of oats sometimes contained nine bushels. The bushel was a unit of volume, equal to eight gallons. Since the mass of grains varied between crops and with the degree of ripeness of grain, it is impossible to provide precise modern equivalents, but 1 ton an acre equates to roughly 37 bushels an acre (approximately 33.5 hectolitres a hectare). The final figure in each entry is the valuation in £ *s d* (12*d* = 1*s*, 20*s* = £1).
4 HCRO inventory 1686/A/84.
5 HCRO inventory 1621/B/24.
6 The possibility that conventional standard valuations were made of growing crops has been rejected for the major cereal crops in all the areas studied. Both simple and complex forms of conventional valuation are considered and rejected in P. Glennie, 'The plausibility of crop yields inferred from probate inventories', unpublished manuscript, 1990.

$$v = y \cdot p. \tag{1}$$

Rearranging Equation 1 gives a measure of 'yield',[7]

$$y = v/p. \tag{2}$$

v is calculated from areas and values given in inventories, so knowledge of p enables the calculation of y. While direct comments from appraisers about their price expectations are lacking, the valuations made of harvested grain in farmers' barns are known from inventories appraised later in the year. Overton used these valuations of harvested grain to calculate p, making the assumption that appraisers were broadly accurate forecasters of prices.[8] Thus, trends in yields are inferred by comparing valuations per acre of growing grain in pre-harvest months with valuations per bushel of stored grain after the same harvest.[9]

Overton acknowledged that his results understate the *level* of crop yields because factors such as tithe and harvesting costs were not taken into account. These costs caused the value of a field of grain to be less than the gross value of the crop, but their exclusion should not obscure the chronology of yield *trends*. He found that East Anglian wheat yields increased between the late sixteenth century and about 1660, while barley yields increased both then and later, until at least 1730. Increased barley yields were accompanied by an expansion in barley cultivation which further increased total arable yields per acre, as barley replaced lower-yielding rye and wheat. Rising yields per sown acre were clearly not due to the diffusion of clover and turnip cultivation, since both were insignificant before c.1660, and were not grown on large areas until after 1700.

Glennie applied Overton's method to Hertfordshire, also finding 'yield' increases, especially after c.1660 and particularly for barley.[10]

---

7 Throughout this paper yield (y) is used to refer to unadjusted inventory valuations converted to bushels/acre, whereas yield (Y) refers to gross yields, i.e. yield adjusted by an estimate for costs, using the equations described later in this section.

8 That this assumption is reasonable is best illustrated by the pattern of valuations of stored grain month by month. Typically, these vary during the growing months, systematically moving towards the actual post-harvest price of grain.

9 In practice, the calculation was more complicated than this because Overton sought to compensate for the non-normality of valuation distributions. He took the average of the reciprocals of per bushel valuations, rather than the reciprocal of the average, as the multiplicand of the average per acre valuation.

10 With a minor modification, that mean yields for each year were calculated separately before being combined to provide decadal estimates: Glennie, 'Continuity and change II', Appendix 1.

Fodder crop innovations came too late to account for increased yields, which instead were ascribed to increased levels of ground preparation (such as summer ploughing of fallows, and dunging) similar to the labour-intensive techniques responsible for high aggregate yields on some medieval demesnes.[11] Glennie also extended Overton's work by investigating the locations and types of individual farms achieving high yields.

A major innovation has been suggested by Allen.[12] He attempts to allow for appraisers' third estimate: that is, the costs of harvesting, getting the crop from the field to the barn, and also the tithe, which a rector would be entitled to take. If these can be estimated accurately, the gross yields of crops can be calculated, not just their net 'yield'. Allen argues both that appraisers did assess these yet-to-be-incurred costs realistically, and that historians can reconstruct what these costs were. Allen's suggestion has great potential since absolute yields per acre derived from inventories could be compared with equivalent figures derived from other sources. Overton's yield trends would no longer be a 'floating series', but would fill part of the gap between medieval yields calculated from manorial accounts, and modern yields from government statistics.

Allen's attempt to estimate seventeenth-century costs displays considerable ingenuity. He begins with harvesting costs in 1806 recorded by T. Batchelor. These are adjusted for differences in winter wage rates between earlier years and 1806.[13] An allowance is made for tithe, which is assumed to have been exactly one tenth, although actual tithe renders were rarely precise.[14] These steps are summarised in Equation 3:

$$v = 0.9(pY - tY - c) - r \qquad (3)$$

where,

v = value of standing crop (per acre)

p = price of grain in the barn (per bushel)

11 B. M. S. Campbell, 'Agricultural progress in medieval England: some evidence from eastern Norfolk', *EcHR*, XXXVI, 1983, pp. 26–46.
12 Allen, 'Inferring yields'.
13 T. Batchelor, *General view of the agriculture of the County of Bedfordshire*, London, 1808, pp. 70–160, especially pp. 108–12; P. J. Bowden, 'Statistical appendix', pp. 814–70 in Thirsk, *The agrarian history of England and Wales*, IV, *1500–1640*, 1967; *idem*, 'Statistical appendix', pp. 827–902 in Thirsk, *The agrarian history of England and Wales*, Vii, *1640–1750: agrarian change*, 1984. Equation 3 assumes that farmers paid for reaping, but that tithe owners paid other costs.
14 E. Evans, *The contentious tithe: the tithe problem and English agriculture, 1750–1850*, London, 1976, illustrates the great variety of tithing practices and the varying levels of the tax.

Y = gross yield per acre (bushels)
t = cost of threshing and dressing grain (per bushel)
c = cost of carting grain from fields to ricks to barn (per acre)
r = cost of reaping and binding grain, and cutting haulm (per acre).

This equation, to compare with Overton's original, can be rewritten:

$$Y = \frac{v + r + 0.9c}{0.9(p - t)} \tag{4}$$

as compared with Overton's original equation:

$$y = v/p. \tag{2}$$

The cost terms for a period (t) are produced by calculations of the form:

$$r_t = W_t / W_{1806} \cdot r_{1806} \tag{5}$$

where,

r = cost of reaping, etc
W = winter wage rate.

Allen applies his method to a sample of inventories from Oxfordshire. Predictably, since the numerator of Equation 4 is larger than that of Equation 2, and its denominator smaller, Allen's method produces high estimates compared with Overton's. He estimates wheat yields in late-seventeenth-century Oxfordshire at 21 bushels an acre, and barley yields at 25 bushels an acre. Yields at these levels leave little room for further increases between c.1700 and the early nineteenth century.[15] Allen then claims to have demonstrated the existence of two discrete phases of agricultural progress in early modern England. The first, 'the yeomen's revolution', saw substantial increases in crop yields, which by c.1700 had raised yields to levels still not exceeded by the early nineteenth century. The second phase, 'the landlords' revolution', saw greatly enhanced labour productivity, largely as a result of economies of scale in arable agriculture on large, consolidated farms, but without any further improvements in crop yields.[16] This neat dichotomy of chronology is linked to dichotomised causal relationships: yield increases were the achievement of yeomen farmers, whereas the

15 Allen, 'Inferring yields', pp. 123–5, *idem* and C. Ó Gráda, 'On the road again with Arthur Young: English, Irish and French agriculture during the industrial revolution', *JEH*, XLVIII, 1988, pp. 97–102.
16 Allen, 'The growth of labour productivity', p. 143; above pp. 236–54.

eighteenth-century enclosure movement redistributed agricultural profits, but did not raise land productivity.[17]

The potential significance of Allen's conclusions makes a detailed scrutiny of his assumptions and methods an important issue. Does this procedure, both in its principles and its specific assumptions, offer a generally applicable procedure? Unfortunately Allen does not provide such a scrutiny. Moreover, his sample of inventories is extremely small, which both constitutes a precarious basis for sweeping conclusions, and introduces several problems into the method – problems which become apparent only through detailed investigation of a large body of data.

II Inferring absolute yields: commentary and revisions

Briefly stated, the argument in this section is that the general structure of Allen's method is sound, but that its present form is flawed in ways which cause crop yields to be systematically overestimated. A number of revisions are suggested to counter the problems identified. It is appropriate, though, to make two general observations. First, not all the problems identified are soluble: to some there is no single 'right' answer. Secondly, flaws and biases in method, and questionable conclusions, cannot detract from the fact that Allen has sought to answer vitally important questions. As D. Cannadine remarks, fertile error is often more fruitful and stimulating than trivial truth.[18]

Subsection II.i examines the difficult problem of how to identify and eliminate COPVs. The remaining subsections identify ways in which Allen's method overestimates yield. These are: how average yields for time periods are calculated (II.ii), deciding what terms to include in the equation (II.iii), how 'real' costs are estimated (II.iv), and the assumption that contemporaries accurately perceived and took account of costs (II.v). The conclusions are briefly summarised at the end of this section.

II.i *Eliminating 'cost of production' valuations (COPVs)*
Appraisers gave valuations of an area of crop either by listing costs incurred in bringing the crop to its current condition (COPVs), or by estimating the likely yield and multiplying this by an estimate of what

---

17 R. C. Allen, 'The efficiency and distributional consequences of eighteenth-century enclosures', *Economic Journal*, LXLII, 1982, pp. 937–53; *idem*, 'The growth of labour productivity'; above pp. 252–4.

18 D. Cannadine, 'British history: past, present – and future?', *Past and Present*, CXVI, 1987, p. 178.

grain would be worth (ASPVs).[19] The former method produced relatively low valuations, was more likely to be used early in the farming year, and, in some areas at least, was becoming less common during the seventeenth century.[20]

Overton, Allen and Glennie all agree that COPVs should be excluded since they do not incorporate an estimate of yield, but it is unclear precisely how this can be done. Overton and Glennie excluded all inventories from early in the year (before May) and any later ones which were explicitly based on costs.[21] Allen suggests the use of a threshold 'yield' of 5 bushels an acre, below which valuations are ignored. The difficulty here is that low ASPVs arising from anticipated poor yields, and the higher COPVs, form two overlapping distributions rather than two discrete ones. Any threshold is likely to be exceeded by the higher COPVs, and to exclude genuine but low ASPVs. On the one hand, 'it is straightforward to work out plausible cost of production estimates that imply yields in the 5 to 15 bushels per acre range, but one is loath to exclude observations from the data set on those grounds alone'.[22] On the other hand, some very low valuations are definitely assessments of a poor crop's worth. In June 1603 some 'very thin wheat' was worth only 10 shillings an acre, and throughout the period low valuations attached to crops described as 'very coarse', 'very bad smutty wheat', or the like.[23] It is thus difficult to argue for too high a threshold.

Moreover, even very low valuations per acre can produce plausible estimates of absolute yield. For example, in the 1690s a net wheat 'yield' of just under 5 bushels an acre would produce an estimated gross yield of nearly 8 bushels an acre by Allen's method (consistent with a sowing rate of 2.5 bushels an acre and yield per seed of just over 3). Whilst low, this is a level which medievalists judge plausible in poor harvests.[24] Moreover, sowing rates may have been lower during successive poor harvests such as the 1690s.

19 There was no actual market for standing grain, and so no direct way in which standing grain could be valued at the price for which it might be sold at any given moment in time (Allen, 'Inferring yields', p. 118). Bob Allen has, however, pointed out that not very much later, Daniel Defoe refers to merchants viewing grain in the fields and making provisional agreements to buy on this basis, in his *The Complete English Tradesman*, 2 vols., London, 1725–27.
20 Overton, 'Estimating crop yields'; Allen, 'Inferring yields', p. 122.
21 In his revised calculations Overton excludes those inventories made before June. See below pp. 302–3.
22 Allen, 'Inferring yields', p. 122.
23 HCRO inventories 1603/B/37, 1641/A/122, 1690/ad/109.
24 For example, J. Z. Titow, *Winchester yields: a study in medieval agricultural productivity*, Cambridge, 1972, pp. 1–35; B. M. S. Campbell, 'Arable productivity in medieval England: some evidence from eastern Norfolk', *JEH*, XLIII, 1983, pp. 382–9.

The effect of the 5-bushels threshold varies for different grains, due to differences in sowing rates. For wheat, typically sown at 2 to 3 bushels an acre, a threshold of 5 bushels will exclude most COPVs which take account of seed alone, or of seed and ploughing. Only valuations which also include other ground preparation or dung will amount to 5 bushels an acre or more. However, the usual sowing densities of barley and oats were higher at 3–4 and 4–5 bushels an acre respectively. Consequently, even COPVs based on seed costs and ploughing will exceed the 5-bushels threshold, especially for oats. This problem is tellingly illustrated in poor harvest years which produce many inventories apparently containing a COPV for wheat, and ASPVs for oats. This is an undesirable inconsistency. Thus different thresholds may be appropriate for different crops, with higher thresholds applied to oats, and possibly barley, than to wheat, to allow for denser sowing rates. Yet the higher the threshold, the greater the upward bias in yield estimates, since genuine ASPVs producing 'yields' under the higher threshold are excluded. Comparisons between studies will also be hindered where each employs different thresholds.

A constant threshold over time also obscures changes in the costs that appraisers recognised. Allen notes that COPVs change during the seventeenth century. Typical early-century COPVs included costs of seed, and perhaps ploughing, but little else. After mid-century, COPVs often included seed, ploughing and the cost of dung (or other soil additions), and labour costs in ground preparation. For example, at Tothill (Romsey) in February 1695, appraisers recorded costs for 'the carrying out of dung and spreading' at £2 14s 0d, 'seed wheat upon the ground' at £5 0s 0d, and 'the sowing of the wheat crop' at £3 9s 0d.[25] Nevertheless, this tendency to more inclusive COPVs never becomes a universal phenomenon. The 1680s and 1690s provide numerous simple 'seed and ploughing' COPVs alongside more complex examples. In Hampshire in the 1690s, 46 per cent of wheat valuations were equivalent to under 5 bushels an acre, which hardly corroborates Allen's observation that COPVs were 'abandoned by the middle of the seventeenth century and thereafter deflated valuation was rarely less than 5 bushels per acre'.[26] And, of course, a threshold which increases over time makes it likely that the yields estimated will also increase over time. It seems preferable to retain a constant threshold for each crop, but to recognise that later yields may be slightly underestimated where they contain more COPVs.

25 HCRO inventory 1694/ad/12.
26 Allen, 'Inferring yields', p. 122.

To summarise. The overlapping distributions of COPVs and ASPVs mean that there can be no unambiguous separation of the two types of valuation. An appropriate threshold offers a basis for consistency, but must compromise between being set too high (excluding genuine, but low, ASPVs), and being set too low (incorporating COPVs). There are arguments for variable thresholds for different crops and time periods, but each alteration is at the cost of spatial and temporal comparability. In Section III, like Allen, thresholds have been used of 5 bushels an acre for wheat and barley throughout the study period, as opposed to 8 bushels an acre for oats, again throughout.

II.ii *Weighting of yield estimates for harvest years*
The use of constant thresholds affects the likelihood of valuations from different years being accepted as genuine ASPVs, because the thresholds exclude a varying proportion of inventories according to harvest quality. The overlap between distributions of COPVs and ASPVs varies with harvest quality. More inventories are likely to exceed the threshold from years when yields were high than from poor harvest years. For the latter there are more low ASPVs at similar values to COPVs, and they are eliminated by the threshold.

For example, Figure 10.1 compares histograms of valuations per acre converted to bushels for above-average and below-average wheat harvests in the 1680s and 1690s.[27] It strikingly demonstrates how the 5-bushels threshold excludes far more inventories from the poor harvest years, than from the good harvest years. This is important when period average yields are being calculated. The sample of valuations from a given period which pass the threshold will derive mainly from the above-average harvest years. The average of this sample is very likely to be higher than when the average yield calculated for each year is given equal weight in the calculation of a period average, but the latter is a truer reflection of mean yields. This pattern is clear from large-scale analysis, but not from Allen's small sample of Oxfordshire inventories.[28] Allen groups inventories in 25-year periods, but the largest of these samples contains just eight farms. The majority of years in each quarter-century cannot be represented at all, and it is possible that several inventories from a period date from the same year.[29] An

27 The 'above-average' harvest years are 1685, 1687, 1688 and 1694; the 'below-average' harvest years are 1693, 1695, 1697 and 1698.
28 Space precludes detailed elaboration of this point. A summary of relevant data can be obtained from the author if required.
29 Overton, below, p. 301.

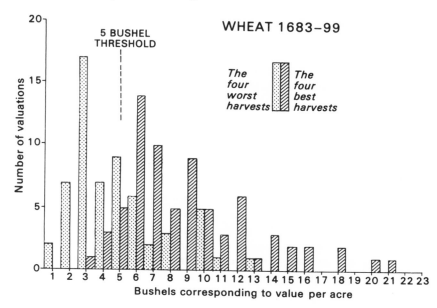

Figure 10.1 *Hampshire, 1683–99: wheat valuation equivalents per acre in bushels for good and bad harvest years from probate inventories*

alternative interpretation would be that imminent poor harvests made appraisers more 'defensive' when valuing standing crops. In other words, appraisers made cost-based valuations when they anticipated a poor harvest, in contrast to selling-price-based estimates when good harvests were expected. Yet this is unlikely since it would imply that different crops in the same inventory were valued in different ways.

Yield estimates should therefore be weighted to allow all years to contribute equally to a period average, to avoid overrepresentation of a disproportionate number of inventories from years with good harvests. It follows that where inventory samples are small, and represent only a few years within a period, a simple average 'yield' is susceptible to upward bias.

II.iii *Factors included in the equation*

Two elements of Equation 4 require scrutiny. The first applies equally to Equation 2. This is the distinction between 'crop' and grain. It is easy to overlook the fact that grain was not the only product from a growing arable crop. The major by-product was straw, although it was very much less valuable than grain. It may be presumed that per-acre valuations of standing crops normally took straw into account, since in a few inventories grain valuations specifically exclude the value of straw. Thus ASPVs may include the value of straw as well as grain, although straw is of low worth when valued on its own in inventories (its high market price reflects its bulk and hence high transport costs).[30] So Equations 2 and 4 will overstate yields where valuation per acre includes straw, although not by much.

Equation 4 also overestimates costs, and hence yields, because in the denominator the cost of dressing grain is deducted, along with threshing costs, from valuations of stored grain. Yet grain in barns is never referred to as dressed. Moreover, some grain in barns had not yet been threshed, so it is pointless to deduct estimated costs of threshing and dressing from the valuations of stored grain.[31] In Section III, no allowance is made for dressing grain under the heading threshing costs. Where valuations of stored crops refer to unthreshed grain, the denominator of Equation 4 will be too low, thus slightly overestimating y.[32] Both these features lead Allen's equation to overestimate yields, a tendency exacerbated by the mechanics of calculating costs.

II.iv *Estimating harvesting and other costs*

Several assumptions are made in estimating harvest costs retrospectively from 1806. These require closer examination than they have hitherto received, including evaluation against contemporary wage data. Inaccuracies in specifying wages have a straightforward impact on the yields estimated by Equation 4. If wage estimates are too high, yields will be overestimated. Conversely, underestimating wages means underestimating yields.

Allen's central assumption is that reaping, binding, and carting costs were constant per acre, independent of yield.[33] That 'the labour requirements of most tasks in cereal production depended on the acreage involved and not on the volume of grain harvested' is an eccentric view, albeit to some extent forced by the form in which Batchelor records wages. Batchelor gives wage rates *per acre* for carting,

---

30 Michael Turner made this point at the Bellagio conference.
31 From seventeenth-century farm accounts, grain was normally threshed shortly prior to its being taken to market, rather than following its arrival in the barn. If this was normal, the vast majority of valuations of stored grain are of unthreshed grain.
32 Overton's revised method differs by not including the threshing term. See below, p. 299.
33 Allen, 'Inferring yields', p. 119. The next quote is from *idem*, 'The growth of labour productivity', p. 139.

reaping, binding, and cutting haulm, but rates *per bushel* for threshing and dressing grain. Most other commentators related harvesting costs to yield. They thought that 'most harvest labour was for cutting and carting crops ... the necessary labour inputs depended more on the bushels of grain harvested than on the area harvested'.[34]

This is important because Batchelor actually states that his cost estimates are based on yields per acre of 25 bushels for wheat, 36 bushels for barley, and 40 bushels for oats.[35] So he does *not* claim that costs are independent of yield; he gives costs for one particular yield level. But by applying these costs to all yield levels, Allen builds into his estimates of seventeenth-century costs the assumption that yield levels were as high as in Batchelor's time. This causes Allen to overestimate wage costs. Seventeenth-century wage data (as distinct from schedules laid down by Justices of the Peace) are sparse, but can be found in farm accounts. For example, the mean wages paid by the Reverend John Crakanthorp for threshing and reaping at Fowlmere, Cambridgeshire, during the decade after 1700 were as follows: reaping wheat 36*d* an acre, threshing wheat 15*d* a quarter, threshing barley 9*d* a quarter, and threshing oats 8*d* a quarter.[36] Actual wages run well below the rates estimated using Allen's method, which are respectively 67.5*d*, 26.4*d*, 18.5*d*, and 16*d*. Allen's estimated harvesting costs are also much higher relative to grain prices in the seventeenth century than in 1806. At the latter date costs amounted to 12 per cent of the market price for wheat, 15 per cent for barley, and 19 per cent for oats. Yet his estimated seventeenth-century costs run at double this level. This is too high to be credible.

Since Batchelor states the yields he assumed, harvesting costs per bushel can be calculated from his data, and the implications of alternative yield assumptions explored. For example, if yields per acre were 16 bushels (rather than 25) for wheat, Equation 5 might be modified thus:

$$r_t = W_t / W_{1806} \cdot r_{1806} \cdot 16/25. \tag{6}$$

---

34 G. Clark, above, p. 222. The exact composition of harvesting costs may have changed over time because of changes in labour intensity, discussed by *idem*, 'Productivity growth without technical change in European agriculture before 1750', *JEH*, XLVII, 1987, pp. 422–4.

35 Batchelor, *County of Bedfordshire*, p. 112.

36 P. Brassley, A. Lambert and P. Saunders, eds., *Accounts of the Reverend John Crakanthorp of Fowlmere 1682–1710*, Cambridgeshire Records Society, VIII, 1988, pp. 121–265.

Similarly, if barley yield was 25 bushels an acre (rather than 36), and oats yield 30 bushels an acre (rather than 40), harvesting costs are estimated at 60–75 per cent of Allen's figures. These revised cost estimates, although still on the high side, correspond more closely to wage rates paid by farmers than do Allen's original estimates. The numerator of Equation 4 is thereby reduced, and the denominator increased, resulting in smaller yield estimates.

While this level of costs may be appropriate to early modern farms, the model still treats them as independent of yields, whereas costs were partly fixed and partly variable. A more realistic model would assume that certain fixed costs were incurred however meagre the harvest, and that above a certain point, increments in yield caused proportional extra costs. Equation 7 still utilises Batchelor's data, but takes 60 per cent of costs as fixed, which is consistent with the comments on costs made in other Board of Agriculture reports. Additional costs are incurred above thresholds of 10 bushels an acre for wheat and barley, and 15 bushels an acre for oats. Y_t from Equation 4 provides a first estimate of yield. Thus, for the reaping cost of wheat:

$$r_t = \frac{W_t}{W_{1806}} \cdot \left[0.6 r_{1806} + \left(\frac{Y_t - 10}{15} \cdot 0.4 r_{1806} \right) \right] \tag{7}$$

subject to the constraint that,

$$\frac{Y_t - 10}{15} \cdot 0.4 r_{1806} = 0 \quad \text{for } Y_t < 10$$

Other cost terms in Equation 4 can be estimated similarly, and Equations 4 and 7 iterated to reach stability. Costs are now treated partly as fixed, and partly as a function of yield. The cost estimates used in producing the Hampshire yields are shown in Table 10.1.

Equation 7 thus produces lower costs than Equation 5 and is more consistent with evidence on seventeenth-century wages. Consequently, using Equation 7 to calculate terms in Equation 4 produces lower yield estimates than Allen's method (see Table 10.2). However, the calculated costs still exceed those paid by Crakenthorp. If his costs were typical of arable farmers, the yields calculated by Equations 4 and 7 remain overestimates. In any case, equations which approximate empirical evidence on wages will only be relevant if appraisers took these costs fully into account when valuing growing crops. How, then, did appraisers recognise and conceptualise costs?

Table 10.1 *Costs used in revised calculations of Hampshire grain yields, 1600–99*

	Reaping (d per acre)		Carting (d per acre)		Threshing (d per bushel)
	[a]	[b]	[a]	[b]	
Wheat					
1600s	38.5	64.1	20.2	33.6	1.27
1620s	44.5	74.1	23.3	38.8	1.48
1640s	51.1	85.2	26.8	44.6	1.69
1660s	48.9	81.5	25.6	42.7	1.62
1680s	49.5	82.5	25.9	43.2	1.64
1690s	50.1	83.5	26.3	43.8	1.66
Barley					
1600s	15.9	26.5	23.8	39.7	0.90
1620s	18.4	30.6	27.5	45.9	1.04
1640s	21.1	35.2	31.6	52.7	1.19
1660s	20.2	33.7	30.3	50.5	1.13
1680s	20.5	34.2	30.7	51.1	1.15
1690s	20.8	34.6	31.1	51.8	1.16
Oats					
1600s	15.8	26.4	23.8	39.7	0.77
1620s	18.4	30.6	27.5	45.9	0.89
1640s	21.1	35.1	31.6	52.7	1.02
1660s	20.2	33.6	30.3	50.5	0.98
1680s	20.4	34.0	30.7	51.1	0.99
1690s	20.7	34.5	31.1	51.8	1.00

Notes

Two figures for reaping and carting costs are given to convey the two-part model of these costs discussed above and summarised in Equation 7. The figure under [a] represents the fixed costs of each operation, and are incurred regardless of yield, up to yields of 10 bushels per acre for wheat and barley, and of 15 bushels per acre for oats. Above these yields, further costs were incurred with rising yields. The figures under [b] represent the costs at the levels of yield assumed by Batchelor in 1806, that is to say, 25 bushels per acre for wheat, 36 bushels for barley, and 40 bushels for oats. Intermediate totals can easily be calculated from these figures.

Source See text.

K

II.v *Appraisers' perceptions of costs*

Is it reasonable to assume that appraisers perceived and took account of costs in the rather modern way described by Allen? It is clear from several aspects of inventories that appraisers were aware of costs, most obviously when they list costs in COPVs. The central question there-fore, is not whether they recognised costs at all, but whether they apprehended them at their actual level. The answer to this question affects yield estimates, since, if contemporaries underestimated the true level of costs compared with those being 'added back in', the yield estimates obtained will be too high even where real costs have been correctly determined. This question can be explored by comparing valuations for grain before and after particular processes with evidence on wages for the relevant tasks.

Whether stored grain is threshed or unthreshed is recorded in sufficient inventories in some years to compare valuations before and after threshing. There are even some inventories where separate valuations appear for threshed and unthreshed grains, although in several, threshed and unthreshed wheat and barley were given the same valuation![37] Differences between valuations can be compared with wages for threshing. Where valuations differed, threshed grains are valued more highly than unthreshed grains, but only by a few pence a quarter – below the actual wage rates which farmers paid. This comparison suggests that contemporaries made only a marginal incor-poration of threshing costs in valuing grain. Had they done otherwise, the difference between threshed and unthreshed valuations would have been greater.[38]

Another indicator of appraisers' perceptions are valuations in the form 'the wheat from 90 acres now in the barn'. These can be compared with near simultaneous valuations of standing crops (in some cases, an inventory from the same parish in the same month, with some of the appraisers in common). Of twenty-two such valuations of wheat, seven

37 They were presumably valued separately because they were in different places in the barns. Examples include HCRO inventories 1604/A/40 and 1689/ad/116.
38 There is scope, given abundant data, to explore this pattern further. Yields could be calculated using only unthreshed valuations in the Equation 4, and compared with calculations using only valuations of threshed grain minus threshing costs. Alternatively, the difference between mean unthreshed- and threshed-grain valuations could be used in the denominator, as a direct measure of perceived cost, instead of estimating a wage rate. The last suggestion might be appropriate if appraisers' allowances were lower than actual costs because they expected threshing to be done by annual servants, whose labour would not incur marginal costs at the rates of labourers' pay.

are more than 15 per cent above the year's mean valuation of standing crops in the same year, nine are above average by less, and six are below average. This pattern also suggests that appraisers recognised costs, but the former type of valuation did not exceed the latter by enough to indicate that costs were allowed for at their 'real' level.[39] Overall, it appears that contemporaries found identification of costs not unproblematic, and their allowances usually underestimate 'true' costs.

The arguments rehearsed in this section demonstrate that Allen's method overestimates costs. The lack of equal weighting for each year in a period causes good harvests to be overrepresented in the inventory sample. A variety of factors inflate the numerator in Equation 4 and decrease the denominator. The presence of some terms in the equation is unjustified, or insufficiently specified, and the cost elements are overestimated. In addition, appraisers incorporated costs at below their true level. Individually, some of these criticisms are minor, but all point in the same direction: Allen's method exaggerates costs, so yields are exaggerated also. The total scale of overestimation is considerable. In Section III, the revisions suggested in Sections II.i–iv have been applied.

III Crop yields in seventeenth-century Hampshire

This section presents results of a large-scale analysis of data from Hampshire, to set alongside existing case studies. Hampshire provides a useful study area. Much is already known about medieval yields in the county from the remarkable harvest record of the estates of the bishopric of Winchester, 24 of whose demesnes were located here.[40] These indicate generally low rates of yield both per acre and per seed.[41] Subsequently, the county is the classic location for E. L. Jones's influential account of the processes, chronology, and geography of early modern agricultural change.[42] Jones argues that the mid- and late-seventeenth-century depression in grain prices stimulated a range

---

39 An allowance for straw, as discussed in Subsection II.iii, has only a marginal effect on these figures.
40 Titow, *Winchester yields*; D. L. Farmer, 'Grain yields on the Winchester manors in the later middle ages', *EcHR*, XXX, 1977, pp. 555–66.
41 See K. Biddick, above, pp. 95–8.
42 E. L. Jones, *Agriculture and economic growth in England, 1650–1815*, London, 1967; *idem, Agriculture and the industrial revolution*, Oxford, 1974. See also R. V. Jackson, 'Growth and deceleration in English agriculture, 1660–1790', *EcHR*, XXXVI, 1985, pp. 333–51.

of responses, including changing land-use specialisations and innovations designed to raise arable crop yields. Farmers whose income was being threatened were forced into these changes to avoid impoverishment. Which changes occurred where, and hence the geographical pattern of changes, reflected both ecological settings (how feasible were alternative product specialisms?) and local social institutions (for example, the degree of enclosure and of co-operative constraints on individual behaviour). However, Jones's work was based mainly on records of large estates and contemporary observation, with only limited anecdotal use of inventories to examine the more typical farms of yeomen and husbandmen which concern this paper.

Opportunity exists alongside motive: a huge volume of probate documents survive for Hampshire. The information analysed here comes from an examination of over 7,500 inventories, from the periods 1600–09, 1620–28, 1640–46, 1660–69, 1683–99 and 1690–1700.[43] Of course, only a minority referred to active farmers during the summer months. Over 1,500 inventories provide valuations of standing crops, while a larger number provide valuations of stored grain. Like Allen, farms with fewer than ten arable acres are disregarded, to prevent smallholdings obscuring trends amongst farms.

Table 10.2 summarises wheat, barley, and oat yields during the seventeenth century. Figures are given for yields by Overton's original method, by Allen's method, and by the revised method described above. In comparison with Overton's original 1979 method, Allen's method produces yields which are on average 59 per cent higher than yields for wheat, 58 per cent higher for barley, and no less than 92 per cent higher for oats: the equivalent figures for the revised method are 35 per cent, 38 per cent, and 54 per cent respectively.[44] Yields per sown acre increased substantially between the 1600s and 1680s, less so for oats than for wheat and barley, but the 1690s are a sharp reminder

43 The surviving Hampshire probate archives are very extensive, covering a large area (consisting not only of the mainland county and the Isle of Wight, but also of parts of Surrey and a small area of Wiltshire) over a long period (from before 1550 until the 1710s, after which date the volume of material is much diminished). This study uses inventories from both archdeaconry and consistory courts of the Winchester diocese, and also draws on inventories preserved in the files of administrations.

44 The additions for individual decades using Allen's method range from 51–64 per cent for wheat, to 49–66 per cent for barley, and 75–110 per cent for oats. The equivalent figures for the revised method are 22–44 per cent, 32–44 per cent, and 38–72 per cent respectively.

Table 10.2 *Alternative estimates of Hampshire crop yields, 1600–99 (bushels per sown acre)*

	Net	Allen	Revised	N
Wheat				
1600–09	8.0	13.1	11.1	83
1619–28	9.1	14.5	12.2	53
1639–46	9.1	15.1	12.2	49
1659–69	10.2	15.4	14.1	46
1683–89	11.0	16.9	15.8	27
1690–99	8.6	13.8	10.5	49
Barley				
1600–09	9.3	15.4	13.4	65
1619–28	12.4	19.5	16.4	42
1639–46	11.2	18.0	15.4	40
1659–69	13.1	19.5	17.7	37
1683–89	14.7	22.7	20.1	23
1690–99	10.6	16.9	14.7	49
Oats				
1600–09	10.9	23.9	18.7	56
1619–28	12.1	24.0	19.4	33
1639–46	12.3	23.9	19.3	36
1659–69	14.6	25.8	21.1	26
1683–89	16.0	28.0	22.1	14
1690–99	11.8	23.1	17.7	28
Equations	(2)	(4)+(5)	(4)+(7)	

Note N is the number of yield estimates.

Source See text.

that extreme weather conditions could still wreak havoc with the harvest.[45]

Figures representing average yields per acre over periods of several years have obvious utility in the investigation of long-term trends in crop yields. But there are considerable benefits in examining results from single years, albeit with caution where samples rarely exceed 20 inventories per crop per year. Annual yields can provide clues about how long-term increases were achieved. Higher yields might

45 Overton, 'Weather and agricultural change'.

result from a reduced incidence of very poor harvests, or from an increase in production in abundant harvests, or less dramatically from an increase in the produce of near-average harvests. Which patterns underlie long-term changes in yields may have implications for the mechanisms responsible.

There are differences among the crops, but at no stage were really poor harvests absent. Even in the 1680s, when the highest decadal average yields were recorded, the worst harvest years were poor by any historical standard, especially for wheat and oats. Higher average crop yields did not at this time bring with them an escape from the risk of periodic very poor harvests. Yield improvements in years of difficult conditions contributed little to raising long-term average yields. By contrast, there were dramatic increases in yields in the better harvests each decade, at least before the 1690s. Better 'good' harvests, together with improvements in 'near-average' harvests (especially for barley), contributed to long-term yield increases.

Results from single years also provide a check on the plausibility of the results obtained. It would obviously be disconcerting to find that high yields are estimated for harvests following which prices were high, and low yields for harvests after which prices were low. For periods in which there was no clear secular trend in the general price level, estimated yields can be compared with prices. Given that stored grain also influenced market supply, that inventoried grain might vary widely in quality, and that the market was far from perfect, some variation can be expected in the relation between the two. It is therefore reassuring that, when estimated yield is plotted against wheat prices at Winchester for the periods 1660–69 and 1683–99, a familiar pattern emerges whereby deviations below normal yields produce price increases larger than the price falls which follow abundant harvests.[46]

Disaggregating further, the pattern of yields can be explored at the level of individual farms. This is a second area where Allen's approach advances Overton's focus on groups of inventories. The chief attraction of focusing on individual inventories is in uncovering patterns of association between yields and other attributes of farms. In this way, the 'ecological problem' to which simple comparisons of groups of inventories (for example, from particular decades or particular districts)

---

46 E. A. Wrigley, 'Some reflections on corn yields and prices in pre-industrial economies', pp. 92–130 in *idem, People, cities and wealth: the transformation of traditional society,* Oxford, 1987.

are prone, can be avoided.[47] This is because associations between farm characteristics at aggregate level need not be produced by associations on individual farms.

One way of investigating this is by grouping farms according to particular features and comparing the yields of the different groups. A comparison of yields on farms with fodder crops and those without during the period 1683–99 is consistent with the belief that fodder-crop innovations produced higher yields (though whether innovations actually caused higher yields merits more detailed investigation). Figure 10.2 demonstrates that yields were higher for those farms devoting an above-average proportion of their farm enterprise to fodder crops. Yet, as in other areas, the yield increases of the seventeenth century were clearly not a simple product of the oft-stressed new fodder crops and leguminous grasses. Turnips occurred only extremely infrequently in seventeenth-century Hampshire inventories. New grass substitutes were more numerous, but also appeared too late and over too restricted an area to have brought about these yield increases. Other explanations must be sought. When farms are classified according to the capital balance of crops, fodder, and various livestock, it transpires that high yields characterised relatively large mixed farms, especially grain–cattle farms, with some fodder. Further analysis of this type is important in corroborating or modifying the views of many agrarian historians, who stress particular types of farm as pivotal to agricultural progress. For example, the large sheep–corn farms emphasised by Jones (group D in Figure 10.2) do not appear to have achieved higher yields than other farms at this time.

A second strategy is to regress yields on attributes of farms such as size, livestock density, and crop mix, as suggested by Allen.[48] In such cases, however, large bodies of data are needed so that regression models can be specified for individual years. If farms from several years of differing harvest quality are mixed, variations in harvest quality will be a major source of variation in yields, and it will not be surprising if relationships between yields and farm attributes seem weak or non-existent.[49] Nor can the ecological problem be entirely avoided in

---

47 The ecological fallacy is defined as 'The problem of inferring characteristics of individuals from aggregate data referring to a population': R. J. Johnston, D. J. Gregory and D. M. Smith, eds., *The dictionary of human geography*, Oxford, 2nd edn., 1986, p. 115.
48 Allen, above, pp. 246–9.
49 See Overton, below, pp. 309–14.

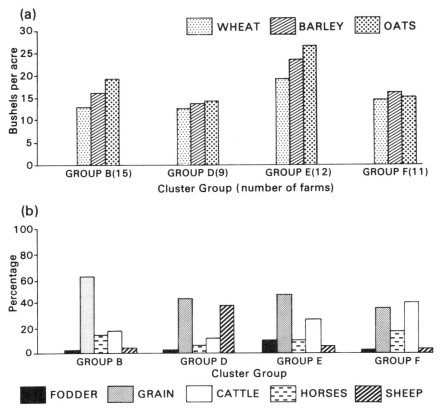

Figure 10.2 *Hampshire, 1683–99: (a) farm types and grain yields, and (b) farm-type characteristics*

exploring the determinants of yields. Because each inventory refers to one particular time of year, some types of information (for example, husbandry practices specific to a particular season) are only found in inventories at certain times. Yet yields can only be estimated from summer inventories. Necessary though examination of the relationship between the two is, it is only possible at an aggregate level by, for example, comparing their respective geographical patterns.[50]

50 For example, Glennie, 'Continuity and change II', pp. 152–5; Overton, below, p. 316.

IV Towards a regional geography of crop yields

Long-term improvements in understanding of agricultural change are likely to come from increasingly sensitive disaggregations of farms and their productivity by locality, social and economic status, and type of farm enterprise. In the meanwhile, some assessment of current views on the timing and geography of agricultural productivity change can be made at the scale of county units. Given the widespread survival of probate inventories in large numbers, it might be supposed that comparable exercises would constitute the basis for systematic maps of early modern English yields. Whether increasing regional product-specialisation was associated with regional divergences in yields might thereby be investigated. For example, did improved yields derive from higher productivity in areas of heightened specialisation, or from the operation of comparative advantage consequent upon growing spatial integration?[51]

Unfortunately, the scope for comprehensive maps is limited by more than inventory survival. Many collections of inventories include a narrower range of detail about crops than might be wished. The Weald, Cumbria, and Lancashire are the most notable of a number of areas abundantly represented by extant inventories for which there is little prospect of applying some form of the Overton–Allen method.[52] The deficiency lies in the fact that few inventories distinguish, quantify, and separately value specific types of grain. As a broad guide, growing or stored crops were individually distinguished in valuations only in areas of commercial grain farming. Comparisons between yields in commercial grain-producing areas and elsewhere are likely to founder because the inventories from less commercial areas are insufficiently detailed.

In order to facilitate comparison with Oxfordshire, the results for Hampshire and Hertfordshire have been recalculated using Allen's method. When this is done a striking contrast emerges between Oxfordshire and the other two counties. Yields in the latter were significantly lower in the late seventeenth century than in *c.*1800: given

---

51 See Overton and Campbell, above, pp. 19–22.
52 M. Zell, 'A wood pasture agrarian regime: Wealden agriculture in the sixteenth century', *Southern History*, VII, 1985, pp. 69–93; J. Marshall, 'Agrarian wealth and social structure in pre-industrial Cumbria', *EcHR*, XXXIII, 1980, pp. 503–21; J. Swain, *Industry before the industrial revolution: north-east Lancashire, c.1500–1640*, Chetham Society, 3rd series, XXXII, Manchester, 1986, chapter 2.

Table 10.3 *A comparison of Hertfordshire, Hampshire and Oxfordshire grain yields using Allen's method, 1550–1800 (bushels per acre)*

	Wheat			Barley		
	Oxon	*Hants*	*Herts*	*Oxon*	*Hants*	*Herts*
1550–74			12.0	12.9		16.3
1575–99	15.0			15.2		
1580–1609			13.5			15.5
1600–24	14.5			14.5		
1600s		13.1			15.4	
1610–39			12.1			16.2
1620s		14.5			19.5	
1625–49	13.1			13.6		
1640s		15.0			18.0	
1640–69			17.4			19.7
1650–74	14.8			17.8		
1660s		15.4			19.5	
1675–99	21.8		19.0	24.9		28.3
1680s		16.9			22.7	
1690s		13.8			16.9	
1700–27	21.5			18.3		
*c.*1800	22.0	21.0	24.0	30.0	30.0	36.0

Note
These are calculated according to Allen's method and are therefore different to the yields in Table 10.2 and Figure 1.2.

Source
1550–1727 probate inventories, see text. *Circa* 1800: M. E. Turner, 'Agricultural productivity in England in the eighteenth century: evidence from crop yields', *EcHR*, XXXV, 1982, pp. 489–510.

the exact comparability in method of estimation there can be little doubt that the shortfall is genuine. Moreover, as Table 10.2 demonstrates, this gap is 25–40 per cent larger when the modifications recommended in Section II are implemented.

Allen's chronology of yield increases, and his two-phase productivity increase, are thus undermined even on his own method. Either the experience of Oxfordshire is exceptional, or Allen's result is a distortion produced by a tiny sample. On the revised method, Allen's claim no longer holds even for Oxfordshire. The notion that 'we can conceive of productivity growth in early modern English agriculture as a two part development' is at best an over-simplified, and at worst a misleading, guide to trends in crop yields.[53]

V Crop yields and arable land productivity

Yet a further complication is that the productivity of arable land depends on much more than yields per sown acre of particular crops. Even if the problems outlined in Section II could be avoided, we would still be some way from understanding land productivity. As medievalists led by B. M. S. Campbell have demonstrated, there are numerous interposing factors.[54] Key influences on arable-land productivity include the frequency with which land is cultivated, the mix of crops grown and their relative importance, changes in the extent of the cultivated arable area, plus, of course, the output of livestock and animal products directly or indirectly supported by the arable.[55] Inventory data alone, referring to farms at a single instant, cannot illuminate some important factors, and can address others only indirectly.

The frequency of cultivation as opposed to fallowing is perhaps the most important. If land is cultivated four years out of five, rather than two years out of three, with no reduction in yields, land productivity has been substantially enhanced. Some important changes in agricultural practice involve longer rotations, rather than higher yields per sown acre. For example, it may be premature to write off the importance of pulses, on the grounds of a poor correlation with yields per acre. If leguminous crops replaced fallow courses in rotations, and yields per sown acre of other crops held up, legumes were contributing to higher land productivity by enabling land to be cropped more often.[56]

Rotational changes are also important because changes in the position of particular crops within rotations have consequences for their yield. For example, the inventory of a Hertfordshire yeoman in 1671 values 'tilth barley' (barley sown following fallowing and ground preparation) at £2 3s 4d an acre, while 'edge barley' (barley

---

53 Allen, 'The growth of labour productivity', p. 143.
54 Campbell, 'Agricultural progress', pp. 28–35; *idem*, 'Arable productivity', pp. 390–6.
55 See P. Solar and M. Goossens, below, p. 372.
56 Allen, above, p. 247; G. P. H. Chorley, 'The agricultural revolution in northern Europe, 1750–1880: nitrogen, legumes, and crop productivity', *EcHR*, XXXIV, 1981, pp. 71–93.

sown following a previous crop) was worth £1 6s 8d an acre.[57] Similarly, medievalists have explained changing yields per sown acre as
consequences of changes in rotations.[58] Some changes in seventeenth-
century yields probably reflect this sort of changing practice. Unfortunately, it is difficult to investigate rotations from inventories, and
indeed from most early modern sources.

The mix of crops grown is significant where the yields of different
arable crops are changing at different rates. It is then possible for
farmers to increase the productivity of their arable by converting land
from crops whose yields are stationary or increasing only slowly, to
those which are growing more rapidly. In both East Anglia and
Hertfordshire, for example, farmers expanded their barley cultivation
after *c*.1660, at a time when barley yields were increasing more rapidly
than those of wheat, oats and rye.[59] Information on crop acreages is
available from a sizeable minority of probate inventories, so this factor
is easier to investigate.

Changes in the extent of the arable area, *especially at the level of the
individual farm*, will also affect yields if the choice of land to till is
related to 'land quality'.[60] Comparisons between individual farms at
different times may not be comparing like with like. Aggregate measures
are more robust in this regard, since the scale of yield changes across
a large sample of farms which could be produced by shedding land
from, or adding land to, the arable area is limited. Estate documentation, field books, and surveys can provide an indication of broad
trends in the arable extent.

Overall, then, to suppose that yields per sown acre of various
crops equate directly to 'arable productivity' is a considerable oversimplification. The identification of trends in crop yields per sown acre
is a significant step forward, but it is not an answer to questions about
overall land productivity. These new yield estimates form only a starting
point for a synthesis of all the factors affecting arable land productivity.

57 HCRO inventory H23/448.
58 For oats, Campbell, above, p. 164, and for barley, D. L. Farmer, 'Grain yields on
   Westminster Abbey manors, 1271–1410', *Canadian Journal of History*, XVIII, 1983,
   pp. 344–5.
59 Overton, 'Agricultural revolution?', pp. 130–1; Glennie, 'Continuity and change
   II', p. 147.
60 'Land quality' is placed in quotes to indicate that it is a contextually-dependent
   property of parcels of land, not an absolute and unchanging property. Thus the
   quality of land could vary over time as technology changed, or to some extent,
   depending on the size and resources of the farm of which it was part.

VI Concluding comments

Claims that absolute levels of crop yields can be simply and reliably calculated from probate inventory valuations and estimated costs are exaggerated. A range of inherent and contingent problems are encountered. But whilst estimating absolute yields is difficult and uncertain, it is neither so difficult nor so uncertain that the results are arbitrary or meaningless. Inventory-based studies of yields are potentially very valuable at both aggregate and individual levels of investigation. They can assist in establishing trends in yields, the relations between yield increases and other sources of increased land productivity, and the institutional and geographical settings of productivity gains. All these facets of agricultural productivity contribute to an ability to make inferences about the *causes* of the long-term increases in agricultural productivity that were central to English economic development.

There remains considerable scope for comparable analyses. For example, the rise of specialised agricultural localities in association with proto-industrial textiles and metalworking is well documented, but little is known of yields or other productivity measures there.[61] Unfortunately, it may prove difficult to investigate yields in less commercial grain economies, since specific crops were rarely quantified and valued separately in inventories. For future comparative analyses, four refinements to Allen's method are recommended: the use of larger samples of inventories; critical appraisal of actual and perceived costs (which may be very difficult); equal weighting of data from each year in the periods over which yields are averaged; and exploration of the sensitivity of results to different thresholds for the exclusion of suspected 'cost of production' valuations. It is unlikely that all the uncertainties involved in calculating and explaining yields will ever be resolved, but this is precisely why a critical examination of the methods of analysis is important.

Analysis of data from individual inventories enables detailed exploration of both the geography of yields and the temporal, spatial, and socio-economic correlates of variations in them. Nevertheless, to advocate individual-level analyses as an advance on exploratory aggregate

---

61 P. Large, 'Urban growth and agricultural change in the west midlands during the seventeenth and eighteenth centuries', pp. 169–89 in P. Clark, ed., *The transformation of English towns, 1600–1800*, London, 1984; P. Kriedte, H. Medick and J. Schlumbohm, *Industrialisation before industrialisation*, Cambridge, 1981, pp. 24–5; P. Kriedte, *Peasants, landlords and merchant capitalists: Europe and the world economy, 1500–1800*, Leamington Spa, 1983, p. 160.

studies is in no way an argument for the use of minute samples of information. Those who urge 'farm reconstitution' analogous to family reconstitution need to remember that it is micro-level detail and large volumes of data in combination which are valuable, not the former alone. Also, as has been seen from debates on appropriate frameworks for regression models, the limits of legitimate inference in the analysis of data from populations of individual inventories are still uncertain. Further substantive studies can do much to clarify them.

Amongst aggregate-scale studies thus far, a relatively consistent picture of yield trends is appearing. This pattern features substantial yield increases at various times during the seventeenth and early eighteenth centuries, but with further increases still to come before *c.*1800. Even using Allen's original method, with its upward bias, yields in three major areas of commercial grain farming *c.*1700 were significantly below their levels in the parliamentary reports of the 1790s, the 1801 crop returns, and the tithe commutations of the 1830s. His conclusion that improvements in crop yields in the eighteenth century did not take place cannot be sustained.

Revising current ideas about trends in yields has implications for explanations of their causes. The chronologies of yield increases and of agricultural innovations suggest that the former were not produced by the latter for most of the seventeenth century. New fodder crops (such as turnips) and grass substitutes (such as clover) were innovated too late, over too small an area, and in too small quantities to have been responsible. This does not deny the fact that on some individual farms they were beginning to be associated with higher yields, and may well have increased in importance thereafter.[62] The eighteenth century consequently remains important for three reasons. First, there is direct evidence of increasing yields.[63] Second, estimated yields *c.*1700 imply further increases before *c.*1800 linked to more effective systems of cycling soil nitrogen.[64] Finally, other developments raised land productivity without raising yield per sown acre.

The results indicate that the simple picture of a two-phase 'agricultural revolution', with increases in crop yields confined to the period prior to 1700, cannot be sustained. In the areas examined here, both the seventeenth and the eighteenth centuries witnessed substantial gains in crop yields, although these may have had different causes. It

---

62 Figure 10.2; Overton, below, pp. 312–14.
63 Overton, below, pp. 301–5.
64 See R. Shiel, above, pp. 62–75.

is undeniable that substantial yield increases were obtained by a yeoman tenantry prior to the vigorous eighteenth-century enclosure movement. Allen's point that a yeoman tenantry was not an insuperable barrier to certain increases in land productivity is well made. However, to argue that crop yields remained stagnant through the eighteenth century is as unjustifiable as earlier views which dogmatically ruled out higher yields before the mid eighteenth century because of monocausal assumptions about the preconditions for agricultural growth.

Crop yields rose in several phases during the early modern period. These phases of rising yields seem to have had various causes and varying ecological, social and geographical impacts. Improved methods of estimating yields can help to elucidate these impacts, as a step towards specifying and interpreting the relative importance of causes of higher yields. In this way it may prove possible to uncover exactly how yields were increased under various conditions of landowning structure and property rights. Furthermore, in so far as views on English agricultural and industrial revolutions influence contemporary preconceptions about agricultural development in general, the conclusion of this particular historical debate is unlikely to be without its lessons. Already it is clear that monocausal theories of the determinants of agricultural productivity should be rejected as a basis for either 'historical truth' or 'development myths'.

The determinants of crop yields in early modern England

In 1795 William Marshall wrote: 'No dung – no turnips – no bullocks – no barley – no clover – nor ... wheat'.[1] He was describing a rotation that became known as the Norfolk four-course which was regarded by contemporary agricultural writers as responsible for unprecedented improvements in crop yields and farm output. It is not surprising therefore, that the rotation is regarded by historians as the cornerstone of an 'agricultural revolution' which took place in north-western Europe, although their analyses of the rotation have rarely advanced beyond Marshall's description.[2] Indeed, their emphasis on the Norfolk four-course as the means of raising crop yields has led to the neglect of the many other ways by which grain yields may have been improved during the early modern period.

This chapter is an attempt to redress the balance, by examining the influences on land productivity – output per unit area – in the early modern period. The issue is tackled from two directions. First, possible influences on crop yields are considered in general terms utilising the findings of agronomists which are applicable to early

I am grateful to the participants at the Bellagio conference for their comments on the original draft of this paper and owe particular thanks to Robert Shiel, Paul Glennie and Bruce Campbell. My apologies to those participants whose advice I have stubbornly ignored. Some work included in this chapter was carried out during a Social Science Research Council Grant, D00242003 held during 1984–85. The Lincolnshire data were collected with the help of an Economic and Social Research Council grant B00232211 held during 1987–89. I am grateful to Brenda Webster and Linda Crust for gathering material from the Lincolnshire inventories, and to Meemee Wong for 'cleaning' the data for Norfolk and Suffolk. I must also thank the University of Newcastle for a contribution towards travel expenses.

1 W. Marshall, *The rural economy of Norfolk*, 2 vols., London, 1787, I, pp. 262–3.
2 The most important exception is G. P. H. Chorley, 'The agricultural revolution in northern Europe, 1750–1880: nitrogen, legumes and crop productivity', *EcHR*, XXXIV, 1981, pp. 71–93. See also M. Overton, 'Agricultural revolution? Development of the agrarian economy in early modern England', pp. 118–39 in A. R. H. Baker and D. J. Gregory, eds., *Explorations in historical geography: interpretative essays*, Cambridge, 1984, pp. 125–6.

modern farming systems. The Norfolk four-course rotation is discussed, but in the context of a more general model of the determinants of crop yields. Second, new evidence of crop yields and farm enterprises from Norfolk, Suffolk and Lincolnshire is presented, and the attempt is made to relate changes in yields to changes in farming practice as far as historical sources will allow. This new evidence is derived from probate inventories, but for the first time crop and livestock statistics from inventories are compared with two nineteenth-century surveys; the tithe files of the 1830s and the agricultural statistics collected for Norfolk and Suffolk in 1854. The chapter concludes by bringing the empirical and the more theoretical material together in an exploration of how changes in East Anglian grain yields and output may have come about from the sixteenth to the nineteenth centuries.

I Influences on output per acre

Figure 11.1 is an attempt to represent the orthodox view of how output per acre ('productivity' in the diagram) was brought about by the introduction of two new fodder crops, turnips and clover. Part (a) shows the situation in the period before innovation. Productivity is taken to be a direct reflection of the fertility of the soil, which can be maintained through applications of animal manure and from the 'rest' provided by the fallow period. The quantity of manure is seen as a function of the amount of pasture and meadow, and also of the amount of fallow.[3] Part (b) indicates what happens when the fallow is replaced by turnips and clover. The two new crops now provide extra supplies of fodder thereby increasing the quantity of manure available and hence raising fertility. Moreover, since clover is a legume it contributes directly to fertility by fixing atmospheric nitrogen into the soil. Fallow can be replaced because of these extra sources of fertility, and because turnips are a 'cleaning' crop, meaning that the land can still be kept weed-free while they are being grown.

Important though this rotation was, it was not the only means of raising output per acre. Before discussing it in more detail it is therefore necessary to consider some of the other determinants of yields in the early modern period. It is convenient to divide these into two categories: those over which farmers had some control and those over which they did not. In the latter category by far the most important, as today, is the weather, or, in the longer term, climate.

3 W. Harwood Long, 'The low yields of corn in medieval England', *EcHR*, XXXII, 1979, pp. 464–5, discusses the meanings of the term 'fallow'.

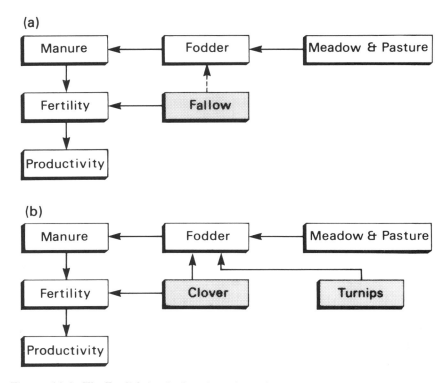

Figure 11.1 *The English 'agricultural revolution'*

Historians of agricultural change in England have paid relatively little attention to the influences of weather and climate on changes in farming practice.[4] The relationships between weather and yields in East Anglia in the early modern period has been the subject of a recent paper which concluded that the effects of the so-called 'Little Ice Age' on farm enterprises in Norfolk and Suffolk may have been considerable, particularly towards the end of the seventeenth century. Low grain yields in the 1690s can be directly related to wet winters and cool summers, and a fall in the mean herd size for both sheep and cattle at the same time may also have been related to the weather more indirectly through a reduction in fodder supplies and the increased

4 Exceptions are E. L. Jones, *Seasons and prices: the role of the weather in English agricultural history*, London, 1964, and P. J. Bowden, 'Agricultural prices, wages, farm profits and rents', pp. 593–695 in Thirsk, *The agrarian history of England and Wales*, Vii, *1640–1750: agrarian change*, 1985, pp. 45–62.

incidence of disease, especially for sheep. Of more significance is the possibility that bad weather could have prompted lasting changes in farm enterprises by encouraging farmers to introduce new fodder crops in order to mitigate the consequences of a failure in conventional fodder supplies.[5]

While farmers could do nothing to alter the weather, there was a wide range of influences on output per acre over which they did have some control. Figure 11.2 is an attempt to indicate those of most relevance in an early modern context. It does not aim to be comprehensive, and for the sake of clarity the diagram does not show all the links between the elements; rather, it is designed to stress the range of influences on output per acre and thus direct attention to the ways in which output might have been increased through changes in husbandry practice.[6] The elements in Figure 11.2 will be discussed firstly in general terms, and secondly with reference to historical evidence of farming practice.

As with Figure 11.1, the application of manure and the presence of a fallow are seen as contributing directly to soil fertility. Manure provides crop nutrients (mainly nitrates) while a bare fallow also results in the addition of nitrogen to the soil through the action of soil bacteria.[7] The more important role of the fallow, however, (especially a bare fallow), lies in removing weeds (particularly perennial ones) which compete with crops and hence lower output per acre. Increasing the quantity of manure has little benefit unless the acidity of the soil can be controlled since this determines the extent to which crop nutrients can be taken up by growing crops. Acid soils also inhibit the bacterial action which breaks down farmyard manure, and can severely

---

5 M. Overton, 'Weather and agricultural change in England, 1660–1739', *Agricultural History*, LXIII, 1989, pp. 77–88.

6 The following is based on a selection of farming texts which describe nineteenth-century farming practice. Thus they incorporate the scientific discoveries about fertility made during that century, but are not tainted with the methods of late-twentieth-century farming. They include; R. Patrick Wright, ed., *The standard cyclopaedia of modern agriculture and rural economy*, 12 vols., London, 1908; W. Fream, *Elements of agriculture*, London, 2nd edn., 1892; J. A. S. Watson and R. A. More, *Agriculture: the science and practice of British farming*, London, 11th edn., 1962 (1st edn., 1924); A. D. Hall, *Fertilisers and manures*, London, 1909; E. J. Russell, *The fertility of the soil*, Cambridge, 1913; R. Ede, *The principles of agriculture*, London, 1945.

7 R. S. Loomis, 'Ecological dimensions of medieval agrarian systems: an ecologist responds', *Agricultural History*, LII, 1978, pp. 480–1. H. V. Garner and G. V. Dyke, 'The Broadbalk yields', *Rothamsted Experimental Station Report for 1968*, Harpenden, 1969, pp. 26–49.

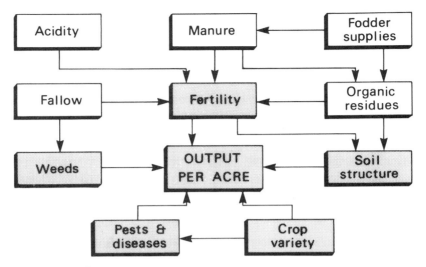

Figure 11.2 *Influences on crop output per acre*

inhibit the development of certain crops. Management of soil acidity is also a means of controlling certain crop diseases.[8]

In addition to recycling nitrogen through animals, crops can also contribute to soil fertility more directly through the organic residues they leave in the soil. Organic residues improve soil structure by providing a favourable environment for soil bacteria which release nitrogen, and by assisting in both drainage and the retention of moisture. Crops can therefore benefit from additional nitrogen, from a better moisture balance, and from deeper root penetration. The soil structure can also be improved by other means such as deep ploughing, more frequent cultivations, and by improving drainage with surface or deep drains.

The impact of the two remaining factors in Figure 11.2 has been considerable in the twentieth century but the extent of their influence before 1850 is uncertain. It is estimated that a fifth of the world's grain output is currently lost to pests and diseases and it is obvious that such losses must also have been considerable in the past, probably exceeding

8 H. W. Gardner and H. V. Garner, *The use of lime in British agriculture*, London, 1953.

this proportion.[9] Finally, although crop variety is by far the most important factor determining yield today, the extent of its significance in the past is also uncertain.[10]

Given the nature of the historical record it is impossible to quantify the effects of these influences on yields in the past, or even to assess their relative importance. Nevertheless, it is possible to demonstrate how early modern farmers adopted a variety of strategies to maintain or increase yields through the mechanisms suggested by Figure 11.2.[11]

Most agricultural writers of the early modern period list at some length the varieties of manures or fertilisers that could be added to the land.[12] They include such things as bones, rags, seaweed and malt dust, though there is no way of knowing the extent to which these more esoteric substances were used. Nor is there much information about the ways in which orthodox manure supplies were employed. If livestock grazed permanent pasture then their manure would fertilise the grass but would have no effect on arable land. Rotating grass around the farm would give some benefit to arable crops, as would moving the animals from pasture to arable at night.[13] Most productive of all would have been a move to stall-feeding livestock, particularly cattle, so that their manure could be collected and deposited where it was needed.[14] Some farmers might also have grown crops to provide green manure simply to be ploughed in for the benefit of a following crop. Buckwheat, for example, was introduced into East Anglian farming in the fifteenth and sixteenth centuries and came to be grown quite widely in eastern

9 D. B. Grigg, *The dynamics of agricultural change*, London, 1982, p. 125.
10 V. Silvey, 'The contribution of new varieties to increasing cereal yield in England and Wales', *Journal of the National Institute of Agricultural Botany*, XIV, 1975, pp. 367–84; D. G. Dalrymple, 'Changes in wheat varieties and yields in the United States, 1919–1984', *Agricultural History*, CXII, 1988, pp. 20–36.
11 The best general discussion is J. Thirsk, 'Farming techniques', pp. 161–99 in *idem, The agrarian history of England and Wales*, IV, *1500–1640*, 1967. See also R. V. Lennard, 'English agriculture under Charles II', *Economic History Review*, IV, 1932, pp. 23–45. G. E. Fussell, *Crop nutrition: science and practice before Liebig*, Lawrence, Kansas, 1971, describes the scientific principles which underlay contemporary understanding.
12 J[ohn] W[orlidge], *Systema agriculturae*, London, 4th edn., 1697, pp. 66–85. See also E. Kerridge, *The agricultural revolution*, London, 1967, pp. 240–4.
13 R. Shiel, above, pp. 62–7. Historians have documented many examples of such systems, particularly for sheep. J. Thirsk, 'The farming regions of England', pp. 1–112 in *idem, Agrarian history* IV; Kerridge, *Agricultural revolution*; Thirsk, *Agrarian history Vi: regional farming systems*.
14 B. A. Holderness, 'East Anglia and the fens', pp. 197–238 in Thirsk, *Agrarian history* Vi, pp. 234–6, describes the early development of the stall-feeding of bullocks.

Norfolk.[15] Although there is little evidence of how the crop was used, agricultural writers considered it was often grown as green manure.[16]

One of the most problematic issues is that of crop variety. Scientific plant breeding is a twentieth-century phenomenon, but farmers in the early modern period were certainly aware of the benefits of selecting seed. Contemporaries described several types of wheat: John Houghton devoted several issues of his *Collections* to the description of wheat and quotes Robert Plot who described thirteen varieties being grown in Oxford.[17] The notion that certain varieties were more suited to certain types of land seems to have been well established, as was the principle that fresh seed should be bought on to the farm fairly frequently.[18] Random mutations must have produced more productive varieties of cereal crops and it is likely that farmers would have selected these in preference to others. The development of Chevallier barley by this process of selection in the early nineteenth century is described by P. Pusey.[19] What impact this had on cereal yields remains an open question, although R. C. Allen suggests that improved seeds might have been responsible for a rise in grain yields in seventeenth-century Oxfordshire.[20]

Not only was the proportion of land under fallow being reduced from the sixteenth century onwards, but evidence also suggests that fallows were being cultivated more carefully, and not simply left as a mass of weeds for livestock to forage. Evidence from probate inventories, for example, indicates that as the seventeenth century progressed farmers were increasing the cultivations of their land, and P. Glennie has concluded from his recent study of Hertfordshire that higher yields may have been due to more careful and systematic ground and seed-bed preparation.[21] Inventories also indicate the spread of iron-shod

---

15 M. Overton and B. M. S. Campbell, 'Five centuries of farming: agricultural change in medieval and early modern Norfolk, *c.*1250–*c.*1750', unpublished paper presented to the Annual Conference of the Economic History Society, Liverpool, 1990. Table 11.8 below.

16 Worlidge, *Systema agriculturae*, p. 41. It was also used as food for poultry.

17 J. Houghton, *A collection for the improvement of husbandry and trade*, IV, number 77, London, 1695. See also IV, numbers 85 and 86.

18 Worlidge, *Systema agriculturae*, pp. 39 and 56; D. Woodward, ed., *The farming and memorandum books of Henry Best of Elmswell, 1642*, Records of Social and Economic History, new series, VIII, London, 1984, pp. 48 and 92; Lennard, 'English agriculture under Charles II', p. 37.

19 P. Pusey, 'On the present state of the science of agriculture in England', *Journal of the English Agricultural Society*, I, 1839, p. 11.

20 R. C. Allen, above, pp. 248–9.

21 P. Glennie, 'Continuity and change in Hertfordshire agriculture, 1550–1700: II – trends in crop yields and their determinants', *AHR*, XXXVI, 1988, pp. 145–61.

ploughs, which would have been more efficient in the preparation of the land, and contemporary commentators also mentioned the virtues of deep ploughing, and discussed the types of plough most suitable for such activity.[22]

Soil drainage was, however, perhaps the most important way of improving soil structure. Successful underdraining on a large scale had to wait until the nineteenth century with the introduction of the tile drain. Before then ridge and furrow was the principal means of surface drainage, but from the seventeenth century onwards hollow drains seem to have been more frequently employed, whereby stones or bushes were put into trenches and covered with soil.[23] Nevertheless, A. D. M. Phillips concludes that very little effective underdraining had been carried out by 1800. Once underdraining got under way on a large scale in the nineteenth century significant increases in yields were possible.[24]

Aside from draining, farmers were also aware of the improvements that could be made through the addition of lime or marl to the land even if they had little idea of the biological and chemical processes involved.[25] E. Kerridge has gone so far as to describe the increase in the use of lime after 1590 as 'revolutionary'.[26] Liming became particularly important as turnips were introduced since they are very intolerant of an acid soil. Reducing soil acidity could also reduce the incidence of certain crop diseases, but on the whole early modern farmers were helpless in the face of these problems, and seem to have regarded them, with the weather, as Acts of God over which they had no control.[27] Crop rotation was the most important way of preventing

22 Worlidge, *Systema agriculturae*, pp. 35–8. On the contribution of improved plough technology to rising cereal productivity after 1750 see G. Grantham, below, pp. 354–5.

23 E. Kerridge, 'A reconsideration of some former husbandry practices', *AHR*, III, 1955, pp. 26–40.

24 A. D. M. Phillips, *The underdraining of farmland in England during the nineteenth century*, Cambridge, 1989, pp. 45–9, 224–8.

25 Worlidge, *Systema agriculturae*, pp. 65 and 212; Marshall, *Rural economy of Norfolk*, II, p. 364, and I, p. 259; M. A. Havinden, 'Lime as a means of agricultural improvement: the Devon example', pp. 104–34 in *idem* and C. W. Chalklin, eds., *Rural change and urban growth*, London, 1974; H. C. Prince, 'England *circa* 1800', pp. 389–464 in H. C. Darby, ed., *A new historical geography of England*, Cambridge, 1974, p. 416.

26 Kerridge, *Agricultural revolution*, pp. 248–50.

27 E. L. Jones, 'Afterword', pp. 327–36 in *idem* and W. N. Parker, eds., *European peasants and their markets: essays in agricultural history*, New Haven, 1975, pp. 344–9; G. E. Mingay, ed., *The agrarian history of England and Wales*, VI, *1750–1850*, Cambridge, 1989, pp. 311–13.

disease being passed from crop to crop. 'Take-all', for example, is a disease that affects both wheat and barley, but rarely oats, which might explain why oats were often in the middle of a rotation.[28] Aside from rotations, a variety of methods were adopted to combat diseases, the most prevalent of which was the steeping of seed prior to sowing.[29]

Some pests could be controlled quite simply by increasing the amount of labour expended on a crop – by scaring birds, trapping vermin, and keeping the land free from weeds.[30] Indeed, increasing labour inputs was the major means of improving yields in the ways described above. Direct evidence of the utilisation of labour on early modern farms is scarce, but enough farm accounts are extant, especially for the eighteenth century, for some assessments to be made of the fluctuations in intensity of labour input, and possibly the relationship of this to levels of yields. Such a relationship has been demonstrated for the middle ages to great effect.[31] If the medieval pattern were repeated in the early modern period it seems reasonable to suggest that under conditions of population pressure in the sixteenth century, when food prices were high and wage rates relatively low, increasing labour inputs would have been the principal means of raising output per acre. It is likely, however, that this would have been at the expense of falling labour productivity, although once again there is, as yet, no direct evidence.

This discussion demonstrates that early modern farmers had a wide range of options open to them for increasing yields per acre. Although it is possible to show that the opportunities to exercise these options existed, and to cite general instances of their application, specific information of their respective contributions to productivity changes awaits further research. Yet the whole was greater than the sum of the parts and, as Figure 11.2 makes clear, many of the developments described above were mutually reinforcing. Some might have involved a degree of technological innovation, but in many cases they could be found in the husbandry of medieval England.[32] Perhaps

28 Watson and More, *Agriculture*, 1962, pp. 215–16.
29 Lennard, 'English agriculture under Charles II', pp. 37–8. J. Worlidge, *Dictionarium rusticum and urbanicum*, London, 1704, lists many crop diseases and their supposed cures.
30 E. L. Jones, 'The bird pests of British agriculture in recent centuries', *AHR*, XX, 1972, pp. 107–25.
31 B. M. S. Campbell, 'Arable productivity in medieval England: some evidence from Norfolk', *JEH*, XLIII, 1983, pp. 379–404.
32 Liming, marling, manuring, folding, applying urban manure, weed from rivers, seaweed, and seasand, weeding, bird-scaring, buying-in seed, draining, stall-feeding, the multiple ploughing of fallows, and systematic rotation of crops, are all well documented from medieval sources. See B. M. S. Campbell, above, pp. 159–78.

of more significance in the long run, therefore, were those changes in husbandry systems which enabled a break with the past, not only by raising output per acre to unprecedented levels, but by doing so without suffering a fall in labour productivity as a consequence. Two systems have been singled out by historians as being of particular significance in making such a break.

The most significant is held to be the Norfolk four-course, but before considering that rotation it is necessary to consider the inno-vation in cropping which lies at the heart of Kerridge's 'agricultural revolution' of the sixteenth and seventeenth centuries, namely, 'con-vertible' or 'up-and-down' husbandry. He claims that this system, whereby the distinction between permanent grass and permanent arable was broken, and grass was rotated around the farm, could have 'quadrupled output per acre'.[33] On the other hand, E. L. Jones considers that the impact of ley farming on yields would have been minimal.[34] In fact, as R. Shiel has demonstrated, when permanent pasture is ploughed up, the store of nitrogen released can have a dramatic influence on the yield of cereal crops.[35] Nevertheless, within a period of a few years yields fall back to their previous levels as the amount of organic matter decreases, and the soil becomes more acid because of leaching and the production of acids from the decay of organic matter. This might contribute to the explanation of J. Broad's findings of a retreat from 'up-and-down' husbandry in the midlands in the later seventeenth century;[36] so too might have been the difficulties of establishing a grass ley: 'to make a pasture breaks a man, to break a pasture makes a man'.[37] On the other hand, a grass ley would serve to keep down weeds (provided it could be established satisfactorily), leave organic residues when it was ploughed in, and probably serve as a barrier to the transmission of some crop-specific pests and diseases.

Direct evidence of the impact of 'up-and-down husbandry' is hard to find. Although Kerridge cites scattered instances of yield im-provements, the rotation of grass and arable is difficult to detect from available sources in a systematic way. Probate inventories, for example, only give a snapshot of a farm at one point in the year so cannot

33 E. Kerridge, *The farmers of old England*, London, 1983, p. 108.
34 E. L. Jones, 'Agriculture and economic growth in England, 1660–1750: agri-cultural change', *JEH*, XXV, 1965, pp. 1–18, reprinted as pp. 67–84 in *idem, Agriculture and the industrial revolution*, Oxford, 1974, pp. 69–70.
35 Shiel, above, pp. 62–3.
36 J. Broad, 'Alternate husbandry and permanent pasture in the midlands 1650–1800', *AHR*, XXVIII, 1980, pp. 77–89.
37 H. I. Moore, *Grassland husbandry*, London, 3rd edn., 1946, p. 17.

provide evidence of crop rotations, and in any case are inconsistent in the way they record growing grass. As with labour inputs, the most promising sources for further research are surviving farm accounts.[38] Tithe records are equally scarce, but can record crop rotations.[39]

Nevertheless, convertible husbandry might be of considerable significance because it integrated the arable and pasture sectors on the farm. This represents a radical departure from the Middle Ages when the two branches of husbandry were often kept separate. Shiel's model of the yields and output from a farm under permanent arable and permanent pasture assumes that manure is transferred from the pasture to the arable: if this was not in fact the case then yields may well have been lower, and the model may be more representative of some form of convertible husbandry.

With the exception of Kerridge, historians of English agriculture have long been agreed that rotations based on the principles of the Norfolk four-course were by far the most important innovation in English agriculture before the mid nineteenth century.[40] Turnips and clover, when integrated into arable rotations, have an impact on output per acre through almost all the mechanisms shown in Figure 11.2. Turnips can smother weeds, and when sown in rows can easily be hoed, they provide more fodder, leave organic residues when ploughed in, can improve the soil structure because they are deeper rooted than grain crops, and provide a break between grain crops to help prevent the carry-over of disease. Much the same is true of clover, except that the crop is not hoed. By far the most important property of clover, however, is its ability to fix nitrogen from the air and G. P. H. Chorley has estimated that a third of the increase in arable productivity in northern Europe between 1750 and 1850 can be attributed to legumes such as clover.[41]

While acknowledging its importance, historians have hitherto paid little attention to the ways in which the rotation worked in any detail.

---

38 Manorial accounts provide detailed evidence of some late- medieval prototypes of ley farming: T. A. M. Bishop, 'The rotation of crops at Westerham, 1297–1350', *Economic History Review*, IX, 1938, pp. 38–44; E. Searle, *Lordship and community: Battle Abbey and its banlieu, 1066–1538*, Toronto, 1974, pp. 272–86.

39 This source is discussed by R. J. P. Kain and H. C. Prince, *The tithe surveys of England and Wales*, Cambridge, 1985, pp. 208–10. See below, pp. 313–14.

40 Kerridge, *Agricultural revolution*, pp. 32–3. Its crucial significance has been accepted by historians from Lord Ernle, *English farming past and present*, London, 1961, p. 174 (1st edn., 1912), to J. V. Beckett, *The agricultural revolution*, Oxford, 1990, pp. 12–13.

41 Chorley, 'The agricultural revolution'.

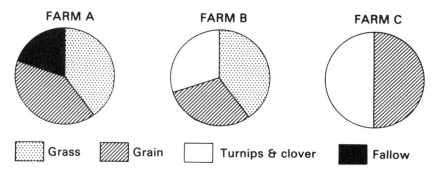

Figure 11.3 *Stages in the adoption of the Norfolk four-course rotation*

Yet, as Shiel has shown in Chapter 2, the workings of the Norfolk four-course are quite complicated.[42] Thanks to his efforts it is now possible to demonstrate the effects that the introduction of the rotation might have had in terms of both increases in land productivity and in the total output of crops and stock. Figure 11.3 illustrates the land-use on three hypothetical farms, each of 100 acres. The first (A) has 40 per cent of its area devoted to grass in the form of permanent pasture and meadow and the remainder under a three-course arable rotation of wheat and oats followed by a fallow.[43] The third (C) has the whole farm devoted to the Norfolk four-course, so that the rotation of wheat, turnips, barley, and clover now covers the entire farm. A wholesale switch from one to the other would have been most unlikely in practice, at least in the early eighteenth century, because of the risks involved in replacing permanent pasture with turnips and clover. Permanent grass was a reliable if low-yielding source of fodder, but the new crops required new cultivation techniques and had a much higher risk of failing. Thus the second farm in Figure 11.3 (B) illustrates the situation where the acreage under grass is retained and the Norfolk four-course is implemented over the arable area previously under a three-course. Although this farm retains the assured source of fodder, the *area* of grain is reduced by 25 per cent (from 40 per cent to 30 per cent of the farm area). Of course, farmers might not have introduced turnips and clover with the intention of increasing grain output or of raising yields at all,

42 Fream, *Elements of agriculture*, pp. 233–7; Shiel, above, pp. 68, 74–5.
43 Results for barley would be similar.

Table 11.1 *The impact of the Norfolk four-course rotation*

Model farm	Grain yields (bush/acre)	Grain output (bushels)	Livestock output[a] (bushels)	Total output (bushels)	% grain
A	11.5	460	400	860	53
B	21.4	642	950	1,492	43
	(23.9)	(717)	(950)	(1,567)	46
C	16.0	800	750	1,550	52
	(18.5)	(925)	(750)	(1,675)	55

Notes
Figures in brackets assume some pest and disease control from the rotation.
The farms are illustrated in Figure 11.1.
[a] Assuming the rotation has all the benefits of fallowing.

Source Tables 2.1, 2.2 and 2.3 above.

but simply desired to increase the output of fodder for their animals.[44] But if farmers did wish to maintain grain output they would have needed great faith that the reduction in grain area would indeed have been offset by higher yields.[45]

Such faith would have been justified. Table 11.1 shows the results in terms of both output and yields of applying Shiel's models discussed in Chapter 2 to the three hypothetical farms.[46] The table demonstrates convincingly that the traditional 'agricultural revolution' could indeed have been responsible for unprecedented (and hence perhaps 'revolutionary') changes in both crop and livestock productivity and output. If a farmer moved from a three-course to a four-course system (farm A to farm B), retaining his area of permanent grass, grain yields would have doubled (a rise of 107 per cent) and total output would have risen by 82 per cent. Grain output would have increased despite the reduction in area because of the dramatic increase in yields, but the major proportion of the increase in total output would have come

44 M. Overton, 'The diffusion of agricultural innovations in early modern England: turnips and clover in Norfolk and Suffolk 1580–1740', *Transactions of the Institute of British Geographers*, new series, X, 1985, pp. 212–14; *idem*, 'An agricultural revolution, 1650–1750', pp. 9–13 in *idem*, E. J. T. Collins, M. E. Turner and D. N. McCloskey, *Agricultural history: papers presented to the Economic History Society Conference*, Canterbury, 1983. Below, p. 320.
45 A point also noted by G. W. Grantham, 'The diffusion of the new husbandry in northern France', *JEH*, XXXVIII, 1978, pp. 326–7.
46 Shiel, above, pp. 70–5. My thanks to Robert Shiel for constructing this table for me.

from the livestock sector. The increases would not have been so dramatic if farm A devoted a higher proportion of its area to pasture. The optimum output under such a system would have been with 77 per cent of the farm devoted to grass (Table 2.1), but the assumption of 40 per cent shown in Table 11.1 is historically the more likely.

If a farm then moved towards system C and devoted an increasing proportion of its area to the four-course, yields would have started to fall (since the grain would lose the benefit of manure from animals grazing the permanent pasture) but grain output would nevertheless have risen because of the additional area under grain. Furthermore, as the arable area encroached on to areas hitherto under pasture the initial rise in yields would have been higher than those indicated in the table because of the utilisation of nitrogen reserves in permanent pasture.[47]

The benefits of the Norfolk four-course were therefore consider-able and will be considered further in the conclusion to this chapter. The rotation also had other advantages. Although it required more labour, especially for hoeing turnips, demand for that labour came at seasons of the year when labour demand was usually slack. Thus it did not affect labour requirements at peak periods and served to even out the demand for labour over the year.[48] On the other hand the rotation was not without its problems. Turnips were subject to club-root disease and to the ravages of the turnip fly, and were not very frost-hardy. In practice clover could not be grown every four years because the land became 'clover sick'. Both turnips and clover require a finer tilth than cereal crops, and turnips cannot tolerate an acid soil.[49]

The foregoing section has been based on a mixture of agronomy and largely anecdotal historical evidence. Such an exercise is valuable both in raising historical questions and suggesting a range of possibilities for the answers, but it is inadequate history on its own. The remainder of this chapter therefore complements these theoretical speculations with some direct historical evidence of changes in farm enterprises in eastern England, though that evidence itself, in part at least, is far from unproblematic.

47 Shiel, above, Table 2.2, p. 73.
48 C. P. Timmer, 'The turnip, the new husbandry, and the English agricultural revolution', *Quarterly Journal of Economics*, LXXXIII, 1969, pp. 375–95.
49 J. B. Lawes and J. H. Gilbert, 'Rotation of crops', *Journal of the Royal Agricultural Society of England*, 3rd series, V, 1894, pp. 584–646; Kerridge, *Agricultural revolution*, p. 32; Mingay, *Agrarian history* VI, pp. 283–4; Watson and More, *Agriculture*, p. 138.

II Calculating crop yields from probate inventories

Estimates of grain yields for Norfolk and Suffolk were published in 1979 in an article which was essentially a methodological exploration.[50] Although the data were tentative, some speculations were made about trends in the absolute levels of yields from the sixteenth to the eighteenth centuries, although no actual figures of yields were published, and the data were presented as graphs which were intended to suggest trends in yields rather than their absolute levels. Despite the warnings in the article, these results have been used as indications of absolute yields.[51] Recently the method adopted to estimate yields has been subjected to comment and criticism by Allen and Glennie, and in the light of these some new yield estimates are presented here.[52]

The original method for estimating yields made the assumption that $v = py$ where v is the valuation per acre of growing grain, p is the price per bushel after the harvest, and y is the yield in bushels per acre. Thus yield becomes

$$y = v/p. \tag{1}$$

The actual calculation was more complicated and resulted in a yield estimate that was an average for a ten-year period and yields for individual farms were not calculated. Equation 1 makes the major assumption that the appraisers of an inventory valued standing grain according to yield and post-harvest price, and, furthermore, made a reasonable forecast of future prices.

Allen has two major criticisms of this procedure. First, he points out that valuations of standing grain could be based on the costs of production rather than on the forecasts of future yields and prices. He is quite correct in this. Evidence of such valuations were cited in the 1979 article and care was taken to exclude valuations made on a cost-of-production basis.[53] Second, and of more significance, Allen argues that appraisers would have deducted harvesting costs and possibly tithe

---

50 M. Overton, 'Estimating crop yields from probate inventories: an example from East Anglia 1585–1735', *JEH*, XXXIX, 1979, pp. 363–78.

51 For example, by Grigg, *The dynamics of agricultural change*, p. 186; N. F. R. Crafts, *British economic growth during the industrial revolution*, Oxford, 1985, p. 44.

52 R. C. Allen, 'Inferring yields from probate inventories', *JEH*, XLVIII, 1988, pp. 117–25; Glennie, 'Crop yields and their determinants'; *idem*, above, pp. 255–83. A correction factor was added to the original estimates in M. Overton, 'Agricultural productivity in eighteenth-century England: some further speculations', *EcHR*, XXXVII, 1984, p. 250, n. 37. My reply to Allen is M. Overton, 'Re-estimating crop yields from probate inventories', *JEH*, L, 1990, pp. 931–5.

53 Overton, 'Estimating crop yields', pp. 370 and 374.

from the expected sale price. He is undoubtedly right, and the original article was in error for not making some allowance for this. When harvesting costs are deducted the relationship now becomes

$$v = py - r - c \qquad (2)$$

or,

$$v = 0.9 \ (py - c) - r \qquad (3)$$

taking account of tithe when the rector paid for carting but not for reaping, where r is the cost of reaping per acre and c the costs of leading and stacking grain per acre.

The question then arises as to which prices the appraisers had in mind when forecasting the sale price of the crop. There are three alternatives here: wholesale market prices, inventory barn prices of unthreshed grain, and inventory barn prices less threshing costs (since grain would be threshed before it was sold). There are strong arguments for preferring inventory barn prices to wholesale prices. The quality of grain in the fields is more accurately represented by grain in farmers' barns rather than by that sold in the market. Not all grain harvested was fit to be sold for human consumption as bread or beer. Thus some of the grain valued standing in the field would have been of such low quality that it would have been kept for feeding livestock rather than sold at market. Using inventory barn prices has other advantages. Marketing costs are uncertain and difficult to calculate but can be ignored since they do not have to be deducted from grain still on the farm in the barn. Likewise, threshing costs can largely be ignored since most of the grain in the barn after the harvest would be unthreshed.[54]

For the new yield calculations, inventory prices for harvested grain have been used, so the formula becomes

$$v = 0.9 \ (p_{I+t} - ty - c) - r \qquad (4)$$

where p_I represents inventory prices. Since threshing costs cancel out, the equation for calculating yields is

$$y = (0.9c + r + v)/0.9p_I. \qquad (5)$$

Table 11.2 shows the cost estimates used in the calculation of these new yields for Norfolk, Suffolk and Lincolnshire, based on a wide variety of sources, including inventories themselves and farm accounts. The yield estimates are, however, fairly insensitive to changes in these

54 Glennie, above, pp. 265–6.

Table 11.2 *Costs used in revised calculations of grain yields in Norfolk, Suffolk and Lincolnshire, 1584–1739*

A. *Reaping or mowing, binding and stacking (shillings per acre)*

	Wheat	Rye	Barley	Oats
1584–1599	3.5	3.5	1.6	1.6
1628–1739	5.0	5.0	2.0	2.0

B. *Carting costs (shillings per acre)*

1584–1599	1.0
1628–1739	1.5

Source
P. J. Bowden, 'Agricultural prices, farm profits, and rents', pp. 593–685 in Thirsk, *The agrarian history of England and Wales*, IV, *1500–1640*, 1967, p. 662; *idem*, 'Agricultural prices, wages, farm profits and rents', pp. 593–695 in Thirsk, *The agrarian history of England and Wales*, Vii, *1640–1750: agrarian change*, 1985, pp. 88–9; University of Reading Library Farm Accounts, NORF 14/1 for 1685–98; P. Brassley, A. Lambert and P. Saunders, eds., *Accounts of the Reverend John Crakanthorp of Fowlmere 1682–1710*, Cambridgeshire Records Society, VIII, Cambridge, 1988; G. E. Fussell, ed., *Robert Loder's farm accounts 1610–1620*, Camden Society, 3rd series, LIII, London, 1936.

costs. Table 11.3 and Figure 1.2 show the results of calculating yields for Norfolk and Suffolk, and Table 11.4 and Figure 1.2 for Lincolnshire, from Equation 5.[55] The yields are gross: they are not net of seed, nor of tithe, and, unlike the original 1979 estimates, are means of harvest-year averages. They are not directly comparable with Allen's Oxfordshire yields but are calculated in a similar way to Glennie's, differing only in the threshing term in the equation and in the cost estimates they employ.[56]

Judgements about the merits of these various estimates must depend on two sets of considerations; the theoretical basis on which they have been calculated and individual empirical factors specific to each series. The theoretical aspects have already been reviewed with the conclusion that yields calculated from Equation 5, which incorporates most of Allen's modifications to the original method, are probably the most representative of absolute yield levels. On average

---

55 The results for Lincolnshire must be regarded as preliminary since the analysis of the inventories is not yet complete.
56 Glennie, above, pp. 260, 268, Equations 4 and 7.

they are 25 per cent higher than estimates calculated with the original 1979 method.[57] Probably the most important factor for each series is the number of farms on which it is based. Allen's data is the least plausible in this respect for his average yields for each 25-year period are based on between two and eight inventories. Given that yields fluctuated from year to year, from village to village, and from plot to plot, it is difficult to put much faith in them at all, particularly since the actual years to which they refer are not mentioned in his articles.[58] Glennie concludes that when his Hampshire and Hertfordshire yields are calculated using Allen's method, so that they are exactly comparable with the results for Oxfordshire, the Oxfordshire yields are still much higher.[59] The same is true of a comparison with Norfolk and Suffolk yields. From 1675 to 1729 Allen's wheat yields (calculated from fifteen inventories) are over 5 bushels per acre higher than yields for Norfolk and Suffolk calculated in the same way (from 110 inventories).

If these new yield estimates are indicative of absolute yields then they can be compared with other yields derived from different sources, both before and after the period for which inventories survive.[60] Lincolnshire is well represented by the 1801 crop return, but unfortunately, insufficient evidence is available for Norfolk and Suffolk.[61] All three counties are represented in the tithe files, and R. J. P. Kain has compiled evidence of yields from 675 tithe districts in Norfolk and Suffolk and from 124 for Lincolnshire. The 1854 crop returns also give yield information, but only for Norfolk. These statistics were not compiled for Lincolnshire so an estimate for 1861 is used which comes from the results of a survey carried out by the *Mark Lane Express*.[62] The other sources in Tables 11.3 and 11.4 must be less reliable than these

57 See Glennie, above, pp. 272–3.

58 Allen, 'Inferring crop yields'; *idem*, above, p. 247.

59 Above, pp. 277–9.

60 Campbell, above, pp. 178–82, gives a longer-term perspective on Norfolk yields. M. Overton, 'Agriculture', pp. 34–53 in J. Langton and R. Morris, eds., *An atlas of industrializing Britain 1780–1914*, London, 1986, combines estimates from the 1801 crop return, the tithe files, and the agricultural statistics for 1871 and 1911 in a series of maps of grain output for Britain as a whole.

61 D. B. Grigg, *The agricultural revolution in south Lincolnshire*, Cambridge, 1966, pp. 58–62, discusses yield evidence for south Lincolnshire.

62 The statistical sources are referenced in Tables 11.3 and 11.4. See also P. Dodd, 'The agricultural statistics for 1854: an assessment of their value', *AHR*, XXXV, 1987, pp. 159–70; *idem*, 'Norfolk agriculture in 1853–4', *Norfolk Archaeology*, XXXVI, 1976, pp. 253–64; H. M. E. Holt and R. J. P. Kain, 'Land use and farming in Suffolk about 1840', *Proceedings of the Suffolk Institute of Archaeology*, XXXV, 1982, pp. 123–39.

L

Table 11.3 *Norfolk and Suffolk: gross grain yields, 1584–1854 (bushels per acre)*

	Wheat	Rye	Barley	Oats	WACY[a]	Index[b]
1584–1599	11.4 (45)	11.4 (31)	12.2 (74)	16.3 (22)	8.1	100
1628–1640	14.5 (37)	11.0 (18)	13.0 (69)	21.7 (24)	9.4	116
1660–1679	14.5 (40)	13.8 (13)	14.6 (55)	19.3 (4)	9.3	116
1680–1709	15.9 (26)	8.6 (5)	16.1 (33)	16.8 (10)	9.2	114
1710–1739	19.2 (70)	13.8 (13)	20.8 (75)	22.6 (33)	13.0	161
1660–1699	15.3 (54)	13.5 (14)	15.1 (70)	17.2 (5)	9.5	118
1700–1739	18.5 (82)	12.5 (17)	20.2 (93)	22.1 (42)	12.5	155
1760s[c]	26.5 (20)	25.0 (2)	32.5 (20)	36.7 (11)		
c.1800[d]	23.0		34.0	37.0		
c.1800[e]	22.4	21.3	32.0	32.5		
c.1836[f]	23.3		32.0	36.3	21.0	260
1854[g]	30.0		38.0	46.0	25.5	317

Notes

The figures following each yield estimate refer to the number of farms for which a yield may be estimated 1584–1739 and to the number of observations on which Young's 1760 estimate is based. The inventory yields are means of harvest-year means for all farms with an acreage valuation made from June to August.

[a] Weighted aggregate cereal yield given by $\sum (y_i \cdot p_i / p_w \cdot a_i / \Sigma a)$ where y_i is the yield of crop i in bushels per acre, p_i is the price of the crop per bushel, p_w is the price of wheat per bushel, a_i is the acreage under crop i.
[b] Index of weighted aggregate gross yield per cereal acre. 1584–99 = 100.

Source

1584–1739 calculated from Norfolk Consistory Court probate inventories (see text).
[c] Calculated from A. Young, *The farmer's tour through the east of England*, 4 vols., London, 1771, IV, pp. 230–45.
[d] A. Young, *General view of the agriculture of the county of Norfolk*, London, 1804, p. 303; *idem, General view of the agriculture of the county of Suffolk*, London, 1813, pp. 72, 74 and 75.
[e] House of Lords Record Office, *Second report of the Lord's committee on the dearth of provisions*, 1801, Appendix I.
[f] R. J. P. Kain, *An atlas and index of the tithe files of mid-nineteenth-century England and Wales*, Cambridge, 1986, pp. 43, 72. But see also J. Fletcher, 'Contributions to the agricultural statistics of the eastern counties', *Journal of the Statistical Society of London*, VI, 1843, pp. 130–3, who reports higher yields for the harvests of 1837–38.
[g] *Reports by the poor law inspectors on agricultural statistics (England)*, BPP, LIII, 1st series Cd.1928, London, 1854–55, pp. 34–55 (Norfolk only).

statistics if only because they are based on such a small sample of farms. Although Arthur Young's figures for the 1760s are based on averages from a selection of farms it is possible that his selection is biased. From their context here they seem too high, unless yields fell from the 1760s to the 1830s, which bears on the debate about the reliability and representativeness of his figures.[63]

63 Compare E. Kerridge, 'Arthur Young and William Marshall', *History Studies*, I, 1968, pp. 43–65, and G. E. Mingay, *Arthur Young and his times*, London, 1975, pp. 15–16. R. C. Allen and C. Ó Gráda, 'On the road again with Arthur Young: English,

Table 11.4 *Lincolnshire: gross grain yields, 1550–1861 (bushels per acre)*

	Wheat		Rye		Barley		Oats		WACY[a]	Index[b]
1550–1574	10.6	(41)	13.0	(2)	19.0	(54)	13.1	(7)	10.5	100
1575–1599	11.1	(19)	20.6	(4)	13.9	(29)	12.8	(4)	9.2	87
1600–1624	12.4	(19)	20.1	(3)	17.3	(21)	17.0	(4)	10.5	100
1625–1649	16.5	(12)	13.2	(5)	17.3	(19)	21.6	(7)	10.1	96
1650–1674	15.1	(11)	28.4	(5)	20.8	(19)	18.5	(8)	10.0	95
1675–1699	14.7	(16)	19.4	(6)	19.8	(18)	18.3	(10)	10.5	99
1700–1724	16.5	(5)	16.7	(3)	18.4	(18)	23.2	(13)	10.9	103
1725–1749	18.7	(21)	31.8	(3)	18.5	(19)	25.2	(9)	12.8	122
1550–1599	10.8	(60)	18.1	(6)	16.8	(83)	13.0	(11)	10.1	95
1600–1649	14.4	(31)	15.5	(8)	17.2	(40)	19.9	(11)	10.2	97
1650–1699	14.8	(27)	23.9	(11)	20.3	(37)	18.4	(14)	10.2	97
1700–1749	18.1	(26)	24.2	(6)	18.4	(37)	24.1	(20)	12.0	114
1760s[c]	21.4	(5)	22.0	(2)	34.0	(5)	28.7	(3)		
c.1800[d]	28.0				34.0		52.0			
c.1800[e]	24.0				34.0		42.0			
1801[f]	21.0				31.0		39.0		15.8	150
c.1836[g]	22.9				31.1		38.0		20.0	190
1861[h]	31.0				39.5		54.5			

Notes

The figures following each yield estimate refer to the number of farms for which a yield may be estimated 1550–1749 and to the number of observations on which Young's 1760 estimate is based. The inventory yields are means of harvest-year means for all farms with an acreage valuation made from June to August.

[a] Weighted aggregate cereal yield, see Table 11.3, note [a].

[b] Index of weighted aggregate gross yield per cereal acre. 1550–74 = 100.

Source

1550–1749 calculated from Lincolnshire probate inventories (see text).

[c] Calculated from A. Young, *The farmer's tour through the east of England*, 4 vols., London, 1771, IV, pp. 230–45.

[d] A. Young, *General view of the agriculture of the county of Lincoln*, London, 1813, p. 149.

[e] See Table 11.3 note [c].

[f] M. E. Turner, 'Agricultural productivity in England in the eighteenth century: evidence from crop yields', *EcHR*, XXXV, 1982, p. 509; *idem*, 'Arable in England and Wales: estimates from the 1801 crop return', *Journal of Historical Geography*, VII, 1981, p. 294.

[g] R. J. P. Kain, *An atlas and index of the tithe files of mid-nineteenth-century England and Wales*, Cambridge, 1986, p. 87.

[h] The results of a survey by *The Mark Lane Express*, reproduced in P. G. Craigie, 'Statistics of agricultural production', *Journal of the Royal Statistical Society*, XLVI, 1883, pp. 40–2.

Irish, and French agriculture during the industrial revolution', *JEH*, XLVIII, 1988, pp. 97–104, consider Young's yields to be representative although they do not compare them with either inventory or tithe evidence, or any other contemporary material. W. Marshall, *The review and complete abstract of the county reports to the Board of Agriculture from the eastern department*, York, 1818, p. 150, considers that Young's Lincolnshire figures 'cannot be useful to the public'.

Table 11.5 *Norfolk, Suffolk and Lincolnshire: changes in crop yields, sixteenth to nineteenth centuries (percentage change per annum)*

Period	Wheat		Barley	
	gross	*net*	*gross*	*net*
A. Norfolk and Suffolk				
1584–99 to 1628–40	0.68	0.87	0.16	0.24
1628–40 to 1660–99	0.12	0.15	0.36	0.52
1660–99 to 1700–39	0.52	0.62	0.84	1.15
1700–39 to c.1800	0.27	0.31	0.73	0.91
c.1800 to c.1836	0.11	0.12	0.00	0.00
c.1836 to 1854	1.31	1.46	0.85	0.97
B. Lincolnshire				
1550–99 to 1600–49	0.67	0.87	0.05	0.06
1600–49 to 1650–99	0.06	0.07	0.36	0.47
1650–99 to 1700–49	0.45	0.54	−0.19	−0.23
1700–49 to c.1800	0.21	0.25	0.91	1.17
c.1800 to c.1836	0.28	0.32	0.01	0.01
c.1836 to 1861	1.22	1.37	0.93	1.07

Note
Net yields are calculated by deducting 2.5 bushels per acre for wheat and 4 bushels per acre for barley for seed.

Source Tables 11.3 and 11.4.

Table 11.5 shows the annual percentage rates of increase in yields for the three counties for selected periods, for both gross yields and yields net of seed, although the seeding rates are merely assumptions without direct confirmation from inventories.[64] Wheat yields rose from the late sixteenth century to the early seventeenth century but rose little over the remainder of the seventeenth century. Thereafter they rose again in the early eighteenth century, breaking through to unprecedentedly high levels after 1700.[65] From the mid eighteenth century the rate of increase slowed (ignoring Young's estimates) until the 1830s, when another sharp rise took place. These trends contradict

64 E. A. Wrigley, 'Some reflections on corn yields and prices in pre-industrial economies', pp. 92–139 in *idem, People, cities and wealth: the transformation of a traditional society,* Oxford, 1987, pp. 123–39, stresses the importance of considering yields net of seed. Assumed rates are 2.5 bushels per acre for wheat and 4 bushels per acre for barley.
65 Unprecedented, that is, in comparison with the middle ages. Campbell, above, pp. 179–82.

both Kerridge ('at the end of the eighteenth century, yields were hardly more than in the early seventeenth') and Allen, who argues for yield increase over the seventeenth century on the basis of his Oxfordshire evidence.[66] In Norfolk and Suffolk barley yields did rise over the seventeenth century, but as with wheat the rate of increase steepened in the early eighteenth century. During the latter century the rise for barley was evidently greater than for wheat, but thereafter yield trends of the two crops moved together. In Lincolnshire the picture for barley was different. Barley yields actually fell in the early eighteenth century, but then rose dramatically to around 1800, slumped again, and then rose in harmony with wheat from the 1830s to the 1850s. In fact, in all three counties it was during the second quarter of the nineteenth century that wheat and barley yields both rose most rapidly.

III Grain yields and farm enterprises in Norfolk and Suffolk

The fluctuations in yields derived from probate inventories can be related to changes in husbandry practice reconstructed from the same source.[67] The difficulties of using inventories to measure agricultural change have been discussed elsewhere and will not be repeated here.[68] It is worth stressing, however, that inventories exclude crops grown without 'the industry and manurance of man', and thus make no reference to standing timber, fallow, permanent pasture and most meadow.[69] They do not comprise a census of all the crops and stock on a farm over the year, but merely give a snapshot of a farm's enterprise at one point in time. Nor are all sizes of farm equally well represented, since the inventories used here for Norfolk and Suffolk include few of the largest farms of all. Compounding the difficulties of the source

66 Kerridge, *Agricultural revolution*, p. 331; Allen, above, p. 247.
67 Unfortunately other agricultural information is not available for Lincolnshire since only valuations were extracted from the inventories.
68 M. Overton, 'English probate inventories and the measurement of agricultural change', *A. A. G. Bijdragen*, XXIII, Wageningen, 1980, pp. 205–15; *idem*, 'Probate inventories and the reconstruction of agrarian landscapes', pp. 167–94 in M. Reed, ed., *Discovering past landscapes*, London, 1984; *idem*, 'Computer analysis of an inconsistent data source: the case of probate inventories', *Journal of Historical Geography*, III, 1977, pp. 317–26; *idem*, 'Computer analysis of probate inventories: from portable micro to mainframe', pp 96–104 in D. Hopkin and P. Denley, eds., *History and computing*, Manchester, 1987; *idem*, 'Computer standardization of probate inventories', pp. 145–51 in J-P. Genet, ed., *Standardisation et échange des bases de données historiques*, Paris, 1988.
69 J. S. Burn, *Ecclesiastical law*, London, 3rd edn., 1775, IV, p. 240.

Table 11.6 *Norfolk and Suffolk: crop combinations, 1584–1854*

	1584–99	1628–40	1660–99	1700–39	c.1836	1854
% grain area						
Wheat	23.0	27.4	29.9	26.7	48.7	49.1
Rye	21.2	10.9	10.9	7.3		1.2
Maslin	1.8	1.9	2.1	0.8		0.0
Barley	46.8	46.7	47.8	54.0	46.8	42.1
Oats	7.2	13.1	9.4	11.2	4.5	7.6
% cropped area						
Legumes	7.8	10.7	16.4	11.9	27.8	25.6
Fodder[a]	10.4	12.3	13.8	15.1	51.4	45.2
Turnips[b]	0.0	0.0	0.9	8.2	20.4	19.6
Clover	0.0	0.0	0.1	2.8	23.6[c]	19.1
% legumes						
Vetches	30.7	48.0	17.9	10.3		3.4
Clover	0.0	0.0	0.3	22.3	85.0	74.8
Bare fallow as					5.9	3.9
% cropped area						
% grass[d]						26.9

Notes
Data for 1584–1739 are for all farms with inventories made in June and July.
[a] Legumes and roots.
[b] Mean turnip acreage August–December as a per cent of mean cropped acreage
June and July.
[c] 'Seeds'.
[d] Meadow, permanent and rough pasture (excluding clover) as a percentage of
grass and arable.

Source
1584–1739: Norfolk and Suffolk probate inventories.
Circa 1836: see Table 11.3 note [f].
1854: *Reports by the poor law inspectors on agricultural statistics (England)*, *BPP*, LIII, 1st
series Cd.1928, London, 1854–55.

itself are the decisions that have to be made about how measures of
farm enterprises are to be calculated. It should be evident that
inventories can only shed light on some of the factors influencing
yields shown in Figure 11.2. They provide little information on exactly
how farming operations were carried out, and furnish no details of
actual crop rotations. With these qualifications, Tables 11.6 to 11.9
give a variety of measures of farm enterprises in Norfolk and Suffolk

Table 11.7 *Norfolk and Suffolk: percentages of farms growing particular crops, 1584–1739*

	1584–99	1628–40	1660–99	1700–39
Wheat	62.9	52.0	62.8	73.3
Rye	47.6	33.3	37.4	31.6
Maslin	12.9	12.0	10.8	4.8
Barley	74.2	66.7	67.0	75.3
Oats	37.3	29.7	28.9	45.2
Legumes	61.1	45.9	46.0	55.7
Vetches	31.8	31.2	24.8	21.0
Clover	0.0	0.0	1.1	17.2
Turnips[a]	0.5	0.6	7.1	40.8

Note
Data are for all farms with inventories made in June and July, except [a] which is from August–December inventories.

Source Norfolk and Suffolk probate inventories.

Table 11.8 *Norfolk and Suffolk: percentages of farms with particular crops, 1584–1739*

	1584–99	1628–40	1660–99	1700–39
Buckwheat	16.3	12.6	9.6	10.2
Turnips[a]	0.5	1.3	9.4	49.1
Clover	0.0	0.0	2.9	23.1
Vetches	33.5	36.5	26.0	21.8
Leys	0.0	0.0	2.5	8.8
Grass	13.7	22.5	22.8	26.5

Note
Unlike Table 11.7 any mention of the crop, growing or otherwise is used.
Data are for all farms with inventories made in June and July, except [a] which is from August–December inventories.

Source Norfolk and Suffolk probate inventories.

derived from inventories, and, where possible, comparable statistics from the tithe files and the 1854 crop return.

The tables showing crop proportions are reasonably straightforward, since all crops (with the exception of root crops) should be in the ground during June and July. Livestock statistics are more problematic. Sheep are probably under-represented in the inventories since some of the very large sheep flocks would have been owned by

Table 11.9 *Norfolk and Suffolk: livestock statistics, 1584–1854*

	1584–99	1628–40	1660–99	1700–39	1854
% livestock units[d]					
Cattle	57.4	63.4	61.8	66.7	38.4
Horses	30.1	26.8	27.9	25.6	24.2
Sheep	5.8	4.6	5.9	4.7	32.0
Swine	5.7	4.5	3.8	3.1	5.3
Immature : adult cattle[a] [c]	0.86	1.13	1.53	1.55	
Immature : adult cattle[b] [c]	0.81	1.06	1.07	1.18	
Sheep:cattle[b]	1.5	1.3	3.2	1.6	8.5
Beasts per 100 cereal acres					
Livestock[a][d]	102.1	145.4	127.1	114.0	
Livestock[b][d]	60.2	101.7	80.5	70.9	56.0
Cattle[b]	39.4	71.6	42.7	51.1	21.0
Horses[b]	16.7	22.6	16.6	15.5	13.6
Sheep[b]	51.0	99.2	198.2	82.6	179.5
Swine[b]	33.7	25.9	25.4	19.2	29.9

Notes
Data are for all farms with inventories made in June and July.
[a] Means of farm ratios.
[b] Aggregate means.
[c] Minimum cattle herd size of 10.
[d] Livestock units (horses × 1.0) + (oxen, cows, and bulls × 1.2) + (immature cattle × 0.8) + (sheep × 0.1) + (swine × 0.1).

Source See Table 11.6.

farmers who had their probate proved in the Prerogative Court of Canterbury rather than the Consistory Court of Norwich.[70] The calculation of livestock ratios involves some arbitrary decisions, and can be calculated as means of individual farm ratios or as aggregate measures, dividing the mean number of beasts by the mean cereal acreage.

Information on absolute acreages and livestock numbers has been published elsewhere.[71] These show a drop in the mean cropped acreage per farm from the end of the sixteenth century to the early seventeenth century, but a doubling from the 1660s to the 1730s, mainly accounted for by a more than threefold rise in the mean acreage of barley on farms.[72] This doubling of the cropped acreage could be the consequence

70 Overton, 'Reconstructing agricultural landscapes', p. 171; K. J. Allison, 'The sheep–corn husbandry of Norfolk in the sixteenth and seventeenth centuries', *AHR*, V, 1957, pp. 12–30.
71 Overton, 'The diffusion of agricultural innovations', p. 213.
72 Slight differences in the method of calculation and in the inventories used to calculate the statistics mean there is a slight difference between the crop proportions given here and those previously published. The present ones are to be preferred.

of several processes. It might reflect a change in the representativeness of the surviving inventories, a reduction in the proportion of fallow and permanent pasture, or an increase in overall farm size.

If farm sizes were increasing, then the rise in yields might simply be due to that. Modern studies of the relationship between farm size and yield in less developed countries have concluded that there is no consistent relation between the two except that very small farms often have higher-than-average yields.[73] Some historians, on the other hand, have argued that yields were higher on larger farms. This may be because they have followed either Karl Marx or Arthur Young. Marx equated large farms with capitalist farming, and capitalist farming with higher output and therefore higher yields. Young thought that large farms had higher yields on the basis of evidence he collected for his *Tours*, yet Allen and C. Ó Gráda have recently shown how he misinterpreted his evidence.[74] Until the nineteenth century and the application of capital in the form of machinery or large-scale drainage, there is no reason to assume that small farms were at a disadvantage.[75]

There are a number of ways of attempting to demonstrate the relationship between yields and farm size. Thanks to Allen's improvements to the original 1979 method of estimating yields, it is now possible to relate yields on individual farms to other aspects of farm enterprises. Allen adopts a regression approach, but the problem here is in countering the effects of seasonal fluctuations in the weather.[76] Seasonal effects do not necessarily display a linear trend, so a linear model is not appropriate.[77] A more straightforward approach is simply to calculate yields for farms of particular size groups, provided enough inventories are available. Table 11.10 does this for Norfolk and Suffolk, and Table 11.11 for Lincolnshire. The results from this exercise should not be pushed too far given the sample sizes on which they are based, yet the Tables do not indicate a strong relationship between cropped acreage and yield, which accords with Allen's findings for Oxfordshire.[78] On the other hand, whereas Allen finds a slight tendency for yields to increase

73 See Allen, above, pp. 252–3.
74 Allen and Ó Gráda, 'On the road again'.
75 But see the arguments of M. M. Postan, 'Medieval agrarian society in its prime: England', pp. 549–632 in *idem*, ed., *The Cambridge economic history of Europe*, I, *The agrarian life of the middle ages*, Cambridge, 2nd edn., 1966, pp. 600–4.
76 R. C. Allen, *Enclosure, capitalist agriculture, and the growth of corn yields in early modern England*, University of British Columbia, Department of Economics Discussion Paper No. 86–39, 1986.
77 Glennie agrees, above, pp. 275–6.
78 Cropped acreage is not the same as total farm size which inventories cannot measure.

Table 11.10 *Norfolk and Suffolk: gross yields of wheat and barley by farm size[a], 1584–1739 (bushels per acre)*

	<20 acres	20–75 acres	>75 acres	All farms[b]
A. Wheat				
1584–1599	12.6 (24)	12.8 (18)		12.9 (82)
1628–1639	14.9 (19)	13.8 (14)		14.5 (37)
1660–1699	15.9 (26)	16.1 (19)	10.9 (8)	15.3 (54)
1700–1739	16.0 (26)	18.7 (43)	15.9 (12)	18.5 (82)
B. Barley				
1584–1599	12.8 (41)	11.4 (28)	11.9 (5)	12.2 (74)
1628–1639	13.4 (40)	11.4 (23)	12.9 (6)	13.0 (69)
1660–1699	15.9 (39)	14.6 (26)	10.8 (5)	15.1 (70)
1700–1739	20.1 (29)	19.9 (52)	16.9 (12)	20.1 (93)

Notes
The numbers following the yields are the number of inventories from which they are derived.
[a] Measured in terms of cropped acres recorded in inventories. This excludes grass (except clover) and fallow.
[b] Since the cropped acreage for some farms cannot be calculated the number of inventories used in this column may exceed the sum of those used in the previous three.

Source Norfolk and Suffolk probate inventories.

with farm size, in the three counties considered here there was a slight tendency for them to fall.[79] The change in yields cannot therefore be attributed to changes in average farm size.

More direct evidence of influences on yields can be gleaned by relating yield levels to specific aspects of farm enterprises. As with farm size, a regression approach is not the most suitable method of demonstrating relationships, so Table 11.12 employs a different strategy. Farms with yield information are divided into two categories; those with yields below the lower quartile of the distribution of yields for a harvest year, and those with yields above the upper quartile.[80] Table 11.12 reinforces the earlier finding that yields were not strongly related to farm size by showing the mean acreage of corn for the two categories of farms. Neither, as Allen finds for Oxfordshire, is there a relationship between yields and the proportion of the farm under pulses.[81] Although

79 Allen, above, p. 247. He uses regressions with 35 farms. My tables are based on 399 for wheat and 505 for barley.
80 This is the strategy adopted by Glennie, 'Crop yields and their determinants'.
81 Allen, above, p. 247.

Table 11.11 *Lincolnshire: gross yields of wheat and barley by farm size[a],*
1550–1749 (bushels per acre)

	<20 acres	20–75 acres	>75 acres	All farms[b]
A. Wheat				
1550–1599	11.0 (41)	9.7 (18)		10.8 (60)
1600–1649	14.5 (23)	13.0 (8)		14.4 (31)
1650–1699	15.4 (14)	13.8 (12)		14.8 (27)
1700–1749	18.4 (10)	18.3 (14)		18.1 (26)
B. Barley				
1550–1599	17.7 (18)	12.1 (22)		16.8 (83)
1600–1649	17.1 (8)	18.0 (12)		17.3 (40)
1650–1699	20.4 (12)	20.4 (15)		20.3 (37)
1700–1749	21.9 (14)	16.8 (20)		18.9 (39)

Notes
The numbers following the yields are the number of inventories from which they
are derived.
[a] Measured in terms of cropped acres recorded in inventories. This excludes
grass and fallow.
[b] Since the cropped acreage for some farms cannot be calculated the number of
inventories used in this column may exceed the sum of those used in the previous
three.

Source Lincolnshire probate inventories.

Table 11.12 *Norfolk and Suffolk: crop and livestock statistics for farms with yields*
below the lower quartile yield for a harvest year and for those with yields above the
upper quartile yield, 1584–1739

	Corn acreage	Pulses as % of cropped acres	Livestock units/ corn acres[a]	Immature: adult cattle
A. Wheat				
Below lower quartile	27.1	12.3	90.2	1.647
Above upper quartile	24.7	10.8	153.8	0.796
B. Barley				
Below lower quartile	31.8	10.1	94.7	1.194
Above upper quartile	27.9	12.8	116.6	1.565

Notes
[a] See Table 11.9 note [d].
For details of the statistics see Tables 11.6 and 11.9 above.

Source Norfolk and Suffolk probate inventories.

pulse crops (mainly peas, beans and vetches) fix nitrogen from the air, they do not necessarily give a net gain in nitrogen. In comparison with clover the crops are in the ground for a much shorter period of time, and the nitrogen in the crop is less likely to be returned to the soil if the crops are used for human consumption.[82] On the other hand there is a strong relationship between the level of yield and the ratio of livestock to cereal acres, especially for wheat, which is to be expected if the density of livestock represents the density of manure. The fourth column in Table 11.12 shows the ratio of immature to adult cattle, which is an indication of whether the cattle on a farm were mainly for dairying (a low ratio) or for fattening (a high ratio). The measure is used in an attempt to see whether higher yields are related to bullock-fattening enterprises. On the face of it, there was no apparent relation between the two, since many of the largest cattle-fattening enterprises had little or no arable and were found in the fens and marshes of the two counties. Repeating the analysis for mixed farms alone, however, tells a different story, for on these farms bullock fattening does appear to have gone hand-in-hand with higher yields.[83]

The adoption of clover and turnips, the new ingredients of the Norfolk four-course rotation, is shown dramatically in Tables 11.6, 11.7 and 11.8. By the early decades of the eighteenth century over 20 per cent of farmers with a surviving inventory had clover on their farm, and nearly 50 per cent had turnips (Table 11.8), though the proportions of inventories actually mentioning them as being grown are slightly smaller (Table 11.7). Less impressive are the proportions of the cropped area recorded as being under the two crops – respectively, 3 per cent for clover and 8 per cent for turnips. Over the next hundred years these crops made rapid strides so that the tithe files indicate proportions of over 20 per cent of the cropped area for both, which was roughly the same as the proportions in 1854 (Table 11.6). Thus, although the new crops were quite prevalent in the early eighteenth century, their impact on overall yields could not have been very great. That impact must have been achieved by the 1830s (assuming the crops were rotated), though in the absence of evidence for the intervening period the period of decisive breakthrough cannot, alas, be pin-pointed.

Searching for an exact Norfolk four-course rotation is a rather pointless exercise, for, as Kerridge has pointed out, the rotation was rarely practised in its pure form. Instead, what is of significance is the

82 Shiel, above, p. 70.
83 This relationship is explored more fully in Overton and Campbell, 'Five centuries of farming'.

identification of rotations based on its principle of integrating grass and grain, along with evidence of the proportion of land devoted to both turnips and clover: the former as an indication of the extent to which fallows could be abandoned, and the latter as an indication of the extent of nitrification. In the early eighteenth century few farmers seem to have been employing anything resembling a fully-fledged Norfolk four-course. Some inventories are suggestive of rotations based on its principles, the main one being the alternation of fodder crops with grain crops, but, as has already been stated, inventories do not report rotations.[84] One point that does emerge from inventories, however, is that turnips are rarely mentioned as growing before July or August, suggesting they were being grown as a catch crop after the harvest rather than being sown in the spring as they were supposed to be under a proper four-course rotation. Contemporaries were well aware that the crop could be sown at two seasons of the year, and a guide to valuing turnips for tithe purposes, published in 1807, gives two valuations: one for spring-sown or fallow turnips at 5s per acre and the other for etch or stubble turnips at 3s per acre.[85] There is comparatively little additional evidence as to how turnips were grown, although it is possible to identify a precocious farmer hoeing turnips in Norfolk as early as 1662.[86]

Other independent evidence of the rotation of these crops before the endless examples cited by Young is rare.[87] Tithe accounts are, however, potentially quite revealing. A good set covering the parish of Hunstanton in north-east Norfolk survive for the period 1705–11 recording each crop grown by 50 farmers over seven years on 493 plots of land. Turnips accounted for about 2 per cent of the cropped acreage, and clover about 9 per cent, though the 312 different rotations bear little resemblance to the Norfolk four-course or anything like it. Several grain crops were still often taken in succession, as had commonly been the practice in this locality in the middle ages, and turnips tended to be grown in closes rather than in the open-field strips. One of the earliest direct pieces of evidence of the Norfolk four-course rotation (wheat, turnips, barley, clover, repeated for two years in succession)

84 For example, Norfolk Record Office (NRO), Consistory Court inventories 73/24 and 78/30.
85 Worlidge, *Systema agriculturae*, p. 46; J. Paul, *The law of tythes*, London, 2nd edn., 1807, p. 183.
86 NRO, Consistory Court inventory 50/97; Reading University Library MSS NORF 14/1.
87 Young, *Eastern tour; idem, General view Norfolk; idem, General view Suffolk.*

Table 11.13 *Norfolk and Suffolk: mean yields on farms growing selected crops, 1710–39 (bushels per acre)*

	Buckwheat		Turnips		Clover	
	NG[a]	G[a]	NG	G	NG	G
Wheat	17.4	16.5	17.4	16.8	16.8	18.3
Barley	19.4	19.9	18.2	22.3	19.0	20.5

Note
[a] *NG* not growing; *G* growing.

Source Norfolk and Suffolk probate inventories.

comes, in fact, from East Suffolk, and then not until 1787–94, though there must be earlier ones.[88]

In comparison with the nineteenth century, therefore, the cultivation of turnips and clover was not on such a scale, nor of such a manner, as to have had a great impact on yields per acre. Yet, as Tables 11.3–11.5 demonstrate, the breakthrough in yield levels does coincide with their introduction.

Table 11.13 shows the mean yields of wheat and barley for farmers growing turnips and for those growing clover, for a period when the rate of innovation was roughly stationary (grain yields for farmers growing buckwheat are also shown with reference to the possible benefits of green manuring). The results indicate that wheat yields were significantly higher on farms growing clover, but not on those growing turnips. For barley, the situation was reversed: yields were higher on farms growing clover but not on those growing turnips. The proportion of cropped acreage under turnips and clover on the farms growing them was of course much higher than the average for all farms, reaching 18 per cent for clover, and nearly 20 per cent for turnips, and evidently the new crops were having some influence on yields. Nevertheless, other influences must also have been at work, since the yields on farms without the crops were still significantly higher than they had been at the end of the seventeenth century, as indicated in Table 11.3.[89]

88 NRO, L'Estrange, BH4. Mr Thompson of Culpho Hall farm north of Ipswich. Suffolk Record Office, Ipswich Branch, HA 54 970. An earlier example is at Cosgrove in Northamptonshire, cited in T. Bedford Franklin, *British grasslands from the earliest times to the present day*, London, 1953, p. 90.
89 In fact, the mean wheat yield for all farms in Table 11.3 is higher than the mean of the figures in Table 11.13. Table 11.13 uses a smaller selection of farms than Table 11.3 and does not weight each harvest year.

Table 11.14 *Norfolk and Suffolk: grain yields and population density*

A. *1590–99, 1628–40 (mean population density in 1603: 114 persons per 1,000 acres)*

	Density	CV%[a]
Wheat yields 25% above mean	114	−1.2
Barley yields 25% above mean	125	12.4
Wheat yields 25% below mean	117	3.3
Barley yields 25% below mean	108	−6.8

B. *1660–1739 (mean population density in the 1670s: 119 persons per 1,000 acres)*

	Density	CV%[a]
Wheat yields 25% above mean	156	45.3
Barley yields 25% above mean	114	29.2
Wheat yields 25% below mean	77	−53.7
Barley yields 25% below mean	146	32.9

Note
[a] The coefficient of variation expressed as a percentage.

Source Norfolk and Suffolk probate inventories and J. H. C. Patten (see note 90).

The argument has already been advanced that increased labour input may well have contributed to rises in yields. In order to examine this properly, information is needed on the actual labour force working on particular farms and the manner in which they were employed. Unfortunately, such information is extremely rare, and early modern historians can only look with envy at the sources available to medievalists. All that is available on a wide scale are estimates of population densities for 1603 and the 1670s, derived from the Communicants' Returns, the Hearth Tax, and the Compton Census.[90] These data do not constitute a measure of the proportion of the population employed in agriculture, let alone labour employed on particular farms. Moreover, relating the population density of a parish to the yield on a farm in that parish ignores the problem of inter-parish migration. So the attempt may be doomed from the start.

Table 11.14 shows mean population densities for parishes with wheat and barley yields in one of four categories. The population

90 These data were kindly supplied by John Patten. The methodology of their use is described in M. Overton, 'Agricultural change in Norfolk and Suffolk, 1580–1740', unpublished University of Cambridge Ph.D. thesis, 1981, pp. 216–17.

density for each group is expressed as a deviation from the average for all rural parishes using the coefficient of variation. Before 1640 no relationship is apparent, except that high yields of barley occurred in parishes with higher-than-average population densities. After 1660, some sort of a relationship does appear to have existed, since above-average yields for both wheat and barley tended to be associated with above-average population densities, and below-average wheat yields with parishes whose population densities were well below average. This could be interpreted as showing that higher yields were more likely where more labour was available. But there are other plausible explanations. Most obviously, lower population densities were also associated with areas of poorer soils (and vice versa), so that yields may have been lower simply because the quality of the land was poor.

Perhaps more than any other, this attempt to relate yields to population density as a surrogate for labour supplies demonstrates how difficult it is to relate yields to their determining factors in the early modern period. Probate inventories are the best source on which to base generalisations, but once a collection of farmers' inventories is disaggregated in the attempt to relate yields to other aspects of husbandry systems at the farm level, the number that can be used becomes perilously small. There are, for instance, too few usable inventories for Norfolk and Suffolk to relate yields to farm types in the manner adopted by Glennie for Hampshire.[91] Glennie also suggests that an aggregate geographical approach can supplement studies of individual farms.[92] Figure 11.4 shows the distribution of farms in Norfolk and Suffolk with particularly high or particularly low yields (those farms with yields below the lower quartile and above the upper quartile for a particular harvest year). Higher yields were to be found in eastern Norfolk and in central Suffolk. These were areas of better soils, but were also the areas associated with the introduction of clover and other innovations such as the growing of buckwheat. Moreover, notwithstanding the lack of a relationship between bullock fattening and higher yields in Table 11.12, there was a regional association between the higher yields of eastern Norfolk and the fattening of bullocks.[93]

91 Above, pp. 275–6. See also M. Overton, *Agricultural regions in early modern England: an example from East Anglia*, University of Newcastle upon Tyne, Department of Geography Seminar Paper, XLII, 1983, for the identification of farm types in Norfolk and Suffolk, and *idem*, 'Diffusion of agricultural innovations', where innovation is related to farm types.

92 Above, pp. 276, 280.

93 Space precludes maps of these other variables. They can be found for Norfolk in Overton and Campbell, 'Five centuries of farming'.

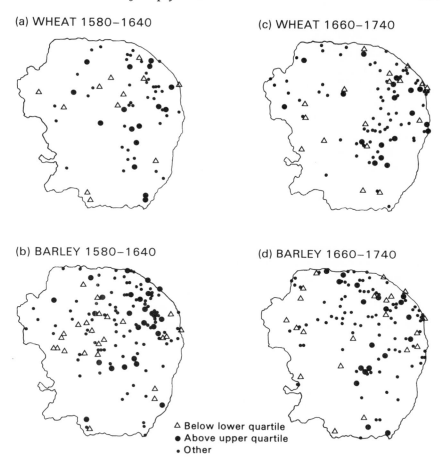

(a) WHEAT 1580–1640

(c) WHEAT 1660–1740

(b) BARLEY 1580–1640

(d) BARLEY 1660–1740

△ Below lower quartile
● Above upper quartile
· Other

Figure 11.4 *Distribution of extreme grain yields in Norfolk and Suffolk*

While Section I posed a range of questions about the determinants of yields and suggested some answers using historical examples in a rather anecdotal way, Section III has only been able to shed systematic light on a limited assortment of issues. The final section of the chapter therefore draws together the theoretical and empirical in an attempt to describe how yield changes were brought about in East Anglia from the sixteenth to the nineteenth centuries.

IV Conclusion: possible paths to productivity increases

From at least the mid sixteenth century onwards farmers were under pressure to increase output. This is obvious from what is known of population trends and the movement of agricultural prices relative to other prices.[94] In response to these pressures, yields of both wheat and barley increased, though exactly how cannot yet be determined from the historical record: certainly, there was no conspicuous innovation of fodder crops. It is possible that average farm sizes fell (at least the mean cropped acreage in inventories fell) and that livestock densities increased, including the density of working horses, thus providing more manure and more animal power for husbandry operations. In addition more grassland was ploughed up, and the arable area extended, most conspicuously in the fens.[95] Most likely, given the trend of population and wage-rates, labour inputs were increased, raising land productivity in the ways discussed above in the first section of the chapter, but probably depressing labour productivity. It must nevertheless be emphasised that this is a very speculative conclusion.[96] What is more certain, however, is that both yields and output increased, through a variety of mechanisms, but without major technological innovation to boost yields beyond their medieval maxima.[97]

From the mid seventeenth to the mid eighteenth centuries, demand slackened as population growth ceased and grain prices levelled off. Yields rose little if at all before the end of the seventeenth century, but thereafter they rose relatively sharply to unprecedented levels. Farmers began to introduce both turnips and clover to augment their fodder supplies, and although these crops were grown by a large proportion of farmers they were not, on the vast majority of farms, part of a rotation resembling the Norfolk four-course. On some farms they might well have led to considerable increases in yields, but yields on farms not growing these crops were also increasing.

It has been argued elsewhere that the most startling feature of farming in Norfolk and Suffolk after 1660 was a threefold increase in

94 E. A. Wrigley and R. S. Schofield, *The population history of England 1541–1871: a reconstruction*, London, 1981; R. S. Schofield, 'The impact of scarcity and plenty on population change in England, 1541–1871', pp. 67–94 in R. I. Rotberg and T. K. Rabb, eds., *Hunger and history*, Cambridge, 1985; P. J. Bowden, 'Agricultural prices, farm profits and rents', pp. 593–695 in Thirsk, *Agrarian history* IV; idem, 'Agricultural prices, wages, farm profits and rents', pp. 593–695 in Thirsk, *Agrarian history* Vii.
95 H. C. Darby, *The draining of the fens*, Cambridge, 1940; idem, *The changing fenland*, Cambridge, 1983.
96 Above, pp. 287–94.
97 See V. H. T. Skipp, *Crisis and development: an ecological case study of the forest of Arden 1570–1674*, Cambridge, 1978, for an excellent survey of the responses to population pressure in a group of Warwickshire parishes in the early seventeenth century.

the mean farm acreage under barley. Although this may have reflected increasing farm sizes, the expansion was much lower for the other grains and probably reflects a genuine increase in the area devoted to barley at the expense of permanent pasture or fallow. This is a rather perverse response to a relative fall in grain prices but can be explained by the development of new forms of marketing for barley, and perhaps also by the promotion of malt exports by the government.[98]

Extension of arable cultivation could well have resulted in increases in yields without the addition of new crops to rotations as Shiel has demonstrated, and could help to explain why yields increased for farms not cultivating new crops. But there are other possibilities. C. Lane considers that 'grass' on a farm in the sixteenth century usually consisted of natural grasses which were not selected and sown – the pasture land being left uncultivated. By the end of the seventeenth century selected grasses (not just clovers) were increasingly sown on land that had been cultivated and might therefore have produced higher yields. Inventories cannot be persuaded to provide grass yields, but from the mid seventeenth century onwards they increasingly record 'leys' and 'summerlays'. The fact that they were recorded suggests they were made 'with the industry and manurance of man' and hence that labour had been expended in producing them.[99] It is highly probable (though inventories cannot reveal it directly) that these leys were part of an arable rotation, and therefore indicate the presence of convertible husbandry. Table 11.8 shows how leys (including summerleys) and grass were increasingly recorded in Norfolk and Suffolk inventories, which echos Glennie's findings for Hertfordshire.

In some areas, where pasture land was too light to sustain grain crops without improvement, turnips could have been important in helping to reclaim newly-ploughed-up land. They did this by taking nutrients from the soil (up to five times the amount of cereal crops) and, since their roots were deeper in the ground, from a deeper level in the soil. These nutrients could be recycled, either as manure, or through crop residues left in the soil. Barley yields can thus be expected to have been higher on those farms growing turnips – which they were, as Table 11.13 shows. On the other hand, there was no difference between the mean yields of wheat for the two groups of farms.

Clover had rather a different role in rotations since in addition to providing more fodder the crop added nitrogen. Contemporaries

98 Overton, 'Diffusion of agricultural innovations', p. 213.
99 Above, p. 305.

recognised the beneficial effects of clover for a following grain crop and may have been sowing it as a preparation for wheat.[100] Wheat was the dominant crop in eastern Norfolk – an area which had long been in the vanguard of agricultural improvement – which was also the area where clover first appears in East Anglia.[101] Here at least, the crop may have been grown with the intention of raising yields. As Table 11.13 shows, wheat yields were significantly higher on farms with clover.

In addition to producing more barley, the price environment was favouring livestock, so farmers might simply have been growing new fodder crops to produce more meat. The exercise in Section I demonstrated that replacing a three-field system by a Norfolk four-course while retaining the area of permanent grass on the farm would increase livestock output dramatically. Thus the initial benefits of such a system would favour livestock husbandry, so that the gain in grain yields and output could have been unintended benefits of a strategy aimed at increasing livestock production. Farmers had other incentives to increase their fodder supplies other than as a response to price movements. Indeed, it has recently been argued that historians have over-emphasised the significance of prices in determining farmers' behaviour in the early modern period.[102] Of much more immediate impact were short-term changes in the weather. The weather impinged directly on farmers' experience and was probably regarded as the direct determinant of prices.

A variety of sources indicate that the weather of the 1670s, '80s, and '90s was particularly bad for hay.[103] Local evidence is provided by the weather diary kept by Samuel Clark of Rainham, Norfolk, for the years 1659–85. His observations clearly indicate that the months of May and June were much drier than average with over 40 per cent of those months in the 27-year period noted for being exceptionally dry.[104] In 17 of those 27 years (or over 60 per cent) either the weather was noted as being dry or the spring as backward. These drought conditions, coupled with low temperatures, would have given farmers every incentive

---

100 W. Blith, *The English improver improved*, London, 1652, pp. 184–5; Worlidge, *Systema agriculturae*, p. 26.
101 Overton, 'Diffusion of agricultural innovations'.
102 Overton, 'Weather and agricultural change', pp. 82–4.
103 T. H. Baker, *Records of the seasons, prices of agricultural produce and phenomena observed in the British Isles*, London, 1883. Baker's records are also included in J. M. Stratton, *Agricultural records AD 220–1968*, London, 1969, and in Jones, *Seasons and prices*.
104 Royal Society MSS of Samuel Clark of Rainham, Norfolk.

to search for other sources of fodder, and may therefore, in part, explain why turnips were adopted so rapidly from the 1670s when they had been known to farmers as a field crop from the 1620s and perhaps even earlier. Turnips could be sown as late as August to provide winter feed, so immediate action could be taken to mitigate the consequences of reduced yields of hay. Alternative 'grass' crops such as clover also increased the variety of fodder sources and so mitigated against a complete failure of supplies, as J. Worlidge recognised.[105]

While dry and backward springs encouraged farmers to grow turnips, the very hard winters of the 1690s were detrimental to the success of the crop. Although the proportion of farmers growing turnips continued to rise into the eighteenth century, the mean acreage they grew fell after the 1690s, which might well have been a consequence of hard winters. It was not until swedes replaced turnips towards the end of the eighteenth century that a root crop could be grown with more security.[106]

From the mid eighteenth to the mid nineteenth century the proportion of arable under turnips rose from around 9 per cent to around 20 per cent, and for clover from around 2.5 per cent to 20 per cent. By the 1830s the elements of the Norfolk four-course, which had existed in the late seventeenth century, had finally come together in fully-fledged rotations. Yet the growth in yields was *less* rapid over this period than it had been in the previous fifty years or so: a finding that demands some explanation.

After 1700 the differential rate of yield increase for wheat and barley (Table 11.5) might be explained in terms of a change in the relative proportions of the two crops. From being predominantly barley counties in the early eighteenth century, wheat and barley were grown in roughly the same proportions in Norfolk and Suffolk by the 1830s. A fall in the barley acreage and an extension of the wheat could have resulted in wheat cultivation extending on to less suitable soils while barley cultivation retreated from them. Another possibility is that grain output was expanding more rapidly than livestock output. If the balance

105 Worlidge, *Systema agriculturae*, p. 26.
106 F. W. Macro, 'The culture of turnips, recommended to those counties where they are not yet common', *Annals of Agriculture*, III, 1785, pp. 297–304; T. Southwell, 'An account of the severe winter of 1739–40 and its effects in the county of Norfolk', *Transactions of the Norwich Naturalists Society*, II, 1875, pp. 125–30; MSS diary of Daniel Gwilt of Icklingham, Suffolk, East Suffolk Record Office, Redstone S6/1/1.1; N. Harvey, 'The coming of the swede to Great Britain: an obscure chapter in farming history', *Agricultural History*, XXIII, 1949, pp. 286–8.

between arable and pasture was moving towards arable, and the area of the Norfolk four-course was being extended, then yields per acre may well have been sacrificed in the interests of an overall expansion in grain output, as the differences between Farm B and Farm C in Table 11.1 show. Further yield rises could also have been held back because the reserves of nitrogen exploited in the ploughing-up early in the eighteenth century were now running out. A final possibility is that, thanks to the spread of the Norfolk four-course, nitrogen was no longer the limiting factor in crop yields.[107] Turnips make high demands on phosphates and it could have been a shortage of these that was keeping yields down. The use of phosphate fertilisers increased rapidly after the 1830s, which may account for the subsequent jump in yields to mid-century.[108]

The explanation of yield change in the two counties of Norfolk and Suffolk is not a simple one. While, in theory, diffusion of the Norfolk four-course could have had dramatic effects, the period of its most rapid spread does not synchronise with the most rapid rise in yields. From the mid eighteenth to the mid nineteenth centuries, the index of gross yields doubled, as Table 11.3 shows. Output must have risen by much more than this since the cultivated area rose, and the greatly improved fodder supplies increased livestock output considerably. In Norfolk and Suffolk, therefore, agricultural output must have risen by more than the doubling recently attributed to English agriculture as a whole.[109] This rise in output and land productivity was accompanied, probably for the first time in English agrarian history, by a rise in the productivity of labour. But that is another story.[110]

107 Shiel, above, pp. 51–2.
108 Russell, *Fertility of the soil*, p. 50; Watson and More, *Agriculture*, p. 282; F. M. L. Thompson, 'The second agricultural revolution, 1815–1880', *EcHR*, XXI, 1968, pp. 62–77.
109 B. A. Holderness, 'Prices, productivity and output', pp. 84–189 in Mingay, *Agrarian history* VI, p. 174.
110 M. Overton, 'The critical century? The agrarian history of England and Wales 1750–1850', *AHR*, XXXVIII, 1990, pp. 185–9; Overton and Campbell, above, pp. 30–7.

Energy availability and agricultural productivity

This paper is largely speculative. It will have served a useful purpose if it leads to a reconsideration of existing empirical evidence, and still more if it provokes a search for new material, but it has been cast in a largely deductive form, using only a scattering of illustrative data. Its starting point is the commonplace observation that agriculture is necessarily a very energy-intensive activity. Ploughing the land (or turning it over with a hoe) requires a large number of foot-pounds of effort per acre. Manuring is apt to be an equally back-breaking job, and there are many aspects of harvesting which involve heavy labour: using a sickle or scythe, stooking, forking up to a cart, and, later, beating out the grain. Moreover, because agricultural production, unlike most forms of industrial production, is always scattered over a large area, running up to some hundreds of acres in the case of a large farm, a great deal of energy must be expended on transport within the farm; in carting hay, grain and roots from the field to the barn, in taking cartloads of manure from the farmyard to the field, and so on. Not for nothing was it enjoined upon men that they must live by the sweat of their brow. Nor is it surprising that physical strength was a prized asset. A strong man could produce considerably more in the course of a year than a weakling, in contrast with the situation in most forms of employment today when there is seldom any benefit to be gained from unusual strength.

Energy availability for agricultural operations had a close connection with output per head, and hence with the possible scale of economic activity outside agriculture in any pre-industrial society. The higher the level of manpower productivity in agriculture, the higher the proportion of the labour force that could engage in secondary or tertiary activities and still be adequately fed. The manpower productivity limitations of traditional agriculture tended to restrict, often severely, the proportion of the population that could make a living outside the agricultural sector.

In view of its great strategic importance, it is well to recall that the opportunities for improving productivity levels by the classic route described by Adam Smith were far more limited in agriculture than in industry, as Smith himself emphasised. When he told the parable of the pinmakers early in the first chapter of *The wealth of nations*, he suggested that the specialisation of function made possible by the division of labour could give rise to truly immense increases in output per head.[1] And he was explicit in suggesting that what was attainable in pin manufacture was also possible in many other branches of industry. But he was careful to stress that the paradigm was much less applicable to agriculture because 'the ploughman, the harrower, the sower of seed, and the reaper of corn' were often perforce one and the same.[2]

Yet if economies were ever to put behind them the constraints implied by the low real incomes characteristic of traditional societies, a rise in output per head in agriculture was essential. Agriculture was such a dominant element in all pre-industrial economies that this assertion is virtually a truism. In this connection, it is easy to overlook the fact that the land was not only the source of almost all food both for man and beast, but also much the most important source of industrial raw materials. Without exception the industries that employed a large labour force before the industrial revolution were industries dependent upon organic raw materials. Weavers and spinners, butchers and bakers, shoemakers and glovers, tailors and cappers, carpenters and coopers, all used organic raw materials. Even those relatively few workers engaged in working metals were indirectly heavily dependent on the productivity of the land. Iron manufacture was as likely to be prevented from further expansion by a shortage of wood for charcoal as by any other factor.

Before the advent of the steam engine in the middle decades of the nineteenth century and of the internal combustion engine at the end of the century, almost all the mechanical energy used on the farm to perform productive tasks came from human or animal muscle.[3] Although what might be termed potential human muscle power per

---

1 Adam Smith believed that in the small pin manufactory that he had visited the ten men there employed were producing at least 240 times as many pins per man as each would have been able to produce if he had been working individually and in isolation. Indeed he seems to have thought that the true figure was probably far higher. A. Smith, *An inquiry into the nature and causes of the wealth of nations*, ed. R. Campbell and A. Skinner, 2 vols., Oxford, 1976, I, p. 15.
2 Smith, *Wealth of nations*, p. 16.
3 There were, of course, some minor exceptions to this generalisation. Wind power, for example, might be employed in the drainage or irrigation of fields.

head may not have varied greatly between different populations, in the sense that the average energy output of well-fed individuals would have been similar, the amount of energy that could be realised day by day was strongly affected by any significant variations in levels of nutrition. As a rough-and-ready rule about 1,500 calories a day are needed to maintain basic bodily functions. If daily intake falls much below this level over a substantial period the effects of malnutrition will become evident and may ultimately prove fatal even if no physical labour is performed. Above the 1,500-calorie-per-day level there is a broadly straight line relationship between additional calorie intake and the ability to exert energy in order to carry out a productive task. Thus, twice as much labour can be performed by a man regularly receiving 3,000 calories a day as by a man regularly receiving only 2,250. The relationship holds up to an intake level of about 4,000 calories a day.[4]

In principle there could clearly be major differences in output per head in agriculture as a function of the level of nutrition prevailing in a population. Since the amount of work performed largely determines the level of output per head, other things being equal, a population in which poor nutrition was an endemic condition would be apt for that reason to suffer from low productivity per head. Moreover, it would also be likely to become firmly clamped into a state of misery and wretchedness since low output per head tends to ensure poor nutrition, just as the reverse relationship holds true, thus engendering a vicious circle.

At the bottom end of the scale of agricultural productivity the issue of human nutritional levels may well have been of great importance in the past. At the opposite end of the scale, however, other considerations prevailed. Even the stoutest and best-fed man is still feeble compared with an ox or a horse. A man working with a hoe or a spade, for example, can prepare for sowing only a small fraction of the area that the same man can prepare if he has a horse and plough to assist him. Without the help of draught animals it may be difficult for a farmer to do more than feed his family on the produce that he can secure by a year's labour. Indeed, it may be difficult for one man to cultivate a sufficiently large area for any other result to be possible, given the traditional crops and prevalent environmental circumstances of western Europe. But the situation can be transformed by the use of

---

4 These are only rough orders of magnitude. Views vary. See, for example, E. Cook, *Man, energy and society*, San Francisco, 1976, pp. 27–8; F. Cottrell, *Energy and society*, New York, 1955, pp. viii and 18.

draught animals. They can raise the level of mechanical energy available to the average person working on the land to the point where one man may be able to feed, not only his own family, but others as well.

Man and ox or horse are, of course, in constant competition with one another. The same fixed area of farmland must provide food for both, and, though the energy output of draught animals may be high, they have appetites to match. Each working horse needs the fodder produced by about 5 acres of land to keep it in good condition over the working year.[5] If the tension between the food needs of people and their animals becomes sufficiently acute, the needs of people will be given priority. In the short run this strategy may bring relief, but in the longer term the result may be a lowering of output per head and therefore greater poverty.

If, however, an agricultural economy is so structured that there is a favourable ratio between draught animals and workers on the land, the possibility exists of a relatively high level of output per worker with all the benign implications that this will have for the economy as a whole. A study of Mexican agriculture in the recent past affords a good illustration of the extent of the advantages that may flow from a situation in which draught animals are employed to assist in agricultural production. The study covered both areas where only human labour was used, and others where oxen were also employed in farm work. Empirical data about maize cultivation showed that every hour of ox labour saved about 3.8 hours of human labour. Those areas in which maize was cultivated solely by hand therefore involved much greater inputs of human labour than those where draught animals were common. In the former case, the tilling and cultivation of a hectare of maize needed 1,140 man-hours of labour; where oxen were used, 380 man-hours sufficed, since they were supplemented by 200 ox-hours of work.[6] Since horses work faster than oxen, each hour of labour by a horse can save more man-hours than can be saved by an ox, perhaps in the ratio of three to two.

I England and France compared

By the standards of pre-industrial economies, output per head was unusually high in English agriculture at the end of the eighteenth

5 J. R. McCulloch, *A statistical account of the British Empire*, 2 vols., London, 1837, I, pp. 489–90.
6 D. Pimentel, 'Energy flow in the food system', pp. 1–23 in *idem* and C. W. Hall, eds., *Food and energy resources*, London, 1984, pp. 5–6.

century. At the time of the 1801 census only about 36 per cent of the labour force were engaged in agriculture, forestry and fishing, at a time when the comparable percentage in continental European countries was usually in the range between 60 and 75.[7] Yet the country was broadly self-sufficient in its main foodstuffs, and standards of nutrition were probably not inferior to those elsewhere in Europe and may well, indeed, have been slightly higher than in neighbouring countries.[8] The contrast is so marked that it is impossible not to conclude that productivity per head must have been substantially higher in England than elsewhere. Similar estimating procedures suggest both that output per head of those employed in agriculture doubled between the early sixteenth century and 1800 in England, and that by the latter date agricultural productivity per worker was between 50 and 100 per cent higher in England than in France.[9]

Given that animal power can be substituted for human labour in many agricultural operations, including several of those which demand most time in the course of the annual cycle of farm work, it is possible in principle that differences in the ratio of draught animals to farm workers may have accounted for a major part of the difference in agricultural manpower productivity between England and France, and also that the same factor could explain a substantial part of the rise in productivity taking place in England between the sixteenth and nineteenth centuries.[10] What of the empirical evidence?

7 E. A. Wrigley, *People, cities and wealth: the transformation of traditional society*, Oxford, 1987, p. 189. See also Table 13.1 below, p. 341.

8 Fogel estimates that the final height reached by men in Great Britain in the last quarter of the eighteenth century and again in the first quarter of the nineteenth century was greater than that in the other European countries for which he has assembled contemporary data (Sweden, France, Denmark and Hungary). Since achieved final height closely reflects the cumulative effect of nutrition in childhood and adolescence, these data, if accurate, strongly suggest that British nutritional standards were relatively good. R. W. Fogel, *Second thoughts on the European escape from hunger: famines, price elasticities, entitlements, chronic malnutrition, and mortality rates*, National Bureau of Economic Research working paper series on historical factors in long-run growth, I, Cambridge, Mass., 1989, Table 9, p. 50.

9 Wrigley, *People, cities and wealth*, pp. 186–9. For labour productivity in French agriculture see G. Grantham, below, pp. 340–63. The rise in labour productivity within English agriculture is discussed by R. C. Allen, above, pp. 250–2. G. Clark, above, pp. 228–31, argues that labour productivity in English agriculture was already high by the late sixteenth century.

10 Pounds' description and analysis of labour usage on estates belonging to the Buller family and cultivated directly by them in the middle decades of the eighteenth century show very clearly what a high proportion of the total of working days recorded was spent in aspects of farm work where constant use was made of draught animals. At Keveral Barton, a manor in the east of the county,

Neither topic can be investigated with great confidence because of the weakness of the available data. F. M. L. Thompson's recent work suggests that there were about 700,000 farm horses in England and Wales in 1811 at a time when the total number of adult males employed in agriculture was close to one million.[11] On the assumption that each horse did work equivalent to that performed by five men, each man-hour of work done by a man was assisted by 3.5 'man-hours' of work performed by a horse.[12] Just over a century earlier, Gregory King estimated the number of 'cart and plough' horses in England and Wales at 502,000.[13] The agricultural labour force was perhaps 10 per cent smaller in the 1690s than in 1811, suggesting that in King's time the level of animal power per man in agriculture was more than 20 per cent lower than a century later (i.e. 2.75 'man-hours' of horse power per man compared with 3.5 'man-hours' at the later date).[14] This

---

for example, 626 out of a total of 2,567 working days, or almost a quarter, were spent in carrying and spreading manure, ploughing, sowing and harrowing. Only sowing among these operations would not have involved a fairly constant use of draught animals. A further 846 working days (33 per cent) were devoted to harvesting and haymaking, occupations for which a considerable amount of animal power was also needed. The data for Morval Barton suggest an equal or greater dependence on draught animals, while even at Golden Barton, further to the west and less engaged in arable cultivation, work with draught animals also figured prominently in the graphical representation of the weekly division of male and female labour at various tasks for the years 1754–55. The importance of manuring, ploughing, and driving oxen and horses is plain. Equally noticeable is the way in which any slack in labour usage in the winter months, and especially from late September to mid-December, was taken up in spreading sand, lime and manure. This was an effective way of securing a long-term improvement in the land, in effect capital investment, and feasible only by the employment of many horses. N. J. G. Pounds, 'Barton farming in eighteenth-century Cornwall', *Journal of the Royal Institution of Cornwall*, new series, VII, 1973, pp. 55–75.

11 F. M. L. Thompson, 'Nineteenth-century horse sense', *EcHR*, XXIX, 1976, p. 80; and E. A. Wrigley, 'Men on the land and men in the countryside: employment in agriculture in early nineteenth-century England', pp. 295–336 in L. Bonfield, R. M. Smith and K. Wrightson, eds., *The world we have gained: histories of population and social structure*, Oxford, 1986, Table 11.12, p. 332. The reason for reducing Thompson's estimate of 800,000 horses for Britain to 700,000 for England and Wales is given in E. A. Wrigley, *Continuity, chance and change: the character of the industrial revolution in England*, Cambridge, 1988, pp. 41–2.

12 This approximate calculation does not involve the assumption that horses worked the same number of hours per day as men, rather that horses worked roughly half as many.

13 G. King, 'The LCC Burns Journal', a manuscript notebook containing workings for several projected works (composed c.1695–1700), in P. Laslett, comp., *The earliest classics: John Graunt and Gregory King*, Farnborough, 1973, p. 200.

14 Wrigley, *People, cities and wealth*, Table 7.4, p. 170, gives estimates of the rural agricultural population in 1700 and 1801.

calculation has a fragile empirical base in the light of present knowledge, and unfortunately it is not possible even to venture a 'guesstimate' of the extent of change during the seventeenth century. Given the probable scale of the shift from arable to pasture in the seventeenth century, however, it is quite possible that the proportionate increase in the ratio of animal power to man power in the seventeenth century was greater than in the eighteenth, and that therefore over the whole period from 1600 to 1800 the rise in this ratio might constitute a proximate cause explaining much of the apparent gain in output per head in agriculture.[15]

Any comparison of England and France at the start of the nineteenth century must also necessarily be tentative in view of the quality of the available data, but the contrast is sufficiently marked to leave little doubt that differences in animal draught power per head were significant. The estimation of the total number of 'horses' employed in French agriculture is complicated by the fact that in France, unlike England, large numbers of oxen were still in use in the early nineteenth century. Assuming that three oxen may be taken as the equivalent of two horses, contemporary estimates suggest that the number of horse equivalents at work in agriculture in France in 1820 was about 1.87 million.[16] The male labour force engaged in French agriculture was about 4.5 million,[17] and therefore, on these assumptions, a French farm worker would have had at his disposal only 2.08 'man-hours' of horse power compared with the English figure of 3.5. Combining the effort made by each man with the effort made on his behalf by his draught animals, therefore, the energy exerted in the production process by each French farm worker each hour was 3.08 man-hours, while the comparable English figure was 4.5.[18]

It does not necessarily follow, of course, that the ratio between these two figures captures the difference in overall productivity between farm workers in the two countries, nor that if it did the congruence in

15 There is much useful information to be had about draught animals, and especially about the horse, in J. Langdon, *Horses, oxen and technological innovation: the use of draught animals in English farming from 1066 to 1500*, Cambridge, 1986; and in F. M. L. Thompson, ed., *Horses in European economic history: a preliminary canter*, Reading, 1983.
16 Wrigley, *Continuity, chance and change*, p. 41.
17 J.-C. Toutain, *Le Produit de l'agriculture française de 1700 à 1958: II, la Croissance*, in J. Marczewski, ed., *Histoire quantitative de l'économie française (2)*, Cahiers de l'Institut de Science Économique Appliquée, supplement CXV, Paris, 1961, Table 141, pp. 200–1. Toutain's estimate relates to the male population engaged in agriculture.
18 Wrigley, *Continuity, chance and change*, pp. 40–2.

the two ratios could be attributed to differences in energy per head available. For energy differences to be persuasive as an explanation of overall productivity differences, it would be necessary to show that it could be safely assumed that other things were equal. Patently this was not the case. There were, for example, substantial differences in types of land tenure and in the size of holdings between the two countries. Both may have influenced the prevailing level of output per head. And many other factors might be adduced as playing a part in accounting for productivity differences. Furthermore, even if differences in energy availability per farm worker could be conclusively shown to be the chief reason for differences in productivity per head, this would still only provide a proximate cause for the contrast. A satisfactory explanation would need to probe deeper. Nor should it be overlooked that this line of argument is serviceable chiefly in regard to cereal agriculture and is less weighty where animal husbandry is concerned.

Nevertheless, the difference in the energy ratios suggested for England and France does correspond fairly closely with the apparent differences in agricultural productivity per head between the two countries, and, pending further investigation, it is reasonable to regard differences in available animal power as important in explaining the wide gap between output per head in agriculture in England and France.

II Circumstances favouring the use of draught animals

If the ratio between draught animals and men on the land exercised a strong influence on manpower productivity in the past, and if this in turn was a key element in governing opportunities for economic growth and change, it is natural to attempt to discover why some agricultural systems achieved a favourable ratio while others did not.

Discussions of the determinants of the balance between arable and pastoral usage of the land tend to stress the importance of ecological and economic factors, either separately or in combination. Regions in which rainfall is relatively abundant, with a long growing season but only moderate summer heat, are favourable to the growth of grass but are less suited to cereal culture, because the grain does not ripen satisfactorily in poor summers and harvesting may be difficult and laborious. Such regions are certainly at a comparative disadvantage in cereal production if there are other regions with warmer and drier summers within the same market network. Thus, once a national market for agricultural produce had been established, the contrast between the balance of arable and pasture in the west midlands and East Anglia may reasonably be referred to the comparative advantages bestowed on the two areas by their differing agricultural ecologies, especially when soil types are also taken into account.

The overall balance of arable and pastoral activity, however, is a distinct issue from the question of the ratio of draught animals to men in agriculture. It will be determined chiefly by the relative importance of meat, wool and dairy products on the one hand, and cereal cultivation on the other. Within the total of livestock units on the farm, draught animals may characteristically represent only a small fraction, at least in areas specialising in pastoral agriculture.[19]

That the relative abundance of draught animals is not simply a matter of the suitability of the local environment for supporting livestock is suggested by English medieval economic history. Climate and soils were much the same in the thirteenth century as in the seventeenth. The ecological elements of a successful pastoral economy were present in the earlier no less than in the later period. But livestock farming in medieval times, it has been argued, came under pressure because of rising population which brought with it an imperative necessity to increase the output of food grain, with a consequent decline in the proportion of land devoted to pasture.[20] Whether there was a similar falling tendency in the ratio of draught animals to farm workers (or to a unit area of arable land) is less clear and would repay greater attention. That there should be some tendency of this sort, however, is plausible, both in that fodder probably became scarcer and more expensive, and in that the price of human labour fell as real wages were squeezed by competition among an over-abundant labour force.[21]

Considerations of this sort suggest that, while the ratio of draught animals to farm workers may have been a major proximate determinant

19 The concept of the livestock unit is used to reduce totals of livestock of many different types to a common measure, large animals like the horse and the cow being treated as equivalent to several smaller animals such as the pig or the sheep.

20 For example, the argument is set out in the form of a feedback diagram in C. T. Smith, *An historical geography of western Europe before 1800*, London, 1967, Figure 4.5, p. 206. As Smith observes (p. 210): 'Beyond a certain point ... the extension of arable at the expense of pasture, meadow and woodland grazings would lead to progressive impoverishment of the village community and a vicious circle of declining yields as draught-power and supplies of manure were prejudiced by shortage of stock.'

21 See, for example, the evidence about the course of real wages in the later thirteenth and early fourteenth centuries in H. Phelps Brown and S. V. Hopkins, *A perspective of wages and prices*, London, 1981, Appendix B, Table 3, pp. 28–9.

of the level of agricultural productivity per head, at one remove the demographic characteristics of the human population of a country were important. Some draught animals were a virtual necessity in the heavy-plough areas of northern and western Europe. Without them, the primary preparation of the soil to receive seed was difficult to the point of impracticability (though when a new crop with rice-like yield capacity appeared in the form of the potato, Irish peasants found it possible to make a living on lazy-bed plots dug over with the spade). But there were many other agricultural activities in which energy supplied by animal muscle could be substituted for human effort, and the scale of such substitution varied substantially according to the relative abundance of draught animals. This affected both current output per head and also what might be termed the capital account of agriculture. Not only was the ease and speed with which many energy-intensive agricultural operations could be performed influenced by the number of draught animals available, but in addition an area blessed with plenty of draught animals could undertake capital improvements that were impractical elsewhere.

Agricultural improvement in eighteenth-century England, for example, frequently involved very heavy expenditures of energy. Arthur Young referred quite casually to the advantages of marling farmland in light soil areas at the rate of 100 to 150 tons per acre.[22] Assuming by way of illustration that 100 acres were marled in this way, and, conservatively, that the marl was brought an average of two miles from the marl pit to the field, then treating such an acreage in this way would have meant providing 30,000 ton-miles of transport, an operation only feasible if vast quantities of fodder were available to 'fuel' the horses needed to perform the task. Where it was possible to marl in this way, however, a significant and semi-permanent improvement in soil quality and therefore in yields could be secured, thus bringing about a capital improvement of importance. Since each farm horse needed about five acres of land for maintenance, and there were some 700,000 farm horses by the beginning of the nineteenth century, they pre-empted the output from 3.5 million acres for their fodder by that date, a 'luxury' that might not have been possible if the pressure to maximise food production had been more severe.

Considerations of this sort suggest that one of the most valuable by-products of the adoption of rotational systems involving fodder crops

22 A. Young, *Travels in France during the years 1787, 1788 and 1789*, ed. J. Kaplow, New York, 1969, p. 314. He made the remark in the course of a panegyric about the advantages of large-scale over small-scale farming.

may have been the encouragement that this afforded to the keeping of draught animals no less than of animals kept for meat or wool. To be able to secure higher cereal output per acre, and perhaps some increase in aggregate cereal output from a given area, while at the same time simultaneously increasing fodder production, overcame an energy-supply difficulty as well as solving a food supply problem, and did so in a manner likely also to increase productivity per head.

It can be shown that the institution of marriage played a central role in determining the relationship between the demographic characteristics and the economic constitution of England in the early modern period. Fertility levels were almost exclusively governed by the timing and incidence of marriage, and fertility changes were more influential than mortality changes in changing the rate of population growth.[23] For reasons lucidly set forth by Malthus in his *Essay on population*, a marriage regime that reflects 'prudence' on the part of would-be brides and grooms is consonant with a substantially higher standard of living, even within the inhibiting circumstances of a pre-industrial economy, than one in which marriage is early and universal.[24] Marriage practice in early modern England was situated towards the prudent end of the spectrum of possibilities represented in the marriage practices of pre-industrial societies generally. The nature of the prevailing marriage regime should therefore not be left out of account in attempting to identify the reasons for the exceptionally successful agricultural economy of England in the seventeenth and eighteenth centuries. A 'low-pressure' demographic regime reduces any potential tension between the food needs of the population and the fodder needs of its draught animals. It would be absurd to propose the English marriage regime as a sufficient cause of the higher manpower productivity that was gradually achieved, but it may find a place as one of a number of necessary causes for the advance that occurred.

III Rising productivity per head in early modern English agriculture

The history of the agricultural economy of England between the sixteenth and nineteenth centuries was most unusual when compared with that of her continental neighbours. During this period the

23 E. A. Wrigley and R. S. Schofield, *The population history of England 1541–1871: a reconstruction*, London, 1981, pp. 236–48.
24 *The works of Thomas Robert Malthus*, ed. E. A. Wrigley and D. Souden, London, 1986, III, *Essay on population*, 6th edn., 1826, book 4, chapters 1, 2, 3 and 14.

M

population of England rose very much faster than that of any other major country of western Europe (between 1550 and 1820 the population of England rose by about 280 per cent whereas in France, Germany, Italy, Spain and Holland the rise was in the range between 50 and 70 per cent).[25] Throughout the period, however, England remained largely self-sufficient in basic foodstuffs and, in addition to meeting the rapidly growing demand for human food, large increases in other agricultural outputs were secured, providing raw materials for industry and sustaining a steadily rising number of draught animals at work outside the agricultural sector. Evidently great strides must have been made in increasing output per acre since the total area in agricultural use grew far less than total output.

With an unchanged material technology, the logic of Ricardo's argument about the inevitability of declining marginal returns both at the intensive and extensive margins of agriculture is hard to resist.[26] At some point, as demand for food and other agricultural products rises, it seems inevitable that larger inputs of labour and capital will be necessary to secure a unit increase in output. It may be possible to continue to obtain increases in gross output over quite a wide production horizon, but to do so only by paying the penalty so lucidly expounded by Ricardo. For example, B. M. S. Campbell has shown both that notably high yields were sometimes secured and sustained in medieval Norfolk and that they were associated with very high labour inputs.[27] It is not, therefore, the fact that there were significant increases in output per acre in seventeenth- and, especially, eighteenth-century England that should occasion surprise, even in the absence of great changes in agricultural techniques, but that the increases were obtained from an agricultural labour force that probably grew only very modestly between 1600 and 1800.[28]

A rough doubling of output per arable acre, such as took place in England over the seventeenth and eighteenth centuries, is a striking

---

25 Wrigley, *People, cities and wealth*, pp. 215–16.
26 D. Ricardo, *On the principles of political economy and taxation* in *The works and correspondence of David Ricardo*, ed. P. Sraffa with the collaboration of M. H. Dobb, Cambridge, 1951, I, chapter 6, 'On profits', especially pp. 125–6.
27 B. M. S. Campbell, 'Agricultural progress in medieval England: some evidence from eastern Norfolk', *EcHR*, XXXVI, 1983, pp. 26–46; *idem*, above, pp. 173–7.
28 Wrigley, *People, cities and wealth*, Table 7.4, p. 170, provides estimates suggesting that the rural agricultural population in England grew from 2.87 million to 3.14 million between 1600 and 1800. The apparent precision is spurious, but the accompanying text provides some reasons for supposing that the order of magnitude of the change may be broadly correct.

achievement in any agricultural system before the advent of artificial fertilisers, pesticides, powerful and ingenious machinery, and modern methods of improving seeds and breeds. Starting from a roughly similar level in the sixteenth century, the increase in output per acre appears to have been much greater in England than was normal on the continent over the two succeeding centuries.[29] It is not surprising, therefore, that agricultural historians should have devoted so much attention to the better measurement of rising output per acre and to the attempt to explain it satisfactorily. But if success in raising output per unit area was remarkable, securing such increases from an agricultural labour force whose size did not greatly change was an even more remarkable achievement, and one of far greater significance in preparing the ground for the changes which have come, in retrospect, to be referred to as the industrial revolution.

The evidence and arguments associated with the view that there was little growth in the number working on the land over the period 1600–1800 are not beyond dispute.[30] More work on this topic would be very welcome, but no future revision of the estimates is likely to place in doubt the inference that there must have been a large rise in output per head in agriculture. This follows directly from the fact that only about a third of the national labour force was engaged in agriculture in 1800, combined with the virtual certainty that the comparable figure 200 years earlier must have been about twice as large.[31]

The increases in output per head in agriculture that took place were no doubt the result of many different influences. It is possible that the development of a more fully capitalist organisation of the industry assisted in this respect. Under-employment of labour is often found in traditional systems of agriculture. For example, if the prevailing conventions of a society encourage peasant families to retain their sons on their holdings until the *average* product falls to the level of subsistence rather than when the *marginal* product does so, there is likely to be a

29 But R. C. Allen and C. Ó Gráda, 'On the road again with Arthur Young: English, Irish, and French agriculture during the industrial revolution', *JEH*, XLVIII, 1988, pp. 93–116, argue that by the close of the eighteenth century yields per acre in Ireland and on the better soils of northern France were broadly comparable with those obtained in England.

30 The figures given in note 28 were obtained by multiplying the national population totals at the two dates by two ratios; first by estimates of the proportion of the population living in towns to eliminate urban populations, and then by estimates of the proportion of the rural population engaged in non-agricultural pursuits. This left, finally, a residuum which was both rural and agricultural.

31 But see Clark, above, pp. 228–30, for a dissentient view.

substantial measure of agricultural under-employment. Malthus pointed out long ago that in a capitalist agricultural system it can never be in the interest of the farmer to retain in his employment any worker who does not produce at least an output equivalent to that necessary to maintain a family of average size at the standard of life accepted by the society in question as appropriate for the labouring class.[32] To the degree, therefore, that sixteenth-century agriculture, still retaining many husbandmen/virgators and only partially market-orientated, may have continued practices that interfered with an optimal allocation of labour by keeping too many men in agricultural employment or by distributing them inefficiently, some of the subsequent rise in labour productivity may have resulted from the reduction or elimination of such practices.

Labour productivity may also have benefited from success in mitigating the problem of meeting a high peak in the demand for labour at times like harvest without also suffering from prolonged periods of under-employment at other seasons of the year. A part of the significance of the shift towards new systems of crop rotation, of the introduction of new fodder crops, and of the heavy labour requirement for marling, liming and manuring, may lie in its effect in evening out the distribution of the demand for labour in the course of the farming year.[33]

Sometimes the adoption of new tools may have helped to increase productivity. Presumably the substitution of the scythe for the sickle, for example, must have contributed to this effect. Other comparable changes in technology will have had comparable beneficial effects. Again, although Adam Smith was probably right in discounting the possibility of obtaining large increases in output per head in agriculture through the division of labour on the pin-maker model, a different form of the division of labour, that arising from geographical specialisation, may have helped the cause of higher labour productivity substantially.[34] There is strong evidence of an increased integration of English regions into a single market area in the course of the seventeenth century, provoked in large measure by the pressure of demand from London.[35] Such a change is likely not only to have increased aggregate output but also to have improved output per head.

32 *Works of Malthus, Essay on population,* p. 405.
33 C. P. Timmer, 'The turnip, the new husbandry, and the English agricultural revolution', *Quarterly Journal of Economics,* LXXXIII, 1969, pp. 375–95.
34 For a discussion of the medieval economy which stresses the productivity benefits of greater regional specialisation see K. G. Persson, *Pre-industrial economic growth, social organization and technological progress in Europe,* Oxford, 1988.
35 A. Kussmaul, 'Agrarian change in seventeenth-century England: the economic historian as paleontologist', *JEH,* XLV, 1985, pp. 1–30.

It remains doubtful, however, whether the changes just enumerated, and others like them, are sufficient to account for the very large apparent increase in labour productivity that took place, especially as the agricultural economy was swimming against the tide, so to speak, in attempting to improve labour productivity, for it is hard not to suppose that some Ricardian drag was experienced as a largely unchanging area of farmland was induced to yield a steadily rising annual output.

Unhappily, it is impossible to quantify the contribution of each factor that may reasonably be supposed to have tended to raise agricultural labour productivity, impossible even to suggest a plausible ranking list of such factors. It is therefore patently foolhardy, and in any strict sense unjustifiable, to assert the pre-eminence of a particular influence on the rising trend of labour productivity. Unfortunately, neither the scale of the change to be explained nor the relative importance of the several factors contributing to the change can be established with any precision. If only to provoke argument, however, the thesis is advanced here that energy input into the agricultural process has not only been a conspicuously neglected topic, but is a strong candidate for the role of leading actor on the agricultural stage of early modern England.

Just as Adam Smith's pin-maker paradigm has a very wide application, in the sense that wherever division of function can be practised it is likely to mean that, for example, the joint output of ten men will be much more than ten times the output of a single man, so it is also generally true that in any process of production which is energy-intensive to a significant degree, increasing the availability of energy per worker will increase his output. Take a simple, imaginary case. If peasants in an area of hoe agriculture were suddenly miraculously endowed with twice their normal bodily strength without any change in their food consumption, they would not find it difficult to cultivate much larger plots of land than they could previously have managed and they would therefore be able to increase the annual output from their farms, especially if there were sufficient land available to enable them to put their new-found additional strength to good use.

In circumstances of widespread chronic malnutrition, as has been noted, a comparatively modest proportional rise in food intake may effect a large proportional increase in the amount of energy that average peasants are able to devote to their work, and so improve their productivity. This represents a possibility analogous to the imaginary case just described, but one which had direct relevance at times in the past, as it still has in some parts of the Third World today. It is improbable, however, that change of this sort had other than a marginal impact on labour productivity in England between 1600 and 1800. The diet of farm labourers in the later eighteenth and early nineteenth centuries was arguably less good than a century earlier, and perhaps no better than in late-sixteenth-century England.[36]

Yet agriculture was undeniably an energy-intensive activity and individual output was therefore closely geared to the energy supply at the disposal of the individual worker. Because animal muscle could be directly substituted for human muscle, an abundance of draught animals not only allowed an increase in output per head, but also the release of labour from the land without sacrifice of output. For example, in the Mexican case referred to above, it required 5.48 man-years of work to cultivate 10 hectares of maize if all the work involved was done by hand (assuming a 40-hour working week sustained through all 52 weeks of the year). Where oxen were also employed as in the alternative case, however, the corresponding figure was only 1.83 man-years of work. The switch to oxen-assisted maize cultivation could therefore release many men from the land without loss of production, while raising output per head substantially.

In the case of seventeenth- and eighteenth-century England there was a substantial increase in output per head among those engaged in agriculture but no fall in employment on the land, a less straightforward case. What the Mexican example demonstrates, however, is that increasing the scale of the input of animal energy into farm operations is capable of producing a change in output per head of a magnitude to match the change that occurred in early modern England.[37] With many of the other possible explanations it is difficult to see how such large gains in agricultural productivity could have been secured in the circumstances of the day. The attractiveness of the 'energy' hypothesis is enhanced by the close correspondence, when comparing England and France in the early nineteenth century, between the implications

36 Direct evidence is very slight, but the evidence of real-wage trends suggests that the standard of living of agricultural labourers fell during the second half of the eighteenth century, at least in the south of England and the midlands. The same evidence (i.e. the Phelps Brown and Hopkins real-wage estimates) suggests that the later decades of the sixteenth century and the Revolutionary and Napoleonic War period were broadly alike. Wrigley and Schofield, *Population history of England*, Table A9.2, pp. 642–4.

37 This assertion can be made with fair confidence as far as cereal agriculture is concerned. In the pastoral sector, however, any benefits would have been slighter and less direct.

of the differences in the ratio of draught animal power to the labour force and the apparent gap in the productivity of agricultural labour between the two countries. The same considerations may also go far towards explaining the contrast in the productivity of agricultural manpower between England in 1600 and England in 1800, especially when the big changes in the quality as well as the quantity of farm horses is noted. Perhaps man's best friend was his horse rather than his dog.

The growth of labour productivity in the production of wheat in the *Cinq Grosses Fermes* of France, 1750–1929

Few empirical generalisations drawn from the statistical study of western economic growth in the long run are more securely established than the declines in the proportion of the total labour force dedicated to growing food and the share of personal income employed to purchase it. This displacement of economic structure has been mainly due to rising labour productivity in farming, and especially to the increased productivity of labour occupied in raising the cereals that constitute the basis of the western diet. The change proceeded in two great waves, as Table 13.1 demonstrates. The first lasted from the early eighteenth to the early twentieth century and raised labour productivity five- to six-fold, permitting the proportion of the population engaged in farming to fall from over 45 per cent to around 30 per cent. A second and more brutal surge occurred after the Second World War, when the development of pesticides and herbicides, new plant strains, expanded use of fertiliser, and the substitution of the internal combustion machine for horse power drove the number of persons in agriculture below 5 per cent of the work force. This chapter is concerned with the first wave, which coincided with the first long phase of European industrialisation.

Recent studies of the comparative economic performance of the western economies before the twentieth century have emphasised organisational factors in explaining national differences in agricultural labour productivity. P. O'Brien and C. Keyder attribute as much as 60 per cent of England's superior agricultural labour productivity relative to France to the prevalence of family farming in France, which they claim inhibited intersectoral migration and depressed labour productivity in arable farming.[1] N. F. R. Crafts conjectures that the English lead in the early nineteenth century was largely due to the intersectoral

---

1 P. K. O'Brien and C. Keyder, *Economic growth in Britain and France 1780–1914: two paths to the twentieth century*, London, 1978, chapter 4.

Table 13.1 *Agricultural labour as a proportion of the total labour force in selected countries, 1800–1988*

Country	1800	1850	1900–10	1920–30	1950	1988
United Kingdom	35.9	21.7	8.5	6.0	5.0	2.0
Netherlands				22.0	20.0	4.0
USA	80.9	54.8	34.1	22.9	11.2	2.5
Canada		54.2	40.2	35.1	21.7	3.6
Germany		54.6	28.4	23.3		4.5[a]
Belgium			32.0	22.5	16.2	2.8
France	55.0	51.5	42.4	35.3	30.9	3.6

Note
[a] Combined Federal Republic of Germany and German Democratic Republic.

Source
International Labour Office, *International labour documentation*, Geneva, 1988; United Kingdom: P. Deane and W. A. Cole, *British economic growth, 1688–1959*, Cambridge, 2nd edn., 1967; Germany: W. G. Hoffmann, *Das wachstum des Deutschen wirtschaft seit der mitte des 19. jahrhunderts*, Berlin, 1965; Netherlands: B. R. Mitchell, *European historical statistics (1750–1970)*, London, 1975; United States: *Historical statistics of the United States: colonial times to 1970*, Washington, 1975 and S. Lebergott, *Manpower in American economic growth*, New York, 1964; Canada: F. H. Leacy, *Historical statistics of Canada*, Ottawa, 1983.

responsiveness of workers and owners of capital to the country's emerging comparative advantage in manufacturing.[2] R. C. Allen locates the cause in the savings of labour achieved through better organisation of labour on England's large-scale farms.[3] These studies have extended understanding of the institutional determinants of productivity growth, but none directly addresses the question of what was the influence of technological change on productivity growth. To detect that influence it is necessary to employ more sensitive instruments of observation than aggregate agricultural output.[4] One way is to study

2 N. F. R. Crafts, *British economic growth during the industrial revolution*, Oxford, 1985.
3 R. C. Allen, 'The growth of labour productivity in early modern English agriculture', *Explorations in Economic History*, XXV, 1988, pp. 117–46.
4 Britain's high productivity in the eighteenth century is in part due to her specialisation in fodder crops and small grains, to the virtual exclusion of labour-intensive textile plants, dyestuffs, and wine that constituted a large share of continental agricultural output. If data on output and labour-use were available for eighteenth-century Britain (which they are not), analysis of the implied labour intensity of the British crop mix would probably lend strong support to Crafts's conjecture that England's agriculture had evolved in line with the nation's comparative advantage.

the long-term record of productivity growth in a homogeneous class of commodities, where the technological components of change can be identified precisely and their effects measured.

I The technological basis of productivity growth in the first industrial age

Before the twentieth century the realms of thought and experience that constituted the ultimate cause of technological change in agriculture – crudely classified as mechanical, biological and chemical – were housed in separate social and intellectual abodes. Biological and chemical innovation grew from the practices of intensive husbandry. In the early decades of the nineteenth century this empirical body of knowledge was further developed by men at farm schools and experimental farms into an agricultural 'science' that became truly scientific after the discovery in the 1830s of efficient procedures for chemically analysing organic substances.[5] The subsequent establishment of agricultural experiment stations, whose focus of research gradually widened from agricultural chemistry and the analysis of fertilisers to embrace the full range of the biological sciences concerned with agriculture, provided the science whose full consequences were to come only with the merging of genetic and fertiliser research and the discovery of vegetable growth hormones in the twentieth century.[6] This cluster of improvements imposed its direct effect on output per unit of land. Output per unit of labour, on the other hand, was increased by the second stream of improvements that flowed from the application of mechanical technology across the spectrum of farming operations. This body of technique and machinery had its social home in shop and factory and was the industrial expression of the breakthroughs in mechanical and metallurgical technology which occurred between 1770 and 1850. Yet, when the ultimate creations of 'industrial' technology appeared in the form of the tractor and the increasingly complex assemblages of harvest machinery, their efficient employment came

5 G. Grantham, 'The shifting locus of agricultural innovation in nineteenth-century Europe: the case of the agricultural experiment stations', pp. 191–214 in G. Saxonhouse and G. Wright, eds., *Technique, spirit, and form in the making of the modern economies: essays in honor of William N. Parker*, Research in Economic History, Supplement III, Greenwich, Ct. and London, 1984.
6 See D. G. Dalrymple, 'Changes in wheat varieties and wheat yields in the United States, 1919–1984', *Agricultural History*, LXII, 1988, pp. 20–36.

to depend on physiological changes in plants secured by selective breeding.[7] The two streams had become one.

Students of agricultural development have speculated that the relative importance of 'biological' and 'mechanical' innovations might reflect responses of innovators to differences in the relative scarcity of land and labour. In contrast to historical studies that hypothesise institutional barriers to factor mobility as the cause of national differences in the rate of growth of agricultural productivity, theories of 'induced innovation' assert that inducements to invent in one or the other direction are responses to relative factor costs, which in turn reflect economy-wide conditions of factor supply. The line of causation is believed to operate through the invention of new inputs that relieve limitations on the growth of output imposed by inelastic factor supplies.[8] The strongest evidence in support of this hypothesis comes from the recent agricultural history of developed nations, which suggests that bias toward land- or labour-saving innovation has been correlated with land or labour scarcity, respectively.[9] However, these findings may overstate the plasticity of technological possibilities in the nineteenth century, when the scientific and institutional base of agricultural innovation was still primitive.

The chief impediment to investigating the long-term evolution of agricultural productivity is the absence of numerical information about inputs and outputs for periods prior to the middle of the nineteenth century. For France there is enough quantitative and qualitative information to estimate agricultural labour productivity *c.*1800 and to make conjectural estimates of labour productivity in wheat as far back as 1750. Accordingly, productivity indices are here constructed for northern France for the period between 1750 and 1929.[10] Presentation

---

7 See A. G. Bogue, 'Changes in mechanical and plant technology: the corn belt, 1910–1940', *JEH*, XLIII, 1983, pp. 1–27.

8 Y. Hayami and V. W. Ruttan, *Agricultural development, an international perspective*, Baltimore and London, revised edn., 1985.

9 Haymi and Ruttan, *Agricultural development*, chapter 7. For a statistical analysis of nineteenth-century European experience, see W. W. Wade, *Institutional determinants of technical change and agricultural productivity growth: Denmark, France, and Great Britain, 1870–1965*, New York, 1981.

10 The main sources for the study of yields in 1800 are the manuscripts and published documents produced in response to François de Neufchateau's project in Year 9 (1801) to describe France's dominions statistically, the manuscripts of the prefects' estimates of output and area sown in small grains of 1812 and 1813, and the enormous late-eighteenth-century documentation on farming techniques in northern France. The statistics of Year 9 and related documents are inventoried

of the estimates is contained in three sections. The first describes the region studied and outlines its agricultural history as it affected productivity; the second presents the productivity indices and analyses them; the final section offers some reflections about long-run productivity trends and its causes as seen through the lens of France's experience.

II The *Cinq Grosses Fermes*

The *Cinq Grosses Fermes* was so named after the practice of leasing out tax collections in the provinces of northern France that J.-B. Colbert consolidated into a customs union in 1664. This study covers a slightly larger area that includes departments carved from the provinces of Flanders, Artois, Picardie and Lorraine, which were not part of France in 1664, and Brittany, which as a *Pays d'États* had its own fiscal arrangement with the central monarchy. It is almost equal in size to Great Britain and contains a similar range of soil types, endures a more continental climate in the east, and enjoys a warmer wine-supporting climate in the Loire Valley. Paris stood near its centre, and its area extended eastward to Alsace and Lorraine, westward to Brittany, and southward to the confines of Burgundy, Auvergne, the Marche, and the province of Saintonge and Angoumois.

The *Cinq Grosses Fermes* contained France's most productive arable farming districts (see Table 13.2 and Figure 13.1). It was roughly coterminous with the region directly controlled by the medieval French monarchy and had been politically unified since the thirteenth century. In the mid eighteenth century it included three districts where yields often attained 20 hectolitres per hectare, which was high by eighteenth-century standards: the densely populated semi-industrial Flemish lowlands (the present department of Nord), the loams of Brie and the Ile de France near Paris, and a narrow belt of land along the Breton coast

---

in J-C. Perrot, *L'Age d'or de la statistique régionale française (An 4 – 1804)*, Paris, 1977. In preparing the estimates for 1800 in this study, all the published sources and documentation deposited in the French National Archives and a number of departmental archives were consulted. The eighteenth-century literature is inventoried in A. J. Bourde, *Agronomie et agronomes au XVIIIe siècle*, 3 vols., Paris, 1967. Output and area sown in 1812 and 1813 are taken from the 'Etat des Récoltes', A.N. F^{11} 454–67. I am indebted to M. Gilles Postel-Vinay for making available his transcription of these data. Space limitations prevent me from describing the construction of the indices developed for this study. Full details are available from the author upon request.

Table 13.2 *Characteristics of the* Cinq Grosses Fermes *in 1892*

	Hectares	*Percentage of France*
Total area	24,148,707	45.7
Agricultural	22,822,264	45.2
Cultivated	21,956,117	49.6
Pasture	668,558	37.7
Natural meadow	1,957,983	44.5
Arable	14,832,769	57.6
Great Britain	23,000,000	

Source
France, Ministère d'Agriculture, *Statistique agricole de la France. Résultats généraux de l'enquête décennale de 1892*, Paris, 1892.

Figure 13.1 *The regions of northern France studied in this chapter*

fertilised by dressings of shells and kelp.[11] The *Fermes* was a free-trade zone, and by the early eighteenth century regional specialisation in rearing livestock – sheep on the plains of Berri, and cattle in the western departments – had developed in response to the expanding market for wool and a huge Parisian demand for meat. In these districts farmers raised only enough grain to meet local demand. Yields were 7 to 9 hectolitres; in the absence of a stronger demand for grain, farmers had little incentive to do anything costly to make them higher.[12]

The agricultural history of the *Cinq Fermes* between 1750 and 1930 mirrors the general pattern of agricultural development in north-west Europe during the industrial revolution. The first phase was dominated by the demand for food, fodder, and straw generated by the growth and prosperity of the commercial and political capitals of the eighteenth century, and intensified by the emergence of urban-based manufacture in the nineteenth.[13] Between 1750 and 1850, systems of cultivation evolved in the direction of more fodder-intensive rotations and higher stocking levels, increasing the effective supply of farm manure and thereby raising crop yields.[14] By the second decade of the nineteenth century, the availability of new ploughs and other implements to work the soil began to complement demand-side incentives to intensify agricultural practices. The new implements speeded the tasks of turning and stirring the soil, accommodating the labour requirements of more intensive cultivation to the supply of farm labourers. It was in these years also that mechanical threshers made their first appearance. Labour productivity between 1750 and 1850 was thus affected by factors that tended to push it in opposite directions. Market-induced intensification increased labour inputs per hectare, while the mechanical improvements to ploughing and threshing reduced them.

Between 1850 and 1930, labour-saving innovations dominated land-saving ones. The impetus to raise yields that had been imparted by the

---

11 One hectolitre per hectare is equivalent to 1.15 bushels per acres; a 20-hectolitre yield equals 23 bushels per acre.

12 The techniques employed by farmers in the west of France were well adjusted to their natural resources and market outlets, and reflected a sophisticated use of them. See J. Mulliez, 'Du blé, "mal nécessaire". Réflexions sur le progrès de l'agriculture de 1750 à 1850', *Revue d'histoire moderne et contemporaine*, janvier-mars, 1979, pp. 3-47.

13 G. Grantham, 'Agricultural supply during the industrial revolution: French evidence and European implications', *JEH*, XLIX, 1989, pp. 43–72.

14 G. P. H. Chorley, 'The agricultural revolution in northern Europe, 1750–1880: nitrogen, legumes, and crop productivity', *EcHR*, XXXIV, 1981, pp. 71–93.

growth of urban market demand was diluted by the decline in local
and international transport costs. Yields continued to rise, but the
increases were concentrated in the regions that had either only recently begun to raise grain for more distant markets or that virtually
abandoned production when it became possible to import food. By
the end of the century, commercial fertilisers and new plant strains
were beginning to lift crop yields above the practical limits set by
manure-intensive husbandry. On the mechanical front, the main improvements in this period resulted from the diffusion of mechanical
threshing and the replacement of the sickle and the scythe by mechanical reapers and binders.

III The estimates: labour productivity, 1750–1929

Table 13.3 presents estimates of land and labour productivity in
northern France between the middle of the eighteenth century and
the Great Depression. The figures are weighted averages of estimates
of regional productivity. For the period before 1862 separate estimates
have been constructed of labour productivity on heavy and light soils,
to allow for the significant difference in pre-harvest labour inputs
between them. As it is impossible to make a similar adjustment for
crop yields, the indices understate productivity growth on strong soils,
where yields in earlier years were below the departmental averages
used to calculate the indices.[15] By the end of the nineteenth century
most of the difference had been eliminated by amendment or abandonment of the most difficult soils and it is therefore ignored in
constructing indices for 1892 and 1929.

The estimates reveal a steady acceleration of productivity growth
through the whole period. In the first half of the nineteenth century
the annual rate of growth was about 0.7 per cent per year, between
1862 and 1892 it rose above 1.0 per cent, and from 1892 to 1929 it
reached an annual rate of 1.8 per cent. They are therefore inconsistent
with more broadly-based studies of the French agricultural economy,
which indicate a deceleration of productivity growth in the latter part
of the nineteenth century.[16] The rate of growth in the early years was
more pronounced on stiff than on light soils, mainly because the

15 Some light soils were also unproductive. The chalks of Champagne were easily
    worked but gave extremely poor crops.
16 M. Lévy-Leboyer, 'La Decélération de l'économie française dans la seconde moitié
    du 19ᵉ siècle', *Revue d'histoire économique et sociale*, XLIC, 1971, pp. 485–507.

Table 13.3 *Northern France: land and labour productivity for wheat cultivation, 1750–1929*

	Output per man-day in hectolitres		Index (1750 = 100)		Yield (hl/hectare)	Index
	Stiff	*Light*	*Stiff*	*Light*		
1750	0.19	0.24	100	100	11.0	100
1800	0.22	0.27	114	111	12.3	112
1862	0.35	0.41	185	166	17.0	154
1892	0.54	0.54	279	220	18.4	167
1929	1.05	1.05	543	429	25.3	230

Source
Yield estimates are based on published data for departments from 1815, manuscript and published estimates from Year 9 (1801) in the departmental *statistique des préfets*, and a variety of eighteenth-century estimates and reported yields. Labour inputs were derived from estimates given in contemporary agricultural handbooks, descriptions of contemporary practice, and the inputs reported in the manuscripts of the 1852 agricultural census. The underlying data are given in Appendix 13.2. Details of construction are available from the author upon request and will be published shortly.

contraction of the fallow, which was ploughed three to four times prior to being sown with wheat, had a greater effect on the heavy soils where ploughing was slow than on the lighter ones. The estimated growth of labour productivity before 1800 is entirely due to rising yields, as there was little improvement in mechanical techniques in this period.

To take account of large differences in productivity and methods of cultivation existing within northern France at the beginning of the period, the sample was divided into seven sub-regions. The regions are Paris (which includes the Norman departments except for Orne), West (containing the departments carved out of the old provinces of Maine and Anjou, Touraine, plus Deux-Sèvres, Vendée and Loire-Inférieure), Bretagne, Berri, Champagne, Lorraine, and Nord (which contains the Flemish department of the North, and the departments of Pas-de-Calais and Somme). The productivity indices of these regions are given in Table 13.4.

The indices reveal the extent of regional disparities in labour productivity in the eighteenth century. On heavy soils the ratio of labour productivity in the Nord to that in Berri and the West was

Table 13.4 *Northern France: labour productivity in wheat, 1750–1929 (man-days per hectolitre)*

Region	1750	1800	1862	1892	1929
A. *Stiff soils*					
Paris	4.21	3.63	2.00	1.70	0.87
West	7.51	6.67	3.68	1.93	1.00
Bretagne	5.77	5.49	4.28	1.93	0.99
Berri	7.57	6.50	4.18	2.16	1.08
Champagne	4.83	4.19	2.25	1.96	1.00
Lorraine	4.75	3.69	2.86	2.15	1.24
Nord	2.76	2.62	1.77	1.51	0.76
Mean	5.17	4.54	2.79	1.86	0.95
B. *Light soils*					
Paris	3.35	3.01	2.00	1.70	0.87
West	5.70	5.17	2.99	1.93	1.00
Bretagne	4.73	4.57	3.60	1.93	0.99
Berri	5.76	5.05	3.37	2.16	1.08
Champagne	3.94	3.48	2.25	1.96	1.00
Lorraine	3.85	3.08	2.37	2.15	1.24
Nord	2.38	2.34	1.77	1.51	0.76
Mean	4.09	3.69	2.46	1.86	0.95

Source See Table 13.3.

more than two-and-a-half to one. Although harvesting was carried out a little more quickly in the Nord, most of the difference in man-days per unit of output is attributable to regional differences in ploughing time. Mean labour input per hectolitre in departments that used horses exclusively was 4.1 on heavy soils and 3.3 on light soils; in departments that employed oxen it was 7.0 and 4.5, respectively. The effect of differences in draught animals employed dominates the significant, but relatively minor, effect of soil type, which is associated with a 26 per cent advantage in favour of the light-soil regions.

The extension of horse-powered husbandry was one of the important agricultural changes of the nineteenth century. In the middle of the eighteenth century, the employment of horses in the ordinary tasks of arable husbandry was confined to the part of France north of the Loire and east of a line slightly to the west of Chartres.[17] This

17 R. Musset, *L'élévage du cheval en France*, Paris, 1917.

regional separation was the result of two economic factors. The first was the speed of horses in the performance of ploughing and harrowing, which became more important as wages rose and as the cultivation of the main fields intensified. To this must be added the advantages of horses in hauling produce to market. The second reason was the complementarity of ox power with livestock husbandry in the western districts specialising in rearing meat animals. It was because of this that oxen remained the animal of preference in the highly specialised grazing department of Deux Sèvres down to the end of the 1920s.

Despite the gaps in productivity that were evident at the beginning of the nineteenth century, the overall rise in productivity was accomplished not by shifting production from regions of low to regions of high productivity, but by raising productivity everywhere, most rapidly in the more backward regions. Indeed, had regional yields and techniques remained unchanged, the productivity of labour would have declined over the period, as an increasing proportion of total wheat output came to be grown in departments where yields were low in the eighteenth and early nineteenth century.[18] The modest redistribution of output was mainly due to the amending and fertilising of previously infertile soils. The direct gains from trade were modest. In the late eighteenth century, uncultivated land was truly marginal land. The inducement of higher prices for output and lower prices of inputs might lead farmers to clear new land; but efforts on the extensive margin could not fundamentally alter the regional distribution of output, which was locked into crop rotations that reflected both local physical conditions and long-standing patterns of final output. These patterns had been fixed before the middle of the eighteenth century in response to markets whose histories extend back to the thirteenth century. Increased availability of soil amendments and fertilisers in the nineteenth century permitted farmers to grow wheat on land previously too acidic or thin to support it, but it did not alter the basic distribution of livestock husbandry in the west, and grain farming around Paris and the north-east.

IV Partitioning the growth of labour productivity

How much of the overall increase in labour productivity in France was due to mechanical improvements and how much to rising crop yields? To ask this question is to peer through a kaleidoscope of discrete bits

18 See Tables 13.4 and 13.5.

of information that reassemble themselves into new patterns with each tilting of the instrument of observation. To facilitate comparison with other work, a method of analysis has been adopted which was developed by W. N. Parker and J. Klein to study the growth of labour productivity in the small grains in nineteenth-century America.[19] Their method separates farming operations into two orthogonal classes: those in which labour inputs are roughly constant per unit of sown land, such as ploughing or reaping, and those in which they are roughly constant per unit of output, such as binding, stacking, transporting grain to the barn, and threshing. This division permits the effect of changes in crop yields to be distinguished from the effect of labour-saving innovation. It thus facilitates investigation of the relative importance of the two broad streams of technological change discussed above.

One inestimable advantage of Parker and Klein's technique over the widely-employed alternative of estimating statistical production functions is its capacity to absorb endless information about the labour content of individual farm operations. Such information can be classified, averaged, and welded into overall indices of labour productivity. The indices can be further manipulated to estimate the relative contribution of each operation to total labour requirements per hectare and per unit of output. As it gives no play to endogenous factor substitution within operations, the method cannot be used to analyse agricultural supply.[20] Nevertheless, when used with sensitivity to the technological constraints and the historical environment, it is a descriptive device capable of producing historical insight.

In adapting the Parker–Klein method to European conditions, it is necessary to allow for the strong interaction between intensity of cultivation and crop yields, which was largely absent in the extensive farming practice of nineteenth- and early-twentieth-century America. To raise yields in the first half of the nineteenth century required increasing the amount of labour employed in cultivating and manuring the soil; the independence of crop yields and labour inputs per hectare, which is a feature of the Parker–Klein experiment, is thus absent.

19 W. N. Parker and J. L. V. Klein, 'Productivity growth in grain production in the United States, 1840–1860 and 1900–1910', pp. 523–80 in *Conference on research in income and wealth, ouput, employment, and productivity in the United States after 1800,* Studies in Income and Wealth, XXX, New York, 1966.
20 F. M. Fisher and P. Temin, 'Regional specialisation and the supply of wheat in the United States, 1867–1914', *Review of Economics and Statistics,* LII, 1970, pp. 134–49.

Rising yields might well be associated with falling labour productivity, depending on the balance between the labour coefficient in operations where it was fixed per unit of land, and the coefficient in operations where it was proportional to yields. In the estimates below, labour productivity has been 'corrected' by separately accounting for labour employed in manuring, binding, stacking, and transporting grain, all of which were roughly proportional to the size of the crop.[21]

It is also necessary to adjust estimates for the use of inputs that were jointly consumed by different crops in short rotations. Fortunately, in three-course rotations with fallow, manure was applied prior to sowing winter corn, so that the entire labour input can be allocated to winter corn for most of the period before 1850. The allocation is less defensible when row crops and sown meadows replaced the fallow, as the plants absorbed manure and, in the case of sugar beets, could not have been grown without it. In the calculations below, the labour input of manuring has been assigned to winter corn. An analogous problem exists with respect to the preparation of the seed bed. Where fallow was cultivated, the entire labour input has been associated with the subsequent crop of winter corn, in line with contemporary accounting practice. If row crops or fodder leys preceded wheat in the rotation, only the immediate preparation of the seed bed is attributed to the cost of producing winter corn. The economic justification for this allocation is that the crops that replaced fallow paid for the costs of their cultivation. It means, however, that the contraction of fallow, which often *raised* labour inputs per hectare, *reduces* the labour required to grow winter wheat. Two sets of estimates have therefore been prepared, one in which fallow is held constant, and the other in which it is allowed to vary. In isolating the particular contribution of different mechanical operations to the growth of productivity, the first index is the more appropriate.

21 The manure inputs are the labour employed in loading, transporting, discharging and speading manure on the fields. It is assumed that the number of loads per hectare is proportional to yields. This overstates the labour input after 1862, when concentrated commercial fertilisers began to be widely used. The effect of this convention is to reduce the estimated contribution to total productivity of rising yields between 1862 and 1929. It is unlikely that this seriously biases the results of this study, since manure applications rose with yields to the end of the period under study.

Table 13.5 *Northern France: sources of productivity growth (proportional change in total productivity from 1750)*

Factor	1800		1862		1892		1929	
	Stiff	Light	Stiff	Light	Stiff	Light	Stiff	Light
A. *Fallow varies*								
v (output shares)	.00	.00	−.04	−.02	−.04	−.04	−.02	−.02
L ('mechanisation')	.38	.50	.58	.61	.87	.86	.75	.75
y (yields)	.69	.42	.38	.26	.17	.12	.19	.16
v, L	.00	.00	−.01	.00	−.01	−.01	−.01	−.01
v, y	.00	.00	.01	.01	.02	.02	.01	.01
L, y	−.08	.08	.07	.14	−.02	.04	.06	.10
v, L, y	.00	.00	.01	.01	.01	.01	.01	.01
B. *Fallow constant*								
v	.00	.00	−.03	−.02	−.04	−.04	−.02	−.03
L	.44	.45	.52	.54	.82	.79	.69	.67
y	.52	.35	.36	.30	.19	.15	.21	.21
v, L	.00	.00	−.02	.00	−.01	−.01	−.01	−.01
v, y	.00	.00	.02	.01	.02	.02	.01	.01
L, y	.04	.09	.15	.16	.01	.07	.12	.13
v, L, y	.00	.00	.01	.00	.01	.01	.01	.01

Source See Table 13.3.

V Measuring the proximate sources of productivity change

The indices of labour productivity used in this paper are of the form:

$$I = \sum (L_i^1 / y_i + L_i^2) v_i,$$

where L^1 measures labour used in operations where it is constant per hectare, L^2 measures labour in operations where it is fixed per unit of output, y is yield, and v_i is the share of wheat grown in the ith region.[22] By holding different combinations of v, L and y constant a series of eight indices are obtained that can be further combined to yield estimates of the relative contribution of each factor taken singly and in combination with others to the growth of productivity.[23] Thus, in Table 13.5, the first row (factor v) records the proportion of the total change

22 The complete identity and the definition of the variables is in Appendix 13.1.
23 Parker and Klein, 'Productivity growth in grain production'.

in the labour productivity index from the base level of 1750 that is attributable to the shift in the regional distribution of output, holding all other factors constant; the second row (factor L) measures the proportion of change that is due to changes in the labour content of the several farming operations; row three records the proportion of change contributed by the rise in yields. The last four rows measure the 'interaction effects' of the three primary factors. They explain the marginal changes not already accounted for in the first three rows.

Improvements in operations that directly raised productivity in specific operations were the dominant source of rising labour productivity from the middle of the eighteenth century to the 1930s. Rising yields per hectare contributed one-seventh to one-fifth of the increase in output per man-day. The effect of sub-regional redistribution of wheat production (factor v) is consistently negative. The estimates for 1750 and 1800 have been constructed from data on '*bled*', which includes rye as well as wheat, so that the negative values of v are not a result of the higher degree of commercialisation of wheat relative to other cereals in the eighteenth century. This suggests that the prevalence of subsistence farming in the earlier period, which it is alleged reduced labour productivity by sustaining a geographically inefficient distribution of labour, was of minor importance. The period under review was one in which the incidence of subsistence production of wheat was declining, which taken alone, should have caused the value of factor v to rise.

The growth of labour productivity therefore stemmed from reductions in the labour content of farm operations. Holding fallow constant reduces the contribution of labour saving to its mechanical core, by eliminating savings that came from reducing the number of ploughings, but factor L still accounts for more than two-thirds of the total increase and, in interaction with yields, about 80 per cent.

The role of mechanical improvements can be further analysed into the effects of the three classes of farm operations, ploughing and other pre-harvest activities, harvest, and threshing. Partitioning the mechanical sources of productivity growth and holding yields and regional output shares constant, indicates how important the improvements in tillage technology were to the growth of productivity in pre-twentieth-century European farming. Table 13.6 decomposes the productivity index into its mechanical sub-components, analysing the contribution of L on the assumption that yields and regional output shares are fixed at their 1750 levels.

The magnitude of the contribution of improvements in ploughing and soil preparation is not surprising, given that pre-harvest opera-

Table 13.6 *Northern France: relative contribution of improvements in ploughing, harvest, and post-harvest operations to the change in productivity due to all mechanical improvements from 1750*

Factor	1800		1862		1892		1929	
	Stiff	*Light*	*Stiff*	*Light*	*Stiff*	*Light*	*Stiff*	*Light*
a (ploughing)	.83	.64	.43	.22	.41	.26	.30	.22
b (harvest)	.00	.00	.13	.20	.15	.24	.18	.23
c (threshing)	.17	.27	.32	.49	.18	.29	.17	.22
a, b	.00	.00	.02	.01	.09	.06	.12	.10
a, c	.00	.09	.06	.04	.10	.06	.11	.09
b, c	.00	.00	.02	.04	.03	.07	.07	.09
a, b, c	.00	.00	.00	.00	.04	.02	.06	.05

Source See text.

tions consumed half of all labour inputs used to grow wheat in the late eighteenth century. The effect is strongest on stiff soils, where soil preparation took an especially long time. Even so, taken together, harvest and post-harvest operations account for 42 per cent of the rise in labour productivity to 1929 on stiff soils, and fully 54 per cent on the light soils. The figures thus illustrate the powerful thrust of mechanical innovation on agricultural techniques in the late nineteenth and early twentieth century.

The rise in the productivity of pre-harvest labour was due to improved ploughs and plough teams, and to the diminution of ploughing caused by the contraction of fallow. Table 13.7 sorts out the relative importance of these two factors. The contraction of fallow accounts for roughly half of the decline in pre-harvest labour inputs. When the figures in Table 13.7 are combined with those of Table 13.6, it appears that no more than 10 to 15 per cent of the total increase to 1929 in labour productivity attributable to 'mechanical' technology is attributable to changes in crop rotations, and no more than 25 per cent of the increase to 1862, when these changes were most intense.

The timing of the changes outlined above can be further explored by recalculating the indices developed above for each pair of dates. Table 13.8 performs this analysis for 1800–62, 1862–92 and 1892–1929. Mechanical improvements (including the effect of reduction in fallow) were important throughout the whole period. The rise of crop yields made its main contributions in two distinct phases: the first was during

Table 13.7 *Northern France: the sources of pre-harvest labour productivity from 1750*

	1800		1862		1892		1929	
	Stiff	*Light*	*Stiff*	*Light*	*Stiff*	*Light*	*Stiff*	*Light*
Ploughing	.40	.50	.37	.00	.69	.48	.63	.45
Fallow	.60	.50	.63	1.00	.31	.52	.37	.55

Source See text.

the diffusion of the new husbandry between 1800 and 1862; the second was in the early twentieth century, when increased use of commercial fertilisers was the prime mover. These patterns reveal both economic and technological causation. The extraordinary contribution of mechanisation to total growth between 1862 and 1892 surely illustrates the maturation of nineteenth-century mechanical technology, but it indirectly reflects the declining rate of growth of crop yields that resulted from the fall in the world and domestic price of the small grains after 1875.

The temporal patterns of the mechanical contributions to productivity change show a shift from pre-harvest and post-harvest operations towards the harvest. The operational location of the innovations is evident in Table 13.9. Mechanisation of threshing is responsible for a high share of the contribution made by post-harvest operations to mechanical sources of growth between 1800 and 1862. The substitution of the cradle for the sickle explains the improvement in harvest productivity over the same period, the diffusion of the reaper between 1862 and 1892, and the triumph of the binder between 1892 and 1929. The contribution of pre-harvest improvements between 1862 and 1892 is in part a statistical artefact of the suppression of the distinction between stiff and light soils, but the 33 per cent contribution on light soils indicates that progress in ploughing technologies and ploughing technique was considerable.

Tables 13.8 and 13.9 suggest that the current of mechanical improvements flowed strongly through the whole period under review, finding outlets first in the mechanisation of threshing, then in the improvement of ploughs and cultivators, and finally in the mechanisation of the harvest.

Table 13.8 *Northern France: relative importance of yields, regional weights, and mechanisation, 1800–1929*

| | 1800–1862 | | 1862–1892 | | 1892–1929 |
	Stiff	Light	Stiff	Light	
v	.04	−.02	−.07	−.12	.01
L	.82	.57	1.10	.79	.53
y	.23	.26	.06	.36	.33
v, L	.13	.05	.03	−.19	.00
v, y	−.14	.00	−.01	.24	.01
L, y	−.02	.08	−.13	−.14	.13
v, L, y	−.07	.05	−.02	−.01	−.01

Source See text.

Table 13.9 *Northern France: relative importance of pre-harvest, harvest, and post-harvest operations (holding fallow constant), 1800–1929*

| | 1800–1862 | | 1862–1892 | | 1892–1929 |
	Stiff	Light	Stiff	Light	
a (pre-harvest)	.17	.12	.52	.33	.15
b (harvest)	.21	.23	.22	.34	.35
c (post-harvest)	.56	.59	.16	.23	.37
a, b	.01	.02	.05	.03	−.12
a, c	.03	.02	.03	.03	.05
b, c	.03	.03	.02	.02	.07
a, b, c	.01	.00	.00	.01	.14

Source See text.

VI Comparisons and conclusions

It is instructive to compare these results with similar estimates of the growth of labour productivity in nineteenth-century America. Between 1750 and 1929 output of wheat per man-day in France rose 543 per cent on heavy soils and 429 per cent on light ones.[24] On the assumption that about 60 per cent of the soils in the region were 'heavy', the

24 The rates implied by the figures in Table 13.3 differ slightly from those in the text because of rounding.

overall increase would have been about 475 per cent. This compares with a 550 per cent increase in output of wheat per man-hour estimated to have occurred in the United States between 1840 and 1910.[25] Even supposing that output per effective unit of labour input in France increased by 20 per cent between 1750 and 1900 as a result of improved diet and shorter working hours, output per man-hour in wheat production could not have risen more than 300 per cent from 1840 to 1910, or about 60 per cent of the American rate of growth over the same period. These comparisons of nineteenth-century productivity growth in specific crops, which are the only ones now directly available, confirm the exceptional position of the United States in the history of nineteenth-century agriculture. About half of the change in labour productivity in France occurred in the early years of the twentieth century. On stiff soils 45 per cent of the long-term increase was achieved by 1862, and slightly more than half by 1892. In contrast to America, where labour productivity reached a plateau at the end of the nineteenth century as the gains from horse-powered mechanisation began to play themselves out and the extensive frontier shifted northward into the Canadian prairies, French labour productivity accelerated into the twentieth century, presaging the surpluses that were to haunt farmers in the 1920s and 1930s.

What is remarkable about the results of this exercise in accounting is that the share of overall productivity growth attributable to 'mechanisation' in France is higher than it was in the United States. Parker and Klein estimated that about 60 per cent of the total increase in labour productivity between 1840 and 1910 was due to reductions in the labour input requirements of particular operations; in France, the contribution from this source to 1892, which is a periodisation roughly comparable to that in the American study, is between 70 and 85 per cent. Parker and Klein associated their indices with historical 'factors' that constituted historic opportunities whose origins lay outside the sphere of individual farming enterprises. The central factors in nineteenth-century American agrarian history were the westward movement of settlement, which was a peculiarly American phenomenon, and the elaboration of mechanical technology, which was a European cultural phenomenon. In America the relocation of grain production

25 J. Atack and F. Bateman, 'Mid-nineteenth-century crop yields and labor productivity growth in American agriculture: a new look at Parker and Klein', pp. 215–42 in Saxonhouse and Wright, *Technique, spirit and form*, 1984, p. 236. The estimates in this article revise the estimates produced by Parker and Klein in their pioneering work, 'Productivity growth in grain production'.

on to the level plains in the mid-west and west interacted positively with a general advance in mechanical skill to produce what to European observers must have seemed hyper-mechanisation of farming by the early twentieth century. European agrarian history in this period moved in grooves that started from a different initial state: population density was high and there remained little uncultivated land. Increases in total output could only come from increasing yields. Yet even though yields in France increased by 230 per cent in the period under study, three-quarters of growth in the productivity of labour was mechanical in origin. American and European agricultural histories could not help diverging, but their technological histories nevertheless display remarkable parallels. Mechanisation was the supremely powerful technological impulse in the nineteenth century.

Agricultural mechanisation responded to the falling iron prices, improved quality of iron resulting from better control of its physical properties by iron-masters, and to the revolution in machine-tool technology that gave rise to mass production of screws and bolts. These changes permitted the substitution of lighter and stronger iron implements for implements whose mechanical inefficiency derived immediately from the bulkiness of wooden assemblages held together by mortise and tenon joinery. Assembling metal ploughs using bolts reduced their weight and mechanical resistance by more than 50 per cent. Some implements, such as heavy harrows and row cultivators, the working parts of which were subjected to unusually strong forces, would not have been built in the absence of metallurgical improvements. The improved *materiel* of cultivation was thus a central factor permitting farmers to work the land more rapidly and more frequently; where stiff soils had previously necessitated the employment of large teams, improved implements reduced labour requirements by half, since the new implements could be drawn by fewer animals and could be directed by a single ploughman. Threshers and the early models of reapers had wooden frames, but their working parts were metal. Industrial inputs were central to agricultural productivity growth.

The long-run rise of agricultural productivity exhibits a sequence of phases that seem in general to mirror the phases of technological and economic history. In the early modern period, such increases in output per unit of labour as occurred came mainly from the indirect effect of rising crop yields per unit of labour and from whatever economies of labour could be secured by means of more extensive division of labour within farms and between regions. This phase lasted until the early eighteenth century, when a small but deepening stream

of mechanical improvements in ploughs, harrows, and then – in the
nineteenth century – threshing machines and finally reapers came to
be superimposed on the biological technology of the new husbandry,
first in England and then on the European continent. The record of
productivity growth in France in this period reflects the predominance
of mechanical over other branches of agriculturally-related sciences
and technologies. An alternative history can be imagined, in which the
technologies based on soil chemistry and selective breeding preceded
those of the mechanic. Output per unit of labour would have been
perhaps 20 per cent higher in 1930 than it was in 1750. It is impossible
to imagine this alternative economy accompanying an industrial
revolution – not because of the economic constraints imposed by a
lower rate of growth of agricultural output, but because the actual
increase in output per unit of labour and the early industrial revolution
both derived from the same rootstock of technological skill. Both
revolutions had a common cause.

Appendix 13.1 *Definitions of the variables used in calculating indices of labour productivity for northern France, 1750–1929*

Preparing the seed bed
t_p Team days per hectare per ploughing
n_p Number of ploughings (variants, light and stiff soils, fallow and non-fallow course preceding wheat)
m_p Men per team (two variants, light and stiff soils)
f Proportion of wheat land preceded by fallow
L_p Man days per hectare, ploughing
$L_p = t_p \cdot m_p \cdot (n_p \cdot f + 1 - f)$
t_h Team days per harrowing per hectare
n_h Number of harrowings after ploughing
H_p Man-days per hectare: harrowing
S Man-days per hectare: sowing
H_s Man-days per hectare: harrowing in seed

Manuring
l_m Loading manure: man-days per ton (1,000 kilograms)
c_m Carting manure: man-days per load of one ton
m_s Spreading manure: man-days per ton
F Tons per hectare
M Manuring: man-days per hectare
$M = (l_m + c_m + s_m) \cdot F$

Weeding
W Weeding the standing crop: man-days per hectare

Harvest operations
s_i Man-days per hectare in cutting for ith technique
    $i = 1$: sickle
    $i = 2$: scythe
    $i = 3$: reaping hook (sape)
    $i = 4$: mechanical harvester
l_h Man-days per hectolitres-worth of ties for making sheafs
j_h Man-days per hectare: gathering grain into swathes
b_h Man-days per hectolitre: binding sheaves
t_h Man-days per hectolitre: loading, transporting and unloading grain at barn or threshing floor
y Yield in hectolitres per hectare
R Man-days per hectare: harvest operations
$R = s_i + j_h + (l_h + b_h + t_h) \cdot y$

Post-harvest operations
T_h Man-days per hectolitre, threshing
w Man-days per hectolitre, winnowing and screening
$PH = (T_h + w) \cdot y$

Labour productivity index
L = Man-days per hectolitre
$L = (L_p + H_p + S + H_s + M + W + R)/y + PH$

Appendix 13.2 *Yields, regional weights, and labour input coefficients by regions of northern France, 1750–1929*

Region	1750	1800	1820	1840	1862	1892	1929
A. *Wheat yields (hectolitres per hectare)*							
Paris	13	15	15.3	16.7	19.0	20.1	29.1
West	8	10	9.7	12.4	15.9	16.2	25.3
Bretagne	12	12	14.1	14.4	15.6	15.9	21.7
Berri	8	9	7.6	9.8	14.2	17.9	24.7
Champagne	10	10	10.7	11.6	16.3	17.5	21.0
Lorraine	9	10	10.7	11.9	15.0	14.5	16.1
Nord	17	17	18.3	18.7	20.9	21.4	30.4
B. *Regional shares of wheat output*							
Paris	.352	.368	.330	.280	.235	.268	
West	.212	.157	.207	.240	.267	.248	
Bretagne	.089	.069	.061	.059	.076	.095	
Berri	.058	.052	.062	.077	.083	.150	
Champagne	.082	.080	.083	.096	.096	.073	
Lorraine	.088	.112	.109	.122	.067	.039	
Nord	.128	.130	.116	.117	.131	.124	
C. *Pre-harvest operations on stiff soils (ploughing, harrowing, sowing and weeding) in man-days per hectare*							
Paris	28.5	24.7			9.0	5.9	3.6
West	33.5	31.5			27.4	9.2	5.9
Bretagne	35.5	33.5			29.7	8.9	5.5
Berri	34.0	32.0			30.0	13.9	7.9
Champagne	19.5	17.5			8.4	7.0	4.5
Lorraine	20.5	18.5			17.9	8.3	5.8
Nord	14.7	11.9			5.3	2.9	2.7
D. *Pre-harvest operations on light soils (ploughing, harrowing, sowing and weeding) in man-days per hectare*							
Paris	15.5	13.6			9.0	5.9	3.6
West	19.0	18.0			16.5	9.2	5.9
Bretagne	21.0	20.0			19.1	8.9	5.5
Berri	19.5	18.5			18.5	13.9	7.9
Champagne	11.0	10.0			8.4	7.0	4.5

Appendix 13.2 *(cont.)*

Region	1750	1800	1820	1840	1862	1892	1929
Lorraine	11.5	10.5			10.7	8.3	5.8
Nord	8.5	7.1			5.3	2.9	2.7

E. *Manuring operations (loading, transporting to fields and spreading) in man-days per hectare*

Paris	5.5	7.4			12.5	14.5	12.7
West	3.0	3.5			8.3	9.7	11.6
Bretagne	4.2	4.7			9.4	9.4	9.2
Berri	3.0	3.0			7.7	11.4	11.2
Champagne	4.0	4.0			12.3	15.0	10.0
Lorraine	4.0	4.0			10.7	12.2	9.0
Nord	8.1	9.0			13.2	15.1	11.3

F. *Harvest operations (cutting, binding, stooking, transporting from field) in man-days per hectare*

Paris	12.5	12.9			8.4	7.6	4.5
West	13.6	14.0			15.1	7.5	4.0
Bretagne	16.3	16.3			17.0	7.6	3.5
Berri	13.6	13.8			14.8	8.0	3.9
Champagne	13.0	13.0			8.2	6.9	3.4
Lorraine	12.8	13.0			7.9	6.3	2.7
Nord	9.3	9.3			9.1	8.0	4.7

G. *Threshing operations in man-days per hectolitre*

Paris	1.00	0.90			0.43	0.30	0.15
West	1.25	1.25			0.48	0.30	0.15
Bretagne	1.25	1.25			0.68	0.30	0.15
Berri	1.25	1.25			0.48	0.30	0.15
Champagne	1.00	0.90			0.48	0.30	0.15
Lorraine	1.00	0.90			0.41	0.30	0.15
Nord	1.00	0.90			0.41	0.30	0.15

Agricultural productivity in Belgium and Ireland in the early nineteenth century

Belgium and Ireland had the highest rural population densities in Europe during the early nineteenth century. In the early 1840s Belgium was by far the most densely populated country in Europe, with about 390 persons per square kilometre. Ireland, Britain and the Netherlands followed in a group at around 260 persons, but in the last two a much greater share of the population lived in towns.[1] In Ireland and Belgium many who lived in the countryside subsisted on small, even tiny, agricultural holdings and supplemented their incomes through domestic industry. This agrarian system was most pronounced in north-western Belgium (the provinces of East and West Flanders, and adjoining parts of Brabant and Hainaut) and north-eastern Ireland – the most densely populated parts of the two countries. In Flanders and east Ulster domestic linen production was the dominant industrial activity; indeed, they were competitors on the world market.

These structural similarities need qualification on two fronts. First, economic developments outside the linen textile areas were very different in the two countries. In parts of southern Ireland agricultural holdings were much larger, closer in size to those in Britain than to those in southern and eastern Belgium. Industry in southern Ireland also atrophied during the early nineteenth century, while in Wallonia there was rapid and successful industrialisation. A second qualification is that Belgium and Ireland had arrived at their high rural population densities at different rates. The southern Netherlands had been a densely settled part of Europe since the middle ages. Ireland, by contrast, was a sparsely-populated frontier in the sixteenth and seven-

We would like to express our thanks to the Belgian National Foundation for Scientific Research for their support of Martine Goossens' research and to the Ministry of Scientific Policy, the Belgian National Lottery, the National Bank of Belgium and the Belgian Royal Academy for their support of the project on 'Economic growth, structural change and productivity in the Belgian economy, 1790–1990', to which Peter Solar is affiliated.
1 C. McEvedy and R. Jones, *Atlas of world population history*, Harmondsworth, 1978.

teenth centuries, which from the late seventeenth century experienced
extraordinarily rapid demographic growth.

Belgium, with its longer history of high population density, was a
source of agricultural technology and ideas for Ireland. This was most
evident in the cultivation of flax. Flemish flax had long been recognised as a high-quality raw material and was especially in demand in
the late 1820s and 1830s as mills using wet-spinning techniques were
set up in England and Ireland. Irish industrialists and agricultural
improvers repeatedly urged Flemish methods for the cultivation and
preparation of flax on Irish farmers. On several occasions Flemish
farmers were brought to Ireland as instructors or Irish farmers sent to
Flanders as students.[2]

Flax is a highly labour-intensive crop that was typically grown on
small farms in both Belgium and Ireland. For some Irish agricultural
improvers its cultivation in Flanders was just one element in a system
of farming that could serve as a more appropriate model for Ireland
than the large farms of England and Scotland. As William Greig wrote
in his 1821 report on the Gosford Estates in County Armagh, 'the rural
economy of Flanders etc., is a proof that very considerable improvements may be effected on comparatively small farms'.[3] Greig may well
have drawn his picture of Flemish agriculture from the Reverend
Thomas Radcliff's *Report on the agriculture of eastern and western Flanders*.
This detailed study, commissioned by the Farming Society of Ireland
and published in 1819, was based on a lengthy visit in 1817.[4] Another
influential proponent of Flemish methods was William Blacker, the
agent on the Gosford estate. In several publications and in testimony
before parliamentary commissions, Blacker argued for the productive-
ness of small farms when intensively cultivated.[5] Others saw the nature
of tenure and ownership as crucial. George Poulett Scrope thought
'that the small farm system can in Ireland be made as conducive as it
is in Belgium to the comfort of the population and the increase of
production: but that the secret of this comfort and increased production, – in other words, of the industry by which both are created – *lies*

---

2 C. Gill, *The rise of the Irish linen industry*, Oxford, 1925, p. 293; *Belfast mercantile
  register*, 15 November 1842, report of Flax Improvement Society meeting.
3 W. H. Crawford, ed., *General report on the Gosford estates in County Armagh, 1821,
  by William Greig*, Belfast, 1976, p. 164.
4 T. Radcliff, *A report on the agriculture of eastern and western Flanders*, London, 1819.
5 W. Blacker, *An essay on the improvements to be made in the cultivation of small farms,
  by the introduction of green crops and housefeeding the stock thereon* ... , Dublin, 1834.

N

in the possession by the cultivator of a durable and certain interest in the results of his labour'.[6]

Belgians, by contrast, showed little interest in Irish agriculture, except occasionally as an example of what was to be avoided. But they did come to be less optimistic than the Irish were about the success of their own agricultural system. In the 1800s and 1810s a self-satisfied optimism reigned. By the 1840s observers had begun to take a much more pessimistic line, influenced in large part by rising imports of foodstuffs.[7]

Contemporary agriculturalists are not always reliable guides. R. C. Allen and C. Ó Gráda have shown, for example, how Arthur Young's ideas about technical improvements sometimes biased his interpretation of data on English, French and Irish cereal yields.[8] Were Irishmen and other contemporaries right about the superiority of Flemish agriculture? Were its intensively cultivated small farms an appropriate model for Ireland? These questions may be addressed by a systematic comparison of agricultural productivity in the two countries. This will focus on the early 1840s, the earliest date for which the quantitative evidence permits reasonably reliable calculations of land and labour productivity, and will be made primarily at the national level. It would, of course, be more appropriate to compare Flanders and Ulster, but, unfortunately, the statistical material at the regional level in Ireland does not permit reliable estimates to be made for livestock production in Ulster.

I Physical productivity in Belgium and Ireland

A first step in comparing the Belgian and Irish agricultural sectors is to look at several indicators of physical productivity in the early 1840s. Table 14.1 shows values for gross crop yields and various indicators of meat and dairy production per animal. The figures for Belgium and Ireland are the national averages which provide the basis for the estimates of agricultural output in the two countries outlined in Section

---

6 Quoted in R. D. C. Black, *Economic thought and the Irish question, 1817–1870*, Cambridge, 1960, p. 30.

7 See, for example, Belgium, Ministère de l'Interieur, *Agriculture. Recensement général. 15 Octobre 1846*, Brussels, 1850 (hereafter 1846 Census), p. xiii, and the 'Rapports au Ministère de l'Intérieur sur la situation des subsistances', *Bulletin de la Commission Centrale de Statistique*, III, 1847, pp. 107–22 and IV, 1851, pp. 175–81.

8 R. C. Allen and C. Ó Gráda, 'On the road again with Arthur Young: English, Irish, and French agriculture during the industrial revolution', *JEH*, XLVIII, 1988, pp. 93–116.

Table 14.1 *Indicators of physical productivity in Belgium and Ireland in the early 1840s*

	Units	Belgium	Ireland	Flanders	E. Ulster
Crop yields (gross)					
Potatoes	tons/acre	5.0	6.0	5.2	
Wheat	bush./acre	22.0	24.4	24.4	25.6
Oats	bush./acre	37.6	38.7	43.4	38.7
Barley	bush./acre	31.1	38.9	41.1	40.0
Flax	lb./acre	535	546	546	527
Animal husbandry					
Beef per beast	lb.	425	364		
Mutton per sheep	lb.	57	55		
Pork per pig	lb.	123	139		
Wool per sheep	lb.	4.4	5.1		
Butter per cow	lb.	106	112		

Source
Belgium, Flanders: M. Goossens, 'De economische ontwikkeling van de belgische landbouw in regionaal perspectief, 1812–1846. Een analyse op basis van de ontwikkeling van het regionaal landbouwprodukt', unpublished Catholic University of Leuven Ph.D. thesis, 2 vols., 1990, I, part II; Ireland: P. M. Solar, 'Growth and distribution in Irish agriculture before the Famine', unpublished Stanford University Ph.D. thesis, 1987, chapter 9; E. Ulster: average yields, 1847–51, for counties Antrim, Armagh, Down, from *Irish agricultural statistics*, BPP, London, 1847–51.

II. The evidence underlying the crop yields and the Belgian animal weights is quite good. The Irish animal weights, except that for pigs, and the milk yields (here expressed in butter equivalents) for both countries are less firmly based.

On the basis of the figures in Table 14.1 it would be hard to distinguish between the two agricultures. The differences in physical productivity were minimal in the early 1840s, a striking result given their contemporary reputations. Crop yields in Flanders (the provinces of East and West Flanders) and east Ulster (counties Antrim, Armagh and Down) are also given in Table 14.1. Flemish yields were only somewhat higher than the Belgian averages and east Ulster's about the same as the Irish averages, so that the results at the regional level confirm the national picture of broad similarity. Nor do trends in physical productivity during the early nineteenth century show any evidence that Ireland had recently caught up with Belgium. On the contrary, from around 1810 to the 1840s Irish cereal yields rose by at most 10 per cent, whereas in Belgium cereal yields rose by about 20

per cent over the same period, and potato yields by about 30 per cent.
Animal weights and butter yields, on the other hand, exhibited little
upward movement in either country.[9]

These indicators of physical productivity suggest that Belgium
and Ireland were on a par, more or less, in the 1840s and that the
Belgians had, in fact, been catching up to the Irish in the early
nineteenth century. Since the evidence on crop yields is plentiful and
relatively easy to summarise, this result is unlikely to be a statistical
artefact. Were contemporary observers then simply unwilling to face
the facts when commenting on the states of agriculture in the two
countries?

II Aggregate agricultural output in the two countries

Recent estimates of Belgian and Irish agricultural output in the early
1840s enable a more comprehensive examination of aggregate land
and labour productivity in the two countries. This is not the place to
discuss these output estimates in detail, but since neither set has been
widely diffused, certain aspects of them need to be highlighted.

The estimates for Ireland have been put together by P. Solar.[10]
His work builds on P. M. A. Bourke's pioneering efforts to estimate
land-use and cereal and potato yields on the eve of the Famine. Bourke's
estimates for the amount of land in crops have been revised downward
on the basis of J. Mokyr's reworking of the constabulary returns for
potato acreage and of additional evidence on the changes in cereal
cultivation from the early 1840s to the first official agricultural statistics
in 1847.[11] Output from animal husbandry has been estimated with the
help of information from farm, estate, and merchant accounts. The
estimates for both crops and animal products have also benefited from
the availability of new series for Irish trade in grain, butter, eggs, dead
meat and livestock.

---

9 Allen and Ó Gráda, 'On the road again', p. 107. P. M. Solar, 'Growth and
distribution in Irish agriculture before the Famine', unpublished Stanford
University Ph.D. thesis, 1987, pp. 131 and 368–9. This and other information on
Belgian agriculture is drawn from M. Goossens, 'De economische ontwikkeling
van de belgische landbouw in regionaal perspectief, 1812–1846. Een analyse op
basis van de ontwikkeling van het regionaal landbouwprodukt', unpublished
Catholic University of Leuven Ph.D. thesis, 2 vols., 1990.

10 Solar, 'Growth and distribution', chapter 9.

11 J. Mokyr, 'Irish history with the potato', *Irish Economic and Social History*, VIII, 1981,
pp. 8–29.

The Irish estimates, it must be acknowledged, are far from precise. The evidence, particularly on meat and milk yields and the shares of animal stocks that constituted output, is often fragmentary and suggestive of considerable underlying variation. Ó Gráda, working with similar material, came up with figures that put Irish agricultural output on the eve of the Famine 10–20 per cent higher than the estimates used here.[12] Without entering into the differences between the two sets of estimates, using Ó Gráda's figures would thus give a more favourable picture of agriculture in Ireland relative to that in Belgium.

The estimates for Belgian output arise from work by M. Goossens on agricultural development during the early nineteenth century.[13] She has constructed detailed estimates for 1812 from the statistics collected under the French regime and for the mid 1840s from a thorough reworking of material to be found in the 1846 census and elsewhere. Although both 1812 and 1846 were years marked by crop failures and particularly high cereal prices, there is sufficient information in the sources to allow estimates to be made for 'normal' years. The Belgian evidence for both periods is, in general, much better than that available for Ireland in the 1840s. Its weaknesses are similar: the sources are thin on milk yields and on the shares of total output constituted by the potato crop, and by cattle, sheep, and pig stocks.

Nevertheless, it is the relative rather than the absolute level of agricultural output in Belgium and Ireland which is of interest when comparing their respective productivities. In this context, certain discrepancies should be noted in the composition of the two sets of output estimates, mainly due to the absence for one country or the other of detailed estimates for some minor products. For Ireland no estimates are available for rape, hemp, madder, tobacco, hops or chicory, which together accounted for 3–4 per cent of Belgian output in 1846. Some of these were grown in Ireland, but not nearly to the same extent as in Belgium. Conversely, for Belgium no estimates are available for eggs and poultry. On the other hand, these are likely to have been less important than in Ireland, where they accounted for 2–3 per cent of total output, partly because of the large trade in eggs to Britain. Since these items are small and to some extent cancel each other out, they have simply been excluded from the indices of relative output.

12 C. Ó Gráda, 'Irish agricultural output before and after the Famine', *Journal of European Economic History*, XIII, 1984, pp. 149–65.
13 Goossens, 'De belgische landbouw', I, part II.

Two indices of relative agricultural output have been constructed, one weighted by Irish relative prices, the other by Belgian prices. The former uses a potato price which approximates reasonably closely to rural conditions. The latter uses a potato price more representative of urban conditions where, to judge from the situation in Ireland, potatoes were probably dearer relative to cereals than in the countryside. The choice of prices clearly makes a difference: at Irish prices Irish agricultural output was 1.90 times Belgian output, at Belgian prices 2.36 times. The discrepancy is almost entirely due to the price of potatoes and is probably exaggerated, even though potatoes were undoubtedly more expensive in Belgium than in Ireland. As a result, calculations at Belgian prices may overstate productivity in Ireland by more than might be expected from simple index-number bias.

III Land productivity

An attempt can now be made to arrive at a measure of land productivity that is more comprehensive than the yield of a single crop. This requires the derivation of a measure of land input in addition to the measures of relative output obtained in Section II. This is not the place to get involved in problems of assessing the inherent quality of land in Belgium and Ireland. At first glance Belgium might be thought to have the better land. Contemporaries often thought of Flanders, at least, as a fertile region, although this reputation may have been built more on the results that were obtained than on its basic endowment. Radcliff, for one, was struck by the 'natural poverty of the soil' in Flanders.[14] Ireland, by contrast, has some very good land, particularly on its central limestone plain, but it also contains large areas where drainage is poor. It is possible to envisage a detailed comparison of land quality on the basis of modern soil surveys, as P. K. O'Brien and C. Keyder have done for Britain and France, but in the meanwhile, reliance will here be placed on the cruder measures of the land input shown in Table 14.2.[15]

The crudest, and least ambiguous, measure is the total land area of each country. Ireland was 2.85 times larger than Belgium, which implies that Irish land productivity was only 67–83 per cent that of Belgium, depending on which set of prices is used to compare output. A somewhat better measure would exclude all land that was urban,

14 Radcliff, *Report*, pp. 95–6.
15 P. K. O'Brien and C. Keydar, *Economic growth in Britain and France 1780–1914: two paths to the twentieth century*, London, 1978, pp. 109–12.

Table 14.2 *Estimates of land areas in Belgium and Ireland in the early 1840s (1,000s hectares)*

	Belgium	Ireland
Crops	1,163	2,185
Sown grasses and fallow	239	445
Cultivated land	1,402	2,631
Pasture	317	3,358
Agricultural land	1,719	5,989
Other	1,231	2,414
Total land	2,950	8,403

Source
Solar, 'Growth and distribution', chapter 9; Goossens, 'De belgische landbouw', I, part II.

wooded, under water, used for roads, or 'waste'. The problem is how to define this last category. Bourke, who has attempted an estimate of the amount of agricultural land in Ireland on the eve of the Famine, has shown the difficulties that contemporaries faced in drawing the line between agricultural land and waste in Ireland. It is this estimate that is used here, although it should not be regarded as too precise.[16] Whether the Belgians classified land in the same way as the Irish is not clear, but the errors that might result are likely to be smaller. The area classified as waste in the 1840s came to only 325,000 hectares and was highly concentrated in two areas: 48 per cent was in the Ardennes and 38 per cent in the Campine. Yet even this land probably produced some agricultural output. Sheep were grazed on waste in the Campine, and the *terres sarts* in the Ardennes produced a rye crop every eighteen to thirty years and supported a few cattle in other years. In any case, the land classified as either pasture or waste came to only 31 per cent of the Belgian land which was unambiguously agricultural. The comparable figure for Ireland was 67 per cent, which leaves much more scope for error in specifying the land input to agriculture. Certainly, Bourke's estimate probably includes much land that was at best rough grazing and only suitable for rearing young cattle and sheep. Nevertheless, comparing his estimate of agricultural land in Ireland with figures from the 1846 Belgian census show Ireland with 3.48 times

16 P. M. A. Bourke, 'The agricultural statistics of the 1841 Census of Ireland. A critical review', *EcHR*, XVIII, 1965, pp. 382–91.

more agricultural land. This implies an output per unit of land in Ireland only 55–68 per cent that of Belgium, a result which is probably biased against Ireland.

A measure of the land input biased against Belgium would be the land under crops, including sown grasses, since Ireland had only 1.88 times as much land under cultivation. Nevertheless, it had more than ten times as much land under natural (unsown) grass and this pasture, of course, produced output. If it is assumed that all Belgian agricultural output came from the cultivated area, but that in Ireland output of cattle and sheep came exclusively from the grassland and output of crops and pigmeat exclusively from the tilled land, a very rough estimate can be made of the respective productivities of their tilled land. Of course, the underlying assumption is a gross oversimplification: some Irish animals were fed the products of tillage, and much grassland would have been cultivated periodically. But the results are telling. On this supposition, output per unit of tillage in Ireland was still only 67–104 per cent that of Belgium. Again, the true figure is likely to lie below the upper end of this range due to the heavy weighting that Belgian relative prices give to potato output.

It is therefore difficult to come up with a single figure for relative land productivity, but it is likely that the Belgians produced more output per unit of land and that their advantage in land productivity may have been as much as 50 per cent. This result shows the danger of identifying crop yields with land productivity. While yields in Belgium and Ireland were much the same, the Belgian mix of crops resulted in much more output per unit of land. This may answer Allen and Ó Gráda's question as to why Arthur Young chose high rents and new crops, rather than grain yields, as his productivity measure.[17] On the results presented here, he may well have done so because the introduction of roots and leguminous plants permitted farmers to keep more of their land under crops and so produce significantly more final output per unit of land.[18]

IV Labour productivity

One reason why land productivity was higher in Belgium may have been that the Belgians applied more labour to each unit of land. If methods of cultivation were similar in the two countries, this would

17 Allen and Ó Gráda, 'On the road again', p. 115.
18 See also R. Shiel, above, pp. 74–5, and M. Overton, above, pp. 295–7.

have been the case simply because relatively more of their land was in crops instead of pasture. But methods of cultivation were not the same. Radcliff's description of Flemish agricultural practice suggests that they involved more labour in manuring, ploughing and weeding than was the case in Ireland.[19]

As with the land input, there are difficulties in coming up with a comparable measure of the labour input for the two countries in the early 1840s. An obvious choice would be the number of persons recorded in the censuses as having agricultural occupations. The 1841 census in Ireland recorded 1.59 million males and 0.13 million females of 15 years and over working in agriculture, giving a total of 1.72 million.[20]

The Belgian census of 1846 gives two sets of figures for the agricultural labour force, both of which are highly problematic.[21] The census of agriculture recorded 0.66 million males and 0.43 million females as employed in agriculture, but this probably over-states the participation of family members. The population census, on the other hand, enumerated only 0.27 million males and 0.10 million females with agricultural occupations. This is a significant understatement. Many additional agricultural workers were undoubtedly to be found in the large numbers of 'unspecified labourers' and 'servants', who together accounted for almost a third of the occupied population. Opinion varies concerning the shares of these categories which ought to be assigned to the agricultural sector. The 1846 census report put all the unspecified labourers there, which is surely incorrect. B. Verhaegen, at the other extreme, allocated only a third of them to agriculture, which results in a mysteriously large rural non-agricultural labour force. P. Klep's figure of 75 per cent is probably closer to the truth, and draws support from detailed local work done recently by E. Gubin and A. Van Neck.[22] Klep makes this and other adjustments to the data in

19 Radcliff, *Report*, pp. 60 and 225–6.

20 *Report of the Commissioners appointed to take the Census of Ireland for the year 1841*, BPP, XXIV, HC.504, London, 1843 (hereafter 1841 Census), p. 440.

21 The following discussion is based largely on P. M. M. Klep, 'De agrarische beroepsbevolking van de provincies Antwerpen en Brabant en van het Koninkrijk België, 1846–1910. Nieuwe evaluaties van kwantitatief-historisch materiaal', *Bijdragen tot de geschiedenis*, LIX, 1976, pp. 25–69. See also G. L. De Brabander, 'De regionaal-sectoriele spreiding van de economische activiteiten in België, 1846–1910. Een bronkritische benadering', *Bijdragen tot de geschiedenis*, LXI, 1977, pp. 97–195.

22 E. Gubin and A. Van Neck, 'La repartition professionnelle de la population Belge en 1846: un piège statistique', pp. 269–365 in *Acta Historica Bruxellensia IV. Histoire et méthode*, Brussels, 1981.

the 1846 occupational census and arrives at figures of 0.62 million males and 0.23 females working in agriculture, a total of 0.85 million. The size of these adjustments suggests that the estimates ought not to be regarded as too precise. Nevertheless, they are the best currently available and those most comparable to the figures from the Irish census.

One notable feature of these estimates is that the share of women in the agricultural labour force was significantly higher in Belgium. This is not a statistical artefact. Women's participation in agriculture was more important in Belgium, particularly in Flanders, than it was in Ireland. Radcliff stressed that spinning and weaving in Flanders were limited to the 'dead' winter season and that women were occupied in agriculture during the rest of the year.[23] Moreover, the detailed cadastral surveys of the early nineteenth century show that the weeding of grain and potatoes, for which Flemish agriculture was noted, was women's work. Women also helped in planting and harvesting.[24]

The Irish evidence suggests a lesser role for women in agriculture. Most witnesses to the Irish Poor Inquiry in the early 1830s testified that labourer's wives could obtain paid employment for a total of no more than one month in the year. Women were sometimes hired to help with the hay and corn harvests and with setting and digging potatoes, but their main contribution to family income was clearly the sale of eggs and poultry (which is excluded from the output figures used here). Of course, limited involvement with the market did not rule out labour on the family's potato plot, though the testimony in the Poor Inquiry did not stress this.[25]

One indicator of the greater role that women played in Belgian agriculture was that their wage relative to male labourers was higher than the relative wage for female workers in Ireland. Information in the 1846 agricultural census suggests that women's daily wages in Belgian

---

23 Radcliff, *Report*, p. 256.
24 The cadastral surveys were set up during the French period and continued during Dutch rule. Their aim was to fix the value of property in each commune. For farmland this was done by making detailed estimates of gross and net output for a sample of holdings. Gross output was estimated per hectare over an entire rotation of crops, so that information is available concerning rotations, crop yields, and output from animals. Net output was calculated on the basis of detailed investigations of the costs of manuring, ploughing, weeding, harvesting, threshing and winnowing.
25 *First report from Commissioners for inquiring into the condition of the poorer classes in Ireland*, BPP, XXXII, HC.369, London, 1836 (hereafter Poor Inquiry), Appendix D, pp. 84–92.

agriculture were roughly 60 per cent of men's. Irish women did less well. Evidence given to the Poor Inquiry in the early 1830s suggests that women's wages were at best half of those of men.[26]

This information on relative wages may be used to weight the male and female contributions to the agricultural labour force. If each woman is counted as 0.55 and each man as 1.00, then the labour input in Ireland was 2.23 times that in Belgium. This measure leads to the conclusions that the Belgian agricultural sector applied more labour to each unit of land, but that output per unit of labour was more or less the same in the two countries. Labour productivity in Irish agriculture was 85-106 per cent of that in Belgium, depending on the prices used to compare output. As an alternative measure of the labour input, women's work in agriculture can simply be ignored, with the result that the number of male agricultural workers in Ireland was more than two-and-a-half times that in Belgium. In this case Irish labour productivity was only 74–91 per cent of that in Belgium.

Two further corrections may be made in measuring relative labour inputs. First, the seasonal migration of agricultural labourers from Ireland to Britain means that census figures overstate the effective agricultural labour force. During the summer of 1841 a special survey by the census commissioners counted 50,000 men and 7,000 women crossing the Irish Sea for the hay and cereal harvests.[27] These seasonal migrants were generally unavailable for the harvesting of cereal crops in Ireland, though they did return in time for the digging of potatoes.

A second correction arises from the inherent difficulty of assigning one occupation to individuals who undertook several sorts of economic activity. Agricultural labour in both countries was commonly combined with the production of textiles and other non-agricultural goods. In Ireland many linen weavers with holdings of a few acres were probably recorded in the 1841 census as farmers. Most of the 100,000 or so adult males who were recorded as weavers would also have worked in agriculture, either on plots too small to justify the label 'farmer' or as casual labourers. Reports on the linen industry repeatedly mention that markets for yarn and cloth were quiet when weavers were occupied with field work.[28] The situation in Belgium was much the same. Weavers with land were certainly classified as agricultural workers in the census of agriculture; some may have been recorded as such in the

26 1846 Census, p. ccx; Poor Inquiry, Appendix D, pp. 1–74.
27 1841 Census, pp. xxvi-xxvii.
28 Solar, 'Growth and distribution', pp. 387–8.

occupational census. Most of the 50,000 weavers and 21,000 workers in manufacturing industry (primarily textiles) who lived in rural areas would also have worked in agriculture.[29]

These corrections may be incorporated into a third measure of the relative labour input by adjusting the numbers of male agricultural workers in two ways: seasonal migrants have been subtracted in the case of Ireland and male domestic textile workers added in both countries. These adjustments lead to the result that labour productivity in Ireland was 79–99 per cent of that in Belgium.

On the basis of these various calculations it transpires that labour productivity in Belgian agriculture was approximately 10–20 per cent higher than in Irish agriculture. Different methods yield different results hence it is difficult to be more precise. Indeed, on certain calculations Ireland emerges as having had the higher labour productivity, although these are invariably based on output estimates valued according to Belgian prices, which, for the reasons given in Section II, overstate Ireland's output relative to Belgium's.

V Total factor productivity

Since both land and labour productivity were higher in Belgian agriculture, it follows that in the early 1840s Belgium was generally more efficient at producing agricultural goods than Ireland and enjoyed a corresponding advantage in total factor productivity. To quantify that advantage it is necessary to weight the respective contributions of land and labour, for which the factor shares in output will be used. For both Ireland and Belgium the land share has been derived from estimates of the current rental value of all agricultural land. The labour share is then taken as the residual. For Ireland this gives factor shares of 0.31 for land and 0.69 for labour; for Belgium, 0.25 and 0.75 respectively.[30] The values for relative inputs and the results of the total factor productivity calculations are shown in Table 14.3. At Belgian output prices and factor shares, Belgium's advantage was about 5–10 per cent; at Irish prices and factor costs, it is about 30 per cent. Most probably the 'true' value lies nearer the upper end of this range, so that, on balance, Belgium was perhaps 20–30 per cent more efficient than Ireland in turning land and labour, as measured here, into agricultural output.

Why Belgian agriculture was more efficient is a more difficult

29 Gubin and Van Neck, 'La Repartition', pp. 348–51.
30 Solar, 'Growth and distribution', pp. 371–2.

Table 14.3 *Output, inputs, and productivity in Irish agriculture relative to Belgian agriculture in the early 1840s (Belgium = 100)*

	Input	Output or productivity	
		At Irish prices	At Belgian prices
Agricultural output		190	236
Output per unit of labour			
Male and female – weighted	223	85	106
Male	258	74	91
Male (revised)	239	79	99
Output per unit of land			
Total land area	285	67	83
Agricultural land	348	55	68
Cultivated land	188	101	126
Output per weighted unit of labour and land		72–7	90–5

Notes
The entries for labour and land productivity use the output index given at the top of the column and the input index in the same row. Total factor productivity at Belgian prices takes the land input as 330 and the labour input as the range from 220 to 240. The Belgian factor shares – 75 per cent for labour and 25 per cent for land – are used. Total factor productivity at Irish prices takes the same values for the land and labour input, but uses Irish factor shares – 69 per cent for labour and 31 per cent for land.

Source See text.

question, and some informed speculations are all that may be offered. It is unlikely that the Belgian advantage was purely technical. The Belgians do not seem to have been noticeably superior in terms of plant varieties, animal breeds or farm implements. Seed-yield ratios for cereal crops were similar in the two countries.[31] The quality of Irish grain seems to have been only slightly lower than that of British: in the 1840s it sold at only a small discount on the London and Liverpool markets.[32] Almost all flax seed used in both countries was imported, with Belgium and Ireland buying from the same suppliers. As for farm

31 Solar, 'Growth and distribution', chapter 9; Goossens, 'De belgische landbouw', I, part II.
32 The comparison is based on prices quoted during the decade 1840–49 in the following newspapers: *Gore's general advertiser* (Liverpool) and the *London mercantile price current*.

animals, Table 14.1 shows that yields of meat and milk were broadly
similar in the two countries. Radcliff was certainly not impressed by the
quality of Flemish cattle, sheep, and pigs, nor by the quality of the
farm implements he saw.[33]

Contemporary observers were more likely to see Belgian agriculture's superiority in the sophistication of its crop rotation. The central
element here was the cultivation of clover and fodder crops. Clover
was harvested and used to sustain cattle during the summer and autumn;
in the winter and spring they were fed turnips, potatoes, and other
fodder crops. In its most thorough application this system eliminated
pasture entirely. Soil fertility was maintained by the efficient recycling
of dung and urine from farm animals, by purchases of manure from
outside the agricultural sector, and by the nitrogen-fixing properties of
the clover crop.[34]

Yet these Belgian methods were not necessarily technically superior
to those employed in Ireland. First, this sort of intensive cultivation is,
at least in part, a reflection of different factor proportions in the two
countries. Belgium's greater rural population density meant that there
was enough labour to cultivate all but a small share of the land. Second,
these methods were not unknown in Ireland. They were repeatedly
urged upon Irish farmers during the early nineteenth century, and
clover was increasingly cultivated before the Famine. But, as Solar, and
Allen and Ó Gráda have argued, Irish farmers may have had good
reason not to integrate sown clover into the rotation. Irish land had a
natural propensity to regenerate itself in clover. The practice of taking
three or four crops, then returning land to grass, meant that its fertility
would be restored by nitrogen-fixing clover that, to the astonishment
of visiting agriculturalists, was so abundant in Irish pastures.[35] This system
had obvious limits: the share of the cultivated land could not be pushed
too far or the land would not remain under grass long enough for the
soil to be replenished. Intensification of agricultural production would
sooner or later require that clover be cultivated. But, again, this may
not have been necessary given the relative endowments of land and
labour in Ireland in the early 1840s.

33 Radcliff, *Report*, pp. 207–11.
34 See Shiel, above, pp. 74–5.
35 P. M. Solar, 'Agricultural productivity and economic development in Ireland and
    Scotland in the early nineteenth century', pp. 70–88 in T. M. Devine and
    D. Dickson, eds., *Ireland and Scotland 1600–1850: parallels and contrasts in economic
    and social development*, Edinburgh, 1983; Allen and Ó Gráda, 'On the road again',
    p. 108.

If Belgian agriculture was not technically superior, how is its demonstrable productivity advantage to be explained? Part of the explanation undoubtedly lies with other agricultural inputs which have not so far been considered, and of which the Belgians used relatively more. Intermediate inputs of fertilisers and feedstuffs from outside the agricultural sector, the basis for what F. M. L. Thompson has described as the 'second agricultural revolution', are one such unmeasured factor.[36] Ireland was, if anything, a net exporter of these inputs: its oats exports fed British horses and its exports of live cattle, sheep and pigs ultimately became a source of bone manure for British farmers. The Belgian agricultural sector, by contrast, was probably a net importer of fertilisers. The Belgian trade statistics are not very revealing on manures, but they do show imports of oil cakes in the 1840s at a respectable one-seventh of the United Kingdom level.[37] Within Belgium, farmers close to mines and iron works made use of some industrial by-products. And Radcliff noted that:

Manure being in Flanders in some measure an article of trade, the selling price of each description is easily ascertained; and that it should not be infinitely higher, where the demand is so great, can only follow from the numbers occupied in collecting it with unceasing industry. Every substance that constitutes, or is convertible to manure, is sought after with avidity, which accounts for the extreme cleanliness of the Flemish towns and pavements, hourly resorted to, with brooms and barrows, as a source of profit.[38]

Night soil was also used as fertiliser in Ireland, but the Belgians seem to have been more assiduous in its collection and there was, in any case, a larger share of the Belgian population living in towns.

Another input which has not been measured, and for which it would be very difficult to arrive at any comprehensive estimate, is capital. It seems likely that the Belgian farmer was the better endowed. One component of the agricultural capital stock that can be measured is the stock of horses. Belgium had about 275,000 agricultural horses in the mid 1840s; Ireland about 510,000.[39] The Belgians thus had more horses per unit of land and labour, but their advantage was not

36 F. M. L. Thompson, 'The second agricultural revolution, 1815–1880', *EcHR*, XXI, 1968, pp. 62–77.
37 The average imports during the period 1840–45 amounted to 10.5 million kilograms. See Thompson, 'The second agricultural revolution', for the United Kingdom's imports.
38 Radcliff, *Report*, p. 234.
39 Solar, 'Growth and distribution', chapter 9; Goossens, 'De belgische landbouw', I, part II. See also E. A. Wrigley, above, pp. 328–9.

overwhelming. It was probably greater if the quality of the animals is taken into account. As Radcliff observed, 'Flanders has long been noted for its breed of work-horses, and that of England has been considerably improved by frequent importation from there ...'.[40] The superiority of Belgian horses is confirmed by their relative value: the Belgian 1846 census took horses to be worth almost twice as much as cows and oxen; the Irish 1841 census put their average value at less than a quarter more.[41]

A more important explanation for Belgian agriculture's productivity advantage may be that the Belgians simply worked more and harder. It is extremely rare to find comments about Belgian agricultural workers of the following sort: 'an Irish labourer in his own country is decidedly a lazy workman. The long-handled shovel is often put in requisition to prop up his body while the gossip goes round.'[42] Yet such statements abound in the contemporary literature on Irish agriculture. The system of agriculture in Belgium, and particularly that practised in Flanders, seems to have left little time for gossip. Radcliff thought Flanders 'remarkable for the reiterated use of the plough in the production of its crops'.[43] The number of ploughings for particular crops far exceeded what was usual in Britain or Ireland. Land to be planted with oats, for example, was given three ploughings and two harrowings. In Ireland 'oats ... are commonly a very poor, because a very neglected crop; one slovenly ploughing, without harrowing or hackling, being deemed sufficient'.[44] Repeated ploughing in Flanders was combined with careful weeding of all crops. Not so in Ireland: 'still more unpardonable, in a country so abounding with idle hands, is Pat's utter inattention to the general enemy of agricultural industry, weeds. With these, as if he considered indigenous plants to have a native right of possession, he suffers all his ground, save only that which bears potatoes, to be overrun.'[45] It is significant that ploughing and weeding were activities generally undertaken at slack times of the year, so that the Belgians may have put in more hours per year than the Irish.

40 Radcliff, *Report*, pp. 212–16 and also pp. 53–5.
41 1841 Census, pp. xxxi-xxxii; 1846 Census, p. ccxiv.
42 Anonymous, 'On the agricultural state of Ireland', *Quarterly Journal of Agriculture*, II, 1831, p. 737.
43 Radcliff, *Report*, p. 225.
44 H. Townsend, 'On the improvement of Irish Agriculture', *Quarterly Journal of Agriculture*, 1828–29, p. 324.
45 Townsend, 'Improvement', pp. 324–5.

G. Clark has recently suggested work intensity as the major factor behind productivity differences in European agriculture before the twentieth century.[46] Appealing as is Clark's conclusion, the evidence on Ireland and Belgium offers little support for the way in which he reached it. His main quantitative indicator of work intensity is the number of man-days required for threshing wheat. He gives threshing rates for Ireland and Belgium, but they are only indirect observations (calculated from daily wages and wheat yields) and are separated by 60–70 years. Ireland in the first decade of the nineteenth century has a higher value than Belgium in the late 1860s, which offers little support for the hypothesis that the Belgians worked harder. Direct observations on threshing rates in the 1820s and 1830s produce the same result. For Ireland, alas, there is only the contemporary estimate of Martin Doyle that a good worker could thresh 127 kilograms of wheat per day.[47] For Belgium there is an abundance of evidence in the cadastral surveys.[48] Unfortunately, this source groups threshing and winnowing together, so the threshing rate will be somewhat understated. For five communes in Flanders 87–109 kilograms of wheat were threshed and winnowed by a labourer per day, a level which ought to be more or less comparable to that in Ireland. But elsewhere the rates were much lower. In the provinces of Antwerp and Limburg values of only 40–60 kilograms per worker per day were common. This large degree of variation within a small country raises questions about the usefulness of the threshing rate as an indicator of work effort. Preliminary analysis of the Belgian data suggests a strong correlation between the yield of the grain and the quantity that could be threshed in a day. If it was simply much easier to thresh high-yielding grain, then the essential difference may still have been that the Irish were lazy and the Belgians industrious.

On the other hand, the Belgians may have worked harder because they had greater incentives to undertake labour-intensive capital formation. While virtually all Irish land was farmed by tenants, roughly two-thirds of Belgian land was in the hands of owner-occupiers.[49] These owner-occupiers reaped the full benefit from improvements. In pre-Famine Ireland it was the common perception, if not necessarily the reality, that landlords did not invest enough and that they reaped at least part of the benefits from tenant investment. Without entering

---

46 G. Clark, 'Productivity growth without technical change in European agriculture before 1850', *JEH*, XLVII, 1987, pp. 419–32. See also *idem*, above, pp. 231–5.
47 J. Bell and M. Watson, *Irish farming 1750–1900*, Edinburgh, 1986, p. 209.
48 See n. 24, above.
49 1846 Census, p. lxiv.

into the tangled question of whether Irish farmers had security of tenure before the Famine, it may still be suggested that owner-occupiers would have put more effort into building up and maintaining soil fertility than would landlords – who may have faced high costs of labour supervision – or tenants – who feared that the landlord would be the principal beneficiary.[50]

Belgian agriculture may also have involved a greater mobilisation of family labour. Small holdings predominated in Belgium: farms of less than 50 acres accounted for more than half of the agricultural land. In Ireland, by contrast, the share of agricultural land held by farmers with less than 50 acres was less than a third.[51] On small holdings farmers' wives and children were able to make an important contribution to the total labour input, which may account for the much larger share of women recorded as agricultural workers in Belgium. Opportunities off the holding were more limited, since the markets for women's and children's labour in agriculture do not seem to have been particularly well developed, perhaps because of the costs of supervision. Farm size and the organisation of the labour market may be behind the differences in weeding practice. In Belgium all crops were weeded, whereas in Ireland only the potatoes were carefully cleared of weeds. The attention given to the potato crop in Ireland is not surprising since even on large farms it was typically cultivated by labourers on their own account. They received short-term access to land in return for their labour on the other crops. Family labour could thus be brought to bear on the potato crop.

If small farms like those in Belgium could more effectively mobilise labour for agricultural production, why did more Irish landlords not divide farms? One reason may be that the gain in rental income would not have been large enough. Belgium's more intensive agriculture did not seem to have produced a much higher level of rents than that which prevailed in Ireland. The average rent in Ireland in the early 1840s was about £2.5 per hectare, and in Belgium about 72.5 francs.[52] These values can be compared in three ways. At the official exchange rate the Belgian rent works out as equivalent to £2.9. Alternatively, use

50 J. Mokyr, *Why Ireland starved: a quantitative and analytical history of the Irish economy, 1800–1850*, London, 1983, chapter 3.
51 Estimated for Ireland using the farm size distribution in P. M. A. Bourke, 'The extent of the potato crop in Ireland at the time of the Famine', *Journal of the Statistical and Social Inquiry Society of Ireland*, XX, III, 1959, p. 21; for Belgium, see note 49 above.
52 Solar, 'Growth and distribution', chapter 7; 1846 Census, p. cxcix.

can be made of the indices of relative prices that are implicit in the output indices which have been constructed. These show the relative value of rents in the two countries measured in terms of a composite agricultural commodity. With Belgian quantities as weights, deflation by the agricultural price index produces a relative real rent index of 109 (Ireland = 100); with Irish quantities, the index is 85. None of these calculations suggest that Belgian agriculture produced particularly high rents. Of course, not all things are held constant in this comparison. First, differences in land quality would influence the relative level of rents. Second, rents in Ireland may have been higher because Irish agriculture was protected by the system of tariffs and prohibitions centred around the Corn Laws.

The increase in rental income may not in any case have been high enough to compensate for the costs of additional tenants. Direct costs in monitoring tenant behaviour and in collecting rents were already high in the north-east of Ireland.[53] Another consideration in Ireland in the 1830s and 1840s was the cost of a proliferation of small farms in terms of political influence and potential liabilities for poor relief. Landlords could, of course, have sold land off in small holdings, but the shortage of capital among labourers and small tenants would have posed problems in financing such transfers.

It is important to take this social context into account for these results would, at first sight, lend support to Mokyr's argument that Ireland was not overpopulated on the eve of the Famine.[54] The comparison with Belgium suggests that Ireland could have supported a larger rural population by adopting more intensive methods of cultivation. But, on the basis of the argument developed here, this would have required a major change in the structure of landholding. As owner-occupiers of small holdings, Irish men and their families might have achieved Belgian levels of productivity. But this was hardly likely to happen since it would have required a complete overhaul of the political and social structures within which Irish agriculture had developed.

It should also be remembered that agricultural output per worker was not all that high in Belgium and that family incomes were higher in rural Belgium than in rural Ireland for reasons unrelated to the technical efficiency of agriculture. First, Belgian rural households put

53 W. A. Maguire, *The Downshire estates in Ireland 1801–1845*, Oxford, 1972, pp. 66–7.
54 Mokyr, *Why Ireland starved*, chapter 3.

more labour into agricultural production by employing more fully the women and children. Second, rural families who were owner-occupiers received not only the labour share of output, but also the land share. Third, many rural households supplemented their income by domestic industrial production. This last element was particularly important in Flanders. When incomes from linen-spinning and weaving collapsed in the 1840s, rural Flanders became one of the poorest areas of Belgium and a persistent problem for the government.[55] By that time it hardly looked like a model for Ireland to imitate.

55 G. Jacquemyns, *Histoire de la crise économique des Flandres, 1845–1850*, Brussels, 1929.

The poverty of Italy and the backwardness of its agriculture before 1914

Italy's agriculture had at its disposal methods of adjustment that were not available to an equal degree north of the Alpine wall.

A. Gerschenkron, 1962.[1]

I On the backwardness of Italian agriculture

Labour productivity in Italian agriculture may have been the highest anywhere in western Europe during the renaissance. Thereafter, although the population of the Peninsula never suffered severely from Malthusian crises and famines, food supplies probably kept just in step with population growth. The ratio of agricultural to non-agricultural population remained high, particularly in relation to its neighbours in western Europe, especially Holland and France, but above all England.[2]

Between 1780 and 1914, while the workforce available to British agriculture remained stable, agricultural output in Britain rose by 240 per cent.[3] Compared with this remarkable achievement, historians of Italy convey the impression that during the long period of European industrialisation labour productivity in Italian agriculture remained roughly constant.[4] This implies that the gap in real incomes between the rural populations of England and Italy probably widened right

Financial support from CNR (grant number 870122510) is gratefully acknowledged.

1 A. Gerschenkron, *Economic backwardness in historical perspective*, Cambridge, Mass., 1962.

2 E. A. Wrigley, 'Urban growth and agricultural change: England and the Continent in the early modern period', *Journal of Interdisciplinary History*, XV, 1985, pp. 683–728.

3 P. K. O'Brien and C. Keyder, *Economic growth in Britain and France 1780–1914: two paths to the twentieth century*, London, 1978, pp. 92–4.

4 G. Federico, 'Mercantilizzazione e sviluppo economico in Italia (1860–1940)', *Rivista di Storia Economica*, III, 1986, pp. 149–86.

down to the closing decade of the nineteenth century. Only towards the end of the century, during the 'Giolittian' upswing (1896–1913), is there evidence of convergence, when Italy began to 'catch up' with the rest of western Europe.[5]

Italian agriculture has often been held responsible for the country's economic retardation. Its low, and for long periods deteriorating, levels of labour productivity imply that the primary sector could not supply investible funds or provide rural markets required to support more rapid industrialisation and urbanisation.

Well-argued critiques of Italian agriculture can be traced back at least to the Enlightenment: it is well known that reformers maintained that political and economic freedom was a prerequisite for economic progress.[6] Thus, in 1789, upon crossing from France into northern Italy, the fertile and irrigated areas of Lombardy impressed Arthur Young. But as he travelled eastward towards the Veneto, he discovered poverty in the countryside which he found became deeper and more widespread as he moved south into Tuscany. In Young's view – and his perception remained common to almost all English classical economists commenting upon Mediterranean societies – rural poverty and poor agriculture could be connected directly to small holding and to sharecropping. Both institutions operated to restrain investment in animals, soil amelioration, tools and implements.[7]

Several decades later, in 1860, Carlo Cattaneo recommended the farming he found in lower Lombardy as a model for most of northern and central Italy. For Cattaneo, good irrigation, a special feature of the Po Valley, appeared to be a less important source of high yields than Lombardy's emulation of north European crop rotations, a good balance between arable and animal husbandry, and well-functioning markets.[8]

According to the final report of a Parliamentary Committee of Enquiry chaired by S. Jacini, around mid-century and compared with most of Europe, Italian agriculture could not be represented as backward, but it had fallen behind other economies during the Risorgimento when resources and human energies were diverted to political ends. Retardation had, moreover, been exacerbated by other

---

5 G. Toniolo, *An economic history of liberal Italy 1850–1918*, London, 1990.
6 G. M. Galanti, *Nuova descrizione storica e geografica delle Sicilie*, Naples, 1786, pp. vii ff.
7 A. Young, *Travels during the years 1787, 1788, and 1789*, II, *Italy*, Bury St Edmunds, 1792.
8 C. Cattaneo, 'Dell'agricoltura inglese paragonata alla nostra', pp. 269–300 in *idem*, *Memorie di economia pubblica dal 1833 al 1860*, I, Milan, 1860.

and essentially temporary problems, such as phylloxera and other plant diseases which had seriously afflicted the production of grapes, silk cocoons and oranges. Agriculture was also depressed by social unrest in the south, by the return to the gold standard which restrained agricultural exports, and by the heavy tax burdens.[9] But when it focused upon the structural problems of farming *per se*, the report contradicted its otherwise optimistic general view about the potential efficiency of Italy's agriculture and observed that most of the sector remained 'simple in that it basically involved fertile soil and human labour'. Only about 20 per cent of all land was cultivated as a 'rural industry' requiring capital and entrepreneurial skills.[10]

With the passing of the Tariff Act of 1887, discussion on agricultural efficiency shifted into a debate between protectionists and free-traders. The liberal argument rested not merely on the losses from the misallocation of resources but also from the baneful effects of propping up southern latifundia – a form of tenure and organisation regarded as inimical not only to industrial but also to agrarian development itself. Marxist historians later joined with liberals in condemning the tariff of 1887, but more for its dynamic than for its short-run allocative effects. Thus for R. Zangheri – for whom 'agricultural backwardness is the key to understanding many of the distinctive characteristics of the Italian economic development' – the duty on cereals meant a renunciation of agricultural progress based on the north European model 'Italian agriculture remained a deadweight on economic expansion.'[11]

A. Gramsci's explanation of Italian backwardness is both political and institutional in form, since 'the unification of Italy occurred without changes in economic and social conditions that are typical of a bourgeois revolution'.[12] For Gramsci the absence of French-style agrarian reform is at the root of the backwardness of Italian agriculture, especially in the south, a region dominated by an unprogressive *blocco agrario*.[13] According to Gramscian interpretations, the survival of inefficient institutions accounts both for the slow pace of agricultural

9 S. Jacini, *I risultati dell'inchiesta agraria (1884)*, Turin, 1976, pp. 30–9.
10 Jacini, *I risultati*, pp. 84–5.
11 R. Zangheri, 'The historical relationship between agricultural and economical development', pp. 23–41 in E. L. Jones and S. J. Woolf, eds., *Agrarian change and economic development*, London, 1969, p. 25.
12 A. Soboul, 'Risorgimento e rivoluzione borghese: schema di una direttiva di ricerca', pp. 801–16 in Istituto Gramsci, *Problemi dell'Unità d'Italia*, Rome, 1962, p. 81.
13 A. Gramsci, *Il Risorgimento*, Turin, 1950; E. Sereni, *Il capitalismo nelle campagne (1860–1900)*, Turin, 1974.

growth and lack of original accumulation which underlies the mediocre performance of Italian industry for some three to four decades after unification.[14]

R. Romeo was one of the few historians who argued that Italy's tenurial institutions did not restrain growth and capital accumulation in the 1860s and 1870s, particularly in the north and centre of the Peninsula. For Romeo the major constraint on agricultural growth came basically from the 'corn laws' of 1887.[15]

More recently, G. Orlando agreed that more appropriate agrarian policies were required but asserted that neither the *laissez-faire* of the Right, before 1876, nor the more interventionist policies pursued thereafter, created favourable conditions for agricultural development. In his view, liberals, especially after Cavour's death, proved incapable of fostering state investment in social-overhead capital, technical education, and agricultural credit. While the governments of Depretis, Crispi, and Giolitti merely provided farmers with limited subsidies and protection, only towards the end of the century did early experiments in co-operation begin to produce some favourable results before being swept away by Fascism.[16]

To sum up: contemporary observers and most historians present Italian agriculture as backward without, however, providing a systematic definition or any estimates of backwardness. Three main explanations for the poor performance of Italian agriculture have been advanced. Firstly, institutional deficiencies, which include the lack of political and civil liberties, persisting until late into the nineteenth century, as well as inefficient tenurial systems – share-cropping in the north-east and centre of Italy and the maldistribution of landownership with absentee proprietors in the south. Secondly, ill-designed economic policies, particularly the protection of cereal cultivation as well as the state's failure to provide an adequate infrastructure of credit institutions and agrarian education. Thirdly, natural resource deficiencies in the south and the centre of Italy.

This essay confronts Italian historiography with an exercise in productivity comparison across two frontiers. Comparative economic history at macro, sectoral, or micro levels seeks to expose what may be general, particular, or deficient in a country's economic development.

---

14 E. Sereni, *Capitalismo e mercato nazionale*, Rome, 1966; and Zangheri, 'The historical relationship'.
15 R. Romeo, *Risorgimento e capitalismo*, Bari, 1955.
16 G. Orlando, *Storia della politica agraria in Italia dal 1848 ad oggi*, Rome–Bari, 1984.

In this case it is to be expected that the placing of Italian agriculture on a scale for comparison with the most advanced agriculture in Europe should both expose the 'degree' to which the sector was inefficient and help historians to specify the nature and sources of Italian economic backwardness before 1914.

Methodologically, this attempt to analyse the relative efficiency of Italian agriculture in value terms differs from most other exercises in quantification contained in this volume, which are conducted in terms of physical yields and productivities. Values combine volume with price data and explicitly include national consumers' preferences as bounds on the choices faced by producers of food and raw materials. Essentially, the exercise has been designed to ascertain how far and why the value of all the agricultural output produced by Italian farmers (constrained as they were by national patterns of demand, ecology, and institutions, as well as by the inputs of land, labour and capital available to them) fell short of the standards set by farmers operating within a different set of environmental and economic constraints in the United Kingdom.

Economic historians generally use physical indicators (such as kilograms per hectare or per worker) to compare productivity changes through time or across regions. These ratios are clearly useful as measures of how technical possibilities for the cultivation of crops and rearing of farm animals varied over the centuries. They may be used under *ceteris paribus* assumptions about natural conditions to represent institutional or entrepreneurial successes or failures to deploy best-practice techniques. Nevertheless, such ostensibly revealing numbers do not measure differentials in economic efficiency. For example, even an acceptable demonstration that environmental conditions were similar in Lincolnshire and Lombardy and that crop yields (bushels per sown acre) in the English county were way above the levels obtained in northern Italy, has only limited economic meaning. To measure economic efficiency, further information is required on the prices of crops sold and consumed, and on rents, interest, and wages, imputable as costs to the inputs of land, capital, and labour utilised to produce output. Economic efficiency is measured by the ratio between *values* of inputs used to produce a given output (or mix of commodities) and the market *value* of that output.

In this essay relative productivities are estimated and compared as far as possible in economic terms. Ideally, *all* factors should be combined into a weighted index and expressed as a ratio of aggregate output in order to estimate total factor productivities for the two agricultures. Unfortunately, there is no hard information on capital deployed by

Italian or by British farmers, and only partial productivity indicators can be estimated for labour and land. Finally, available figures refer to a rather short span of years immediately preceding the Great War when agricultural censuses happened to be taken. How far the relative productivity of the labour and land used in Italian agriculture *c.*1910 can be used to make inferences about more long-term and persistent facets of Italian backwardness will emerge in the conclusions to this chapter. Meanwhile, methods will be used which have been extensively discussed in modern economics literature to homogenise first outputs and then the inputs of labour and land in order to compare productivities between the most advanced and one of the more backward sectors of European agriculture.[17]

II Outputs in Italian and United Kingdom agricultures valued in pounds and lire, *c.*1910

Theoretically, the problems involved in comparing the values of outputs supplied by United Kingdom and Italian farmers are analogous to more familiar index-number problems implicit in comparing real values of different mixes of outputs separated by time. For example, how much produce a medieval peasant obtained from a 50-hectare plot of land compared with his modern successor cultivating the same plot is a question that can only be tackled by valuing the mix of crops harvested at prices prevailing in medieval and modern times. Similarly, the question of how much output Italian farmers supplied compared with their English counterparts can only be answered by valuing the agricultural outputs produced in the two countries in two sets of national prices.

Equally valid comparisons can then be made in sterling or lire. Differences reflect British and Italian preferences which in turn reflect needs, tastes, income levels and income distribution, productive efficiency and, to go round the circle, the structure of relative prices in the two economies. The conversion of Italian output into sterling equivalents conceptualises Italian agriculture from a British standpoint. The totals purport to measure what Italian farm output might have

17 For example, D. Paige and G. Bombach, *A comparison of national outputs and productivity*, Paris, 1959; I. Kravis, 'A survey of international comparisons of productivity' *Economic Journal*, LXXXVI, 1976, pp. 1–41; I. Kravis, Z. Kenessy, A. Heston and R. Summers, *International comparison of real product and purchasing power*, Baltimore, 1975; I. Kravis, A. Heston and R. Summers, *World product and income*, Baltimore, 1978.

been worth 'if' sold on British markets at British prices. Similar estimates of what British farm output might have commanded in lire on Italian markets conceptualises British agriculture from an Italian standpoint.[18]

In Table 15.1, the quantities of various crops and livestock products produced in the two countries are valued, first in British and then in Italian prices. Several problems emerged including: the quality of the basic price and quantity data; numerous difficulties involved in matching British and Italian outputs product by product; the estimation of shadow prices in sterling for 'unique' crops such as wine, rice and olive oil (not grown in the United Kingdom) and similar prices in lire for hops (uncultivated in Italy).

Essentially, accurate estimates were required of the quantities produced and the prices obtained or potentially obtainable (farm-gate prices) for comprehensive lists of agricultural outputs produced upon farms throughout Italy and the United Kingdom. As always the data turned out to be neither accurate nor comprehensive. For example, no figures were found for rabbits, wild birds or soft fruit produced by Italy's farmers. Some vegetables and horticultural products and timber are missing for both countries.

For United Kingdom quantities and prices, the results of E. Ojala's research were the main source used.[19] His quantities relate to 1904–10 and are from official sources, and his estimates were cross-checked against agricultural censuses for Britain and Ireland.[20] The British census was based upon a survey covering all farm holdings of an acre and above. In a later study, J. Bellerby accepted Ojala's figures but preferred to work with a somewhat lower estimate for meat production based upon different techniques of estimation.[21] United Kingdom farm-gate prices are from the same sources and Ojala's farm-gate prices for 1910–14 are based upon information collected in the census of agricultural production for 1925 and extrapolated backwards using wholesale price indices.[22]

On comparing Ojala's figures with the Agricultural Census, it

---

18 D. Usher, *The measurement of economic growth*, Oxford, 1980.
19 E. M. Ojala, *Agriculture and economic progress*, London, 1952, pp. 192–217.
20 Department of Agricultural and Technical Instruction for Ireland, *The agricultural output of Ireland 1908 (in connection with the Census of Production Act, 1906)*, Dublin, 1912, pp. 4–27.
21 J. R. Bellerby, 'The distribution of farm income in the United Kingdom 1867–1938', *Journal of Proceedings of the Agricultural Economics Society*, X, 1953, reprinted as pp. 259–80 in W. E. Minchinton, ed., *Essays in agrarian history*, II, Newton Abbot, 1968.
22 *Census of agricultural production 1925, BPP*, XXV, Cmd.2815, London, 1927, p. 291.

became clear that the data available for fruit and vegetables, poultry and eggs are likely to be underestimated because such commodities tended to be produced on small holdings where fairly high proportions were consumed by farmers and their families.[23] Despite these and other minor shortcomings, the censuses and other official sources available to Ojala and Bellerby can be accepted with a fair degree of confidence.[24]

Italian data for both quantities and prices are less satisfactory largely because no complete agricultural census was taken in Italy at the time. The source underlying most available data for quantities of crops produced is the *Monthly Bulletin of the Statistical Office of the Ministry of Agriculture, Trade and Industry*, 1911–13. After 1909 (when the results of the '*Catasto Agrario*' were made available) the scope and quality of these sample surveys improved. In the 1950s the Central Statistical Office (ISTAT) produced a volume of historical statistics which included data on quantities and prices for Italy's main agricultural crops and products from 1861 to 1955.[25] These post-war figures suggested a sharp upward revision for outputs of fruit and vegetables compared with the original estimates of the Ministry of Agriculture. ISTAT's figures have been reviewed and amended recently by V. Zamagni who made a computation of the amount of total output that was recycled within the agricultural sector.[26] In constructing Table 15.1 ISTAT and Zamagni were heavily relied upon for 'net' quantities of crops cultivated from 1909 to 1913.[27]

The quantities of meat, poultry, eggs, and dairy produce published by ISTAT can be depended upon with less confidence because neither that publication nor *Annali Statistica* provide information on how estimates for animal produce were compiled, and attempts to trace the figures back through original sources failed. Censuses for the 'stock' of animals go back to 1891 and a census was taken for 1908. But how flows of dead meat were derived from stock figures is not yet clear because no slaughterhouse data appear to have been published before 1939.[28] With reluctance, the estimates published by ISTAT as amended recently by Zamagni were simply accepted. Italian prices are wholesale

23 Department of Agricultural and Technical Instruction for Ireland, *The agricultural output*, pp. 5–9.
24 Ojala, *Agriculture*, pp. 58–60; Ministry of Agriculture and Fisheries and Food, *A century of agricultural statistics*, London, 1968, chapters IV, V, IX.
25 ISTAT, *Sommario di statistiche storiche*, Rome, 1958.
26 V. Zamagni, 'Le radici agricole del dualismo italiano', *Nuova Rivista Storica*, LIX, 1975, pp. 55–99.
27 ISTAT, *Sommario*; Zamagni, 'Le radici agricole'.
28 Gazzetta Ufficiale, *Supplemento straordinario al n. 49*, Rome, 1939.

prices reported by chambers of commerce and other official bodies for major towns. They are summarised into annual averages in ISTAT. No sources were found for farm-gate prices or estimates of differentials between farm and wholesale prices. Price variations from town to town in Italy were probably greater than for comparable regional price variations in the United Kingdom. Mark-ups for transport and distribution are unlikely to be high but the use of unadjusted market prices biases the comparison in favour of Italy. For both countries the quantities quoted in Table 15.1 are expressed net of the volume of gross output 'recycled' as inputs (*reimpieghi*) within agriculture as seed, animal feed, and fertilisers.[29]

Matching Italian and United Kingdom outputs commodity by commodity proved to be feasible in the majority of cases, and it was assumed that most crops under comparison (wheat, potatoes, peas, wool, and so on) were similar in quality. In so far as the quintals of a crop presented in the sources under a particular head contain farm produce of widely different qualities, then variations in average prices and output values simply reflect differences in the mix of crops listed under that given category. For 'other vegetables', 'fruit and nuts', 'meat', 'butter and cheese' and 'poultry and eggs', these 'composite categories' were broken down as far as possible into their constituent sub-components and the quantities of each crop and animal product priced by its own price in sterling and lire. But the sources do not provide the refined breakdowns required for higher accuracy and estimates of the variegated and high-value Italian output presented under these labels are likely to represent lower-bound figures.

Six Italian crops were encountered not cultivated in the United Kingdom: maize, rice, tobacco, silk cocoons, wines and olive oil. Various procedures have been adopted by other investigators to estimate the 'other country's' prices for such 'unique commodities'.[30] The solution preferred here was to begin with United Kingdom imports of these commodities from Italy expressed in (c.i.f.) unit values.[31] The values were then adjusted to exclude the costs of shipping commodities from Italian to British ports and further reduced by 20 per cent to allow for charges for moving goods from Italian farms to Italian ports.[32]

29 Ojala, *Agriculture*, pp. 190–298; Bellerby, 'Distribution of farm income'; Zamagni, 'Le radici agricole', p. 8.
30 Kravis, Kenessy, Heston and Summers, *International Comparison*.
31 *BPP, Accounts and papers*, London, 1909–14.
32 L. Isserlis, 'Tramp shipping cargoes and freight', *Journal of the Royal Statistics Society*, CI, 1938, pp. 73–86.

Table 15.1 *Agricultural outputs of United Kingdom and Italy, c.1909–14 valued in sterling and lire*

	Quantity (quintals)		Prices (per quintal)		Value of production (thousands of pounds)		(millions of lire)	
	UK	Italy	£	Lire	UK	Italy	UK	Italy
Cereals								
Wheat	12,547	46,809	0.693	29.2	8.695	32.439	366	1,367
Barley	13,772	312	0.639	20.9	8.800	0.199	288	7
Oats	8,163	1,023	0.615	21.4	5.020	0.629	175	22
Rye	43	675	0.482	21.7	0.021	0.325	1	15
Maize	0	13,100	0.426	19.4	0.000	5.581	0	254
Rice	0	5,300	0.720	25.5	0.000	3.816	0	135
Vegetables								
Potatoes	46,032	19,068	0.189	12.3	8.700	3.604	566	235
Beans, peas	2061	7,756	0.689	27.1	1.420	5.344	56	210
Other veg.	12,155	30,374	0.348	12.0	4.230	10.570	146	364
Raw materials								
Flax, hemp	75	886	4.920	100.0	0.369	4.359	8	89
Beetroot	0	16,721	0.106	2.7	0.000	1.772	0	45
Wool	1,092	155	3.214	188.0	3.510	0.498	205	29
Tobacco	0	70	0.233	96.0	0.000	0.016	0	7
Hops	187	0	9.679	0.0	1.810	0.000	46	0
Fodder	36,610	12,300	0.770	8.5	28.190	9.471	311	105
Equine					2.400	0.817	60	20
Silk cocoons	0	463	11.400	285.0	0.000	5.278	0	132
Fruit & nuts	18,270	37,090	0.277	19.4	5.061	10.274	354	720
Wine (hl.)	0	50,515	1.260	39.3	0.000	63.649	0	1985
Olive oil (hl.)	0	1,659	2.780	90.0	0.000	4.612	0	149
Meat and dairy products								
Meat	14,804	5,670	5.840	199.1	86.455	33.113	2,947	1,129
Milk (hl.)	52,550	12,260	0.730	20.0	38.362	8.950	1,051	245
Butter, cheese	1,170	2,260	6.580	218.0	7.699	14.871	255	493
Poultry, eggs	1,680	2,890	6.930	185.8	11.642	20.028	312	537
Total					222.384	240.215	7,147	8,294

Notes
All quantities are net of products 'recycled' as agricultural inputs. Aggregate prices are weighted averages of individual components. Wholesale prices in lire for Italy; farm-gate prices in pounds for the UK.

Source
General sources are described in the text. A detailed description of sources and methods are contained in an unpublished appendix, available on request.

These steps provide a proxy for a farm-gate price in Italy for commodities delivered by Italian farmers to United Kingdom consumers. In most cases, and particularly for wines, they in fact sold only the very best qualities to Britain. Thus, United Kingdom prices of, for instance, wine and olive oil exported had to be adjusted downwards to approximate to sterling prices for modal qualities produced and consumed within Italy. The procedure followed was, either, to estimate price ratios of modal to high quality farm produce within Italy (by using Italian prices for diverse qualities) and apply these ratios to the sterling prices of Italian exports as calculated above, or, alternatively, to search for equivalent United Kingdom import prices, adjusted and converted at current rates of exchange. For sound theoretical reasons, utilising the commercial rate of exchange was avoided, but such compromises are less objectionable when modal qualities of the commodity in question (e.g. silk cocoons) were exported from Italy to the United Kingdom.

In textbook theory the British prices used here to represent sterling values for wine, silk cocoons, olive oil, maize, tobacco and rice represent proxies for the marginal utilities to British consumers of these uniquely Italian products. They are not, however, equal to the marginal costs of producing British substitutes for such goods. But given the quantities involved, the choice of any 'plausible' set of prices for unique commodities other than wine would be of no statistical significance for the purpose of this particular exercise, which is to estimate partial productivity indicators for Italian and United Kingdom agriculture.

For wine – a large component of Italian agricultural output – any British price adopted definitely affects the valuation of Italian agricultural output in pounds sterling. For example, it would make a huge difference to the value of Italian farm output priced in sterling if the price selected represented the cost of producing substitute wines in Britain and Ireland in 1910. It is, however, important to realise that there can be no single theoretically correct answer to the question: what is the value of wine consumed in Italy in British prices? First, there is no *ex ante* way of measuring utility which is inferred from expenditures. Why purchases occurred or did not occur historically is a complex matter to explain which would take this argument off towards the study of cultural anthropology, distribution networks, advertising, and traditions. The preferred approach was to find a price that British consumers might have been prepared to pay for modal Italian wine if they had been a nation of wine drinkers, which clearly they were not.

Information is available on the price differentials within Italy between
standard and quality wines and the price that some segments of the
British population were prepared to pay for quality imported Italian
wines. It was assumed that this particular sub-group were likely to have
had similar perceptions of quality differences to Italian consumers.
Thus, the price that English people might have been prepared to pay
for standard Italian wine was estimated by applying the differential in
price between modal and quality wine on the Italian market to the
prices of Italian wines sold on British markets adjusted for mark-ups for
transport and distribution costs.

   Alternative and equally plausible solutions to the problem were
also tried. They included comparisons of the price British consumers
might have been prepared to pay for beverages with comparable
alcoholic content. The alcoholic content of a modal litre of English
beer and the alcoholic content of a litre of standard Italian wine are
known. That differential was applied to the price of beer in order to
proxy a hypothetical evaluation by British consumers of Italian wine.
Another approach was to price wine in terms of the differential between
beer and wine prices in countries (such as Germany and Austria) where
both beverages were in mass consumption. Both methods generated
higher sterling values than the preferred solution, which then emerged
as a lower-bound numerical solution to the problem of how to price
unique and significant Italian products such as wine in sterling.

   Table 15.1 presents a breakdown of the aggregated values produced by Italian and United Kingdom farmers weighted by the prices
that their crops, raw materials, meat, dairy produce, fruit, and vegetables commanded on their respective home markets or might have
commanded on the domestic market of the other country. Italian
output in sterling thus measures the total value of agricultural output
produced in Italy and hypothetically sold to British consumers, and
vice versa.

III Inputs of labour

In order to estimate equivalents for hours of labour-time employed in
producing United Kingdom and Italian agricultural outputs, information was required on:

(a)   numbers of males, females, and children enumerated in censuses
      as available for work in agriculture;
(b)   numbers of days per year and hours per day worked by fully-
      employed agricultural workers;

(c)   the degree to which the days and hours worked by different categories of people classified as agricultural workers fell below full employment levels;

(d)   differences in output per hour of labour input between prime male adult workers on the one hand and females, children, and elderly males on the other.[33]

Italian workers were not employed on Sundays (except at harvest times), on holidays of obligation, or, obviously, on days lost through inclement weather and ill health. Italian farm workers were potentially available for employment for up to 265 days a year. Although farm workers in the United Kingdom enjoyed less time off for religious festivals they almost certainly lost more days through bad weather. Hours worked per day varied in both economies from 14 or 15 at harvest to around five in mid-winter. No reliable figures have been published on the average length of the working day for British or Italian agricultural workers, but their hours can be expected to be comparable.[34]

Converting available workforces into labour inputs can only be a matter of guesswork. The hypothesis that in both economies a fully-employed agricultural worker could have been engaged for 265 days a year for comparable hours each day provides a beginning. Although a majority of male adult workers in the United Kingdom probably remained fully employed throughout the year, that assumption cannot be applied either to female and child labour engaged on farms in the United Kingdom or to the Italian workforce as a whole. Before 1914 the massive and endemic under-employment which afflicted most men, women, and children employed in Italian agriculture varied region by region and was probably related to the terms upon which families obtained access to land. Involuntary unemployment was certainly more severe among landless labourers (*braccianti*) and their dependents than among farmers and their families who owned or hired land, regardless of the form of tenure.[35] In an attempt to formulate plausible estimates for the numbers of days worked per year by males, females, and children employed as family or as wage labour, official and private investigations

33 J. T. Dunlop and V. T. Diatchenko, *Labour productivity*, New York, 1964; E. Dennison, *Why growth rates differ?*, Washington, 1967.

34 R. C. O. Matthews, C. H. Feinstein and J. Odling-Smee, *British economic growth 1856–1973*, Oxford, 1982, pp. 563–6; A. Maddison, *Economic growth in the west*, New York, 1964; *idem*, *Phases of capitalist development*, Oxford, 1982.

35 A. Serpieri, *Il contratto agrario e le condizioni di vita dei contadini nell'alto milanese*, Milan, 1910; G. Medici and G. Orlando, *Agricoltura e disoccupazione. I braccianti nella bassa padana*, Rome, 1951; INEA, *Monografie di famiglie agricole*, Rome, 1933.

P

Table 15.2 *The labour force and labour inputs utilised in Italian agriculture in 1911*

Categories of farm labour	Labour force (000s) [a]	Estimated days of labour supplied per head for 1911	Productivity conversion coefficients	Labour input converted to fully-employed male-equivalents (000s)
Male Farmers aged 15 to 65	2,235	265	1.0	2,235
Landless male labourers (*braccianti*) aged 15–65	2,608	220	1.0	2,165
Males aged 10–15	675	120	0.5	153
Males over 65	607	120	0.6	165
Females aged 15–65	3,410	120	0.6	926
Females aged 10–15	341	120	0.5	77
Totals (upper-bound)	9,876			5,721

Note
[a] O. Vitali, *La popolazione attiva in agricoltura attraverso i censimenti italiani*, Rome, 1973, pp. 10–21.

Source See text.

into under-employment in Italian agriculture were surveyed. On this evidence the following assumptions were made which provide the basis for the estimates set out below:

(a)   male farmers aged 15–65 (including owner-occupiers, tenants and share-croppers) owned or rented sufficient land to keep themselves fully employed for 265 days a year;
(b)   *braccianti* (landless male labourers) worked 220 days a year;
(c)   females, children, and elderly males worked 120 days a year regardless of their status as family or landless labour.

The figures for days worked during the year presented in column two of Table 15.2 are definitely too high. More defensible estimates have been published for particular regions and categories of workers. For current purposes it was appropriate to select published figures which represented upper-bound figures of the days actually worked by farmers, labourers, and their families in agriculture for 1911 in order to bias the calculation against Italy.

Table 15.3 *The labour force and labour inputs utilised in United Kingdom agriculture in 1908*

Categories of farm labour	Labour force (000s)	Estimated days of labour supplied per head in 1908	Productivity conversion coefficients	Labour input converted to fully-employed male-equivalents (000s)
Male farmers and labourers aged 15+	2,080	265	1.0	2,080
Female family labour aged 15+	235	133	0.6	71
Female workers aged 15+	145	265	0.6	87
Male and female workers under 15	109	133	0.5	27
Total	2,569			2,265

Source
See text. Fuller details on data and assumptions are contained in an unpublished appendix, available on request.

Finally, in converting the days of labour time supplied by females, children and elderly men into 'male equivalents', conversion coefficients were utilised. Procedures of this kind rest upon the premise that females, children and elderly men were on average less skilled, were weaker in terms of physical capacities for hard work, and diverted more of their potential working time to leisure, to household tasks and to manufacturing activities inside and outside the home.

Estimates for the agricultural workforce and labour input for the United Kingdom in Table 15.3 above were constructed from data in the British and Irish agricultural censuses.[36] Working assumptions were:

(a) all males aged 15 and above (and non-family female workers), regardless of occupational status, were fully employed throughout a working year of 265 days;
(b) female family workers aged 15 and above worked half of the year producing farm output;

36 Department of Agricultural and Technical Instruction for Ireland, *The agricultural output*, pp. 17–19, 18, 25.

(c) workers classified by the agricultural censuses as 'person temporarily employed' worked half the working year on the production of farm output;

(d) young workers (under 15 years of age and regardless of their occupational status) worked half the working year on the production of farm output;

(e) the same productivity-conversion coefficients were employed as those applied to the Italian work force.

No doubt, other assumptions could be made to convert workforces classified as 'available for employment' in agriculture into labour inputs. There is certainly a wide gap between the Italian agricultural workforce – listed in the population census to include nearly 10 million men, women and children – and the labour input, estimated as 5.7 million man-years, 'required' to produce total farm output for 1911. The difference reflects the extent of under-employment in the Italian countryside which was described in numerous secondary sources as well as in major official reports on conditions of employment among the rural population for 1911, 1933 and the early 1950s.[37]

That particular gap was far narrower in the United Kingdom, where male and female adults are presumed to have been fully employed. The United Kingdom economy offered many more jobs outside farming, and by 1911 agricultural workers formed less than a tenth of the total workforce, compared with over half in the Italian case.

IV Land

To define and to measure the input of land utilised for agricultural production is far from simple, largely because of the uncertainties which surround the areas of rough and mountain pasture used to support farm animals (as well as the considerable variations in the quality of the soil used for both arable and animal husbandry). In Table 15.4 the total amount of land utilised for agricultural purposes is classified under comparable categories. Ideally, all land inputs should be transformed into equivalent units of arable land. Unfortunately, the existing data do not allow a procedure to be followed which is similar to that used above to estimate labour inputs. Simple and arbitrary

37 *Inchiesta Parlamentare*, 1909; Serpieri, *Capitalismo*; INEA, *Monografie*; *Inchiesta Parlamentare*, 1953–4; G. Toniolo and F. Piva, 'Unemployment in the 1930s: the case of Italy', pp. 221–45 in B. Eichengreen and T. Hatton, eds., *Interwar employment in international perspective*, London, 1988.

Table 15.4 *Hectares of land utilised for agricultural production in the United Kingdom and Italy, c.1907–09*

	Italy (000s)	GB (000s)	Ireland (000s)	UK (cols. 2+3) (000s)
1. Arable land	13,233	5,988	1,895	7,883
2. Permanent pasture	6,080	7,048	4,091	11,139
3. Tree crops (vines, fruit trees, olive trees, etc.)	1,486			
4. Total land inputs (1+2+3)	20,799	13,036	5,986	19,022
5. Rough grazing		5,181		5,181
6. Mountain grazing			999	999
7. *Incolto produttivo* (marginal land)	1,035			
8. Woodlands	4,564	1,126	122	1,248
Total agricultural land (4+5+6+7+8)	26,398	19,343	7,107	26,450

Source See text.

solutions are usually adopted by economists. For example, E. Dennison converts permanent pasture into arable land at a ratio of three to one and omits rough grazing from his productivity estimates.[38] J. Hayami and V. Ruttan utilise an 'unweighted aggregation of arable and pasture'.[39] Both these methods tend to underestimate land inputs used by the agricultural sector of the United Kingdom, because 'rough-grazing' land certainly supported considerable numbers of sheep and other livestock.[40] For purposes of calculating yields per hectare, total land inputs as given in Table 15.4 represent 'agricultural land'.

V Productivity: Italy compared with the United Kingdom

It is now possible to present estimates of agricultural product per unit of labour and per unit of land in the two countries. As Table 15.5

38 Dennison, *Why growth rates differ?*, pp. 183–4.
39 J. Hayami and V. Ruttan, *Agricultural development, an International Perspective*, Baltimore, 1975, pp. 312–13.
40 Ministry of Agriculture, *Agricultural statistics*, pp. 5–15.

Table 15.5 *Gross output per unit of labour and land in United Kingdom and Italian agriculture, 1909–14*

	Output per worker (fully employed male-equivalent units)		Output per hectare of cultivated land	
	At British prices (£)	At Italian prices (lire)	At British prices (£)	At Italian prices (lire)
United Kingdom	98	3,156	11.7	376
Italy	42	1,449	11.5	399
Ratio Italy/UK	42.8%	45.9%	98.2 %	106.1%

Source Tables 15.1–15.4.

shows, a fully-employed British agricultural worker produced more than twice as much as his Italian counterpart, and this gap turns out to be slightly wider when measured in English prices. A unit of land yielded in the United Kingdom a mix of agricultural produce roughly comparable in value to that yielded by a unit of Italian land. Since labour inputs for Italy are overestimated, the ratios represent upper-bound estimates of the gap in product per man that existed between Italy and the United Kingdom on the eve of World War I.

By excluding rough grazing, land inputs will underestimate the land actually used to produce animal and raw-material outputs in the United Kingdom and will therefore bias the comparison of gross output per hectare against Italy.

In order to estimate value added (net output) per worker and per hectare, the value of inputs purchased outside the agricultural sector should be subtracted from the gross-output values set out in Table 15.1. Unfortunately, no estimates exist for the quantities and prices of such inputs commodity by commodity. Plausible but macro guesstimates must rely entirely upon the work of Ojala and Zamagni who put the aggregate value of industrial inputs at 37 per cent and 11 per cent of the value of gross agricultural output in the two economies respectively.[41] Accepting their percentages, estimates of value added per worker and per unit of land can then be compared in the two countries (Table 15.6).

The numerical results in Table 15.5 are sensitive to the methods

41 Ojala, *Agriculture*; Zamagni, 'Le radici agricole'.

Table 15.6 *Value added per unit input of labour and land into United Kingdom and Italian agriculture, 1904–14*

	Net output per worker (fully employed male-equivalent units)		Net output per hectare of cultivated land	
	At British prices (£)	At Italian prices (lire)	At British prices (£)	At Italian prices (lire)
United Kingdom	62	1,988	7.4	237
Italy	37	1,290	10.2	355
Ratio Italy/UK	59.7%	64.9%	137.8%	149.8%

Source Tables 15.1–15.5.

employed to convert people 'available for work in the countryside' into fully-employed male equivalents. If gross outputs are divided instead by agricultural workforces, as listed in censuses of population, output per worker in Italian agriculture declines to about one-third of British levels. This ratio does not approximate to a productivity but rather to a welfare differential between farmers and their dependents in the two societies. It is this index that captures the poverty of the Italian rural population which so struck travellers from England in the late nineteenth century. But they mistakenly equated rural poverty with backward agriculture. That is why it is important to emphasise the current price estimates of gross and net output per hectare of cultivated land. These yield ratios capture the radically different soil conditions, terrain, hydrology, and climate found within the borders of the Peninsula compared to the United Kingdom. They also encapsulate differences in the mix of crops produced, techniques of cultivation, variable farm sizes, contrasting tenurial institutions, government policies, and agrarian social-overhead capital.

Partial productivity indicators are perhaps even more difficult to interpret than they are to measure. But comparisons between Italy and the most advanced agricultural sector in Europe are consistent with the presumption that Italian farmers made an efficient use of the resources available to them. At the very least, these numbers shift the *onus of proof* on to those who maintain that an unhealthy, illiterate peasantry, deficient tenurial institutions, and defective policies seriously constrained Italian agriculture from operating close to its production-possibility frontier.

Agrarian historians are aware of the varieties of agriculture and farming regions encompassed within the Peninsula and to some degree within the United Kingdom. There are few countries in Europe where soil, irrigation and climate vary as they do in Italy. From the Alps to Sicily, the traveller finds the well-irrigated and developed Po Valley, the rough Appennines, the vines and olives of Tuscany and Umbria, the intensive vegetable farming of Latium and Campania, the poor pastures of Abruzzo, the rich Tavoliere, and the wheat and citrus groves of Sicily.

Not long before the period under discussion, the whole of southern Italy (Mezzogiorno) was a large independent kingdom with its own traditions, culture and legal system. A large body of Italian historiography perceives the Mezzogiorno as a major drag on the overall development of Italy. Lombardy, on the other hand, has long been praised for an agriculture held to be the equal of the most advanced farming systems found in England, Holland and northern France. It is therefore illuminating to compare gross agricultural output per unit of labour input across three regions of Italy against the standard set for labour productivity found in the agriculture of the United Kingdom.

First, a word about data. According to the 1911 census figures (revised by O. Vitali), one-third of the Italian labour force resided in provinces previously territory of the Kingdom of Naples and in Sardinia (hereafter the 'South'), a region where 61 per cent of the labour force was employed in agriculture. For Italy as a whole, the ratio of the labour force in agriculture to the total labour force was about 57 per cent, and for Lombardy alone, 41 per cent. Following procedures adopted above, it can be estimated that 2.189 million fully-employed male-equivalent units approximated to the labour input into southern agriculture. The methods used to derive gross output for the South are less accurate than those for the Peninsula as a whole. Total gross output of the South can be estimated at £77.7 million or at Lire 2,932 million. No attempt was made to provide value-added estimates because no reliable figures for inputs purchased from outside agriculture exist on a regional basis. Assuming that such inputs would be higher in the north than in the South, the 'gap' between the two areas measured in value-added rather than in gross-output terms would then be narrower than the estimates suggested in Table 15.7.

Table 15.7 suggests that on this index the backwardness of Italian agriculture cannot be attributed, except in an entirely marginal sense, to the weight of a 'retarded' South. The productivity of labour – and presumably of land – seems to have been roughly on a par with the rest of Italy, despite the supposed deficiencies of its *latifundia*.

Table 15.7 *Output per unit of labour in three main Italian regions, c.1911*

	Output per man (lire)	Index (UK = 100)
Lombardy	1,593.7	51.4
North and Central Italy	1,518.6	49.0
South	1,341.4	43.3

Source See text.

VI The backwardness of Italian agriculture in a comparative perspective

Between the French Revolution and the last decades of the nineteenth century, output per worker and the contingent standard of living among Italy's rural population deteriorated (perhaps markedly) compared with the United Kingdom where the labour force available for work in agriculture remained roughly constant while output went up by a multiple of around 2.4. Unfortunately, the data do not allow for the measurement of output or productivity change in Italy until the boom of 1897–1913, when labour productivity seems to have increased at the remarkable rate of 2 to 3 per cent per annum.[42] Before that upswing (which also witnessed the massive migration of landless labourers to the Americas) it is likely that the agricultural production barely kept pace with a rural population and workforce growing at around 0.7 per cent per annum.

Thus, over the very long run British agriculture had released (or expelled) redundant labour from work on the land, while Italian agriculture absorbed more labour than it could employ. The differentials in rural incomes and consumption standards widened. To English travellers who visited Italy at the end of the nineteenth century, not only did the peasantry suffer from a poverty more widespread and dire than anything observed in the United Kingdom, but these observers suggested that the country's tenurial institutions, its illiterate and unskilled farmers, indifferent landowners, and misplaced governmental policies could be held responsible for conditions in the countryside. The poverty and relative deprivation they observed becomes evident on the basis of an index constructed by dividing agricultural incomes by the agricultural population as listed in the Population Census for

42 G. Fuà, ed., *Lo sviluppo economico in Italia*, III, Milan, 1968; Toniolo, *An economic history*.

1911: the level of rural income per capita was £24 a year in Italy compared with £85 in the United Kingdom. But this gap does not mean that Italian agriculture can be indicted for widespread failures to adapt best-practice techniques of cultivation or for a serious misallocation of resources. Historians have blamed successive governments for not undertaking reforms to property rights and institutions required to expel far more redundant labour from the countryside. Tampering with property rights was not, however, on the political agenda of most parts of western Europe for more than a century after the French Revolution had run its course. More realistic critiques focused upon the lack of courage displayed by successive Italian governments from 1878 to 1914 in not resisting demands for protection against imports of American grain. But it is unlikely that a more open trading regime in agriculture would have prompted more rapid emigration from the countryside to the towns and the Americas.

Apart from the imposition of tariffs, Italian statesmen preferred to leave rural populations to do the best they could with the supplies of land, capital and skills at their disposal. These endowments seem meagre by British and French standards. For example, by 1911 the land to labour ratio in Italy amounted to 2.1 cultivable hectares per agricultural worker, compared with 5.4 hectares in France and nearly 9 hectares in the United Kingdom.[43] British farmers also utilised far greater quantities of machinery, energy, chemicals, and other industrial inputs purchased from outside agriculture (see Section V).

Despite the small supplies of land and capital at their disposal, Italian farmers emerge from these exercises in productivity measurement with a creditable record. When placed on a scale which allows for limited but nevertheless revealing comparisons with farmers in the most advanced economy in Europe, they appear to have performed well enough to undermine suggestions that widespread failures of an institutional, market, policy, or entrepreneurial kind had depressed Italian agricultural output well below some optimal and attainable level. Just before the Great War, value added per unit of labour input stood at 60 per cent of the standard achieved by farmers in the United Kingdom. And even in that poorly-endowed and much maligned agrarian economy of the Mezzogiorno, labour productivity was not far below the average for Italy as a whole.

Operating with an abundance of labour, Italian farmers had obviously intensified their efforts to maximise yields from the land

43 O'Brien and Keyder, *Economic growth*, p. 105.

they cultivated. Their 'success' is gauged in Tables 15.5 and 15.6 which show gross output per hectare cropped (measured in pounds or lire) to be around United Kingdom levels. In terms of net value added per hectare, they performed better than their more educated, capitalised, and industrialised counterparts in Britain and Ireland. While releasing labour, United Kingdom farmers still obtained relatively high yields per hectare by utilising greater quantities of machinery, energy, and chemicals, while Italians relied above all on highly-priced crops cultivated with ample supplies of cheap labour to raise the aggregate value of agricultural output. That strategy maintained people on the land (at tolerable levels of subsistence), minimised outlays on intermediate goods, economised on capital, and depressed output per worker.

In Mediterranean agriculture, intensifying labour inputs could not raise the physical yields per hectare for major field crops such as grains, potatoes and pulses to the standards set by England, Holland and northern France. The environmental constraints (soils, precipitation, elevations) were simply too strong to be overcome by human toil. Unfortunately, that bundle of knowledge and techniques which successfully raised yields for grain and fodder crops in north-western Europe could not be diffused over large areas of the Italian peninsula. New fodder and root crops inserted into rotations in England, northern France and the Low Countries supported higher animal populations and generated increased supplies of organic manure and draught power. These new crops required a certain minimal amount of rainfall during their short growing season and particularly over the summer months when they lose moisture through transpiration. And during the Italian wet season the hours of sunshine were usually too few for the new crops to survive. Furthermore, the higher-yielding varieties of wheat seeds which had proved successful in north-western Europe could not survive Mediterranean drought. To retain moisture in summer and arrest soil erosion during the months of heavy rainfall in winter, Italian farmers planted three crops (olives, vines and fruit) around and across their fields – a response to nature which, together with a hilly terrain, made deeper ploughing difficult – except on the irrigated plains of the Po Valley.[44]

This 'inter-cropping' not only made ecological sense, it provided Italian farmers with a mix of high-value produce to compensate for their lower grain yields and small populations of farm animals. Through

44 F. Galassi, 'Stasi e sviluppo dell'agricoltura toscana 1870–1914', *Rivista di Storia Economica*, new series, III, 1986, pp. 304–37.

a process of trial and error they had (like managers of the land in
Britain and Ireland) adapted cropping patterns and techniques of
cultivation to local variations in soil climate and terrain in order to
optimise yields. The Peninsula contained land and environmental
conditions naturally suited to the cultivation of such high-value and
labour-intensive crops as vines, tobacco, flax, silk cocoons, olives,
vegetables and fruit. Through their long involvement in networks of
trade with towns and with international commerce, Italian farmers
were responsive to demand. Indeed, by the late nineteenth century
something like 70 per cent of agricultural output was traded on markets,
and foodstuffs and agricultural raw materials dominated the nation's
exports.[45]

Given the relatively high levels of gross- and net-value-added
achieved per hectare of land cultivated in Italy, and recognising the
real constraints imposed by soil, climate and terrain on the diffusion
of north European agronomic techniques, there are grounds for
believing that the value of Italian agricultural output may not have
fallen far short of the optimal obtainable.

What, then, can be concluded about the undeniable poverty
experienced by Italian peasants before the Great War? The answer to
this question should be sought primarily in the demographic history
of the Peninsula over the previous three centuries. By 1911 the total
labour force available for work in agriculture amounted to nearly 10
million men, women and children, working on average well below full
employment levels (see Table 15.2). Despite the mass emigration
witnessed over the previous three decades, and the accelerated growth
of production experienced after 1896, the classical problem of excess
population in the countryside remained visible and serious right down
to the war.

Italian agriculture had adapted to this situation by concentrating
upon a mix of crops that maximised the utilisation of labour. From an
area of land comparable to that cultivated in Britain and Ireland, Italian
farmers wrested an agricultural net output that was in value terms
about 40 per cent higher than the agricultural product of the United
Kingdom. But that income had to be shared through institutional
arrangements, such as the extended family, among an agricultural
population three to four times larger than the population sustained on
the land of their more fortunate European neighbours to the north in
the United Kingdom.

45 Federico, 'Mercantilizzazione'.

   Some historians continue to blame Italian agriculture for the retardation of the economy and the slow pace of structural change. In the light of this exercise in comparative economic history an alternative hypothesis appears more plausible, namely that the agriculture was caught in what M. Elvin refers to as a 'high level equilibrium trap'.[46] The poverty of the rural population before 1914 may be more realistically attributed to the fact that Italy's industrial and urban economy (and the international economy as a whole) had not developed rapidly enough to pull under-employed labour from the countryside of Mediterranean Europe.

46 M. Elvin, *The pattern of the Chinese past*, London, 1973.

Agricultural output and productivity in post-Famine Ireland

Agricultural historians of post-Famine Ireland are blessed with an array of annual agricultural statistics which in their diversity leave their British counterparts envious. The English and Welsh June Returns, which began in 1866, are a rich source of evidence and are widely used, but the Irish Returns preceded them by a clear twenty years.[1] For an investigation of output the latter provide, in gross terms, acreages under crops, average crop yields, and animal numbers, which distinguish within animal groups those of different ages, and other 'vital' statistics. This information is available annually from 1847 to the moment of Irish Partition in the early 1920s, at which point Northern Ireland and the Irish Free State made separate arrangements.[2] Furthermore, the data are available at the level of the county, of which there are 32; at the level of Poor Law Unions, of which there were roughly 160; and, up to the 1870s, at the Barony level, of which there were over 300. In addition, and separately collected, price material is available. It is mostly

My thanks to the Nuffield Foundation for the award of a Research Fellowship during the year 1985–86 when most of the data for this chapter were collected. My thanks to Bob Dodgshon for his discussant's comments at the Bellagio conference. My thanks also to Peter Solar who read an earlier and much expanded version of this paper and made valuable suggestions with regard to language and estimating procedures. I am further grateful to him for allowing me to see a substantial extract from his thesis. Finally, my thanks to Cormac Ó Gráda for constant encouragement.

1 For England and Wales see, for example, J. T. Coppock, *An agricultural atlas of England and Wales*, London, 1964; E. M. Ojala, *Agriculture and economic progress*, London, 1952, pp. 191–217; T. W. Fletcher, 'The Great Depression of English agriculture, 1873–96', *EcHR*, XIII, 1961, pp. 417–32. The Irish Agricultural Returns are reported annually in *BPP*.

2 Returns for 1848 are incomplete because of political disturbances. An excellent summary of Irish statistics – giving, amongst other things, crop acreages, yields, and livestock numbers – can be found in Saorstat Eireann, *Agricultural statistics 1847–1926: reports and tables*, Dublin, 1930. There is no equivalent for the Northern Ireland counties of Ulster, though see J. P. Huttman, 'Institutional factors in the development of Irish agriculture, 1850–1915', unpublished University of London Ph.D. thesis, 1970, for distributions of farm sizes, crop acreages, animal numbers, and so on, at the national and provincial level.

based on Dublin prices, but it can and has been used as a long-run national price series for use with crop and animal data to calculate the value of Irish agricultural output.[3]

In historic times it is precisely the absence of measures of output which has encouraged historians to look for direct, and, more often, indirect, measures of productivity, which are often expressed as yield per acre. By contrast, the nineteenth-century Irish data allow the direct estimation of output. This chapter will therefore begin with the essential data for productivity studies – production and output – and then proceed to assess labour productivity over time for Ireland which will be compared with trends for Great Britain. Finally, the output estimates are used to review some aspects of both land and total factor productivity over time.

I Valuing net agricultural output

Given data on gross agricultural output and prices, it should be a short and simple step to obtain the value of output over time for what was the main source of Irish income in the nineteenth century. It might be a short step in terms of archival research, but as a number of commentators have discovered, it is not simple. The main problem lies in

---

3 See T. Barrington, 'Review of Irish agricultural prices', *Journal of the Statistical and Social Inquiry Society of Ireland*, XV, 1927, pp. 249–80; R. M. Barrington, 'The prices of some agricultural produce and the cost of farm labour for the last fifty years', *Journal of the Statistical and Social Inquiry Society of Ireland*, IX, 1887, pp. 137–53. These prices are in turn based on the Cowper Commission, *Report of the Royal Commission on Land Law (Ireland) Act 1885*, BPP, XXVI, C.4969, London, 1887, for prices up to 1881. For official prices thereafter see, for example, *Agricultural statistics, Ireland, 1907–8, return of prices of crops, livestock and other Irish agricultural products*, BPP, CXXI, Cd.4437, London, 1908, pp. 24–5, for the period 1888–1907; and *Agricultural statistics, Ireland, 1915, return of prices of crops, livestock and other Irish agricultural products*, BPP, XXXVI, Cd.8452, London, 1917, pp. 14–15, for the overlapping period 1896–1915. On the use of the price data with the annual agricultural data see Huttman, 'Institutional factors', pp. 469–505; C. Ó Gráda, 'Post-Famine adjustment, essays in nineteenth-century Irish economic history', unpublished University of Columbia Ph.D. thesis, 1973, pp. 128–43; *idem*, 'Irish agricultural output before and after the Famine', *Journal of European Economic History*, XIII, 1984, pp. 149–65; B. Solow, *The land question and the Irish economy, 1870–1903*, Cambridge, Mass., 1971, pp. 170–3 and 213–17; W. E. Vaughan, 'Agricultural output, rents and wages in Ireland, 1850–1880', pp. 85–97 in L. M. Cullen and F. Furet, eds., *Ireland and France 17th–20th centuries*, Paris, 1980; C. Ó Gráda, *Ireland before and after the Famine: explorations in economic history, 1800–1925*, Manchester, 1988, pp. 128–31 and 149–50; M. E. Turner, 'Towards an agricultural prices index for Ireland 1850–1914', *The Economic and Social Review*, XVIII, 1987, pp. 123–36.

the definition of crop, livestock, and livestock product output; that is, the net value added output as distinct from the gross product. For example, a proportion of seed from the previous year's harvest would be retained for the current year's crop, so in one sense, part of each year's crop does not realise its value until a succeeding year. In this initial equation, acreage and yield per acre are known, but not the seeding ratio. After seed retained for future use was deducted there were other calls on the output of the major crops before the producers were left with the final net output which was marketed at the prices for which data are available. Much of the gross output was retained on the farm for subsequent consumption by animals and people. That consumed by people should really be included as net output because it would otherwise have been purchased at the market, but that proportion consumed by animals realised its value when the animals were milked, slaughtered, sold for fattening overseas, or disposed of in other ways. For crops alone, therefore, what was the marketed produce? The answer is that the non-marketed proportion varied both over time and across different crops. Within the animal sector there are similar problems of estimating the marketed proportion of output. Some animals and their products were consumed on the farm and should rightly form part of total net output. Conversely, some products were recycled on the farm and should not be counted towards net output. For example, a certain amount of milk production was retained for rearing calves and some was fed to pigs, and a certain proportion of animals enumerated at the annual census never realised their value or their full value because of premature mortality.

In recent years a number of historians have tackled this problem of value-added Irish agricultural output. They have used a variety of net output estimating procedures, involving different weights and parameters, producing inconsistencies in the output estimates thereby obtained.[4] Appendix 16.1 gives some idea of these differences and suggests the fragility of what economic historians and economists are trying to do. It has been constructed from a number of sources and includes the estimates given in this chapter. For comparison, results have been extracted to conform with the years that other estimators have used, together with the five-year averages which surround those years. While at times there is comparability among the estimates of different historians, there are also wide divergencies, implying significant

4 Vaughan, 'Agricultural output'; Solow, *The land question*; Ó Gráda, 'Irish agricultural output'; *idem, Ireland before and after the Famine*; Turner, 'Agricultural prices index'.

underlying differences in the weighting of individual crop and livestock components.

In any study of temporal trends the representativeness of the years taken as starting and terminal dates also exercises some influence upon the results obtained. The present study appears to be the first to attempt an uninterrupted long-run series for the period 1850–1914, with the merit that this allows short-run fluctuations to be seen in perspective. For example, in the mid 1850s there was a sharp upturn in the value of output. This estimation of value is based on a simple equation, but, as W. E. Vaughan has demonstrated, it involves volatile elements: annual acreages and yields which both fluctuated; prices, which themselves were partly responsive to sown acres and yields, and other, external, factors. He estimated the value of tillage in 1851 at £7.3 million. It fell to £6.9 million in 1852, but then leapt to £11.3 million in 1853, £11.9 million in 1854, and £12.9 million in 1855, before falling to £8.7 million in 1856.[5] At face value this was the most volatile five or six years in the 30-year period 1851–83. What makes it doubly important is that both Vaughan and C. Ó Gráda use the year 1854 or the period 1852–54 in comparisons with other periods – the former as a base, the latter as a terminus. The result, in Vaughan's case, is an exaggerated base for his comparison with 1874, and, in Ó Gráda's, an exaggerated terminus for his comparison with pre-Famine Ireland.[6] On the other hand, there is now evidence to suggest that the early annual agricultural census returns were under-enumerated, in which case the doubts about using a year like 1854 are unfounded. Possibly 1854 may be sufficiently far from 1847 for the learning process attending data collection on such a scale to be complete, or as near complete as makes little difference.[7] Nevertheless, as Appendix 16.1 reveals, it is for

5 W. E. Vaughan's estimates as reported in T. W. Moody, *Davitt and Irish revolution 1846–82*, Oxford, 1981, p. 369. Vaughan excluded hay and potatoes and therefore his estimates are not wholly comparable with those of others. For this reason they have been omitted from Appendix 16.1, but they may still be used to illustrate this important point.

6 The consequences of supply problems for market prices during the Crimean War period were great. See S. H. Cousens, 'Emigration and demographic change in Ireland', *EcHR*, XIV, 1961, p. 277, who identifies the effect of the Crimean War on wheat prices. See also C. S. Orwin and E. H. Whetham, *History of British agriculture 1846–1914*, Newton Abbot, 1971, p. 96 for the effect of a reccurrence of potato blight on British supply prices in 1853 and 1854. In Ireland in these years potato prices approached those of the Famine years, for which see T. Barrington, 'A review of prices', p. 251.

7 C. Ó Gráda, 'Slices of Irish agricultural history: output and productivity pre-Famine and post-Famine', unpublished paper presented to a meeting of the Irish Agricultural Economics Society, May 1989.

the early 1850s that historians' estimates of the value of agricultural output exhibit the greatest divergencies.

Whilst estimating the value of certain tillage products poses problems, the equivalent exercise for livestock and their products is yet more complicated. It is more complicated because the net output parameters concerned entail more guesswork. For instance, how large was a pig, or rather how much bacon did it produce? How large was a sheep and how big was the wool clip per head? How many head of cattle of different ages were sold and for what purpose? If slaughtered they should be equated with beef prices (in which case, how big was the carcass?), but if sold on the hoof the relevant prices are those of live animals. Moreover, how much milk did a cow produce, how much was sent to market, and how much was fed to calves and how much to pigs? To compound the problem, all estimates of milk output must be translated into butter equivalents, because butter rather than milk prices are available. The greater complications and uncertainties surrounding estimates for this side of the industry are well exemplified by the range of estimates summarised in Appendix 16.1.

II Trends in net agricultural output

The examination of existing histories of Irish agricultural output shows that it is difficult to have precise rules about the net output parameters applied to the different components which make up net agricultural output, but that having chosen certain rules it is possible to estimate agricultural output. At the end of the exercise there seems to be a fair measure of agreement between other historians over the size of total agricultural output. As yet, however, no complete set of annual assessments is available either of total output or of the components which make up total output.[8] The time has come, therefore, to step back from existing estimates and produce a new series for the long-run period 1850–1914. In so doing it is necessary to be mindful of Vaughan's telling truism that the methods of calculation 'are based in the end, on more or less arbitrary estimates of the value of the commodities sold or consumed by Irish farmers'.[9]

---

8 But see Vaughan's partial breakdown of output for the period 1851–83 in Moody, *Davitt*, pp. 369–70. See also W. E. Vaughan, 'A study of landlord and tenant relations between the Famine and the Land War, 1850–78', unpublished National University of Ireland Ph.D. thesis, 1973, pp. 33–5 and 336–58; Huttman, 'Institutional factors', pp. 471–6 and 483–505.

9 Vaughan, 'Agricultural output', p. 95.

The method employed in making these annual estimates may seem no less arbitrary than those of previous estimators. On occasion variable parameters have been used.[10] These have been applied to the annual statistics of crops and livestock in association with the index of prices given by T. Barrington. The resultant annual estimates can be found in Appendix 16.2.[11] It is an easy task to convert Barrington's index back into proper prices by referring back to the original prices reported in Parliamentary Papers. The enumeration of milch cows as distinct from all cattle over two years of age was not made by the census enumerators until 1854, but over the period 1854–59 the proportion of milch cows to all cattle over two years of age was fairly constant, and it has been assumed that this proportion prevailed earlier in the decade.[12] In truth, however, these first years after the Famine were somewhat disrupted and it was not until the mid 1850s that the reliability of the annual statistics is affirmed.[13]

Unfortunately, due to data deficiencies, the current estimates are no freer from subjective decisions than those made by previous authorities. The degree of subjectivity increases for the estimates made for periods further back in time from the first official estimate of 1908. The latter formed one element in the calculations made towards the contemporary Census of Production in fulfilment of the Census of Production Act of 1906.[14] Subsequently, in 1952, a long-run attempt at estimating value added output was made by E. M. Ojala, but this began in the period 1867–69 and thereafter was only undertaken for groups of years of unequal duration up to 1935–39.[15] Unfortunately he treated his estimates on a United Kingdom basis, subsuming the whole of

10 A brief explanation of the weights which have been employed can be found in Turner, 'Agricultural prices index', pp. 133–4. Since they were published, the weights for oats and pigs have been revised. Notwithstanding that the weights of individual components will have varied over time, change from one parameter to another has for simplicity been assumed to be constant.
11 T. Barrington, 'A review of prices', pp. 251–3.
12 In those years it varied from a low of 66.7 per cent in 1857 to a high of 68.4 per cent in 1854, giving a mean over six years of 67.5 per cent.
13 See Ó Gráda, 'Irish agricultural output', p. 154.
14 Department of Agriculture and Technical Instruction for Ireland, *The agricultural output of Ireland 1908 (in connection with the Census of Production Act, 1906)*, Dublin, 1912.
15 Ojala's methodology is set out in an appendix in *idem, Agriculture*, pp. 191–217. His groupings of years from 1867–1913 are based on those defined by C. Clark, *National income and outlay*, London, 1937, p. 246. These groups begin three years after the peak of each main trade cycle. Ojala's estimates are partially dependent on extrapolation backwards from the early 1880s to 1867 due to the lack of yield and price data early on, a problem which is not present for Ireland.

Ireland under that head before 1922, and subsequently Northern Ireland. In addition he did not provide an adequate specification of his estimating procedures, which cannot now be replicated. Nevertheless, at present this provides the sole opportunity for a comparison between Ireland and the United Kingdom, although likely discrepancies in estimating procedures render this an exercise of doubtful reliability.[16]

Appendix 16.2 represents the outcome of applying the chosen net output parameter weights to the annual agricultural statistics of Ireland for the period 1850–1914. In broad terms the contribution of tillage fell from £21 million in 1850 to £7–8 million by 1900, before recovering slightly to £10 million by the start of the Great War (see Figure 16.1). Against this long-term trend, the value of tillage output rose to £33–4 million in both 1854 and 1855. This period, above all others, appears as the most dramatic of the short-term fluctuations and, notwithstanding distortions arising from under-estimation in the early years of the annual census, probably reflects a genuine supply response to the price rise induced by the Crimean War. In other respects 1854 is a natural year to begin a study such as this since it was the first year when milch cows were distinguished from other cattle over two years of age. Two years later, in 1856, the enumeration was standardised as a June return.

As Figure 16.1 illustrates, the comparable trend in livestock and livestock product output rose from £10 million in 1850 to an initial peak of £31–3 million in the mid 1870s, fell back to £24 million in the mid 1880s before recovering to a plateau of £27–8 million in the mid 1890s, and finally rose to a new peak of £39–41 million by the outbreak of the Great War.[17] The rise through the 1850s was steep but,

---

16 See also the attempt at calculating agricultural output in L. Drescher, 'The development of agricultural production in Great Britain and Ireland from the early nineteenth century', *The Manchester School*, XXIII, 1955, pp. 153–75, with a 'Comment' by T. W. Fletcher, pp. 176–83. See also Fletcher, 'The Great Depression', p. 432, for a critique of both Drescher and Ojala. Correspondence with Ojala reveals that any notes on the procedures he followed in making his estimates have been lost. See also J. R. Bellerby, 'The distribution of farm income in the United Kingdom 1867–1938', *Journal of Proceedings of the Agricultural Economic Society*, X, 1953, reprinted as pp. 259–80 in W. E. Minchinton, ed., *Essays in agrarian history*, II, Newton Abbot, 1968, pp. 264 and 276–7.

17 According to the method of estimation there was 'zero output' of cattle less than two years of age up to 1854. The explanation may lie partly in under-enumeration, but this was also a period when stocks were replenished in the wake of the Famine and this would have depressed sales. This is not to say that no cattle were sold, but rather that the method of calculation reveals 'negative' sales.

unlike tillage output, formed part of a long-term trend rather than a short-term aberration. It originated as a post-Famine production shift out of tillage and into pastoral activities: an adjustment which came early and persisted until at least the Great War.[18] In 1902 the body which administered the annual agricultural census – the Department of Agriculture and Technical Instruction for Ireland – attributed this trend to a labour supply constraint arising directly from the Famine and subsequently from the high rate of emigration.[19] During the agricultural depression of 1859–64, as throughout much of the period 1850–1914, the value of livestock production proved significantly more buoyant than that of tillage.[20]

Aggregating arable and pastoral production reveals that value-added total agricultural output stood at £31–2 million in 1850. This rose to a temporary peak of £52 million in the mid 1850s – induced largely by a combination of earlier under-enumeration and exceptional tillage values during the period of the Crimean War – before stabilising at around £35–45 million for the next ten years. By the mid 1870s output had recovered to £45–9 millions but it thereafter fell progressively to a low of about £33 million in the mid 1880s. There was then some slight recovery until, following a further temporary downturn in 1896–97, a sustained rise took the value of total output to a new high of £50–1 million on the eve of the Great War (see Figure 16.1).

18 The derived demand for livestock products came mainly from Britain. In 1908 it was calculated that 58 per cent of the net value of livestock output came from exports. In the 1850s 35–40 per cent of the cattle which 'disappeared' each year from the annual enumeration were exported to Britain, rising to 50 per cent in the mid 1860s, over 60 per cent by the early 1870s, and finally 70 per cent throughout the last quarter of the nineteenth century. The respective proportions of fat cattle, store cattle, and calves were 40 : 53 : 7 during the years 1875–91. Store-cattle prices have been used throughout, but using beef prices makes little difference to the final result. Between 1850 and 1875 30–50 per cent of sheep, over 30 per cent of pigs, and an untold proportion of bacon were exported. *The agricultural output of Ireland 1908*, p. 6; export figures are reported in *Agricultural statistics of Ireland for the year 1891*, BPP, LXXXVIII, C.6777, London, 1892, p. 23. See also R. Perren, *The meat trade in Britain 1840–1914*, London, 1978, pp. 96–7, for 1865–89, and Huttman, 'Institutional factors', pp. 538–40, for 1850–1915.

19 *Agricultural statistics of Ireland, with detailed report for the year 1901*, BPP, CXVI, Cd.1170, London, 1902, p. viii. Simple investigations of the agricultural labour force tend to assume full employment throughout the year. Nevertheless, using standard man-days to investigate labour inputs across various sectors of agriculture suggests that livestock farming was not as labour-saving as might at first sight appear to be the case.

20 See J. S. Donnelly, 'The Irish agricultural depression of 1859–64', *Irish Economic and Social History*, III, 1976, p. 34.

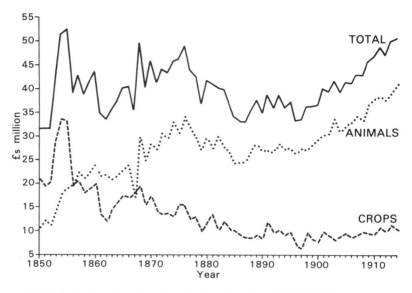

Figure 16.1 *Ireland: net value of agricultural output, 1850–1914*

Table 16.1 summarises the annual trend of Irish agricultural output in 13 half-decades from 1850–54 to 1910–14. In conjunction with Figure 16.1 it will be seen that three broad phases emerge of roughly equal duration. First, a period of generally rising output down to the mid 1870s, which was held in check partly by the declining contribution from cash crops. Second, a middle period of steadily declining output down to the mid 1890s. Third, a final phase lasting until the Great War, when output exhibited a pronounced upturn. Comparing 1850–54 with 1910–14, the contribution of crops to value-added total output fell by nearly 60 per cent whereas animal output increased by 192 per cent, giving an overall increase of nearly 30 per cent. Since the early agricultural returns are of uncertain accuracy a better comparison might be between 1855–59 and 1910–14. This shows a fall of 54 per cent in crop output and rises of 86 per cent and 14 per cent respectively for livestock and total output. Nevertheless, regardless of the basis on which the comparison is made, there is no denying the fact that tillage gave way to livestock from 1857 onwards. The tillage-created peak of £52 million in 1854–55 was just about the only period when tillage dominated total output.

The picture thus far presented is set in terms of current prices and historians of price history will notice some familiarity in the trends.

Table 16.1 *Annual average value added in Irish agricultural output, 1850–54 to 1910–14*

Period	Crops	Animals	Total
A. £ million			
1850–54	24.8	13.2	38.0
1855–59	22.1	20.8	42.8
1860–64	15.1	21.9	37.0
1865–69	17.5	23.7	41.1
1870–74	14.3	29.7	44.0
1875–79	13.2	30.5	43.8
1880–84	11.6	28.3	39.9
1885–89	9.0	25.6	34.7
1890–94	9.8	27.1	36.9
1895–99	8.2	27.2	35.3
1900–04	8.7	30.8	39.4
1905–09	9.2	33.7	42.9
1910–14	10.2	38.6	48.8
B. Percentage changes			
1850–54 to 1870–74	−42.3	125.0	15.8
1870–74 to 1890–94	−31.7	−8.6	−16.1
1890–94 to 1910–14	4.4	42.3	32.2
1850–54 to 1910–14	−58.9	192.7	28.4
1855–59 to 1910–14	−53.8	86.1	14.0

Source Appendix 16.2.

In particular, the general prices peak of the early to mid 1870s is mirrored in both the animal and total output trends, as is the general prices depression down to the mid 1890s (though with a greater absolute fall in the mid 1880s), and the progressive recovery of prices thereafter. The correlation is not, of course, exact, but then price is only one variable in the output equation. It nevertheless demonstrates the need to evaluate the impact of price variations upon the computed trend of value-added total output. This can be done with two quite different results for assessments of the output and productivity performance of Irish agriculture. The value of agricultural output can be equated, first, with the volume of agricultural production, and second, with the income of agricultural producers. Making the assumption that the estimated value of agricultural output is equivalent to volume and individual agricultural income, Figure 16.2 shows output deflated

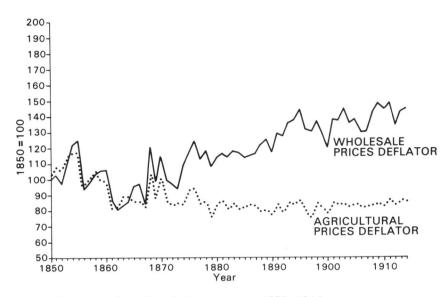

Figure 16.2 *Ireland: 'real' agricultural output, 1850–1914*

in two ways, the deflators being indexes of agricultural and wholesale prices.[21]

Taking output in farmers' agricultural income terms and deflating by a wholesale price index reveals that while short-term fluctuations were the norm, the long-term trend was unmistakably upwards. Notwithstanding sharp two- to three-year variations, livestock output increased in real terms virtually throughout the entire period. The depression of the early 1860s was probably the most pronounced short-term aberration, but overall the increase in livestock output was in excess of 300 per cent from 1850 to 1914. In real terms the apparent depression in livestock output value from the mid 1870s to the mid 1890s depicted in Figure 16.1 was illusory. Moreover, because livestock output overwhelmed the tillage sector from the mid 1850s, what was true for livestock was more or less true for agriculture as a whole. The depressed state of tillage output softened the overall impact of the upward trend in livestock output so that between 1850 and 1914

21 The agricultural prices index is a revised version of that published in Turner, 'Agricultural prices index'. The wholesale-prices index is that given in Barrington, 'A review of prices', pp. 251–3. The latter has been used by others, notably Vaughan, 'Agricultural output', p. 85, in an exercise on living standards, and Huttman, 'Institutional factors', pp. 370–1.

the 'real' rise in total output was of the order of 150 to 160 per cent. The depression of the early 1860s was the only major interruption to the steady progress made by the industry, although it was only from *c.*1873 that real gains in agricultural output took place continuously. This is in direct contrast to the situation in Britain. Indeed, from *c.*1870 the industry in Ireland appeared to run contra-cyclically in comparison with western European price history.

While the value of livestock output superseded that of tillage output from the mid 1850s, tillage remained a large enough proportion of total agricultural output to make 'real' improvements in total agricultural output appear small or even non-existent for the first two or three decades after the Famine. Throughout this period tillage remained depressed in real terms at 45 to 60 per cent of its early 1850s level. Seen in this light, the adjustment over the next half-century to a pastoral economy was a perfectly rational response by Irish farmers to changing terms of trade.

But there is another and perhaps more revealing way to investigate real output. This is by looking at the agricultural industry from within, so to speak, by comparing the value of output with the price trend of agricultural products. This has been achieved by constructing a composite agricultural product prices index as the deflator. The result is also shown in Figure 16.2. It can be read as a measure of the 'real' volume of agricultural output. While the wholesale prices deflator shows that farmers' real incomes may have improved, this was achieved through favourable price changes. By contrast, the real volume of agricultural output exhibited little overall improvement. Give or take short-term fluctuations and possible doubts over the accuracy of the early agricultural returns, there would appear to have been a decline in real volume down to the early 1860s, a rise to about 1870, and a renewed decline to about 1880. Thereafter real output levelled off.[22]

The distribution of output over time among its individual components throws up some interesting patterns. At the macro level tillage represented over 60 per cent of total output until the mid 1850s (with a half-decade average of 65.1 per cent in 1850–54), but thereafter slumped more or less progressively to a level of 21 per cent by 1900, and remained at between 20 and 25 per cent until the Great War.

22 I am grateful to Professor Kieran Kennedy of the Economic and Social Research Institute in Dublin and Cormac Ó Gráda for advice on more effective use of the agricultural prices index as a deflator when measuring agricultural performance. See also K. A. Kennedy, T. Giblin and D. McHugh, *The economic development of Ireland in the twentieth century*, London, 1988, pp. 20, 28n.

Table 16.2 *Composition of Irish agricultural output, 1850–54 to 1910–14 (annual average percentages)*

Period	Cash crops[a]	Oats	Potatoes	Tillage[b]	Cattle	Milk/ butter	Pigs	Sheep[c]	Eggs	Livestock
1850–54	17.4	15.8	30.4	65.1	9.1	12.0	9.3	2.5	2.0	34.9
1855–59	15.2	12.7	21.0	50.9	12.0	17.9	11.3	5.6	2.4	49.1
1860–64	13.6	11.4	13.6	40.4	17.9	18.3	12.3	7.7	3.3	59.6
1865–69	15.9	11.1	14.1	42.7	13.1	19.2	13.4	8.4	3.2	57.3
1870–74	9.1	8.7	12.9	32.6	20.9	20.2	13.0	9.7	3.7	67.4
1875–79	8.8	8.5	10.7	30.1	23.4	18.9	13.8	9.1	4.8	69.9
1880–84	7.2	8.2	11.6	29.0	25.9	16.6	14.0	8.3	6.2	71.0
1885–89	6.0	7.0	11.2	26.2	27.5	16.0	15.5	7.4	7.4	73.8
1890–94	5.7	7.6	10.0	26.4	26.2	16.8	14.8	8.0	7.7	73.6
1895–99	4.1	5.8	10.8	23.1	29.6	16.6	14.4	7.7	8.6	76.9
1900–04	4.1	5.4	9.9	22.0	30.7	16.5	15.0	7.3	8.5	78.0
1905–09	4.0	4.9	9.9	21.4	29.1	16.8	14.4	7.0	11.3	78.6
1910–14	4.0	4.3	10.2	20.9	28.8	16.1	15.1	6.2	13.0	79.1

Notes
[a] Wheat, barley, rye and flax.
[b] Includes hay and straw.
[c] Includes wool.

Source See Table 16.1.

Conversely, the share of the livestock and livestock product sector rose from approximately 35 per cent in the early 1850s to nearly 80 per cent by the close of the century. As Ó Gráda has observed, 'the humble farmyard hen and duck were adding more to agricultural output than wheat, oats, and potatoes combined, crops which in the early 1840s accounted for more than half of output'.[23] This may be an exaggeration, but as Table 16.2 confirms, the general point about the shifting balance of agricultural output is well made.

III Output and productivity in Britain and Ireland

Until Partition in 1922 Irish agriculture formed part of agricultural output in the United Kingdom as a whole, estimates of which have been published by Ojala.[24] As already observed, the method by which he derived these results remains unclear. Nor, more importantly, does he provide a regional or national breakdown of his results. Hence it

23 Ó Gráda, 'Irish agricultural output', p. 154.
24 See above, pp. 415–16.

is impossible to check the Irish component of his United Kingdom estimates against the independent estimates presented here. With this important caveat, Table 16.3 presents a comparison of United Kingdom output (including Ojala's built-in estimate for Ireland) with the new Irish estimates. In the absence of disaggregated annual totals, this is done on the basis of the same groupings of years as those employed for the post-1867 period by Ojala. These were based on C. Clark's identification of the late-nineteenth-century trade cycle; that is, the periods 'commence three years after each main cyclical peak of economic activity'.[25]

From the onset of the Great Depression in British agriculture in the 1870s, the share of the United Kingdom's tillage output coming from Ireland rose from 15 per cent to nearly 19 per cent by 1913. This was an impressive rise, the more so as Ireland's tillage acreage was in absolute decline. It testifies, in fact, to the very poor performance of mainly English tillage output from c.1870–1913, and thereby underlines the Great Depression's impact upon English arable farmers. Within the pastoral sector Ireland's contribution to livestock output also rose, from about 20 per cent in 1870 to 23 per cent by the Great War. This was a modest increase in monetary terms but, again, a significant indicator of the depressed performance of British agriculture at the time. Overall, therefore, Irish agriculture would seem to have contributed about one-sixth or one-fifth of the United Kingdom's agricultural output in the 1860s, rising to one-fifth to one-quarter on the eve of the Great War. At face value this seems a substantial achievement, though in part a function of the straitened times facing British agriculture during this period. Indeed, the Irish achievement may have been even better than these figures suggest, for Ojala's United Kingdom estimates include the value of marketed fruit and vegetables (calculated by Ojala as contributing £5 million and £4–5 million respectively throughout the period 1867–1913), whereas the Irish figures exclude fruit entirely because of lack of data, and assume all root and green crops were sent as fodder to the animal sector. Nor do the Irish estimates take account of the output of horses or poultry, both of which are included in Ojala's figures. Thus, he calculated that the value of United Kingdom horse output rose from a low of £0.4 million in the 1860s to £3 million 1877–93 before falling to £2.3 million in 1911–13. Over the same period the value of poultry meat rose from £1.1 million to £3.5 million. If these elements are deleted from Ojala's global estimates the

Table 16.3 *United Kingdom and Irish value-added agricultural output, 1850–66 to 1911–13*[a]

Period	UK tillage	Irish tillage	UK livestock	Irish livestock	UK total	Irish total
A. *Annual averages 1850–66 to 1911–13 in £s million*						
1850–66		20.2		19.2		39.4
1867–69	104.2	17.7	125.7	24.0	229.8	41.6
1870–76	95.0	14.7	152.2	30.4	247.2	45.1
1877–85	76.0	11.5	143.2	28.2	219.2	39.7
1886–93	56.8	9.4	131.1	26.6	187.8	36.0
1894–03	49.8	8.5	133.0	28.6	182.8	37.1
1904–10	50.7	9.1	150.1	33.9	200.8	43.0
1911–13	56.2	10.5	165.9	38.3	221.1	48.8
B. *Irish output as a percentage of United Kingdom output*						
1850–66						
1867–69		16.9		19.1		18.1
1870–76		15.4		20.0		18.2
1877–85		15.1		19.7		18.1
1886–93		16.6		20.3		19.2
1894–03		17.0		21.5		20.3
1904–10		18.0		22.6		21.4
1911–13		18.7		23.1		22.1

Notes
Subject to rounding errors.
[a] Where output is defined as sales off farm plus consumption in farm houses.

Source
E. M. Ojala, *Agriculture and economic progress*, Oxford, 1952, p. 208, and tables in this chapter.

contribution of Irish output is necessarily adjusted upwards, the whole rising from about 19 per cent around 1870 to 24 per cent in 1913.[26]

The implied productivity differences between Ireland and the United Kingdom in general are reinforced when crude income/labour

26 In his defence of British agriculture as a 'depressed' sector T. W. Fletcher reworked Ojala's estimates using what he considered to be improved data. The arable estimate remained unchanged except that for 1894–1903 it rose to £61.95 million, mainly by adding about £4 million to both the oats and potato estimates. On this new estimate the contribution of Ireland falls to 14 per cent of United Kingdom tillage output for that period. Fletcher's livestock estimates for 1867–69 and 1870–76 scarcely differ from those made by Ojala, but for 1894–1903 they rose to £146.18 million as compared with Ojala's £133 million. On these figures the contribution of Irish livestock falls to 19.5 per cent of United Kingdom

productivity estimates are examined.[27] This is demonstrated in Tables 16.4 and 16.5. The average annual data from both the new Irish estimates and Ojala's United Kingdom estimates are reworked, centred on seven time periods on or about the year of the decennial population census. Additionally, the Irish estimates have been deducted from Ojala's United Kingdom estimates to provide estimates for Great Britain only. Finally, from data contained in the census reports for England, Wales, and Scotland, and from estimates for Ireland, an attempt is made to isolate the agricultural workforce from the total population. For Ireland this is achieved in several ways: by looking at the agricultural labour force as given in the census; by using J. P. Huttman's separate estimate of the agricultural labour force; and by using the latter's estimate of the farm population (i.e. that part of the population which was directly dependent on agriculture).[28] Whichever procedure is followed, there is no doubt as to the improving relative position of Irish agricultural labour productivity.

In terms of the total population, Irish agricultural output per head improved over the whole period whereas British output per head declined. In addition, the value of output per head in Ireland was always higher than in Britain, rising to twice as much immediately prior to the Great War. At the level of the supposed agricultural labour force the picture is more complicated. Irish 'agricultural incomes' increased up to the mid 1860s and then remained roughly level until the mid 1890s, when they began to increase once more. In Britain, by contrast, although the level of income per capita of the agricultural work force was consistently higher than in Ireland – by 180 per cent early on, and still by over 100 per cent on the eve of the Great War – there was in fact a decline in that income during the period of the Great Depression. So great was the decline that, notwithstanding two decades of relatively buoyant prices, mean incomes had still not recovered to their pre-Depression level by the eve of the Great War. Measured against this experience, Irish agriculture seemingly performed relatively well.

---

livestock output in 1894–1903 and 18 per cent overall. Fletcher only reported the three periods 1867–69, 1870–76, and 1894–1903 (with separate English-only estimates for 1867–71 and 1894–98). Had he reworked other periods in a similar way it is probable that the United Kingdom totals would progressively have risen, bringing about a corresponding reduction in the relative contribution of Ireland. Fletcher, 'The Great Depression', p. 432.

27 In effect these measure per capita contribution to net agricultural-output values.
28 Huttman, 'Institutional factors', pp. 384–7 and 414.

Table 16.4 *Agricultural output per head of population and per head of the agricultural workforce in Ireland and Britain, 1850–54 to 1904–10 (average output per head in £s)*

Period	\[a\]	\[b\]	\[c\]	\[d\]	\[e\]	\[f\]
	Irish output				British output	
1850–54	5.8	26.1	7.6	24.1		
1855–66	6.9	33.9	9.3	31.6		
1867–76	8.1	41.5	11.7	39.6	7.5	113.0
1877–85	7.7	40.2	11.6	39.4	6.0	110.6
1886–93	7.6	38.3	12.1	39.0	4.6	99.0
1894–03	8.3	42.3	13.9	44.4	3.9	103.9
1904–10	9.8	56.4	17.3	54.0	4.1	111.5

Notes
\[a\] Output per head of population based on Census.
\[b\] Output per head of agricultural labour force based on Census.
\[c\] Output per head of 'farm' population based on Huttman.
\[d\] Output per head of agricultural labour force based on Huttman.
\[e\] Output per head of population based on Census.
\[f\] Output per head of agricultural labour force based on Census.

Source
Derived from tables in this chapter; Census of 1911; E. M. Ojala, *Agriculture and economic progress*, Oxford, 1952, p. 208; J. P. Huttman, 'Institutional factors in the development of Irish agriculture, 1850-1915', unpublished Ph.D. thesis, University of London, 1970, pp. 384–7 and 414.

Taking this approach a step further, it is possible to estimate the 'real' movement in Irish agricultural output per capita. This is demonstrated in Table 16.5. When deflated against a wholesale-prices index, total per capita agricultural incomes appear to improve in 'real' terms, and this remains the case whether set against total population or estimates of farm or labour force populations (columns \[a\] to \[d\] of Table 16.5).[29] Regardless of the definition of population in ques-

29 Ideally a retail prices index should be used as the deflator but such an index does not exist. This is not a standard of living exercise even though it is couched in per capita income terms. The incomes in question are not wages or salaries or combinations of the two, but, rather, proxies for the performance of the agricultural sector. In this respect an index of wholesale prices provides a plausible substitute.
 Official sources tend to confirm the impression that Irish agriculture's performance underwent a real improvement, at least from 1881, when an index of official weighted agricultural prices is available. When compared with wholesale prices, as calculated by 'official' procedures, 'real' agricultural prices kept con-

Table 16.5 *Real agricultural output per capita in Ireland and Britain, 1850–54 to 1904–10 (1867–76 = 100)*

Period	[a]	[b]	[c]	[d]	[e]	[f]	Deflator
A. Using a wholesale-price index deflator							
1850–54	84.6	74.3	76.9	72.0			84.7
1855–66	85.3	82.3	80.4	80.4			99.4
1867–76	100.0	100.0	100.0	100.0	100.0	100.0	100.0
1877–85	113.7	117.1	120.0	119.9	96.3	118.2	82.9
1886–93	135.0	133.0	148.6	141.4	87.8	125.9	69.6
1894–03	155.1	154.8	180.9	170.4	78.5	139.6	65.9
1904–10	156.7	177.3	192.5	177.4	70.4	128.5	76.8
B. Using an Irish agricultural-price index deflator							
1850–54	101.2	89.0	92.0	86.1			70.7
1855–66	97.4	94.0	91.8	91.8			87.0
1867–76	100.0	100.0	100.0	100.0	100.0	100.0	100.0
1877–85	96.1	99.0	101.4	101.4	81.4	99.9	98.0
1886–93	103.6	102.0	114.0	108.5	67.4	96.6	90.7
1894–03	110.7	110.5	129.1	121.6	56.0	99.7	92.3
1904–10	110.2	124.7	135.3	124.7	49.5	90.3	109.2

Notes
[a] Ireland – real output per head of population.
[b] Ireland – real output per head of agricultural labour force.
[c] Ireland – real output per head of 'farm' population.
[d] Ireland – real output per head of agricultural labour force.
[e] Britain – real output per head of population.
[f] Britain – real output per head of agricultural labour force.

Source Derived from Table 16.4.

tion, per capita output almost doubled from the mid 1860s to the Great War. By comparison, the level of British agricultural income per capita fell dramatically over the same period (column [e] Table 16.5), though per capita of the agricultural workforce it improved throughout the supposed Agricultural Depression before falling in Edwardian times. Yet although per capita incomes of British agricultural labour – as defined and measured in this exercise – were consistently higher than their Irish counterparts, and improved in real terms from the

---

sistently ahead of wholesale prices from 1881. They were 20 per cent ahead by 1900, and remained so until the Great War. Calculated from *Agricultural statistics, Ireland, 1915, return of prices of crops, livestock, and other Irish agricultural products, BPP*, XXXVI, Cd.8452, London, 1917, pp. 5–8. See also Turner, 'Agricultural prices index'.

1860s to the turn of the century, the gap between the two countries clearly narrowed.

Deflating per capita output against an Irish agricultural prices index, as might be expected from earlier use of this deflator, changes this picture significantly. In Ireland the improvement in real output per capita (or per unit of agricultural labour force) is still evident but now much reduced, indicating a 10 to 20, or at most 30, per cent improvement over the period 1867–76 to 1904–10 according to which definition of population or labour force is used. But using the Irish agricultural price index to deflate British per capita output reveals quite the opposite: a 10 per cent decline in real output per unit of agricultural labour, a decline which reached its nadir during the first decade of the new century.

Given that the amount of land under cultivation did not change very much one way or the other, what was true for labour productivity was also true to a large extent for land productivity. That is to say, short-term fluctuations excepted, the value of Irish output per acre rose modestly from *c.*£2.2 per acre *c.*1850 to a little under £3 by the mid 1870s, then fell back to £2.4 towards the end of the century before rising steeply to £3.5 per acre by the Great War. In farmers' real income terms (i.e. deflated against a wholesale prices index), there was an initial decline down to the early 1860s but a continuous improvement thereafter. By contrast, in real volume terms (i.e. deflated against an agricultural prices index), there was an initial decline down to and including the 1859–64 depression, a rise to *c.*1870, a further decline to *c.*1880, and a levelling-off thereafter. Thus, whereas in income terms productivity advanced, in volume terms the trend was less encouraging.

IV Output and income per occupier

In addition to their output data the annual agricultural statistics include much information on landholdings, specifying for much of the period up to nine categories of landholding from less than 1 acre to over 500 acres. The number of holdings within each size category is enumerated both for each county and the country at large (given that some holdings straddle county boundaries), and, from 1861, equivalent figures are given for the number of occupiers of holdings (allowing that some occupiers occupied more than one holding). Thus, the *c.*573,000 holdings in 1891 were in the hands of only *c.*527,000 occupiers.[30] As

---

30 *The agricultural statistics of Ireland for 1891, BPP*, LXXXVIII, C.6777, Dublin 1892, p. 10.

the original enumerators recognised, it is doubtful whether the smallest holdings of all, especially those of less than 1 acre, should be regarded as agricultural at all since many of them can have been little more than gardens, although their elimination does little to alter overall trends.

During an initial period of land rationalisation the number of occupiers fell from *c*.550,000 in the early 1860s to 537,000 by the end of the decade, and thence to 521,000 by 1884. Under the influence of subsequent tenurial changes their numbers then recovered to *c*.550,000 by 1905 at which level they remained until 1914. On these figures the value of net output per occupier rose from an estimated £60 to £90 over the period *c*.1860–76, fell back to a little over £60 by 1887, rose and then fell again between 1887 and 1897, and finally rose steadily to reach over £90 by 1914. This last period of expansion coincides in part with significant changes in tenurial relations and land law and a general move towards offering tenants the opportunity to become owner-occupiers and therefore independent men.[31] Whereas in 1906 tenants and owner-occupiers numbered 423,000 and 175,000 respectively, in 1914 – a mere nine years later – the corresponding figures were 217,000 and 349,000. Under the influence of land rationalisation prior to the mid 1880s occupiers thus managed to achieve at least some initial improvement in the gross value of their output, although it was arguably the strong move to greater tenurial independence from the mid 1890s which apparently delivered the most genuine and durable gains.

Converting the value of output per occupier into a measure of real output by volume using the agricultural prices index nevertheless reveals a rather different story. Thus, apart from outstanding improvements in the 1860s and mid 1870s, real output per occupier by volume effectively declined, or at best stood still, from the mid 1870s to the Great War. Any productivity gains during this period were thus monetary rather than physical. Deflating the value of output per occupier against the wholesale-prices index provides a measure of associated changes in farmers' incomes. These generally rose to the mid 1890s but then fell from 1895 to the Great War. The apparent productivity improvements detected in the value of output in the two decades or so before the Great War thus emerge as illusory in real terms, both with respect to the income and the output volume of individual farmers.

These observations nevertheless fail to take account of the influence of factor costs on output, notably rent and labour costs. Current knowledge on these matters has recently been reviewed by K. T. Hoppen

---

31 For an up-to-date and succinct summary see K. T. Hoppen, *Ireland since 1800: conflict and conformity*, London, 1989, pp. 94–8.

Q

Table 16.6 *Ireland: land, labour, and gross farming profits, 1852–54 to 1905–10*

Date	Output	Rent	Labour	Gross farming profits
In £s million				
1852–54	42.3	10.0	9.3	23.0
1872–74	44.4	12.0	10.6	21.8
1882–84	39.0	11.5	11.0	16.5
1905–10	43.6	8.0	10.6	25.0
In real terms, 1852–54 = 100				
1852–54	100.0	100.0	100.0	100.0
1872–74	89.9	102.7	97.6	81.2
1882–54	104.7	130.6	134.4	81.5
1905–10	125.1	97.1	138.4	131.9

Source
Derived from Appendix 16.2; K. T. Hoppen, *Ireland since 1800: conflict and conformity*, London, 1989, p. 100.

and from summary information which he provides, combined with the output estimates presented here, estimates of the respective output shares of land, labour, and gross farming profits have been made (Table 16.6).[32] The time periods in question, although not ideal, are determined by those chosen by Hoppen. On this evidence, between 1852–54 and 1905–10, output remained fairly stable and the gross rental and labour bills likewise fluctuated within relatively narrow limits. As far as the impact of the Land War is concerned, the major point to notice is the difference between the early 1870s and the early 1880s, when gross output declined by more than any compensating adjustments in costs (rent and wages) and, indeed, the wages bill actually rose. Under these circumstances farm profits collapsed, and they only subsequently recovered with the advent of more widespread owner-occupancy and its concomitant substantial reduction in the rent bill (see Table 16.6). In 'real' terms output decreased between 1852–54 and 1872–74 without any compensating decrease in farming costs; on the contrary, rent actually rose modestly. Real farming profits therefore slumped dramatically and remained depressed in 1882–84. By 1905–10, however, they had made a dramatic recovery notwithstanding continuing high

32 Hoppen, *Conflict and conformity*, p. 100.

labour costs. The explanation lies in rising land productivity (as meas-ured this way) coupled with a much reduced national rent bill.

V Total factor productivity

Discussion thus far has focused upon partial factor productivity measures since, apart from the data on agricultural output, information on the factor inputs of land and labour is available in terms of quantity rather than value. The question of capital inputs also arises. Fortunately, enough fragmentary information is available for the estimation of total factor productivity to be attempted. Given data limitations this has been undertaken on a decennial basis for the 1850s, 1870s, 1890s and 1910s only. The results are summarised in Table 16.7.

The output values employed are averages of the annual values for the respective decades. The mean cultivated area per decade is simi-larly calculated, while the labour factor input is derived from Huttman's measure of the agricultural labour force.[33] The respective values of land (rent) and labour (wages) are taken from Hoppen's summary estimates for 1852–54, 1872–74, 1882–84 and 1905–10, extrapolated to provide decennial means.[34] These probably lead to some overstatement of rent levels in the 1890s and 1910s but the result is not serious, for minor adjustments to these figures make little difference to the final total factor productivity estimates.

Given that the main adjustment in Irish agriculture from the Famine down to the Great War was a relative switch from tillage to livestock and their products, a surrogate measure of capital input has been utilised based upon total livestock numbers. These are measured in unit equivalents according to the respective feed requirements of the various animals with the decennial means derived from the weighted annual totals.[35] These are then valued using a price index of yearling store cattle. The estimated annual addition to stock for each decade is taken as the difference between the total value of stock in decade *t* and

---

33 Substituting alternative figures from the census makes little difference to the outcome of the estimates.

34 Hoppen, *Conflict and conformity*, p. 100

35 The weights are: milch cattle 1.0; beef cows 0.8; other cattle greater than two years old 0.75; cattle between one and two years 0.5; cattle under one year 0.25; sows for breeding 0.5; boars 0.4; other pigs 0.25; breeding ewes 0.2; rams 0.1; other sheep 0.066; poultry over six months 0.02; poultry under six months 0.005. See J. T. Coppock, *An agricultural geography of Great Britain*, London, 1971, p. 150. Also K. Biddick, B. M. S. Campbell, C. Thornton, R. C. Allen and G. Clark, above, pp. 115–16, 156–7, 198–9, 213, 245.

Table 16.7 *Total factor productivity in Irish agriculture, 1850s to 1910s*

A. *Output values and factor inputs*

Date	Output Q (£m, current prices)	Output Q (£m, constant prices)	Labour L (millions)	Land N (millions of acres)	Capital K (millions of LUEs)
1850s	40.431	40.431	1.575	15.015	4.734
1870s	43.895	33.072	1.112	15.598	5.182
1890s	36.136	30.878	0.923	15.165	5.340
1910s	48.835	32.147	0.797	14.681	5.803

Annual rates of change

	ΔQ	ΔQ	ΔL	ΔN	ΔK
1850s–70s	0.412	−0.999	−1.725	0.191	0.453
1870s–90s	−0.968	−0.343	−0.927	−0.141	0.150
1890s–1910s	1.517	0.202	−0.731	−0.162	0.416

B. *Factor values and shares*

Factor values (in £m)			Annual wages	Annual rent	Annual additions to stock
1850s			9.300	10.000	0.962
1870s			10.600	12.000	1.900
1890s			11.000	11.500	0.220
1910s			10.600	8.000	1.890

Factor shares			l	n	k
1850s			0.459	0.494	0.047
1870s			0.433	0.490	0.078
1890s			0.484	0.506	0.010
1910s			0.517	0.390	0.092

(Table 16.7 *cont. facing page*)

C. *Total factor productivity*	$R^* = \Delta Q - l\Delta L - n\Delta N - k\Delta K$

(i) Using starting decades for factor shares
1850s–70s $R^* =$ 1.088
1870s–90s $R^* =$ −0.509
1890s–1910s $R^* =$ 1.949
1850s–1910s $R^* =$ 0.836

(ii) Using terminal decades for factor shares
1850s–70s $R^* =$ 1.030
1870s–90s $R^* =$ −0.449
1890s–1910s $R^* =$ 1.920
1850s–1910s $R^* =$ 0.882

In real volume terms
(i) Using starting decades for factor shares
1850s–70s $R^* =$ −0.323
1870s–90s $R^* =$ 0.116
1890s–1910s $R^* =$ 0.634
1850s–1910s $R^* =$ 0.139

(ii) Using terminal decades for factor shares
1850s–70s $R^* =$ −0.381
1870s–90s $R^* =$ 0.176
1890s–1910s $R^* =$ 0.605
1850s–1910s $R^* =$ 0.186

Notes
For sources and methods of calculation see text.
LUEs refers to Livestock Unit Equivalents.

decade t_{-1}, annualised on a ten-year basis. For example, livestock had a total value of £61.218 million in the 1890s and £58.999 million in the 1880s, giving an annual addition to capital in the 1890s of only £0.22 million, and so on. This implies that additions to stock took ten years to realise their full potential, which is probably too long, but the constraint of working within decadal units leaves little alternative. In the absence of information for the 1840s, the figure for the 1850s is obtained by extrapolation from the 1860s on the grounds that both are documented as decades of replenishment.

The use of rent, wages, and capital additions allows the derivation of factor weights for the total factor productivity calculation. Unfortunately, the estimates of capital addition are gross rather than net for they fail to take account of the cost of providing specialist equipment – byres, dairies, milking and butter-making equipment, etc. – associated with the shift from tillage into livestock production. Nevertheless, at best the share of capital is only ever 9 per cent.[36]

The results reported in Table 16.7 confirm the established tripartite pattern of growth, followed by stagnation, and finally a period up to the Great War of stronger growth. The period of stagnation is represented by negative total factor productivity and is associated with a lowered value of output per unit of labour and land. As with earlier measurements, however, this may reflect price effects rather than genuine productivity changes. Controlling for these using the agricultural prices index as a deflator and re-estimating total factor productivity in real volume terms ensures that physical output is compared with physical inputs. This reveals lower annual rates of productivity growth in all three time periods but with a cumulative gain in productivity across the entire span from the 1850s to the 1910s, suggesting a steady improvement in efficiency.

VI Conclusion

Any conclusions drawn from this study of Irish agricultural output and productivity should be drawn with caution. The caution arises from the methodological problem of deciding what is the correct method of estimating net output. This is an area upon which much work remains to be done. In the meanwhile, the absolute estimates of output and productivity are likely to prove less reliable than the relative trends which they reveal. In this respect they do, perhaps, provide a basis for inter-sector and inter-country comparisons. The lasting conclusion must be that at a time of considerable change within west European agriculture in general, let alone the specific upsets and changes within Ireland itself, the Irish agricultural industry seems to have made a mostly successful adjustment to those changes. Progress was by no means smooth and consistent, but overall there were nevertheless certain real gains in land, labour, and total factor productivity.

36 This accords well with Ó Gráda who calculates capital's share of agricultural income in 1854, 1876 and 1908 as 6, 7 and 8 per cent respectively: Ó Gráda, *Ireland before and after the Famine*, p. 130. Crops, it will be noted, are omitted from the measure of capital employed here. Moreover, although their value fell over time, inputs of machinery are nevertheless likely to have risen and to have done so more rapidly than the increase in livestock numbers. To a degree these are compensating biases. Yet, even if capital stock were underestimated by as much as 100 per cent, the most that total-factor productivity would change would be a modest 8 per cent.

Appendix 16.1 *Different estimates of gross value-added output in Irish agriculture, c.1854–1914, in £m.*

Date	Crops	Live-stock	Total	Notes	Source
1854	19.9	19.7	39.6	[a]	Vaughan
1854	20.8	24.2	45.0	[b]	Ó Gráda (1)
1854	33.8	17.8	51.6	[c]	Turner
1852–56	27.3	16.4	43.7	[c]	Turner
1856–60	15.0	25.4	40.4	[b]	Solar
1856–60	19.4	21.7	41.1		Turner
1869–71	15.5	29.1	44.6		Ó Gráda (2)
1869–71	15.7	26.7	42.4		Turner
1874	14.6	34.8	49.4	[a]	Vaughan
1874	13.0	32.8	45.8		Turner
1876	11.9	35.2	47.1	[b]	Solow
1876	15.5	33.6	49.1		Turner
1873–77	14.0	31.7	45.6		Turner
1881	9.4	29.0	38.4	[b]	Solow
1881	13.4	27.5	40.9		Turner
1879–83	11.5	28.4	39.9		Turner
1886	6.1	24.2	30.3	[b]	Solow
1886	8.9	24.1	33.1		Turner
1884–88	9.3	25.3	34.6		Turner
1908	5.5	36.3	41.8	[d]	Census
1908	9.7	33.4	43.1		Turner
1906–10	9.1	34.9	44.0		Turner
1912	14.9	45.2	60.1	[e]	Ó Gráda (3)
1912	9.6	37.6	47.3		Turner
1910–14	10.2	38.6	48.8		Turner

Notes
[a] Does not include a hay/straw estimate.
[b] For comparability, unspecified 'other' items excluded.
[c] Inflated by exceptional potato values in the mid 1850s.
[d] For comparability certain items excluded.
[e] Includes items not separately specified and therefore excluded from the estimates by Turner.

Source
Department of Agriculture and Technical Instruction for Ireland, *The agricultural output of Ireland 1908 (in connection with the Census of Production Act, 1906)*, Dublin, 1912, p. 18.
C. Ó Gráda (1), *Ireland before and after the Famine: explorations in economic history*, Manchester, 1988, p. 68.
C. Ó Gráda (2), 'Post-Famine adjustment, essays in nineteenth-century Irish economic history', unpublished University of Columbia Ph.D. thesis, 1973, p. 137.
C. Ó Grada (3), 'Irish agriculture north and south since 1900', *this volume*, p. 444.
P. M. Solar, 'Growth and distribution in Irish agriculture before the Famine', unpublished Stanford University Ph.D. thesis, 1987, p. 359.
B. Solow, *The land question and the Irish economy, 1870–1903*, Cambridge, Mass., 1971, p. 171.
Turner, this chapter, Appendix 16.2.
W. E. Vaughan,'Agricultural output, rents and wages in Ireland, 1850–1880', pp. 85–97 in L. M. Cullen and F. Furet, eds., *Ireland and France 17th-20th centuries*, Paris, 1980, p. 97.

Appendix 16.2 *The value of Irish agricultural output, 1850–1914 in £000s*

Year	Crops	Livestock	Total
1850	21,185	10,420	31,605
1851	19,499	12,156	31,655
1852	20,268	11,286	31,554
1853	29,375	14,308	43,683
1854	33,806	17,804	51,610
1855	33,304	19,087	52,391
1856	19,578	19,437	39,016
1857	20,615	22,086	42,701
1858	17,965	20,952	38,917
1859	18,973	22,206	41,179
1860	19,787	23,793	43,579
1861	13,228	21,570	34,797
1862	11,739	21,756	33,495
1863	14,667	20,937	35,604
1864	15,906	21,481	37,386
1865	17,463	22,763	40,226
1866	16,825	23,793	40,618

Appendix 16.2 *(cont.)*

Year	Crops	Livestock	Total
1867	17,661	17,565	35,226
1868	19,766	29,719	49,485
1869	15,538	24,645	40,184
1870	17,401	28,338	45,739
1871	14,130	27,172	41302
1872	13,433	30,595	44,028
1873	13,684	29,581	43,265
1874	13,006	32,772	45,778
1875	15,543	30,839	46,382
1876	15,461	33,641	49,103
1877	12,293	31,530	43,822
1878	12,779	29,721	42,500
1879	10,055	26,978	37,033
1880	12,034	29,646	41,680
1881	13,439	27,494	40,933
1882	10,136	29,962	40,098
1883	12,068	27,835	39,903
1884	10,351	26,775	37,126
1885	10,023	24,093	34,116
1886	8,941	24,135	33,077
1887	8,566	24,372	32,938
1888	8,448	27,113	35,562
1889	9,271	28,390	37,661
1890	8,251	26,826	35,077
1891	11,842	26,914	38,757
1892	9,500	26,591	36,091
1893	10,433	28,125	38,557
1894	8,902	27,256	36,158
1895	9,871	27,292	37,163
1896	7,239	26,080	33,319
1897	6,389	27,186	33,576
1898	9,365	26,960	36,325
1899	8,082	28,260	36,342
1900	7,652	29,089	36,741
1901	9,940	30,148	40,088
1902	8,986	30,365	39,351
1903	8,120	33,494	41,614

Appendix 16.2 *(cont.)*

Year	Crops	Livestock	Total
1904	8,690	30,765	39,455
1905	9,432	32,031	41,463
1906	8,507	32,711	41,218
1907	8,900	34,161	43,061
1908	9,685	33,403	43,088
1909	9,338	36,441	45,779
1910	9,199	37,731	46,930
1911	10,676	38,255	48,931
1912	9,696	37,593	47,289
1913	11,199	38,964	50,163
1914	10,292	40,571	50,863

Source See text.

Irish agriculture north and south since 1900

There is the Ireland of the north, where the land is, comparatively speaking, poor land and the climate cold, where the farmers are shrewd, intelligent men, who have made the most of their circumstances. The farms are trim and well kept. The land is well tilled. There is an air of prosperity about the country. There is the Ireland of the south, where the land is better and the climate milder, and the people, possibly to some extent because nature has done so much for them, less energetic; where the steadings are ill-kept and the land badly tilled, and waste and neglect are much in evidence.

John Sinclair, 1906.[1]

The preceding chapters by P. Solar and M. Goossens, and by M. Turner confirm the more favourable picture of nineteenth-century Irish agriculture emerging from recent research.[2] Solar and Goossens's comparison may show Belgium to have held a slight edge over Ireland in the early 1840s, but it must be borne in mind that Belgian farmers at this stage were supporting a successful industrial revolution. Turner's comparison of Irish and British productivity growth is in Ireland's favour, belying stagnation in Irish agriculture either before or during the Land War. The analysis of this chapter is also comparative, but now it is the creation of two Irelands in 1921 that affords scope for such a perspective.

The notion that northern Irish (or Ulster) agriculture is 'superior to' or 'more efficient than' southern has a long history. In the past, this northern edge was linked to the alleged advantages of its tenurial

The comments of Gerry Boyle, Alan Matthews, Des Norton, and those present at Bellagio on a preliminary draft are much appreciated. My thanks, too, to Bob O'Connor, T. F. Stainer and P. W. Kelly for supplying relevant data. For reasons of space the data appendices to the Bellagio paper have been omitted here; they are in C. Ó Gráda, *Irish agriculture north and south*, University College Dublin, Centre for Economic Research, Working Paper 89/1, 1989.

1 J. Sinclair, *Report of the Scottish Commission on Agriculture to Ireland*, Edinburgh, 1906, p. 34.
2 See P. Solar and M. Goossens, above, pp. 364–84; and M. E. Turner, above, pp. 410–38.

system. By allowing farmers considerable discretion in disposing of their investment in the land, the Ulster variant of landlordism was supposed to have provided the economic advantages of peasant proprietorship, which southern farmers lacked before the end of the nineteenth century. Ulster farmers were accordingly considered more progressive and more mobile.

This traditional interpretation of Ulster superiority is no longer widely accepted. The association between tenant right and improvement across Ulster turns out to be by no means clear cut; the case of County Donegal, much of it agriculturally backward though faithfully observing Ulster Custom, has been stressed by B. Solow, and E. D. Steele has shown that 'Ulster Custom' was somewhat of a misnomer, at least in the nineteenth century, since tenant right was a good deal more widespread by then than the name implies.[3] Nor can the existence of the considerable capitalised sum obtained by farmers on ceding their tenancies really be put down to investment: rather, it suggests that landlords could not (or, less likely, would not) exact their full Ricardian rents.[4] However, D. J. Johnson and L. Kennedy show that Ulster farmers fared no better than others before the Famine, in the sense that the rents they paid were no lower than elsewhere, and this was also the case around the turn of the century.[5]

There are more direct hints that the traditional story is exaggerated. The 'weed-census' data of the mid 1850s show Ulster in a relatively bad light, better than only Connacht in the provincial stakes.[6] And the common assertion that 'where the linen manufacture spreads the tillage is very bad', must have applied more to Ulster than anywhere else in the nineteenth century, though it also implies that Ulster's farming may have improved relatively with rural de-industrialisation.[7]

A further problem is definitional. The 'Ulster' implied by some accounts is the Northern Ireland component of the United Kingdom,

---

3 B. Solow, *The land question and the Irish economy 1870–1903*, Cambridge, Mass., 1971, chapter 1; E. D. Steele, *Irish land and British politics*, Cambridge, 1970, pp. 19 and 21.

4 W. E. Vaughan, *Landlords and tenants in Ireland 1848–1904*, Dublin, 1984, p. 20.

5 D. J. Johnson and L. Kennedy, 'George O'Brien', unpublished manuscript, The Queen's University of Belfast, 1987.

6 W. E. Vaughan, 'Landlord and tenant relations in Ireland between the Famine and the Land War, 1850–70', pp. 216–26 in L. M. Cullen and T. C. Smout, eds., *Comparative aspects of Scottish and Irish economic and social history 1600–1900*, Edinburgh, 1977, pp. 222–3.

7 A. Young, *Tour in Ireland: with general observations on the present state of that kingdom: made in the years 1776, 1777 and 1778, and brought down to the end of 1779*, 2 vols., London, 1780, I, p. 151.

which excludes counties Cavan, Donegal and Monaghan. In what follows the six-county political unit is allowed to determine the discussion, whose main concern is with the effect of governmental policy on the agricultural sector. Indeed, government policy prompts another explanation for differential performance. For a full decade after Partition in 1921, southern farmers enjoyed continued free access to the United Kingdom market; in some accounts, the period is still remembered as a kind of golden age.[8] Not so the 1930s and 1940s, an era of high tariffs, and a world in depression or at war. A productivity slow-down in southern agriculture is only to be expected. In the post-war period, northern farmers continued to benefit from more generous subsidies and price supports through the British deficiency-payments system, but at least southern farmers again gradually gained freer access to British, and later European, markets. Since membership of the European Economic Community in 1973, southern policy has been very pro-farmer, while United Kingdom (and hence Northern Ireland) policy has been broadly pro-consumer.[9]

This chapter is by no means the first examination of this issue: where it differs from others is in its greater reliance upon macro-productivity data. It also takes a closer look at conditions before Partition, in order to gain added perspective.

I A long-term perspective

The main focus of the present study is the agricultural sector in the two Irelands since Partition in 1921. For most of this period, farmers in Northern Ireland and the Irish Free State (since 1947 the Irish Republic) have been subject to very different price, tariff, and subsidy regimes. Between 1932 and the late 1960s in particular, southern farmers faced less favourable markets, and government policy in the south had a marked bias towards tillage. Several comparisons have suggested that northern farmers out-performed southern, either in output or efficiency terms, after Partition and especially after 1931.[10] But a key question,

8 G. O'Brien, 'Patrick Hogan', *Studies*, XXV, 1936, pp. 353–68; J. F. Meenan, *The Irish economy since 1922*, Liverpool, 1971, pp. 91–5 and 303–7. But see also D. Hoctor, *The Department's story: a history of the Department of Agriculture*, Dublin, 1971, pp. 126–7 and 163–4.

9 M. Cuddy and M. Doherty, *An analysis of agricultural developments in the north and south of Ireland and of the effects of integrated policy and planning*, Dublin, 1984.

10 For example, S. Sheehy, J. T. O'Brien and D. McClelland, *Agriculture in Northern Ireland and the Republic of Ireland*, Dublin and Belfast, 1981; Cuddy and O'Doherty,

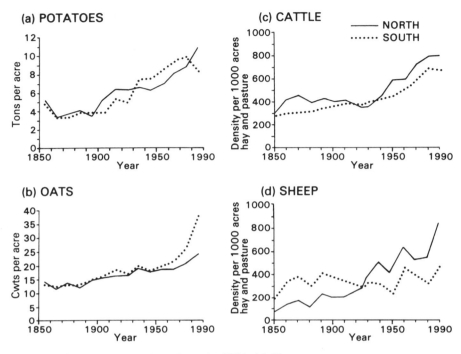

Figure 17.1 *Ireland north and south, 1851–1945: potato output per acre, oats output per acre, cattle density per 1,000 acres of hay and pasture, and sheep density per 1,000 acres of hay and pasture*

addressed only fleetingly, or not at all, in these studies, is whether the gap in performance changed after the 1920s relative to before.

Here, comparative performance is first gauged by crop and livestock ratios, then by labour-productivity measures. Figures 17.1(a)– 17.1(d), derived from the official statistics available annually from 1847, address this question but fail to provide a clear-cut answer. Figures

Agricultural developments; R. Johnston and A. Conway, 'Factors associated with growth in farm output', *Proceedings of the Agricultural Economics Society of Ireland*, 1976, pp. 52–102; G. W. Furness and T. F. Stainer, 'Economic performance in agriculture in Northern Ireland and the Irish Republic', *Annual Report on Research and Technical Work*, Belfast, 1981; E. A. Attwood, 'Agricultural developments in Ireland, north and south', *Journal of the Statistical and Social Inquiry Society of Ireland*, XXI, 1966, pp. 9–34; E. A. Attwood and M. O'Sullivan, 'Some aspects of agricultural development in Ireland north and south since accession to the EEC', *Proceedings of the Agricultural Economics Society of Ireland*, 1983–84, pp. 137–72; O. Mangan, 'Irish agriculture 1926–1987', unpublished University College, Dublin MA term paper, 1987.

17.1(a) and 17.1(b) report trends in potato and oat yields in the two Irelands from the mid nineteenth century. Potatoes and oats were chosen because both were widely cultivated in both Irelands throughout the period. Figures 17.1(c) and 17.1(d) describe cattle and sheep densities per acre since 1850. Taken together, these trends permit no strong inferences: but tillage would seem to have done better in the south after 1921 relative to earlier, pasture in the north. Unfortunately for the south, tillage accounted for a small and generally declining share of output in the two Irelands.

The earliest official estimates of Irish agricultural output date from 1908 and 1912.[11] A recent study by R. O'Connor and C. Guiomard uses the second set of estimates to calculate southern output, thereby allowing an evaluation of output and labour productivity growth north and south between 1912 and the mid 1920s.[12] The result is reported in Table 17.1, which also includes data for 1938. The comparison required certain adjustments to the raw data. The first problem concerns bog peat or turf, a major item in Irish farmers' output. Although as long ago as 1636 coal was supposed to be 'almost the only material used for firing along this coast all the winter from Knockfergus to Youghal', a 1918 survey found that on nearly two-thirds of farmsteads turf was the sole fuel.[13] No wonder Dubliners referred to their rural compatriots as 'bogmen'.

It might be argued that turf should be excluded because it is non-reproducible, except in the very long run. Yet national accounts everywhere include marine, forest, and mineral products, regardless of resource-depletion considerations. Semantics aside, excluding turf would badly distort north–south labour productivity comparisons. Yet neither the 1908 nor the 1912 estimate allowed for it. The first to do so was the official estimate for the south in 1926, which put turf output at 5.9 million tons, worth over £6 million, or almost 10 per cent of total

11 It should be noted that the 1908 and 1912 estimates are not entirely consistent. In particular, the gap in the output of dairy products is far greater than could be explained by the (small) difference between the size of the dairy herds in the two years. The valuation put on potatoes was twice as high in 1912 as in 1908. Though I have used the earlier estimate in other work (see also Solow, *The land question*, pp. 171–4), here, R. O'Connor and C. Guiomard, 'Agricultural output in the Irish Free State area before and after independence', *Irish Economic and Social History*, XII, 1985, pp. 89–97, are followed in using the 1912 estimate.

12 O'Connor and Guiomard, 'Agricultural output'. I am grateful to Robert O'Connor for providing me with his worksheets and related material.

13 *Calender of State Papers Ireland 1633–47*, p. 130, quoted in O. Wood, *West Cumberland coal 1600–1982/3*, Cumberland and Westmorland Antiquarian and Archaeological Society, extra series, XXIV, Kendal, 1988, p. 5; P. Purcell, *The peat resources of Ireland*, Fuel Research Board, special report II, London, 1920, p. 12.

Table 17.1 *Irish agriculture north and south: the value of output, 1912, 1925–26 and 1938–39 (in £ million)*

	All-Ireland	26-Counties	6-Counties
A. 1912			
Livestock	45.2	37.2	8.0
Crops	14.9	10.1	4.8
Total	60.1	47.3	12.8
Labour force (millions)	0.977	0.765	0.212
Output per worker (£)	60	62	60
B. 1925–26			
Livestock	60.2	48.4	11.8
Crops	14.3	11.1	3.2
Total	74.5	59.6	15.0
Labour force (millions)	0.847	0.648	0.199
Output per worker (£)	88	92	75
C. 1938–39			
Livestock	52.0	38.9	13.0
Crops	15.1	13.0	2.2
Total	67.1	51.9	15.2
Labour force (millions)	0.761	0.586	0.175
Output per worker (£)	88	89	87

Source See text.

gross value added.[14] That estimate relied in part on a 1918 inquiry.[15] However, subsequent estimates of southern turf production were more conservative: output was put at 3.6 million tons in 1929 and at 3.3 million in 1939.[16] The estimates in Table 17.1 assume, first, that the south produced nine-tenths of all turf throughout; northern output has been adjusted accordingly. Second, O'Connor and Guiomard's estimate for 1912 is used instead of the higher official figure. Third, the turf price implicit in that estimate – £0.85 per ton at a time when the wholesale price of coal, with more than twice the calorific power, was less than that – seems implausibly high.[17] Fourth, O'Connor and

14 *Statistical abstract*, Dublin, 1931, p. 48.
15 Commission of Inquiry into the resources and industries of Ireland, *Report on peat*, R.10/6, Dublin, 1921; see also Purcell, *Peat resources*.
16 For further details see Ó Gráda, *Irish agriculture*.
17 The average price listed for imported coal in Department of Agriculture and Technical Instruction for Ireland, *Report on the trade in imports and exports at Irish ports*, Dublin, 1911–13, was £0.65 per ton.

Guiomard's volume estimate of 3.9 million tons is nevertheless probably conservative. Accordingly, the value of turf output used here – £3 million – is a compromise.

A separate problem concerns the agricultural labour force in Northern Ireland in the late 1930s. The figure used in Table 17.2 relates the index in K. S. Isles and N. Cuthbert to official post-war data.[18] The comparison produces an unexpected result: evaluating output in both areas at domestic prices, agricultural output per worker was slightly higher in the south in both 1912 and 1926. The result is perhaps less surprising when the smaller average farm size in the north is remembered. In 1911, 76 per cent of Ulster farms were less than 30 acres, compared with 64 per cent in the other three provinces.[19] Indeed, the gap widened between those dates, but during the subsequent decade or so the south lost most or all of its advantage.[20] But since southern food prices had been driven about 10 per cent below northern during the 1930s, it is likely that the south maintained its advantage in volume terms even then.[21] Excluding turf revises the story somewhat: the south maintains its edge up to the 1920s, but may well have lost it by the 1930s.

Although no formal calculation is attempted here, the south's advantage can hardly have stemmed from a greater endowment of physical capital. The difference in farm buildings and outhouses may have been trivial – their rateable value per worker was about £10 per male worker both north and south before the Great War – but the agricultural census of 1908 implies that northern farmers had considerably more machinery at their disposal.[22] The north's share of the all-Ireland male labour force was about 22 per cent, but the north contained 30.2 per cent of all steam or gas engines, 71.6 per cent of horse sprayers, 70.7 per cent of threshing mills, 38.5 per cent

---

18 K. S. Isles and N. Cuthbert, *An economic survey of Northern Ireland*, Belfast, 1957, p. 61.
19 See L. Kennedy, 'The rural economy 1820–1914', pp. 1–61 in L. Kennedy and P. Ollerenshaw, eds., *An economic history of Ulster 1820–1939*, Manchester, 1985, pp. 20–1.
20 In the 1920s about one-third of the gap is explained by the very low price put on potato output in Northern Ireland. Adjusting for this (see below, p. 448), output per worker in the north would have been £81.
21 See below, pp. 447–8.
22 The 1911 census of population (Table 164) provides the basis for an estimate of the value of farm buildings and outhouses by county, using Griffith's valuation. The outcome is an aggregate figure of £2.1 million for the north and £7.3 million for the south.

Table 17.2 *Irish agriculture, north and south: output and labour-input change,*
1926–82

	ΔQ/Q	ΔL/L
A. *North*		
1926–38	+29	−7.2
1938–48	+12	−7.0
1948–62	+72	−32.3
1926–62	+149	−42
B. *South*		
1926–38	+5.3	−10.5
1938–48	+1.0	−7.0
1948–62	+22	−14.5
1926–62	+30	−29

Source
Northern agricultural output is defined as gross output. In the south, R. O'Connor
and C. Guiomard's data form the basis for the 1926–38 estimate; agricultural output
between 1938 and 1962 is net output, excluding farm materials such as fertilisers,
feeding stuffs and seeds (*Statistical abstract*, Dublin, 1966, p. 89).

of cultivators and grubbers, 26.2 per cent of ploughs, 40.8 per cent of
drill ploughs, and 25.1 per cent of reapers and mowers.[23]

The trend in output per head in constant prices is also of interest.
While Table 17.2 fails to confirm the link proposed by R. D. Crotty
between the switch to peasant proprietorship and outright agricultural
stagnation, it shows how strikingly trends have diverged between north
and south since partition.[24] Between the mid 1920s and the early 1960s,
output per worker almost doubled in the north, and grew by somewhat
more than half in the south.

II The economic war

The mid 1930s marked the nadir of southern-Irish farmer welfare in
the present century. The plunge in conacre or eleven-month rents, a
sensitive indicator of farmer expectations, tells the story. Conacre rents

23 Department of Agricultural and Technical Instruction for Ireland, *The agricul-*
tural output of Ireland 1908 (in connection with the Census of production Act, 1906),
Dublin, 1912.
24 R. D. Crotty, *Irish agricultural production: its volume and structure*, Cork, 1966.

in the Limerick area fell from nearly £2 per acre in 1930–32 to just over £1 in 1934–35.[25] The world-wide downturn in agricultural prices after 1929 was blow enough, but far more serious from the farmers' standpoint was the Anglo-Irish 'Economic War' which lasted from 1932 to 1938. This dispute was sparked off by the refusal of the newly-elected Fianna Fail administration to transfer to London certain payments worth £5 million annually, payments made without demur by its predecessor. Westminster countered by recouping the money through special duties on Irish exports. The effect of this policy is captured in the agricultural-output data summarised in Table 17.3, although no attempt is made to correct for output quality differences. This table implies that the south 'lost' about £6 million or 10 per cent of output value through lower prices in 1935–36, on the assumption that northern prices would still have been available had there been no Economic War. The sum is close to the £5 million raised by the United Kingdom's Treasury in special duties.

Another feature of southern agriculture in the 1930s – the greater impact of the crisis on the livestock sector – is not fully reflected in these official output data. This is mainly due to the very low valuation put on potatoes in Northern Ireland in 1925–26: £2.7 per ton compared with £5.1 in the south.[26] Note now the substantial rise in the tillage-to-livestock price ratio between the mid 1920s and mid 1930s. Nevertheless, while the £6 million represented a direct loss to Irish farmers, the loss to Ireland was not commensurate. Holding the annuities meant that the Dublin government could enjoy both higher revenue and lower taxation. Still, the British duties entailed a deadweight efficiency loss in farming.[27] But did the anti-livestock distortion result in a further loss?

In this period the agricultural labour force was declining both north and south; could the price shift towards labour-intensive tillage have placed the south at a relative disadvantage? This argument founders on an index-number problem. But J. Johnston provided another reason in 1937 why a shift in the price of crops relative to livestock might reduce productivity.[28] This argument has its origin in

25 D. Nunan, 'Price trends for agricultural land in Ireland 1901–1986', *Irish Journal of Agricultural Economics and Rural Sociology*, XII, 1987, p. 69.
26 The values used in 1935–36 were £3.8 and £3.4 per ton.
27 J. P. Neary and C. Ó Gráda, *Protection, economic war, and structural change: Ireland in the 1930s*, University College Dublin, Centre for Economic Research, working paper XXX, 1986.
28 J. Johnston, 'Price ratios in recent Irish agricultural experience', *Economic Journal*, XLVII, 1937, pp. 680–5.

Table 17.3 *Ireland: twenty-six-county output in its own prices and six-county prices, 1926–27, 1935–36 and 1948–49 (in £ million)*

Year	(1) 26-County prices	(2) 6-County prices	Price ratio (2)/(1)
1926–27[a]			
Tillage	11.2	9.8	0.875
Livestock	46.7	50.4	1.079
Total	57.9	60.2	1.039
1926–27[b]			
Tillage	11.2	11.4	1.018
Total	57.9	61.8	1.067
1935–36			
Crops	11.6	11.2	0.966
Livestock	30.9	37.2	1.204
Total	42.6	48.4	1.137
1948–49			
Crops	33.7	31.6	0.938
Livestock	85.9	83.1	0.967
Total	119.6	114.7	0.959

Notes
[a] Potatoes valued according to 26-County prices and 6-County prices
[b] Potatoes in the 6 Counties valued at 26-County prices.

Source
Calculated from official output data, using the implicit prices where possible. Otherwise (e.g. turf, 'other vegetables'), (2) was evaluated at southern prices.

a statement by Adam Smith in *The wealth of nations* about the consequences for Scottish agriculture of union with England:

The price of butcher's meat … and consequently cattle must gradually rise till it gets so high, that it becomes as profitable to employ the most fertile and best cultivated lands in raising food for them as for raising corn … Till [the price of cattle] has got to this height, it seems scarce possible that the greater part, even of those lands which are capable of the highest cultivation, can be completely cultivated. In all farms too distant from any town to carry manure from it, that is, in the far greater part of those of every extensive country, the quantity of well-cultivated land must be in proportion to the quantity of manure which the farm itself produces; and this again must be in proportion to the quantity of cattle raised on it … The increase of stock and the improvement of land are two events which must go hand in hand ... Of all the commercial advantages ... which Scotland has derived from the union with England, this rise in the price of cattle is perhaps the greatest.[29]

If the Union benefited Scotland by increasing the viability of livestock, according to Johnston Ireland suffered after 1932 for the opposite reason. The sharp rise in the ratio of tillage to livestock prices after 1932 brought structural dislocation. Hence, in Johnston's view, 'Adam Smith's contention is abundantly illustrated'.[30] Now there is nothing automatic about this outcome, since world prices need not reflect the ratio of pasture to tillage prices required by resources and technology. However, perhaps the point is saved by noting that Ireland has long been 'by nature counted a great soil of pasture', so that any price shift towards tillage would have been injurious.[31] In other words, until 1932–33 a free market in agricultural produce generated something closer to the near-constant ratio of grain to livestock prices required by technology. Thereafter, however, politics drove the ratio out of kilter, making Johnston conclude with the rather apocalyptic prediction of 'a gradual but increasingly rapid decline of our national agriculture'.[32]

E. Hoffman and J. Mokyr have also applied this argument to Irish agriculture.[33] Their study refers to the pre-Famine period, an era of draught animals and natural fertilisers, where the trade-off is most plausible. Even in the 1930s, when tractors were still few and artificial fertilisers less relied on, this characterisation carries some conviction. The argument is set out diagrammatically in Figure 17.2. In the short run the trade-off between livestock and grain outputs might be generous as with DD in Figure 17.2, but not so in the long run. Suppose the long-run trade-off is EE: in that case the shift from G induced by a corresponding shift in relative prices might be to H in the short run, but to J (inside the original production-possibility frontier) in the long run. The latter, while a plausible representation of what both Smith

29 A. Smith, *An inquiry into the nature and causes of the wealth of nations*, ed. R. Campbell and A. Skinner, 2 vols., Oxford, 1976, I, pp. 238–40.
30 Johnston, 'Price ratios', p. 685.
31 E. Spencer, *A view of the present state of Ireland in 1596*, ed. W. L. Renwick, Oxford, 1986, p. 158.
32 Johnston, 'Price ratios', p. 685. See also *idem, The nemesis of economic nationalism*, Dublin, 1934; *idem, Irish agriculture in transition*, Dublin, 1951.
33 E. Hoffmann and J. Mokyr, 'Peasants, potatoes and poverty: transactions costs in pre-Famine Ireland', pp. 115–45 in G. Saxonhouse and G. Wright, eds., *Technique, spirit and form in the making of modern economies: essays in honour of W. N. Parker*, Greenwich, Ct., 1984, pp. 120 and 124–5.

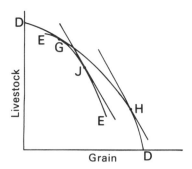

Figure 17.2 *The long- and short-run trade-off between tillage and pasture sectors*

and Johnston seem to mean, implies a high degree of myopia on the part of government, if not of farmers. No formal attempt to test this model will be made here. Note, however, that while the model may help explain the problems of the mid 1930s, it does not account for the subsequent poor performance of southern agriculture.

III The record since 1960

Research on this period, particularly on the years since accession to the European Economic Community, has been plentiful, but the verdict on north–south performance keeps changing. In their assessment of the 1970s, S. Sheehy, J. T. O'Brien and S. D. McClelland concluded that the 'poor performance of northern agriculture in the EEC has been a great disappointment', and 'the disparity in performance in favour of the south has been particularly striking'.[34] The output figures seem to support this: net output in Northern Ireland declined during the 1970s, while in the Irish Republic net output grew by twelve per cent between 1970 and 1979 (both average years). However, just two years later E. A. Attwood and M. O'Sullivan flatly denied this, claiming that 'northern agriculture has performed strikingly better than that of the south'.[35] Nor does it end there. T. F. Stainer shows that net product per hectare was higher in the north in 1973, but higher in the

34 Sheehy, O'Brien and McClelland, *Agriculture*, pp. 64–5.
35 Attwood and O'Sullivan, 'Aspects of agricultural development', pp. 137–8. Seamus Sheehy has pointed out to me that the difference is largely explained by a revision in the Northern Ireland statistics in 1978 and the extraordinary performance of northern agriculture in 1979–82. Compare Attwood and O'Sullivan, Table 6, with Sheehy, O'Brien and McClelland, *Agriculture*, Figure 2.2.

Table 17.4 *Irish agriculture north and south: output per worker, 1969–71 and 1984–86*

	North		South	
	1969–71	*1984–86*	*1969–71*	*1984–86*
1. Net output (Ir £)	65.3	216.2	202.8	1,177.4
2. Labour force (000s)	37.0	26.8	275.6	73.0
3. 1/2 (Ir £)	1,765	8,067	736	6,786

Note
The subsidy element in 'net income arising from agriculture' has been removed from the southern figures. In both cases, estimates of the full-time male labour force only have been used. The 1984–86 Northern Ireland estimate has been converted to Ir £.

Source
Statistical abstract, Dublin; *Ninth report of the agricultural statistics of Northern Ireland 1966/7 to 1973/4,* Belfast, 1977; *46th annual general report of the Department of Agriculture in the year ended 31 March 1987,* Belfast, 1987.

south in each year since then. By this criterion, southern has been much better than northern performance since 1973. Certainly, comparing labour productivity in 1969–71, on the eve of accession to the EEC, and 1984–86 suggests an improvement in southern performance (see Table 17.4).[36]

In theory, since both Irelands were subject to the Common Agricultural Policy, farmers should have faced a common price regime. In practice, the southern government was much more willing (at least before membership of the European Monetary System in 1979) than the northern to avail of Green Pound devaluations, while northern farmers benefited from the Meat Industry Employment Scheme (1975–80) and from Milk Aid.[37] Yet the reasons given for the south's better performance during the 1970s generally emphasise other factors: the less wasteful use of machinery in the south in the 1970s, a delayed

36 The change is highlighted in T. Ferris, 'Changing productivity and living standards: 1971–1986', *Irish Banking Review,* 1989, pp. 32–9. However, Ferris's conclusion that southern output per worker in the 1980s exceeded northern rests on an inflated estimate of the northern agricultural labour force. Compare also Cuddy and O'Doherty, *Agricultural developments.*
37 D. A. G. Norton, *Ireland, the Common Agricultural Policy, trade distortion and induced smuggling activity,* Dublin, 1983; T. F. Stainer, 'Recent developments in agriculture in Northern Ireland', unpublished paper presented to the Agricultural Economics Society of Ireland, October 1987, p. 19.

return in the 1980s on earlier machinery investment, or the south's more favourable output mix.[38]

Finally, consider plain 'efficiency'. So far, comparisons have been in terms of land and labour productivity. A comparison of total factor productivity growth is a preliminary to sorting out the various arguments. G. E. Boyle's productivity-growth calculations for the south since the 1960s show healthy growth (over 1 per cent) up to the late 1970s, and stagnation since then.[39] But so far there have been no measures of total factor productivity performance for the north, although an official series is contemplated.[40] This chapter eschews sophisticated measurements, suggesting instead two indirect but simple ways of evaluating performance north and south in the last few decades.[41] Poor or noncomparable data are a problem: the north's net-product series has already been noted. One standard means of comparing productivity is to estimate for the areas being analysed:

$$A^j = -p^j + a_i^j w_i^j \tag{1}$$

Here A^j is productivity change in country j, p is the proportionate change in an index of output prices, w_i the proportionate change in input price i, and a_i the factor share of i. Provided production technology is similar in the areas compared, some data requirements may be finessed and tentative results offered of productivity changes since the 1950s using two alternative approaches.

The first draws upon evidence of trends in land prices north and south, since, unlike labour and fertilisers, land is immobile. Granted that northern and southern output were similar, and factor markets reasonably competitive, then most of any relative productivity gain in one area should accrue to the fixed factor, and that should be reflected in its price.[42] In other words, if farmers remain in business, and yet can

38 Furness and Stainer, 'Economic performance'; Attwood and O'Sullivan, 'Aspects of agricultural development'; J. M. Whittaker and J. E. Spencer, *The Northern Ireland agricultural industry: its past development and medium-term prospects*, London, 1986.
39 G. E. Boyle, 'Essays on the measurement of technological efficiency in Irish agriculture', unpublished National University of Ireland Ph.D. thesis, 1986; *idem*, 'Measurement of the total factor productivity of Irish agriculture 1960–1987', *Irish Journal of Agricultural Economics and Rural Sociology*, XII, 1987, pp. 29–49.
40 Stainer, 'Recent developments'.
41 For example, Boyle, 'Essays'.
42 Compare D. N. McCloskey, 'The enclosure of the open fields: preface to a study of its impact on the efficiency of English agriculture in the eighteenth century', *JEH*, XXXII, 1972, pp. 15–35.

afford to pay progressively higher prices in one area relative to another, the most plausible reason must be their greater efficiency.[43]

The difference in productivity performance may be gauged by calculating $A^{North} - A^{South}$. Under a common price regime this would be approximated by $b(r^{North} - r^{South})$, where r is the rate of change in the return on land, and b rent's share of output. Unfortunately, the data here are not good. Rental data in time series are not available for the north, and although land *price* data are available, it is possible that they reflect anticipated more than past performance. Fortunately, the record in the south suggests that this is not such a problem. D. Nunan's analysis of the land market in the Limerick region since 1900 shows that except for 1957–70, movements in the price of land mirrored closely those in rents.[44] On this justification land prices are here used as a proxy for rent movements, although even these are subject to qualification. Thus, Northern Ireland boasts an official series stretching back to 1959 whereas the available southern data are unofficial, and quite patchy before the late 1970s.[45] It is therefore necessary to make do with what there is. P. W. Kelly provides a good series based on valuation-office data from 1978.[46] For earlier years a simple average of Nunan's Limerick series, the Irish Land Commission series, and Kelly's pre-1978 data have been relied upon.[47] All three series follow the same broad trends, but are subject to substantial year-to-year fluctuations. Since the Irish Land Commission generally paid a lower price for land, all were indexed at 100 in 1970. Official agricultural price indices are used, with one correction: in 1978–80 the Meat Industry Employment Scheme paid farmers about 21.5 per cent of the Northern Ireland cattle reference price, effectively adding almost 10 per cent to northern prices.[48]

Here it is assumed that rent's share of output (b) is 0.1 – 0.3. The implied rates of productivity change (A^j) are given below. Note,

43 In the short run, differences in expectations or credit availability could muddy the picture.
44 Nunan, 'Price trends', pp. 55–7.
45 Nunan, 'Price trends'; P. W. Kelly, 'Price of land in the Republic of Ireland 1978–1981', *Agricultural Institute Situation and Outlook, Bulletin*, V, 1983. Kelly's 1983 series is brought forward to 1986 in An Foras Taluntais, 'The land market in 1986', Information Update Series, XXVI, Dublin, 1986.
46 Kelly, 'Price of land'.
47 The Irish Land Commission series is reported by Nunan, 'Price trends', and Kelly, 'Price of land'.
48 Norton, *Ireland*, p. 157.

Table 17.5 *Irish agriculture north and south: output and land prices,*
1960s to 1980s (percentage change per annum)

	South	North
A. *1959–61 to 1983–85*		
Land prices	15.8	12.4
Output prices	8.8	6.9
B. *1969–71 to 1983–85*		
Land prices	18.5	15.0
Output prices	12.7	11.3
C. *1969–71 to 1978–80*		
Land prices	29.5	24.6
Output prices	16.4	16.5

Source
Southern land prices from D. Nunan, 'Price trends for agricultural land in Ireland
1901–1986', *Irish Journal of Agricultural Economics and Rural Sociology*, XII, 1987,
pp. 51–77; P. W. Kelly, 'Price of land in the Republic of Ireland 1978–1981',
Agricultural Institute Situation and Outlook, Bulletin, V, 1983. Kelly's valuation-derived
data are used from 1978. The Northern Ireland data sources for land values are
given in J. M. Whittaker and J. E. Spencer, *The Northern Ireland agricultural industry:*
its past development and medium-term prospects, London, 1986. The output prices are
taken from Nunan, 'Price trends' and official Northern Ireland sources. The
1978–80 northern output price was adjusted upwards by the average Meat Industry
Employment Scheme premium in those years (21.5 per cent), weighted by the share
of cattle and pigs in the agricultural price index (0.457).

however, that simply comparing land price movements amounts to
assuming the same movement in output prices north and south (see
Table 17.5), whereas policy toward Green Pound devaluations in the
two Irelands differed. Moreover, output mix may have influenced
output-price movements differently north and south. In order to correct for the possibility that the movement in land prices was merely a
reaction to different output price movements, and not different productivity movement, it is necessary to deflate the index of land prices
by an index of output prices north and south, as in Equation 2:

$$A^N - A^S = b(r_n - r_s) - (p_n - p_s) \tag{2}$$

The result of so doing is given in Table 17.6. This shows that both over
1960–85 and 1969–71 to 1983–85, productivity growth was greater in
the north. However, the gap was quite narrow, and during the 1970s
the south performed better by this measure.

Table 17.6 *Irish agriculture north and south: the gap in productivity growth as implied by land-price movements, 1960s to 1980s*

	Rental share of output (b)		
	b = 0.1	*b = 0.2*	*b = 0.3*
1959–61 to 1983–85	1.6	1.2	0.9
1969–71 to 1983–85	1.1	0.7	0.4
1969–71 to 1978–80	0.6	0.1	−0.4

Source See text.

An alternative approach would be to focus on the change over time in an index of real net output (i.e. after subtracting for transport, fertiliser, machinery, and other intermediate inputs) relative to that in the farm labour force. More precisely:

$$R = Q_i - g \cdot L_i \qquad (3)$$

where Q is the proportionate net-output change at constant prices, L the change in labour input, and g a factor weight. Netting-out measurable inputs leaves something loosely comparable to the 'residual' in standard calculations. The results are given in Table 17.7 and confirm the earlier story of faster productivity gains in the south.

Table 17.7 *Irish agriculture north and south: annual growth rate of real net output, 1956–58 to 1984–86 (per cent)*

Period	South		North	
	g = 0.4	*g = 0.6*	*g = 0.3*	*g = 0.6*
1956–58 to 1984–86	3.2	3.8		
1956–58 to 1964–66	2.4	2.6		
1964–66 to 1984–86	2.8	3.1	6.4	7.0
1970–72 to 1978–80	3.1	3.8	3.9	4.4
1978–80 to 1984–86	4.4	5.1	6.1	6.5

Note
g = a factor weight.

Source See text.

IV Conclusion

It is commonplace to point out that differences in definitions and data-gathering procedures make growth-rate comparisons more reliable than those of levels taken at a given date. In the present context, this applies more perhaps to recent data than to that of 1912. Nevertheless, bearing data limitations in mind, the message relayed by comparing rates and levels is broadly consistent. This chapter began by showing that, contrary to expectation, output per worker in southern Irish agriculture was higher than in northern at the beginning of the century. The north took the lead during the ensuing protectionist decades of the 1930s to the 1950s, but since then productivity has once more grown faster in the south. By 1985, both net product per hectare and net product per worker were higher in the south than in the north, but the latter still possibly had the edge in terms of total factor productivity.[49]

49 Stainer, 'Recent developments', Figure 8.

Bibliography

A Official publications

Agricultural labourers: return of the average rate of weekly earnings of agricultural labourers in the unions of England and Wales, BPP, L, HC.14, London, 1861.
Agricultural statistics of Ireland for the year 1891, BPP, LXXXVIII, C.6777, London, 1892.
Agricultural statistics of Ireland, with detailed report for the year 1901, BPP, CXVI, Cd.1170, London, 1902.
Agricultural statistics, Ireland, 1907–8, return of prices of crops, livestock and other Irish agricultural products, BPP, CXXI, Cd.4437, London, 1908.
Agricultural statistics, Ireland, 1915, return of prices of crops, livestock and other Irish agricultural products, BPP, XXXVI, Cd.8452, London, 1917.
BPP, Accounts and papers, London, 1909–14.
Census of agricultural production 1925, BPP, XXV, Cmd.2815, London, 1927.
Census of Great Britain, 1851. Population tables II, BPP, LXXXVIII, 1st series 1691, London, 1852–53.
Commission of Inquiry into the Resources and Industries of Ireland, *Report on peat*, R.10/6, Dublin, 1921.
Cowper Commission, *Report of the Royal Commission on Land Law (Ireland) Act 1885*, BPP, C.4969, XXVI, London, 1887.
Department of Agricultural and Technical Instruction for Ireland, *The agricultural output of Ireland 1908 (in connection with the Census of Production Act, 1906)*, Dublin, 1912.
Department of Agriculture and Technical Instruction for Ireland, *Report on the trade in imports and exports at Irish ports*, Dublin, 1911–13.
First report from Commissioners for inquiring into the condition of the poorer classes in Ireland, BPP, XXXII, HC.369, London, 1836.
Forty-sixth annual general report of the Department of Agriculture in the year ended 31 March 1987, Belfast, 1987.
ISTAT, *Sommario di statistiche storiche*, Rome, 1958.
Ministry of Agriculture and Fisheries and Food, *A century of agricultural statistics*, London, 1968.
Ministry of Agriculture and Fisheries and Food, *Fertiliser recommendations*, London, 1973.
Ninth report of the agricultural statistics of Northern Ireland 1966/7 to 1973/4, Belfast, 1977.
Report of the Commissioners appointed to take the Census of Ireland for the year 1841, BPP, XXIV, HC.504, London, 1843.
Reports by the poor law inspectors on agricultural statistics (England), BPP, LIII, 1st series 1928, London, 1854–5.
Returns relating to live stock in the United Kingdom, BPP, LX, 1st series 3655, London, 1866.
Returns relating to the acreage of crops in the United Kingdom, BPP, LX, 1st series, 3727, London, 1866.
Smith, E., *Food of the lowest fed classes, appendix VI, conditions of nourishment*, pp. 216–329 in *Sixth report of the medical officer of the Privy Council*, BPP, XXVIII, 1st series 3416, London, 1864.
Statistical abstract, Dublin, 1931.
Statistical abstract, Dublin, 1966

B Other works

Abel, W., *Agricultural fluctuations in Europe from the thirteenth to the twentieth centuries*, trans. O. Ordish, London, 1980.

Alexander, M., *Introduction to soil microbiology*, New York, 1961.
Allen, D., 'Excavations in Bierton, 1979. A late iron age "belgic" settlement and evidence for a Roman villa and a twelfth- to eighteenth-century manorial complex', *Records of Buckinghamshire*, XXVIII, 1986, pp. 1–120.
Allen, R. C., 'The efficiency and distributional consequences of eighteenth-century enclosures', *Economic Journal*, LXLII, 1982, pp. 937–53.
Allen, R. C., *The 'capital intensive farmer' and the English agricultural revolution: a reassessment*, Discussion Paper 87–11, Department of Economics, University of British Columbia, 1987.
Allen, R. C., 'Inferring yields from probate inventories', *JEH*, XLVIII, 1988, pp. 117–25.
Allen, R. C., 'The growth of labour productivity in early modern English agriculture', *Explorations in Economic History*, XXV, 1988, pp. 117–46.
Allen, R. C. and Ó Gráda, C., 'On the road again with Arthur Young: English, Irish, and French agriculture during the industrial revolution', *JEH*, XLVIII, 1988, pp. 93–116.
Allen, R. C., 'Enclosure, farming methods, and the growth of productivity in the south midlands', pp. 69–88 in Grantham, G. and Leonard, C., eds., *Agrarian organization in the century of industrialization: Europe, Russia, and North America*, Research in Economic History, Supplement V, Greenwich, Ct. and London, 1989.
Allison, K. J., 'The sheep–corn husbandry of Norfolk in the sixteenth and seventeenth centuries', *AHR*, V, 1957, pp. 12–30.
An Foras Taluntais, 'The land market in 1986', *Information Update Series*, XXVI, Dublin, 1986.
Anderson, J., *General view of the agriculture of Aberdeenshire*, Edinburgh, 1794.
Anonymous, 'On the agricultural state of Ireland', *Quarterly Journal of Agriculture*, II, 1831, pp. 733–82.
Applebaum, S., 'The agriculture of the British early iron age, as exemplified at Figheldean Down, Wiltshire', *Proceedings of the Prehistoric Society*, XX, 1954, pp. 103–14.
Applebaum, S., 'Roman Britain', pp. 3–277 in Finberg, *The agrarian history of England and Wales*, Iii, AD *43–1042*, 1972.
Armitage, P. L., 'A preliminary description of British cattle from the late twelfth to the early sixteenth century', *Ark*, VII, 1980, pp. 405–13.
Ashbee, P., Smith, I. F. and Evans, S. G., 'Excavations of three long barrows near Avebury', *Proceedings of the Prehistoric Society*, XLV, 1979, pp. 207–300.
Aston, T. H. and Philpin, C. H. E., eds., *The Brenner debate: agrarian class structure and economic development in pre-industrial Europe*, Cambridge, 1985.
Atack, J. and Bateman, F., 'Mid-nineteenth-century crop yields and labour productivity growth in American agriculture: a new look at Parker and Klein', pp. 215–42 in Saxonhouse, G. and Wright, G., eds., *Technique, spirit, and form in the making of the modern economies. Essays in honour of William N. Parker*, Research in Economic History, Supplement III, Greenwich, Ct., 1984.
Attwood, E. A., 'Agricultural developments in Ireland, north and south', *Journal of the Statistical and Social Inquiry Society of Ireland*, XXI, 1966, pp. 9–34.
Attwood, E. A. and O'Sullivan, M., 'Some aspects of agricultural development in Ireland north and south since accession to the EEC', *Proceedings of the Agricultural Economics Society of Ireland*, 1983–84, pp. 137–72.
Bailey, M., *A marginal economy? East Anglian Breckland in the later middle ages*, Cambridge, 1989.
Bailey, M., 'Sand into gold: the evolution of the foldcourse system in west Suffolk, 1200–1600', *AHR*, XXXVIII, 1990, pp. 40–57.
Bairoch, P., 'Agriculture and the industrial revolution, 1700-1914', pp. 452–506 in

Cipolla, C. M., ed., *The Fontana economic history of Europe*, III, *The industrial revolution*, London, 1973.

Bairoch, P., 'Niveau de développement économique de 1810 à 1910', *Annales, Économies, Sociétés, Civilisations*, XX, 1965, pp. 1091–6.

Bairoch, P., *De Jéricho à Mexico. Villes et économie dans l'histoire*, Paris, 1985.

Bairoch, P., *Cities and economic development: from the dawn of history to the present*, trans. C. Braider, Chicago, 1988.

Bairoch, P., 'Les trois révolutions agricoles du monde développé: rendements et productivité de 1800 à 1985', *Annales, Économies, Sociétés, Civilisations*, XLIV, 1989, pp. 317–53.

Baker, A. R. H., 'Evidence in the *Nonarum Inquisitiones* of contracting arable lands in England during the early fourteenth century', *EcHR*, XIX, 1966, pp. 518–32, reprinted as pp. 85–102 in *idem*, Hamshere, J. D. and Langton, J., eds., *Geographical interpretations of historical sources: readings in historical geography*, Newton Abbot, 1970.

Baker, A. R. H. and Butlin, R. A., eds., *Studies of field systems in the British Isles*, Cambridge, 1973.

Baker, T. H., *Records of the seasons, prices of agricultural produce and phenomena observed in the British Isles*, London, 1883.

Banks, F. J., 'Monastic agriculture: a farmer's view, with special reference to Byland Abbey', *Ryedale Historian*, XV, 1990–91, pp. 16–20.

Barker, G., *Prehistoric farming in Europe*, Cambridge, 1985.

Barrington, R. M., 'The prices of some agricultural produce and the cost of farm labour for the last fifty years', *Journal of the Statistical and Social Inquiry Society of Ireland*, IX, 1887, pp. 137–53.

Barrington, T., 'Review of Irish agricultural prices', *Journal of the Statistical and Social Inquiry Society of Ireland*, XV, 1927, pp. 249–80.

Batchelor, T., *General view of the agriculture of the county of Bedfordshire*, London, 1808.

Bayldon, J. S., *The art of valuing rents and tillages*, London, 1827.

Bayliss-Smith, T., *The ecology of agricultural systems*, Cambridge, 1982.

Beckett, J. V., *The agricultural revolution*, Oxford, 1990.

Bedford Franklin, T., *British grasslands from the earliest times to the present day*, London, 1953.

Behre, K. E., *Anthropogenic indicators in pollen diagrams*, Rotterdam, 1986.

Belgium, Ministère de l'Intérieur, *Agriculture. Recensement général. 15 Octobre 1846*, Brussels, 1850.

Belgium, Ministère de l'Intérieur, 'Rapports au Ministère de l'Intérieur sur la situation des subsistances', *Bulletin de la Commission Centrale de Statistique*, III, 1847, pp. 107–22, and IV, 1851, pp. 175–81.

Bell, J. and Watson, M., *Irish farming 1750–1900*, Edinburgh, 1986.

Bell, M., 'Valley sediments and environmental change', pp. 75–91 in Jones and Dimbleby, *The environment of man*, 1981.

Bell, M., 'Pedogenesis during the later prehistoric period in Britain', pp. 114–26 in Harding, A. F., ed., *Climatic change in later prehistory*, Edinburgh, 1982.

Bellerby, J. R., 'Distribution of farm income in the United Kingdom 1867–1938', *Journal of Proceedings of Agricultural Economics Society*, X, 1953, reprinted as pp. 259–80 in Minchinton, W. E., ed., *Essays in agrarian history*, II, Newton Abbot, 1968.

Bennett, H. S., *Life on the English manor: a study of peasant conditions 1150–1400*, Cambridge, 1937.

Bennett, J., 'Examination of turret 10A and the wall and *vallum* at Throckley, Tyne and Wear, 1980', *Archaeologia Aeliana*, 5th series, XI, 1983, pp. 61–78.

Bennett, M. K., 'British wheat yield per acre for seven centuries', *Economic History* (a supplement of *The Economic Journal*), III, 1935, pp. 12–29, reprinted as pp. 54–72 in Minchinton, W. E., ed., *Essays in agrarian history*, I, Newton Abbot, 1968.

Beresford, M., 'Habitation versus improvement: the debate on enclosure and agreement', pp. 40–69 in Fisher, F. J., ed., *Essays in the economic and social history of Tudor and Stuart England in honour of R. H. Tawney*, Cambridge, 1961.

Berry, R. A. and Cline, W. R., *Agrarian structure and productivity in developing countries*, Baltimore, 1979.

Bersu, G., 'Excavations at Little Woodbury, Wiltshire. Part 1: the settlement as revealed by excavation', *Proceedings of the Prehistoric Society*, VI, 1940, pp. 30–111.

Beveridge, W., 'The yield and price of corn in the middle ages', *Economic History* (a supplement of *The Economic Journal*), I, 1927, pp. 155–67.

Beveridge, W., 'The Winchester rolls and their dating', *Economic History Review*, II, 1929, pp. 93–114.

Beveridge, W., *Prices and wages in England from the twelfth to the nineteenth century*, I, London, 1939.

Beynon, V. H. and Houston, A. M., *Productivity, the concept, its measurement and a literature review*, National Economic Development Office, 1969.

Bharadwaj, K., *Production conditions in Indian agriculture*, Cambridge, 1974.

Biddick, K., 'Pig husbandry on the Peterborough-Abbey estate from the twelfth to the fourteenth century AD', pp. 161–77 in Clutton-Brock, J., and Grigson, C., eds., *Animals and archaeology*, BAR, supplementary series, CCXXVII, Oxford, 1985.

Biddick, K., *The other economy: pastoral husbandry on a medieval estate*, Berkeley and Los Angeles, 1989.

Biddick, K., 'People and things: power in early English development', *Comparative Studies in Society and History*, XXXII, 1990, pp. 3–23.

Biddle, M., ed., *Winchester in the early middle ages*, Oxford, 1976.

Bishop, T. A. M., 'The rotation of crops at Westerham, 1297–1350', *Economic History Review*, IX, 1938, pp. 38–44.

Black, R. D. C., *Economic thought and the Irish question, 1817–1870*, Cambridge, 1960.

Blacker, W., *An essay on the improvements to be made in the cultivation of small farms, by the introduction of green crops and housefeeding the stock thereon ...*, Dublin, 1834.

Bliss, C. J. and Stern, N. H., *Palanpur: the economy of an Indian village*, Oxford, 1982.

Blith, W., *The English improver improved*, London, 1652.

Bogue, A. G., 'Changes in mechanical and plant technology: the corn belt, 1910–1940', *JEH*, XLIII, 1983, pp. 1–27.

Bökönyi, S., 'The development of stockbreeding and herding in medieval Europe' in Sweeney, D., ed., *People of the plough: land and labour in medieval Europe*, State College, Pa., forthcoming.

Boon, G. C., *Silchester: the Roman town of Calleva*, Newton Abbot, 1974.

Booth, A. and Sundrum, R. M., *Labour absorption in agriculture*, Oxford, 1985.

Boserup, E., *The conditions of agricultural growth: the economics of agrarian change under population pressure*, London, 1965.

Boserup, E., *Population and technology*, Oxford, 1981.

Bourde, A. J., *Agronomie et agronomes au XVIIIᵉ siècle*, 3 vols., Paris, 1967.

Bourke, P. M. A., 'The extent of the potato crop in Ireland at the time of the Famine', *Journal of the Statistical and Social Inquiry Society of Ireland*, XX, III, 1959, pp. 1–35.

Bourke, P. M. A., 'The agricultural statistics of the 1841 Census of Ireland. A critical review', *EcHR*, XVIII, 1965, pp. 382–91.

Bowden, P. J., 'Agricultural prices, farm profits, and rents', pp. 593–685 in Thirsk, *The agrarian history of England and Wales*, IV, *1500–1640*, 1967.

Bowden, P. J., 'Statistical appendix', pp. 814–70 in Thirsk, *The agrarian history of England and Wales*, IV, *1500–1640*, 1967.

Bowden, P. J., 'Agricultural prices, wages, farm profits and rents', pp. 593–695 in Thirsk, *The agrarian history of England and Wales*, Vii, *1640–1750: agrarian change*, 1985.

Bowden, P. J., 'Statistical appendix', pp. 827–902 in Thirsk, *The agrarian history of England and Wales*, Vii, *1640–1750: agrarian change*, 1985.

Bowen, H. C. and Fowler, P. J., eds., *Early land allotment in the British Isles: a survey of recent work*, BAR, British series, XLVIII, Oxford, 1978.

Boyle, G. E., 'Essays on the measurement of technological efficiency in Irish agriculture', unpublished National University of Ireland Ph.D. thesis, 1986.

Boyle, G. E., 'Measurement of the total factor productivity of Irish agriculture 1960–1987', *Irish Journal of Agricultural Economics and Rural Sociology*, XII, 1987, pp. 29–49.

Bradley, R., *The prehistoric settlement of Britain*, London, 1978.

Brandon, P. F., 'Demesne arable farming in coastal Sussex during the later middle ages', *AHR*, XIX, 1971, pp. 113–34.

Brandon, P. F., 'Cereal yields on the Sussex estates of Battle Abbey during the later middle ages', *EcHR*, XXV, 1972, pp. 403–20.

Brandon, P. F., 'Farming techniques. South-eastern England', pp. 312–24 in Hallam, *The agrarian history of England and Wales, II, 1042–1350*, 1988.

Branigan, K., *Gatcombe*, Oxford, 1977.

Brassley, P., *The agricultural economy of Northumberland and Durham in the period 1640–1750*, New York, 1985.

Brassley, P., Lambert, A. and Saunders, P., eds., *Accounts of the Reverend John Crakanthorp of Fowlmere 1682–1710*, Cambridgeshire Records Society, VIII, Cambridge, 1988.

Breeze, D., 'Plough-marks at Carraburgh on Hadrian's Wall', *Tools and Tillage*, II, 1974, pp. 188–90.

Brenner, R., 'Agrarian class structure and economic development in pre-industrial Europe', *Past and Present*, LXX, 1976, pp. 30–75, reprinted as pp. 10–63 in Aston and Philpin, *The Brenner debate*, 1985.

Brenner, R., 'The agrarian roots of European capitalism', *Past and Present*, XCVII, 1982, pp. 16–113, reprinted as pp. 213–327 in Aston and Philpin, *The Brenner debate*, 1985.

Bridbury, A. R., *Economic growth: England in the later middle ages*, London, 1962.

Britnell, R. H., 'The proliferation of markets in England, 1200–1349', *EcHR*, XXXIV, 1981, pp. 209–21.

Broad, J., 'Alternate husbandry and permanent pasture in the midlands 1650–1800', *AHR*, XXVIII, 1980, pp. 77–89.

Brothwell, D., 'Palaeodemography and earlier British populations', *World Archaeology*, IV, 1972, pp. 75–87.

Burn, J. S., *Ecclesiastical law*, London, 3rd edn., 1775.

Caird, J., *English agriculture, 1850–1*, London, 1853.

Campbell, B. M. S., 'The extent and layout of commonfields in eastern Norfolk', *Norfolk Archaeology*, XXXVIII, 1981, pp. 5–32.

Campbell, B. M. S., 'The regional uniqueness of English field systems? Some evidence from eastern Norfolk', *AHR*, XXIX, 1981, pp. 16–28.

Campbell, B. M. S., 'Agricultural progress in medieval England: some evidence from eastern Norfolk', *EcHR*, XXXVI, 1983, pp. 26–46.

Campbell, B. M. S., 'Arable productivity in medieval England: some evidence from Norfolk', *JEH*, XLIII, 1983, pp. 379–404.

Campbell, B. M. S., 'The complexity of manorial structure in medieval Norfolk: a case study', *Norfolk Archaeology*, XXXIX, 1986, pp. 225–61.

Campbell, B. M. S., 'Arable productivity in medieval English agriculture', unpublished paper presented to the UC – Caltech conference, 'Pre-industrial developments in peasant economies: the transition to economic growth', 1987.

Campbell, B. M. S., 'The diffusion of vetches in medieval England', *EcHR*, XLI, 1988, pp. 193–208.

Campbell, B. M. S., 'Towards an agricultural geography of medieval England', *AHR*, XXXVI, 1988, pp. 24–39.

Campbell, B. M. S., 'Ecology versus economics in late thirteenth- and early fourteenth-century English agriculture', in D. Sweeney, ed., *People of the plough: land and labour in medieval Europe*, State College, Pa., forthcoming.

Campbell, B. M. S., 'People and land in the middle ages, 1066–1500', pp. 69–121 in Dodgshon, R. A. and Butlin, R. A., eds., *An historical geography of England and Wales*, London, 2nd edn., 1990.

Campbell, B. M. S. and Power, J. P., 'Mapping the agricultural geography of medieval England', *Journal of Historical Geography*, XV, 1989, pp. 24–39.

Cannadine, D., 'British history: past, present – and future?', *Past and Present*, CXVI, 1987, pp. 169–91.

Capstick, M., *The economics of agriculture*, London, 1970.

Cattaneo, C., 'Dell'agricoltura inglese paragonata alla nostra', pp. 269–300 in *idem, Memorie di economia pubblica dal 1833 al 1860*, I, Milan, 1860.

Chambers, J. D. and Mingay, G. E., *The agricultural revolution 1750–1880*, London, 1966.

Chambers, J. D., *Population, economy and society in pre-industrial England*, Oxford, 1972.

Chapman, J. C., 'The "Secondary Products Revolution" and the limitations of the neolithic', *Bulletin of the Institute of Archaeology, University of London*, XIX, 1982, pp. 107–22.

Chapman, J. C. and Mytum, H. C., eds., *Settlement in north Britain 1000 BC–AD 1000: papers presented to George Jobey, Newcastle upon Tyne, December, 1982*, BAR, British series, CXVIII, Oxford, 1983.

Chartres, J. C., 'The marketing of agricultural produce', pp. 406–502 in Thirsk, *The agrarian history of England and Wales*, Vii, *1640–1750: agrarian change*, 1985.

Cherry, J. F., Gamble, C. and Shennan, S., *Sampling in contemporary British archaeology*, BAR, British series, L, Oxford, 1978.

Childe, V. G., *New light on the most ancient Near East: the oriental prelude to European prehistory*, London, 1934.

Chisholm, M., *Rural settlement and land-use: an essay on location*, London, 1962.

Chorley, G. P. H., 'The agricultural revolution in northern Europe, 1750–1880: nitrogen, legumes and crop productivity', *EcHR*, XXXIV, 1981, pp. 71–93.

Cipolla, C., *Before the industrial revolution*, New York, 1976.

Clark, C., *National income and outlay*, London, 1937.

Clark, G., 'Productivity growth without technical change in European agriculture before 1850', *JEH*, XLVII, 1987, pp. 419–32.

Clark, G., 'Productivity growth without technical change in European agriculture: reply to Komlos', *JEH*, XLIX, 1989, pp. 979–91.

Clark, G., 'Yields per acre in English agriculture 1266–1860: evidence from labour inputs', *EcHR*, XLIV, 1991.

Clay, C., *Economic expansion and social change: England 1500–1700*, Cambridge, 1984.

Cole, S., *The neolithic revolution*, London, 1970.

Coles, W., *Adam in Eden, or nature's paradise*, London, 1657.

Collins, E. J. T., 'The age of machinery', pp. 200–13 in G. E. Mingay, ed., *The Victorian countryside*, I, 1981.

Cook, E., *Man, energy and society*, San Francisco, 1976.

Cooke, G., *The control of soil fertility*, London, 1967.

Cooter, W. S., 'Ecological dimensions of medieval agrarian systems', *Agricultural History*, CII, 1978, pp. 458–77.

Cooper, J. P., 'In search of agrarian capitalism', pp. 138–91 in Aston and Philpin, *The Brenner debate*, 1985.

Coppock, J. T., *An agricultural atlas of England and Wales*, London, 1964.

Coppock, J. T., *An agricultural geography of Great Britain*, London, 1971.

Coppock, J. T., 'Mapping the agricultural returns: a neglected tool of historical geography', pp. 8–55 in Reed, M., ed., *Discovering past landscapes*, London, 1984.

Copus, A. K., 'Changing markets and the development of sheep breeds in southern England, 1750–1900', *AHR*, XXXVII, 1989, pp. 36–51.

Cottrell, F., *Energy and society*, New York, 1955.

Courti, M. A., Golberg, P. and Macphail, R., *Soils and micromorphology in archaeology*, Cambridge, 1990.

Cousens, S. H., 'Emigration and demographic change in Ireland', *EcHR*, XIV, 1961, pp. 275–88.

Crafts, N. F. R., 'Income elasticities of demand and the release of labour by agriculture during the British industrial revolution, *Journal of European Economic History*, IX, 1980, pp. 153–68.

Crafts, N. F. R., 'British economic growth 1700–1831: a review of the evidence', *EcHR*, XXXVI, 1983, pp. 177–99.

Crafts, N. F. R., *British economic growth during the industrial revolution*, Oxford, 1985.

Crafts, N. F. R., *British industrialization in an international context*, University of Leeds, School of Economic Studies, Discussion Paper Series A:87/7, 1987.

Crafts, N. F. R., 'British industrialization in its international context', *Journal of Interdisciplinary History*, XXIX, 1989, pp. 415–28.

Crafts, N. F. R., 'The new economic history and the industrial revolution', pp. 25–43 in Mathias P. and Davis, J. K., eds., *The first industrial revolutions*, Oxford, 1990.

Craigie, P. G., 'Statistics of agricultural production', *Journal of the Royal Statistical Society*, XLVI, 1883, pp. 1–58.

Crawford, W. H., ed., *General report on the Gosford estates in County Armagh, 1821, by William Greig*, Belfast, 1976.

Crossley, A., ed., *The Victoria history of the County of Oxford*, IV, Oxford, 1979.

Crotty, R. D., *Irish agricultural production: its volume and structure*, Cork, 1966.

Cuddy, M. and Doherty, M., *An analysis of agricultural developments in the north and south of Ireland and of the effects of integrated policy and planning*, Dublin, 1984.

Cunliffe, B. W. and Rowley, R. T., eds., *Oppida, the beginnings of urbanisation in barbarian Europe: papers presented to a conference at Oxford, October 1975*, BAR, supplementary series, XI, Oxford, 1976.

Cunliffe, B. W., 'Settlement and population in the British iron age: some facts, figures and fantasies', pp. 3–24 in *idem* and Rowley, R. T., eds., *Lowland iron age communities in Europe: papers presented to a conference of the Department for External Studies held at Oxford, October, 1977*, BAR, supplementary series, XLVIII, Oxford, 1978.

Cunliffe, B. W., *Danebury: an iron age hillfort in Hampshire*, 2 vols., Council for British Archaeology Research Report, LII, London, 1984.

Currie, C. R. J., 'Early vetches: a note', *EcHR*, XLI, 1988, pp. 114–16.

Dahl, G. and Hjort, A., *Having herds: pastoral growth and household economy*, Stockholm Studies in Social Anthropology, II, 1976.

Dalrymple, D. G., 'Changes in wheat varieties and wheat yields in the United States, 1919–1984', *Agricultural History*, LXII, 1988, pp. 20–36.

Darby, H. C., *The draining of the fens*, Cambridge, 1940.

Darby, H. C., 'The changing English landscape', *Geographical Journal*, CXVII, 1951, pp. 377–94.

Darby, H. C., *Domesday England*, Cambridge, 1977.

Darby, H. C., *The changing fenland*, Cambridge, 1983.

Davenport, F. G., *The economic development of a Norfolk manor, 1086–1565*, Cambridge, 1906.

Darby, H. C., 'The changing English landscape', *Geographical Journal*, CXVII, 1951, pp. 377–94.

David, P. A., 'Labour productivity in English agriculture, 1850–1914: some quantitative evidence on regional differences', *EcHR*, XXIII, 1970, pp. 504–14.

De Brabander, G. L., 'De regionaal-sectoriele spreiding van de economische activiteiten in België, 1846–1910. Een bronkritische benadering', *Bijdragen tot de geschiedenis*, LXI, 1977, pp. 97–195.

De Vries, J., *The Dutch rural economy in the golden age, 1500–1700*, New Haven, 1974.

Deane, P. and Cole, W. A., *British economic growth, 1688–1959*, Cambridge, 2nd edn., 1967.
Defoe, D., *The Complete English Tradesman*, 2 vols., London, 1725–27.
Dennison, E., *Why growth rates differ?*, Washington, 1967.
Derville, A., *Histoire de Saint-Omer*, Lille, 1981.
Derville, A., 'Le Nombre d'habitants des villes de l'Artois et de la Flandre Wallone 1300–1450', *Revue du Nord*, LXV, 1983, pp. 277–99.
Derville, A., 'Dimes, rendements du blé et révolution agricole dans le nord de la France au moyen âge', *Annales, Économies, Sociétés, Civilisations*, XLII, 1987, pp. 1,411–32.
Derville, A., 'Les Greniers des Pays-Bas médiévaux', *Revue du Nord*, LXIX, 1987, pp. 267–80.
Desportes, P., 'Les Communes picardes au moyen âge: une évolution originale', *Revue du Nord*, LXX, 1988, pp. 265–84.
Dewey, C. J., 'The rehabilitation of the peasant proprietor in nineteenth-century economic thought', *History of Political Economy*, VI, 1974, pp. 17–47.
Dimbleby, G. W., *The development of British heathlands and their soils*, Oxford, 1962.
Dimbleby, G. W., *The palynology of archaeological sites*, London, 1985.
Dobson, R. B., ed., *The Peasants' Revolt of 1381*, London, 2nd edn., 1981.
Dodd, P., 'Norfolk agriculture in 1853–4', *Norfolk Archaeology*, XXXVI, 1976, pp. 253–64.
Dodd, P., 'The agricultural statistics for 1854: an assessment of their value', *AHR*, XXXV, 1987, pp. 159–70.
Donnelly, J. S., 'The Irish agricultural depression of 1859–64', *Irish Economic and Social History*, III, 1976.
Drescher, L., 'The development of agricultural production in Great Britain and Ireland from the early nineteenth century', *The Manchester School*, XXIII, 1955, pp. 153–75, with a 'Comment' by T. W. Fletcher, pp. 176–83.
Drew, J. S., 'Manorial accounts of St Swithun's Priory, Winchester', *English Historical Review*, LXII, 1947, reprinted as pp. 12–30 in Carus-Wilson, E. M., ed., *Essays in economic history*, II, London, 1962.
Du Boulay, F. R. H., 'Who were farming the English demesnes at the end of the middle ages?', *EcHR*, XVII, 1965, pp. 443–55.
Duby, G., *The early growth of the European economy*, trans. H. B. Clarke, Ithaca, NY, 1974.
Dudley-Stamp, L., ed., *The land of Britain: the report of the Land Utilisation Survey of Britain*, London, 1936–8.
Dunford, M. and Perrons, D., *The arena of capital*, London and Basingstoke, 1983.
Dunlop, J. T. and Diatchenko, V. T., *Labour productivity*, New York, 1964.
Dury, G. H., 'Crop failures on the Winchester manors 1232–1349', *Transactions of the Institute of British Geographers*, new series, IX, 1984, pp. 401–18.
Dyer, C. C., *Lords and peasants in a changing society: the estates of the Bishopric of Worcester, 680–1540*, Cambridge, 1980.
Dyer, C. C., 'English diet in the later middle ages', pp. 191–216 in Aston, T. H., Coss, P. R., Dyer, C. C. and Thirsk, J., eds., *Social relations and ideas: essays in honour of R. H. Hilton*, Cambridge, 1983.
Dyer, C. C., 'Changes in nutrition and the standard of living in England, 1200–1500', pp. 35–44 in Fogel, R. W., ed., *Long-term changes in nutrition and the standard of living*, Section B7, the proceedings of the Ninth International Economic History Congress, Bern, 1986.
Dyer, C. C., *Standards of living in the later middle ages: social change in England, c.1200–1520*, Cambridge, 1989.
Ede, R., *The principles of agriculture*, London, 1945.
Elvin, M., *The pattern of the Chinese past*, London, 1973.
Erdtman, G., *Handbook of palynology*, Copenhagen, 1969.
Ernle, Lord, *English farming, past and present*, London, 1912.

Evans, E., *The contentious tithe: the tithe problem and English agriculture, 1750–1850*, London, 1976.

Evans, J. G., *Land snails in archaeology*, London, 1972.

Everton, A. and Fowler, P. J., 'Pre-Roman ard-marks at Lodge Farm, Falfield, Avon: a method of analysis', pp. 179–85 in Bowen and Fowler, *Early land allotment*, 1979.

Faith, R. J., 'The "Great Rumour" of 1377 and peasant ideology', pp. 43–73 in Hilton, R. H. and Aston, T. H., eds., *The English Rising of 1381*, Cambridge, 1984.

Farmer, D. L., 'Some grain price movements in thirteenth-century England', *EcHR*, X, 1957–58, pp. 207–20.

Farmer, D. L., 'Some price fluctuations in Angevin England', *EcHR*, IX, 1956–57, pp. 34–43.

Farmer, D. L., 'Some livestock price movements in thirteenth-century England', *EcHR*, XXII, 1969, pp. 1–16.

Farmer, D. L., 'Grain yields on the Winchester manors in the later middle ages', *EcHR*, XXX, 1977, pp. 555–66.

Farmer, D. L., 'Crop yields, prices and wages in medieval England', *Studies in Medieval and Renaissance History*, VI, 1983, pp. 117–55.

Farmer, D. L., 'Grain yields on Westminster Abbey manors, 1271–1410', *Canadian Journal of History*, XVIII, 1983, pp. 331–48.

Farmer, D. L., 'Two Wiltshire manors and their markets', *AHR*, XXVII, 1989, pp. 1–11.

Federico, G., 'Mercantilizzazione e sviluppo economico in Italia (1860–1940)', *Rivista di Storia Economica*, III, 1986, pp. 149–86.

Feinstein, C. H., 'Capital formation in Great Britain', pp. 28–96 in Mathias, P. and Postan, M. M., eds., *The Cambridge economic history of Europe*, VII, *The industrial economies: capital, labour, and enterprise*, part 1, Cambridge, 1978.

Feinstein, C. H., 'Agriculture', pp. 267–80 in *idem* and Pollard, S., eds., *Studies in capital formation in the United Kingdom, 1750–1920*, Oxford, 1988.

Fenoaltea, S., 'Transaction costs, Whig history, and the common fields', *Politics and Society*, XVI, 1988, pp. 171–240.

Ferris, T., 'Changing productivity and living standards: 1971–1986', *Irish Banking Review*, 1989, pp. 32–9.

Finberg, H. P. R., *Tavistock Abbey: a study in the social and economic history of Devon*, Cambridge, 1951.

Finberg, H. P. R., ed., *The agrarian history of England and Wales*, Iii, AD *43–1042*, Cambridge, 1972.

Fisher, F. J., 'The development of the London food market, 1540–1640', *Economic History Review*, V, 1935, pp. 46–64, reprinted as pp. 135–51 in Carus-Wilson, E. M., ed., *Essays in Economic History*, I, London, 1954.

Fisher, F. M. and Temin, P., 'Regional specialisation and the supply of wheat in the United States, 1867–1914', *Review of Economics and Statistics*, LII, 1970, pp. 134–49.

Fitzherbert, *Surveyenge* (1539), pp. 22–5 in Tawney, R. H. and Power, E., eds., *Tudor economic documents, being select documents illustrating the economic and social history of Tudor England*, III, London, 1924.

Fleming, A., *The Dartmoor reaves*, London, 1988.

Fletcher, J., 'Contributions to the agricultural statistics of the eastern counties', *Journal of the Statistical Society of London*, VI, 1843, pp. 130–3.

Fletcher, T. W., 'The Great Depression of English agriculture, 1873–96', *EcHR*, XIII, 1961, pp. 417–32.

Floud, R. and McCloskey, D. N., eds., *The economic history of Britain since 1700*, 2 vols., Cambridge, 1981.

Fogel, R. W., *Second thoughts on the European escape from hunger: famines, price elasticities, entitlements, chronic malnutrition, and mortality rates*, National Bureau of Economic

Research working paper series on historical factors in long-run growth, I, Cambridge, Mass., 1989.

Fossier, R., *La Terre et les hommes en Picardie jusqu'à la fin du XIIIe siècle*, Paris, 1968.

Fowler, P. J. and Evans, J. G., 'Plough marks, lynchets and early fields', *Antiquity*, XLI, 1967, pp. 289–301.

Fox, H. S. A., 'Local farmers' associations and the circulation of agricultural information in nineteenth-century England', pp. 43–63 in *idem* and Butlin, R. A., eds., *Change in the countryside: essays on rural England, 1500–1900*, Institute of British Geographers Special Publication, X, London, 1979.

Fox, H. S. A., 'Some ecological dimensions of medieval field systems', pp. 119–58 in Biddick, K., ed., *Archaeological approaches to medieval Europe*, Kalamazoo, 1984.

Fox, H. S. A., 'The alleged transformation from two-field to three-field systems in medieval England', *EcHR*, XXXIX, 1986, pp. 526–48.

France, Ministère d'Agriculture, *Statistique agricole de la France. Résultats généraux de l'enquête décennale de 1892*, Paris, 1892.

Fream, W., *Elements of agriculture*, London, 2nd edn., 1892.

Fuà, G., ed., *Lo sviluppo economico in Italia*, III, Milan, 1968.

Furness, G. W. and Stainer, T. F., 'Economic performance in agriculture in Northern Ireland and the Irish Republic', *Annual Report on Research and Technical Work*, Belfast, 1981.

Fussell, G. E., 'Population and wheat production in the eighteenth century', *The History Teachers' Miscellany*, VII, 1929, pp. 65–8, 84–8, 108–11, and 120–7.

Fussell, G. E., ed., *Robert Loder's farm accounts 1610–1620*, Camden Society, 3rd series, LIII, London, 1936.

Fussell, G. E., 'Social change but static technology: rural England in the fourteenth century', *History Studies*, 1968, pp. 23–32.

Fussell, G. E., *Crop nutrition: science and practice before Liebig*, Lawrence, Kansas, 1971.

Galanti, G. M., *Nuova descrizione storica e geografica delle Sicilie*, Naples, 1786.

Galassi, F., 'Stasi e sviluppo dell'agricoltura toscana 1870–1914', *Rivista di Storia Economica*, new series, III, 1986, pp. 304–37.

Gallman, R. E., 'Changes in total US factor productivity growth in the nineteenth century', *Agricultural History*, XLVI, 1972, pp. 191–210.

Gardner, H. W. and Garner, H. V., *The use of lime in British agriculture*, London, 1953.

Garner, H. V. and Dyke, G. V., 'The Broadbalk yields', *Rothamsted Experimental Station Report for 1968*, Harpenden, 1969, pp. 26–49.

Garnier, R. M., 'The introduction of forage crops into Great Britain', *Journal of the Royal Agricultural Society of England*, 3rd series, VII, 1896, pp. 82–97.

Gazzetta Ufficiale, *Supplemento straordinario al n. 49*, Rome, 1939.

Geertz, C., *Agricultural involution: the process of ecological change in Indonesia*, Berkeley, 1963.

Gerschenkron, A., *Economic backwardness in historical perspective*, Cambridge, Mass., 1962.

Gibbs, J. P. and Martin, W. T., 'Urbanization, technology and the division of labour', *American Sociological Review*, XXVII, 1962, pp. 667–77.

Gibson, A. J. S., 'The size and weight of cattle and sheep in early modern Scotland', *AHR*, XXXVI, 1988, pp. 162–71.

Gill, C., *The rise of the Irish linen industry*, Oxford, 1925.

Glennie, P., 'A commercialising agrarian region: late medieval and early modern Hertfordshire', unpublished University of Cambridge Ph.D. thesis, 1983.

Glennie, P., 'Continuity and change in Hertfordshire agriculture, 1550–1700: II – trends in crop yields and their determinants', *AHR*, XXXVI, 1988, pp. 145–61.

Glennie, P., 'The plausibility of crop yields inferred from probate inventories', unpublished manuscript, 1990.

Goddard, N., 'Agricultural literature and societies', pp. 361–83 in Mingay, *The agrarian history of England and Wales*, VI, *1700–1850*.

Godwin, H., *History of the British flora*, Cambridge, 2nd edn., 1975.

Goossens, M., 'De economische ontwikkeling van de belgische landbouw in regionaal perspectief, 1812–1846. Een analyse op basis van de ontwikkeling van het regionaal landbouwprodukt', unpublished Catholic University of Leuven Ph.D. thesis, 2 vols., 1990.

Gowlett, J. A. J. and Hedges, R. E. M., eds., *Archaeological results from accelerator dating: research contributions drawing on radiocarbon dates produced by the Oxford radiocarbon accelerator based on papers presented at the SERC sponsored conference 'Results and prospects of accelerator dating' held at Oxford in October 1985*, Oxford University Committee for Archaeology/monograph, XI, Oxford, 1986.

Gramsci, A., *Il Risorgimento*, Turin, 1950.

Grant, A., 'Animal resources', pp. 149–87 in *idem* and Astill, G., eds., *The countryside of medieval England*, Oxford, 1988.

Grantham, G. W., 'The diffusion of the new husbandry in northern France', *JEH*, XXXVIII, 1978, pp. 311–37.

Grantham, G., 'The shifting locus of agricultural innovation in nineteenth-century Europe: the case of the agricultural experiment stations', pp. 191–214 in Saxonhouse, G. and Wright, G., eds., *Technique, spirit, and form in the making of the modern economies. Essays in honour of William N. Parker*, Research in Economic History, Supplement III, Greenwich, Ct., 1984.

Grantham, G., 'Agricultural supply during the industrial revolution: French evidence and European implications', *JEH*, XLIX, 1989, pp. 43–72.

Grantham, G., 'Jean Meuvret and the subsistence problem in early modern France', *JEH*, XLIX, 1989, pp. 184–200.

Gray, H. L., *English field systems*, Cambridge, Mass., 1915.

Greig, J., 'The palaeoecology of some British hay meadow types', pp. 213–26 in Van Zeist, W. and Casparie, W., eds., *Plants and ancient man*, Rotterdam, 1984.

Greig, J., 'Some evidence of the development of grassland plant communities', pp. 39–54 in Jones, *Archaeology and the flora of the British Isles*, 1988.

Grigg, D. B., *The agricultural revolution in south Lincolnshire*, Cambridge, 1966.

Grigg, D. B., 'The changing agricultural geography of England: a commentary on the sources available for the reconstruction of the agricultural geography of England 1770–1850', *Transactions of the Institute of British Geographers*, XLI, 1967, pp. 73–96.

Grigg, D. B., *Population growth and agrarian change: an historical perspective*, Cambridge, 1980.

Grigg, D. B., *The dynamics of agricultural change*, London, 1982.

Gubin, E. and Van Neck, A., 'La Répartition professionnelle de la population belge en 1846: un piège statistique', pp. 269–365 in *Acta Historica Bruxellensia IV. Histoire et méthode*, Brussels, 1981.

Habakkuk, H. J., 'The agrarian history of England and Wales: regional farming systems and agrarian change, 1640–1750', *EcHR*, XL, 1987, pp. 281–96.

Hall, A. D., *An account of the Rothamsted experiments*, London, 1905.

Hall, A. D., *Fertilisers and manures*, London, 1909.

Hall, A. D., *The feeding of crops and stock*, London, 1911.

Hallam, H. E., 'Some thirteenth-century censuses', *EcHR*, X, 1958, pp. 340–61.

Hallam, H. E., *Rural England 1066–1348*, London, 1981.

Hallam, H. E., 'The climate of eastern England 1250–1350', *AHR*, XXXII, 1984, pp. 124–32.

Hallam, H. E., ed., *The agrarian history of England and Wales*, II, *1042–1350*, Oxford, 1988.

Hanson, H., Borlaug, N. E. and Anderson, R. G., *Wheat in the Third World*, Colorado, 1982.

Hare, J. N., 'The demesnes lessees of fifteenth-century Wiltshire', *AHR*, XXIX, 1981, pp. 1–15.

Harper, F. R., 'Crop production in England and Wales 1950–1980', *Journal of the Royal Agricultural Society of England*, CXLII, 1981, pp. 42–54.

Hartlib, S., *His legacie, or an enlargement of the husbandry used in Brabant and Flanders*, London, 1651.

Harvey, B. F., 'Draft letters of manumission and pardon for the men of Somerset in 1381', *English Historical Review*, LXXX, 1965, pp. 89–91.

Harvey, B. F., 'The leasing of the Abbot of Westminster's demesnes in the later middle ages', *EcHR*, XXII, 1969, pp. 17–27.

Harvey, N., 'The coming of the swede to Great Britain: an obscure chapter in farming history', *Agricultural History*, XXIII, 1949, pp. 286–8.

Harvey, P. D. A., *A medieval Oxfordshire village: Cuxham 1240–1400*, Oxford, 1965.

Harvey, P. D. A., 'Agricultural treatises and manorial accounting in medieval England', *AHR*, XX, 1972, pp. 170–82.

Harvey, P. D. A., 'The Pipe Rolls and the adoption of demesne farming in England', *EcHR*, XXVII, 1974, pp. 345–59.

Harvey, P. D. A., 'Introduction, Part II, accounts and other manorial records', pp. 12–71 in *idem, Manorial records of Cuxham, Oxfordshire circa 1200–1359*, 1976.

Harvey, P. D. A., ed., *Manorial records of Cuxham, Oxfordshire, circa 1200–1359*, Oxfordshire Record Society, L, London, 1976.

Harvey, S., 'Domesday England', pp. 45–138 in Hallam, *The agrarian history of England and Wales*, II, *1042–1350*, 1988.

Harwood Long, W., 'The low yields of corn in medieval England', *EcHR*, XXXII, 1979, pp. 459–69.

Haselgrove, C. C., Millett, M. and Smith, I., *Archaeology from the ploughsoil: studies in the collection and interpretation of field survey data*, Sheffield, 1985.

Hassan, F. A., *Demographic archaeology*, London, 1981.

Havinden, M. A., 'Agricultural progress in open-field Oxfordshire', *AHR*, IX, 1961, pp. 73–83.

Havinden, M. A., 'Lime as a means of agricultural improvement: the Devon example', pp. 104–34 in *idem* and Chalklin, C. W., eds., *Rural change and urban growth*, London, 1974.

Hayami, Y. and Ruttan, V. W., *Agricultural development, an international perspective*, Baltimore and London, revised edn., 1985.

Higgs, E. S. and Vita-Finzi, C., 'Prehistoric economies: a territorial approach', pp. 27–36 in Higgs, *Papers in economic prehistory*, 1972.

Higgs, E. S., ed., *Papers in economic prehistory: studies by members and associates of the British Academy major research project in the early history of agriculture*, Cambridge, 1972.

Higgs, E. S., ed., *Palaeoeconomy: being the second volume of papers in economic prehistory by members and associates of the British Academy major research project in the early history of agriculture*, Cambridge, 1975.

Higounet-Nadal, A., 'La Démographie des villes françaises au moyen âge', *Annales de Démographie Historique*, 1980, pp. 187–211.

Hill, C., *The world turned upside down*, London, 1972.

Hillman, G. C., 'On the origins of domestic rye – *secale cereale*: the finds from a ceramic Can Hasan III in Turkey', *Anatolian Studies*, XXVIII, 1978, pp. 157–74.

Hillman, G. C., 'Interpretation of archaeological plant remains: the application of ethnographic models from Turkey', pp. 1–47 in Van Zeist, W. and Casparie, W., eds., *Plants and ancient man*, Rotterdam, 1984.

Hilton, R. H., 'Peasant movements in England before 1381', *EcHR*, II, 1949, pp. 117–36.

Hilton, R. H., 'Medieval agrarian history', pp. 145–98 in *Victoria County History of Leicestershire*, II, London, 1954.

Hilton, R. H., *A medieval society: the west midlands at the end of the thirteenth century*, London, 1966.

Hilton, R. H., 'Rent and capital formation in feudal society', pp. 174–214 in *idem, The English peasantry in the later middle ages*, Oxford, 1975.

Hilton, R. H., *The decline of serfdom in medieval England*, London and Basingstoke, 2nd edn., 1983.

Historical statistics of the United States. Colonial times to 1970, Washington, 1975.

Hoctor, D., *The Department's story: a history of the Department of Agriculture*, Dublin, 1971.

Hoffmann, E. and Mokyr, J., 'Peasants, potatoes and poverty: transactions costs in pre-Famine Ireland', pp. 115–45 in Saxonhouse, G. and Wright, G., eds., *Technique, spirit and form in the making of modern economies: essays in honour of W. N. Parker*, Greenwich, Ct., 1984.

Hoffmann, W. G., *Das wachstum des Deutschen wirtschaft seit der mitte des 19. jahrhunderts*, Berlin, 1965.

Hogan, M. P., 'Clays, *culturae* and the cultivator's wisdom: management efficiency at fourteenth-century Wistow', *AHR*, XXXVI, 1988, pp. 117–31.

Holderness, B. A., 'Capital formation in agriculture', pp. 159–83 in Higgins, J. P. P. and Pollard, S., eds., *Aspects of capital investment in Great Britain, 1750–1850: a preliminary survey*, London, 1971.

Holderness, B. A., 'Credit in a rural community, 1660–1800', *Midland History*, III, 1975–76, pp. 94–115.

Holderness, B. A., 'Credit in English rural society before the nineteenth century, with special reference to the period 1650–1720', *AHR*, XXIV, 1976, pp. 97–109.

Holderness, B. A., 'East Anglia and the fens', pp. 197–238 in Thirsk, *The agrarian history of England and Wales*, Vi, *1640–1750: regional farming systems*, 1984.

Holderness, B. A., *British agriculture since 1945*, Manchester, 1985.

Holderness, B. A., 'Agriculture, 1770–1860', pp. 9–34 in Feinstein, C. H. and Pollard, S., eds., *Studies in capital formation in the United Kingdom, 1750–1920*, Oxford, 1988.

Holderness, B. A., 'Prices, productivity and output', pp. 84–189 in Mingay, *The agrarian history of England and Wales*, VI, *1750–1850*, 1989.

Holmes, C. J., 'Science and the farmer: the development of the agricultural advisory service in England and Wales, 1900–1939', *AHR*, XXXVI, 1988, pp. 77–86.

Holmes, G. A., *The estates of the higher nobility in the fourteenth century*, Cambridge, 1957.

Holt, H. M. E. and Kain, R. J. P., 'Land use and farming in Suffolk about 1840', *Proceedings of the Suffolk Institute of Archaeology*, XXXV, 1982, pp. 123–39.

Hoppen, K. T., *Ireland since 1800: conflict and conformity*, London, 1989.

Hoskins, W. G., 'The Leicestershire farmer in the sixteenth century', pp. 123–83 in *idem*, ed., *Essays in Leicestershire history*, Liverpool, 1950.

Hoskins, W. G., 'The Leicestershire farmer in the seventeenth century', pp. 149–169 in *idem*, ed., *Provincial England*, London, 1963.

Houghton, J., *A collection for the improvement of husbandry and trade*, IV, number 77, London, 1695.

Howell, C., *Land, family and inheritance in transition: Kibworth Harcourt 1280–1700*, Cambridge, 1983.

Howell, M., *Regalian right in medieval England*, London, 1962.

Hudson, K., *Patriotism with profit: British agricultural societies in the eighteenth and nineteenth centuries*, London, 1972.

Hueckel, G., 'Agriculture during industrialisation', pp. 182–203 in Floud and McCloskey, *Economic history of Britain*, I, 1981.

Hunt, E. H., 'Quantitative and other evidence on labour productivity in agriculture, 1850–1914', *EcHR*, XXIII, 1970, pp. 515–19.

Huttman, J. P., 'Institutional factors in the development of Irish agriculture, 1850–1915', unpublished University of London Ph.D. thesis, 1970.

Hybel, N., *Crisis or change. The concept of crisis in the light of agrarian structural reorganization in late medieval England*, trans. J. Manley, Aarhus, 1989.

INEA, *Monografie di famiglie agricole*, Rome, 1933.

International Labour Office, *International labour documentation*, Geneva, 1988.

Isles, K. S. and Cuthbert, N., *An economic survey of Northern Ireland*, Belfast, 1957.

Isserlis, L., 'Tramp shipping cargoes and freight', *Journal of the Royal Statistics Society*, CI, 1938, pp. 73–86.

Jacini, S., *I risultati dell'inchiesta agraria (1884)*, Turin, 1976.

Jackson, R. V., 'Growth and deceleration in English agriculture, 1660–1790', *EcHR*, XXXVI, 1985, pp. 333–51.

Jacquemyns, G., *Histoire de la crise économique des Flandres, 1845–1850*, Brussels, 1929.

Jenkinson, D. S., 'Soil organic matter and its dynamics', pp. 589–91 in Wild, A., ed., *Russell's soil conditions and plant growth*, London, 11th edn., 1988.

John, A. H., 'Statistical appendix', pp. 972–1,155 in Mingay, *The agrarian history of England and Wales*, VI, *1750–1850*, 1989.

Johnson, D. J. and Kennedy, L., 'George O'Brien', unpublished manuscript, The Queen's University of Belfast, 1987.

Johnston, J., *The nemesis of economic nationalism*, Dublin, 1934.

Johnston, J., 'Price ratios in recent Irish agricultural experience', *Economic Journal*, XLVII, 1937, pp. 680–5.

Johnston, J., *Irish agriculture in transition*, Dublin, 1951.

Johnston, R. J., Gregory, D. J. and Smith, D. M., eds., *The dictionary of human geography*, Oxford, 2nd edn., 1986.

Johnston, R. and Conway, A., 'Factors associated with growth in farm output', *Proceedings of the Agricultural Economics Society of Ireland*, 1976, pp. 52–102.

Jones, E. L., *The development of English agriculture, 1815–1873*, London, 1968.

Jones, E. L., 'Agriculture and economic growth in England, 1660–1750: agricultural change', *JEH*, XXV, 1965, pp. 1–18, reprinted as pp. 67–84 in *idem, Agriculture and the industrial revolution*, Oxford, 1974.

Jones, E. L., *Seasons and prices: the role of the weather in English agricultural history*, London, 1964.

Jones, E. L., *Agriculture and economic growth in England, 1650–1815*, London, 1967.

Jones, E. L., 'The bird pests of British agriculture in recent centuries', *AHR*, XX, 1972, pp. 107–25.

Jones, E. L., *Agriculture and the industrial revolution*, Oxford, 1974.

Jones, E. L., 'Afterword', pp. 327–36 in *idem* and Parker, W. N., eds., *European peasants and their markets: essays in agricultural history*, New Haven, 1975.

Jones, M. K., 'The development of crop husbandry', pp. 97–107 in *idem* and Dimbleby, *The environment of man*, 1981.

Jones, M. K. and Dimbleby, G. W., eds., *The environment of man: the iron age to the Anglo-Saxon period*, BAR, British series, LXXXVII, Oxford, 1981.

Jones, M. K., 'Crop production in Roman Britain', pp. 97–107 in Miles, D., ed., *The Romano-British countryside: studies in rural settlement and economy*, BAR, British series, CIII, Oxford, 1982.

Jones, M. K., ed., *Integrating the subsistence economy*, BAR, supplementary series, CLXXXI, Oxford, 1983.

Jones, M. K., 'The ecological and cultural implications of selected carbonised seed assemblages from southern Britain', unpublished University of Oxford D.Phil. thesis, 1985.

Jones, M. K., 'Towards a model of the villa estate', pp. 38–42 in Miles, D., ed., *Archaeology at Barton Court Farm, Abingdon, Oxon.*, London, 1986.

Jones, M. K., *England before Domesday*, London, 1986.

Jones, M. K., ed., *Archaeology and the flora of the British Isles: human influence on the evolution of plant communities*, Oxford University Committee for Archaeology monograph, XIV, and Botanical Society of the British Isles conference report, XIX, Oxford, 1988.

Jones, M. K., 'Agriculture in Roman Britain: the dynamics of change', pp. 127–34 in Todd, M., *Research on Roman Britain 1960–1989*, Britannia monograph, XI, London, 1989.

Kain, R. J. P. and Prince, H. C., *The tithe surveys of England and Wales*, Cambridge, 1985.
Kain, R. J. P., *An atlas and index of the tithe files of mid-nineteenth-century England and Wales*, Cambridge, 1986.
Keene, D., *Survey of medieval Winchester*, Winchester Studies, II, Oxford, 1985.
Keene, D., 'Medieval London and its region', *The London Journal*, XIV, 1989, pp. 99–111.
Keil, I., 'The estates of the Abbey of Glastonbury in the later middle ages', unpublished University of Bristol Ph.D. thesis, 1964.
Kelly, P. W., 'Price of land in the Republic of Ireland 1978–1981', *Agricultural Institute Situation and Outlook, Bulletin*, V, 1983.
Kennedy, K. A., Giblin, T. and McHugh, D., *The economic development of Ireland in the twentieth century*, London, 1988.
Kennedy, L., 'The rural economy 1820–1914', pp. 1–61 in Kennedy, L. and Ollerenshaw, P., eds., *An economic history of Ulster 1820–1939*, Manchester, 1985.
Kenyon, N., 'Labour conditions in Essex in the reign of Richard II', *EcHR*, IV, 1932–34, pp. 429–51, reprinted as pp. 91–111 in Carus-Wilson, E. M., ed., *Essays in economic history*, II, London, 1962.
Kerridge, E., 'A reconsideration of some former husbandry practices', *AHR*, III, 1955, pp. 26–40.
Kerridge, E., *The agricultural revolution*, London, 1967.
Kerridge, E., 'Arthur Young and William Marshall', *History Studies*, I, 1968, pp. 43–65.
Kerridge, E., *The farmers of old England*, London, 1983.
Kershaw, I., *Bolton Priory: the economy of a northern monastery, 1286–1325*, Oxford, 1973.
Klep, P. M. M., 'De agrarische beroepsbevolking van de provincies Antwerpen en Brabant en van het Koninkrijk België, 1846–1910. Nieuwe evaluaties van kwantitatief-historisch materiaal', *Bijdragen tot de geschiedenis*, LIX, 1976, pp. 25–69.
Komlos, J., 'Agricultural productivity in America and eastern Europe: a comment', *JEH*, XLVIII, 1988, pp. 655–64.
Kosminsky, E. A., *Studies in the agrarian history of England in the thirteenth century*, Oxford, 1956.
Kravis, I., Kenessy, Z., Heston, A. and Summers, R., *International comparison of real product and purchasing power*, Baltimore, 1975.
Kravis, I, 'A survey of international comparisons of productivity', *Economic Journal*, LXXXVI, 1976, pp. 1–41.
Kravis, I., Heston, A. and Summers, R., *World product and income*, Baltimore, 1978.
Kravis, I., 'Comparative studies of national income and prices', *Journal of Economic Literature*, XXII, 1984, pp. 1–44.
Kriedte, P., Medick, H. and Schlumbohm, J., *Industrialisation before industrialisation*, Cambridge, 1981.
Kriedte, P., *Peasants, landlords and merchant capitalists: Europe and the world economy, 1500–1800*, Leamington Spa, 1983.
Kula, W., *An economic theory of feudalism*, trans. L. Garner, London, 1976.
Kussmaul, A., 'Agrarian change in seventeenth-century England: the economic historian as paleontologist', *JEH*, XLV, 1985, pp. 1–30.
La Roncière, C.-M., *Prix et salaires à Florence au XIVᵉ siècle*, Rome, 1982.
Lamb, H. H., *The changing climate*, London, 1966.
Lamb, H. H., *Climate, history and the modern world*, London, 1982.
Lambrick, G. and Robinson, M., 'The development of flood-plain grassland in the upper Thames Valley', pp. 55–75 in Jones, *Archaeology and the flora of the British Isles*, 1988.
Lane, C., 'The development of pastures and meadows during the sixteenth and seventeenth centuries', *AHR*, XXVIII, 1980, pp. 18–30.
Langdon, J. L., 'Horse hauling: a revolution in vehicle transport in twelfth- and thirteenth-century England', *Past and Present*, CIII, 1984, pp. 37–66.

Langdon, J. L., *Horses, oxen and technological innovation: the use of draught animals in English farming from 1066–1500*, Cambridge, 1986.

Langton, J. and Hoppe, G., *Town and country in the development of early modern western Europe*, Historical Geography Research Series, XI, Norwich, 1983.

Large, P., 'Urban growth and agricultural change in the west midlands during the seventeenth and eighteenth centuries', pp. 169–89 in Clark, P., ed., *The transformation of English towns, 1600–1800*, London, 1984.

Laslett, P., comp., *The earliest classics: John Graunt and Gregory King*, Farnborough, 1973.

Lawes, J. B. and Gilbert, J. H., 'Rotation of crops', *Journal of the Royal Agricultural Society of England*, 3rd series, V, 1894, pp. 584–646.

Le Roy Ladurie, E., *Peasants of Languedoc*, Urbana, Ill., 1974.

Le Roy Ladurie, E., 'The end of the middle ages: the work of Guy Bois and Hugues Neveux', pp. 71–92 in *idem* and Goy, J., *Tithe and agrarian history from the fourteenth to the nineteenth centuries: an essay in comparative history*, Cambridge, 1982.

Leacy, F. H., *Historical statistics of Canada*, Ottawa, 1983.

Lebergott, S., *Manpower in American economic growth*, New York, 1964.

Lennard, R. V., 'English agriculture under Charles II', *Economic History Review*, IV, 1932, pp. 23–45.

Lévy-Leboyer, M., 'La Decélération de l'économie française dans la seconde moitié du 19ᵉ siècle', *Revue d'histoire économique et sociale*, XLIX, 1971, pp. 485–507.

Liebig, J. von, *Organic chemistry in its applications to agriculture and physiology*, ed. L. Playfair, London, 1840.

Limbrey, S., *Soil science and archaeology*, London, 1975.

Lindert, P., 'English occupations, 1670–1811', *JEH*, XLV, 1980, pp. 685–712.

Link, A. N., *Technological change and productivity growth*, London, 1987.

Lipsey, R. G., *An introduction to positive economics*, London, 1972.

Lomas, R. A., 'The Priory of Durham and its demesnes in the fourteenth and fifteenth centuries', *EcHR*, XXXI, 1978, pp. 339–53.

Loomis, R. S., 'Ecological dimensions of medieval agrarian systems: an ecologist responds', *Agricultural History*, LII, 1978, pp. 478–83.

Loudon, J. C., *An encyclopaedia of agriculture*, London, 6th edn., 1866.

Lynch, J. M. and Woods, M., 'Interaction between plant roots and micro-organisms', pp. 534–50 in Wild, *Russell's soil conditions and plant growth*, 1988.

McCloskey, D. N., 'The enclosure of the open fields: preface to a study of its impact on the efficiency of English agriculture in the eighteenth century', *JEH*, XXXII, 1972, pp. 15–35.

McCloskey, D. N., 'The industrial revolution 1780–1860: a survey', pp. 103–27 in Floud and McCloskey, eds., *The economic history of Britain*, I, 1981.

McCloskey, D. N., 'The open fields of England: rent, risk, and the rate of interest, 1300–1815', pp. 5–51 in Galenson, D. W., ed., *Markets in history: economic studies of the past*, Cambridge, 1989.

McCloskey, D. N. and Nash, J., 'Corn at interest: the extent and cost of grain storage in medieval England', *American Economic Review*, LXXIV, 1984, pp. 174–87.

McCulloch, J. R., *A statistical account of the British Empire*, 2 vols., London, 1837.

Macdonald, S., 'Agricultural response to a changing market during the Napoleonic Wars', *EcHR*, XXXIII, 1980, pp. 59–71.

McEvedy, C. and Jones, R., *Atlas of world population history*, Harmondsworth, 1978.

Macguire, D. J., 'The identification of agricultural activity using pollen analysis', pp. 5–18 in Jones, *Integrating the subsistence economy*, 1983.

McIntosh, M. K., *Autonomy and community: the royal manor of Havering, 1200–1500*, Cambridge, 1986.

Macphail, R., 'Soil and botanical studies of the "Dark Earth"', pp. 309–31 in Jones and Dimbleby, *The environment of man*, 1981.

Macro, F. W., 'The culture of turnips, recommended to those counties where they are not yet common', *Annals of Agriculture*, III, 1785, pp. 297–304.

Maddison, A., *Economic growth in the west*, New York, 1964.

Maddison, A., *Phases of capitalist development*, Oxford, 1982.

Maguire, W. A., *The Downshire estates in Ireland 1801–1845*, Oxford, 1972.

Mangan, O., 'Irish agriculture 1926–1987', unpublished University College Dublin MA term paper, 1987.

Manning, W. H., 'The native and Roman contribution to the development of metal industries in Britain', pp. 111–21 in Burnham, B. C. and Johnson, H. B., eds., *Invasion and response: the case of Roman Britain*, BAR, British series, LXXIII, Oxford, 1979.

Mantoux, P., *La Révolution industrielle au XVIII' siécle*, Paris, 1905.

Marshall, G., 'The "Rotheram" plough', *Tools and Tillage*, III, 1978, pp. 149–67.

Marshall, J., 'Agrarian wealth and social structure in pre-industrial Cumbria', *EcHR*, XXXIII, 1980, pp. 503–21.

Marshall, W., *The rural economy of Norfolk*, 2 vols., London, 1787.

Marshall, W., *The review and abstract of the county reports to the Board of Agriculture, III, Eastern Department*, York, 1818.

Mate, M., 'High prices in early fourteenth-century England: causes and consequences', *EcHR*, XXVIII, 1975, pp. 1–16.

Mate, M., 'Profit and productivity on the esates of Isabella de Forz (1260–92)', *EcHR*, XXXIII, 1980, pp. 326–34.

Mate, M., 'The farming out of manors: a new look at the evidence from Canterbury Cathedral Priory', *Journal of Medieval History*, IX, 1983, pp. 331–44.

Mate, M., 'Medieval agrarian practices: the determining factors?', *AHR*, XXXIII, 1985, pp. 22–31.

Mate, M., 'The agrarian economy of south-east England before the Black Death: depressed or buoyant?', pp. 78–109 in Campbell, B. M. S., ed., *Before the Black Death: studies in the 'crisis' of the early fourteenth century*, Manchester, 1991.

Matthews, R. C. O., Feinstein, C. H. and Odling-Smee, J. C., *British economic growth, 1856–1973*, Oxford, 1982.

Mathias, P., *The first industrial nation*, London, 2nd edn., 1983.

Mayhew, N. J., 'Money and prices in England from Henry II to Edward III', *AHR*, XXXV, 1987, pp. 121–32.

Medici, G. and Orlando, G., *Agricoltura e disoccupazione. I braccianti nella bassa padana*, Rome, 1951.

Meenan, J. F., *The Irish economy since 1922*, Liverpool, 1971.

Merrington, J., 'Town and country in the transition to capitalism', *New Left Review*, LXLIII, 1975, pp. 452–506, reprinted as pp. 170–95 in Hilton, R. H., ed., *The transition from feudalism to capitalism*, London, 1976.

Mill, J. S., *Principles of political economy*, ed. W. J. Ashley, New York, 1965.

Miller, E. and Hatcher, J., *Medieval England: rural society and economic change 1086–1348*, London, 1978.

Millett, M. J., *The Romanisation of Britain*, Cambridge, 1990.

Mingay, G. E., 'The size of farms in the eighteenth century', *EcHR*, XIV, 1962, pp. 469–88.

Mingay, G. E., *Arthur Young and his times*, London, 1975.

Mingay, G. E., ed., *The agrarian history of England and Wales*, VI, *1750–1850*, Cambridge, 1989.

Mitchell, B. R. and Deane, P., *Abstract of British historical statistics*, Cambridge, 1962.

Mitchell, B. R., *European historical statistics (1750–1970)*, London, 1975.

Mokyr, J., 'Irish history with the potato', *Irish Economic and Social History*, VIII, 1981, pp. 8–29.

Mokyr, J., *Why Ireland starved: a quantitative and analytical history of the Irish economy, 1800–1850*, London, 1983.

Mokyr, J., 'Has the industrial revolution been crowded out? Some reflections on Crafts and Williamson', *Explorations in Economic History*, XXIV, 1987, pp. 293–391.

Mols, R., *Introduction à la démographie historique des villes d'Europe du XIVe au XVIIIe siècle*, 3 vols., Louvain, 1954–56.

Moody, T. W., *Davitt and Irish revolution 1846–82*, Oxford, 1981.

Moore, H. I., *Grassland husbandry*, London, 2nd edn., 1943, and 3rd edn., 1946.

Moore, P. D. and Webb, J. A., *An illustrated guide to pollen analysis*, London, 1978.

Moore, P. D., 'The development of woodlands and upland mires', pp. 116–22 in Jones, *Archaeology and the flora of the British Isles*, 1988.

Morgan, M., *The English lands of the Abbey of Bec*, Oxford, 1946.

Morton, J. C., *A cyclopaedia of agriculture*, 2 vols., Glasgow, 1851 and 1855.

Mueller, J. W., *Sampling in archaeology*, Tucson, Arizona, 1975.

Mulhall, M. G., *A dictionary of statistics*, London, 1892.

Mulliez, J., 'Du blé, "mal nécessaire". Réflexions sur le progrès de l'agriculture de 1750 à 1850', *Revue d'histoire moderne et contemporaine*, janvier-mars, 1979, pp. 3–47.

Musset, R., *L'Elevage du cheval en France*, Paris, 1917.

National Economic Development Office, *Farm productivity: a report by the Agriculture EDC on factors affecting productivity at the farm level*, London, 1973.

Neary, J. P. and Ó Gráda, C., *Protection, economic war, and structural change: Ireland in the 1930s*, University College, Dublin, Centre for Economic Research, working paper XXX, 1986.

Nerlove, M., *The dynamics of supply: estimation of farmers' response to prices*, Johns Hopkins University Studies in Historical and Political Science, series LXVI, II, 1958.

Neveux, H., *Les Grains du Cambrésis, fin du XIVe–début du XVIIe siècles. Vie et déclin d'une structure économique*, Paris, 1980.

Nicholas, D., *Town and countryside: social, economic and political tensions in fourteenth-century Flanders*, Bruges, 1971.

Nicholas, D., 'Structure du peuplement, fonctions urbaines et formation du capital dans la Flandre médiéval', *Annales, Économies, Sociétés, Civilisations*, XXXIII, 1978, pp. 501–27.

Nicholas, S., 'Total factor productivity growth and the revision of post-1870 British economic history', *EcHR*, XXXV, 1982, pp. 83–98.

Nicholas, S., 'British economic performance and total factor productivity growth, 1870–1940', *EcHR*, XXXVIII, 1985, pp. 576–82.

Nightingale, P., 'The evolution of weight standards and the creation of new monetary and commercial links in northern Europe from the tenth century to the twelfth century', *EcHR*, XXXVIII, 1985, pp. 192–209.

Norton, D. A. G., *Ireland, the Common Agricultural Policy, trade distortion and induced smuggling activity*, Dublin, 1983.

Nunan, D., 'Price trends for agricultural land in Ireland 1901–1986', *Irish Journal of Agricultural Economics and Rural Sociology*, XII, 1987, pp. 51–77.

Ó Gráda, C., 'Post-Famine adjustment, essays in nineteenth-century Irish economic history', unpublished University of Columbia Ph.D. thesis, 1973.

Ó Gráda, C., 'Agricultural decline 1860–1914', pp. 175–97 in Floud and McCloskey, *Economic history of Britain*, II, 1981.

Ó Gráda, C., 'Irish agricultural output before and after the Famine', *Journal of European Economic History*, XIII, 1984, pp. 149–65.

Ó Gráda, C., *Ireland before and after the Famine: explorations in economic history, 1800–1925*, Manchester, 1988.

Ó Gráda, C., 'Slices of Irish agricultural history: output and productivity pre-Famine and post-Famine', unpublished paper presented to a meeting of the Irish Agricultural Economics Society, May 1989.

Ó Gráda, C., *Irish agriculture north and south*, University College Dublin, Centre for Economic Research, Working Paper 89/1, 1989.

O'Brien, G., 'Patrick Hogan', *Studies*, XXV, 1936, pp. 353–68.

O'Brien, P. K. and Keydar, C., *Economic growth in Britain and France 1780–1914: two paths to the twentieth century*, London, 1978.

O'Connor, R. and Guiomard, C., 'Agricultural output in the Irish Free State area before and after independence', *Irish Economic and Social History*, XII, 1985, pp. 89–97.

Ohkawa, K. and Rosovsky, H., 'The significance of the Japanese experience', pp. 617–84 in Ogura, T., ed., *Agricultural development in modern Japan*, Tokyo, 1963.

Ojala, E. M., *Agriculture and economic progress*, London, 1952.

Orlando, G., *Storia della politica agraria in Italia dal 1848 ad oggi*, Rome–Bari, 1984.

Orwin, C. S. and Whetham, E. H., *History of British agriculture 1846–1914*, Newton Abbot, 1971.

Oschinsky, D., *Walter of Henley and other treatises on estate management and accounting*, Oxford, 1971.

Osmaston, H., 'Crop failures on the Winchester manors 1232–1349 AD: some comments', *Transactions of the Institute of British Geographers*, new series, X, 1985, pp. 495–8.

Outhwaite, R. B., 'Progress and backwardness in English agriculture, 1500–1650', *EcHR*, XXXIX, 1986, pp. 1–18.

Overton, M., 'Computer analysis of an inconsistent data source: the case of probate inventories', *Journal of Historical Geography*, III, 1977, pp. 317–26.

Overton, M., 'Estimating crop yields from probate inventories: an example from East Anglia, 1585–1735', *JEH*, XXXIX, 1979, pp. 363–78.

Overton, M., 'English probate inventories and the measurement of agricultural change', *A. A. G. Bijdragen*, XXIII, Wageningen, 1980, pp. 205–15.

Overton, M., 'Agricultural change in Norfolk and Suffolk, 1580–1740', unpublished University of Cambridge Ph.D. thesis, 1981.

Overton, M., 'Agricultural productivity in eighteenth-century England: some further speculations', *EcHR*, XXXVII, 1984, pp. 244–51.

Overton, M., 'An agricultural revolution, 1650–1750', pp. 9–13 in *idem*, Collins, E. J. T., Turner, M. E. and McCloskey, D. N., *Agricultural history: papers presented to the Economic History Society Conference*, Canterbury, 1983.

Overton, M., *Agricultural regions in early modern England: an example from East Anglia*, University of Newcastle upon Tyne, Department of Geography seminar paper, XLII, 1983.

Overton, M., 'Agricultural Revolution? Development of the agrarian economy in early modern England', pp. 118–39 in Baker, A. R. H. and Gregory, D., eds., *Explorations in historical geography: interpretative essays*, Cambridge, 1984.

Overton, M., 'Probate inventories and the reconstruction of agrarian landscapes', pp. 167–94 in Reed, M., ed., *Discovering past landscapes*, London, 1984.

Overton, M., 'The diffusion of agricultural innovations in early modern England: turnips and clover in Norfolk and Suffolk 1580–1740', *Transactions of the Institute of British Geographers*, new series, X, 1985, pp. 205–21.

Overton, M., 'Agriculture', pp. 34–53 in Langton, J. and Morris, R., eds., *An atlas of industrializing Britain 1780–1914*, London, 1986.

Overton, M., 'Depression or revolution? English agriculture 1640–1750', *Journal of British Studies*, XXV, 1986, pp. 344–52.

Overton, M., 'Computer analysis of probate inventories: from portable micro to mainframe', pp. 96–104 in Hopkin, D. and Denley, P., eds., *History and Computing*, Manchester, 1987.

Overton, M., 'Computer standardization of probate inventories', pp. 145–51 in Genet, J-P., ed., *Standardisation et échange des bases de données historiques*, Paris, 1988.

Overton, M., 'Agricultural revolution? England, 1540–1850', pp. 9–21 in Digby, A. and Feinstein, C., eds., *New directions in economic and social history*, London and Basingstoke, 1989.

Overton, M., 'Weather and agricultural change in England, 1660–1739', *Agricultural History*, LXIII, 1989, pp. 77–88.

Overton, M., 'Re-estimating crop yields from probate inventories', *JEH*, L, 1990, pp. 931–5.

Overton, M., 'The critical century? The agrarian history of England and Wales 1750–1850', *AHR*, XXXVIII, 1990, pp. 185–9.

Overton, M. and Campbell, B. M. S., 'Five centuries of farming: agricultural change in medieval and early modern Norfolk, *c.*1250–*c.*1750', unpublished paper presented to the Annual Conference of the Economic History Society, Liverpool, 1990.

Paige, D. and Bombach, G., *A comparison of national outputs and productivity*, Paris, 1959.

Parker, W. N., 'Productivity growth in American grain farming: an analysis of its nineteenth-century sources', pp. 175–86 in Fogel, R. W. and Engerman, S. L., eds., *The reinterpretation of American economic history*, New York, 1971.

Parker, W. N. and Klein, J. L. V., 'Productivity growth in grain production in the United States, 1840–60 and 1900–10', pp. 523–80 in *Conference on research in income and wealth, output, employment, and productivity in the United States after 1800*, National Bureau of Economic Research, Studies in Income and Wealth, XXX, New York, 1966.

Patrick Wright, R., ed., *The standard cyclopaedia of modern agriculture and rural economy*, 12 vols., London, 1908.

Paul, J., *The law of tythes*, London, 2nd. edn., 1807.

Pawson, H. C., *Cockle Park Farm*, Oxford, 1960.

Payne, R. C., 'Agrarian conditions on the Wiltshire estates of the Duchy of Lancaster, the Lords Hungerford and the Bishopric of Winchester in the thirteenth, fourteenth and fifteenth centuries', unpublished University of London Ph.D. thesis, 1940.

Penn, S., 'Female wage-earners in late fourteenth-century England', *AHR*, XXXV, 1987, pp. 1–14.

Perren, R., *The meat trade in Britain 1840–1914*, London, 1978.

Perrot, J.-C., *L'Age d'or de la statistique régionale française (An 4–1804)*, Paris, 1977.

Persson, K. G., *Pre-industrial economic growth, social organization and technological progress in Europe*, Oxford, 1988.

Persson, K. G., *Aggregate output and labour productivity in English agriculture 1688–1801. A novel approach and comforting new results*, Discussion Papers from the Institute of Economics, 89–06, University of Copenhagen, 1989.

Phelps Brown, H. and Hopkins, S. V., 'Seven centuries of building wages', *Economica*, XXII, 1955, pp. 195–206.

Phelps Brown, H. and Hopkins, S. V., 'Seven centuries of the prices of consumables compared with builders' wage-rates', *Economica*, XXIII, 1956, pp. 296–314.

Phelps Brown, H. and Hopkins, S. V., *A perspective of wages and prices*, London, 1981.

Phillips, A. D. M., *The underdraining of farmland in England during the nineteenth century*, Cambridge, 1989.

Pimentel, D., 'Energy flow in the food system', pp. 1–23 in *idem* and Hall, C. W., eds., *Food and energy resources*, London, 1984.

Pirenne, H., *Les Villes flamandes avant le XIIe siècle*, Paris, 1905.

Plot, R., *The natural history of Oxfordshire*, Oxford, 1677.

Poos, L. R., 'The rural population of Essex in the later middle ages', *EcHR*, XXXVIII, 1985, pp. 515–30.

Postan, M. M., 'Village livestock in the thirteenth century', *EcHR*, XV, 1962, pp. 219–

49, reprinted as pp. 214–48 in *idem, Essays on medieval agriculture and general problems of the medieval economy*, Cambridge, 1973.

Postan, M. M., 'Medieval agrarian society in its prime: England', pp. 549–632 in *idem*, ed., *The Cambridge economic history of Europe*, I, *The agrarian life of the middle ages*, Cambridge, 2nd edn., 1966.

Postan, M. M., 'Investment in medieval agriculture', *JEH*, XXVII, 1967, pp. 576–87.

Postan, M. M., *The medieval economy and society*, London, 1972.

Pounds, N. J. G., 'Barton farming in eighteenth-century Cornwall', *Journal of the Royal Institution of Cornwall*, new series, VII, 1973, pp. 55–75.

Prestwich, M., 'Currency and the economy of early fourteenth-century England', pp. 45–58 in Mayhew, N. J., ed., *Edwardian monetary affairs, 1279–1344*, BAR, British series, XXXVI, Oxford, 1977.

Prevenier, W., 'Bevolkingscijfers en professonele strukturen der bevolking van Gent en Brugge in de XIVde eeuw', pp. 269–303 in *Album offert à Charles Verlinden à l'occasion de ses trente ans de professorat*, Ghent, 1975.

Prevenier, W., 'La Démographie des villes du comté de Flandre aux XIVᵉ et XVᵉ siècles. État de la question. Essai d'interpretation', *Revue du Nord*, LXV, 1983, pp. 255–75.

Prince, H. C., 'The origins of pits and depressions in Norfolk', *Geography*, XLIX, 1964, pp. 15–32.

Prince, H. C., 'England *circa* 1800', pp. 389–464 in Darby, H. C., ed., *A new historical geography of England*, Cambridge, 1974.

Prince, H. C., 'The changing rural landscape, 1750–1850', pp. 7–83 in Mingay, *The Agrarian history of England and Wales*, VI, *1750–1850*, 1989.

Purcell, P., *The peat resources of Ireland*, Fuel Research Board, special report II, London, 1920.

Pusey, P., 'On the present state of the science of agriculture in England', *Journal of the English Agricultural Society*, I, 1839, pp. 1–21.

Radcliff, T., *A report on the agriculture of eastern and western Flanders*, London, 1819.

Raftis, J. A., *The estates of Ramsey Abbey*, Toronto, 1957.

Rao, C. H. H., *Technological change and distribution of gains in Indian agriculture*, Delhi, 1975.

Raynbird, W. and H., *The agriculture of Suffolk*, London, 1849.

Rees, S., *Agricultural implements in prehistoric and Roman Britain*, 2 vols., Oxford, 1979.

Renouard, Y., *Les Villes d'Italie de la fin du Xᵉ siècle au début du XIVᵉ siècle*, 2 vols., Paris, 1969.

Reynolds, P. J., *Iron age farm: the Butser experiment*, London, 1979.

Ricardo, D., *On the principles of political economy and taxation* in *The works and correspondence of David Ricardo*, ed. P. Sraffa with the collaboration of M. H. Dobb, Cambridge, 1951.

Richard, J. M., 'Thierry d'Hireçon, agriculteur artésien', *Bibliothèque de l'Ecole des Chartes*, LIII, 1892, pp. 383–416 and 571–604.

Ritson, C., *Agricultural economics: principles and policy*, London, 1980.

Roberts, B. K., Turner, J. and Ward, P., 'Recent forest history and land use in Weardale, northern England', pp. 207–21 in Birks, H. and West, R., eds., *Quaternary plant ecology: 14th symposium of the British Ecological Society*, Oxford, 1973.

Robinson, M. A., 'Arable/pastoral ratios from insects?', pp. 19–55 in Jones, *Integrating the subsistence economy*, 1983.

Robo, E., *Medieval Farnham: everyday life in an episcopal manor*, Farnham, 1935.

Rogers, J. E. Thorold, *A history of agriculture and prices in England*, 7 vols., Oxford, 1866–1902.

Romeo, R., *Risorgimento e capitalismo*, Bari, 1955.

Roper, D. C., 'The method and theory of site catchment analysis: a review', pp. 119–40 in Schiffer, M. B., ed., *Advances in archaeological method and theory*, II, London, 1979.

Russell, E. J., *A history of agricultural science in Great Britain*, London, 1966.

S

Russell, E. J., *The fertility of the soil*, Cambridge, 1913.

Russell, E. J., *Soil conditions and plant growth*, London, 9th edn., 1961.

Russell, J. C., *British medieval population*, Albuquerque, New Mexico, 1948.

Russell, J. C., *Medieval regions and their cities*, Newton Abbot, 1972.

Russell, N., *Like engend'ring like: heredity and animal breeding in early modern England*, Cambridge, 1986.

Ryden, J. C., 'The flow of nitrogen in grassland', *Proceedings of the Fertiliser Society*, CCXXIX, London, 1984, 44 pp.

Saorstat Eireann, *Agricultural statistics 1847–1926: reports and tables*, Dublin, 1930.

Scaife, R. G., 'The elm decline in the pollen record of south-east England and its relationship to early agriculture', pp. 21–33 in Jones, *Archaeology and the flora of the British Isles*, 1988.

Schofield, R. S., 'The impact of scarcity and plenty on population change in England, 1541–1871', pp. 67–94 in Rotberg, R. I. and Rabb, T. K., eds., *Hunger and history*, Cambridge, 1985.

Searle, E., *Lordship and community: Battle Abbey and its banlieu, 1066–1538*, Toronto, 1974.

Sen, A. K., 'Size of holdings and prouu tivity', *The Economic Weekly*, XVI, 1964, pp. 323–6.

Sereni, E., *Capitalismo e mercato nazionale*, Rome, 1966.

Sereni, E., *Il capitalismo nelle campagne (1860–1900)*, Turin, 1974.

Serpieri, A., *Il contratto agrario e le condizioni di vita dei contadini nell'alto milanese*, Milan, 1910.

Sheehy, S., O'Brien, J. T. and McClelland, D., *Agriculture in Northern Ireland and the Republic of Ireland*, Dublin and Belfast, 1981.

Sherratt, A. G., 'Plough and pastoralism: aspects of the secondary products revolution', pp. 261–305 in Hodder, I., Isaac, G. and Hammond, N., eds., *Pattern of the past*, Cambridge 1976.

Shiel, R. S., 'Variation in amounts of carbon and nitrogen associated with particle size fractions from the Palace Leas meadow hay plots', *Journal of Soil Science*, XXXVII, 1986, pp. 249–57.

Shiel, R. S. and Batten, J. C., 'Redistribution of nitrogen and phosphorus on Palace Leas meadow hay plots as a result of aftermath grazing', *Grass and Forage Science*, XLIII, 1988, pp. 105–10.

Silvey, V., 'The contribution of new varieties to increasing cereal yield in England and Wales', *Journal of the National Institute of Agricultural Botany*, XIV, 1975, pp. 367–84.

Simmons, I. G., *The ecology of natural resources*, London, 1974.

Sinclair, J., *Report of the Scottish Commission on Agriculture to Ireland*, Edinburgh, 1906.

Sivéry, G., *Structures agraires et vie rurale dans le Hainaut à la fin du moyen âge*, 2 vols., Lille, 1973.

Skipp, V. H. T., *Crisis and development: an ecological case study of the forest of Arden 1570–1674*, Cambridge, 1978.

Slicher van Bath, B. H., 'The rise of intensive husbandry in the Low Countries', pp. 130–53 in Bromley, J. S. and Kossmann, E. H., eds., *Britain and the Netherlands: papers delivered to the Oxford–Netherlands historical conference 1959*, London, 1960.

Slicher van Bath, B. H., *Yield ratios, 810–1820*, A. A. G. Bijdragen, X, Wageningen, 1963.

Slicher van Bath, B. H., *The agrarian history of western Europe* AD *500–1850*, trans. O. Ordish, London, 1963.

Slicher van Bath, B. H., 'The yields of different crops, mainly cereals in relation to the seed *c.*810–1820', *Acta Historiae Neerlandica*, II, Leiden, 1967, pp. 78–97.

Slota, L., 'Law, land transfer and lordship on the estates of St Albans Abbey in the thirteenth and fourteenth centuries', *Law and History Review*, VI, 1988, pp. 119–38.

Smith, A., *An inquiry into the nature and causes of the wealth of nations*, ed. R. Campbell and A. Skinner, 2 vols., Oxford, 1976.

Smith, C. T., *An historical geography of western Europe before 1800*, London, 1967.

Smith, R. A. L., *Canterbury Cathedral Priory*, Cambridge, 1943.

Smith, R. M., 'Human resources', pp. 188–212 in Astill, G. and Grant, A., eds., *The countryside of medieval England*, Oxford, 1988.

Smith, R. M., 'Demographic developments in rural England 1300–48: a survey', pp. 25–77 in Campbell, B. M. S., ed., *Before the Black Death: studies in the 'crisis' of the early-fourteenth century*, Manchester, 1991.

Soboul, A., 'Risorgimento e rivoluzione borghese: schema di una direttiva di ricerca', pp. 801–16 in Istituto Gramsci, *Problemi dell'Unità d'Italia*, Rome, 1962.

Solar, P. M., 'Agricultural productivity and economic development in Ireland and Scotland in the early nineteenth century', pp. 70–88 in Devine, T. M. and Dickson, D., eds., *Ireland and Scotland 1600–1850: parallels and contrasts in economic and social development*, Edinburgh, 1983.

Solar, P. M., 'Growth and distribution in Irish agriculture before the Famine', unpublished Stanford University Ph.D. thesis, 1987.

Solow, B., *The land question and the Irish economy 1870–1903*, Cambridge, Mass., 1971.

Somerville, W., *Agriculture*, London, *c*.1910.

Southwell, T., 'An account of the severe winter of 1739–40 and its effects in the county of Norfolk', *Transactions of the Norwich Naturalists Society*, II, 1875, pp. 125–30.

Speed, A., *Adam out of Eden*, London, 1659.

Spencer, E., *A view of the present state of Ireland in 1596*, ed. W. L. Renwick, Oxford, 1986.

Spratt, D. and Burgess, C., eds., *Upland settlement in Britain: the second millennium BC and after*, BAR, British series, CXLIII, Oxford, 1985.

Spufford, M., *Contrasting communities: English villagers in the sixteenth and seventeenth centuries*, Cambridge, 1974.

Stacey, R. C., 'Agricultural investment and the management of the royal demesne manors, 1236–1240', *JEH*, XLVI, 1986, pp. 919–34.

Stainer, T. F., 'Recent developments in agriculture in Northern Ireland', unpublished paper presented to the Agricultural Economics Society of Ireland, October 1987.

Stanhill, G., 'Trends and deviations in the yield of the English wheat crop during the last 750 years', *Agro-Ecosystems*, III, 1976, pp. 1–10.

Steele, E. D., *Irish land and British politics*, Cambridge, 1970.

Stephenson, M. J., 'The productivity of medieval sheep on the great estates, 1100–1500', unpublished University of Cambridge Ph.D. thesis, 1987.

Stephenson, M. J., 'Wool yields in the medieval economy', *EcHR*, XLI, 1988.

Stern, D. V., 'A Hertfordshire manor of Westminster Abbey: an examination of demesne profits, corn yields, and weather evidence', unpublished University of London Ph.D. thesis, 1978.

Stigler, G. J., 'The early history of empirical studies of consumer behaviour', *Journal of Political Economy*, LXII, 1954, pp. 95–113.

Stitt, F. B., 'The medieval minister's account', *Society of Local Archivists Bulletin*, XI, 1953, pp. 2–8.

Stone, E., 'The estates of Norwich Cathedral Priory, 1100–1300', unpublished University of Oxford D.Phil. thesis, 1956.

Stratton, J. M., *Agricultural records AD 220–1968*, London, 1969.

Sullivan, R., 'Measurement of English farming technological change, 1523–1900', *Explorations in Economic History*, XXI, 1984, pp. 270–89.

Sutcliffe, D., 'The financial condition of the See of Canterbury 1279–1282', *Speculum*, X, 1935, pp. 53–68.

Swain, J., *Industry before the industrial revolution: north-east Lancashire, c.1500–1640*, Chetham Society, 3rd series, XXXII, Manchester, 1986.

Sykes, J. D., 'Agriculture and science', pp. 260–72 in Mingay, G. E., ed., *The Victorian countryside*, I, London, 1981.

Tawney, A. J. and R. H., 'An occupational census of the seventeenth century', *Economic History Review*, V, 1935, pp. 98–103.

The works of Thomas Robert Malthus, III, *Essay on population*, 6th edn., 1826, ed. E. A. Wrigley and D. Souden, London, 1986.

Thirsk, J., 'Farming techniques', pp. 161–99 in idem, *The agrarian history of England and Wales*, IV, *1500–1640*, 1967.

Thirsk, J., 'The farming regions of England', pp. 1–112 in idem, *The agrarian history of England and Wales*, IV, *1500–1640*, 1967.

Thirsk, J., ed., *The agrarian history of England and Wales*, IV, *1500–1640*, Cambridge, 1967.

Thirsk, J., ed., *The agrarian history of England and Wales*, Vi, *1640–1750: regional farming systems*, Cambridge, 1984.

Thirsk, J., ed., *The agrarian history of England and Wales*, Vii, *1640–1750: agrarian change*, Cambridge, 1985.

Thomas, B., 'Escaping from constraints: the industrial revolution in a Malthusian context', *Journal of Interdisciplinary History*, XV, 1985, pp. 729–53.

Thomas, B., 'Feeding England during the industrial revolution: a view from the celtic fringe', *Agricultural History*, CVI, 1982, pp. 328–42.

Thomas, C., 'Types and distributions of pre-Norman fields in Cornwall', pp. 7–15 in Bowen and Fowler, *Early land allotment*, 1979.

Thomas, M., 'Accounting for growth, 1870–1940: Stephen Nicholas and total factor productivity measurements', *EcHR*, XXXVIII, 1985, pp. 569–75.

Thompson, F. M. L., 'The second agricultural revolution, 1815–1880', *EcHR*, XXI, 1968, pp. 62–77.

Thompson, F. M. L., 'Nineteenth-century horse sense', *EcHR*, XXIX, 1976, pp. 60–81.

Thompson, F. M. L., ed., *Horses in European economic history: a preliminary canter*, Reading, 1983.

Thornton, C. C., 'The demesne of Rimpton, 938 to 1412: a study in economic development', unpublished University of Leicester Ph.D. thesis, 1989.

Thünen, J. H. von, *Der isolierte staat*, trans. by C. M. Wartenberg as *Von Thünen's isolated state*, ed. P. Hall, Oxford, 1966.

Timmer, C. P., 'The turnip, the new husbandry, and the English agricultural revolution', *Quarterly Journal of Economics*, LXXXIII, 1969, pp. 375–95.

Titow, J. Z., 'Evidence of weather in the account rolls of the Bishopric of Winchester 1209–1350', *EcHR*, XII, 1960, pp. 365–91.

Titow, J. Z., 'Some evidence of thirteenth-century population increase', *EcHR*, XIV, 1961, pp. 216–31.

Titow, J. Z., 'Land and population on the Bishop of Winchester's estates 1209–1350', unpublished University of Cambridge Ph.D. thesis, 1962.

Titow, J. Z., *English rural society 1200–1350*, London, 1969.

Titow, J. Z., 'Le Climat à travers les rôles de compatibilité de l'évêché de Winchester (1350–1450)', *Annales, Economies, Sociétés, Civilisations*, XXV, 1970, pp. 312–50.

Titow, J. Z., *Winchester yields: a study in medieval agricultural productivity*, Cambridge, 1972.

Tits-Dieuaide, M.-J., 'Cereal yields around Louvain, 1404–1729', pp. 97–105 in Van der Wee, H. and Van Cauwenberghe, E., eds., *Productivity of land and agricultural innovation in the Low Countries (1250–1800)*, Leuven, 1978.

Toniolo, G. and Piva, F., 'Unemployment in the 1930s: the case of Italy', pp. 221–45 in Eichengreen, B. and Hatton, T., eds., *Interwar employment in international perspective*, London, 1988.

Toniolo, G., *An economic history of liberal Italy 1850–1918*, London, 1990.

Toutain, J.-C., *Le Produit de l'agriculture française de 1700 à 1958: II, La Croissance*, in Marczewski, J., ed., *Histoire quantitative de l'économie française (2)*, Cahiers de l'Institut de Science Économique Appliquée, supplement CXV, Paris, 1961.

Townsend, H., 'On the improvement of Irish Agriculture', *Quarterly Journal of Agriculture*, I, 1828–29, pp. 310–25.

Toynbee, A., *Lectures on the industrial revolution in England*, London, 1884.

Tribe, K., *Land, labour and economic discourse*, London, 1978.

Trow-Smith, R., *A history of British livestock husbandry to 1700*, London, 1957.

Turner, J., 'The anthropogenic factor in vegetational history', *New Phytologist*, LXIII, 1964, pp. 73–90.

Turner, J., 'A contribution to the history of forest clearance', *Proceedings of the Royal Society*, series B, CLXI, 1965, pp. 343–54.

Turner, J., 'The vegetation', pp. 67–73 in Jones and Dimbleby, *The environment of man*, 1981.

Turner, M. E., 'Arable in England and Wales: estimates from the 1801 crop return', *Journal of Historical Geography*, VII, 1981, pp. 291–302.

Turner, M. E., 'Agricultural productivity in England in the eighteenth century: evidence from crop yields', *EcHR*, XXXV, 1982, pp. 489–510.

Turner, M. E., 'Agricultural productivity in eighteenth-century England: further strains of speculation', *EcHR*, XXXVII, 1984, pp. 252–7.

Turner, M. E., 'English open fields and enclosures: retardation or productivity improvements', *JEH*, XLI, 1986, pp. 669–92.

Turner, M. E., 'Towards an agricultural prices index for Ireland 1850–1914', *The Economic and Social Review*, XVIII, 1987, pp. 123–36.

Usher, D., *The measurement of economic growth*, Oxford, 1980.

Van der Veen, M. and Haselgrove, C., 'Evidence for pre-Roman crops from Coxhoe, Co. Durham', *Archaeologia Aeliana*, 5th series, XI, 1983, pp. 23–5.

Van der Wee, H., 'Introduction – the agricultural development of the Low Countries as revealed by the tithe and rent statistics, 1250–1800', pp. 1–23 in *idem* and Van Cauwenberghe, E., eds., *Productivity of land and agricultural innovation in the Low Countries (1250–1800)*, Leuven, 1978.

Van Werveke, H., *Miscellanea mediaevalia*, Ghent, 1968.

Van Zanden, J. L., *De economische ontwikkeling van de Nederlandse landbouw in de negentiende eeuw, 1800–1914*, A. A. G. Bijdragen, XXV, Wageningen, 1985.

Vaughan, W. E., 'A study of landlord and tenant relations between the Famine and the Land War, 1850–78', unpublished National University of Ireland Ph.D. thesis, 1973.

Vaughan, W. E., 'Landlord and tenant relations in Ireland between the Famine and the Land War, 1850–70', pp. 216–26 in Cullen, L. M. and Smout, T. C., eds., *Comparative aspects of Scottish and Irish economic and social history 1600–1900*, Edinburgh, 1977.

Vaughan, W. E., 'Agricultural output, rents and wages in Ireland, 1850–1880', pp. 85–97 in Cullen, L. M. and Furet, F., eds., *Ireland and France*, Paris, 1980.

Vaughan, W. E., *Landlords and tenants in Ireland 1848–1904*, Dublin, 1984.

Verhulst, A., 'La Laine indigène dans les anciens Pays-Bas entre le XIIᵉ et le XVIIᵉ siècle', *Revue historique*, DIV, 1972, pp. 281–322.

Verhulst, A., *Neue Ansichten über die Entstehung der Flämischen Städte am Beispiel von Gent und Antwerpen*, Studia Historica Gandensia, CCLV, 1983.

Vitali, O., *La popolazione attiva in agricoltura attraverso i censimenti italiani*, Rome, 1973.

Wade, W. W., *Institutional determinants of technical change and agricultural productivity growth: Denmark, France, and Great Britain, 1870–1965*, New York, 1981.

Walton, J. R., 'Agriculture 1730–1900', pp. 239–66 in Dodgshon, R. A. and Butlin, R. A., eds., *An historical geography of England and Wales*, London, 1978.

Walton, J. R., 'Mechanisation in agriculture: a study of the adoption process', pp. 23–42 in Fox, H. S. A. and Butlin, R. A., eds., *Change in the countryside: essays on rural England, 1500–1900*, Institute of British Geographers special Publication, X, London, 1979.

Walton, J. R., 'The diffusion of the improved shorthorn breed of cattle in Britain during the eighteenth and nineteenth centuries', *Transactions of the Institute of British Geographers*, new series, IX, 1984, pp. 22–36.

Warren, R. G. and Johnson, A. E., *Rothamsted Experimental Station annual report for 1963*, Harpenden, 1964.

Watson, J. A. S. and More, J. A., *Agriculture: the science and practice of British farming*, Edinburgh, 1st edn., 1924, and 11th edn., 1949.

White, R. E., *Introduction to the principles and practice of soil science*, Oxford, 1979.

Whitney, M., 'The yield of wheat in England over seven centuries', *Science*, CVIII, 1923, pp. 320–4.

Whittaker, J. M. and Spencer, J. E., *The Northern Ireland agricultural industry: its past development and medium-term prospects*, London, 1986.

Wild, A., ed., *Russell's soil conditions and plant growth*, London, 11th edn., 1988.

Willerding, U., 'Zum Ackerbau in der jüngeren vorrömischen Eisenzeit', pp. 309–30 in *Festschrift Maria Hopf*, Cologne, 1979.

Willerding, U., 'Anbaufrüchte der Eisenzeit und des frühen Mittelalters, ihre Anbauformen, Standortsverhältnisse und Erntemethoden', pp. 126–96 in Beck, H. and Jankuhn, H., eds., *Untersuchungen zur eisenzeitlichen und früh-mittelalterlichen Flur in Mitteleuropa und ihrer Nutzung*, Göttingen, 1980.

Williams, M., 'The enclosure and reclamation of waste land in England and Wales in the eighteenth and nineteenth centuries', *Transactions of the Institute of British Geographers*, CI, 1970, pp. 58–69.

Wilson, C., *England's apprenticeship 1603–1763*, London, 2nd edn., 1984.

Wilson, D. R., *Aerial reconnaissance for archaeology*, London, 1975.

Wood, O., *West Cumberland coal 1600–1982/3*, Cumberland and Westmorland Antiquarian and Archaeological Society, extra series, XXIV, Kendal, 1988.

Woodward, D., ed., *The farming and memorandum books of Henry Best of Elmswell, 1642*, Records of Social and Economic History, new series, VIII, London, 1984.

Wordie, J. R., 'Social change on the Leveson-Gower estates', *EcHR*, XXVII, 1974, pp. 593–609.

Worlidge, J., *Systema agriculturae*, London, 4th edn., 1697.

Worlidge, J., *Dictionarium rusticum and urbanicum*, London, 1704.

Wrigley, E. A., 'The supply of raw materials in the industrial revolution', *EcHR*, XV, 1962, pp. 1–16.

Wrigley, E. A., 'A simple model of London's importance in changing English society and economy, 1650–1750', *Past and Present*, XXXVII, 1967, pp. 44–70.

Wrigley, E. A. and Schofield, R. S., *The population history of England, 1541–1871: a reconstruction*, London, 1981.

Wrigley, E. A., 'Urban growth and agricultural change: England and the continent in the early modern period', *Journal of Interdisciplinary History*, XV, 1985, pp. 683–728.

Wrigley, E. A., 'Men on the land and men in the countryside: employment in agriculture in early nineteenth-century England', pp. 295–336 in Bonfield, L., Smith, R. M. and Wrightson, K., eds., *The world we have gained: histories of population and social structure*, Oxford, 1986.

Wrigley, E. A., 'Early modern agriculture: a new harvest gathered in', *AHR*, XXXV, 1987, pp. 65–71.

Wrigley, E. A., 'The classical economists and the industrial revolution', pp. 21–45 in *idem, People, cities and wealth*, 1987.

Wrigley, E. A., 'Some reflections on corn yields and prices in pre-industrial economies', pp. 92–130 in *idem, People, cities and wealth*, 1987.

Wrigley, E. A., *Continuity, chance and change: the character of the industrial revolution in England*, Cambridge, 1988.

Wrigley, E. A., *People, cities and wealth: the transformation of traditional society*, Oxford, 1987.

Yelling, J. A., 'Probate inventories and the geography of livestock farming: a study of east Worcestershire, 1540–1750', *Transactions of the Institute of British Geographers*, LI, 1970, pp. 111–26.

Yelling, J. A., *Common field and enclosure in England, 1450–1850*, Hamden, Ct., 1977.

Young, A., *Six weeks tour through the southern counties of England and Wales*, London, 1768.

Young, A., *A six months' tour through the north of England*, London, 2nd edn., 1771.

Young, A., *The farmer's guide in hiring and stocking farms*, I, Dublin, 1771.

Young, A., *The farmer's tour through the east of England*, 4 vols., London, 1771.

Young, A., *Political arithmetic*, London, 1774.

Young, A., *A tour in Ireland with general observations on the present state of that kingdom made in the years 1776, 1777, and 1778 and brought down to the end of 1779*, 2 vols., Dublin, 1780.

Young, A., *Travels during the years 1787, 1788, and 1789*, II, *Italy*, Bury St Edmunds, 1792.

Young, A., *General view of the agriculture of the county of Norfolk*, London, 1804.

Young, A., *General view of the agriculture of the county of Lincoln*, London, 1813.

Young, A., *General view of the agriculture of the county of Suffolk*, London, 1813.

Young, A., *Travels in France during the years 1787, 1788 and 1789*, ed. J. Kaplow, New York, 1969.

Zamagni, V., 'Le radici agricole del dualismo italiano', *Nuova Rivista Storica*, LIX, 1975, pp. 55–99.

Zangheri, R., 'The historical relationship between agricultural and economical development', pp. 23–41 in Jones, E. L. and Woolf, S. J., eds., *Agrarian change and economic development*, London, 1969.

Zell, M., 'A wood pasture agrarian regime: Wealden agriculture in the sixteenth century', *Southern History*, VII, 1985, pp. 69–93.

Index